LESSONS FROM COVID-19

LESSONS FROM COVID-19

Impact on Healthcare Systems and Technology

Edited by

ARTURAS KAKLAUSKAS

Department of Construction Economics and Property Management, Vilnius Gediminas Technical University, Vilnius, Lithuania

AJITH ABRAHAM

Machine Intelligence Research Labs (MIR Labs), Scientific Network for Innovation and Research Excellence, Auburn, WA, United States

KINGSLEY OKOYE

Writing Lab, Institute for Future of Education, Tecnológico de Monterrey, Monterrey, Nuevo Leon, Mexico

SHANKRU GUGGARI

Department of Computer Science and Engineering, B.M.S. College of Engineering, Bengaluru, India

ELSEVIER

ACADEMIC PRESS

An imprint of Elsevier

Academic Press is an imprint of Elsevier
125 London Wall, London EC2Y 5AS, United Kingdom
525 B Street, Suite 1650, San Diego, CA 92101, United States
50 Hampshire Street, 5th Floor, Cambridge, MA 02139, United States
The Boulevard, Langford Lane, Kidlington, Oxford OX5 1GB, United Kingdom

ISBN 978-0-323-99878-9

For information on all Academic Press publications
visit our website at https://www.elsevier.com/books-and-journals

Publisher: Stacy Masucci
Acquisitions Editor: Rafael E. Teixeira
Editorial Project Manager: Mica Ella Ortega
Production Project Manager: Niranjan Bhaskaran
Cover Designer: Miles Hitchen

Typeset by STRAIVE, India

Contents

Contributors

Ashok Kumar Ahirwar
Department of Biochemistry, UCMS, Delhi, India

W. Regis Anne
PSG College of Technology, Coimbatore, India

Peter A. Arockiam
St. Xavier's College (Autonomous), Kolkata, West Bengal, India

Senthil Kumar Arumugam
Department of Professional Studies, School of Commerce, Finance and Accountancy, Christ University, Bangalore, Karnataka, India

Sailesh Bajpai
Regional Center for Biotechnology, Faridabad, India

Sourav Banerjee
Kalyani Government Engineering College, Kalyani, India

Saloni Bhatia
Department of Biotechnology, B.M.S. College of Engineering, Bengaluru, Karnataka, India

Sourav Chakraborty
Department of Food Engineering and Technology, Tezpur University, Tezpur, Assam, India

Mukesh Chouhan
Department of Computer Science and Engineering, Government Polytechnic College, Sheopur, India

Giuseppe Ciaburro
Department of Architecture and Industrial Design, Università degli Studi della Campania Luigi Vanvitelli, Borgo San Lorenzo, Aversa, Italy

Milton Costa
St. Xavier's College (Autonomous), Kolkata, West Bengal, India

Saptashish Deb
Center for Rural Development and Technology, Indian Institute of Technology Delhi, New Delhi, India

Onur Dogan
Department of Industrial Engineering; Research Center for Data Analytics and Spatial Data Modeling (RC-DAS), Izmir Bakircay University, Izmir, Turkey

Bhagwati Garg
Union Bank of India, Branch, Gwalior, India

Shankru Guggari
Machine Intelligence Research Labs, Auburn, WA, United States

M.A. Jabbar
Vardhaman College of Engineering, Hyderabad, India

M. Harini Jaya
Adhiyamaan College of Agriculture and Research (ACAR), Hosur, Tamil Nadu, India

S. Carolin Jeeva
Karunya Institute of Technology and Sciences, Coimbatore, India

K.R. Jolvis Pou
Department of Bioresource Engineering, McGill University, Sainte-Anne-de Bellevue, Montreal, QC, Canada

Sarina Kabade
Government Science College (Autonomous) affiliated to Bangalore University, Bangalore, Karnataka, India

Vijayakumar Kadappa
Department of Computer Applications, B.M.S. College of Engineering, Bengaluru, Karnataka, India

V. Kakulapati
Sreenidhi Institute of Science and Technology, Hyderabad, Telangana, India

Teesta Katte
Department of Biotechnology, B.M.S. College of Engineering, Bengaluru, Karnataka, India

Joseph Kulandai
St. Xavier's College (Autonomous), Kolkata, West Bengal, India

Nitesh Kumar
Centurion University of Technology and Management, R. Sitapur, Odisha, India

Ravi Kumar
Department of Computer Science and Engineering, B.M.S. College of Engineering, Bengaluru, India

S.N. Kumar
Department of EEE, Amal Jyothi College of Engineering, Kanjirappally, Kerala, India

Thabisa E. Mabusela
Department of Psychology, Nelson Mandela University, Gqeberha, South Africa

Vinod Mahor
Department of Computer Science Engineering, IPS College of Technology and Management, Gwalior, India

Santanu Malakar
Department of Food Engineering, National Institute of Food Technology Entrepreneurship and Management, Sonipat, Haryana, India

Ram N. Manas
Department of Biotechnology, B.M.S. College of Engineering, Bengaluru, Karnataka, India

Samuel S. Mitra
St. Xavier's College (Autonomous), Kolkata, West Bengal, India

Mohona Munshi
Department of Chemical Engineering, Vignan Foundation for Science, Technology, and Research, Vadlamudi, Guntur, Andhra Pradesh, India

Prathibha Narayanan
Department of Biotechnology, B.M.S. College of Engineering, Bengaluru, Karnataka, India

Magnolia B. Ngcobo-Sithole
Department of Psychology, Nelson Mandela University, Gqeberha, South Africa

Ruby Mary Notts
St. Xavier's College (Autonomous), Kolkata, West Bengal, India

Fernando Ortiz-Rodriguez
Universidad Autonoma de Tamaulipas, Ciudad Victoria, Mexico

Kiran Pachlasiya
Department of Computer Science Engineering, NRI Institute of Science and Technology, Bhopal, India

Vijay K. Patel
Institute of Pharmaceutical Sciences, Guru Ghasidas University; Dr. C.V. Raman Institute of Pharmacy, Dr. C.V. Raman University, Bilaspur, India

Rashmi Rai
School of Business and Management, CHRIST University, Bengaluru, Karnataka, India

Harish Rajak
Institute of Pharmaceutical Sciences, Guru Ghasidas University, Bilaspur, India

Avinash Arvind Rasalkar
Prabhat-Advanced Life Tech Analytics, Dharwad, Karnataka, India

Sachin B. Rathod
Department of Physiology, Indira Gandhi Government Medical College, Nagpur, Maharashtra, India

Romil Rawat
Department of Computer Science Engineering, Shri Vaishnav Vidyapeeth Vishwavidyalaya, Indore, India

Divijendra Natha S. Reddy
Department of Biotechnology, B.M.S. College of Engineering, Bengaluru, Karnataka, India

Sheri Mahender Reddy
Otto-Friedrich University of Bamberg, IsoSySc, Bamberg, Germany

Joshi Manisha S.
Department of Medical Electronics Engineering, B.M.S. College of Engineering, Bengaluru, India

Shishir Kumar Shandilya
School of Computing Science and Engineering, VIT Bhopal University, Bhopal, India

Aarti Mehta Sharma
Symbiosis Centre for Management Studies, Bengaluru, Karnataka; Symbiosis International (Deemed University), Pune, Maharashtra, India

Anuj Sharma
All India Institute of Medical Sciences, Nagpur, Maharashtra, India

Ashok Kumar Shettihalli
Department of Biotechnology, B.M.S. College of Engineering, Bengaluru, Karnataka, India

Ekta Shirbhate
Institute of Pharmaceutical Sciences, Guru Ghasidas University; Dr. C.V. Raman Institute of Pharmacy, Dr. C.V. Raman University, Bilaspur, India

Priyanka Singh
School of Management and Commerce, Poornima University, Jaipur, Rajasthan, India

Anusha Sonar
Department of Medical Electronics Engineering, B.M.S. College of Engineering, Bengaluru, India

Smita R. Sorte
Department of Physiology, All India Institute of Medical Sciences, Nagpur, Maharashtra, India

Neha Sreedharala
Department of Medical Electronics Engineering, B.M.S. College of Engineering, Bengaluru, India

Shrikant Telang
Department of Information Technology, Shri Vaishnav Vidyapeeth Vishwavidyalaya, Indore, India

Sanju Tiwari
Universidad Autonoma de Tamaulipas, Ciudad Victoria, Mexico

Umadevi V.
Department of Computer Science and Engineering, B.M.S. College of Engineering, Bengaluru, India

Anandhu Venu
Department of EEE, Amal Jyothi College of Engineering, Kanjirappally, Kerala, India

Saisha Vinjamuri
Department of Biotechnology, B.M.S. College of Engineering, Bengaluru, Karnataka, India

About the editors

Arturas Kaklauskas is Professor at Vilnius Gediminas Technical University, in Lithuania; Member of the Research Council of Lithuania; Member of the Science Europe working group on data sharing and supporting infrastructures; Head of the Department of Construction Management and Property; Laureate of the Lithuanian Science Prize; Member of the Lithuanian Academy of Sciences, Editor-in-Chief of the *Journal of Civil Engineering and Management*; Editor of the international journal titled *Engineering Applications of Artificial Intelligence*; and Associate Editor of the journal *Ecological Indicators*. He has contributed to nine Framework and five Horizon 2020 programs and participated in more than 30 other projects in the European Union, the Unite States, Africa, and Asia. The Belarusian State Technological University (Minsk, Belarus) awarded him an Honorary Doctorate in 2014. His publications include 9 books and 150 papers in Web of Science journals. A total of 15 PhD students successfully defended their theses under his supervision. The Web of Science h-Index of Prof. A. Kaklauskas is 29. Web of Science journals have cited him 2724 times, and average citations per article are 18.16. His areas of interest include affective computing, neuromarketing, and intelligent tutoring systems; affective intelligent tutoring systems; massive open online courses (MOOCs); affective Internet of Things; smart built environment; intelligent event prediction; opinion mining, intelligent decision support systems; life cycle analyses of built environments; energy; climate change; resilience management; healthy houses; sustainable built environments; big data and text analytics; intelligent library; Internet of Things; etc.

Dr. Ajith Abraham is the Director of Machine Intelligence Research Labs (MIR Labs), a not-for-profit scientific network for innovation and research excellence connecting industry and academia. The network with HQ in Seattle, USA has currently more than 1,500 scientific members from over 105 countries. As an investigator/co-investigator, he has won research grants worth over US$100 Million. Currently he holds two University Professorial appointments. He works as a Professor of Artificial Intelligence at Innopolis University, Russia and is the Yayasan Tun Ismail Mohamed Ali Professorial Chair in Artificial Intelligence of UCSI, Malaysia. Dr. Abraham works in a multi-disciplinary environment and he has authored/co-authored more than 1,400+ research publications out of which there are 100+ books covering various aspects of computer science. One of his books was translated to Japanese and a few other articles were translated to Russian and Chinese. Dr. Abraham has more than 47,000 academic citations (h-index of 102 + as per google scholar). He has given more than 150 plenary lectures and conference tutorials (in 25 + countries). Dr. Abraham was the Chair of IEEE Systems Man and Cybernetics Society Technical Committee on Soft Computing (which has over 200 + members) during 2008-2021 and served as a Distinguished Lecturer of IEEE Computer Society representing Europe (2011-2013). Dr. Abraham was the Editor-in-Chief of Engineering Applications of Artificial Intelligence (EAAI) during 2016-2021 and serves/served on the editorial board of over 15 International Journals indexed by Thomson ISI. Dr. Abraham received the Ph.D. degree in Computer Science from Monash University, Melbourne, Australia (2001) and a Master of Science degree from Nanyang Technological University, Singapore (1998).

Dr. Kingsley Okoye received his PhD in software engineering from the University of East London, United Kingdom, in 2017. He completed his MSc in technology management in 2011 and his BSc in computer science in 2007. He is an MIET member at the Institution of Engineering and Technology, United Kingdom, and a graduate member of the IEEE. He is a devoted researcher in industry and academia in both hardware and software fields of computing in areas such as Data Science, Machine Learning, Artificial Intelligence, Big Data and Advanced Analytics, Software Development and Programming, and Business Process Management. Dr. Kingsley has had the opportunity to do case studies and work in interdisciplinary and cross-cultural teams of various business and academic units that serve multiple industries. This includes serving as a software programming lab tutor for undergraduate students. He has also served as a principal organizer and participated in organizing special session workshops, presentations, research methods, and statistical analysis topics in several conferences and workshops. He also serves as an editorial board member and a reviewer for journals and conferences of international repute and has contributed to research and project outcomes by assessing and evaluating their impacts upon the scientific and industrial communities. Dr. Kingsley is Data Architect in the Writing Lab of Tecnologico de Monterrey. He is also a member of the Machine Intelligence Research Labs, United States, and a member of the IEEE SMCS Technical Committee (TC) on Soft Computing. It is Dr. Kingsley's personal mission to foster sustainable technical research and provide solutions through critical thinking, creative problem solving, and cross-functional collaboration. The outcomes of his research have been published as journal articles, books, book chapters, and conference proceedings in high indexed and reputable journals, publications, and conferences in the areas of computing and educational innovation. His research interests include process mining and automation, learning analytics and systems design, semantic web technologies, knowledge engineering and data management, computer education, educational innovation, Internet applications, and ontologies.

Dr. Shankru Guggari obtained his PhD in computer science and engineering. He is currently working on building robust classification techniques. Recently, Dr. Shankru has won the best research paper award in the international conference. His areas of research interest include pattern recognition, IOT, and machine learning. He has published some of his research works in international conferences and reputed journals published by Elsevier, Springer, etc. He has more than 4 years of industry experience and 2 years of academic research experience. Currently, Dr. Shankru is serving as a lead editor for edited book, which will be published by Elsevier. He has delivered technical talks in various platforms. He also served as a guest editor for few special issues related to AI and ML domains.

Preface

The COVID-19 pandemic disrupted many sectors of the humans, organizations', and the underlying operational processes and livelihood worldwide. This ranged from its global impact on the health and well-being of people and dramatic loss of human lives (Tandon, 2020; WHO, 2020; Murphy et al., 2021), to the technological impact (Chick et al., 2020; IEEE, 2020a; Kummitha, 2020; Woolliscroft, 2020), and the millions of organizations or enterprises that faced an existential threat or risked losing their businesses and workforce (Juan Ricardo Márquez, 2020; WHO, 2020; Alsamhi et al., 2021; ILO, 2021; IEEE, 2020a), including the social, economic, education, policy, and governance disruptions caused by the pandemic (Aristovnik et al., 2020; Crawford et al., 2020; OECD, 2020; Reimers et al., 2020; Tran et al., 2020; UNESCO, 2020; Pokhrel and Chhetri, 2021; UN, 2021b). For example, while the cost estimated for low- and middle-income countries to provide an effective healthcare response to the pandemic was approximately US$52 billion monthly, the United Nations (UN) estimated that it would cost the global economy around US$2 trillion during the peak of the pandemic, and a decrease of nearly US$8.5 trillion in output over the next 2 years due to the COVID-19 pandemic (Kaye et al., 2020; UN, 2021a). Besides, at the end of 2020, the World Health Organization (WHO) confirmed that the COVID-19 virus had infected over 82 million people and killed more than 1.8 million people worldwide (WHO, 2021).

Some of the main challenges experienced by the different organizations during the COVID-19 pandemic were the lack of preparedness of the several healthcare and information technology (IT) companies or institutions and the struggles they encountered practically and technically around the world (Kaye et al., 2020; Salloml, 2020; Sohrabizadeh et al., 2021). In the healthcare system, there was the problem of short supplies of items and facilities such as personal protective equipment (PPE), hospital equipment, and medical and drug supplies (Kaye et al., 2020). There was also the challenge of how to take care of the patients and provide them with non-stop healthcare and management (Juan Ricardo Márquez, 2020; Montenegro et al., 2021). Moreover, although technological approaches such as telemedicine proved inevitable, indispensable, and effective during the crises, the issue of digital skills, literacy, and training for the medical professionals was also a barrier to its wide use and ample adoption in the healthcare system (Heinzelmann et al., 2005; ATA, 2006; Wootton, 2008; Ryu, 2012; Juan Ricardo Márquez, 2020; Tandon, 2020; Woolliscroft, 2020; UN, 2021b). New innovations and healthcare models will also emerge as telehealth services and standards proliferate (IEEE, 2021). Moreover, it is also noteworthy to mention that the COVID-19 pandemic has spanned the necessity of *data* and *science* in reinstating or building back a more resilient and robust healthcare system toward equitably accelerating a shared development and sustainable global health goal or ecosystem (WHO, 2021). Therefore, there is a need for disentangling and bridging the health gap between the populations who have missed the necessary care during this time and in the future from those who had access to quality healthcare systems (Moynihan et al., 2021).

With regard to the technology sector, the COVID-19 disruptions have inadvertently caused an acceleration or heightening of almost "virtual-everything," e.g., remote working, telemedicine/teleconsultation, virtual learning (Bao, 2020; Chick et al., 2020; WHO, 2020; Woolliscroft, 2020; Alsamhi et al., 2021; Benabdallah and Bourgault, 2021; Evans, 2020). It has also, on the other hand, led different organizations to focus swiftly on reevaluating and de-risking of the end-to-end value chains, business operations, and/or policies (Salloml, 2020; ILO, 2021). Moreover, there has also been a significant or challenge-based impact on the technology sector, ranging from issues affecting the supply of raw materials and disruption of the electronics value chain, e.g., hardware and software, semiconductors, networks equipment, IT services, causing an inflationary risk on products (Salloml, 2020), to more direct methods or efforts that are purportedly required to support contact tracing, and providing high-performance computing resources for COVID-19-related research or projects (Evans, 2020; Moynihan et al., 2021; Sohrabizadeh et al., 2021). The Organization for Economic Cooperation and Development (OECD) has also highlighted in its policy responses to COVID-19, the long-term effects that the COVID-19 crisis could have on the future of science, technology, and innovation (STI) (OECD, 2021). The main themes that have emerged in these topics or technological areas include the challenges that have to do with accelerating digital transformation, literacy, and skills; increased importance of technology in the economy and society; prevalence of inequalities in access to and the use of technology; unequal effects of the crisis on research and development (R&D) across the different sectors; and changes in the openness, inclusiveness, and agility of research and innovation ecosystems (OECD, 2020, 2021; UNESCO, 2021, IEEE, 2020b).

Indeed, the editors note that the aforementioned affirmations must have raised concerns across the different organizations or sectors that are directly or indirectly involved, or yet, affected by the impact of the COVID-19 outbreak. In other words, some lessons were theoretically and practically learned from the COVID-19 pandemic, which the several organizations and stakeholders concerned would, consequently, build on, adopt, adapt, and implement to tackle the aftermath of the pandemic on the "healthcare system and technology," which is the main focus of this book. The stakeholders, *per se*, would also supposedly leverage the resultant *innovations* to ensure that such crises do not unveil the unpreparedness of the different sectors and/or inadequate measures being put in place to handle global pandemics (OECD, 2020; UNESCO, 2020; Moynihan et al., 2021; Sohrabizadeh et al., 2021; UN, 2021a).

Thus, this book uncovers the impact that COVID-19 has had on the healthcare and technology industry. The content covers state-of-the-art case studies, empirical research, and new trends or solutions that have spanned during the pandemic to help inform and guide the concerned sectors and readers in understanding the disruptions and effects that the COVID-19 outbreak has had across the healthcare system and technology sectors.

Scientifically, this book discusses both the positive and negative impacts of the COVID-19 pandemic on the aforementioned sectors (healthcare and technology). Current studies showed that the COVID-19 outbreak has caused most of the healthcare and technology industries to close their in-person operations and in turn migrate to the remote way of continuing their business operations (Bunch et al., 2020; Kaye et al., 2020; Kummitha, 2020; Salloml, 2020; Viner et al., 2020; WHO, 2020; Woolliscroft, 2020; Alsamhi et al., 2021). Although the different e-health and technology-mediated solutions and contingency plans have been remarkable, there is evidence that many of the resultant *innovations* that have emerged during this period will stay and remain part of the different organizations' strategic and decision-making processes (Woolliscroft, 2020; Sohrabizadeh et al., 2021), especially with the primary aim of sustaining, tracking, and managing in the aftermath of the COVID-19 pandemic (WHO Global Observatory for e-Health, 2010; UNESCO, 2016; WHO, 2021). Therefore, the editors note that now is the time for the medical professionals and IT experts to not only embrace the existing and emerging technology-mediated or e-health solutions, but to also rapidly act in ensuring that the innovations and alternative solutions that were created during this period are developed, nurtured, and sustained to fill the voids (e.g., safe face-to-face interactions of patients and health professionals, adequate digital technology literacy and infrastructure, efficient supply chain and vaccination) that the pandemic has purportedly created. Some of the areas in which the COVID-19 outbreak has disrupted, but to name a few, include virtual learning (VL) platforms to telemedicine (Juan Ricardo Márquez, 2020; Woolliscroft, 2020). Thus, augmented reality (AR) and virtual reality (VR) are fast becoming the next frontier in clinical and technological programs, research, and development (Woolliscroft, 2020; Díaz et al., 2021). We note that the main challenge, particularly for the health professionals and researchers, has been in developing turn-around policies or innovative measures that incorporate coping mechanisms for the stakeholders, managing continuity of the different services offered, and improving/accelerating the healthcare systems and technology in general (OECD, 2020; Debre and Dijkstra, 2021; Okoye et al., 2021). It is noteworthy to mention the speculations on how disproportionate the implications of COVID-19 have been on the healthcare, engineering, and informatics sectors due to age, ethnicity, gender, demographic and linguistic distribution, cultural and socio-economic status, and other factors (WHO, 2020, 2021).

Therefore, the aim of this book is primarily to bring to light state-of-the-art research and technologies, from the perspective of the healthcare and technology industries, that can not only be used to inform the readers about the current trends and studies on the lessons learned during COVID-19, but can also be applied by the different sectors to foster future innovations in response to the pandemic (in terms of the lesson learned pre-COVID-19, during COVID-19, and post-COVID-19). Thus, the chapters collected in this book expound on both the theoretical and technological advancements that have occurred during the COVID-19 pandemic, as well as state-of-the-art methods and technologies that are being put in place in preparedness for the post-COVID-19 era, or the "new normal" *per se*.

This book can be considered as a reference material, particularly for scholars, practitioners, and experts within the healthcare system and technological sector, in addressing the challenges and embracing the innovations that have emerged due to the COVID-19 disruptions. The editors believe that the book's chapters, written by experts and scholars from around the world in their different areas of specialty, will help inform and facilitate the operations of the different industries, process owners, and research in healthcare systems and technology, particularly as it concerns the lessons from the COVID-19 pandemic, which justifies the title of this book, *Lesson from COVID-19: Impact on Healthcare System and Technology.*

With the help of this book, readers will be able to:

(1) understand the effects of COVID-19 on the healthcare and technology sectors;

(2) obtain a comprehensive view of the case studies and methodologies, state-of-the-art research, technologies, and effective practices that have impacted the different sectors during COVID-19;

(3) work on effective hypotheses to test the disruptions and changes that have spanned across the duration of COVID-19 in preparedness for what is next;

(4) bridge the practical and theoretical gaps or lessons learned during the COVID-19 pandemic, particularly within the healthcare system and technology sector.

This book includes both original research and case studies from a diverse range of authors within their different areas of interests and specialty, with a focus on the impact of COVID-19 on the healthcare system and technology sectors. Each submitted chapter was reviewed by peer reviewers and the editors, and after assessing the relevance of the submitted chapters and the review process, during which some chapters went through several rounds of revisions, 16 chapters were selected for inclusion in this book. The selected chapters present groundbreaking and in-depth studies of practical issues and challenging problems that deal with or reveal "lesson learned from COVID-19," particularly within the wider spectrum of the "healthcare system and technology."

A brief description of the 15 chapters in this book follows.

In Chapter 1, titled "COVID-19: Origin, Epidemiology, Virology, Pathogenesis, and Treatment" and written by Sharma, Ahirwar, Sorte, and Rathod, the authors examined the promising and alternative measures taken by practitioners during the pandemic and the preventive measures that are to be taken until it fizzles out. This includes a discussion of the viral morphology and pathogenesis, asymptomatic stages of the COVID-19 disease, and laboratory diagnosis for screening and diagnosis of patients with COVID-19.

In Chapter 2, titled "Coronavirus Reinfections: An Outlook on Evidences and Effects" and written by Patel, Shirbhate, and Rajak, the authors discussed various aspects of COVID-19 reinfection, including its severity, frequency, immunopathogenesis, immune responses, effect on vaccine development, corona waves and herd immunity, management, and prevention strategies. Their study notes that the deep, extensive, rapid, and real-time whole-genome sequencing studies, as well as an enhanced vaccination drive and rigorous adherence to COVID-19 appropriate behavior, would be critical in limiting the severity of transmission and reinfection of the virus.

In Chapter 3, titled "Effect of Yoga Mudras in Improving the Health of Users: A Precautionary Measure Practice in Daily Life for Resisting the Deadly COVID-19 Disease" and written by Kumar, Venu, and Jaya, the authors studied the role of Yoga (mudras) in improving the health condition of both infected and noninfected persons during the COVID-19 pandemic. Their study showed that consistent practice of mudras with a breathing exercise for 30 min each (morning and evening) paved the way toward a healthy life. Thus, they proposed a set of mudras with a breathing exercise that focuses on the improvement of immunity and minimizes respiratory issues.

In Chapter 4, titled "Blockchain: Opportunities in the Healthcare Sector and Its Uses in COVID-19" and written by Arumugam and Sharma, the authors examined how best to manage and protect electronic medical records and personal health records data using blockchain technology. To this end, they analyzed issues in healthcare, blockchain implementation, and its uses during the COVID-19 pandemic. The authors put forward the idea that even after the world is free of the coronavirus, there will be pressure on the healthcare industry, and that blockchain technology is the way to alleviate this pressure. To note, the chapter purports that with secure access, blockchain-distributed ledgers can help in exchange of health information securely without complex intermediation of trust. And with scarcity of time and resources, adaptation of blockchain technology will help mitigate the pressures on existing infrastructure.

In Chapter 5, titled "The Impact of COVID-19 on Functioning, Disability, and Health in African Countries: The Case of Cameroon" and written by Nganji, Ngeh, and Cockburn, the authors examined the impact of COVID-19 in low- and medium-income countries (LIMCs) in Africa in the areas of disabilities and rehabilitation services, with a particular focus on Cameroon. They utilized the International Classification of Functioning, Disability and Health (ICF) framework to analyze and organize the information and to develop different themes: (1) preventing loss of function, (2) contracting the virus, (3) diagnosing and assessing impairments and functioning, (4) treatment including rehabilitation, (5) impacts on engagement in activities, (6) collective efforts and social participation, and (7) government actions against COVID-19. Theoretically, the study provided insight on COVID-19 in Cameroon and can help to inform decisions on how to manage it effectively.

In Chapter 5, titled "COVID-19 and Its Impact on Cancer, HIV, and Mentally Ill Patients" and written by Rasalkar, Bhatia, Katte, Narayanan, Vinjamuri, Shettihalli, Kabade, Manas, Kadappa, and Reddy, the authors found that while COVID-19 patients with other comorbid conditions face severe health complications irrespective of their gender or age, the management of COVID-19 patients is consuming health resources and that it is becoming difficult to treat patients suffering from other dreadful diseases like cancer, HIV, and mental health issues. In their study, the authors discussed the effects of COVID-19 and management of cancer patients considering the main cancer subtypes (e.g., breast, lung, and blood cancers) and patients affected with HIV and mental health issues. Finally, they have added a perspective on Ayurvedic treatment and its efficacy on COVID-19 patients.

In Chapter 6, titled "Revisiting the Efficacy of the Policies in Indian Primary Healthcare Sector: Interventions and Approaches During the COVID-19 Pandemic" and written by Rai and Singh, the authors opined that gaining self-dependency in research and development, technology, raw materials, and production cannot be overlooked particularly amidst the recent COVID-19 pandemic. To this end, the authors conducted a cohesive review of the literature and all available secondary data from international databases to unfold the paradigm shift in India's primary healthcare industry due to the pandemic during the last one and a half years. They put India's experience with the coronavirus in context considering the first and second waves, and also looked at public health difficulties during the COVID-19 era, both from a national and worldwide perspective. In addition, the study critically covered the primary healthcare sector's role during the pandemic and the government's policies and processes to deal with COVID-19 and any other unforeseen situations that the host country may encounter in the future.

In Chapter 7, titled "Benefits and Use of Blockchain Technology to Support Supply Chain During COVID-19" and written by Ciaburro, the author analyzed the basic blockchain concepts and the use of the technology in addressing the COVID-19 emergency. A blockchain-based model for vaccine supply chain was explained in relation to management of a pandemic situation by adopting innovative technologies such as blockchain, ranging from the identification of outbreaks of contagion, to the supply and distribution of personal protective equipment (PPE), to the problematic campaign of administering anti-COVID-19 vaccines.

In Chapter 8, titled "Novel Coronavirus Disease (COVID-19): Emergence, Early Infection Rate, and Deployment Strategies for Preventive

Solutions" and written by Munshi, Deb, Malakar, Pou, and Chakraborty, the authors discussed in detail the various epidemics and pandemics (plague, cholera, Spanish flu, etc.) in the history of human civilization. They applied a principal component analysis (PCA) to interpret the COVID-19 spreading kinetics during the first wave (in the year 2020). The numbers of confirmed, recovered, active, and deceased cases were considered for the mapping of the PCA within different countries. Their study can be used as an informative approach for anticipating and strategy-making in connection with COVID-19 or other pandemics in the future. In addition, the potential use of herbal medicines, dietary remedies, and allopathic therapy to fight COVID-19 and various preventive measures used to combat the pandemic during the first wave are also discussed in the chapter.

In Chapter 9, titled "Challenges and Opportunities in the Provision of Mental Healthcare Services During the COVID-19 Pandemic and Beyond" and written by Ngcobo-Sithole and Mabusela, the authors noted that, in the case of South Africa, the change from face-to-face to online service provision has been disruptive, and at times resulted in people not being able to access the resultant healthcare services. They described specifically the use of online psychological service delivery pre-COVID-19 and during the lockdown. To this end, the authors conducted a literature review exploring the delivery of psychological services through online channels pre-COVID-19 and during the lockdown. In turn, they highlighted lessons learned and opportunities for psychological service provision beyond the pandemic, and concluded that online service platforms can increase access to psychological services and identification of strategies that can be adopted to strengthen service provision.

In Chapter 10, titled "Applications of Machine Learning Approaches to Combat COVID-19: A Survey" and written by Tiwari, Dogan, Jabbar, Shandilya, Ortiz-Rodruiguez, Bajpai, and Banerjee, the authors critically examined the appropriateness and contribution of artificial intelligence and/or machine learning methods to COVID-19 datasets, particularly in enhancing the understanding to apply these methods for quick analysis and verification of pandemic databases. While the study noted that the COVID-19 outbreak had a rapid growth, it was not easy to predict the patients affected and the resources needed within a specified time. The authors opined that machine learning is a strong approach in the fight against pandemics like COVID-19. They showed the importance of machine learning in predicting the susceptible, infected, recovered, or exposed persons and how it could assist the control strategies to block the spread of infections.

In Chapter 11, titled "Machine Learning Modeling Techniques and Statistical Projections to Predict the Outbreak of COVID-19 with Implication to India" and written by Anne and Jeeva, the authors used machine learning regression models such as Least Absolute Shrinkage and Selection Operator (Lasso), Linear Regression, Ridge, Elastic-Net, Random Forest, Adaptive Boosting (AdaBoost), Light Gradient Boosted Machine (LGBM), Extreme Gradient Boosting (XGBoost), and Facebook Prophet Model to study and predict the impact of the COVID-19 outbreak and the exponential increase in mortality rate, number of confirmed cases, and recovery rate, using data collected in a university setting. The outcome of their study showed that concerned representatives can infer the necessary measures that can be adopted to control the outbreak of the COVID-19 pandemic.

In Chapter 12, titled "Lexical Modeling and Weighted Matrices for Analyses of COVID-19 Outbreak" and written by Kakulapati, Reddy, and Kumar, the authors analyzed the diagnostic methods for COVID-19 outbreak using mathematical modeling. They proposed an SVM optimal diagnostics model to identify the probable corona patient category with an enhanced AUC. The experimental and computational analyses demonstrated that the diagnosis of potential COVID-19 patients can be supported by adopting machine learning algorithms that learn linguistic diagnostics especially from the interpretation of verbal information obtained from elderly persons. Thus, they opined that such techniques can help in decision-making through useful predictions about issues such as treatment protocols and interference and can minimize the spread of COVID-19.

In Chapter 13, titled "Design of IoT-Enabled, Scalable Mobile Application for ASHA Workers in COVID-19 Data Management" and written by Manisha, Umadevi, Guggari, Ravikumar, Sonar, and Sreedharala, the authors described the development of an IoT-enabled mobile application (ASHA Bot) for fast data gathering and its management by Accredited Social Health Activist (ASHA) workers owing to the ineffectiveness of the data collection and submission process by ASHA's frontline workforces in rural and urban India. Their integrated solution consisted of a portable handheld device to capture body temperature with no direct contact and SpO_2 during the mass screening. The developed device was interfaced with the ASHA Bot mobile app and shown to be scalable for other statistical needs, such as field data collection and its management by zonal officers, and could be used by the stakeholders for COVID-19 data management.

In Chapter 14, titled "Reflecting on the Impact of COVID-19 on Healthcare and IT Sector with Special Emphasis on India: A Collection of Multifarious Cases with Few Empirical Evidences" and written by Mitra, Arockiam, Joseph, Costa, and Notts, the authors deliberated on the effects triggered by COVID-19 on the healthcare and technology sectors in India. To strengthen the impact of their study, the authors conducted a few surveys in selected districts through which robust empirical insights were obtained.

In Chapter 15, titled "Modeling of Cyber Threat Analysis and Vulnerability in IoT-Based Healthcare Systems During COVID" and written by Rawat, Mahor, Garg, Chouhan, Pachlasiya, and Telang, the authors proposed an IoT-attributes and threat analyzer for tracing malicious traffic in smart sensor environment, which they called IoT-ATATMT, to address the challenge of security of IoT devices, particularly in the healthcare industry, using IoT-Flock, an open-source sensor data-generating tool. The outcome of their study also includes an open-source application for transforming IoT-recorded Flock's traffic into an IoT dataset and studying different machine learning algorithms for detecting cyber threats to safeguard the e-healthcare system datasets.

The editors hope that this book and its contents will serve as a practical reference and scholarly material that will be beneficial for the healthcare and technology sectors, and the scientific community at large, ranging from industry and process innovators to computer and information systems designers, researchers, and students, to general consumers within the overlapping context of the COVID-19 pandemic and its impact on the aforementioned sectors. With this book, the editors hope to bridge the practical and theoretical gaps with lessons learned during the COVID-19 pandemic, particularly within the healthcare and technology sectors, so the book is aptly titled *Lessons from COVID-19: Impact on Healthcare Systems and Technology*.

We, the editors, thank the authors for their dedicated, expert, and impactful chapters and discussions that have formed the main scientific contributions and rich contents of this book. We also thank the production manager and the editorial team at Elsevier, especially Mica Ella Ortega and Rafael Teixeira, for their professional commitment and support in ensuring the successful coordination and completion of this book project.

Arturas Kaklauskas, Editor[a]
Ajith Abraham, Editor[b]
Kingsley Okoye, Editor[c]
Shankru Guggari, Editor[b]
[a]Vilnius Gediminas Technical University, Vilnius, Lithuania
[b]Machine Intelligence Research Labs, Auburn, WA, United States
[c]Tecnologico de Monterrey, Monterrey, Mexico

References

Alsamhi, S.H., Lee, B., Guizani, M., Kumar, N., Qiao, Y., Liu, X., 2021. Blockchain for decentralized multi-drone to combat COVID-19 and future pandemics: framework and proposed solutions. Trans. Emerg. Telecommun. Technol. 32. https://doi.org/10.1002/ETT.4255, e4255.

Aristovnik, A., Keržič, D., Ravšelj, D., Tomaževič, N., Umek, L., 2020. Impacts of the COVID-19 pandemic on life of higher education students: a global perspective. Sustainability 12 (20), 8438. https://doi.org/10.3390/SU12208438.

ATA, 2006. Telemedicine, Telehealth, and Health Information Technology an ATA Issue Paper Patient Care Health Provider. The American Telemedicine Association.

Bao, W., 2020. COVID-19 and online teaching in higher education: a case study of Peking University. Hum. Behav. Emerg. Technol. 2 (2), 113–115. https://doi.org/10.1002/HBE2.191.

Benabdallah, G., Bourgault, S., 2021. Remote learners, home makers: how digital fabrication was taught online during a pandemic. In: Conference on Human Factors in Computing Systems - Proceedings., https://doi.org/10.1145/3411764.3445450.

Bunch, A., Ardila, F., Castaño, R., Quiñonez, S., Corzo, L., 2020. Through the storm: automated peritoneal dialysis with remote patient monitoring during COVID-19 pandemic. Blood Purif., 1–4. https://doi.org/10.1159/000511407.

Chick, R.C., Clifton, G.T., Peace, K.M., Propper, B.W., Hale, D.F., Alseidi, A.A., Vreeland, T.J., 2020. Using technology to maintain the education of residents during the COVID-19 pandemic. J. Surg. Educ. 77 (4), 729–732. https://doi.org/10.1016/j.jsurg.2020.03.018.

Crawford, J., Butler-Henderson, K., Rudolph, J., Malkawi, B., Glowatz, M., Burton, R., Magni, P., Lam, S., 2020. COVID-19: 20 countries' higher education intra-period digital pedagogy responses. J. Appl. Learn. Teach. 3 (1), 1–20. https://doi.org/10.37074/jalt.2020.3.1.7.

Debre, M.J., Dijkstra, H., 2021. COVID-19 and policy responses by international organizations: crisis of liberal international order or window of opportunity? Global Pol. 12, 443–454. https://doi.org/10.1111/1758-5899.12975.

Díaz, C., Hincapié, M., Zapata-Cárdenas, M.-I., Toro-Rios, H.D.J., Valencia, D., Güemes-Castorena, D., 2021. Augmented reality mobile apps for cultural heritage reactivation. Comput. Electr. Eng. 93. https://doi.org/10.1016/j.compeleceng.2021.107281, 107281.

Evans, C., 2020. The coronavirus crisis and the technology sector. Bus. Econ. 55 (4), 253–266. https://doi.org/10.1057/s11369-020-00191-3.

Heinzelmann, P.J., Lugn, N.E., Kvedar, J.C., 2005. Telemedicine in the future. J. Telemed. Telecare 11, 384–390. https://doi.org/10.1177/1357633x0501100802.

IEEE, 2020a. COVID-19 Made Internet Access, Broadband and Hotspots an Educational Necessity, IEEE Transmitter. Available at: https://transmitter.ieee.org/covid-19-made-internet-access-broadband-and-hotspots-an-educational-necessity/. (Accessed 9 June 2020).

IEEE, 2020b. How COVID-19 is Affecting Industry 4.0 and Innovation. IEEE Transmitter. Available at: https://transmitter.ieee.org/how-covid-19-is-affecting-industry-4-0-and-the-future-of-innovation/. (Accessed 4 June 2020).

IEEE, 2021. Laying the Groundwork for the Future of Telehealth – IEEE Transmitter. Available at: https://transmitter.ieee.org/laying-the-groundwork-for-the-future-of-telehealth/. (Accessed 10 September 2021).

ILO, 2021. Global Impact and Policy Recommendations (COVID-19 and the World of Work).

Juan Ricardo Márquez, V., 2020. Teleconsultation in a pandemic due to coronavirus: Challenges for telemedicine in the post-COVID-19 era. Rev. Colomb. Gastroenterol. 35 (Suppl. 1), 5–16. https://doi.org/10.22516/25007440.543.

Kaye, A.D., Okeagu, C.N., Pham, A.D., Silva, R.A., Hurley, J.J., Arron, B.L., Sarfraz, N., Lee, H.N., Ghali, G.E., Gamble, J.W., Liu, H., Urman, R.D., Cornett, E.M., 2020. Economic impact of COVID-19 pandemic on healthcare facilities and systems: international perspectives. Best Pract. Res. Clin. Anaesthesiol. 35 (3), 293–306. https://doi.org/10.1016/J.BPA.2020.11.009.

Kummitha, R.K.R., 2020. Smart technologies for fighting pandemics: the techno- and human-driven approaches in controlling the virus transmission. Gov. Inf. Q. 37, 101481. https://doi.org/10.1016/j.giq.2020.101481.

Montenegro, P., Pinillos, L., Young, F., Aguilar, A., Tirado-Hurtado, I., Pinto, J.A., Vallejos, C., 2021. Telemedicine and the current opportunities for the management of oncological patients in Peru in the context of COVID-19 pandemic. Crit. Rev. Oncol. Hematol. 157, 103129. https://doi.org/10.1016/j.critrevonc.2020.103129.

Moynihan, R., Sanders, S., Michaleff, Z.A., Scott, A.M., Clark, J., To, E.J., Jones, M., Kitchener, E., Fox, M., Johansson, M., Lang, E., Duggan, A., Scott, I., Albarqouni, L., 2021. Impact of COVID-19 pandemic on utilisation of healthcare services: a systematic review. BMJ Open 11 (3). https://doi.org/10.1136/BMJOPEN-2020-045343, e045343.

Murphy, L., Markey, K., Donnell, C.O., Moloney, M., Doody, O., 2021. The impact of the COVID-19 pandemic and its related restrictions on people with pre-existent mental health conditions: a scoping review. Arch. Psychiatr. Nurs. 35 (4), 375–394. https://doi.org/10.1016/J.APNU.2021.05.002.

OECD, 2020. Regulatory Quality and COVID-19: Managing the Risks and Supporting the Recovery (Note by the Secretariat in consultation with the Chairs and the Bureaus of the Regulatory Policy Committee and the Network of Economic Regulators), Organisation for Economic Co-operation and Development. Available at: https://www.oecd.org/regreform/regulatory-policy/Regulatory-Quality-and-Coronavirus%20-(COVID-19)-web.pdf. (Accessed 30 August 2021).

OECD, 2021. How will COVID-19 Reshape Science, Technology and Innovation? OECD Policy Responses to Coronavirus (COVID-19). Available at: https://www.oecd.org/coronavirus/policy-responses/how-will-covid-19-reshape-science-technology-and-innovation-2332334d/. (Accessed 21 September 2021).

Okoye, K., Rodriguez-Tort, J.A., Escamilla, J., Hosseini, S., 2021. Technology-mediated teaching and learning process: a conceptual study of educators' response amidst the Covid-19 pandemic. Educ. Inf. Technol. 26, 7225–7257. https://doi.org/10.1007/s10639-021-10527-x.

Pokhrel, S., Chhetri, R., 2021. A literature review on impact of COVID-19 pandemic on teaching and learning. High. Edu. Future 8 (1), 133–141. https://doi.org/10.1177/2347631120983481.

Reimers, F., Schleicher, A., Saavedra, J., Tuominen, S., 2020. Supporting the Continuation of Teaching and Learning During the COVID-19 Pandemic, Annotated Resources for Online Learning © OECD 2020. Available at: https://www.oecd.org/education/Supporting-the-continuation-of-teaching-and-learning-during-the-COVID-19-pandemic.pdf. (Accessed 23 August 2020).

Ryu, S., 2012. Telemedicine: opportunities and developments in member states: report on the second global survey on eHealth 2009 (global observatory for eHealth series, volume 2). Healthc. Inform. Res. 18 (2), 153. https://doi.org/10.4258/hir.2012.18.2.153.

Salloml, P., 2020. Understanding COVID-19's impact on the technology sector | Deloitte Global, Respond: Guidance for Technology Executives. Available at: https://www2.deloitte.com/global/en/pages/about-deloitte/articles/covid-19/understanding-covid-19-s-impact-on-the-technology-sector-.html. (Accessed 31 August 2021).

Sohrabizadeh, S., Yousefian, S., Bahramzadeh, A., Vaziri, M.H., 2021. A systematic review of health sector responses to the coincidence of disasters and COVID-19. BMC Public Health 21 (1), 1–9. https://doi.org/10.1186/S12889-021-10806-9.

Tandon, P.N., 2020. COVID-19: impact on health of people & wealth of nations. Indian J. Med. Res. 151 (2–3), 121. https://doi.org/10.4103/IJMR.IJMR_664_20.

Tran, T., Hoang, A.-D., Nguyen, Y.-C., Nguyen, L.-C., Ta, N.-T., Pham, Q.-H., Pham, C.-X., Le, Q.-A., Dinh, V.-H., Nguyen, T.-T., 2020. Toward sustainable learning during school suspension: socioeconomic, occupational aspirations, and learning behavior of Vietnamese students during COVID-19. Sustainability 12 (10), 4195. https://doi.org/10.3390/SU12104195.

UN, 2021a. COVID-19 to Slash Global Economic Output by $8.5 Trillion Over Next Two Years | United Nations. Available at: https://www.un.org/en/desa/covid-19-slash-global-economic-output-85-trillion-over-next-two-years. (Accessed 30 August 2021).

UN, 2021b. Everyone Included: Social Impact of COVID-19. Department of Economic and Social Affairs. Available at: https://www.un.org/development/desa/dspd/everyone-included-covid-19.html. (Accessed 30 August 2021).

UNESCO, 2016. UNESCO Strategy on Education for Health and Well-Being: Contributing to the Sustainable Development Goals - UNESCO Digital Library. Available at: https://unesdoc.unesco.org/ark:/48223/pf0000246453. (Accessed 27 June 2020).

UNESCO, 2020. Covid-19 Education: From Disruption to Recovery. School Closures Caused by Coronavirus (Covid-19). Available at: https://en.unesco.org/covid19/educationresponse. (Accessed 9 September 2020).

UNESCO, 2021. Global Education Coalition. Available at: https://en.unesco.org/covid19/educationresponse/globalcoalition. (Accessed 17 August 2021).

Viner, R.M., Russell, S.J., Croker, H., Packer, J., Ward, J., Stansfield, C., Mytton, O., Bonell, C., Booy, R., 2020. School closure and management practices during coronavirus outbreaks including COVID-19: a rapid systematic review. Lancet Child Adolesc. Health 4 (5), 397–404. https://doi.org/10.1016/S2352-4642(20)30095-X.

WHO, 2020. Impact of COVID-19 on People's Livelihoods, Their Health and our Food Systems. Available at: https://www.who.int/news/item/13-10-2020-impact-of-covid-19-on-people's-livelihoods-their-health-and-our-food-systems. (Accessed 30 August 2021).

WHO, 2021. The Impact of COVID-19 on Global Health Goals. Available at: https://www.who.int/news-room/spotlight/the-impact-of-covid-19-on-global-health-goals. (Accessed 30 August 2021).

WHO Global Observatory for e-Health, 2010. Opportunities and Developments Report on the Second Global Survey on eHealth Global Observatory for eHealth Series-Volume 2 TELEMEDICINE in Member States. Available at: https://www.who.int/goe/publications/goe_telemedicine_2010.pdf. (Accessed 21 March 2021).

Woolliscroft, J.O., 2020. Innovation in response to the COVID-19 pandemic crisis. Acad. Med. 95 (8), 1140–1142. https://doi.org/10.1097/ACM.0000000000003402.

Wootton, R., 2008. Telemedicine support for the developing world. J. Telemed. Telecare 14 (3), 109–114. https://doi.org/10.1258/jtt.2008.003001.

Acknowledgments

We express our gratitude to all the authors for submitting their novel work for this edited book. Without their support, this work would not have been possible. We are thankful to the following respected reviewers for their timely support and valuable inputs to improve the quality of the book.

Prof. Dr. Ing. Dipl. Math. Radu-Emil Precup
Corresponding member of The Romanian Academy
Senior Member, IEEE
Faculty of Automation and Computers, Department of Automation and Applied Informatics, Politehnica University of Timisoara, Timisoara, Romania

Prof. Tzung-Pei Hong
Chair Professor, Department of Computer Science and Information Engineering, AI Research Center, National University of Kaohsiung, Nan-Tzu District, Kaohsiung, Taiwan

Prof. Dr. Laura García Hernández
Area of Project Engineering, University of Córdoba, Spain

Prof. Onur Seref, PhD
Associate Professor, Business Information Technology, Virginia Tech, Blacksburg, VA, United States

Prof. Fabio Scotti
Department of Computer Science, Università degli Studi di Milano, Milano, Italy

Prof. Laith Abualigah
Assistant Professor, Software Engineering Department, Amman Arab University, Jordan

Finally, we convey our sincere thanks to all those who helped us directly or indirectly to complete this work.

Editorial Team

CHAPTER ONE

COVID-19: Origin, epidemiology, virology, pathogenesis, and treatment

Anuj Sharma[a], Ashok Kumar Ahirwar[b], Smita R. Sorte[c], and Sachin B. Rathod[d]

[a]All India Institute of Medical Sciences, Nagpur, Maharashtra, India
[b]Department of Biochemistry, UCMS, Delhi, India
[c]Department of Physiology, All India Institute of Medical Sciences, Nagpur, Maharashtra, India
[d]Department of Physiology, Indira Gandhi Government Medical College, Nagpur, Maharashtra, India

1 Introduction

COVID-19 (or Coronavirus Disease) originated in China (Hubei provenance, Wuhan city). The first recorded illness occurred in December 2019. It has affected all parts of the world, and the WHO designated the COVID-19 illness, caused by the new Coronavirus SARS-CoV-2, a pandemic on March 11, 2020 (Cucinotta and Vanelli, 2020). It now accounted for the worse-hit and most dreaded pandemic after the Spanish flu in 1920. From December 18, 2019, to December 29, 2019, 5 patients were hospitalized with acute respiratory distress syndrome (ARDS), and one died in China. This progressed to 41 confirmed cases of COVID-19 by January 2, 2020 (most of the patients were suffering from other comorbidities like hypertension, diabetes, or cardiovascular diseases). By January 22, 2020, 571 cases were positive in 25 provinces of China. By January 25, 2020, 1975 positive cases with 56 deaths were reported. By January 30, 2020, this progressed to 7731 cases in China, and along with this, 90 more cases were reported from other countries including India. This progressed to 31,161 cases in China on February 7, 2020 (Zhu et al., 2020; Singhal, 2020; Wu et al., 2020a; Sohrabi, 2020).

The initial source of origin of COVID-19 is unclear, but many possible theories are being proposed. Notable cases have been natural selection in an animal source followed by zoonotic transmission, natural selection in a human source followed by zoonotic transfer, selection during the passage, and genetically modified organisms artificially manufactured in the laboratory. The primitive theory suggested the spread from the Hunan seafood

Lessons from COVID-19
https://doi.org/10.1016/B978-0-323-99878-9.00012-1

market of China probably from an animal source. The COVID-19 caused by the SARS-CoV-2 virus (Severe Acute Respiratory Syndrome Coronavirus-2), and the Coronavirus isolated from bats have 96% similarity, while the Coronavirus isolated from pangolins has 85.5 to 92.4% similarity to SARS-CoV-2, according to research. An examination of the phylogenetic relationship of SARS-CoV-2 suggested that it may have evolved from bats or pangolins. Some debatable speculations suggest that it is a man-made virus, intentionally synthesized in the laboratory but was unintentionally emancipated from a laboratory of Wuhan, China though this theory is not fully supported (Sun et al., 2020).

Coronavirus has been responsible for numerous outbreaks, including the SARS-CoV-1 (severe acute respiratory syndrome) epidemic in China in 2003, which resulted in 8098 cases and 774 fatalities (Pal et al., 2020); moreover, other outbreaks in Saudi Arabia (2012) included the Middle East respiratory syndrome MERS, which resulted in 2143 laboratory-confirmed cases with 750 fatalities in 24 countries (Park, 2020).

The pandemic is straining healthcare systems all over the world. Even the developed nations are finding it difficult to cope up with the situation. USA, UK, Spain, and Italy have engaged the assistance of retired health professionals in the battle against the Pandemic. In developing countries like India, the situation is even worse. The Pandemic is posing a significant challenge to the already fragile healthcare system of the country. India is a developing country struggling to provide quality and affordable healthcare facilities with inadequate health personnel, limited financial resources, and unavailable medications (Agampodi et al., 2015; McGregor et al., 2014). The ongoing Pandemic further worsens the situation. The health care system was under tremendous pressure due to the increased infectivity of the SARS-Cov-2 virus. The testing capacity was inadequate for the large Indian population. In order to control the pandemic situation, the government implemented certain tough decisions like the closure of public places, mass lockdown, restricted people's movement, enlisted containment zones, mobilization of health personnel to treat patients of the COVID-19 infection. Government converted hospitals, hotels, and many complexes to COVID care centers, COVID Isolation centers, and COVID wards for COVID-suspected and -infected patients. This has presented a significant issue for chronic illnesses, which requires regular visits, check-ups, and prescriptions since it became difficult for them to visit healthcare facilities and meet their physicians in lockdown (Kretchy et al., 2021). Health care workers (HCW) were undergoing tremendous physical and mental stress due to long working hours and were at the risk of acquiring COVID-19 due to increased virus load exposure.

For prevention of infection, to deliver state of the art patient care and treatment, and reduce the load on the health care system, it is necessary to understand in depth the viral morphology, pathogenesis, clinical features, diagnosis, targeted drugs, and vaccine.

2 Viral morphology

SARS-CoV-2 is an affiliate of the genus *Beta-coronaviruses*, sub-*sarbeco virus*, *coronaviridae* family. It has two subfamilies, *orthrocoroanviridae* and *Toroviridae*. SARS-CoV-2 belongs to the subfamily *orthrocoronaviridae*; order *Nidovirales* belongs to the genus of *Betacoronaviridae* (Pal et al., 2020).

SARS-CoV-2 is an enclosed virus with positive-sense RNA that is single-stranded (ssRNA), and under electron microscopy, Coronavirus appears as coroneted round or elliptical, often polymorphic form with a 70 to 90 nm diameter. Its carrier's dub, petal, or crown-shaped peplomer spikes give the solar Corona's appearance; it has helical symmetry, as shown in Fig. 1.

Coronaviruses have a genomic size ranging from 26 to 32 kilobases. The hemagglutinin-esterase gene is absent in the SARS-CoV-2 genome: genome expresses structural proteins, nonstructural proteins, and accessory proteins such as ORFs. The virus has four main structural proteins: spike surface glycoprotein (S), transmembrane protein (M), nucleocapsid protein (N), and envelope polypeptide (E). It has 16 nonstructural proteins (nsps); the critical nonstructural proteins are 3-chymotrypsin-like protease (3CL), Papain-like Protease (P.L.), helicase (H), and RNA-dependent

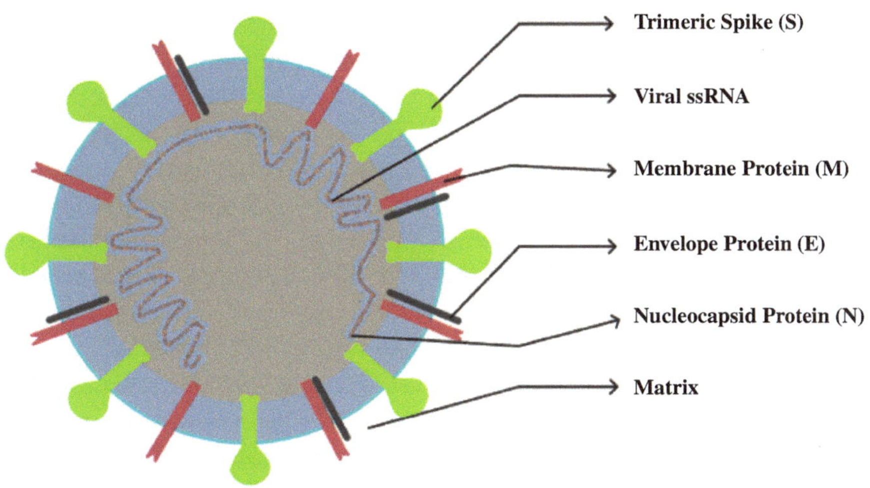

Fig. 1 SARS-CoV-2 structure. *(Credit: Drawn by Author Dr. Ashok Ahirwar.)*

RNA Polymerase (RDRP) are the most significant. A lipid bilayer is formed from the host membrane, the Coronavirus surface protein- spike, membrane, and envelope are encased, with the helical nucleocapsid holding viral RNA enclosed within it (Kumar et al., 2020).

The M and E proteins are needed for the assembly and budding of the virus to be replicated. The fusion viral glycoprotein S comprises two subassemblies, S1 and S2, that interact with the ACE2 receptor to internalize the virus into the host cell and form virions and its assembly. S protein also governs host tropism and transmission capability. (N) protein serves as a structural component of the helical nucleocapsid. It is necessary for the pathogenesis, replication, and packaging of viral RNA. Coronavirus is UV- and heat-sensitive. This virus is inactivated by lipid solvents, including ethanol, chlorine disinfectants, chlorhexidine, peroxyacetic acid, and chloroform (Pal et al., 2020).

3 Viral pathogenesis

The key element determining the COVID infection is the triumphant entry of the virus in the host cell followed by its replication and multiplication in the host cell utilizing the host cellular apparatus followed by spreading the virus by shedding out of the host cells. The viral envelope of SARS-CoV has spike (S) protein. The S protein has a receptor-binding region that demonstrates an intense binding affinity for the extracellular region of angiotensin-converting enzyme 2 (ACE2) of host cells of various organs, mainly the lungs and the heart. As the S protein connects with the ACE2 receptor, the host serine two transmembrane protease TMPRSS2 induces splitting of S protein to produce S1 and S2 subunits. This is essential for fusing the virus membrane with the host cell membrane and endocytosis-mediated internalization of the complex (Hoffman et al., 2020; Iwata-Yoshikawa et al., 2019). The virus-encoded proteinases are released into the host cytoplasm, where they translate the viral RNA and transform it into the polyprotein replicator polyproteins pp1a and pp1b, which are then broken down into smaller proteins by virus-encoded proteinases. Following the triumphant entry of the virus in the host cell, the virus replicates and multiplication using host cellular equipment and apparatus. The replicated virus then breaks the host cell and gets shed off to infect the other tissues. The spike protein also activates ADAM-17/TACE, which increases the release of TNF-α (Heurich et al., 2014). The disease's incubation period is 5 to 7 days, i.e., the time between viral entry in the body and the appearance of symptoms. Depending upon the multiple factors, including individual genetic makeup and the immune response, the person can be asymptomatic or develop symptomatic diseases, which may progress to various stages of COVID-19.

4 Stages of COVID-19

Stage 1-Asymptomatic stage

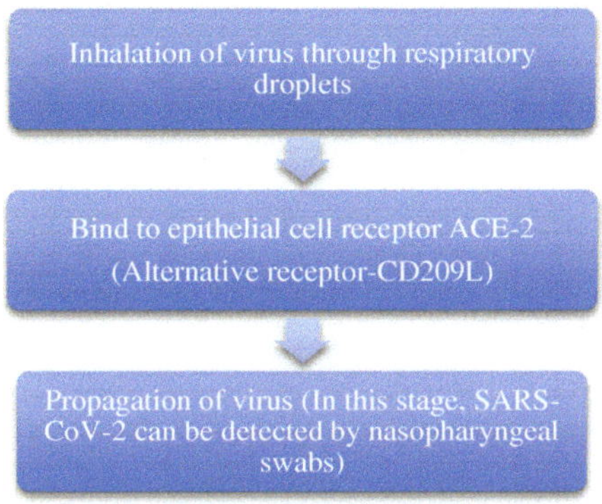

During this stage, the virus multiplies in the body. The person does not develop any symptoms.

Stage 2 – Response of upper airway and conducting airway

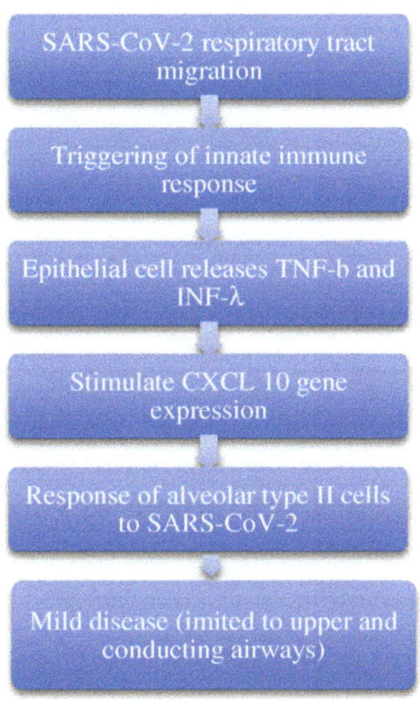

After five days of contact with the symptomatic patient or entry of the virus into the body, the person can be tested positive on RT-PCR tests. COVID-19 illness primarily affects the respiratory system, although it may manifest in other extrapulmonary organs like the nervous system, gastrointestinal system, liver, heart, and kidney. Clinical manifestations are seen in this stage. COVID-19 symptoms range from mild to severe dry cough, fatigue, fever, headache, sore throat, myalgia or arthralgia, chills, loss of taste, loss of smell (anosmia), nausea, vomiting, diarrhea, hemoptysis, nasal congestion, conjunctival congestion, rhinitis, metabolic acidosis, septic shock, coagulation dysfunction, lymphopenia, and hypoxemia (Baj et al., 2020).

Stage 3 – Hypoxia and ground glass infiltration in lungs and progression to ARDS (20% patients progress to this stage.)

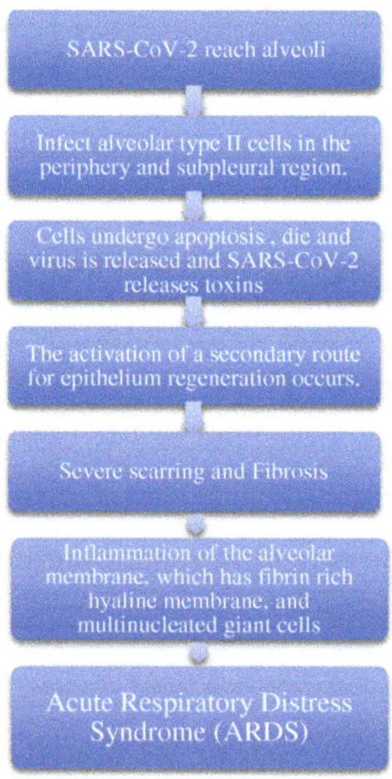

Although most people's symptoms vary from mild to moderate, the disease's severity and medical complications may vary. The case fatality rate is approximately 2.2%. As the disease progress to this stage, pneumonia develops on the 9th day of infection. Other complications include pneumonia, acute respiratory distress syndrome (ARDS), superimposed viral and bacterial infections, thrombosis and embolism, acute renal damage, gastrointestinal illness, hepatocellular damage, ketosis, hyperglycemia, neurological complications, ocular complications, dermatologic manifestations, cardiac abnormalities, myocardial dysfunction, myocarditis, acute coronary syndrome, multiple organ dysfunction syndromes (Sarkesh et al., 2020).

The development of poor outcomes and mortality among patients with comorbidities such as obesity, diabetes mellitus, hypertension, cardiovascular disease, renal disease, and cancer is more likely. SARS-CoV-2 induces the innate immune system and the adaptive immune system. The activated immune system releases many cytokines into the body, including interleukin 6 (IL-6), often known as a "cytokine storm" or cytokine released syndrome (CRS). The term "cytokine storm" refers to raised inflammatory markers, particularly cytokines 5 and 6 (Chau et al., 2020). Many patients with severe COVID-19 have been diagnosed with cytokine released syndrome, which had resulted in the deaths of COVID-19 patients (Zhang et al., 2020). The essential factor in preventing the progression of diseases and reducing mortality is the early detection of disease, which helps clinicians provide necessary and timely patient care and treatment.

5 Laboratory diagnosis for screening and diagnosis of patients with COVID-19

Membrane protein (M), Spike protein (S), nucleocapsid protein (N), and envelope protein (E) are the structural proteins of the COVID virus. The test detects antibodies against S protein. Lateral flow immunoassays are being developed to find COVID-19 virus antigens or antibodies in a short period. Immunoassays are designed to detect COVID-19 monoclonal antibodies IgM or IgG against COVID-19 infection. Nevertheless, these methods have poor sensitivity. Serology is helpful but nonspecific, and several weeks are required for specific IgG responses. Time is crucial in diagnosis hence serology detection may not be beneficial in active case diagnosis but can be used to find the previous exposure via infection or vaccine. The use of cell culture for diagnostic purposes is not advised (la Marca et al., 2020). Randomization of the amplification deep sequencing techniques is useful for the identification of COVID-19 in its early stages. These technologies will discover future mutations of the virus, but they are currently impractical for diagnosis. RT-PCR is a molecular diagnostic test (Tang et al., 2020). Amplification occurs in closed systems, which reduces the number of false-positive outcomes. ssRNA, structural proteins such as helicase protein (HEL), an envelope protein (E), transmembrane protein (M), and nucleocapsid protein (N) can be employed in PCR experiments.

Additionally, accessory genes such as RNA-dependent RNA polymerase (RdRp), hemagglutinin-esterase (HE), open reading frames ORF 1a, and ORF 1b can be targeted. High viral loads in specimens obtained from the upper and lower respiratory tracts may be identified within 5 to 6 days after the onset of symptoms. For diagnosis of COVID-19, the preferred site for specimen collection in the upper respiratory tract is nasopharynx swab or oropharynx swab and lower respiratory tract is sputum or bronchoalveolar lavage after intubation. Due to the inherent quality control, oropharyngeal (O.P.) swabs are more used than nasopharyngeal (N.P.) swabs. The greatest concentration of COVID-19 viral is obtained in bronchoalveolar lavage. Following collection, these samples are placed into a universal viral transport medium kept refrigerated (Tang et al., 2020).

Enteric involvement in individuals with severe Coronavirus infection was associated with high viral RNA levels in fecal material and late sledding from the respiratory system. As a result, a stool sample or a rectal swab may be employed. The SARS Coronavirus was also discovered inside erythrocytes (Cheng et al., 2007).

In contrast to the Centers for Disease Control and Prevention, which recommends screening with two nucleocapsid proteins (N1 and N2), the World Health Organization recommends screening with the E gene first, followed by the RdRp gene. It is preferable to have at least one conserved area and one unique region to guard against the effects of genetic drift, which is especially essential when the virus grows inside a new population (Tang et al., 2020).

Blood tests: Leukocytosis, raised serum ferritin, D-dimer, C-reactive protein, raised concentrations of plasma proinflammatory cytokines like IL-1B**,** IL-1RA**,** IL-2, IL-7,8,9,10**,** basic PGF 2**,** GCSF**,** GMCSF**,** IPN-ϒ**,** TNF-α**,** and VEGF-A are seen in COVID-19-infected person (Costela-Ruiz et al., 2020).

X-ray findings of COVID-19: Chest X-ray (CXR) is an essential noninvasive supporting diagnostic for detecting SARS-COV-2 infection in patients. X-ray of the patient's chest reveals patchy reticulonodular or reticulonodular opacities, multifocal, bilateral ground-glass opacities, and extensive pulmonary consolidations in the lungs, consistent with the diagnosis of COVID-19 (Chandra et al., 2021).

CT scan findings of COVID-19: Bilateral diffusely distributed rounded nodules, ground-glass appearance, and small patchy shadows are seen in pulmonary parenchymal. Sometimes, irregular interlobular pleural thickening and pleural effusion are also evident in COVID-19-infected patients.

Histopathology of COVID-19: On biopsy of lung tissue, specific characteristic findings are seen such as infiltration of mononuclear inflammatory cells into the interstitial space, development of hyaline membranes, and desquamation of pneumocytes, multinucleated giant cells along with atypically enlarged pneumocytes featured with large and prominent nuclei, and amphiphilic granular cytoplasm in interalveolar spaces, which all suggests viral cytopathology (Cheung et al., 2004; Tian et al., 2020).

6 Drugs used in COVID-19 till now with newer drug possibilities tried for infection

To date, there are no single drugs against COVID-19, but they can be combated pharmacologically with combinations of drugs, interferon therapies, oligonucleotides, peptides, monoclonal antibodies, and supportive treatments with steroids, antibiotics, antiparasitic, anticoagulants, multivitamin, and oxygen therapy. The combination of drugs treatment varies according to the severity of diseases and blood oxygen levels (Spo2) of the patient.

RT-PCR-positive and asymptomatic patients need home or institution quarantine with supportive treatments with multivitamins, viz., vitamin D, vitamin C, vitamin E, and minerals like Zinc.

Vitamins A, C, D, and E play potentially beneficial function like immunomodulation, antioxidant effects, augmenting local paracrine signaling and enhancing natural barriers in the fight against COVID-19 (Jovic et al., 2020). Vitamin D (1,25(O.H.)2D3) demonstrates potent antimicrobial and antiinflammatory effects. It may exhibit immunomodulatory effects by regulating both adaptive and innate immunity in COVID-19 patients. Vitamin D can inhibit interleukin IL-2 and IL-17, the inflammatory T cell cytokines. Vitamin D can inhibit toll-like receptors found on the surface of monocytes. Vitamin D supplementation at high doses lowers the levels of the pro-inflammatory cytokine IL-6, which is produced by peripheral mononuclear cells (PMNs) (Cutolo et al., 2020; Leaf and Ginde, 2021). Zinc has been claimed to augment the ability of polymorphonuclear cells to combat infection. Zinc plays an essential role in pathogen removal signal transduction pathways and stimulating cell-mediated immunity by controlling differentiating factors (Gammoh and Rink, 2017).

Depending on the severity of the patient, a symptomatic patient needs to be transferred to a COVID care center or admitted to COVID hospital and needs a combination of drugs, interferon therapies, oligonucleotides, peptides, monoclonal antibodies, and supportive treatments with steroids, antibiotics, antiparasitic, anticoagulants, multivitamin, and oxygen therapy. Based on the mechanisms of action, the anti-COVID drugs can be divided into following categories: Viral entry inhibitors, those that inhibit RNA polymerase or RNA synthesis by acting on work on viral proteins and enzymes or human enzymes or receptors; Inhibitors of viral protein synthesis; those that work on membrane, nucleocapsid, or envelope proteins; drugs that target structural proteins, such as those that impede self-assembly or those that prevent the virus from attaching itself to ACE2 (Wu et al., 2020b).

Viral entry inhibitors—It is believed that aminoquinolines, such as hydroxychloroquine and chloroquine, prevent viral particles from adhering to cell surface receptors by interfering with the glycosylation of these receptors. This results in the cell not being able to accept COVID-19 into the cell. The medication operates on quinone reductase-2, similar to UDP-*N*-acetylglucosamine 2-epimerases (UNEs), and inhibits quinone reductase-2 by binding to the enzyme. The synthesis of sialic acid involves the use of UNEs in the process. In cell transmembrane proteins, sialic acids are structural components of sugar molecules that are accessible for binding, and they are essential factors in recognizing ligands by the protein. It is also possible that chloroquine hinders the pH-dependent access of COVID viruses into endosomes, preventing virus cell fusion (Devaux et al., 2020). For the fusion of endosomal and viral membranes, the pH of the cell must be acidic. This results in the transport of the SARS-CoV genome to the cytoplasm of the cell. Absent an antiviral medication, the virus enters the cell and travels to the lysosome, where the combination of enzymatic activity and low pH causes the virus to be cleaved, releasing replication enzymes and viral RNA. In addition to the rapid increase in endosomal pH, the inhibition of endocytosis and the disruption of endosome-virus fusion have all been hypothesized to be the mechanisms of chloroquine's antiviral effect (Colson et al., 2020). These medications have been associated with the side effects of nausea, vomiting, anorexia, uncontrolled itching, epigastric discomfort, unease, trouble adjusting to new surroundings, and headaches. Using this product for an extended period can result in vision loss owing to retinal damage; corneal deposits can also form; hearing loss; rashes; photo allergies; mental abnormalities; myopathy; and graying of the hair. It should be avoided in the presence of liver damage, severe gastrointestinal symptoms (including diarrhea), neurological, retinal, and hematological illnesses. Attacks of seizure, porphyria, and psoriasis are all possible side effects of this medication. The drug should never be administered in conjunction with mefloquine, amiodarone, or other antiarrhythmic medications (Geleris et al., 2020).

6.1 Viral RNA polymerase inhibitors/RNA synthetase inhibitors

Favipiravir (T-705) is a synthetic prodrug, Guanosine nucleotide analog, enzyme RNA-dependent-RNA-polymerase (RdRp) inhibitor. RdRp is a protease enzyme involved in RNA replication from an intermediate template (Lung et al., 2020). The RNA virus converts favipiravir into an active phosphoribosylated form; it is mistaken by the enzyme RNA-dependent RNA-polymerase (RdRp) and replaces purine nucleotide. It gets amalgamated in the viral RNA strand, preventing further extension. Thus inhibits the activity and terminates the viral protein synthesis (Jean et al., 2020; McKee et al., 2020). As a chain terminator, the medication prevents the creation of viral genomic RNA (Shiraki and Daikoku, 2020). It is approved in Japan for treating the emergency influenza infections pandemic in the year 2014.

Remdesivir (RDV) is a 10-cyano-substituted adenosine analog, a phosphoramidite prodrug, and an enzyme that blocks RdRp and hampering viral nucleic acid amalgamation by establishing a link with the active region of RdRp (Jean et al., 2020). In addition, the exoribonuclease of SRS-CoV-2, which is involved in the prevention of proofreading, is involved in the action of RDV. The viral RNA transcription is prevented from progressing further than necessary (Cao et al., 2020). Ribavirin, Sofosbuvir, Galidesivir, and Tenofovir are other effective medicines against SARS-CoV-2 with a strong affinity for its RdRp (Elfiky, 2020).

6.2 Inhibitors of viral protein synthesis

Lopinavir is a protease inhibitor that may prevent the activity of 3CLpro, hence interrupt viral replication and liberation from host cells. It is an antiretroviral drug used for the treating of HIV.

Ritonavir increases the half-life of lopinavir by inhibiting its metabolizing enzyme cytochrome P450 3A (Dorward et al., 2020). The protease inhibitors target enzymes involved in virus replication like 3C-like protease and papain-like protease (Jean et al., 2020).

6.3 Immunomodulators

Ivermectin is an FDA-approved antiparasitic medication with a broad spectrum of activity. After 48 h of SARS-CoV-2 infection, this medication reduced viral RNA by up to 5000-fold by preventing nuclear of host and viral proteins via inhibition of importin (Caly et al., 2020). Combining Ivermectin with doxycycline (antibiotic) improved the recovery and prevented the progression of diseases to severe outcomes in adults with COVID-19 infection (Mahmud et al., 2021).

Tocilizumab (TZM) is a monoclonal antibody against membrane-bound and soluble interleukin-6 receptors. The drug blocks signal transduction through the mIL-6R and sIL-6R, which are found on the membrane of the immune system (Mihara et al., 2005).

Itolizumab is a monoclonal antibody anti-CD6 *humanized IgG1*. CD-6 plays a vital role in grooming, stimulation, and T-cell differentiation. Itolizumab binds to domain-1 of CD-6, thus drastically decreases the T-cell proliferation and downregulation of cytokines/chemokines production. Steroids are known for their antiinflammatory property hence beneficial in the treatment of COVID-19 (Dogra et al., 2017). Additionally, leronlimab (PRO140), a C—C chemokine receptor type 5 (CCR5) antagonist, and a humanized monoclonal antibody are being investigated as an experimental new medication to treat COVID-19 (Agresti et al., 2021). A serine protease is a type of enzyme that breaks down amino acids. TMPRSS2 is a host cell factor that is required for the priming of S proteins. The serine protease inhibitor "camostat mesylate," which inhibits the activity of the TMPRSS2 enzyme, has been licensed for human use in Japan (Zhou et al., 2015; Kawase et al., 2012).

7 Potential sites for the target for vaccine and drug development

A vaccine strategy may be used to reduce illness severity, limit viral transmission, and prevent future infections. It is also effective in preventing future infections. The critical target for vaccine development is structural proteins, positive-sense RNA of the virus, DNA, and biopolymers. The targets for protein vaccine are two subunits S1 and S2 of S protein (Spike) protein of Coronavirus that facilitate virus entry using ACE-2, E protein embedded in an envelope of the virus, Matrix (M) protein responsible for budding of the virus, Nucleocapsid protein which encapsulates the genetic material ssRNA of virus and also facilitates RNA synthesis (Naz et al., 2020).

Vaccines are often designed to elicit humoral immunity and cell-mediated immunity via T killer cells that detect and destroy contaminated cells. A straightforward technique is to introduce a virus into the body after being inactivated using chemicals, gamma irradiation, or heat. The expressed proteins or the degraded viral surface act as an antigen and triggered neutralizing antibiotics (Gilbert, 2012).

Another approach is to introduce weakened or attenuated copies of the virus that replicate exclusively inside the host cell but still include enough antigens to trigger an immune response from the host cell itself. While employing a nonvirulent organism for demonstration purposes is less safe than using an inactivated virus and has been linked to disease outbreaks, it is preferable to generate the mild infection necessary for developing an efficient adaptive immune response (Lee et al., 2012).

The type of immune response produced and its intensity depend on the strain of the virus used. A more targeted approach induces an adaptive immune response immunogenic viral protein, or their fragments are introduced into the body to stimulate humoral immunity as well as cell-mediated immunity. Another method can be targeting RNA of virus for the vaccine, i.e., RNA-specific vaccines of Coronavirus can be developed. However, the limitations and difficulties are the high mutation rates of the virus, antigenic drift seen in viruses, and genetic variability. The selection of the most appropriate viral genome sequence is of tremendous significance. Because a virus is an obligatory intracellular parasite that needs the presence of a matched host cell in order to reproduce, all vaccine development methods should aim to prevent the virus from attaching itself to the host cell or from being recognized by the host cell's receptors (Pandey et al., 2020). Also, safer attenuated vaccines can be tried for vaccine development via recombinant DNA technology; replicating vectors can be adenoviruses, measles virus, poxviruses, and vesicular stomatitis viruses, which are earlier used as vectors for vaccine delivery to target sites earlier. Previously, these viruses were not dangerous to humans and did not have a genetically changed genome. The genome is changed to contain the coding sequence for the protein/subunit antigen required for optimal expression, assembly, and packaging into the recombinant virus throughout the recombinant viral production process. The creation of mRNA vaccines is similar to the creation of DNA viruses; however, they run the risk of being integrated into the host genome. They might be conventional mRNA vaccinations or ones that utilize mRNA amplifying vaccines. Nonetheless, developing a vaccine resistant to a pandemic like SARS-CoV-2 is critical for humanity's protection, particularly for infectious diseases. As a result, work must be done on these issues (Tse et al., 2020).

8 Conclusion

According to phylogenetic analysis, the SARS-CoV-2 virus may have originated from bats or pangolins, which had affected millions with the severity of symptoms like pulmonary edema, ARDS, sepsis, metabolic syndrome, acidosis, coagulation, lymphopenia, hypoxemia, multiorgan failure, and eventually mortality. Medications, interferon treatments, oligonucleotides, peptides, and monoclonal antibodies may be used to treat COVID-19 pharmacologically. There have been a variety of antivirals used in the treatment of COVID-19, including Favipiravir, Remdesivir (an RNA dependent RNA polymerase inhibitor), Lopinavir and Ritonavir (Retroviral protease inhibitors), Tocilizumab (TZM), Itolizumab, and the combination of doxycycline (an antibiotic) and Ivermectin (antiparasitic). Ribavirin, Sofosbuvir, Galidesivir, and Tenofovir are some of the other effective medicines against SARS-CoV-2. In order to prevent the spread of the pandemic, world health agencies have advised preventive measures such as hand washing, the use of face masks and hand sanitizer, and keeping a safe distance. However, vaccination is a possible strategy to prevent the pandemic from spreading.

References

Agampodi, T.C., et al., 2015. Measurement of social capital in relation to health in low- and middle-income countries (LMIC): a systematic review. Soc. Sci. Med. 1982 (128), 95–104. https://doi.org/10.1016/J.SOCSCIMED.2015.01.005.

Agresti, N., et al., 2021. Disruption of CCR5 signaling to treat COVID-19-associated cytokine storm: case series of four critically ill patients treated with leronlimab. J. Translat. Autoimmun. 4. https://doi.org/10.1016/J.JTAUTO.2021.100083, 100083.

Baj, J., et al., 2020. COVID-19: specific and non-specific clinical manifestations and symptoms: the current state of knowledge. J. Clin. Med. 9, 1753. https://doi.org/10.3390/JCM9061753.

Caly, L., et al., 2020. The FDA-approved drug ivermectin inhibits the replication of SARS-CoV-2 in vitro. Antiviral Res. 178. https://doi.org/10.1016/J.ANTIVIRAL.2020.104787.

Cao, Y., Deng, Q., Dai, S., 2020. Remdesivir for severe acute respiratory syndrome coronavirus 2 causing COVID-19: an evaluation of the evidence. Travel Med. Infect. Dis. 35. https://doi.org/10.1016/J.TMAID.2020.101647, 101647.

Chandra, T.B., et al., 2021. Coronavirus disease (COVID-19) detection in chest X-ray images using majority voting-based classifier ensemble. Expert Syst. Appl. 165. https://doi.org/10.1016/J.ESWA.2020.113909, 113909.

Chau, V.Q., et al., 2020. The imperfect cytokine storm: severe COVID-19 with ARDS in a patient on durable LVAD support. JACC. Case Rep. 2, 1315–1320. https://doi.org/10.1016/J.JACCAS.2020.04.001.

Cheng, V.C., et al., 2007. Severe acute respiratory syndrome coronavirus as an agent of emerging and reemerging infection. Clin. Microbiol. Rev. 20, 660–694. https://doi.org/10.1128/CMR.00023-07.

Cheung, O.Y., et al., 2004. The spectrum of pathological changes in severe acute respiratory syndrome (SARS). Histopathology 45, 119–124. https://doi.org/10.1111/J.1365-2559.2004.01926.X.

Colson, P., et al., 2020. Chloroquine and hydroxychloroquine as available weapons to fight COVID-19. Int. J. Antimicrob. Agents 55. https://doi.org/10.1016/J.IJANTIMICAG.2020.105932, 105932.

Costela-Ruiz, V.J., et al., 2020. SARS-CoV-2 infection: the role of cytokines in COVID-19 disease. Cytokine Growth Factor Rev. 54, 62. https://doi.org/10.1016/J.CYTOGFR.2020.06.001.

Cucinotta, D., Vanelli, M., 2020. WHO declares COVID-19 a pandemic. Acta Biomedica 91, 157–160. https://doi.org/10.23750/abm.v91i1.9397.

Cutolo, M., Paolino, S., Smith, V., 2020. Evidences for a protective role of vitamin D in COVID-19. RMD Open 6, e001454. https://doi.org/10.1136/RMDOPEN-2020-001454.

Devaux, C.A., et al., 2020. New insights on the antiviral effects of chloroquine against coronavirus: what to expect for COVID-19? Int. J. Antimicrob. Agents 55. https://doi.org/10.1016/J.IJANTIMICAG.2020.105938, 105938.

Dogra, S., Uprety, S., Suresh, S.H., 2017. Itolizumab, a novel anti-CD6 monoclonal antibody: a safe and efficacious biologic agent for management of psoriasis. Expert Opin. Biol. Ther. 17, 395–402. https://doi.org/10.1080/14712598.2017.1279601.

Dorward, J., et al., 2020. The protease inhibitor lopinavir, boosted with ritonavir, as treatment for COVID-19: a rapid review. Antivir. Ther. 25, 365–376. https://doi.org/10.3851/IMP3385.

Elfiky, A., 2020. Ribavirin, remdesivir, sofosbuvir, galidesivir, and tenofovir against SARS-CoV-2 RNA dependent RNA polymerase (RdRp): a molecular docking study. Life Sci. 253, 117592. https://doi.org/10.1016/J.LFS.2020.117592.

Gammoh, N.Z., Rink, L., 2017. Zinc in infection and inflammation. Nutrients 9, 624. https://doi.org/10.3390/NU9060624.

Geleris, J., et al., 2020. Observational study of hydroxychloroquine in hospitalized patients with Covid-19. N. Engl. J. Med. 382, 2411–2418. https://doi.org/10.1056/NEJMOA2012410.

Gilbert, S.C., 2012. T-cell-inducing vaccines—what's the future. Immunology 135, 19. https://doi.org/10.1111/J.1365-2567.2011.03517.X.

Heurich, A., et al., 2014. TMPRSS2 and ADAM17 cleave ACE2 differentially and only proteolysis by TMPRSS2 augments entry driven by the severe acute respiratory syndrome coronavirus spike protein. J. Virol. 88, 1293–1307. https://doi.org/10.1128/JVI.02202-13.

Hoffman, M., et al., 2020. SARS-CoV-2 cell entry depends on ACE2 and TMPRSS2 and is blocked by a clinically proven protease inhibitor. Cell 181, 271–280.e8. https://doi.org/10.1016/J.CELL.2020.02.052.

Iwata-Yoshikawa, N., et al., 2019. TMPRSS2 contributes to virus spread and immunopathology in the airways of murine models after coronavirus infection. J. Virol. 93. https://doi.org/10.1128/JVI.01815-18, e01815-18.

Jean, S.S., Lee, P.I., Hsueh, P.R., 2020. Treatment options for COVID-19: the reality and challenges. J. Microbiol. Immunol. Infect. Wei mian yu gan ran za zhi 53, 436–443. https://doi.org/10.1016/J.JMII.2020.03.034.

Jovic, T.H., et al., 2020. Could vitamins help in the fight against COVID-19? Nutrients 12, 1–30. https://doi.org/10.3390/NU12092550.

Kawase, M., et al., 2012. Simultaneous treatment of human bronchial epithelial cells with serine and cysteine protease inhibitors prevents severe acute respiratory syndrome coronavirus entry. J. Virol. 86, 6537–6545. https://doi.org/10.1128/JVI.00094-12.

Kretchy, I.A., Asiedu-Danso, M., Kretchy, J.-P., 2021. Medication management and adherence during the COVID-19 pandemic: perspectives and experiences from low-and middle-income countries. Res. Social Adm. Pharm. 17, 2023. https://doi.org/10.1016/J.SAPHARM.2020.04.007.

Kumar, S., et al., 2020. Morphology, genome organization, replication, and pathogenesis of severe acute respiratory syndrome coronavirus 2 (SARS-CoV-2). Coronavirus Dis. 2019 (COVID-19), 23. https://doi.org/10.1007/978-981-15-4814-7_3.

la Marca, A., et al., 2020. Testing for SARS-CoV-2 (COVID-19): a systematic review and clinical guide to molecular and serological in-vitro diagnostic assays. Reprod. Biomed. Online 41, 483. https://doi.org/10.1016/J.RBMO.2020.06.001.

Leaf, D., Ginde, A.A., 2021. Vitamin D3 to treat COVID-19: different disease, same answer. JAMA 325, 1047–1048. https://doi.org/10.1001/JAMA.2020.26850.

Lee, N.H., et al., 2012. A review of vaccine development and research for industry animals in Korea. Clin. Exp. Vaccine Res. 1, 18. https://doi.org/10.7774/CEVR.2012.1.1.18.

Lung, J., et al., 2020. The potential chemical structure of anti-SARS-CoV-2 RNA-dependent RNA polymerase. J. Med. Virol. 92, 693–697. https://doi.org/10.1002/JMV.25761.

Mahmud, R., et al., 2021. Ivermectin in combination with doxycycline for treating COVID-19 symptoms: a randomized trial. 49 (5). https://doi.org/10.1177/03000605211013550, 3000605211013550.

McGregor, S., Henderson, K.J., Kaldor, J.M., 2014. How are health research priorities set in low and middle income countries? A systematic review of published reports. PLoS One 9, e108787. https://doi.org/10.1371/JOURNAL.PONE.0108787.

McKee, D.L., et al., 2020. Candidate drugs against SARS-CoV-2 and COVID-19. Pharmacol. Res. 157. https://doi.org/10.1016/J.PHRS.2020.104859, 104859.

Mihara, M., et al., 2005. Tocilizumab inhibits signal transduction mediated by both mIL-6R and sIL-6R, but not by the receptors of other members of IL-6 cytokine family. Int. Immunopharmacol. 5, 1731–1740. https://doi.org/10.1016/J.INTIMP.2005.05.010.

Naz, A., et al., 2020. Designing multi-epitope vaccines to combat emerging coronavirus disease 2019 (COVID-19) by employing immuno-informatics approach. Front. Immunol. 11. https://doi.org/10.3389/FIMMU.2020.01663.

Pal, M., et al., 2020. Severe acute respiratory syndrome coronavirus-2 (SARS-CoV-2): an update. Cureus 12, e7423. https://doi.org/10.7759/CUREUS.7423.

Pandey, S.C., et al., 2020. Vaccination strategies to combat novel corona virus SARS-CoV-2. Life Sci. 256, 117956. https://doi.org/10.1016/J.LFS.2020.117956.

Park, S.E., 2020. Epidemiology, virology, and clinical features of severe acute respiratory syndrome -coronavirus-2 (SARS-CoV-2; coronavirus disease-19). Clin. Exp. Pediatr. 63, 119–124. https://doi.org/10.3345/CEP.2020.00493.

Sarkesh, A., et al., 2020. Extrapulmonary clinical manifestations in COVID-19 patients. Am. J. Trop. Med. Hyg. 103, 1783. https://doi.org/10.4269/AJTMH.20-0986.

Shiraki, K., Daikoku, T., 2020. Favipiravir, an anti-influenza drug against life-threatening RNA virus infections. Pharmacol. Ther. 209. https://doi.org/10.1016/J.PHARMTHERA.2020.107512, 107512.

Singhal, T., 2020. A review of coronavirus Disease-2019 (COVID-19). Indian J. Pediatr. 87, 281–286. https://doi.org/10.1007/S12098-020-03263-6.

Sohrabi, C., 2020. World Health Organization declares global emergency: a review of the 2019 novel coronavirus (COVID-19). Int. J. Surg. 76, 71–76. https://doi.org/10.1016/J.IJSU.2020.02.034.

Sun, Z., et al., 2020. Potential factors influencing repeated SARS outbreaks in China. Int. J. Environ. Res. Public Health 17, 1633. https://doi.org/10.3390/IJERPH17051633.
Tang, Y.W., et al., 2020. Laboratory diagnosis of COVID-19: current issues and challenges. J. Clin. Microbiol. 58. https://doi.org/10.1128/JCM.00512-20, e00512-20.
Tian, S., et al., 2020. Pulmonary pathology of early-phase 2019 novel coronavirus (COVID-19) pneumonia in two patients with lung cancer. J. Thorac. Oncol. 15, 700–704. https://doi.org/10.1016/J.JTHO.2020.02.010.
Tse, L.V., et al., 2020. The current and future state of vaccines, antivirals and gene therapies against emerging coronaviruses. Front. Microbiol. 11. https://doi.org/10.3389/FMICB.2020.00658.
Wu, C., et al., 2020b. Analysis of therapeutic targets for SARS-CoV-2 and discovery of potential drugs by computational methods. Acta Pharm. Sin. B 10, 766–788. https://doi.org/10.1016/J.APSB.2020.02.008.
Wu, Y.-C., Chen, C.-S., Chan, Y.-J., 2020a. The outbreak of COVID-19: an overview. J. Chin. Med. Assoc. 83, 217. https://doi.org/10.1097/JCMA.0000000000000270.
Zhang, C., et al., 2020. Cytokine release syndrome in severe COVID-19: interleukin-6 receptor antagonist tocilizumab may be the key to reduce mortality. Int. J. Antimicrob. Agents 55. https://doi.org/10.1016/J.IJANTIMICAG.2020.105954, 105954.
Zhou, Y., et al., 2015. Protease inhibitors targeting coronavirus and filovirus entry. Antiviral Res. 116, 76. https://doi.org/10.1016/J.ANTIVIRAL.2015.01.011.
Zhu, N., et al., 2020. A novel coronavirus from patients with pneumonia in China, 2019. N. Engl. J. Med. 382, 727–733. https://doi.org/10.1056/NEJMOA2001017.

CHAPTER TWO

Coronavirus reinfections: An outlook on evidences and effects

Vijay K. Patel[a,b], Ekta Shirbhate[a,b], and Harish Rajak[a]
[a]Institute of Pharmaceutical Sciences, Guru Ghasidas University, Bilaspur, India
[b]Dr. C.V. Raman Institute of Pharmacy, Dr. C.V. Raman University, Bilaspur, India

1 Introduction

A sudden increase in the number of patients, diagnosed with pneumonia and respiratory distress, more-so-over with unknown etiology were reported in December 2019, from Wuhan city, Hubei province, China. In February 2020, World Health Organization (WHO) announced it as a "Public Health Emergency of International Concern" and termed it COVID-19 (World Health Organization, 2020; Wu and McGoogan, 2020). Coronaviruses (CoVs) belong to the *Coronaviridae* family, the enveloped viruses that own unusually long single-stranded RNA genomes varying from 26 to 32 kilobases in length (Zheng, 2020; Su et al., 2016). The Coronavirus family has shown a high transmission and infection rate in humans; at present seven Coronavirus species have been identified to produce illness in humans. The four members of CoVs family (HCoV-229E, HCoV-OC43, HCoV-NL63, and HCoV-HKU1) are responsible for producing a variety of upper respiratory tract infections with common cold symptoms which are mild, and the remaining three viruses, i.e., Severe Acute Respiratory Syndrome-Coronavirus-1 (nSARS-CoV-1), Middle East Respiratory Syndrome (MERS-CoV) and Severe Acute Respiratory Syndrome-Coronavirus-2 (nSARS-CoV-2) leads to an atypical pneumonia (Su et al., 2016). SARS-CoV was recognized in 2003, began in China spread to more than 30 countries with more than 8000 cases and 774 deaths worldwide (Drosten et al., 2003; Zhong et al., 2003). MERS-CoV was recognized in 2012 in Saudi Arabia and Jordan, spread more than 27 countries with nearly 2500 cases and 850 related deaths (Zaki et al., 2012). SARS-CoV-2 is a novel Coronavirus that has been identified as the causative organism of Coronavirus disease 2019 (COVID-19), which started in late 2019 in Wuhan, China and expanded globally (Su et al., 2016). Currently; as of

Lessons from COVID-19
https://doi.org/10.1016/B978-0-323-99878-9.00013-3

August 05, 2021, the WHO has reported more than 200 million cases and more than 4.26 million deaths globally. The condition of severe pneumonia is visible more likely in the elderly and individuals with clinical irregularities like hypertension, diabetes, CHF, renal failure, etc. All the COVID-19 treatment options of prescribing drugs are based on the experiences gained from SARS, MERS or other new influenza viruses. Hence, there is a crucial need to diminish the spread of the virus by adopting all kinds of preventive and control methods, like social distancing, wearing masks and gloves etc.

2 Coronavirus reinfection

The Coronavirus reinfection means a person was infected once, recovered, and then again became infected due to reactivation of the virus in patient body or attack of genetically different mutant virus. The reinfection was confirmed by epidemiological, clinical, serological, and genomic analyses of continual viral shedding from the first infection (To et al., 2020). The COVID-19 reinfection cases were reported in various regions of the world such as Hong Kong, South Korea, China, Taiwan, Japan, Russia, United States of America, Qatar, Belgium, Ecuador, Brazil, Mexico, Israel, Canada, Switzerland, Sweden, Colombia, Germany, European countries, and India (BNO News, 2021). The world's first COVID-19 reinfection was documented/confirmed in Hong Kong in an adult patient, 33-year old male (To et al., 2020) and the second case was confirmed in Belgium in a 50-year old woman on the same day with the asymptomatic and mild symptoms (Table 1).

The next four cases of Coronavirus reinfections were documented in Netherlands with mild to severe infection. The first case of reinfection in United States was confirmed on August 28, 2020, in a 25-year old man infected with serious symptoms (Tillett et al., 2021). The second case of reinfection in the United States was reported in 45-year old man with notable worse reinfection (Larson et al., 2020). An Indian scientist reported the two genetically confirmed cases of reinfection, one is 25-year old man and second is 28-year old woman, and both were asymptomatic (Gupta et al., 2020). Four additional cases of reinfection were reported with Indian health workers involved in the treatment of COVID-19 patients at Mumbai, who suffered from mild symptoms during the reinfection (Shastri et al., 2020) (Table 1). As per COVID-19 reinfection tracker data published by BNO news, there were 84 cases, 03 deaths, 59 recovered patients, along with more than 40,000 suspected cases and more than 100 deaths till June 02, 2021

Table 1 Reported cases of reinfection (first 30) in world.

S. No.	Reported date[a]	Location	Patient Age/Sex	Interval[b]	Symptoms (1 Case)	Symptoms (2 Case)
1	24 Aug 2020	Hong Kong	33/M	123 days	Mild	None
2	24 Aug 2020	Belgium	51/F	93	Mild	Mild
3	24 Aug 2020	Netherlands	60+	NA	NA	NA
4	26 Aug 2020	Netherlands	60+	60 days	NA	NA
5	26 Aug 2020	Netherlands	80/M	21	Mild	Mild
6	26 Aug 2020	Netherlands	60/M	12 days	Mild	Serious
7	28 Aug 2020	United States	25/M	31 days	Mild	Serious
8	30 Aug 2020	Euador	46/M	47 days	Mild	Moderate
9	15 Sept2020	India	28/F	100 days	None	None
10	15 Sept 2020	India	25/M	101 days	None	None
11	23 Sept 2020	United States	42/M	51 days	Mild	Serious
12	23 Sept 2020	India	24/F	48 days	Mild	Mild
13	23 Sept 2020	India	27/M	13 days	None	Mild
14	23 Sept 2020	India	31/M	59 days	None	Mild
15	23 Sept 2020	India	27/M	60 days	Mild	Mild
16	29 Sept 2020	Qatar	20/M	54 days	NA	NA
17	29 Sept 2020	Qatar	40/F	87 days	NA	NA
18	29 Sept 2020	Qatar	40/M	70 days	NA	NA
19	29 Sept 2020	Qatar	20/M	45 days	NA	NA
20	30 Sept 2020	Belgium	30/M	143 days	Mild	Mild
21	30 Sept 2020	Belgium	25/F	115 days	Mild	Mild
22	12 Oct 2020	Netherland	89/F	54 days	Moderate	Serious
23	14 Oct 2020	Spain	62/M	147 days	Mild	Serious
24	16 Oct 2020	Sweden	53/F	120 days	Mild	Mild
25	10 Nov 2020	Belgium	30/F	185 days	Mild	Mild
26	21 Nov 2020	South Korea	21/F	10 days	Mild	Mild
27	09 Dec 2020	Brazil	37/F	116 days	Mild	Mild
28	11 Dec 2020	Peru	6/F	97 days	Mild	Mild
29	16 Dec 2020	Brazil	41/F	145 days	Mild	Mild
30	17 Dec	Mexico	M	64 days	Mild	Mild

[a]The month in which reinfection is made public. Due to the time needed to establish reinfection, the actual case may have happened weeks or months earlier.
[b]The length of time between the first case's recovery and the second case's start of symptoms, if known. Unless otherwise specified, the number of days between confirmed cases.
https://bnonews.com/index.php/2020/08/covid-19-reinfection-tracker/.

(BNO News, 2021). The Qatar research team has confirmed four cases of reinfection in the world's largest investigation till date with more than 130,000 positive tests and these findings suggested that SARS-CoV-2 reinfection can occur, but it is an exceptional observation in which the majority of infected persons develop immunity against reinfection that remains for a period of few months after primary infection (Abu-Raddad et al., 2020). The studies of the Indian Council of Medical Research (ICMR) have found that 4.5%, (58 of the 1300 individuals) could be most probable cases of reinfection of SARS-CoV-2 in India (Mukherjee et al., 2021). People who suffered from COVID-19 have got 84% protection from COVID-19 reinfection and 93% protection from COVID-19 symptomatic infection during 7 months of follow-up as per studies in healthcare workers in England (Hall et al., 2021).

3 Reinfection and genome sequence

The virus that causes COVID-19, SARS-CoV-2, is one of many viruses that mutate throughout time. Most changes have little or no impact on the virus's properties. On the other hand, specific changes may affect the virus's features, such as the ease with which it spreads, the severity of the illness it causes, or the effectiveness of vaccines, therapeutic medicines, diagnostic instruments, and other public health and social interventions (World Health Organization, 2021). The study of COVID-19 whole genome sequencing (WGS) data has provided valuable information regarding the growth, functioning, and mutation of organisms; it can be applied for diagnosis, control, treatment, and development of vaccine. The genome of Coronavirus is the largest among identified RNA viruses (27 to 31.5 kb) with 29,903 nucleotides and it is polycistronic, consisting of sub-genomic RNAs with regular 5 and 3 sequences (Li et al., 2005; Paraskevis et al., 2020). The first complete genome sequence of the SARS-CoV-2 isolated from human cases from China was reported on January 05, 2020 by China (Wu et al., 2020b) and currently, thousands of genomes sequences have been reported till date. The various scientific investigations has reported that both times COVID-19 patients were infected with the viruses had differences in some of their genes caused by antigenic drift, antigenic shift, and recombination known as natural mutations (Baxi and Saxena, 2020). The Hong Kong case provides the first documentary evidence and confirmed that different viral strains are responsible for reinfection (To et al., 2020). The reinfection was reported from Nevada, in the US, where five nucleotides are muted from the first SARS-CoV-2 Coronavirus genomes, i.e., five single point mutations were found as compared to the reference genome sequence from the first infection (Tillett et al., 2021). There is, however, an indication of SARS-CoV-2 reinfection without changes in the virus's spike protein (Kulkarni et al., 2021). The WHO and its worldwide expert networks are monitoring viral evolution, searching for variations that represent a greater danger to global public health and are designated as Variants of Concern (VOC) or Variants of Interest (VOI) (Table 2). The WHO defines VOC as a rise in transmissibility or detrimental transformation in COVID-19 epidemiology and a surge in virulence or a reduction in diagnostic, vaccine, or treatment efficacy. The WHO defines VOI as viruses that have undergone genetic modifications that are expected or reported to affect virus attributes such as infectivity, disease severity, immune escape, diagnostic or therapeutic escape, and have been identified as causing major community transmission in numerous nations (Table 2). The Alpha, Beta, Gamma, and Delta variants fall under VOC, whereas Eta, Iota, Kappa, and Lambda fall under VOI (World Health Organization, 2021). The B.1.1.7 variant and B.1.1.28 SARS-CoV-2 variant viruses have been circulated in numerous countries and caused reinfection in Brazil, United Kingdom and South Africa (Toovey et al., 2021). The delta variant (B.1.617.2) of Coronavirus which was in circulation during the second wave pandemic in India is significantly less sensitive to immunity from a previous infection or vaccination. According to Public Health England (PHE), the risk of reinfection with delta variant is 46% higher than the Alpha variant, with the highest risk

Table 2 The WHO designated variants of concern (VOC), and variants of interest (VOI).

WHO class	WHO label	Pango lineages	Earliest documented samples	Date of designation
Variant of Concern (VOC)	Alpha	B.1.1.7	United Kingdom, Sep-2020	18-Dec-2020
	Beta	B.1.351, B.1.351.2, B.1.351.3	South Africa, May-2020	18-Dec-2020
	Gamma	P.1, P.1.1, P.1.2	Brazil, Nov-2020	11-Jan-2021
	Delta	B.1.617.2, AY.1, AY.2	India, Oct-2020	VOI: 4-Apr-2021, VOC: 11-May-20
Variants of Interest (VOI)	Eta	B.1.525	Multiple countries, Dec-2020	17-Mar-2021
	Iota	B.1.526	United States of America, Nov-2020	24-Mar-2021
	Kappa	B.1.617.1	India, Oct-2020	4-Apr-2021
	Lambda	C.37	Peru, Dec-2020	14-Jun-2021

seen six months after a first infection. The delta variant second infection was 2.37 times more common than with Alpha.

The possibility of reinfection may be raised in the coming time as the immune system does not have any memory of variant strains of SARS-CoV-2. Therefore, genome sequencing of SARS-CoV-2 is necessary to understand why this virus is behaving differently. As a significant number of people reinfected from COVID-19 infection are asymptomatic, without under surveillance and lack of genomic sequencing studies may make it impossible to estimate the real numbers of reinfections. The reinfection or reactivation of COVID-19 patient with asymptomatic or mild symptom unintentionally spread the virus in the environment and leads to infection of other healthy people. Intensive research on COVID-19 reinfection is urgently needed to elucidate the probability, frequency, severity, and effect on immunity and vaccine development. Hence, this chapter focuses on recent progress on COVID-19 reinfection, its severity, frequency, immunopathogenesis of Coronavirus infection, immune response on reinfection and its effect on the development of vaccine and herd immunity.

4 Immunopathogenesis of Coronavirus infection

The SARS-CoV-2 initiates its response and causes severe damage to the respiratory tract. The spike glycoprotein of the virus binds with the ACE2 receptors on the alveolar epithelium infecting respiratory tract cells, epithelial hair cells of airways and type 2 alveolar pneumocytes, causing immune cells (monocytes, macrophages and neutrophils) infiltration and release of pro-inflammatory cytokines (IL-1, Il-6, IL-12, TNF, TNF-α, INF-γ) and chemokines (CCL2, CXCL, CXL10). These events (generally known as cytokine storm) seem to be responsible for causing diffused alveolar damage through edema, fibrosis, hyaline membrane formation, and ultimately alveolar collapse, desquamation of epithelial and alveolar cells, and multiple organ injury (Fig. 1) (Chen et al., 2020; Wang et al., 2020).

When antigen-presenting cells (dendritic cells or macrophages) identify the SARS-CoV-2 virus, T-lymphocytes become stimulated and produce inflammatory mediators (IFN-I, TNF-, IL-1, IL-6, CCL2), as well as perforin and granzyme B (Kumar et al., 2020). Lymphopenia is mostly identified in the acute phase of infection (Fathi and Rezaei, 2020). However, in severe cases, excessive release of inflammatory mediators (cytokine storm) intensifies the inflammatory response causing lung injuries leading to respiratory collapse, organ failure and eventually death (Song et al., 2020). This is

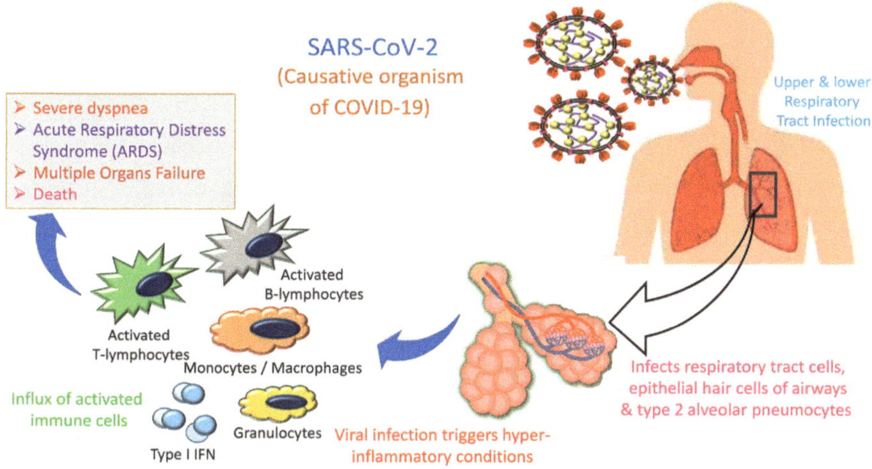

Fig. 1 Human immune response during SARS-CoV-2 infection.

also supported through inflammatory infiltration, carried out by macrophages and neutrophils. The prevalence of immune response directed by immune cells becomes severe in the latter stage of the infection. Basically, immune cells participate in an innate immunity and activate adaptive immune response. The immune response fails to activate T cells during SARS-CoV-2 infection (Oliveira et al., 2020). The constant stimulus initiated by viral infection urges the cells to generate inflammatory mediators to diminish the viral replication, though the event end up exaggerating the pathogenesis with severe tissue damage (Fig. 2) (Shirbhate et al., 2020).

5 Reinfection and immune response

The immune system becomes activated on infection, wherein initially innate immunity fights against infection. If infection still persists, the adaptive immunity plays its role for abolishing the infection. All the infections, primarily activates innate immunity wherein, white blood cells causes inflammation and produces primary antibodies to kill the virus from body. If infection persists for a longer time then adaptive immunity (antigen-specific immune response) involving T cells and B cells identifies the antigens derived from virus. The role of T cells is to sense and kill the infected cells, whereas B cells produce antibodies that kill the virus. In a healthy adult, the coordinated $CD4^+$ T cell, $CD8^+$ T cell and antibody responses are protective against infection, but this coordination frequently fails in the aged

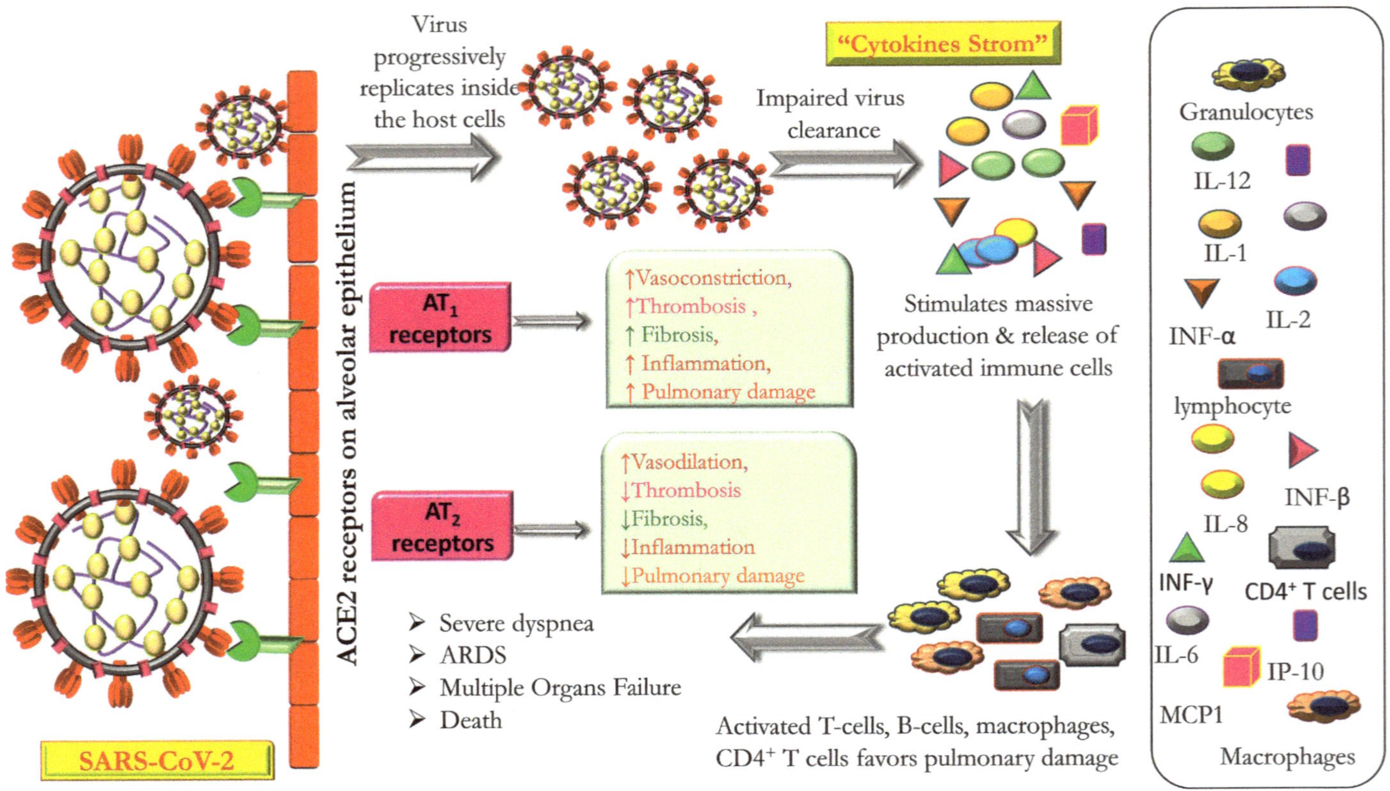

Fig. 2 Mode of action of SARS-CoV-2.

population, leading to impaired adaptive immune response to SARS-CoV-2. The milder symptoms of COVID-19 infection are associated with $CD4^+$ T cells and $CD8^+$ T cells (Fig. 2) (Moderbacher et al., 2020). Some of these T cells and B cells, known as memory cells exist for a longer duration after recovery from infection. Thus, adaptive immunity includes memory that ensures future responses against SARS-CoV-2 reinfection.

Scientific research on the humoral immune response to SARS-CoV-2 indicates that adequate antibody levels are present and they do not decline during the period of three to four months after the diagnosis of COVID-19 in a person thus there is no clinical reinfection within this period (Gudbjartsson et al., 2020; Mumoli et al., 2020; Van Elslande et al., 2020). Additionally, some scientific reports indicate that protective immunity is only for a short period of time and leaves us more exposed to the virus reinfection (Table 1). Edridge et al. studied the duration of acquired immunity suffered from four seasonal Coronaviruses (HCoV-NL63, HCoV-229E, HCoV-OC43 and HCoV-HKU), and reinfection was observed regularly at 12 months after infection (Edridge et al., 2020).

6 Severity and risk of Coronavirus reinfection

The spreading ability rate of different genetically or mutant Coronavirus will increase with time and could lead to increased COVID-19-reinfected patients. The majority of COVID-19 reinfection cases have been described as asymptomatic or with lesser illness severity than the first infection, confirming the notion that natural immunity may mitigate disease incidence even when it does not completely avert reinfection (Van Elslande et al., 2020; Long et al., 2020). However, some COVID-19 reinfection cases have been disclosed with moderate and severe reinfection (Table 3) symptom along with 03 deaths reported in the Netherlands, Israel, and Brazil (BNO News, 2021). The people suffering from COVID-19 infection may not be protected for a longer period against the virus reinfection due to low immunity, tapered antibody response, and increased susceptibility to virus infections. The interval between the first and second infection varied from 10 days to 334 days in reported cases (Table 3) (BNO News, 2021). Various scientists reported that the antibodies stay for 3–6 months after COVID-19 infection. The COVID-19 asymptomatic or mild symptomatic patients are at the most risk of reinfection because those patients activate only innate immunity, which provides partial protection against COVID-19 reinfection. When patients have significant viral replication in their bodies,

Table 3 COVID-19 infections and treatment guidelines.

S. No.	Class of COVID-19	Symptom	Treatment
1	Asymptomatic or Presymptomatic infection of COVID-19	No symptoms	Complete home isolation, nutrient diet and antioxidant-rich beverages. Immunity-boosting supplements comprising of zinc, multivitamins, vitamin C. Routine check-up of temperature and oxygen saturation (SpO_2) level and informing health authorities, if they have low saturation (less than 94) or high temperature.
2	Mild infection of COVID-19	Fever, cough, sore throat, malaise, headache, muscle pain, vomiting, diarrhea, loss of taste and smell. Not have shortness of breath, dyspnea, or abnormal chest imaging.	Self-isolation at home, manage treatment through telemedicine or telephone visits. Symptomatic treatment such as antipyretics for fever and pain, multivitamins, adequate nutrition and appropriate rehydration.
3	Moderate infection of COVID-19	Lower respiratory disease during clinical assessment or imaging and who have an oxygen saturation (SpO_2). 90% to <93% on room air at sea level. Respiratory rate > 24/min, breathlessness, not require emergency interventions or hospitalization.	Isolation is necessary. High risk patients at deterioration, isolation in hospital is preferred. If bacterial pneumonia or sepsis is suspected, empiric antibiotic treatment should be used followed by regular re-evaluation of the patient. Antibiotics should be avoided, if there is no bacterial infection.
4	Severe infection of COVID-19	Obstructed breathing, severe respiratory distress, central cyanosis, shock, coma and/or	Immediate supply of oxygen to patients with emergency signs. If secondary bacterial

Table 3 COVID-19 infections and treatment guidelines—cont'd

S. No.	Class of COVID-19	Symptom	Treatment
		convulsions. The patients have $SpO_2 < 90\%$, a ratio of arterial partial pressure of oxygen to fraction of inspired oxygen (PaO_2/FiO_2) < 300 mmHg, respiratory rate > 30 breaths/min, or lung infiltrates >50%.	pneumonia or sepsis is there antibiotics may be used till any infection persists. Fluid management is required in patients with COVID-19 without tissue hypoperfusion and fluid responsiveness.
5	Critical infection of COVID-19	Respiratory failure, septic shock, and/or multiple organ malfunction.	Application of non-invasive or high-flow nasal oxygen (HFNO) systems. Management of medical condition that has resulted in ICU admission and other comorbidities and hospital acquired infections.

adaptive immunity is activated, and they have a difficult recovery but acquire long-term immunity (Li et al., 2020; García, 2020). The immune compromised persons have impaired antibody response, may not develop sufficient antibodies after infection, having higher risk of COVID-19 reinfection. A Diabetes patient who have had a previous COVID-19 infection have a faster fading immunity, putting them at a greater risk of reinfection than those who do not have diabetes (Pal and Banerjee, 2021). Thyroid disease which affects hormonal and immune system function, reduces the body's capacity to fight infections and other pathogens, increasing the chance of reinfection with COVID-19. The treatment of thyroid can suppress the immune system functioning, make a person vulnerable to catching frequent illnesses (Lisco et al., 2021). Obese people infected with COVID-19 raise inflammatory levels in the body, disrupt essential functioning, and make it much more difficult for the immune system to generate sufficient antibodies, especially after recovering from COVID-19 infection. However, if obese persons receive the vaccination, the outcomes may not able to generate sufficient antibodies. As a result, they are at the greatest risk of reinfection and difficulties following recovery (Mohammad et al., 2021; Popkin et al., 2020). Frontline and healthcare workers are more exposed to COVID-19 virus variants than the general public, putting them at higher risk of reinfection.

7 Management strategies and guidelines for COVID-19 reinfection

Re-infection should be treated similarly to the first COVID-19 infection. Patients infected with SARS-CoV-2 should be classified according to the degree of their illness, with cases being classified as asymptomatic/presymptomatic, mild, moderate, severe, or critical infections and treated appropriately. The standards for each group might overlap or differ in clinical guidelines and trials. Moreover, the clinical condition of a patient might vary with time. COVID-19 reinfected patients always possess severe infection along with compromised lung situation, so they necessitate additional care and examination as compared to primary infected patients.

7.1 Asymptomatic or pre-symptomatic infection of COVID-19

The asymptomatic or pre-symptomatic patients do not possess any primary symptoms, but they are still carriers of the COVID-19 infection and may put other people's lives at risk. These patients need strict home isolation with no contact with any family members, nutrient-rich diet with plenty of fruits and vegetables, and drinking fluids rich in antioxidants. The patients should take immunity-boosting supplements containing zinc, multivitamins, especially vitamin C. The patient should also regularly monitor the temperature and oxygen saturation (SpO_2) and inform to health authorities, if they have low saturation (less than 94%) or higher body temperature.

7.2 Mild infection of COVID-19

The patients with mild infections show a range of symptoms such as fever, sore throat, cough, loss of taste and smell, headache, muscle pain, malaise, nausea, vomiting, diarrhea etc. These patients do not have choking of breath, dyspnea on hard work, or atypical imaging. The majority of mildly infected patients can be treated at home in self-isolation. The telemedicine or telephone visits could be used to treat symptomatic patients using antipyretics for fever and pain, multivitamins, sufficient nutrition, and appropriate rehydration. The health monitoring team should observe elderly patients and susceptible persons directly until clinical recovery is attained.

7.3 Moderate infection of COVID-19

Patients with moderate infection exhibit lower respiratory illness (such as bronchitis or pneumonia) on clinical examination or imaging, an oxygen saturation (SpO_2) level of 90% to 93% on room air at sea level, a respiratory rate more than 24 breaths per minute, and dyspnea. As lungs disease deteriorates rapidly in patients with COVID-19, so they should be monitored closely. If moderately infected COVID-19 patient have bacterial pneumonia or sepsis, then following steps should be considered: (i) empiric antibiotic treatment should be administered, (ii) the patient should be re-evaluated every day, and (iii) When there is no evidence of bacterial infection, antibiotics should be reduced or discontinued. If the condition of COVID-19 deteriorates, isolation in hospital is preferred.

7.4 Severe infection of COVID-19

Patients infected with COVID-19 are classified as having a severe infection if they meet one or more of the following criteria: (i) SpO_2 level less than 90% on room air at sea level, (ii) a respiratory rate more than 30 breaths/min, (iii) PaO2/FiO2 less than 300 mmHg, or lung infiltrates higher than 50%. These patients may have fast clinical worsening. Medical oxygen should be administered instantly by means of a nasal cannula or a high-flow oxygen apparatus. Standard drug therapy for COVID-19 patients is recommended as per specific therapy guidelines prescribed by local authorities. If severe infected COVID-19 patient have bacterial pneumonia or sepsis then following steps should be considered: (i) empiric antibiotic treatment should be administered, (ii) the patient should be re-evaluated every day, and (iii) When there is no evidence of bacterial infection, antibiotics should be reduced or discontinued.

7.5 Critical infection of COVID-19

Critically ill person may include short term respiratory distress syndrome, virus-induced distributive shock, cardiac malfunction, precipitation of inflammatory condition, and/or worsening of comorbidities. The patients with critical infection may have disorders of the respiratory, cardiac, hepatic, renal, and central nervous system. The critically ill patients admitted to intensive care unit (ICU) requires proper clinical treatment of both the medical condition that primarily disease and other comorbidities including hospital acquired infections (if any).

8 COVID-19 reinfection and vaccine development

The vaccination of humans mimics the primary infection through antigens that attack on adaptive immune system and produces memory cells that could be stimulated quickly in the case of actual infection. Hundreds of vaccine candidates are being tested in clinical trials to evaluate their safety and efficacy. At present, 17 vaccines are approved across several countries out of them 06 vaccines are approved by WHO (Covid19 Vaccine Tracker, 2021) (Table 4). The Immunologists reported that the immune response to Coronaviruses is complex. Immune cells play an vital role in remembering the previous infection and shielding the patient from demising to reinfection, as the time progress immunity will fade, leaving us more exposed to the Coronavirus reinfection (Yan et al., 2021). The reinfected COVID-19 patients have asymptomatic or milder infection in the second time; this indicates that the immune system is responding, while not defending us against it for the longer duration. At present, a number of cases have been reported who were vaccinated but suffered from COVID-19, indicating that existing vaccines do not provide protection against infection,

Table 4 List of approved vaccine by at least one country.

S. No.	Vaccine name	Company	Type	Approval
1	AZD1222	Oxford-AstraZeneca	Non Replicating Viral Vector vaccines	WHO, 119 Countries
2	BNT162b2	Pfizer-BioNTech	RNA vaccines	WHO, 97 Countries
3	Ad26.COV2·S	Johnson & Johnson	Non Replicating Viral Vector vaccines	WHO, 56 Countries
4	mRNA-1273	Moderna	RNA vaccines	WHO, 64 Countries
5	BBIBP-CorV	Sinopharm (Beijing)	Inactivated virus vaccines	WHO, 59 Countries
6	Covishield	Serum Institute of India	Non Replicating Viral Vector vaccines	WHO, 45 Countries

Table 4 List of approved vaccine by at least one country—cont'd

S. No.	Vaccine name	Company	Type	Approval
7	RBD-Dimer	Anhui Zhifei Longcom	Protein subunit vaccines	2 Countries
8	Covaxin	Bharat Biotech	Inactivated virus vaccines	9 Countries
9	KoviVac	Chumakov Center	Inactivated virus vaccines	1 Country
10	EpiVacCorona	FBRI	Protein Subunit vaccines	2 Countries
11	Ad5-nCoV	CanSino	Non Replicating Viral Vector	8 Countries
12	Sputnik V	Gamaleya	Non Replicating Viral Vector	70 Countries
13	QazVac	Kazakhstan RIBSP	Inactivated virus vaccines	1 Country
14	SARS-CoV-2 Vaccine	Minhai Biotechnology Co	Inactivated virus vaccines	1 Country
15	Inactivated (Vero Cells)	Sinopharm (Wuhan)	Inactivated virus vaccines	1 Country
16	CoronaVac	Sinovac	Inactivated virus vaccines	39 Countries
17	TAK-919	Takeda	RNA vaccines	1 Country
18	CIGB-66	Center for Genetic Engineering and Biotechnology	Protein Subunit vaccines	1 Country
19	MVC-COV1901	Medigen	Protein Subunit vaccines	1 Country
20	COVID-19 Inactivated Vaccine	Shifa Pharmed Industrial Co	Inactivated virus vaccines	1 Country
21	Sputnik Light	Gamaleya	Non Replicating Viral Vector	12 Countries

while it provide protection against the severity of COVID-19 illness. This makes the existing vaccines capable of reducing serious complications of COVID-19, the need for hospitalization and mortality. Recent research suggests that prior COVID-19 infection may not completely protect children and adolescents from reinfection, and immunization is still required to enhance immune responses, minimize reinfection, and decrease spread (Letizia et al., 2021).

The COVID-19 reinfection arise questions for the developers of COVID-19 vaccines, i.e., efficacy of genetically different stain and mutant viruses, durability of immunity and safety (immune response can facilitate future infections). The Coronavirus mutations occurring in T-cell and B-cell epitopes or in proteins as component of the host-viral interactome, might hinder vaccine or drug effectiveness in limited people (Singh et al., 2020). The researchers need to develop new generations of vaccines able to prevent from antigenic drift and shift, as performed with the flu. During the 2009 pandemic of a rising influenza A virus (IAV; H1N1pdm09), scientists found that in the months, when both the rhinovirus and the influenza virus were active, the influenza virus was absent if the rhinovirus was present (Wu et al., 2020a). These outcomes showed that one respiratory virus can obstruct the infection with another by activating the antiviral defenses in the respiratory epithelium, confirming the fact that intervention from rhinovirus disrupted the 2009 IAV pandemic in Europe. Later findings showed that viral intervention might possibly have an effect on the course of an epidemic, and this approach could be considered during the design of interventions for continuing COVID-19 pandemic. Recent studies of dengue antibodies may lend some level of immunity against the novel Coronavirus (Nicolelis et al., 2020). Another approach is to design vaccine with seasonal shots of vaccine with periodic administration for protection against newer strains.

9 COVID-19 waves and reinfections

The COVID-19 waves can be described as curve of infections that develop during a pandemic, the number of infections rises and then drops; this every cycle is one "wave" of COVID-19. The exact cause of Coronavirus wave is unknown, however it has afflicted a number of nations including Kyrgyzstan, Australia, South Korea, Israel, New Zealand, India, Japan, Spain, United State of America, and United Kingdom. A few new Coronavirus strains, including the UK virus, the South African virus, the B.1.617 variation, and the double mutant form of SARS-CoV-2, may have generated the outbreaks in the United States and the United Kingdom. These Coronavirus mutations are highly contagious and have the ability to evade the human immune system. A recent studies in Denmark found that risk of COVID-19 reinfection is 0.65% (72 of 11,068 tested positive in PCR test again) during the first wave between March and May 2020, while in the second wave 3.3% (16,819 of 514,271 tested positive in PCR test again) during September to December 2020. The rate of reinfection was five times higher during the second wave as compared with previous COVID-19 infections (Hansen et al., 2021).

10 Herd immunity and COVID-19 reinfection

Herd immunity is a public health terminology to describe the notion that when an adequate public in a society have immunity from Coronavirus, then society will be protected from the outbreak of that disease. This can happen either because these people got vaccinated or had already been infected and have developed protective antibodies against future infection. The theory of herd immunity sticks only for same type of virus. However, the theory of herd immunity does not apply to new or mutant variants of the original virus strain because these new variants may bypass or cheat the immune system. At present, thousands of new virus variants are available, so herd immunity could not provide protection from different types of virus variants.

11 Prevention against COVID-19 reinfection

The possibility of reinfection also depends on the chances of re-exposure to infectious cases of COVID-19. The increased transmission of the COVID-19 virus also increases the possibility that reinfections may occur. A recent population level observational study in Denmark assessed the protection against reinfection with SARS-CoV-2 and found that a first infection with COVID-19 provides only 47% protection against a COVID-19 reinfection for elder person (65 years and over), compared with 80% protection across all age groups. The study also found that the level of protection against reinfection stayed stable for more than six months. These outcomes highlight the importance of physical distancing and vaccinations, even among those who have already had COVID-19 (Hansen et al., 2021). The following preventive measures for COVID-19 infection are suggested as main approach during this pandemic.

1. Strict obedience to COVID-19-appropriate behavior (CAB), i.e., in public settings, wear a mask and keep a distance of about 6 ft from other individuals wash your hands, restrict your travel, avoid eating or drinking in public places, avoid crowds and confined spaces, and self-quarantine, if sick.

2. Deep, extensive, rapid and real-time whole-genome sequencing studies are required to recognize new mutations and variants of concern to provide valuable information regarding growth, functioning, transmission capacities, and mutation of organisms. This information can be applied to diagnosis, control, treatment, and development of vaccines.
3. COVID-19 vaccinations offer a higher grade of immunity, a greater number of antibodies, and a longer duration of protective immunity than spontaneous infection with SARS-CoV-2. Increased immunization rates are critical for limiting the severity of reinfection. However, the vaccination is not a full assurance for protection against reinfection so the person should be obedient to CAB.

12 Implication on COVID-19 reinfection studies

COVID-19 reinfection has been reported all across the world and it is noteworthy that it can occur with or without changes in the virus's spike protein. The rate of reinfection was five times higher during the second wave as compared with previous COVID-19 infections. The risk of reinfection with delta variant (B.1.617.2) is 46% higher than the Alpha variant. Asymptomatic or mildly symptomatic patients, immune impaired people, diabetic patients, thyroid disease patients, obese people, frontline and healthcare professionals are all at increased risk of COVID-19 reinfection.

The present work suggests several implications for possible control of COVID-19 reinfection in the society and may guide the future research in this field are as follows: (a) The management of reinfection should be the same as the treatment of the first COVID-19 infection. (b) Strict adherence to COVID-19-appropriate behavior to avoid reinfection with COVID-19. (c) The medical history of patients should be considered, while treating the COVID-19-reinfected cases. (d) The majority of the COVID-19 reinfection cases are due to novel variant of viruses while few are without mutated virus. Thus deep, extensive, rapid and real-time whole-genome sequencing studies are required to estimate the real numbers of reinfections and treat them accordingly with modified the management/therapeutic strategies. (e) The vaccination against COVID-19 has been established as a proven approach for reducing the risk of reinfection. The vaccination leads to diminished transmission of SARS-CoV-2 (and its new variants also) infection in the society, thus an increased rate of vaccination drive would be crucial to control the severity of re-infection.

13 Conclusion

The accelerated spread of COVID-19 disease has created noteworthy challenges for the economies and healthcare systems of the world. The condition has advanced very rapidly and, till date, there is a high degree of ambiguity about the future consequences of the pandemic (Malkov, 2020). A person recovered from COVID-19, may again get infected with COVID-19 after a time interval due to reactivation of virus in patients bodies or attack of genetically different mutant virus is known as COVID-19 reinfection. The COVID-19 reinfection cases were reported by researchers in various regions, more importantly these are asymptomatic or mild, lack of surveillance and genomic sequencing studies make it difficult to estimate the real numbers of reinfections. Both times COVID-19 patients were infected with the viruses; they had differences in some of their genes caused by antigenic drift, antigenic shift, and recombination, known as natural mutations. The world's first COVID-19 reinfection was documented/confirmed in Hong Kong on August 24, 2020, currently, 78 cases, 03 deaths, 56 recovered patients have been reported along with more than 40,000 suspected cases and more than 100 deaths being reinfected with COVID-19. The various scientific reports indicate that the reinfection with COVID-19 occurred due to new variant of viruses, while few are without any mutations. Exposure to SARS-CoV-2 variant virus strains in the future may increase the likelihood of reinfection since the immune system is not sensitive to them. Therefore, genome sequencing of SARS-CoV-2 is necessary to understand why this virus is behaving differently.

The immune system T cells ($CD4^+$ T cell, $CD8^+$ T cell), B cells and antibody responses protect the person from reinfection for some time, but as the time spent immunity fades up, leaving us more susceptible to the Coronavirus reinfections. The COVID-19 reinfection arises several questions for the developers of COVID-19 vaccines, i.e., efficacy of genetically different stain and mutant viruses, durability of immunity and safety. At present, number of cases have been reported who have been vaccinated but get suffered from COVID-19 disease, indicating that the existing vaccines do not provide protection against infection, while it protect against the person from the severity of next COVID-19 infection, if it occurs. Recent research indicates that infection with COVID-19 may not completely protect children and adolescents from reinfection, and immunization is still required to enhance immune responses, prevent reinfection, and decrease transmission. The risk of

COVID-19 reinfection was 0.65% during the first wave, while it was 3.3% in the second wave. It could be stated that the rate of reinfection has increased during the second wave. The management of reinfection should be in accordance with the treatment of the first COVID-19 infection. The strict obedience to COVID-19 appropriate behavior, deep, extensive, rapid and real-time whole-genome sequencing studies and an increased rate of vaccination drive would be crucial to controlling the severity of re-infection.

References

Abu-Raddad, L.J., et al., 2020. Assessment of the risk of SARS-CoV-2 reinfection in an intense re-exposure setting. medRxiv 2020. https://doi.org/10.1101/2020.08.24.20179457.

Baxi, P., Saxena, S.K., 2020. Emergence and reemergence of severe acute respiratory syndrome (SARS) coronaviruses. In: Coronavirus Disease 2019 (COVID-19): Epidemiology, Pathogenesis, Diagnosis, and Therapeutics, pp. 151–163, https://doi.org/10.1007/978-981-15-4814-7_13.

BNO News, 2021. Covid-19-Reinfection-Tracker. https://bnonews.com/index.php/2020/08/covid-19-reinfection-tracker/. (Accessed 2 June 2021).

Chen, N., et al., 2020. Epidemiological and clinical characteristics of 99 cases of 2019 novel coronavirus pneumonia in Wuhan, China: a descriptive study. Lancet 395 (10223), 507–513. https://doi.org/10.1016/S0140-6736(20)30211-7.

Covid19 Vaccine Tracker, 2021. Covid19 Vaccine Tracker. https://covid19.trackvaccines.org/. (Accessed 2 June 2021).

Drosten, C., et al., 2003. Identification of a novel coronavirus in patients with severe acute respiratory syndrome. N. Engl. J. Med. 348 (20), 1967–1976. https://doi.org/10.1056/NEJMoa030747.

Edridge, A.W.D., et al., 2020. Seasonal coronavirus protective immunity is short-lasting. Nat. Med. 26, 1691–1693. https://doi.org/10.1038/s41591-020-1083-1.

Fathi, N., Rezaei, N., 2020. Lymphopenia in COVID-19: therapeutic opportunities. Cell Biol. Int. 44 (9), 1792–1797. https://doi.org/10.1002/cbin.11403.

García, L.F., 2020. Immune response, inflammation, and the clinical spectrum of COVID-19. Front. Immunol. 11, 1441. https://doi.org/10.3389/fimmu.2020.01441.

Gudbjartsson, D.F., et al., 2020. Humoral immune response to SARS-CoV-2 in Iceland. N. Engl. J. Med. 383, 1724–1734. https://doi.org/10.1056/NEJMoa2026116.

Gupta, V., et al., 2020. Asymptomatic reinfection in two healthcare workers from India with genetically distinct SARS-CoV-2. Clin. Infect. Dis. 73, e2823–e2825. https://doi.org/10.1093/cid/ciaa1451. doi:10.1016/S0140-6736(21)00675-9.

Hall, V.J., et al., 2021. SARS-CoV-2 infection rates of antibody-positive compared with antibody-negative health-care workers in England: a large, multicentre, prospective cohort study (SIREN). Lancet 397 (10283), 1459–1469. https://doi.org/10.1016/S0140-6736(21)00675-9.

Hansen, C.H., et al., 2021. Assessment of protection against reinfection with SARS-CoV-2 among 4 million PCR-tested individuals in Denmark in 2020: a population-level observational study. Lancet 397 (10280), 1204–1212. https://doi.org/10.1016/S0140-6736(21)00575-4.

Kulkarni, O., et al., 2021. Evidence of severe acute respiratory syndrome coronavirus 2 (SARS-CoV-2) reinfection without mutations in the spike protein. Clin. Infect. Dis. 73, e1239–e1241. https://doi.org/10.1093/cid/ciab136.

Kumar, S., Nyodu, R., Maurya, V.K., Saxena, S.K., 2020. Host immune response and immunobiology of human sars-cov-2 infection. In: Coronavirus Disease 2019 (COVID-19): Epidemiology, Pathogenesis, Diagnosis, and Therapeutics, pp. 43–53, https://doi.org/10.1007/978-981-15-4814-7_5.

Larson, D., et al., 2020. A case of early re-infection with SARS-CoV-2. Clin. Infect. Dis. 73, e2827–e2828. https://doi.org/10.1093/cid/ciaa1436.

Letizia, A.G., et al., 2021. SARS-CoV-2 seropositivity and subsequent infection risk in healthy young adults: a prospective cohort study. Lancet Respir. Med. 9, 712–720. https://doi.org/10.1016/S2213-2600(21)00158-2.

Li, F., Li, W., Farzan, M., Harrison, S.C., 2005. Structure of SARS coronavirus spike receptor-binding domain complexed with receptor. Science 309 (5742), 1864–1868. https://doi.org/10.1126/science.1116480.

Li, G., et al., 2020. Coronavirus infections and immune responses. J. Med. Virol. 92 (4), 424–432. https://doi.org/10.1002/jmv.25685.

Lisco, G., et al., 2021. Thyroid and COVID-19: a review on pathophysiological, clinical and organizational aspects. J. Endocrinol. Invest. 44, 1801–1814. https://doi.org/10.1007/s40618-021-01554-z.

Long, Q.X., et al., 2020. Clinical and immunological assessment of asymptomatic SARS-CoV-2 infections. Nat. Med. 26 (8), 1200–1204. https://doi.org/10.1038/s41591-020-0965-6. doi:10.1038/s41591-020-0965-6.

Malkov, E., 2020. Simulation of coronavirus disease 2019 (COVID-19) scenarios with possibility of reinfection. Chaos, Solitons Fractals 139. https://doi.org/10.1016/j.chaos.2020.110296, 110296.

Moderbacher, C.R., et al., 2020. Antigen-specific adaptive immunity to SARS-CoV-2 in acute COVID-19 and associations with age and disease severity. Cell 183, 996–1012.e19. https://doi.org/10.1016/j.cell.2020.09.038.

Mohammad, S., et al., 2021. Obesity and COVID-19: what makes obese host so vulnerable? Immun. Ageing 18 (1), 1. https://doi.org/10.1186/s12979-020-00212-x.

Mukherjee, A., et al., 2021. SARS-CoV-2 re-infection: development of an epidemiological definition from India. Epidemiol. Infect. 149. https://doi.org/10.1017/S0950268821000662, e82.

Mumoli, N., Vitale, J., Mazzone, A., 2020. Clinical immunity in discharged medical patients with COVID-19. Int. J. Infect. Dis. 99, 229–230. https://doi.org/10.1016/j.ijid.2020.07.065.

Nicolelis, M.A.L., Raimundo, R.L.G., Peixoto, P.S., Andreazzi, C.S.D., 2020. How super-spreader cities, highways, hospital bed availability, and dengue fever influenced the COVID-19 epidemic in Brazil'. medRxiv 2020. https://doi.org/10.1101/2020.09.19.20197749, 20197749.

Oliveira, D.S., Medeiros, N.I., Gomes, J.A.S., 2020. Immune response in COVID-19: what do we currently know? Microb. Pathog. 148, 104484. https://doi.org/10.1016/j.micpath.2020.104484.

Pal, R., Banerjee, M., 2021. Are people with uncontrolled diabetes mellitus at high risk of reinfections with COVID-19? Prim. Care Diabetes 15 (1), 18–20. https://doi.org/10.1016/j.pcd.2020.08.002.

Paraskevis, D., et al., 2020. Full-genome evolutionary analysis of the novel corona virus (2019-nCoV) rejects the hypothesis of emergence as a result of a recent recombination event. Infect. Genet. Evol. 79. https://doi.org/10.1016/j.meegid.2020.104212, 104212.

Popkin, B.M., et al., 2020. Individuals with obesity and COVID-19: a global perspective on the epidemiology and biological relationships. Obes. Rev. 21 (11), 13128. https://doi.org/10.1111/obr.13128.

Shastri, J., et al., 2020. Whole genome sequencing confirmed SARS-CoV-2 reinfections among healthcare workers in India with increased severity in the second episode. Lancet. https://doi.org/10.2139/ssrn.3688220.

Shirbhate, E., et al., 2020. Synthetic and semi-synthetic drugs as promising therapeutic option for the treatment of COVID-19. Mini Rev. Med. Chem. 21 (8), 1004–1016. https://doi.org/10.2174/1389557520666201204162103.

Singh, J., Singh, H., Hasnain, S.E., Rahman, S.A., 2020. Mutational signatures in countries affected by SARS-CoV-2: implications in host-pathogen interactome. bioRxiv 2020. https://doi.org/10.1101/2020.09.17.301614, 301614.

Song, P., et al., 2020. Cytokine storm induced by SARS-CoV-2. Clin. Chim. Acta 509, 280–287. https://doi.org/10.1016/j.cca.2020.06.017.

Su, S., et al., 2016. Epidemiology, genetic recombination, and pathogenesis of coronaviruses. Trends Microbiol. 24 (6), 490–502. https://doi.org/10.1016/j.tim.2016.03.003.

Tillett, R.L., et al., 2021. Genomic evidence for reinfection with SARS-CoV-2: a case study. Lancet Infect. Dis. 21 (1), 52–58. https://doi.org/10.1016/s1473-3099(20)30764-7.

To, K.K.W., et al., 2020. COVID-19 re-infection by a phylogenetically distinct SARS-coronavirus-2 strain confirmed by whole genome sequencing. Clin. Infect. Dis. 73, e2946–e2951. https://doi.org/10.1093/cid/ciaa1275.

Toovey, O.T.R., Harvey, K.N., Bird, P.W., Tang, J.W.T., 2021. Introduction of Brazilian SARS-CoV-2 484K.V2 related variants into the UK. J. Infect. 82 (5), 23–24. https://doi.org/10.1016/j.jinf.2021.01.025.

Van Elslande, J., et al., 2020. Symptomatic SARS-CoV-2 reinfection by a phylogenetically distinct strain. Clin. Infect. Dis. 73, 354–356. https://doi.org/10.1093/cid/ciaa1330.

Wang, D., et al., 2020. Clinical characteristics of 138 hospitalized patients with 2019 novel coronavirus–infected pneumonia in Wuhan, China. JAMA 323 (11), 1061–1069. https://doi.org/10.1001/jama.2020.1585.

World Health Organization, 2020. Coronavirus Disease 2019 (COVID-19): Situation Report-72. World Health Organization. https://apps.who.int/iris/handle/10665/331685. (Accessed 17 September 2021).

World Health Organization, 2021. Tracking SARS-CoV-2 Variants. https://www.who.int/en/activities/tracking-SARS-CoV-2-variants/. (Accessed 17 September 2021).

Wu, A., Mihaylova, V.T., Landry, M.L., Foxman, E.F., 2020a. Interference between rhinovirus and influenza a virus: a clinical data analysis and experimental infection study. Lancet Microbe 1, 254–262. https://doi.org/10.1016/S2666-5247(20)30114-2.

Wu, F., et al., 2020b. A new coronavirus associated with human respiratory disease in China. Nature 579 (7798), 265–269.

Wu, Z., McGoogan, J.M., 2020. Characteristics of and important lessons from the coronavirus disease 2019 (COVID-19) outbreak in China: summary of a report of 72314 cases from the chinese center for disease control and prevention. JAMA 323 (13), 1239–1242. https://doi.org/10.1001/jama.2020.2648.

Yan, Y., et al., 2021. The COVID-19 vaccines: recent development, challenges and prospects. Vaccines 9 (4), 349. https://doi.org/10.3390/vaccines9040349.

Zaki, A.M., et al., 2012. Isolation of a novel coronavirus from a man with pneumonia in Saudi Arabia. N. Engl. J. Med. 367 (19), 1814–1820. https://doi.org/10.1056/NEJMoa1211721.

Zheng, J., 2020. SARS-CoV-2: an emerging coronavirus that causes a global threat. Int. J. Biol. Sci. 16 (10), 1678–1685. https://doi.org/10.7150/ijbs.45053.

Zhong, N.S., et al., 2003. Epidemiology and cause of severe acute respiratory syndrome (SARS) in Guangdong, People's Republic of China, in February, 2003. Lancet 362 (9393), 1353–1358. https://doi.org/10.1016/s0140-6736(03)14630-2.

CHAPTER THREE

Effect of yoga mudras in improving the health of users: A precautionary measure practice in daily life for resisting the deadly COVID-19 disease

S.N. Kumar[a], Anandhu Venu[a], and M. Harini Jaya[b]
[a]Department of EEE, Amal Jyothi College of Engineering, Kanjirappally, Kerala, India
[b]Adhiyamaan College of Agriculture and Research (ACAR), Hosur, Tamil Nadu, India

1 Introduction

The word yoga was derived from the Sanskrit word yuj and its meaning is "to connect." Yoga links the individual consciousness with the universal consciousness (Raub, 2002). The yoga practice generates a perfect harmony between body, mind, and nature. Yoga comprises asanas, mudras, and meditation. The asanas and mudras involve stretching of legs and hands, mudras utilize fingers for making postures (Ramos-Jimenez et al., 2009). The yoga practice has significant effects on obesity, cholesterol, blood pressure, diabetes, and cardiac diseases (Innes and Vincent, 2007; Yang, 2007; Gordon et al., 2008). Yoga plays vital role in physical and mental health care, Islamic prayer Salah/Namaaz along with yoga was found to be proficient in improving mental health (Sayeed and Prakash, 2013). The mudras for lung specific diseases especially asthma was highlighted in Saravanan et al. (2019). A systematic study was carried out in Bir (2016) for the clinical applications of yoga in the pediatric population (Birdee et al., 2009). The importance of yoga in emotion, embodiment, and gentrification was explored in (Kern, 2012). The effect of yoga in enhancing cognitive-communication skills was discussed in Namratha et al. (2017). Yoga therapy enhances the physiological functions of the heart and lung and makes the body elastic, induce stem cell trafficking from bone marrow to peripheral blood vessel for potential repair and regeneration of tissues (Shree and Bhonde, 2016).

Lessons from COVID-19
https://doi.org/10.1016/B978-0-323-99878-9.00001-7

The increased hectic schedule of life generates stress and the yoga practice nadi-shodhana pranayama reduces stress. The benefits of postoperation therapy using nadi-shodhana pranayama along with physiotherapy are effective in improving lung function and reducing depression, stress, anxiety are highlighted in Kinabalu (2005). Yoga has proven to be beneficial for patients with cardiac arrest or other heart related issues. The severe agitation and apprehension of such events have significant and critical effects on the heart. Pranayama is a type of yogic breathing exercise proven to be efficient in curing lung diseases like asthma, allergic bronchitis, post pneumonia, tuberculosis recovery, and many other occupational diseases. The practice of pranayama modulates cardiac autonomic status and with improvement in cardiac respiratory function, nadi-shodhana pranayama rapidly alters cardiopulmonary response and reduces blood pressure (Shankarappa et al., 2012). The pranayama is the art of control breathing, since it is the only autonomic function of the body that can be consciously controlled (Akhtar et al., 2013). The effect of yoga in enhancing the functionality of anatomical organs is described in Akhtar et al. (2013). The pranayama was meant to improve respiratory functions, but also induce psycho-physical effects in the body. The lung function was found to improve by continuously practicing pranayama (Dhaniwala et al., 2020). The continuous practice of yoga was found to be proficient in increasing alpha and theta frequency activity, it also alleviates cardiovascular and respiratory diseases (Basu-Ray et al., 2021). The yoga practices were found to be efficient in the minimization of stress (Rao et al., 2017). The Bhastrika pranayama has a significant role in the minimization of anxiety and improves the functional connectivity of the brain (Novaes et al., 2020). The specific mudras for improving the respiratory system efficiency and for curing asthma are discussed in Saravanan et al. (2019). Section 2 highlights the materials and methods. The basic mudras for health care are described in Section 2.1. Section 2.2 describes the mudras and breathing exercise for improving the immunity of the body. Section 3 puts forward the yoga health package system for resisting pandemic disease.

2 Materials and methods

Human beings depend on nature for their livelihood and the human body itself comprises water element (blood), air element (breath), earth element (bones and muscles), fire element (heat), and space element (emptiness). The fingers in the hands correspond to panchaboothas and are depicted in Fig. 1A. Out of five fingers, the thumb depicts fire (agni), the

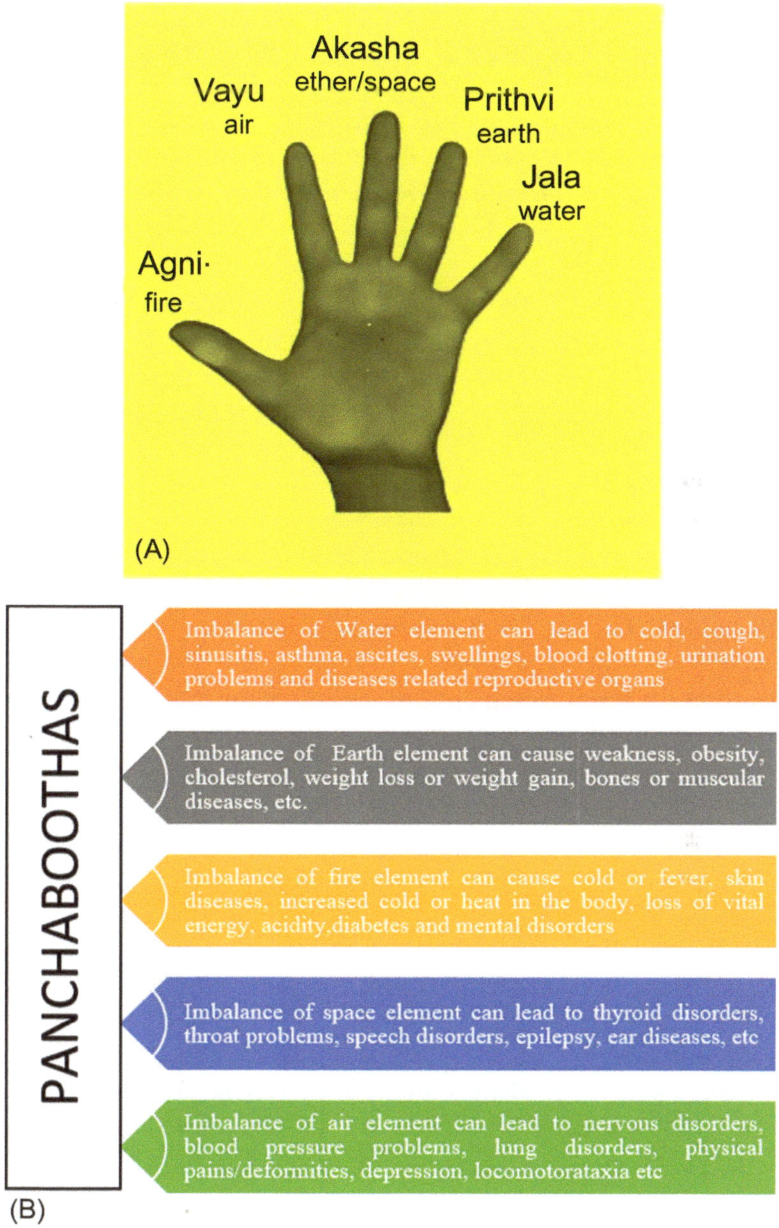

Fig. 1 (A) Panchaboothas in our hand, (B) panchaboothas and their effect on the human body.

index finger depicts air (vayu), the middle finger depicts space (akash), the ring finger depicts earth (prithvi) while the little finger depicts water (jal). The mudras are practiced with fingers, since they are the storehouse of magnetic energy. The practice of mudras helps to balance the energy elements in the body. The imbalance of energy elements is the root cause of diseases and is depicted in Fig. 1B. The mudras regulate the flow of energy elements in the body.

2.1 Basic mudras for health care

Figs. 2 and 3 depict the basic mudras for health care. In Fig. 2, (A) depicts the fingers in stretch out pose, (B) gyan mudra, (C) vayu mudra, (D) shunya mudra, (E) prithvi mudra, (F) surya mudra, (G) varuna mudra.

2.1.1 Gyan mudra

It is also known as the mudra of knowledge and wisdom. It improves the mind concentration during meditation and forms a vital role in pranayama. The consistent practice of this mudra enhances brain activity.

Procedure: The steps in doing the gyan mudra are as follows; sit in a comfortable position, padmasana or vajrasana is the best pose. The hands are placed in the knees facing upward, the tip of the thumb finger touches the tip of the index finger. A slight pressure has to be applied at the tip. The mind concentration should be on our breath and our eyes should be closed. The gyan mudra pose is depicted in Fig. 2B.

Merits: Relieves from stress, anxiety, depression, and tension. Gives better sleep and improves the blood circulation in the nervous system and pituitary gland.

In Fig. 3, the specifications are as follows: (A) prana mudra, (B) apana mudra, (C) apana vayu mudra, (D) adhimudra.

2.1.2 Vayu mudra

It is associated with the air element in the body. It is specifically applicable for those having an imbalance of air element in the body. It reduces the effect of excess gas in the stomach. This mudra was found to be efficient for those having intensified vata.

Procedure: The steps in doing the vayu mudra are as follows; sit in a comfortable position, padmasana or vajrasana is the best pose. The tip of the thumb should touch the middle portion of the index finger, the other fingers are kept straight. Slight pressure is applied and the vayu mudra is depicted in Fig. 2C.

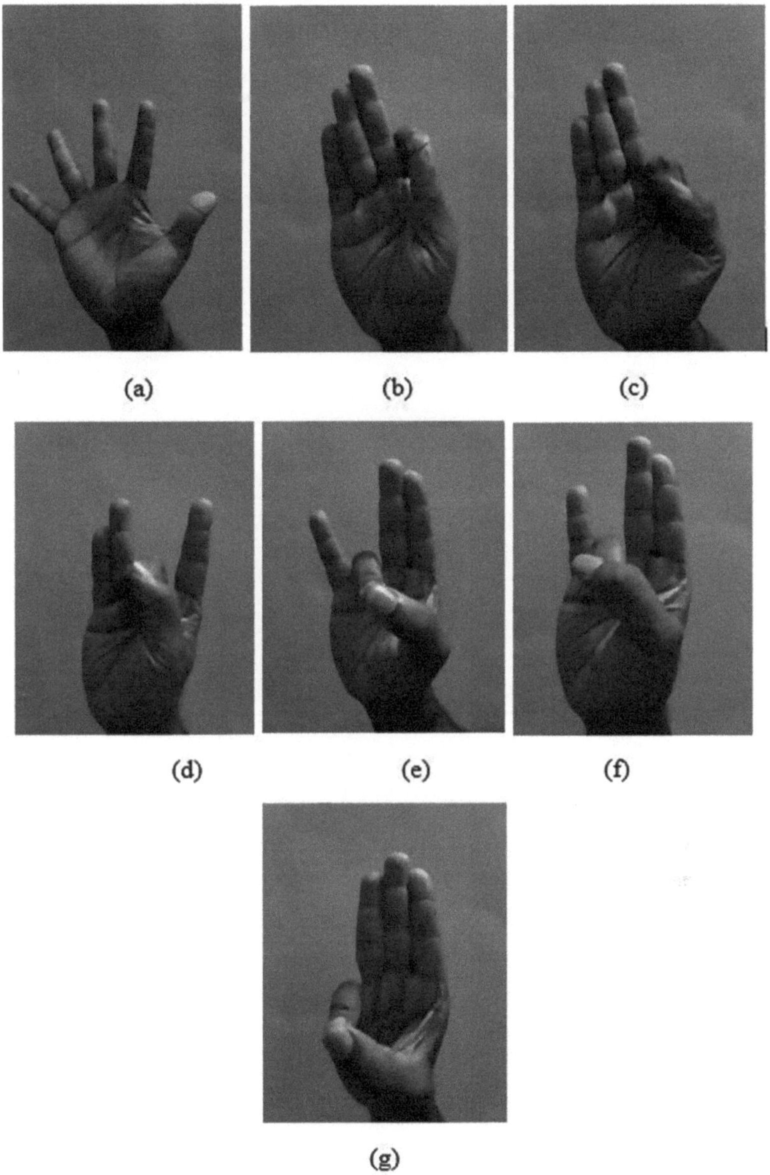

Fig. 2 Yoga mudras for health care—Stage 1.

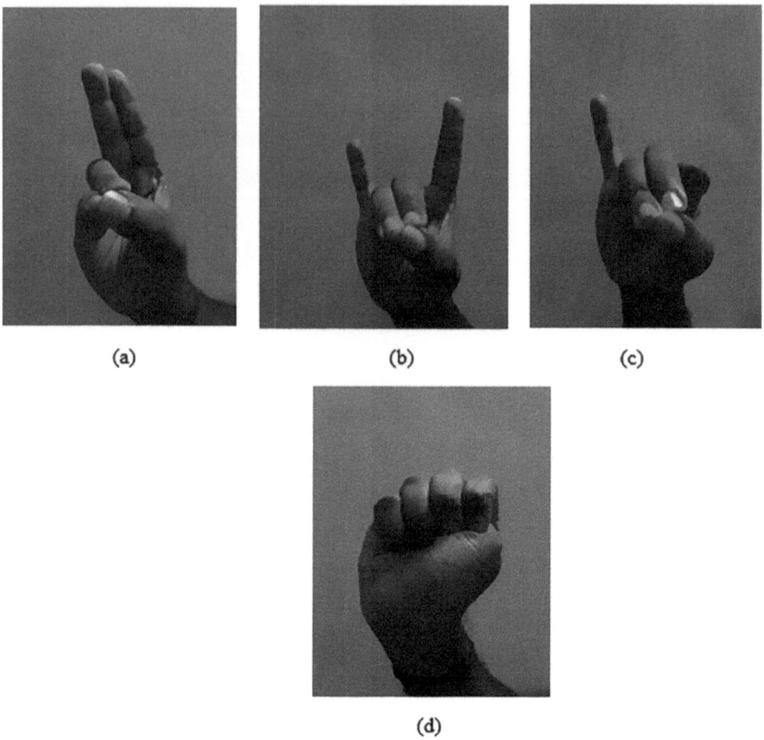

Fig. 3 Yoga mudras for health care—Stage 2.

Merits: Relieves the knee and joint pain, relief in the case of spastic paralysis and Parkinson's disease, alleviates the gas problems in the stomach.

2.1.3 Varuna mudra

It is associated with the water element in the body. It improves blood circulation in the body. This mudra is beneficial for dry mouth, dry eyes, dry skin, and dry hair, as well as a loss of taste and other tongue disorders.

Procedure: The steps in doing the varuna mudra are as follows; sit in a comfortable position, padmasana or vajrasana is the best pose. The hands are placed in the knees facing upward, the tip of the thumb finger touches the tip of the little finger, and the other fingers are kept straight. Slight pressure is applied at the tip and the varuna mudra is depicted in Fig. 2G.

Merits: Cures skin problems, continuous practice of this mudra aids in the maintenance of cholesterol levels in the body.

2.1.4 Surya mudra

It is associated with the heat element in the body. It aids in the dissolving of extra fat and helps to control obesity. This mudra improves metabolism, promoting, weight loss, helps in treating the flu, strengthen the eyes and improves vision.

Procedure: The steps in doing the varuna mudra are as follows; sit in a comfortable position, padmasana or vajrasana is the best pose. The hands are placed in the knees facing upward, the tip of the thumb finger touches the middle of the ring finger, and the other fingers are kept straight. Slight pressure is applied at the tip and the surya mudra is depicted in Fig. 2F.

Merits: It lowers the high LDL cholesterol, minimizes stress and tension, advances metabolic activities in the body, and improves the functioning of the thyroid gland. Hypothyroidism causes obesity, which in turn affects the functioning of the heart.

2.1.5 Prithvi mudra

It is associated with the earth element and has its link with the mooladhara chakra. This mudra is done along with the mediation and is associated with a positive impact on the skin, hair, and bones of the body.

Procedure: The steps in doing the prithvi mudra are as follows; sit in a comfortable position, padmasana or vajrasana is the best pose. The hands are placed in the knees facing upward, the tip of the thumb finger touches the tip of the ring finger, and the other fingers are kept straight. Slight pressure is applied at the tip and the prithvi mudra is depicted in Fig. 2E.

Merits: It is efficient for improving stamina, good for chronic fatigue and Osteoarthritis.

2.1.6 Shunya mudra

It is a simple yoga gesture designed to decrease the space element (akasha) in the body. It can be practiced while seated standing or even walking, as long as the body is relaxed and the posture is symmetrical.

Procedure: The steps in doing the shunya mudra are as follows; sit in a comfortable position, padmasana or vajrasana is the best pose. The hands are placed in the knees facing upward, the tip of the thumb finger touches the middle finger, and the other fingers are kept straight. Slight pressure is applied at the tip and the shunya mudra is depicted in Fig. 2D.

Merits: Cures ear diseases, strengthens muscles, well for the functioning of heart and thyroid gland.

2.1.7 *Apana mudra*

Human health and wellness are dependent on the rapid removal of systemic waste before it turns toxic. It is also called the mudra of digestion and plays a vital role in the regulation of the excretory system.

Procedure: The steps in doing the shunya mudra are as follows; sit in a comfortable position, padmasana or vajrasana is the best pose. The hands are placed in the knees facing upward, the tip of the thumb finger touches the middle finger, and the other fingers are kept straight. Slight pressure is applied at the tip and the apana mudra is depicted in Fig. 3B.

Merits: It regulates diabetes and aids in curing menstrual problems, eliminates the disease related to indigestion such as constipation, piles, vomiting, etc. Good for heart ailments and can be used by those complaining of chest pain due to cardiac malfunction. Useful for pregnant ladies during the 9th month or delayed delivery; it can help in smooth and easy childbirth.

2.2 Mudras and breathing exercise for improving immunity

The mudras and breathing exercise for improving immunity is as follows. Fig. 4 depicts the yoga mudras.

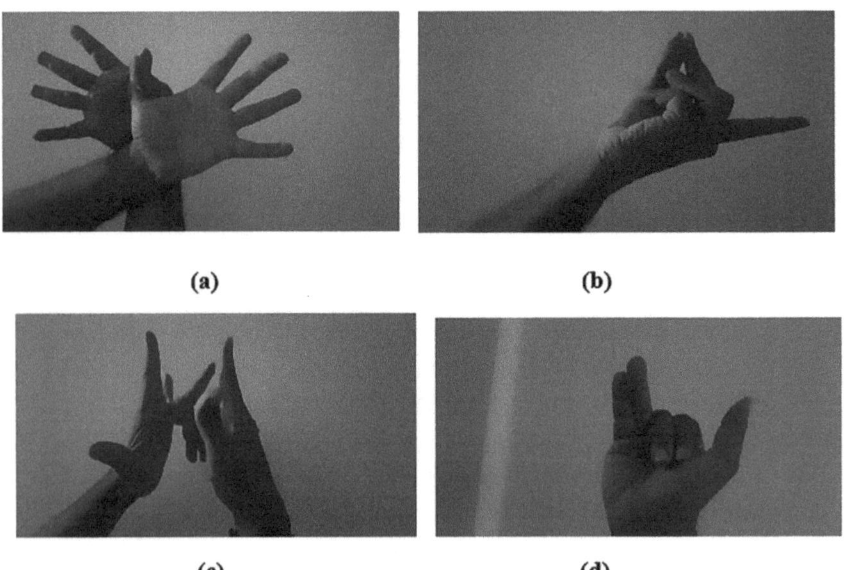

Fig. 4 Yoga mudras for health care—Stage 3.

2.2.1 *Apana vayu mudra*

It is also called mudra of the heart and can be used as a first-aid remedy during a heart attack. It increases the earth element and the fire element decreases the air element in the body. Cleans the body and supplies oxygen to the heart.

Procedure: The steps in doing the apana vayu mudra are as follows; sit in a comfortable position, padmasana or vajrasana is the best pose Touch the tip of the thumb with the tips of middle and ring fingers on both hands. Fold the index finger inward so that its tip touches the base of the thumb on both hands. The little finger is stretched outward. It is depicted in Fig. 3C.

Merits: Cures headache, toothache, backache, neck pain, joint pain, digestion problems, and arthritis. Effective for respiratory diseases, it also improves the functioning of the lungs.

2.2.2 *Prana mudra*

It is also called mudra of vitality. This mudra stimulates the mooladhara or root chakra. It increases the level of earth element, water element and minimizes the fire element.

Procedure: The steps in doing the prana mudra are as follows; sit in a comfortable position, padmasana or vajrasana is the best pose. The tip of the thumb is touched with the ring and the little finger. Slight pressure is applied and the index, the middle finger is stretched out. It is depicted in Fig. 3A.

Merits: Helps in the proper working of the lungs, rejuvenates the heart, and minimizes vitamin deficiency and chronic fatigue. Improves blood circulation and alleviates joint pain, mental tension, and stress.

2.2.3 *Adhi mudra*

This mudra is also called a baby's gesture and is also known as primordial mudra. It is the simplest mudra and the Sanskrit term "Adi" means the first. It had got its name by the hand posture of the fetus inside the mother's womb. It focuses on the breathing pattern and can be practiced with asanas.

Procedure: The steps in doing the shunya mudra are as follows; sit in a comfortable position, padmasana or vajrasana is the best pose. The adhi mudra pose is depicted in Fig. 3D. The hands are placed in thighs with all the fingers closed in such a manner that, thumb is closed first and above which the four fingers are placed.

Merits: Increase the breathing capacity of lungs, enhance the oxygen flow in the body, stimulates the brain, calms the nervous system, enhance the oxygen flow in the body.

2.2.4 *Garuda mudra*

This mudra is also called as eagle pose. It is followed during mediation and pranayama, hence called garuda mudra pranayama.

Procedure: The steps in doing the shunya mudra are as follows; sit in a comfortable position, padmasana or vajrasana is the best pose. Both the thumb are interlocked and the remaining fingers in two hands are stretched out as depicted in Fig. 4A. The thumb represents the fire element in the body, hence this mudra stimulates the fire element and heats the body. This mudra is done at three positions with palms facing us; the lower part of the abdomen, near the navel and above the navel.

Merits: It is practiced in three different regions as stated earlier, hence it improves the functioning of the kidney, lungs, heart, and stomach. Cures respiratory problems and regulates the blood circulation of the body.

2.2.5 *Asthma mudra*

This mudra is practiced with both hands. The middle fingers of the two hands should be in contact, the nails also should touch each other.

Procedure: The steps in doing the asthma mudra are as follows; sit in a comfortable position, padmasana or vajrasana is the best pose Stretch out the fingers of both hands and the middle fingers of two hands are bent inward and are depicted in Fig. 4C. The remaining fingers are stretched out as depicted in the figure.

Merits: Relaxes bronchial tubes and clears bad toxins and blockages. Good for asthma patients, since it eases the muscles that line the respiratory tract.

2.2.6 *Aswini mudra*

This mudra is also known as horse gesture. This mudra directs the prana (life energy) upward along the spine through the sushmna nadi. This mudra focuses on the Muladhara or the root chakra. This mudra should be practiced in a relaxed manner and should not create any redundant tension on other parts of the human body.

Procedure: The steps in doing the asthma mudra are as follows; sit in a comfortable position, padmasana or vajrasana is the best pose, *salamba sarvangasana* (supported shoulder stand) with the knees bent and dropped forward. Relax in chin mudra for 5 min. Take a breath and exhale three times. While inhaling, upright the mouth of anus by feelings and try to keep it for 5 min. While exhaling, relax and contract.

Merits: Expansion and contraction of anus make chakras in our body function in an efficient manner. Wastage in our body will be removed.

2.2.7 Bronchial mudra

This mudra is practiced with four fingers and plays a vital role in minimizing respiratory problems. Bronchial are pipes that transport air through the windpipes at the throat to the lungs in our body. The pipes when diseased, with exposure to irritable substances, cause Bronchitis. This mudra should be avoided by pregnant women.

Procedure: The steps in doing the bronchial mudra are as follows; sit in a comfortable position, padmasana or vajrasana is the best pose. The little finger is placed at the root of the thumb, pressing while curling it inward, the ring finger is positioned on the upper thumb joint, pressing toward the thumb, while curling the finger, then place the middle finger on the tip, of the thumb, pressing against each other, while the index finger is stretch out and is depicted in Fig. 4B.

Merits: Improves breathing, increases the oxygen flow in the body, the function of the lung is enhanced.

2.2.8 Nadi Shuddi pranayama

The human body consists of 72,000 veins. The Nadi Shuddi is a breathing exercise that energizes the veins in the body can be cleaned through our breath. It removes all the dust blocked in our lungs, nostrils, also removes mucous leading to the good functioning of the lungs. The left hand is positioned in chin mudra and the right hand in nasika mudra. It is also called as the anulom-vilom pranayam (alternate nostril pranayam). The nasika mudra pose is as follows; index finger and middle finger is bent, while the remaining fingers are stretched out as depicted in Fig. 4D.

Procedure:

- Sit in Suhasana or Vajrasana or Artha padmasana or Padmasana or Virasana according to one's convenience.
- Press the thumb down on the right nostril and exhale quietly through the left nostril.
- Now inhale from the left nostril and then press the left nostril gently with the ring finger and little finger. Remove the right thumb from the right nostril, exhale from the right.
- Inhale from the right nostril and exhale from the left. The above one is the complete round of Nadi Shodhan pranayama. Continue inhaling and exhaling from alternate nostrils.

Merits: Enhances lung capacity and induces balance in the digestive, nervous, respiratory, cardiovascular systems. The immunity of the body is improved and nerves are purified.

3 Proposed yoga health package model

This research work proposes a health package model that can be followed by every person for improving immunity. The practice of mudras and breathing exercise ensures good physical and mental health. This yoga health package model has to be done before food, preferably after the daily morning routine (nature call). The yoga health package model is depicted in table. The mudras and breathing exercise while practicing in the evening should be before taking food and after a minimum duration of an hour if tea/coffee had been taken. Each mudra can be practiced for a minimum duration of 5 min and a maximum of 20 min. In this proposed health package system, the mudras are grouped into two sections as depicted below in Table 1.

The health package system is depicted in figure, a total of 30 min duration have to be devoted for enhancing the immunity of body during morning and evening session. This system can be practiced by children from the age of 10 to persons above the age of 70. Fig. 5 depicts the proposed yoga health package system.

The Nadi Shuddi pranayama and aswini mudras were incorporated in morning and evening session yoga practice. The seven mudras and a pranayama exercise were considered in this work, the seven mudras are grouped into two sessions based on their effects in improving health. The features of each mudra are detailed in Section 2. A daily practice of this system improves the immunity of the body and ensures physical and mental health thereby resisting the pandemic disease COVID-19.

Table 1 Yoga health package system.

Morning session	Duration (min)	Evening session	Duration (min)
Nadi Shuddi Pranayama	10	Nadi Shuddi Pranayama	10
Prana mudra	5	Apana vayu mudra	5
Garuda mudra	5	Asthma mudra	5
Bronchial mudra	5	Adhi mudra	5
Aswini mudra	5	Aswini mudra	5

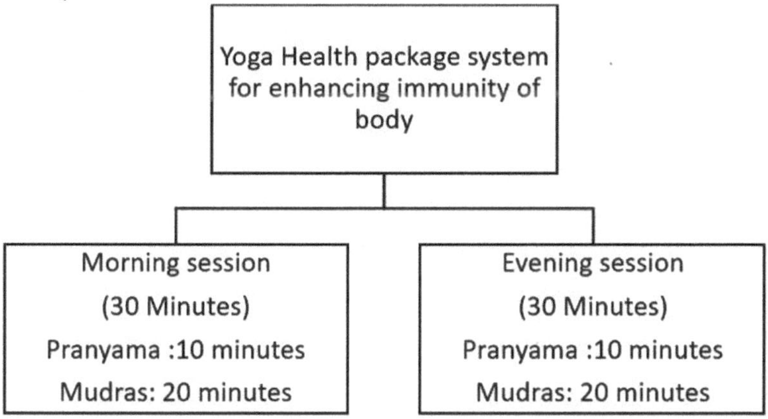

Fig. 5 Yoga health package system for enhancing the immunity of the body.

4 Results and discussion

A set of questionnaire was framed and the survey response was collected. The target audience comprises of population with age criteria from 20 to 60. Out of 24 questions in the Google form, the first four questions was related to personal information. The response was collected through social media apps. The questionnaire was framed through the discussion with experts in yoga and focus group comprises of people who are aware and not aware of yoga principles. A total of 200 participants involved in the survey and the summary of response is also represented here. The questionnaire was highlighted in the Appendix section. The responses are analyzed using pie chart (circular statistical graphical chart) and bar chart, the response with maximum voting by the respondents was taken into account from the survey results.

The response of the questions is analyzed, and the inferences are as follows:

(i) Q1, Q2, and Q3. The 51.1% of the respondents are male and 48.9% are female

(ii) Q4. Many respondents were not ready to share their health problems, however the following response were obtained

(iii) Q5. The 57.4% respondents reported to have stress

(iv) Q6. With respect to the source of stress, the results are depicted in Fig. 6

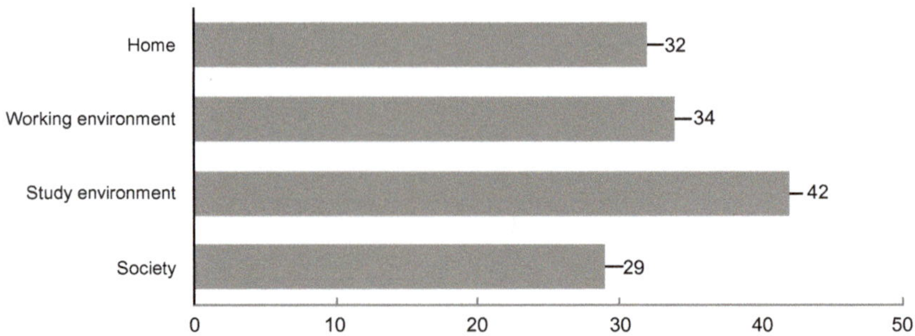

Fig. 6 Source of stress.

(v) Q7. The 31.9% strongly agrees and 44% agrees with the statement that practicing yoga will minimize the stress, the rest 20.6% has neutral response.

(vi) Q8. The preferences in learning yoga principles are depicted below in Fig. 7

(vii) Q9. The 75.9% of target population was aware of pranayama and 24.1% was not aware of pranayama

(viii) Q10. The 21.4% of target population practice pranayama daily, while 78.6% occasionally practice pranayama

(ix) Q11. The 73% of the target population was interested in practicing mudras, while 24% of the target population was not interested in practicing mudras

(x) Q12. The 69.5% of the target population are ready to do yoga practice for 20 min, while the 24.1% of the target population choose 30 min, the rest were ready to spend 1 h

(xi) Q13. The 27.5% of the population often gets angry, the 65.5% of the population occasionally gets angry, while the 7% never gets angry

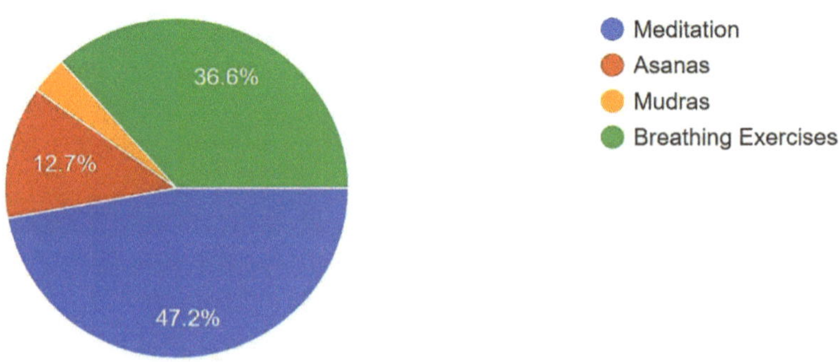

Fig. 7 Pie chart depicting the principles of yoga preferences.

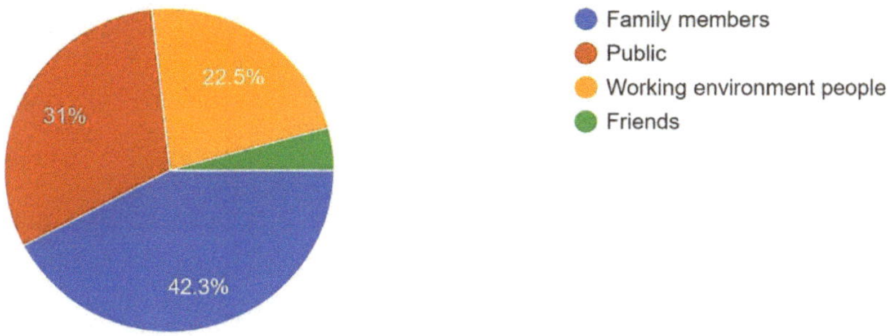

Fig. 8 Response indicating source of provoking a person.

- **(xii)** Q14. The response is depicted below in Fig. 8
- **(xiii)** Q15. The 87.3% of the population was interested in improving immunity to resist COVID-19 through yoga practices
- **(xiv)** Q16. The 85.2% of the population was interested in learning yoga practices
- **(xv)** Q17. The preference in learning yoga practices are depicted below in Fig. 9
- **(xvi)** Q18. The 83.1% of population shows agreement toward the learning of 30 min health package comprising of mudras and pranayama
- **(xvii)** Q19. The 56.3% of population prefer offline technique in learning yoga practices
- **(xviii)** Q20. The 14.8% of population prefer vegetarian food, while 17.6% of population prefer non vegetarian food, the rest prefer veg/ non veg
- **(xix)** Q21. The 90.8% of population are interested in taking a balance diet

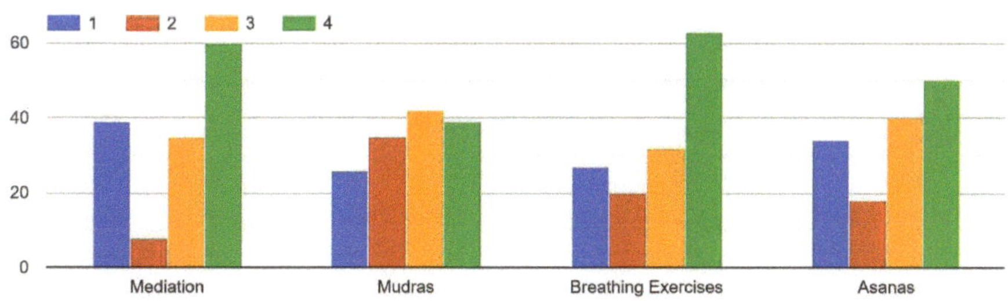

Fig. 9 Preferences in learning yoga practices.

(xx) Q22. The 69% of population are taking medicine to improve immunity

(xxi) Q23. The 52.8% of population are vaccinated for resisting COVID-19 disease

4.1 Implications of the study

The vital implications of the proposed study are highlighted as follows; more than 50% of the respondents are reported to have stress, the stress source of maximum value 42.9% belongs to study environment and the next maximum source of stress value is 34.7% that belongs to working environment. Out of 200 respondents, it was observed that 31.9% strongly agrees and 44% agrees that practicing yoga will minimize the stress. Among the different yoga practices like meditation, asana, breathing exercises, and mudra, the maximum voting preference is for practicing meditation (47.5%). The second maximum voting preference is for practicing breathing exercises. The proposed research work was focused mainly on pranayama and mudra practice, the survey results reveals that 75.9% of the respondents were aware of pranayama, out of which 21.4% of the people practice pranayama regularly. The 73% of the respondents were found to be interested in practicing mudras. This research work proposes a 30 min health package for improving the immunity of the body, the response survey shows that 83.1% of the respondents are willing to take 30 min daily yoga practice.

It was evident from the previous research works (Tillu et al., 2020; Venkatesh et al., 2020) that yoga practices has significant role in improving the immunity of body especially in this current COVID-19 (Bushell et al., 2020) pandemic scenario. By having a balanced diet and proper exercise, the body will be healthy and proper yoga practices will improve the immunity of the body.

5 Conclusion

This chapter focuses on some typical yoga mudras and Nadi Shuddi pranayama for improving the immunity of the body. In this current pandemic COVID-19 scenario, many are subjected to disease because of poor immunity. The vaccination and medicines are there for improving immunity; however, this chapter focuses on the yoga practices that help to resist disease. The scientific benefits of yoga practices were already proved and this work proposes a health package for 30 min in the morning and evening. In the health package, the Nadi Shuddi pranayama and aswini mudra were common for both sessions and the remaining mudras are grouped in such a manner that the total duration is 30 min. The survey results indicate that 83.1% of the focus group shows agreement toward the learning of 30 min health package. Prevention is better than cure, and the outcome of this research work paves a way toward improving the immunity for the welfare of society.

Appendix

The questionnaire is represented below.

Q1. Name:
Q2. Age
Q3. Gender: a. Male, b. Female
Q4. Do you have any health problems?
a. Headache, b. Breathing problem, c. Sinus, d. Joint pains, e. Others
Q5. Do you have stress
a. Yes, b. No
Q6. If you have stress, can you please tick the source of stress
a. Home, b. Working environment, c. Study environment, d. Society
Q7. Do you think Yoga practices had significant role in Health care?
a. Strongly disagree, b. Disagree, c. Neutral, d. Agree, e. Strongly Agree
Q8. What type of yoga practices do you prefer?
a. Meditation, b. Asana, c. Mudras, d. Breathing exercises
Q9. Are you aware of pranayama?
a. Yes, b. No
Q10. If you are practicing pranayama, please indicate your choice?
a. Daily, b. Occasionally
Q11. Are you interested in practicing mudras done by hand for improving health care?
a. Yes, b. No
Q12. How much time you can devote for practicing yoga daily to improve your physical and mental health?
a. 20 minutes, b. 30 minutes, c. 1 hour
Q13. How often do you get angry?
a. Often, b. Occasionally, c. Never
Q14. Who will be troubling you in your daily routine there by making you angry?
a. Family members, b. Public, c. Working environment, d. Friends

Q15. Are you interested in improving immunity of your body to resist COVID-19 through yoga practices?
a. Yes, b. No

Q16. Are you interested in learning yoga practices?
a. Yes, b. No

Q17. Indicate your preference in learning the following practices?
1. Meditation, 2. Mudras, 3. Breathing exercises, 4. Asana

Q18. If a health package of 30 min morning and evening comprising of pranayama and mudras with simple mediation is suggested, are you interested in adopting that for improving your health?
a. Yes, b. No

Q19. Which mode of training you prefer for yoga practices?
a. Online, b. Offline

Q20. Indicate your food preference
a. Vegetarian, b. Non Vegetarian, c. Veg/Non Vegetarian

Q21. Are you interested in following a balance diet to improve your health?
a. Yes, b. No

Q22. Are you taking any medicine to improve your immunity?
a. Yes, b. No

Q23. For improving immunity, which one you follow?
a. Allopathy, b. Ayurveda, c. Homeopathy

Q24. Are you vaccinated to resist COVID-19?
a. Yes, b. No

Acknowledgment

The author SN Kumar would like to acknowledge the support from Sky Yoga Center, Nagercoil, and Schmitt Centre for Biomedical Instrumentation of Amal Jyothi College of Engineering.

References

Akhtar, P., Yardi, S., Akhtar, M., 2013. Effects of yoga on functional capacity and well being. Int. J. Yoga 6 (1), 76.

Basu-Ray, I., et al., 2021. A mechanistic model for yoga as a preventive and therapeutic modality. Int. J. Yoga 14 (2), 152.

Bir, S., 2016. Principles and Practice of Yoga in Health Care. Handspring Publishing Limited.

Birdee, G.S., et al., 2009. Clinical applications of yoga for the pediatric population: a systematic review. Acad. Pediatr. 9 (4), 212–220. https://doi.org/10.1016/j.acap.2009.04.002.

Bushell, W., et al., 2020. Meditation and yoga practices as potential adjunctive treatment of SARS-CoV-2 infection and COVID-19: a brief overview of key subjects. J. Altern. Complement. Med. 26 (7), 547–556. https://doi.org/10.1089/acm.2020.0177.

Dhaniwala, N.K.S., Dasari, V., Dhaniwala, M.N., 2020. Pranayama and breathing exercises – types and its role in disease prevention & rehabilitation. J. Evol. Med. Dent. Sci. 9 (44), 3325–3330. https://doi.org/10.14260/jemds/2020/730.

Gordon, L.A., et al., 2008. Effect of exercise therapy on lipid profile and oxidative stress indicators in patients with type 2 diabetes. BMC Complement. Altern. Med. 8, 1–10. https://doi.org/10.1186/1472-6882-8-21.

Innes, K.E., Vincent, H.K., 2007. The influence of yoga-based programs on risk profiles in adults with type 2 diabetes mellitus: a systematic review. Evid. Based Complement. Alternat. Med. 4 (4), 469–486. https://doi.org/10.1093/ecam/nel103.

Kern, L., 2012. Connecting embodiment, emotion and gentrification: an exploration through the practice of yoga in Toronto. Emot. Space Soc. 5 (1), 27–35. https://doi.org/10.1016/j.emospa.2011.01.003.

Kinabalu, K., 2005. Immediate effect of 'nadi-shodhana pranayama' on some selected parameters of cardiovascular, pulmonary, and higher functions of brain. Thai J. Physiol. Sci. 18 (2), 10–16.

Namratha, H.G., et al., 2017. Effect of yoga and working memory training on cognitive communicative abilities among middle aged adults. Complement. Ther. Clin. Pract. 28, 92–100. https://doi.org/10.1016/j.ctcp.2017.05.007.

Novaes, M.M., et al., 2020. Effects of yoga respiratory practice (Bhastrika pranayama) on anxiety, affect, and brain functional connectivity and activity: a randomized controlled trial. Front. Psych. 11 (May), 1–13. https://doi.org/10.3389/fpsyt.2020.00467.

Ramos-Jimenez, A., et al., 2009. Cardiovascular and metabolic effects of intensive Hatha Yoga training in middle-aged and older women from northern Mexico. Int. J. Yoga 2 (2), 49. https://doi.org/10.4103/0973-6131.60044.

Rao, R.M., et al., 2017. Effect of yoga on sleep quality and neuroendocrine immune response in metastatic breast cancer patients. Indian J. Palliat. Care 23 (3), 253–260. https://doi.org/10.4103/IJPC.IJPC_102_17.

Raub, J.A., 2002. Psychophysiologic effects of Hatha Yoga on musculoskeletal and cardiopulmonary function: a literature review. J. Altern. Complement. Med. 8 (6), 797–812. https://doi.org/10.1089/10755530260511810.

Saravanan, P.S.L., et al., 2019. Lung-specific yoga mudras on respiratory function in asthma patients. Natl. J. Physiol. Pharm. Pharm. 9 (9), 878–883.

Sayeed, S.A., Prakash, A., 2013. The Islamic prayer (Salah/Namaaz) and yoga togetherness in mental health. Indian J. Psychiatry 55 (Spec. suppl), 19–23. https://doi.org/10.4103/0019-5545.105537.

Shankarappa, V., et al., 2012. The short term effect of pranayama on the lung parameters. J. Clin. Diagn. Res. 6 (1), 27–30.

Shree, N., Bhonde, R.R., 2016. Can yoga therapy stimulate stem cell trafficking from bone marrow? J. Ayurveda Integr. Med. 7 (3), 181–184. https://doi.org/10.1016/j.jaim.2016.07.003.

Tillu, G., et al., 2020. Public health approach of ayurveda and yoga for COVID-19 prophylaxis. J. Altern. Complement. Med. 26 (5), 360–364. https://doi.org/10.1089/acm.2020.0129.

Venkatesh, H., et al., 2020. Molecular signature of the immune response to yoga therapy in stress-related chronic disease conditions: an insight. Int. J. Yoga 13 (1), 9. https://doi.org/10.4103/ijoy.ijoy_82_18.

Yang, K., 2007. A review of yoga programs for four leading risk factors of chronic diseases. Evid. Based Complement. Alternat. Med. 4 (4), 487–491. https://doi.org/10.1093/ecam/nem154.

CHAPTER FOUR

Blockchain: Opportunities in the healthcare sector and its uses in COVID-19

Senthil Kumar Arumugam[a] and Aarti Mehta Sharma[b,c]
[a]Department of Professional Studies, School of Commerce, Finance and Accountancy, Christ University, Bangalore, Karnataka, India
[b]Symbiosis Centre for Management Studies, Bengaluru, Karnataka, India
[c]Symbiosis International (Deemed University), Pune, Maharashtra, India

1 Introduction

COVID-19 started from (Fauci et al., 2020; Mishra et al., 2020) Wuhan in China in December 2019 and brought suffering and death to the entire world. There have been two waves so far, and the world is bracing for a third wave. A report by the World Health Organization (WHO, 2021a) in May 2021 said that the rate of COVID patients and fatalities have been more in the South-East Asian countries, particularly devastating for India. As the pandemic rages across the world, it has pushed governments to re-examine their healthcare budgets. Out of 223 countries affected with Coronavirus pandemic at the global level as of June 2021, the top two countries most devastated by the pandemic are the two biggest democracies globally: the USA and India. While the USA suffered in the first wave, India suffered a lot in the second wave during April–June 2021, the second worst-affected country by COVID-19. Table 1 exhibits that as of 15 June 2021, the USA had positioned at the top with 33,140,498 COVID-19 cases, followed by India in second place with 29,510,410 cases at the world level. According to the WHO COVID-19 statistics, on 15 June 2021, 175,847,347 confirmed cases include 3,807,276 confirmed deaths and 2,187,874,534 Vaccine doses administered at the world level. As of 15 June 2021, 29,510,410 confirmed cases, 374,305 deaths, 238,840,635 vaccine doses administered in India (WHO, 2021a). Fig. 1 shows the number of global-level novel Coronavirus deaths at the start of each month from Jan 2020 to July 2021.

Lessons from COVID-19
https://doi.org/10.1016/B978-0-323-99878-9.00002-9

Table 1 Total number of COVID-19-positive cases and total number of deaths (numbers as on 15 June 2021).

Top 15 countries	Country name	Total number of positive COVID cases	Total number of deaths
1	United States of America	33,140,498	594,644
2	India	29,510,410	374,305
3	Brazil	17,412,766	487,401
4	France	5,635,842	109,512
5	Turkey	5,330,447	48,721
6	Russian Federation	5,222,408	126,801
7	The United Kingdom	4,565,817	127,904
8	Italy	4,244,872	127,002
9	Argentina	4,124,190	85,343
10	Colombia	3,753,224	95,778
11	Spain	3,729,458	80,465
12	Germany	3,715,518	89,844
13	Iran (Islamic Republic of)	3,039,432	82,217
14	Poland	2,877,608	74,574
15	Mexico	2,454,176	230,150
16	Ukraine	2,223,978	51,692
17	Peru	2,003,625	188,708
18	Indonesia	1,919,547	53,116
19	South Africa	1,747,082	57,731
20	Netherlands	1,672,744	17,711

Data Source: WHO, 2021a. Coronavirus disease (COVID-19) pandemic. https://www.who.int/emergencies/diseases/novel-coronavirus-2019 (Accessed 15 June 2021).

The WHO also said (WHO, 2021b) that the virus will evolve again. The third wave is expected to hit India by October 2021 (Sharma, 2021a). Thus, it is even more important now to prevent transmission, reduce the occurrence of mutations, and speed up vaccination. If the present disease becomes uncontrollable, it could spread to the animal populations, worsening the fight against the virus. In Vandalur Zoo, Chennai (a city in South India), a nine-year-old lioness died of suspected COVID-19 infection and confirmed positive in other nine lions (Oppili, 2021). Many countries, such as India, the USA, UK, etc., have had to impose lockdowns in their countries, leading to massive economic and social imbalances (Mishra et al., 2020). Governments and societies will take a long time to recover from these imbalances. In India, especially, there are families where both parents have

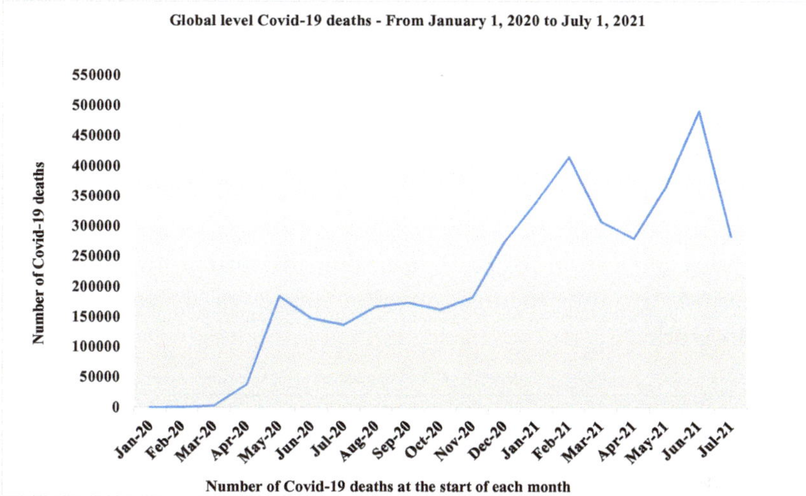

Fig. 1 Global level COVID-19 deaths. *(Data sources: WHO, 2020. Novel Coronavirus (2019-nCoV), Situation Report—6 https://www.who.int/docs/default-source/coronaviruse/situation-reports/20200126-sitrep-6-2019–ncov.pdf?sfvrsn%E2%80%89=%E2%80%89beaeee0c_4 (Accessed 15 July 2021); WHO, 2021a. Coronavirus disease (COVID-19) pandemic. https://www.who.int/emergencies/diseases/novel-coronavirus-2019 (Accessed 15 June 2021); WHO, 2021b. COVID-19 weekly epidemiological update 22 December 2020. World Health Organization, pp.1–3. https://www.who.int/publications/m/item/weekly-epidemiological-update—22-december-2020 (Accessed 12 February 2021).)*

died of COVID, leaving children as orphans. This issue has prompted the Prime minister of India to announce a scheme especially to look after these unfortunate children (TNN, 2021). The future will get even bleaker if the virus is not defeated. For this to happen, vigilance and healthcare are paramount, and so is vaccination. Experts say that the best hope for humanity is if whole countries are vaccinated swiftly, and social distancing is maintained. One way to ensure a quick and error-free vaccination process is by using Blockchain Technology (BCT). While some healthcare providers have been using this technology to maintain records and make supply chains agile, now is the time for more and faster absorption so that this disease can be defeated.

BCT became prominent when cryptocurrency came into the popular realm. BCT applies for various purposes that range from cybercash, financial trading and services, managing risks, trading and services, internet of things, etc., that benefit all sectors in the economy. The business sectors and service companies currently opt for this technology as the best option for accessing vital real-time information shown in a reliable format from trusted sources.

BCT provides authentication, security, transparency, trust, decentralized structure, and privacy for the data communicated through its digital blocks. BCT is otherwise known as "distributed ledger technology" (DLT). It is a secure way to collect, keep and transfer healthcare and its related financial records. It provides a path for individuals to engage openly with others to perform their day-to-day business tasks, services, and fund transfer (Furst, 2020). The present chapter examines the technology, its uses and explains the enormous applications of BCT in healthcare during the COVID pandemic period. It also focuses on the future of healthcare in the blockchain world.

2 Chapter objectives

The WHO has invited researchers and professionals worldwide to accelerate Research and Development (R & D) for providing solutions in "catastrophic" occasions like pandemics, natural disasters, etc. There is an immediate requirement to collect data quickly, share the most advanced existing knowledge, and offer preventive measures quickly at all parts of the universe during outbreaks. In healthcare, it is essential to monitor patients affected during pandemics, tests, medicines, administering vaccines, fees payment, location of medical facilities available, hospital resources, etc. These should be recorded up to date and should take action at the zero-time delay to prevent further pandemic waves. Coordinating all activities globally and integrating and sharing information transparently, the usage of emerging technologies and their applications in healthcare is very much needed, specifically BCT. This chapter aims to identify opportunities in the healthcare sector where blockchain can be applied, particularly in the COVID-19 scenario. Also, it discusses few use cases in which BCT is effectively implemented. The chapter also analyses the implementation challenges in healthcare and how BCT shapes the healthcare industry's future?

3 Research design

The chapter is formed as a meta-synthesis. Secondary data sources such as journal and news articles, reports of Governments, and other recognized organizations were collected and analyzed. In addition, interviews with healthcare officials and blockchain experts were conducted to derive more qualitative inputs related to recent disputes in the healthcare industry and the practicality of emerging technologies.

4 Blockchain technology (BCT)—An overview

In today's world, we maintain records of all kinds of transactions—transferring money, buying goods, paying for electricity or other utilities. Keeping these records is essential for business as they are the data points that lead to better customer service through better recommendations; they help companies forecast the demand of existing products and pave the way for developing new products. This way, they help businesses prepare for the future. Most of these take time to create and maintain and be error-free. If we transact today, the transaction will occur immediately, but the settlement will happen later. For example, if we sell equity stock today or buy mutual funds today, we can sell instantly, but the payment will take time. If we want to sell a house, the negotiation will be done quickly. Still, the registration process (verifying and registering the change in property ownership) will take time and involve lawyers and government employees. Each party maintains its ledger at every stage and is not privy to the other parties' ledgers. This makes the whole process slow and insecure as only each person at each level is privy to their ledger data. On the other hand, if the same transaction were recorded in the blockchain, details of the same such as price, asset, and ownership, would be recorded, verified and settled within seconds across all levels.

Before going any further, it makes sense to understand blockchain (BC) and why it is gaining in popularity. The blockchain came into an alternative to make payments securely and without needing a bank to mediate. The father of blockchain technology, nicknamed Satoshi Nakamoto, described it as "blockchain is a completely peer-to-peer version of electronic money that allows online payments to be sent directly from one party to another without going through a financial institution" (Nakamoto, 2009). It can be said to be an offshoot of people getting used to the internet, shopping, entertaining, communicating, and most of the time for digital cash transactions. "A blockchain is an irreversible distributed ledger that only adds data with a time-ordered set of facts known as transactions. These transactions are further clustered into blocks and structure a cryptographic hash chain. This process is termed a blockchain (Luu et al., 2016). We can think of it as a distributed system for taking down patient details and managing them. The peer-to-peer-based blockchain records are shared, immutable (cannot be changed), and stored in an append-only digital ledger.

There is no single authority in the blockchain. It is an established crypto technique that allows each node (participant) in a chain network for interacting, storing, exchanging, and viewing block information with no prior "trust" between the nodes. Before adding data into the block, miners verify and authenticate the data in the network. The process in the network is well-known by all nodes involved in it (Krawiec et al., 2016). BC is a cloud-centered system storing information and most famously used for cryptocurrencies like Bitcoin, Ethereum, etc. It promotes flexibility, security, and faster data transfer and sharing (Sahu, 2020; Xu, 2016). While the BCT was proposed to store digital data in 1991, it became famous for forming Bitcoin. The reason was that once data shared on it; it cannot be changed. Given in Fig. 2 is a simple transaction made by using BCT.

Each block is a structural and functional unit consisting of transaction details, the hash value of current, and the previous block. A hash value can be considered a digital signature unique to each transaction, hence each block. The hash of the first block is known as "genesis," and this hash is prefixed to all new transactions in a new block, thus creating a unique hash. Each block is connected to the next one, and it thus forms a chain. Depending on the usage of the BC system, the data in a block may differ. Most data in a block are a ledger of transactions. For example, suppose

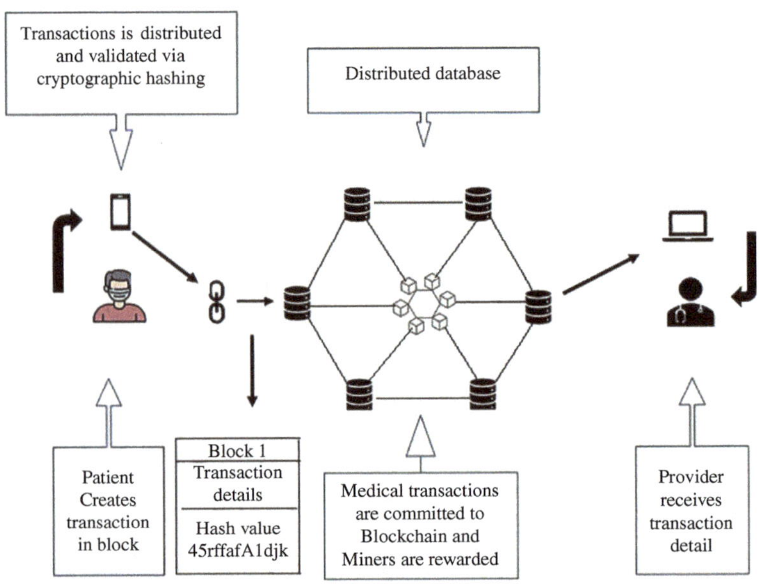

Fig. 2 The flow of a transaction made using a blockchain.

Person A wants to sell Product Z to Person B. In that case, the block will contain data on the seller, the buyer, the good, the time of the transaction, the transaction fee and the digital signature of the transaction with a unique hash. A cryptocurrency, like Bitcoin, works based on BCT, which stores data known as transaction information. A hash is generated in the block for this digital transaction information similar to a fingerprint. Cryptocurrency platforms use different types of hashing algorithms. For example, the algorithm, namely "SHA256," is used by Bitcoin, Ethereum uses the "ethash" algorithm. It mimics a linked list structure, except instead of pointers, it uses hashes. The next block of the chain and other blocks too do not point to this one. If anyone in the BC alters data, the unique hash value of the particular altered block also changes automatically. Hence it proves as a secured system. Users identify tampering through hashes. A hash function converts the different types and length of inputs into a fixed-length output called "hashhash." The hash function generates a fixed hash size even though the original data set size varies. The set of lengths may be the bit of 32 or 64 or 128 or 256 length (Frankenfield, 2021). Further security is added by users having public and private keys.

BCT uses the peer-to-peer structure, and every user in this group receives a copy of the transaction in BC. If anyone tries to tamper with the network, that person should change the whole chain's information. It is not possible to alter and break the security. So, the technologists say BCT is the emerging technology for secured data transfer. There are many advantages of working with a BCT. They are as follows:

- **(i)** BC reveals the history of data. Users get only the updated data in traditional data structures, but while BC, users can retrieve the entire data path from origin to end. The whole track is visible in BC. It is complicated for anyone to change the data. Hence, it is "immutable."
- **(ii)** BC is decentralized. It stores information in a shared distributed database, and there is no exclusive database; however, participants can take any number of copies of it. Again, this adds to the security of the data, and more people can benefit from it.
- **(iii)** There is no single authority to manage the database in BCT. All nodes of BC can receive all copies of transactions and updated them every time.

Different authors have described this technology through different characteristics. According to Monttechi et al. (2018), the essential properties of BC are that it is decentralized, verified, and immutable. The network does not rely on any central administration. When any transaction adds to the chain database, the member in the peer-to-peer blockchain network receives a copy of it. Before sharing data to members in a group, the members first approve the transactions and sign them using private keys. It is immutable because its consensus method allows creating a new block containing many transactions that all network users can verify. If they disagree on the transactions, then they cannot add the block. Hence it is known as a consensus. According to Ali et al. (2021), the main characteristics of BC are trust and decentralization. They say that a "proof-of-work protocol" secures the network and eliminates outsider's participation to check and enter the transaction. This protocol makes it difficult for hackers to attack the system and makes it virtually unhackable. The main features of BCT are "persistence," "anonymity," and "auditability" (Singh et al., 2021). BC looks like a ledger where every transaction between parties is recorded and uses cryptography for data security. It has a "consensus" procedure for warehousing, even one copy or multiple copies of registers and new entries (Kuner et al., 2018). Transaction data are stored in the block format and not written over. There is no central administrator for the administration of this block data.

Recently, BCT applies across all fields, such as selling art and tattoos as non-fungible tokens (NFT's) and sell items to gamers (Chakraborty, 2021). The banking and finance industry, namely HSBC, Visa, and Barclays, use it. InBev and Unilever use it for their supply chains, Pfizer and CDC use its healthcare, the Netherland government for border control, AIG for insurance, DeBeers to monitor diamonds' movement. Other companies that have absorbed this are the government of Dubai, Siemens, Nestle, Sony Music, etc. The number of users is growing day by day and contains the who's who of the business world and governments worldwide who need fast and transparent systems (Iredale, 2020; Lauren et al., 2021; Zago, 2018).

In simple, BC is a system that stores and shares various types of secure information among participants in the network. Each block in BC has two parts, in which the block's data stores in the first part, and the other part contains a dependent link. Without a third party's intervention, participants (nodes) of the network add and transfer the data to others. This technology provides solutions for enhancing healthcare applications such as mobile healthcare applications, medical device monitoring, managing electronic data and records, data generated in clinical trials, patient insurance details, etc. Before December 2019, there were only limited researches in blockchain healthcare applications. However, recently, blockchain specialists are trying to solve all healthcare issues using BCT collaborating with the hospital industry.

5 Challenges and opportunities in the healthcare sector

Today, citizens have access to multiple healthcare options; for example, we can use smart watches, smart bands, fitness apps, online doctor consultations, face-to-face doctor consultations, medicine delivery apps, and sometimes stints in hospitals. All these are nodes in our healthcare system and are disconnected from each other. If they could be bound together chronologically, it would be beneficial to patients and doctors alike. However, the absorption by healthcare leaving a few has not been great, whereas considering that healthcare is such that there is a need for a distributed ledger, it should have been much more. In today's world, a single patient in India generates records in multiple places. Few examples, on apps like a Practo for doctors' consultation, on watches and bands like Fitbit and Redmi, on health apps on the mobile like a Pacer, HealthifyMe, etc., and of course on visits to hospitals. The research survey of KPMG (Arsene, 2020) said that acquiring healthcare data is challenging, disorganized and involve huge costs. Around 38% of the leading health sector's Chief Information Officers have expressed that efficient management of electronic healthcare data and records are the priority of their budgeting planning and consideration in the decision-making process. When healthcare personnel start to maintain and manage these electronic records using BCT, it helps to improve accessibility by all parties, and clients can share documents securely, enlarge interoperability, follow compliance, and valuable in so many ways.

While the healthcare domain needs to share data across all stakeholders to function efficiently, it is challenging to follow them because of an incorrect positive result, replicate records, lack of privacy, etc. (Furst, 2020). Furthermore, lack of trust hinders transparency and efficiency as the stakeholders are reluctant to share data as it may impinge on privacy. An immediate solution to this is to use blockchain technology (BCT), as it allows competitors to transfer patients' details simultaneously to maintain their competitive freedom and privacy. Due to these attributes, it has emerged as a solution provider for various issues in the COVID-19 pandemic and business sectors, giving much importance to healthcare-related data sharing.

There have been malicious attacks on healthcare systems in India (Service, I. A. News, 2019) and abroad (Combs, 2021; Davis, 2020). Hackers have accessed millions of patients' records stored in traditional databases. As governments rush to safeguard and vaccinate citizens against Coronavirus, they use schools, parks, etc., along with hospitals. These temporary arrangements result in security protocols getting strained and making it easier for criminals to hack patient data. Earlier research papers (Mathew, 2019; Xu, 2016) have pointed out that BCT can help prevent malicious attacks, and the healthcare industry now realizes the power of BCT. It is now that BCT can be used to avoid hacking, sharing data securely, and thus providing help and relief to citizens.

Currently, the healthcare industry faces the most significant challenge due to counterfeit or fake drugs plaguing the pharmaceutical supply chain. Poor manufacturing procedures, inadequate storage, medication theft, and the market penetration of poor-quality/counterfeit items in gray markets are all factors that contribute to fake/compromised medication. The World Health Organization estimates that the black-market drugs business is approximately seventy-five billion dollars (Arsene, 2020). but the actual value might be far higher. This is especially true in nations like Bangladesh, where they are spending vast amounts on importing medicines. This is not exceptional to developed countries. Almost all countries are affecting by the healthcare supply chain process due to fake drugs. The Food and Drug Administration issued a caution notice in 2012 to more than a thousand healthcare institutions and health practitioners who may have been victims ofbogus medication rings. They were informed, in particular, that they may have been supplied counterfeit drug "Avastin," one of the most famous anti-cancer treatments on the healthcare market. The BC technology almost fulfills every criterion of FDA compliance such as product authorization, tracking, details of suppliers and agency, drugs verification, etc.

During the pandemic period, the patients' detail from around the world should be available at shared commonplace for enabling the research work by the researchers. The clinical test needs accurate patient details for new vaccine development. The accuracy of research data depends on the healthcare intermediator who provides it. Most medical companies are not sharing their clinical trial details with others and should adhere to the ethical and regulatory requirements. BCT offers a solution to this problem. The data are stored in the common shared database. Any parties in the network can access the decentralized, transparent data.

The governments of the top two COVID-19-affected countries, the USA and India, have decided to spend more on healthcare. The US plans to carve out 20% of its GDP on this field (Daley, 2021), and the Indian government plans to spend 2.5% of its GDP on healthcare (MoF, 2021). This budget is nearly double what it had spent in the previous year. However, as the healthcare industry faces data breaches and problems with supply chains and maintaining patient records, issues arise in government and healthcare institutional administration and successful treatment.

6 Implementation of BC in developing and developed nations

While major business applications will be the same across all countries, it is interesting to observe the differences in BTC adoption between developing and developed countries. Blockchain consumes a lot of electricity; hence adoption in developed countries will be faster (Knowledge@Wharton, 2018). However, developing countries like India, Kenya, Estonia, etc., are highly interested in its applications for social good. Governments are exploring its wide-ranging applications like maintaining land records, keeping accounts of payments, supply chain management, etc. Andhra Pradesh, a State Government of India, is experimenting with maintaining records for land titling with blockchain. Governments of developing countries use blockchain to keep records in land titling, land ownership, healthcare, supply chain, payments, banking and financial services, agriculture, etc. (Martindale, 2018; Zambrano, 2020). As given by Transparency International (2020), a quick look at the most corrupt countries shows that most developing countries are also very corrupt. As blockchain is a technology wherein records once entered cannot be changed, this technology will help root out corruption and improve lives. The Department of Health and Human Services report, United States said that more than five million patients' healthcare records were breached in 2017 (Ugalmugle and Swain, 2019). Therefore, governments that want to do well for their populations examine the benefits that BTC will bring to its citizens. BCT provides enormous opportunities in the healthcare sector of developing and developed nations that will take time to implement. Organizations of these nations should face many technical, institutional, and behavioral challenges before BCT implementations.

The following are the few major challenges faced by developing countries.

- Lack of technical infrastructure for BC implementation
- Shortage of skilled BC professionals
- Absence of essential governing norms and regulatory procedures
- Concerning audit compliance
- Distrust among users and lack of awareness of BCT
- Lack of ability to bring the network together
- Inability to scale

The following are the driving needs of BC implementation in developing countries.

- Rising the risks of fake medicines
- Increasing the rate of breaches of medical data and records
- Increasing of Internet of Things (IoT) applications in the healthcare industry
- Reduction of cost in various healthcare
- Cost-savings in several healthcare functions
- An increasing need to secure medical data
- Rising demand for storing healthcare data
- Rising need to integrate devices and stakeholders

Implementing BC can bring significant benefits to the healthcare industry of developing nations by providing relief for organizations from corruption, reducing intermediaries' prices, and increasing trust among parties involved in medical businesses. The Government of Uganda has collaborated with Medi-connect, UK, a blockchain-based solution provider, to avoid the risks of receiving fake medicines during the supply chain. The BCT in healthcare market share is mainly contributing by pharmaceutical companies, healthcare payers, and healthcare providers. The Global Market Insights Inc. report 2019 said that the BCT in the healthcare market in Canada is estimated at 69.9% Compound Annual Growth Rate (CAGR) during 2019–2025. In 2018, the revenue of the BCT healthcare market in Germany was about USD 2.8 million (Ugalmugle and Swain, 2019). The investment made by start-up companies and the government in implementing BCT is a significant factor for the growth of the healthcare market in developed countries. An agreement was signed between the Gustave Roussy Institute, a foremost European cancer institute, and Embleema Incorporation in March 2019 for BCT-based clinical research and the secure transfer of healthcare records. According to the PwC Global BC survey (PwC, 2018), the United States (29%) was the most progressed region in developing BC projects than China (18%). However, China (30%) will most implement BC-based projects in 2023, followed by the US (18%), Australia (8%), India (6%), Hong Kong (5%), Denmark (5%), Japan (4%) and UK (2%).

7 Blockchain: Uses/applications in healthcare

BCT can correctly transform the healthcare sector includes medicine discovery, development, preclinical research, clinical research, and supply chain process. In the nineteenth centuries, scientists made many clinical trials to find the effective one, and many failed to attain the Food and Drug Administration (FDA) approval stage. The reasons for the failure are pharmaceutical institutes are not acquiring the necessary patient data in an era when people do not trust them.

If BCT implemented well, it could be an excellent solution for enhancing data provenance, integrity, functionality, and, of course, security of a pharma supply chain. The uses of BCT in the healthcare industry are explained below. Fig. 3 also illustrates the various benefits and applications of BCT during the COVID-19 pandemic.

Secured data sharing: A recent report by the European Union Blockchain forum suggests that with this BCT, the patient will own the data and decide whether to share it or not. Also, it can be used for combating the virus by the governments (EUBlockchain, 2021; Lyons, 2020). In our world today, with the technology available, doctors, nurses, and health professionals are limited in the level of care they provided. This is due to the inability to view the complete health records. Medicalchain, a healthcare product company, has introduced a blockchain-based product for quick access to health records. This product keeps electronic data safe and secure in blockchain technology. The BCT layer in the Medicalchain product hosts limited non-personal information. This information access as pointers to

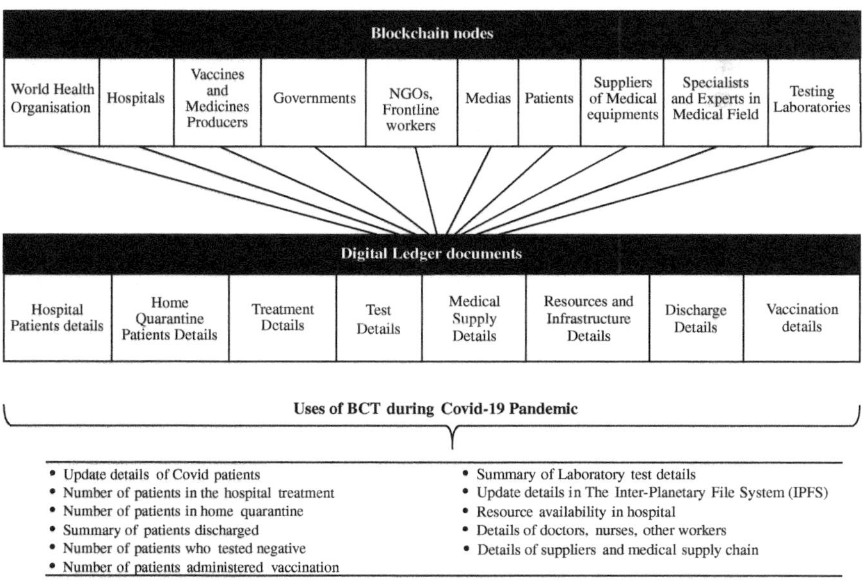

Fig. 3 Uses of BCT during COVID-19 pandemic.

writing the system into encrypted health records. These records help hospitals, universities, and nonprofit organizations regulated and handle sensible data. Only after patient's authorization can one unlock their health records and view the mobile interface. But Medicalchain is much more to view patient's health records using the telemedicine concept available in their device. The doctor can check the patient's medical record and access his medical history. It permits the doctors to access life-saving information with managing vulnerable or unconscious patients. Medicalchain provides peace of mind, and the patient can feel safe, and health data is accessible by the doctor when it matters most.

Secure data of patients: As patients combine data by going to hospitals, consult online or through apps, use fitness apps, etc., they will generate more and more data. This data has to be secured. Last two decades, the world community has an outburst of medical-cum-health related technologies, from maintaining data in electronic format to the Internet of Things (IoT) health device to least-cost whole-genome ordering. The data collected from these devices have met silos primarily in combining the above data sources. BurstIQ, the US-based company established in 2015, solves the silos of integrating data sources in the healthcare industry through blockchain. It creates a path for an end-to-end BC-enabled system for managing big data using BC, adopting cognitive technologies for obtaining data, getting consent and sharing among participants globally, and revenue generation. Similarly, many companies Medicalchain, Factom doing healthcare services using BCT (Daley, 2021; Lyons, 2020; Tandon et al., 2020). Table 2 explains the role of companies in healthcare applications based on blockchain. Healthcare is personalized to each individual based on the beneficiaries' sole genetic, medical, demographic profile, and socio-economic conditions. Healthcare will be available to every place, every individual regardless of the person, location, and money. These companies remove all hurdles in healthcare data management, and it connects all healthcare industry stakeholders at the global level.

Share databases and thus streamline costs: The technology's decentralized nature establishes a common database for patients' data that doctors and healthcare industry officials can access fast and provide effective treatments (Daley, 2021). BCT facilitates quicker diagnoses and personalized action plans (Daley, 2021; Tandon et al., 2020; Zheng et al., 2018). A few healthcare companies that implemented BCT are Simplyvital Health, Coral Health Research & Discovery, Robomed, etc.

Table 2 Companies in blockchain-based healthcare.

Company name	Nature of work
BurstIQ	A US-based company established in 2015 provides an end-to-end BC enabled system that handles big data using BC. It performs data acquiring, authenticating and sharing among customers globally using cognitive technologies and facilitates revenue generation
Chronicled	The MediLedger Network is the ideal bridge between business parties, combining a secured peer-to-peer messaging network with a distributed BC network. It removes chargeback mistakes and disputes by administering agreed business rules.
Blockpharma	This mobile app allows customers to check the legitimacy of the pharmaceutical package they buy in real-time. Medicine can be tracked from the factory to the point of sale. This app employs the most cutting-edge ML (Machine Learning) technology to increase the detection of counterfeit cases.
Tieron	It creates technology and products that diminish the price and trust complication. It offers BC verifiable credentials, confirm the existence and correctness of electronic data and records and regulatory compliance.
DNAtix, Zenome, Luna DNA, EncrypGen	These leading companies have developed BC-based software for the analysis of human genome data. These data help for predictive analysis and to determine a data model for further product development. It assures the safest encryption system for all genome data for maintaining privacy. Some of the other notable companies in the genomic market are Nextcode Genomics, Murrieta Genomics, Gene Blockchain, Longenesis, SimplyVital Health, Neogen, Ripe Technology, Nebula Genomics, GSK, Genobank.io, Merck, Genomes.io, WuXi, Shivom, etc.
HealthVerity	It provides a BC-based centralized platform for the accurate data generation, distribution and secure management of patients, hospitals and healthcare data. It helps in predicting the practices and facilities to be implemented. It solves the existing problems relating to consent from patients in healthcare and supports "consent management."

Continued

Table 2 Companies in blockchain-based healthcare—cont'd

Company name	Nature of work
Kalibrate Blockchain	The firm has developed a BC-based power engine, "Universal Patient Index," for form processing. It supports users in various healthcare activities by providing high clinical relevancy, blood testing, fill-up hospital intake forms and index healthcare. The patient can fill up the form in Kalibrate developed a mobile app and save timing and queuing when visiting hospitals.
TIBCO Software	It has developed a BC driven smart contract system collaborated with Tennessee based "Change Healthcare" company. Their software automates the claim process of payment parties with verifiable and secure features. TIBCO Spotfire software provides data for clinical research, advanced analytics and visualization.
CVS Minute Clinics	This US-based company's BC smart contract system provides drug dispensing, compensation, and settlement processing.
Robomed Networks	A Moscow based company is doing patient-hospital contracts using BCT. Its software facilitates self-executing contract rules, where the insurer, patient and hospital are part of BC. When the patient visits the hospital and meets a doctor, that incident automatically updated the ledger of BC.
Hashed Health	They created a credential verification mechanism using blockchain for doctors and other clinical specialists to show that they are truly licensed to practice medicine. This company has collaborated with other companies such as Accenture, National Government Services, Spectrum Health, Hardenbergh Group, WellCare, and HealthLink Dimensions to create a BC-driven credential system.
IBM	The company has developed a BC system tie-up with insurers such as Aetna, Healthcare Service Corporation (HCSC), Anthem, and PNC Financial Services Group for digital payment operation and interoperability.
St. Joseph Health	This company's platform provides facilities for revenue cycle management using BCT. According to McKinsey Company, the platform uses smart contracts, DLT, and machine intelligence to help decrease inefficiencies in the healthcare revenue process.

Table 2 Companies in blockchain-based healthcare—cont'd

Company name	Nature of work
Guardtime	It is a UK-based health technology company that has developed MyPCR and its partner Healthcare Gateway and Access Medical for improving medication adherence. It is the first BC driven PCR (Personal Care Record) portal. It efficiently manages the rights of General Data Protection Regulation patients' data, integrates it and verifies them automatically.
Medicalchain	It uses BC-driven HLT (hyper ledger technology) to access patients' medical histories and help the healthcare companies and specialists with the other process. It ensures consent management, security, and transparency in the process, prescribes medicines, and solves patients' doubts using their software platform.
Embleema and Hu-manity. co	In the medical field, the researchers typically approach healthcare marketing companies for their research analysis. These companies provide required patients details and issues. This process now simplified using BCT. Here, BC acts as an intermediator. It sells the patients data and their medical issue details to the medical researchers with the consent of the data owners in a suitable market platform. It provides relevant data to generate accurate test results. Also, it allows patients to store their data here and sell it to those who desire to purchase it. It promotes decentralization and selling patients' data legally.
Change Healthcare	The company has developed "the Hyperledger fabric driven BCT platform" for intelligent medical network, where patients/providers can effectively process their forms, audit the details, well known the status of the claim process.
FDA	The FDA's platform helps patients safeguard their test results/trails of clinical activities, genomic and electronic medical records.
DHL	It is one of the BCT-based biggest healthcare companies involved in tracking medical items from production to customer's end-point (supply chain) and its partner company Accenture. As a result, businesses will finally eliminate any counterfeit medicine difficulties that they experience daily.

Continued

Table 2 Companies in blockchain-based healthcare—cont'd

Company name	Nature of work
Centers for Disease Control and Prevention	It offers new BCTs collaborating with IBM for improving the general health of American citizens. It provides security for electronic health records in the encrypted ledger system.
Pfizer	Pfizer is another most giant corporation that has used BCT. The CSBWG (Clinical Supply Blockchain Working Group), coordinated by Biogen and Pfizer, has produced proof of work for keeping patients documents and digital inventory management of medicinal items.
Anthem	In 2019, this insurance company used hyper ledger fabric for customer services. Here, the patients can securely use their platform for sharing their medical records and other details. It is operating from Indiana.
Optum	The company started offering BC-based insurance services in 2018 using Ethereum based BC. Users can enter, share, verify, validate, and audit data within a network in this platform.
Samsung	Nexledger, a BC developed by Samsung SDS, South Korea based company, assists contracting parties in proving their identities and executing agreements. A consortium of eighteen Korean banks is already using the platform through an application called BankSign, which allows banks' retail users to instantly prove who they are, even though they are not an existing customer when they visit there. Nexledger will assist patients in establishing their identification, reducing the time it takes for a health insurance claim to be processed.
Aon	This England based company is developing an "R3 Corda" BCT to speed up insurance procedures to avoid loss from hacker damages. It has developed a platform jointly with RenaissanceRe and EverestRe that will allow large reinsurers to share and cooperate their works on the same system.
Solve.Care	It offers a BC-based worldwide network for the administration and payment of healthcare services. Insurers, regulatory bodies, and healthcare institutions are among the firms that the corporation services.

Table 2 Companies in blockchain-based healthcare—cont'd

Company name	Nature of work
Etheal	This Hungarian-based firm has developed a BC-powered healthcare platform that aims to offer medical services more economical while eliminating inefficiency and lack of transparency.
Mimirium	This software firm creates ecosystems with a primary focus on data gathering, processing, and securely analyzing the data. The firm has made four BCT-based products: personnel surveys, a network, a portal for health management, and smart city data.
Iryo Network	It is a database that stores medical health records on a decentralized basis. It promises to simplify data recording formats by combining fragmented data from numerous sources relating to a specific patient into a single file, obviating the need for fragmentation.

Source: Arsene, C., 2020. The Global "Blockchain in Healthcare" Report: The 2021 Ultimate Guide for every Executive. healthcareweekly.com https://healthcareweekly.com/blockchain-in-healthcare-guide/ (Accessed 14 December 2020); Iredale, G., 2020. List of Top 50 Companies Using Blockchain Technology. 101 blockchains https://101blockchains.com/companies-using-blockchain-technology/ (Accessed 30 May 2021); Lauren, D., Dent, M., Castillo, M.D., Hansen, S., Kauflin, J., Sorvino, C., Tucker, H., 2021. Blockchain 50. In: Castillo, M.D., Schifrin, M. (Eds.), Forbes, https://www.forbes.com/sites/michaeldelcastillo/2020/02/19/blockchain-50/?sh=77cf78b77553 (Accessed 30 May 2021).

Manage supply chain and track the drug: How many of us understand medicine? How can we be sure that the product we are ordering is not damaged until it reaches the user? How to ensure that all drugs come from a genuine supplier? All of the above questions are essential concerns of the supply chain in the medical field that generally arise from everyone. BC is beneficial for making this drug supply chain transparent. BC has severe implications for drug supply chain management. And its virtual decentralization guarantees almost complete transparency in its operation (Daley, 2021; Lyons, 2020; Monttechi et al., 2018). Once medicine produced at the laboratory, information such as the place of origin, the number of quantities, supplier details, date of packing and rate of the medicine are stored in the BC ledger. As the drugs pass each route, their duration and the number of individuals involved in the supply chain have been recorded immediately in BC. Every action recorded in BC is known by each member of that BC immediately. BC helps to reduce costs drastically and avoid intermediaries and their prices.

Currently, Chronicled, the San Francisco based company, supervise and maintain blockchain-based "MediLedger" in the healthcare sector. This foremost BCT model provides results for the medical supply chain issues, revenue management and eases trust and automation between companies. Similarly, other organizations are doing BC-based medical supply process such as Blockpharma, Tieron, and Centers for Disease Control and Prevention (CDC). In a recent poll (GlobalData Healthcare, 2021) conducted among pharmaceutical companies, the supply chain was where pharmaceuticals were expecting to get maximum gains from applying blockchain technology.

Developments in genomics: The genetic potential to improve human health previously a dream has become a scientific and financial reality with the development of current blockchain technology. Beneficiary spent about one billion dollars in 2001 on the human genome process. Currently, the same treatment costs only about a thousand dollars. Nowadays, many companies in the genomics market providing blockchain-based services. Ancestry, Gene blockchain, DNAtix, 23andME, Shivom, WuXi, Neogen, Longenesis, etc., are improving the lives of millions of people through DNA testing. This vast technological development has turned the market into a place where the public can sell their encrypted genetic data to create an extensive database. With this, valuable data is accessed quickly than ever before. All three companies, like DOC.AI, Encrypgen, and Nebula Genomics, use BCT to advance our knowledge of the essential structure of human life.

Clinical trials: Lyons (2020) believes that clinical trials are where blockchain companies could move faster and more securely. The same survey by global healthcare says that this is the second most important area in which blockchain is expected to impact (GlobalData Healthcare, 2021).

8 Blockchain: Implementation challenges and considerations in healthcare

Mainly speaking, two types of data can be maintained in healthcare management. "On-chain" data is directly stored on the blockchain. These are demographic data such as gender, date of birth, place of residence, etc. It does not identify the patient. "Off-chain" data refers to data stored in separate, traditional databases. The blockchain will have links to these sets of data. These data help identify the patient, and the patient can choose to share by using a key, for example, a patient's x-ray or other diagnoses.

Tandon et al. (2020) conducted a systematic literature review and concluded that blockchain is being used and should be used to handle, process, store and share medical data and personal health records. This technology has added significant value through improved efficiency, access control, technological advancement, privacy protection, and security of data management processes. A conceptual model given by (Tandon et al., 2020) in their paper can be used in today's time to fight the COVID pandemic successfully.

Once the information is generated, the data can be stored in a database using blockchain and the patient's permission. This would help the patient get a holistic treatment without having to remember all past and present details. And also, this data would empower doctors to treat the patient better and faster. For a healthcare structure in India that is overburdened, this is like a dream come true. All this data needs to have a single administrator, but all the sources could keep adding information as blocks. Each source would have a key, along with the patient, and each would access the records.

The healthcare industry feels pain from transferring and interchange information due to complicated contracts between stakeholders. Inefficiency in the claim process, errors in documents, and payment process results in waste of money and loss of one's life. After the blockchain transformation, all parties in the healthcare sector access and share the exact version of the information. Blockchain has four key dimensions, as explained in Fig. 4. First, the blockchain is an append-only distributed system of records shared across a business network. Second, smart contracts are business terms both embedded and executed in a transaction database. Third, all parties agree to the validity of a transaction committed to the blockchain. Fourth, it is a secure, authenticated, and verifiable transaction in a consensus mechanism.

Another pain point today is a pendant or denied claims due to missing or inaccurate information such as patient's name, subscriber information, diagnosis and procedure codes. The term clinical attachment is a concept surrounding the need for additional clinical information when a payer adjudicates healthcare claims. The basic premise is that sending a claim without all supporting data is time-consuming, costly and challenging for all parties involved. Luckily a blockchain-enabled claims process provides transparency into the claim requirements and reimbursement rules for all parties if the agreements between providers, patients, payers and government regulators were agreed upon and stored via smart contracts on the blockchain. Providers would know accurately what type of information needed before submitting claims. Proper data format requirements stored on the blockchain would enable providers to format the claim data easily.

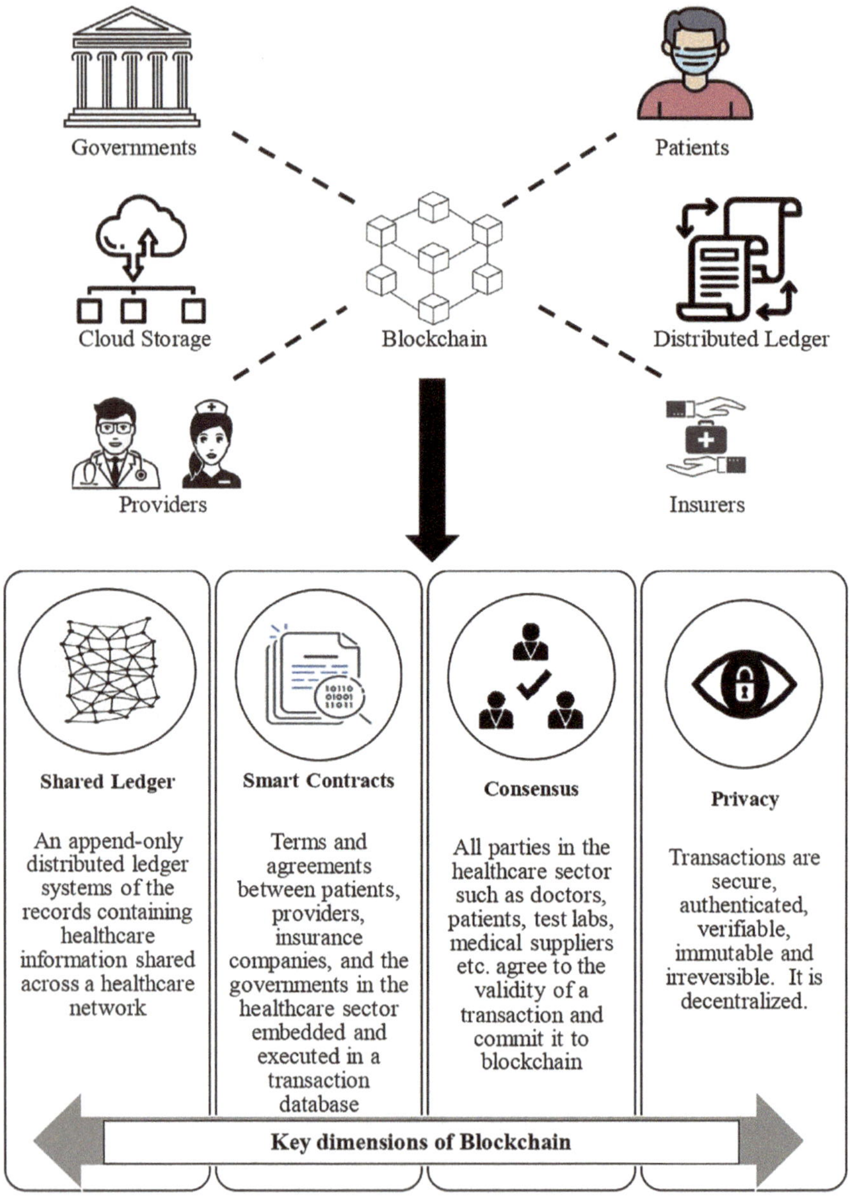

Fig. 4 Role of blockchain technology in the healthcare sector.

To ensure that, he should enter all information correctly. This clarity reduces or eliminates claims being returned due to insufficient data. It saves time and effort for all parties involved.

9 Blockchain: Fight against COVID-19 in healthcare

During the 2020–2021 period, the pandemic has affected people's life drastically. It has upended how we lead our lives, conduct business, study, train, and play while cruelly snuffing our lives. Governments across the world are addressing these problems and urging their populations to stay safe and get vaccinated. BCT is an essential part of this fight to defeat the enemy. It helps establish an efficient and transparent healthcare business model based on higher degrees of accuracy and trust because technology is a tamper-proof public ledger. It cannot prevent the emergence of new viruses itself, but it can create the first line of protection through a network of connected devices whose primary goal is to remain alert about disease outbreaks. It can help prevent future pandemics by enabling the early spotting of epidemics, fast-tracking drug trials, and better management of outbreaks and subsequent treatment (Sharma, 2021b).

This technology helps share real-time information of all transactions between relevant parties in the chain in a secure and immutable fashion. If there been a blockchain with WHO, the Health Ministry of each country and nodal hospitals, the world might have woken up much earlier. We might have seen travel restrictions given sooner, quarantining policies set more shortly, and social distancing implemented faster. And fewer people would have suffered (Banafa, 2020). What every country is doing now fighting this pandemic would have been restricted to fewer countries on a smaller scale.

The following points explain how BCT could have been used to help in stemming the disease:

(a) *Control disease*:

BC can record patients' symptoms and recovery due to the virus (Sharma et al., 2020). Even after the patient recovers, the data stored permanently in the blockchain help to check for after effects. Some patients do not get hospitalized but are isolated and treated at home. BCT facilitates to serve better home-quarantined patients by supplying medicine on time. Also, the data stored in the blockchain can be accessed by drug suppliers, medical stores, and doctors so that the patient will get adequate consultation on time.

(b) *Trace patients and areas*:

Blockchain can trace the contacts of those affected by the disease so that the people contacted can be examined. It can also locate the geographic area, safe zones, infected zones, etc. (Sharma et al., 2020).

(c) *Maintain and ramp up medical supply chains*:

The main challenges running around governments and corporates in a peak COVID pandemic around the globe is to get back the economy to normal. Mainly, the healthcare industry and its supply chain process must be revisited, and it is an immediate requirement to deal with a range of issues and challenges during pandemic times. Legacy procurement system in the medical supply chain breakdown the trust among customers and the public at large. Transforming the medical supply chain to the BCT based solves many problems. Product and manufactures details entered in the block is immutable and irreversible.

The decentralized distributed ledger system in BCT facilitates the parties involved in the supply chain process to get accurate real-time information. The merchant can receive standard medical equipment and track the origin. Companies like IBM and Microsoft are providing solutions for the medical supply chain through BCT. It is essential to supply medicines, medical equipment, ambulances, personnel, and accessories to the designated areas on time during catastrophic events. As blockchain can maintain a current database of designated personnel and equipment in real-time, it can help streamline resource distribution and aid in getting resources in time to those in need (GlobalData Healthcare, 2021; Sharma et al., 2020).

(d) *Make the treatment transparent*:

As the vaccination movement gathers steam, there are many rumors and incorrect reports on the same side effects. Blockchain can help find out where the "fake news" originated and help to curb the same. This will ensure that more and more people get vaccinated and hence help in eradicating the disease.

(e) *Track donations*:

As the world grapples with the pandemic and people lose livelihoods, many organizations have looked at helping those in need by collecting donations in money, food, books, medical supplies, etc. Blockchain specialists said that BCT could help track donations and make sure there is no misuse of funds or equipment (Aarvik, 2020; Banafa, 2020). It uses to check that essential goods are not overpriced or are not counterfeit goods. As it adds blocks from origin to end, goods that start from a point cannot be changed en route. If they are changed, the point at which counterfeit goods are substituted will become clear. In India, various business houses like Amazon, Google, cricket team Royal Challengers, Bangalore, Mahindra etc., have pledged help to victims of COVID-19 (India.com, 2021; PTI, 2021; The Economic Times, 2021). While some companies are helping the families of employees who have suffered from the disease, others support the frontline workers. Governments disburse funds using the direct benefit transfer based on the Aadhaar card, a unique citizen id provided in India (The Economic Times, 2020). BCT will help in making sure that the allotted amount reaches the beneficiary.

(f) *Better Management*:

Most countries have been woefully unprepared for a crisis of this magnitude, which has led to the suffering of a kind never seen before. A shared platform like blockchain would enable early sharing of disease outbreaks with the World Health Organization and major healthcare agencies worldwide (Sharma et al., 2020). It could offer a platform where all concerned authorities, such as governments, health organizations, medical professionals, patients, NGOs, researchers and other connected individuals, can update each other about the situation and prevent it from worsening further.

(g) *Ease of claim process*:

BC enables the claim process and settlement easy. Agreements between patients, hospitals, medical suppliers, insurance companies, and governments are stored via 'smart contracts in blockchain. The provider is aware of precisely the information required for submitting a claim application. BC maintains a proper data format, and it ensures all data entered correctly. BC removes errors in the conventional system. It minimizes and eliminates claims being returned due to insufficient information.

Blockchain use cases: BCT is a well suitable emerging technology for safeguarding every step of the healthcare supply chain. And various use cases for BC in the healthcare supply chain have already arisen, including advancing the efficiency of the IoHT (Internet of Healthy Things), securing internet-connected medical equipment, preventing fake pharmaceuticals, and more. Fig. 5 explains few COVID-19-related use cases for blockchain in healthcare.

There is an emerging need to strengthen the privacy, security, and trust of the developing digital environment specifically for the healthcare industry

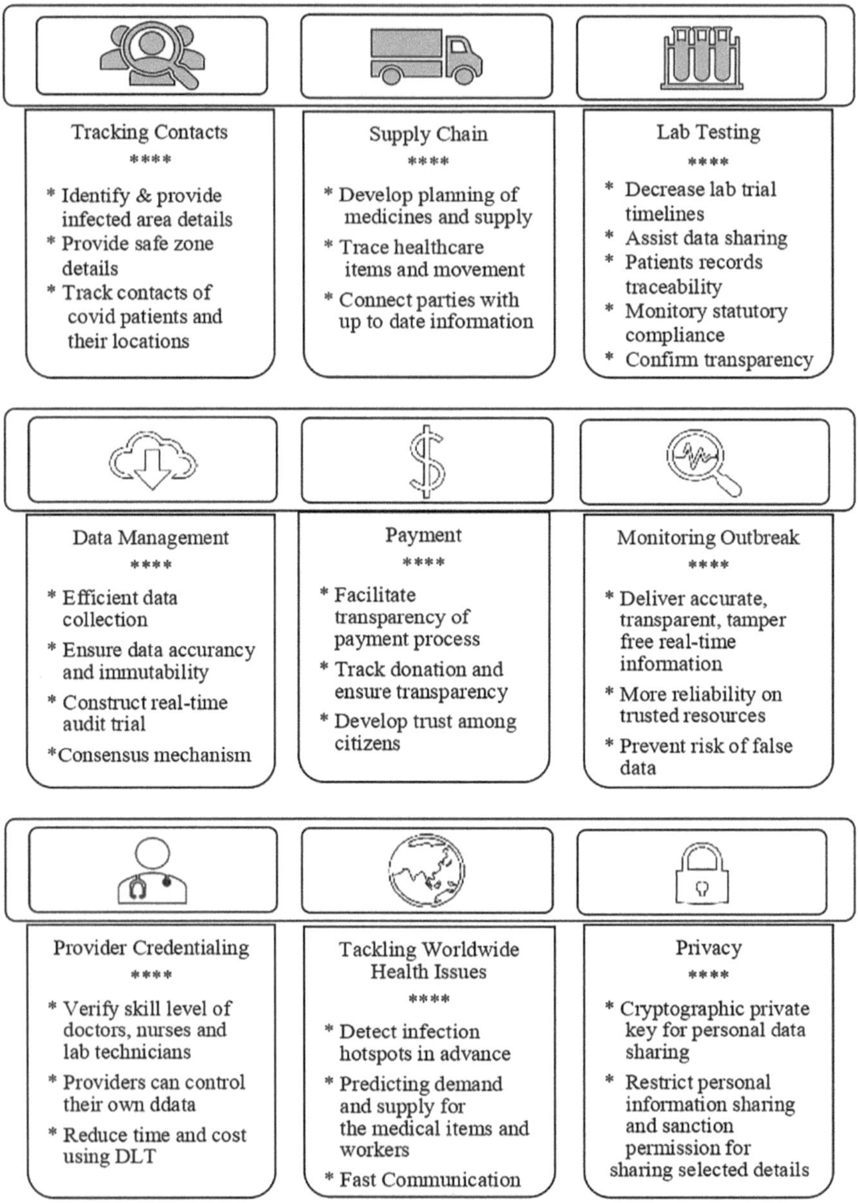

Fig. 5 Some BCT based use cases for fighting the COVID-19 pandemic.

by using BCT, allowing public and mental health experts to proactively monitor treatments, independent of the patients' or healthcare providers' physical location. BC not only improves data consistency and accessibility across different cadres of healthcare providers and social services, but it also uses tokens and digital assets to incentivize healthy behavior. Globally, many companies and network agencies are providing healthcare services using BCT. Table 2 provides the details of few notable companies and their operations in the healthcare sector using BCT.

The most significant benefits offered by BC are associated with greater trust and privacy due to the technology's ability to enable better data accuracy and verification. At its most basic level, blockchain changes ownership and control of data from one centralized source to multiple sources that contribute data (Furst, 2020).

10 Blockchain: Future in healthcare

Healthcare institutions are having problems integrating data at various points, such as maintaining a master database of all records, establishing trust, low costs to keep data, etc. BCT overcomes these problems by maintaining trust between the different stakeholders, lowering costs, and maintaining a trial for whoever has access to the records (Krawiec et al., 2016). The chapter already touched upon the beneficial impact new technologies have on the healthcare sector. When it comes to blockchain, the technology can impact the industry on a fundamental level. It could help build the digital infrastructure of a global healthcare system equipped to address today's issues and confidently face the challenges of tomorrow. It could help ensure fair treatment of patients, efficient medical research, and cost-effective business operations (Kassab et al., 2019; Ribitzky, 2018; Siyal et al., 2019). The possibilities are truly limitless. Some of the far-reaching future uses of BCT in healthcare are:

(i) Managing and maintaining patients' health records: The database can store all kinds of data, whether on blood pressure, cardiac care, height, weight and age, the amount spent in various consultations, insurance premiums etc. It will bring together data from online and offline consultations, apps, prescriptions used etc. This will make it easier for doctors to understand the patient's background and previous treatments and prescribe customized treatments. The doctor will not need to spend time asking the patient to remember historical data, and even if the patient forgets essential information, it will not matter. With its layers of protection and public and private keys, BCT will keep the data safely for the patient.

(ii) Settling Insurance Claims: Unfortunately, there are fraudulent claims made for health insurance companies. BCT can give a complete account of a health insurance petitioner's sickness and subsequent bills. Hence, it will be impossible to fraud a health insurance company.

(iii) Managing the supply chain: Although most governments worldwide have regulations to regulate and protect the integrity of the supply chain, counterfeit drugs make their way into markets. These drugs are harmful to the public and can cause allergies or severe health issues for those taking them. Applying a blockchain to regulate the movement of the drugs from the manufacturer to the end-user will make it easy to pinpoint the node at which a fake drug substituted the actual drug. It will help in arresting the distribution of counterfeit medicines. Another application is to track the drugs' real-time movement to know an accurate "Time of Arrival."

(iv) Research and Development in Pharmaceuticals: The pace of research in the pharmaceuticals industry is phenomenal. Companies are racing against time to find cures to the novel Coronavirus along with other diseases. Whenever any breakthrough is arrived at, it is published in newspapers etc. However, during the research process to come to a breakthrough, there is no sharing of data or research. Here, BC facilitates sharing new drugs, thus making it faster to achieve a cure as companies can share their progress. Also, BC helps to publish medical research so that confirmation received for every research work's validity. Another application of the BC is in the formulation of the drug. Every drug has the formula to be produced. BCT can evaluate, monitor and ensure that the drugs are being manufactured exactly as mapped in the procedure.

(v) Maintaining digital credentials of medical personnel: There is a vast amount of research on various topics in the medical community, especially regarding COVID-19. These research works will not be covered in medical education right away, but doctors will need to know about it. The research output can be disseminated through MOOCs, and healthcare professions can get trained in these and get a digital certificate stored using BCT. Also, storage of traditional degrees can be done using BCT, and as soon as there is an addition to the degree, it can be updated in the database, and all those who have access can view the updated data.

(vi) Clinical Research: Clinical Research is an essential part of knowing how effective new drugs are. However, they are difficult to conduct as there are data privacy issues, data integrity, data sharing, record keeping and patient enrolling. It has been proved that using blockchains makes the whole process transparent, makes transactions faster and leads to the faster enrolment of patients for clinical trials. This leads to quicker drug development.

11 Conclusion and recommendations

In today's world, if we compare a transaction made through a bank and a BC, the transaction made through BCT is faster, cheaper and more secure. While the banking and finance world have looked at this technology keenly and have started utilizing it over the past few years, the healthcare industry has just begun evincing interest in this technology. While BCT has the power to revolutionize the way information about supply chains and patient's health records can be stored and retrieved, very few companies have utilized this. With this technology, healthcare providers can maintain medical records confidentially, update them whenever necessary across numerous facilities and locations in real-time and with security. In today's time, where the healthcare infrastructure is stretched, this would be very useful as it would reduce time in administration and enable redirection toward patient care.

India's public think tank government, called the "Niti Aayog," has carried out pilot studies on BCT use for various projects such as maintaining land records, issuing educational certificates, etc. (Aayog, 2020). This document has explored BC application in two essential healthcare areas: Medical supply chains and the other is the immunization program. The report details out how BCT can streamline and improve the current methods of delivering medicines and vaccinations. The group conducted a pilot study to trace the supply chain of medication from origin to endpoint. The reason was due to combat the entry of counterfeit drugs anywhere during the entire process. The group collaborated with manufacturer, logistics vendors and hospitals. They realized that BCT could vastly improve transparency, efficiency and reliability of the supply of drugs. The second use that the report cites is to use the technology to create a new immunization system enhanced by BCT that would reach all children in India. BCT would help by keeping records of the cold chain supply of the vaccines. It helps to keep a record of births so that vaccination can happen at the right age. It creates an alert system so that parents know when the vaccination is due, and these can be encouraged through incentives to parents and healthcare workers to vaccinate children. Another payoff was that it could help the government to track all its schemes. These payoffs would lead to a healthier and thus wealthier society for a developing country like India.

As with all other technologies, BCT also has a few drawbacks. While they are not insurmountable, it is best to be aware of them before incorporating this technology. The disadvantage of this technology is that adoption and implementation are expensive as it consumes enormous power. However, newer forms of technology are coming forward so that more organizations can make use of it. The security layer that "proof of work" provides consumes a lot of energy and computing power. Newer versions of BCT employ "proof of stake" and "proof of burn," which are less expensive. Also, this technology was designed to store transactions. As its use gets more widespread, it will keep more data, so storage capacity will need to be increased, and as more transactions and more data will be recorded and stored, there will be a need to speed the transactions. BCT will need to be scalable and more resilient.

To practically implement the BCT in healthcare, international standardization authorities will need to be involved to set standards. These standards for technology and healthcare would be helpful to evaluate the size, type of data, and format of the information in the database. This chapter has listed the benefits of BCT as a technology that has immense benefits as it is decentralized, immutable, secure, and auditable. The chances of committing fraud are meager. In the long run, this technology will be cheaper and faster to run and maintain. Like any technology that comes in, setting up will require companies to change mindsets and train people. However, that is a small cost to pay for the immense benefits that BCT brings, and they can save costs.

While adoption by healthcare companies has been slow, there have been some use cases to showcase BCT use in healthcare. By examining more than 20 companies that have incorporated this technology, it is clear that the time for BCT is here and now. As companies look forward to reaching customers faster and increasing efficiencies, BC will become even more essential. The COVID-19-induced pandemic has shown to us that we need healthcare systems that are robust and that can move fast, reach the patient quicker and alleviate suffering. At this juncture in our history, we need to be exceptionally responsive to social needs and BC, Artificial intelligence, the Internet of Healthy Things (IoHT), and plain common sense can help there.

References

Aarvik, P., 2020. Blockchain Technology to Prevent Corruption in Covid-19 Response: How Can it Help Overcome Risks? CMI Chr. Michelsen Institute. https://www.cmi.no/publications/7259-blockchain-technology-to-prevent-corruption-in-covid-19-response-how-can-it-help-overcome-risks. (Accessed 1 June 2021).

Aayog, N.I.T.I., 2020. Blockchain: The India Strategy. http://niti.gov.in/sites/default/files/2020-01/Blockchain_The_India_Strategy_Part_I.pdf. (Accessed 10 April 2021).

Ali, O., Jaradat, A., Kulakli, A., Abuhalimeh, A., 2021. A comparative study: blockchain technology utilization benefits, challenges and functionalities. IEEE Access 9, 12730–12749. https://doi.org/10.1109/ACCESS.2021.3050241.

Arsene, C., 2020. The Global "Blockchain in Healthcare" Report: The 2021 Ultimate Guide for every Executive. healthcareweekly.com. https://healthcareweekly.com/blockchain-in-healthcare-guide/. (Accessed 14 December 2020).

Banafa, A., 2020. Blockchain Technology and COVID-19. Open Mind. https://www.bbvaopenmind.com/en/technology/digital-world/blockchain-technology-and-covid-19/. (Accessed 1 June 2021).

Chakraborty, P., 2021. The Growing World of NFT. The Times of India. https://epaper.timesgroup.com/Olive/ODN/TimesOfIndia/shared/ShowArticle.aspx?doc=TOIM%2F2021%2F05%2F20&entity=Ar00502&sk=2C5FF52B&mode=text#. (Accessed 30 May 2021).

Combs, V., 2021. 177% increase_ Hackers grabbed 21.3 million healthcare records in the second half of 2020. Tech Republic. https://www.techrepublic.com/article/177-increase-hackers-grabbed-21-3-million-healthcare-records-in-the-second-half-of-2020/. (Accessed 26 May 2021).

Daley, S., 2021. How using blockchain in healthcare is reviving the industry's capabilities. builtin.com. https://builtin.com/blockchain/blockchain-healthcare-applications-companies. (Accessed 28 May 2021).

Davis, J., 2020. Update: The 10 Biggest Healthcare Data Breaches of 2020. Xtelligent Healthcare Media. https://healthitsecurity.com/news/the-10-biggest-healthcare-data-breaches-of-2020. (Accessed 26 May 2021).

EUBlockchain, 2021. EU blockchain ecosystem developments. The European Union Blockchain Observatory & Forum, pp. 1–200. https://www.eublockchainforum.eu/sites/default/files/reports/EU%20Blockchain%20Ecosystem%20Report_final_0.pdf. (Accessed 13 June 2021).

Fauci, A.S., Lane, H.C., Redfield, R.R., 2020. Covid-19-navigating the uncharted. N. Engl. J. Med. 382 (13), 1268–1269. https://doi.org/10.1056/nejme2002387.

Frankenfield, J., 2021. Proof of Work (PoW) Definition. Investopedia. https://www.investopedia.com/terms/p/proof-work.asp. (Accessed 2 June 2021).

Furst, B., 2020. How COVID-19 Has Revealed Healthcare's Blockchain Use Cases. hitconsultant.net. https://hitconsultant.net/2020/11/17/covid-19-healthcare-blockchain-use-cases/#.YKJFgqgzY2w. (Accessed 10 June 2021).

GlobalData Healthcare, 2021. Covid-19-induced digital transformation did prioritise blockchain.pdf. Pharmaceutical Technology. https://www.pharmaceutical-technology.com/comment/covid-19-induced-digital-transformation-did-prioritise-blockchain/. (Accessed 22 May 2021).

India.com, 2021. Google's GiveIndia to Provide Cash Assistance to Families Hit Hardest by Covid-19 Crisis. Deets Here. https://www.india.com/technology/googles-giveindia-to-provide-cash-assistance-to-families-hit-hardest-by-covid-19-crisis-deets-here-4616106/. (Accessed 1 June 2021).

Iredale, G., 2020. List of Top 50 Companies Using Blockchain Technology. 101 blockchains. https://101blockchains.com/companies-using-blockchain-technology/. (Accessed 30 May 2021).

Kassab, M.H., DeFranco, J., Malas, T., Laplante, P., Destefanis, G., Graciano, N.V.V., 2019. Exploring research in blockchain for healthcare and a roadmap for the future. IEEE Trans. Emerg. Top. Comput. 1. https://doi.org/10.1109/TETC.2019.2936881.

Knowledge@Wharton, 2018. How the Blockchain Brings Social Benefits to Emerging Economies. Wharton University of Pennsylvania. 28 November https://knowledge.wharton.upenn.edu/article/blockchain-brings-social-benefits-emerging-economies/. (Accessed 24 July 2021).

Krawiec, R.J., Housman, D., White, M., Filipova, M., Quarre, F., Barr, D., Nesbitt, A., Fedosova, K., Killmeyer, J., Israel, A., Tsai, L., 2016. Blockchain: Opportunities for Healthcare. https://www2.deloitte.com/us/en/pages/public-sector/articles/blockchain-opportunities-for-health-care.html. (Accessed 28 May 2020).

Kuner, C., Cate, F., Lynskey, O., Millard, C., Loideain, N.N., Svantesson, D., 2018. Blockchain versus data protection. Int. Data Privacy Law 8 (2), 103–104. https://academic.oup.com/idpl/article/8/2/103/5047578.

Lauren, D., Dent, M., Castillo, M.D., Hansen, S., Kauflin, J., Sorvino, C., Tucker, H., 2021. Blockchain 50. In: Castillo, M.D., Schifrin, M. (Eds.), Forbes. https://www.forbes.com/sites/michaeldelcastillo/2020/02/19/blockchain-50/?sh=77cf78b77553. (Accessed 30 May 2021).

Luu, L., Narayanan, V., Zheng, C., Baweja, K., Gilbert, S., Saxena, P., 2016. A secure sharding protocol for open blockchains. In: Katzenbeisser, S., Weippl, E. (Eds.), Proceedings of the 2016 ACM SIGSAC Conference on Computer and Communications Security. CCS '16. 24–28 October 2016, Vienna, Austria. Association for Computing Machinery, New York, NY, USA, pp. 17–30, https://doi.org/10.1145/2976749.2978389.

Lyons, T.C.L., 2020. Blockchain Use Cases in Healthcare. Frankfurt. www.eublockchainforum.eu/sites/default/files/reports/report_healthcare_v1.0.pd. (Accessed 20 September 2020).

Martindale, J.R., 2018. Merging developing and developed worlds: the blockchain revolution's impact on collective global growth. New Visions Public Affairs 10, 39–47.

Mathew, A.R., 2019. Cyber security through blockchain technology. Int. J. Eng. Adv. Technol. 9 (1), 3821–3824. https://doi.org/10.35940/ijeat.A9836.109119.

Mishra, N.T.P., Das, S.S., Yadav, S., Khan, W., Afzal, M., Alarifi, A., Kenawy, E.-R., Ansari, M.T., Hasnain, M.S., Nayak, A.K., 2020. Global impacts of pre- and post-COVID-19 pandemic: focus on socio-economic consequences. Sens. Int. 1. https://doi.org/10.1016/j.sintl.2020.100042, 100042.

MoF, 2021. Union Budget 2021. Government of India. https://www.indiabudget.gov.in/. (Accessed 28 May 2021).

Monttechi, M., Plangger, K., Etter, M., 2018. It's real, trust me! Establishing supply chain provenance using blockchain. Business Horizons, 1–11. https://doi.org/10.1016/j.bushor.2019.01.008.

Nakamoto, S., 2009. Bitcoin: A Peer-to-Peer Electronic Cash System. https://www.bitcoinpaper.info/bitcoinpaper-html/. (Accessed 25 May 2021).

Oppili, P., 2021. Lioness dies of suspected coronavirus infection in Chennai's Vandalur zoo; nine lions test positive. http://timesofindia.indiatimes.com/articleshow/83228324.cms?utm_source=contentofinterest&utm_medium=text&utm_campaign=cppst. (Accessed 10 June 2021).

PTI, 2021. Amazon India launches COVID-19 financial support for eligible staff. https://www.businesstoday.in/current/corporate/amazon-india-launches-covid-19-financial-support-for-eligible-staff/story/439881.html. (Accessed 1 June 2021).

PwC, 2018. PwC's Global Blockchain Survey. https://www.pwc.com/gx/en/industries/technology/blockchain/blockchain-in-business.html. (Accessed 20 July 2021).

Ribitzky, R., St. Clair, J., Houlding, D.I., McFarlane, C.T., Ahier, B., Gould, M., Flannery, H.L., Pupo, E., Clauson, K.A., 2018. Pragmatic, interdisciplinary perspectives on blockchain and distributed ledger technology: paving the future for healthcare. Blockchain in Healthcare Today, 1. https://doi.org/10.30953/bhty.v1.24.

Sahu, M., 2020. 8 Reasons Why Blockchain Technology Is The Future. UpGrad [Blog]. https://www.upgrad.com/blog/reasons-why-blockchain-technology-is-the-future/. (Accessed 1 June 2021).

Service, I. A. News, 2019. Hackers attack Indian healthcare website, steal 6.8 million records. DataBreaches.net. https://www.databreaches.net/hackers-attack-indian-healthcare-website-steal-68/. (Accessed 26 May 2021).

Sharma, A., Bahl, S., Bagha, A.K., Javaid, M., Shukla, D.K., Haleem, A., 2020. Blockchain technology and its applications to combat COVID-19 pandemic. Res. Biomed. Eng., 1–8. https://doi.org/10.1007/s42600-020-00106-3.

Sharma, M., 2021a. When is a Third Wave of Covid-19 likely to Hit India? Coronavirus Outbreak News. https://www.indiatoday.in/coronavirus-outbreak/story/india-third-wave-of-covid-19-vaccine-prevention-1799504-2021-05-06. (Accessed 2 June 2021).

Sharma, T.K., 2021b. How Blockchain Can Solve Major challenges of COVID-19 Faced by Healthcare Sectors? https://www.blockchain-council.org/blockchain/how-blockchain-can-solve-major-challenges-of-covid-19-faced-by-healthcare-sectors/. (Accessed 2 June 2021).

Singh, S., Hosen, A.S.M.S., Yoon, B., 2021. Blockchain security attacks, challenges, and solutions for the future distributed IoT network. IEEE Access 9, 13938–13959. https://doi.org/10.1109/ACCESS.2021.3051602.

Siyal, A.A., Junejo, A.Z., Zawish, M., Ahmed, K., Khalil, A., Soursou, G., 2019. Applications of blockchain technology in medicine and healthcare: challenges and future perspectives. Cryptography 3 (3), 2–16. https://doi.org/10.3390/cryptography3010003.

Tandon, A., Dhir, A., Islam, A.K.M.N., Mäntymäki, M., 2020. Blockchain in healthcare: a systematic literature review, synthesising framework and future research agenda. Comput. Ind. 122, 103290. https://www.sciencedirect.com/science/article/pii/S0166361520305248. https://doi.org/10.1016/j.compind.2020.103290.

The Economic Times, 2020. Direct benefit transfer: Covid-19: govt to transfer financial assistance only through DBT mechanism. April 16 https://economictimes.indiatimes.com/news/politics-and-nation/covid-19-govt-to-transfer-financial-assistance-only-through-dbt-mechanism/articleshow/75185835.cms?from=mdr. (Accessed 1 June 2021).

The Economic Times, 2021. COVID-19: RCB promises financial help for oxygen support, to also raise funds. The Economic Times. May 6 https://economictimes.indiatimes.com/news/india/covid-19-rcb-promises-financial-help-for-oxygen-support-to-also-raise-funds/articleshow/82351935.cms. (Accessed 1 June 2021).

TNN, 2021. PM Cares to pay for education, care of children orphaned by Covid-19. Times of India. https://timesofindia.indiatimes.com/india/government-to-support-kids-who-lost-parents-to-covid-19-via-pm-cares/articleshow/83065497.cms. (Accessed 30 May 2021).

Transparency International, 2020. Corruption Perceptions Index. https://www.transparency.org/en/cpi/2020/index/nzl. (Accessed 23 June 2021).

Ugalmugle, S., Swain, R., 2019. Blockchain Technology in Healthcare Market Size by Application. Global Market Insights. Report ID: GMI3098 https://www.gminsights.com/industry-analysis/blockchain-technology-in-healthcare-market. (Accessed 20 June 2021).

WHO, 2021a. Coronavirus disease (COVID-19) pandemic. https://www.who.int/emergencies/diseases/novel-coronavirus-2019. (Accessed 15 June 2021).

WHO, 2021b. COVID-19 weekly epidemiological update 22 December 2020. World Health Organization, pp. 1–3. https://www.who.int/publications/m/item/weekly-epidemiological-update—22-december-2020. (Accessed 12 February 2021).

Xu, J.J., 2016. Are blockchains immune to all malicious attacks? Financial Innovation 2 (25). https://jfin-swufe.springeropen.com/articles/10.1186/s40854-016-0046-5#citeas.

Zago, M., 2018. 50+ Examples of How Blockchains are Taking Over the World. https://medium.com/@essentia1/50-examples-of-how-blockchains-are-taking-over-the-world-4276bf488a4b. (Accessed 31 May 2021).

Zambrano, R., 2020. Taming the beast: harnessing blockchains in developing country governments. Front. Blockchain 2, 27. https://www.frontiersin.org/article/10.3389/fbloc.2019.00027. (Accessed 31 May 2021).

Zheng, Z., Shaoan, X., Hongning, D., Xiangping, C.H.W., 2018. Blockchain challenges and opportunities: a survey. Int. J. Web Grid Services 14 (4), 352–375. https://doi.org/10.1504/IJWGS.2018.10016848.

CHAPTER FIVE

COVID-19 and its impact on cancer, HIV, and mentally ill patients

Avinash Arvind Rasalkar[a,*], Saloni Bhatia[b,*], Teesta Katte[b], Prathibha Narayanan[b], Saisha Vinjamuri[b], Ashok Kumar Shettihalli[b], Sarina Kabade[c], Ram N. Manas[b], Vijayakumar Kadappa[d], and Divijendra Natha S. Reddy[b]

[a]Prabhat-Advanced Life Tech Analytics, Dharwad, Karnataka, India
[b]Department of Biotechnology, B.M.S. College of Engineering, Bengaluru, Karnataka, India
[c]Government Science College (Autonomous) affiliated to Bangalore University, Bangalore, Karnataka, India
[d]Department of Computer Applications, B.M.S. College of Engineering, Bengaluru, Karnataka, India

1 Introduction: SARS-COVID-19

The world is reeling from the unprecedented health emergency—COVID-19 disease—caused by the novel Coronavirus-2 infection. Irrespective of the health preparedness of developed and developing or underdeveloped countries, the effect and severity of the disease and its management is being felt at the same magnitude across the world and is testing the limits of health care infrastructure and management. As of July end, 2021, officially 195,886,929 confirmed cases are reported across the globe with an estimate of 4,189,148 deaths worldwide, with a total of 3,830,124,730 vaccine doses administered (WHO, 2021). As COVID-19 is progressing in to its second year, occurrences of second and third waves are creating further panic among the populace and administrations across the world. The resulting lockdowns curtailing the movement of people is creating an economic havoc, pushing untold number of people losing jobs, wages and pushing them in to forced poverty. Although, initially it affected more of the older population with premorbid conditions, however second and third waves of CoV-2 infections are proving to be increasingly effective with accompanied evolution of viral strains (B.1.1.7, i.e., α, B.1.351, i.e., β, P.1, i.e., γ, and B.1.617.2, i.e., δ) over a broader range of age groups

*A.A.R. and S.B. equally contributed to this work.

Lessons from COVID-19
https://doi.org/10.1016/B978-0-323-99878-9.00006-6

including younger population associated with longer recovery periods (long-COVID) (Blomberg et al., 2021; Venkatesan, 2021).

1.1 Pathophysiology of COVID-19: Infection, interactions

SARS-CoV-2 was identified as a causative agent of COVID-19 disease in late 2019 in Wuhan, China. Since its discovery and identification, the disease spread across the globe with almost half a billion infections and more than 4,189,148 deaths (WHO, 2021) reaching the status of a global pandemic. Initially, effects of infection of SARS-CoV-2 seemed to be relatively milder in younger population while older patients and patients with comorbid conditions were more vulnerable for severe disease and ensuing death (Sanyaolu et al., 2020). Although the infection rates are very high, the death rate is considerably low and only higher in older patients (Sanyaolu et al., 2020). Overall death rate is estimated to be around 1%–2% (Baud et al., 2020). Despite low death rate, rapid infectivity, less incubation time and consequent acute respiratory distress symptoms lead to the urgent need of health care facilities for many patients in a short span, causing severe strain and panic among administration and populations. Since the occurrence of COVID-19, intense research has led to the increased basic understanding of the causative agent that is SARS-CoV-2 and its relation to the already existing SARS and MERS viruses (Zhu et al., 2020).

SARS-CoV-2 belongs to the group of Coronaviruses, a diverse group of viruses infecting different variety of animals (Hu et al., 2021a). Most of them cause mild to severe acute respiratory diseases. Of all the Coronaviruses, SARS (2002), MERS (2012), the present SARS-CoV-2 (2019) seem to cause serious diseases (Gorbalenya et al., 2020). Among the Coronaviruses, SARS-CoV-2 is fast spreading and infecting an overwhelmingly larger number of people than either SARS or MERS (Zhu et al., 2020) within very short span of time.

SARS-CoV-2 is a single stranded, positive sense RNA virus with an envelope for protecting its genome (Pal et al., 2020). SARS-CoV-2 genome is 80% similar to SARS-CoV and MERS-CoV (Lu et al., 2020; Zhang and Holmes, 2020; Zhou et al., 2020). The surface of the virus contains matrix (M) glycoprotein, envelope(E) protein and is richly coated with spike(S) protein (Zhang and Guo, 2020) (illustrated in Fig. 1). The transmission of infection is through the viral particles in the air released from the infected person or through contact with the surfaces with active virus particles. Usual mode of entry in the new host is through nasal cavities, eyes or any wounds for effective infection. The spike protein of the virus plays an important role in connecting and binding with receptors expressed on the host cell surface. Spike protein binds to angiotensin-

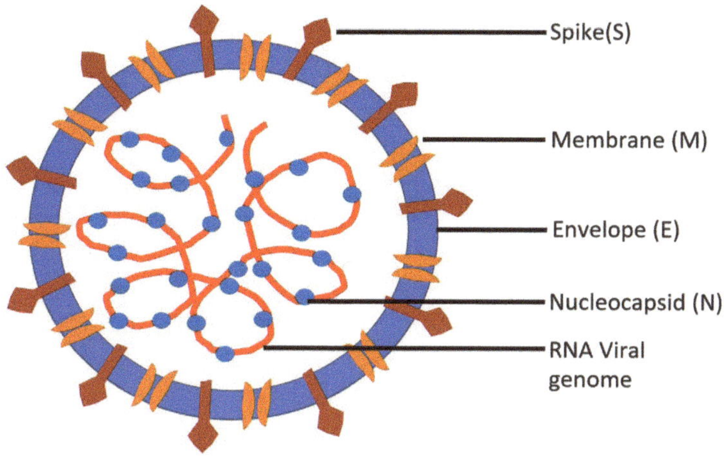

Fig. 1 Schematic diagram of SARS-CoV-2.

converting enzyme 2 (ACE2), a surface receptor highly expressed on the surface of the tracheal epithelial cells of the host. Once the spike protein and ACE2 establishes the binding, another transmembrane host protease, TMPRSS2 cleaves the membrane helping in the internalization of virus by endocytosis. In the endocytic vesicle, proteases from host such as CTSL cleave the spike proteins and other viral surface proteins to release the viral RNA in the cytoplasm of the host cell (Pišlar et al., 2020) (illustrated in Fig. 2). After entering the host cell, the genome gets replicated through RNA dependent RNA polymerase. The viral genome is 30kb, and consists of 14-open reading frames (ORFs) and ORF1a and ORF1b encodes for polyproteins, which produces 16 nonstructural proteins (NSP1–16) upon auto-proteolysis—and forms the replicase and transcriptase activity mainly. The rest of the genome codes for structural proteins; spike, envelop, membrane and nucleocapsid and also 9 putative accessory factors (Gordon et al., 2020). The translation of viral protein is processed in endoplasmic reticulum vesicles leading to the assembly of virion particles, consequently budding off from host cell. Thus, newly formed virions enter in to the interstitial space and thereby the blood circulation and starts to infect new host cells aggravating the infection and onset of the COVID-19 (illustrated in Fig. 2) (Snijder et al., 2006; Perlman and Netland, 2009).

The respiratory tract is the main route of infection for SARS-CoV-2, like for many other Coronaviruses. Airway and alveolar epithelial cells, vascular endothelial cells and alveolar macrophages are the primary target hosts' cells for viral infection (Hamming et al., 2004; Jia et al., 2005; Kuba et al., 2005; Ziegler et al., 2020). The most observable symptoms include

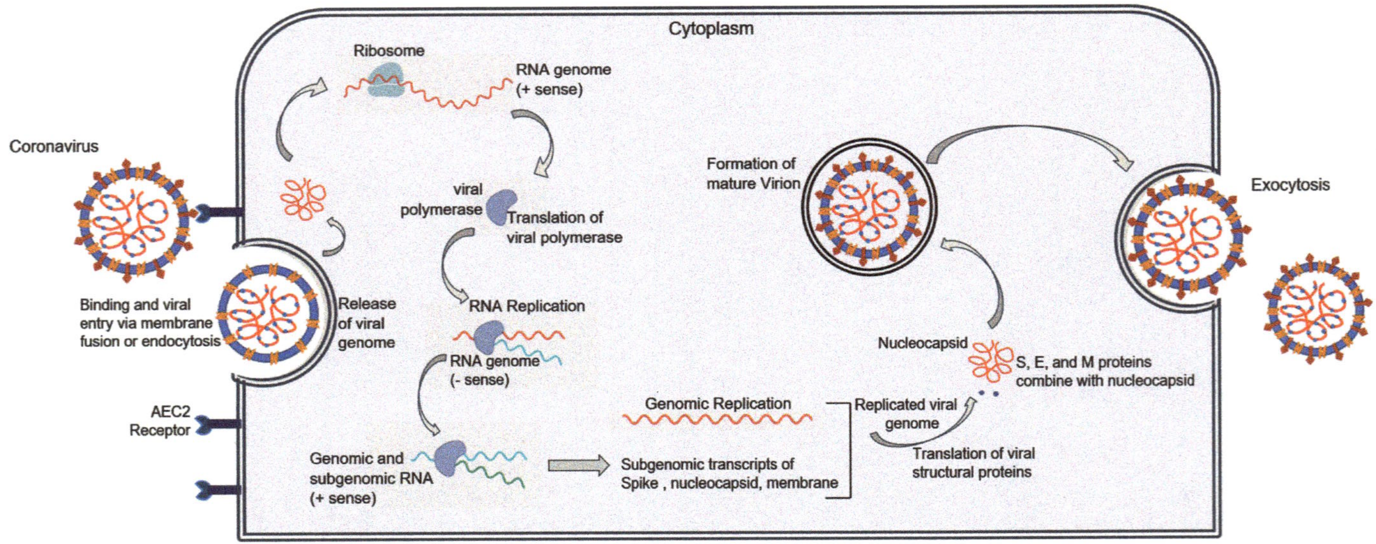

Fig. 2 The life cycle of the SARS-CoV-2 from entry to exit of the host cell.

persistent fever or chills, dry cough, tiredness, fatigue and myalgia for a few days, loss of smell, taste and enteric problems such as diarrhea. The severe symptom includes trouble in breathing, persistent pain or pressure in chest and pale or gray, lips. All or some of them can be present in moderate or severe COVID-19. The disease could be very mild in some patients with very few or none of the above symptoms but they can still act as carriers. SARS-CoV-2 elicits strong immune response and activates all components of the innate and adaptive immune system. In severe COVID-19 cases, the immune system loses the battle to contain the virus and there is considerable reduction in $CD4^+$ T, $CD8^+$ T, NK, and B cell number leading to lymphopenia (Huang et al., 2020; Lippi and Plebani, 2020; Qin et al., 2020; Xu et al., 2020). In severe form of COVID-19, cytokines such as IL-2, IL-4, IL-6, IL-10, TNFα, and TNF-γ elevates up to an alarmingly high level within short span of time and create a pathogenic condition called "cytokine storm" (illustrated in Fig. 3). As the disease progresses, severe acute respiratory distress syndrome (ARDS) occurs leading to shortness of breath requiring external supply of oxygen, hospitalization and in further extreme cases occurrence of multiple organ failure leading to death (Cattaneo et al., 2020; Huang et al., 2020). The current treatment regimens include usage of remdesivir (although its effect seems to be marginal and WHO is contemplating its removal from usage for COVID-19 treatment),

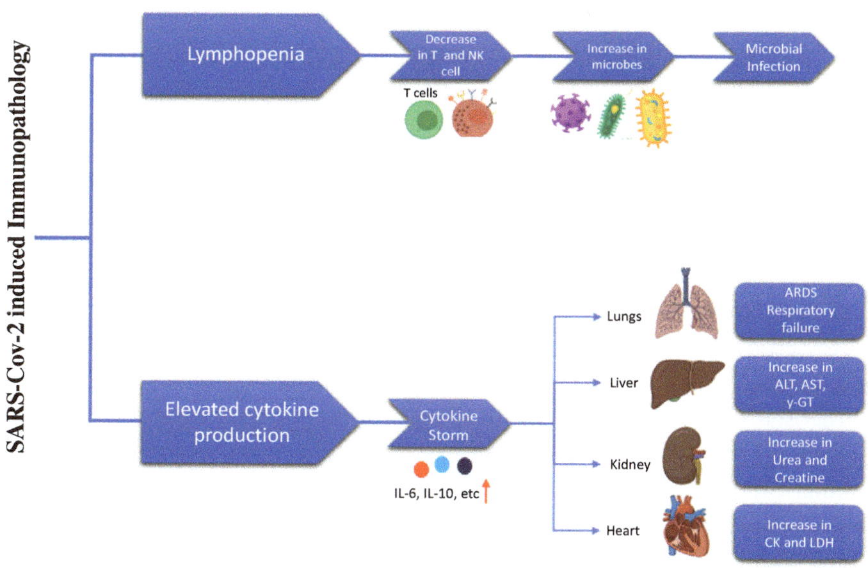

Fig. 3 SARS-CoV-2 induced immunology of severe form of COVID-19.

steroids and antibiotics to reduce the cytokine storm and opportunistic infections in severe cases, respectively. To contain ARDS, either external oxygen supply or ventilation is required in case of severe COVID-19. The rapid increase in infections across the globe and resulting fatalities forced development of vaccines for the disease on a war footing. Within a short span of less than a year, several vaccines have been developed and vaccination is administered rapidly across the globe hoping to achieve herd immunity and there by contain the disease.

In the context of COVID-19 pandemic, the treatment of patients with dreadful diseases like cancer, HIV, mental illness is challenging. In this chapter, we discuss the impact of COVID-19 on these patients and the managing strategies prevailed or emerged during this pandemic. We present the impact of COVID-19 on cancer patients in Section 2. The effect of COVID-19 and its management on HIV patients is discussed in Section 3. Subsequently, we discuss the impact of COVID-19 on mentally ill patients and patient management in Section 4 and present a perspective on Ayurveda and its relevance in the context of COVID-19 treatment in Section 5. Finally, we add a note on the available digital platforms or software tools for managing the COVID-19 patients in Section 6.

2 COVID-19 and cancer

In this section, we review the work related to cancer and its management in COVID-19 patients. More specifically, we present the treatment and managing the COVID-19 patients suffering from major types of cancers such as breast cancer, lung cancer, and hematologic neoplasms and malignancies.

Cancer is one of the prominent and persistent diseases of several types and affect almost all the tissues and organs with few exceptions. Despite intensive research, there is still no cure for many cancers and is one of the highly researched areas of modern medicine. Cancer is characterized by increased cell proliferation in tissues which leads the involved cell, tissue, and organ dysfunctional, leading to broad physiological disturbances in homeostasis of multicellular, multiorgan organisms with a final consequence in death. The cellular homeostasis of a tissue and organ is controlled by four cellular processes, *viz.*, self-renewal, proliferation, differentiation, and apoptosis which are in turn regulated by molecular determinants (gene/protein expression and genomic integrity), cell signaling, and biochemical regulation. Any changes in terms of genomic integrity leading to mutations, gene amplifications, duplications affecting at least two of the cellular control processes, finally manifests into cancer. Thus, cancer is a multistep process which is accompanied by and is the result of the acquisition of the six biological capabilities such as sustenance of proliferative signaling, evasion of growth suppressors, resistance to cell death, replicative immortality, induction of angiogenesis, invasion and metastasis (Hanahan and Weinberg, 2000, 2011). Further to this it has been increasingly evident in the last decade that the progressively growing transformed cells/cancer tissue itself creates a hypoxic and inflamed microenvironment which pushes the cells to reorganize their metabolic states and evade immunity/or suppress it to thrive in the stress—essential for survival, which leads the cell for further transformation, and sets the stage for metastasis (Tennant et al., 2009; Cavallo et al., 2011; Prensner and Chinnaiyan, 2011; Fouad and Aanei, 2017; Tennant et al., 2009; Prensner and Chinnaiyan, 2011; Fouad and Aanei, 2017). The foundation of rationale for drug design/discovery to target at least two or more pathways with effective prognosis to achieve the disease free survival had been evident in last two decades with advent of targeted and semitargeted therapeutics (Fouad and Aanei, 2017). Nevertheless, most of the patients suffering from cancer need to visit the hospitals and also have to undergo various monitored therapeutic regimens which require several visits and hospitalization. However, due to the COVID-19 pandemic and the urgency to treat the patients, it is demanding a majority of the medical resources dedicated for treating COVID-19 patients. Therefore, it is very challenging to manage not only cancer patients but also patients suffering from other medical conditions. In this context we present the risk factors, scenarios and management of various types of cancers patients in COVID-19 pandemic.

2.1 COVID-19 and breast cancer

Breast cancer is prominent cancer type affecting more than 2 million cases across the world (Bray et al., 2018). Breast cancer is the most predominant cancer with very few or negligible number of male breasts cancers. Breast cancer is highly heterogeneous at the molecular level, and requires different treatment approaches for major subtypes (Testa et al., 2020). Breast cancer is classified in subtypes based on the many genetic alterations (Radice and Pierotti, 1997). The most prominent one was proposed a couple of decades ago by Perou and Sorlie (Perou et al., 2000). Based on this classification, breast cancer is divided into various subtypes such as luminal A and luminal B, basal like (with no receptor expression) and

HER2 enriched (without ER expression). Clinical practice uses classification based on histological and molecular characteristics and thus, breast cancer is further classified into various types (do Nascimento and Otoni, 2020). When all the membrane-bound hormone receptors such as ER, PR, and HER2 are being expressed these tumors are called hormone receptor–positive breast cancers and if the receptor expression is completely absent, then those tumors are classified as receptor negative or triple negative breast cancers. Among all these cancer subtypes, targeted therapies are available for hormone positive breast cancers such as HER2 positive breast cancers (von Minckwitz et al., 2019). This cancer subtype can be treated with monoclonal antibodies against HER2 receptors and this therapy is proven to be effective (Baselga, 2001). However, triple negative breast cancers lack expression of any of the hormone receptors and are difficult to treat. Thus, they are more aggressive in recurrence with high fatality rates (Engebraaten et al., 2013).

Although incidence of breast cancer is global, its distribution is skewed toward developed nations, and is more prominent in North America and Europe than in developing countries from Asia and Africa (Ferlay et al., 2015). This could be due to genetic factors as well as availability of better screening facilities for early detection (Winters et al., 2017). Less than 10% breast cancers are hereditary in nature and most prominent being the breast cancer with mutations in BRCA1 and BRCA2 tumor suppressor genes (Pruss et al., 2014). The incidence of breast cancer is also dependent on genetic, environmental, reproductive, and cultural factors (Rojas and Stuckey, 2016). Early pregnancy and breast feeding are shown to be inversely correlated with breast cancer incidences (Kotsopoulos et al., 2012). Obesity, alcohol consumption and less bodily exercises are considered to be positively correlated with occurrence of breast cancer (Australian Institute of Health and Welfare, 2012; Australian Bureau of Statistics, 2009, 2013). The histology and expression of the receptor dictates treatment regimens to be followed to treat various types of breast cancers.

Many breast cancer patients require regular visits to the hospital for consultations, surgeries, for radio or chemotherapies. COVID-19 is not only demanding most of the healthcare resources but also warrants social distancing and therefore cancer patients are advised to minimize hospital exposure to reduce risk of infections. Based on the urgency of requirement they are being categorized into Priority A, B, and C (Dietz et al., 2020). Priority A patients requires urgent hospitalization as the breast cancer is unstable and might result in poor prognosis if not intervened immediately. A short delay in medical intervention may not significantly affect the poor prognosis in category B patients. Nevertheless, they may require hospitalization in the near future and can be subdivided based on the hospitalization requirement. Priority C patients may not require hospitalization for a considerable number of months and can be managed by remote consultations. Hospitalization can be deferred for these patients for a certain duration of time without affecting the outcome of the prognosis. For cancers such as triple negative breast cancer (BC) and HER2 positive cancers, surgery can be deferred by the option of neoadjuvant therapy (Sikov et al., 2015; von Minckwitz et al., 2019). Adjuvant and neoadjuvant therapy may not work with luminal A type, BC patients and they can be administered with endocrine therapy to delay immediate hospitalization. Metastatic breast cancer patients' doses and schedule adjustments could be made to reduce their hospital visits, blood work and side effects. Palliative care could be considered as an option if that relieves painful effects of the metastasis of the cancer. However, if the surgeries or progression of the disease to metastasis are imminent, then hospitalization of patients may be considered under strict COVID-19 guidelines (Dietz et al., 2020; Sheng et al., 2020). Many studies demonstrated that cancer patients that contract COVID-19 may have poor prognosis due to compromised immune system, radiation, and chemotherapies (Liang et al., 2020; Zhang and Guo, 2020). Most of the studies show that BC patients with COVID-19 may not be as vulnerable as other cancer patients to effects of SARS-CoV-2 infection.

2.2 COVID-19 and lung cancer

Lung cancer is highly prevalent next to colorectal and breast cancers with a high rate of fatality. Its high incidence is attributed to hereditary susceptibility, unbalanced diet, smoking, air pollution, radiation exposure, and an occupational exposure (Mao et al., 2016). One of the reasons for high mortality rate include the late detection of lung cancers by which time the cancer is metastatic or at an advanced stage (Spiro and Silvestri, 2005). Traditionally, lung cancers are classified as small cell lung carcinoma (SCLC) and non-small cell lung carcinoma (NSCLC). NSCLC account for more than 80% of cases. SCLCs behave aggressively and are mostly treated nonsurgically, while treatment of NSCLC includes surgery and adjuvant therapies (Zheng, 2016). The diversity of NSCLC and SCLC has led to further subclassifications by World Health Organization (WHO). As per the 2015 WHO classification, lung cancers can be divided broadly into mesenchymal tumors, epithelial tumors, lymphohistiocytic tumors, tumors of ectopic origin, and metastatic tumors. These classes are further subdivided based on their differences in immunohistochemistry (Pelosi et al., 2010). The major types of NSCLC include large cell carcinoma (LCC), squamous cell carcinoma (SSC/LUSC), and adenocarcinoma (ADC/LUAD), whereas SCLC is grouped with other tumors having neuroendocrine differentiation (Zheng, 2016). As mentioned earlier, the entry of SARS-CoV-2 virus into host cells occurs by binding of spike proteins to ACE-2 receptor. Further, the SARS-CoV-2 spike proteins are reported to be activated/primed by a number of mediators like transmembrane protease serine-2 and -4 (TMPRSS-2, TMPRSS-4), neuropilin-1 (NRP1), cathepsin L (CTSL) leading to infection in host cells (Katopodis et al., 2021). The physiological responses triggered by COVID-19 are amplified in the case of lung cancer patients due to the preexisting elevated levels of these molecules (Wan et al., 2010; Qian et al., 2013; Zhang et al., 2020). ACE-2 is primarily expressed in alveolar epithelial cells which play an important role in pulmonary gaseous exchange (Dobbs, 1989). Overexpression of ACE-2 in lung squamous cell carcinoma and lung adenocarcinoma has been reported. Aberrations of DNA methylation is considered as one of the causes for this abnormality in addition to histone modifications and glycosylation. Chai et al. (2020), Zhang et al. (2020), Kong et al. (2020), and Samad et al. (2020) explored the expression of *ACE2* and *TMPRSS2* with prognosis of COVID-19 in LUAD and LUSC. TMPRSS2 is required for the binding of the spike protein (S protein) of SARS-CoV-2 virus to ACE-2. They reported that lung cancer patients at all stages and subtypes are highly prone to COVID-19 of which LUAD patients are highly susceptible. Tang et al. (2020) studied the expression levels of ACE2, TMPRSS2, and AAK1 (endocytic regulator) in LUAD patients. They also studied the correlation of the expression of these genes and levels of immune infiltration caused as well as identified potential therapeutic targets and drugs for ACE2, TMPRSS2, and AAK1. They showed that expression of ACE2 and TMPRSS2 was high in case of LUAD which could be the reason for high susceptibility of these patients to COVID-19. They also reported that these patients showed higher infiltration of B cells, activated dendritic cells, memory T cells, and CD4 cells leading to the development of a "cytokine storm." Hu et al. (2021b) have also reported a positive correlation between ACE2 and *TMPRSS2* gene expression in lung cancer and the rate of immune infiltration.

In addition to the role of ACE2 in COVID-19, the effect of other mediator proteins has also been studied. Yang et al. (2020) have reported the role of interferon gamma-induced protein 10 (IP-10) in COVID-19 infections.

IP-10 also known as CXCL10 (C-X-C motif10) is a proinflammatory cytokine known to be associated with pathological processes like infections and cancer. CXCL10 has been reported to be involved in the "cytokine storm" leading to tissue damage and ARDS. Hence has been also considered as an important biomarker for COVID-19 in addition to ACE2 receptor. Xu et al. (2020) and Mahmood et al. (2021) have analyzed in silico, the expression pattern, functional characterization and mutations of ACE2 and CXCL10 in LUSC and LUAD and have reported these are overexpressed. The overexpression of ACE2 gene might lead to higher degree of binding of the spike protein while high levels of CXCL10 might lead to alveolar collapse because of excessive cytokine secretions leading to increased fatality rate to COVID-19.

Katopodis et al. (2020, 2021) had studied the co-expression of TMPRSS-4 with other key SARS-CoV-2 cell entry mediators like ACE-2, ADAM17, and TMPRSS-2 in the bronchial epithelial cells of passive and active smokers. Further, TMPRSS-4 was found to be elevated in smokers. Zang et al. (2020) have reported the involvement of TMPRSS4 as a mediator for entry of SARS COV2 virus. They have observed that ACE2, TMPRSS2, and TMPRSS4 are co-expressed in cancer patients. Their finding indicates a predisposition to severe COVID-19 in these patients. Hence, a better understanding of the expression levels of these proteins and immune cell infiltration could aid in developing appropriate treatment strategies in cancer patients.

Singh et al. (2020) report a strategy for treatment of lung cancer patients during this pandemic. They report a workflow developed for treatment of NSCLC, SCLC, and lung neuroendocrine tumors (NETs) which relies on use of modern radiotherapy techniques for treatment and personalized treatment options. They recommend using image guided transthoracic biopsies instead of transbronchial biopsies for preliminary diagnosis. They also suggest use of computed tomography or Positron emission tomography for identification over invasive methods currently being used. They recommend mediastinoscopy over bronchoscopy in cases where invasive testing is needed.

For more details, it is recommended to visit websites of medical institutes of repute worldwide like British Columbia Cancer center, the European Society for Medical Oncology (ESMO), National Institute for Excellence in Health and Care (NICE), which have posted detailed information on patient handling and clinical management of lung cancer during the pandemic.

2.3 COVID-19 and the hematologic neoplasms and malignancies

The clinically manifested global infection rate of SARS-CoV-2 is 1%–2% and the rate of mortality in general population (noncancer patients) is 1%–5%, while >30% in cancer patients (Paul et al., 2021). SARS-CoV-2 can infect patients of all types of hematologic diseases. However, in early studies it was found that the risk of acquiring infection is higher for patients on immunosuppressive therapies, however the risk is lower in patients with chronic myeloid leukemia. Cattaneo et al. found that the mortality rate is 39.2%, compared to only 3% in not-infected hematologic controls and 23.5% in nonhematologic patients. The severe degree of respiratory syndrome combined with any type of active hematologic treatment was associated with worst prognostic outcome (Cattaneo et al., 2020).

Leukemia is a cancer of the hematopoietic system (HS). HS comprises the entire cellular compartment of the immune system derived from hematopoietic stem/progenitor cells (HSPCs)—through a tightly regulated interplay of the following cellular processes: (1) self-renewal of HSPCs, (2) proliferation, (3) differentiation and (4) apoptosis (Doulatov et al., 2012; Eaves, 2015; Bernitz et al., 2016; Arends et al., 2018; Zhang et al., 2018). It originates in bone marrow in adults and its mature-differentiated cells are present in the peripheral medium, which is blood, reaching each organ, tissue, and cells of the body. HS consist of the functional effectors and are the final frontiers of action to fight and clear off any foreign material or pathogens. The major cellular compartment of HS consist of HSPCs, multipotent progenitors (MPPs), myeloid (granulocytes), and lymphoid (agranulocytes—T and B cells) cells, which form the strong defense compartment to detect, alarm, digest and induce cellular and humoral immunity for future encounters with the pathogen (Dzierzak and Bigas, 2018; Boehm, 2011). The myeloid cells, i.e., granulocytes (mast cells, basophiles, neutrophils, macrophage, antigen presenting cells, erythrocytes, eosinophils) and the lymphoid cells, i.e., T-cells and B-cells and their differentiated progeny; series of T-effector and regulatory cells, NK cells, and memory and plasma cells, respectively—act through cross-talk with amongst themselves and cells of other tissues and organs, which is mediated through cytokines and chemokines upon interaction with the pathogen (Zhu and Emerson, 2002; Boehm, 2011). Interestingly, the receptor angiotensin converting enzyme 2 (ACE2), which is used by SARS-CoV-2 for entry into host cell (Hoffmann et al., 2020)—is expressed on monocytes, monocyte derived macrophages and also the cells of the bone marrow niche, which puts the entire HS at risk of SARS-CoV-2 infection (Patnaik et al., 2020). HSPCs and progenitors can also stay in the same cellular state without differentiation for prolonged periods—some proportions even throughout lifetime. Thus, if these cells upon infection can lead to the generation of virus-persistence phase, which could stay asymptomatic till the HSPCs are not triggered to differentiate. Therefore, it is anticipated that—patients of Leukemia can serve as reservoirs of virus once these cells are infected with SARS-CoV-2 and also suffer secondary infections during the treatment and in relapse—most of the time leading to viremia and bacteremia. This is a regularly observed fact and is reflected in the patient data (Visentin et al., 2017; Pelland-Marcotte et al., 2020).

Leukemia are grouped and categorized in several groups depending on the cell types involved and the rate of cell division/or latency; for simplicity—here we take only two broad group—lymphoid and myeloid leukemia with acute and chronic category (which depends upon the rate of development of disease) (Arber et al., 2016; Swerdlow et al., 2016), which affect the overall functions of the respective compartment severely and thereby compromise immune functions. Leukemia patients can elicit inflammation or immune response or fail to do so depending on the type of leukemia—e.g., if granulocytes are involved, then these cells (transformed) are present at an alarming numbers—thus they can secrete varying quantities of cytokines needed for the first line of defense or fail to raise humoral immunity in lymphoid leukemia, depending on the proportions of transformed cells. This is complicated by the heterogeneous nature of the disease, that means the cell population also consist of various degrees of transformed cells—from leukemic stem cells, to normal cells to highly transformed cells (Stiehl et al., 2016; Beke et al., 2020). Therefore, the degree of these responses (in terms of overall inflammation) cannot be generalized or predicted, and needs to be monitored closely for each patient and treated accordingly to balance or to restore vitals of physiology for better prognosis and disease outcome.

In case of SARS-CoV-2, this is evident from a case study—of a chronic myelogenous leukemia; patient with immunocompromised state could shed the infectious virus for up to 70 days and the genomic and subgenomic RNA was detected till day 105 (Avanzato et al., 2020). Thus COVID-19, put the patients of leukemia in a unique category with short term personal benefit but at an impending risk to the other normal population, as they can serve as a reservoir of the SARS-CoV-2 (Truong et al., 2021).

This is being evident in patients and is an alarming concern as SARS-CoV-2 infection was found persistent in immunocompromised patients—who can be reservoirs for replication and evolution—by accumulation of mutation and consequent emergence as novel strains which can have increased capacities of infectivity and evasion of immune response. It has been demonstrated in three patients with acute lymphoblastic leukemia (ALL) with persistent SARS-CoV-2 infection monitored by quantitative polymerase chain reaction and viral viability—through viral culture analysis over a period of 162 days. These results demonstrated broad spectrum infectivity and immune response (Truong et al., 2021). In another study consisting of 175 patients with myeloproliferative neoplasm (MPN) with clinically manifested COVID-19, the mortality was 48% with a median follow-up of 50 days compared to the general population. There was a significant co-relation between death and age, male gender bias, decreased number of lymphocytes, comorbidities, and myelofibrosis. This study also highlighted the increased risk for patients who discontinued ruxolitinib treatment during COVID-19 (Barbui et al., 2021).

Treatment and management of leukemia patients in COVID-19 presents us with unique challenges as homeostasis of the immune system—itself is disturbed. Given the cellular homeostasis and the dynamics of molecular regulators and associated chemotherapy (targeted and semitargeted likewise) adds to increase the complexity of the treatment during the window period of risk of SARS-CoV-2 infection. Broadly, for the brief benefit of understanding: the line of treatment of leukemia are general chemotherapy or semitargeted chemotherapy (e.g., tyrosine kinase blockers-Gleevec/imatinib, or cell differentiators-like *trans*-retinoic acid for PML-RAR-α (promyelo monocytic-retinoic acid receptor alpha-leukemia and long list of other chemotherapeutics, etc.) or immunotherapy followed by hematopoietic stem cell transplantation (HSCT) and immunosuppression till graft acceptance (Lo-Coco et al., 2013; Dombret and Gardin, 2016; Piccolomo et al., 2020).

HSCT is a standard and most successful therapeutic treatment applied in all acute and chronic leukemia. This poses a challenge evident from the following cases, wherein the healthy allogenic donors (aged 22 years—a child of patient and 50 years—a sibling of patient) were tested negative—8 days before transplantation; however, they tested positive for SARS-CoV-2 but asymptomatic (RT-PCR tested on nasopharyngeal swabs only) on the day of collection. However, considering the benefit-risk balance in cases of acute myeloid leukemia, transplantation was opted. The recipients (patients of leukemia aged 60 and 64) were found negative and asymptomatic when tested twice a week for SARS-CoV-2 with nasopharyngeal swab and plasma for 4 weeks posttransplantation. Nevertheless, recipients developed fever without any other symptoms-suggestive of COVID-19 (Leclerc et al., 2021).

The immunosuppressive treatment post bone marrow (or hematopoietic stem cell) transplantation, post chemotherapy—has immediate implications in COVID-19 pandemic, given that most of the bone marrow cells and its progeny's do express ACE2 receptor, thereby increasing the rate of infectivity of SARS-CoV-2. Therefore, the donors must be tested for persisting SARS-CoV-2 even in recovered survivor of COVID-19, and individualized decisions must be made depending on the risks of immunosuppression and other vital parameters (Jain et al., 2020; Weinkove et al., 2020; Truong et al., 2021). Thus, although COVID-19 is a life-threatening disease, but manageable compared to aggressive acute and relapsing leukemia—therefore, clinicians will have to weigh the "benefit-risk" assessment at a given point of time and location of patient (considering logistics of transplantation)—and administer the treatment without delay to pass through the window periods of mortal risk—which will definitely help to improve the outcome of leukemia patients with COVID-19.

The other effective front of leukemia treatment involves tyrosine kinase inhibitors (TKIs) and could be found fruitful in patients with leukemia suffering from COVID-19. A study of patients of Philadelphia-positive acute lymphoblastic leukemia (Ph^{+}ALL) and chronic myeloid leukemia (CML) on TKIs (like nilotinib and imatinib) showed upregulation of "antiviral" genes, such as CD28 and IFNγ, while less expression of "proviral" genes—ARG-1, CEACAM1, and FUT4, which is in congruent with the low occurrence of COVID-19 in Ph^{+}ALL and CML patients (Galimberti et al., 2020). However, a conflicting in vitro report demonstrated no activity of imatinib or asciminib on SARS-CoV-2 replication (Zhao et al., 2020). In clinical setting, surveys from the Netherlands and Italian CML network (comprising of over 7000 patient data of CML and ALL) found very low incidences of COVID-19 in patients on TKIs, which is strong suggestive evidence of prospective potential to counter COVID-19 effectively (Ector et al., 2020; Breccia et al., 2020). Interestingly, imatinib's role of immunomodulatory effects are known and its target specific inhibition of ABL1/2 (nonreceptor tyrosine-protein kinase) and ABL1 is known for its function as a regulator of multiple pathological signaling cascades during infection. Imatinib also mediates inhibition of cytokine receptor signaling through PDGFR, c-Kit, and CSF1R (UniProt, 2021). Therefore, it is predicted that it can either inhibit or reduce cytokine-induced inflammatory response and thereby the tissue injury as a consequence of the cytokine storm in COVID-19. This is evident in preclinical models leading to alleviation of acute lung injuries. Similar indication is evident in a report of a COVID-19 patient who presented rapid improvement in pulmonary infiltrates upon treatment with imatinib (Morales-Ortega et al., 2020).

Thus, in summary, leukemia patients can serve as long term transmission hosts. Therefore a general recommendation to reduce the risk has been issued—such as—to assort to telemedicine options, to make only essential visits and minimize the time spent in hospitals and infusions sites and treatment tips including indications to reducing or managing therapy-associated immunosuppression (O'Connell et al., 2020; Cengiz Seval et al., 2021). A surveillance mechanism must be attached with every leukemia ward during and postpandemic time for years till SARS-CoV-2 threat is evident.

The treatment of hematological neoplasm and malignancies have to be personalized depending on the disease risk predicted through the type, molecular signatures of disease, respective chemotherapy and its prognosis, the level of immunosuppression and the rate of community transmission of SARS-CoV-2 (i.e., if the patient is in COVID-19 hotspot zones), related healthcare infrastructure and logistics in the area with respect to the availability of HSCT donors, related diagnostics, associated drugs and cryopreservation for HCTs (Ferrara et al., 2020; Hus et al., 2021; Paul et al., 2021). And every patient of leukemia must to treated on emergency basis not only in COVID-19 but in any pandemic. Perhaps in the coming future of around 5 years a general treatment protocol can be drawn from the experience with respect to each type of leukemia and respective targeted or semitargeted chemotherapy and COVID-19 outcome.

Thus, in summary, it is predicted to a great confidence that patients of leukemia are at greater risk for themselves and as well as for others as they can be the reservoir for viral sustenance. Patient feedback mechanisms (such as telemedicine, mobile apps) must be employed to connect and monitor patient remotely and advice for hospital visits in COVID-19 appropriate guidelines to receive therapy for leukemia and also COVID-19 if contracted. Patients under the influence of immune-suppressors post donor HSC transplantations must be advised for COVID-19 appropriate behavior and monitored by RT-PCR on weekly basis. The use of TKI must be employed actively in consultation with the pulmonologist and every protocol for leukemia therapy, including matching healthy bone marrow transfer must be followed without any delay irrespective of local lockdowns to save and protect as many patients as possible. This will in turn contribute in bringing down the overall mortality during COVID-19 outbreaks in present and future.

As per the European Society for Medical Oncology (EMSO), the prioritization of the cancer patients based on urgency of treatment is determined for hospitalization. As per these guidelines patients are categorized into high priority—when patients are unstable clinically or if situation is life threatening qualifies for this category; medium priority—patient condition may not be critical at the moment but may turn out to be critical after 6 weeks; and low priority—patient condition is stable and can be delayed beyond or for the duration of COVID-19 situation.

3 COVID-19 and HIV

In this section, we present the impact of COVID-19 on patients affected by HIV. We discuss in detail about epidemiology, challenges of diagnosis and management of the HIV-affected patients.

World Health Organization (WHO), have reported 169,597,415 COVID-19–positive cases of which 3,530,582 people lost their lives across the world (WHO COVID-19, accessed on May 30, 2021). Since 1981 from the onset of the HIV/AIDS epidemic, 76 million people were diagnosed with HIV, out of which about 33 million died. Globally, 38 million people were HIV positive by the end of 2019. Approximately, 0.7% of middle-aged adults are living with HIV, although the occurrence and impact has been found to vary as per countries. The African region remains most severely affected, contributing to more than 67% of the People Living with HIV (PLWH) (WHO HIV/AIDS, 2021). Incidentally, it is noted that both COVID-19 and AIDS are due to retro viruses originated from animals. SAR-CoV-2 and HIV virus are distinct in their mode of transmission. Another major difference is in their incubation period. COVID-19 has a shorter incubation period relative to AIDS and spreads at a faster rate within few days (Dawa and Narain, 2021). It was believed initially that HIV positive patients don't have higher risk of getting infected with COVID-19. However, recent studies have observed that PLWH especially diagnosed with depleted $CD4^{+}$ T-cells counts or who have not started any treatments for HIV infection might be more severely affected with COVID-19. Lockdown measures taken due to COVID-19 pandemic led to interruption in HIV treatment services worldwide which poses a life-threatening challenge to PLWH. There is not much information on influence of geographical location on the COVID-19 and HIV co-infections. Some of the observations suggest poor clinical outcomes in PLWH diagnosed with COVID-19, especially with low immunity and deprived of antiretroviral therapy (ART) (Boulle et al., 2020; Geretti et al., 2020; Tesoriero et al., 2021). The aged population and people with chronic disease and poor immune systems have high SARS-CoV-2 infection rate (Johns Hopkins University, accessed on May 30, 2021) (Kalichman et al., 2020; Meyerowitz et al., 2020). Although various parameters that determine the severity of the COVID-19 are still under investigation, compromised immune system and other parallel chronic conditions comprise the predisposing conditions for COVID-19 (Sigel et al., 2020). Additionally, renal disease, which is commonly observed in PLWH can lead to poor COVID-19 outcomes (Center for Disease Control and Prevention, 2021). Furthermore, food insecurity as a consequence of lockdowns can lead to poor nutrition which can impede immune functioning (Shalev et al., 2020).

Apparently, substance use is also predisposing condition for increased COVID-19 morbidity and mortality both in general population and PLWH (Suwanwongse and Shabarek, 2020). Tobacco use and/or smoking, is found to be associated with severity of COVID-19 by interacting with other substances and cause imbalance in the functioning of the immune system (Patel et al., 2020; Vizcarra et al., 2020). Alcohol and other drug use also suppress immune responses (Davies, 2020; Gervasoni et al., 2020; Karmen-Tuohy et al., 2020) particularly among PLWH (Childs et al., 2020). Some studies exhibit that continuous substance use with existing co-morbid conditions extend the complexity of COVID-19 in PLWH (Braunstein et al., 2021; Center for Disease Control and Prevention, 2021).

3.1 The epidemiology of COVID-19 in PLWH

Due to lockdown implemented in several countries in 2020, it is believed that the temporary suspension of HIV treatment services might have resulted in increase in mortality in 2020. Research indicates that PLWH represent around 1% of total hospitalized COVID-19 cases (Blanco et al., 2020 Okoh et al., 2020; Bhaskaran et al., 2021). Occurrence of SARS-CoV-2 infection in PLWH is in the range of 0.68%–1.8%, which is close to that in the general population ranging between 0.6% and 0.8% (Cooper et al., 2020; Mirzaei et al., 2021). Considering the clinical representation in PLWH co-infected with COVID-19, it was noted that approximately 67% presented mild signs, 22% showed acute symptoms, and remaining exhibited serious conditions and were hospitalized (Cooper et al., 2020; Mirzaei et al., 2021). However, there is no evidence of asymptomatic infection rates in PLWH (Cooper et al., 2020). In series of studies in Europe and United States—the clinical outcome was not significantly different, rather similar between PLWH and people without HIV infection (Gervasoni et al., 2020; Härter et al., 2020; Karmen-Tuohy et al., 2020; Patel et al., 2020; Shalev et al., 2020; Sigel et al., 2020; Stoeckle et al., 2020; Vizcarra et al., 2020). In another case study, where more than 95% of the participants were male, not much variation in COVID-19 were found between the HIV positive and the general population (Park et al., 2020). However, in contrast, in other cohort studies with PLWH and COVID-19 in the United Kingdom, United States, and South Africa, showed increased mortality rates (Boulle et al., 2020; Dandachi et al., 2020; Geretti et al., 2020; Bhaskaran et al., 2021; Hoffmann et al., 2021; Tesoriero et al., 2021). The severity of COVID-19 was found to be associated with lower CD4-T lymphocyte cell counts (i.e., <200 cells/mm^3) in patients with HIV and COVID-19. High risk was anticipated even in HIV patients who were treated through ART (Dandachi et al., 2020; Hoffmann et al., 2021). Similar observations were made in New York with higher rates of hospitalization and fatality in PLWH and COVID-19 (Tesoriero et al., 2021).

The epidemiology of COVID-19 in PLWH might be impacted in the future by COVID-19 due to different responses to wide range of available vaccines. In spite of presence of COVID-19 in the general population, more investigations need to be performed to study the interactions between SARS-CoV-2 and HIV (Cooper et al., 2020; Prabhu et al., 2020).

3.2 Role of interferons in natural defense to SARS-CoV-2 proliferations in PLWH

Some studies reveal that the clinical behavior of COVID-19 is associated with class-I interferon responses in addition to antibodies that defend cells by neutralizing effect (Park and Iwasaki, 2020). But opposing to this, other investigations observed that, low or delayed immune responses allow rapid spread of virus leading to pneumonia, lung function failure, and even death (Vardhana and Wolchok, 2020). Few reports obtained from patients with severe COVID-19 suggest that cytokine storm is the result of sustained interferon responses coupled with tumor necrosis factor production in lungs (Lee and Shin, 2020). SARS-CoV-2 has evolved to fight or suppress the interferon responses. There can be several reasons for poor COVID-19 outcomes some of which could be low immunity or rare genetic disorders leading to decreased interferon response, and antiinterferon component release (Bastard et al., 2020). HIV infection in order to control virus multiplication naturally activates interferon responses (Doyle et al., 2015). Some experimental data show that ART treats HIV patients by reducing the damages caused by interferon signaling (Díez-Fuertes et al., 2019). Therefore, immunological response of HIV positive patients to COVID-19 is a matter of concern.

3.3 Antibody generation against SARS-CoV-2 and potential threats in PLWH

Patients with COVID-19 might develop ineffective immune responses triggering lymphopenia, high production of cytokines, and fatigue. Lungs also undergo devastating changes leading to pneumonia and death. Cytokine storm also surfaces in acute HIV infection due to virus replication that amplifies immune response (Stacey et al., 2009; Fenwick et al., 2019). In most of the cases, ART restores normal levels of interferons and cytokines. In general, a complete viral suppression with ART ensures drastic immunity improvement in PLWH. However, despite ART, most of the HIV positive patients showed continuous viral replication, associated with low $CD4^+$ T-cell counts, and elevated concentrations of inflammatory markers, which can lead to rapid COVID-19 disease progression. Additionally, COVID-19 vaccines will not serve the purpose in case of defective B-cell functioning and sufficient number of T-cell counts. It has been observed through few studies that the high survival rates for COVID-19 are associated with early productions of anti-SARS-CoV-2 spike protein-IgG antibodies (Atyeo et al., 2020). Some investigations suggested that both B-cell and T-cell responses which are specific to the antigen help in prevention of COVID-19 development, thereby reducing fatalities (Atyeo et al., 2020). In PLWH, HIV multiplication triggers high production of cytotoxic T-cells which in turn leads to depletion of lymphocytes (Fenwick et al., 2019). In some cases, polyclonal response, abnormalities in B cells and T-cell activity have been reported (Moir and Fauci, 2017). If ART does not restore some of these damages in patients with advanced HIV infection, it can result in poor prognostic outcome with added SARS-CoV-2 infection. A couple of studies identified similarity in the concentration of IgG, IgM, and neutralizing antibodies in response to COVID-19 in PLWH and general population (Alrubayyi et al., 2021; Pallikkuth et al., 2021), however, another study displayed a lower rate of production of antibodies in PLWH (Spinelli et al., 2021). Thus, there are contradictory reports, perhaps they can be attributed to the background inflammations and other co-morbidity or associated environmental factors.

3.4 Challenges of SARS-CoV-2 diagnosis in PLWH

Nasal and throat swab samples are most often collected for diagnosis of COVID-19 (Winichakoon et al., 2020). But SARS-CoV-2 is also identified in other samples such as in blood, stool, and urine (Wang et al., 2020a). In general, the SARS-CoV-2 virus concentration is similar in HIV negative and PLWH. In advanced stages of HIV disease, PLWH might exhibit a longer duration of SARS-CoV-2 expulsion and release of progeny (Aydillo et al., 2020). Not much is known about the COVID-19 disease progression in PLWH receiving ART (Peluso et al., 2020; Hu et al., 2021c). Real-time RT-PCR is currently used for diagnosis of COVID-19 which targets specific genes of the virus. It is a known fact that antibody detection is based on host immune responses to infection but there are chances that antibody response might be impaired in immune-deficient PLWH. There is not much evidence regarding the duration up to which IgG and total antibodies can be detected, virus shedding, and factors affecting antibody response which can include age, comorbidities, and immune-deficient conditions like HIV infection (Hanson et al., 2020).

3.5 Management of COVID-19 and HIV co-infections

Antiretroviral drugs have already been used in treatment of COVID-19. There is evidence that drug tenofovir might be active (Ayerdi et al., 2020; Del Amo et al., 2020) as it binds to RNA-dependent RNA polymerase, a critical SARS-CoV-2 enzyme (Elfiky, 2020). However, some clinical trials and research studies could not demonstrate therapeutic and preventive potential of the drug toward COVID-19 (Ayerdi et al., 2020; Del Amo et al., 2020). Protease inhibitors such as lopinavir-ritonavir and darunavir are tested for anti-SARS-CoV-2 activity. It was reported that darunavir did not show anti-SARS-CoV-2 activity at different concentrations and lopinavir-ritonavir failed to demonstrate significant efficacy in reducing mortality (Horby et al., 2020; WHO Solidarity Trial Consortium, 2021). Some investigations identified that remdesivir, an antiviral drug, when used alone or in combination with baricitinib, a JAK inhibitor, improved recovery time period among patients with advanced stages (WHO Solidarity Trial Consortium, 2021; Beigel et al., 2020; Spinner et al., 2020; Stebbing et al., 2020; Wang et al., 2020b; Kalil et al., 2021). However, the WHO Solidarity trial did not reveal significant survival status after usage of these drugs in patient (WHO Solidarity Trial Consortium, 2021). Thus, these findings oppose the decisions with regard to the emergency use of remdesivir for COVID-19, taken by the Food and Drug Administration (FDA). Also, there is data reporting that the use of plasma from recovered COVID-19 patients and neutralizing antibody prevents disease progression and hospital admission in mild disease compared with placebo (Li et al., 2020b; Chen et al., 2021; Libster et al., 2021; Weinreich et al., 2021). Most of the antiinflammatory drugs, such as systemic corticosteroids, and baricitinib are under studies which show that they might act against inflammation and alleviating cytokine storms in severe COVID-19 (Li et al., 2020a). Dexamethasone when given in lose doses consistently for 1–2 weeks has shown promising results in reducing mortality by inducing cytochrome P450 3A4 in critical patients on ventilation (Horby et al., 2020). Dexamethasone administration in PLWH suffering from COVID-19 should be decided in consultation with HIV specialist. There are no indications that drugs used for inflammations, elevated viral infections in PLWH. Hence, COVID-19 treatment for PLWH need not be different than the HIV negative-general population. In addition, anticoagulation therapy is also administered as a precautionary measure and is recommended in all the patients with severe COVID-19 manifestation including PLWH (Nadkarni et al., 2020).

3.6 Interrelationship between HIV infection and SARS-CoV-2 vaccines

The principle behind most of the approved vaccines is based on effective production of neutralizing antibodies against the virus surface proteins. The same concept has been followed to target the spike protein of SARS-CoV-2 in generation of vaccines to mitigate COVID-19 (Krammer, 2020). To enable rapid results on SARS-CoV-2 vaccinology, some of the HIV preventive models under development such as RNA and adenovirus vectors have been used for the Coronavirus vaccines (Krammer, 2020). Very few PLWH were part of phase 3 vaccine trials, therefore their immune response to vaccines remains unclear (Baden et al., 2021). Predictions regarding the effectiveness of COVID-19 vaccine administration to PLWH are based on several parameters like the damages to the T-cell and B-cell compartment thereby consequently leading to diminished antibody generation in turn reducing the total immune responses to the SARS-CoV-2 spike protein. Several studies have showed that PLWH are not much responsive to most of the vaccines against different virus

(Geretti et al., 2020; Doyle et al., 2015). Therefore, specific recommendations are suggested, one of them being repeated vaccine doses (Ceravolo et al., 2013). People living with comorbidities or reduced CD4+ T-cell levels (less than 200 cells per μL) are more prone to COVID-19, and hence must be advised for COVID-19 vaccination. Therefore, some of the agencies are in support that HIV positive patients must be administered vaccine without delay. Unfortunately, as mentioned earlier very less HIV positive patients volunteered for COVID-19 vaccine trials in PLWH, which included less than 1% participants for Moderna and Pfizer vaccine trials (Libster et al., 2021) Though there is not enough data obtained for vaccine effects on PLWH; nevertheless, it is suggested that during vaccination, ART should be provided.

3.7 Future scope of work in coinfection of SARS-CoV-2 and HIV

Though there are very few research work done on PLWH infected with COVID-19, most of the reports indicate increased risk of death (Hadi et al., 2020). Majority of the observations revealed the associations of low CD4 counts with poor COVID-19 outcomes. Further investigations need to be conducted comparing COVID-19 prognosis in HIV-positive patients and general population with varied geographical status. The WHO Global COVID-19 Clinical Platform (WHO, 2021) has been collecting relevant information from PLWH and the general population undergoing treatment for COVID-19. Though there were conflicting results of drugs on SARS-CoV-2 infection, preexposure prophylaxis (PrEP) should be given for protecting against HIV-infection. Similarly, no data obtained so far suggests PLWH should be diagnosed or treated by distinct methods in case of COVID-19 progression. Lockdown measures have affected working of HIV clinics in many countries. Accessibility to hospitals and to ART should be a priority for HIV patients in the COVID-19 pandemic. No evidence exists right now to prove that the vaccines approved might vary in response or increase the risk of HIV infection. Therefore, a COVID-19 vaccine should be immediately available to PLWH to protect them from COVID-19. With regards to this, further studies must be conducted to know the immune response to all COVID-19 vaccines and to check how many doses would be sufficient to attain the required immunity for PLWH. Though research on COVID-19 and its relation with AIDS is progressing, there exists knowledge gaps which can be a focus and future scope of work for the scientific community across the world.

Over the past 1 year, statistics show that more than a million of people have succumbed to COVID-19 across the globe. It is also a known fact that HIV is a deadly disease and PLWH have higher risk of COVID-19. PLWH can have adverse effects if co-infected with SARS-CoV-2 which can be fatal. HIV positive patients who are under ART also can develop COVID-19. In whichever countries HIV is prominent, government must make sure that HIV patients have access to hospitals, treatment and ART even if lockdown measures are taken to mitigate COVID-19 spread. It would be better if PLWH are vaccinated at the earliest to prevent severe side effects of COVID-19, if at all they are infected. It is the need of the hour that hospitals treating COVID-19 patients are educated and made aware of guidelines set by WHO, Centers for Disease Control and Prevention (CDC) and National institutes of Health (NIH) on how to manage HIV and COVID-19 co-infections. Though, there is not much evidence and research to suggest which COVID-19 vaccines and treatments would work efficiently on HIV positive patients, it is recommended that PLWH be given same COVID-19 diagnostic procedures, vaccines and treatment as the general population until further scientific investigations leads to new outcomes and developments which have contradictions to current instructions for disease management.

People infected with HIV and patients of leukemia are not only at greater risk but also, they can serve as reservoir for the sustenance of SARS-CoV-2, its evolution and long-term shedding. Therefore, they must be attended and administered with disease and individual specific therapeutics with antiretroviral in combination with management of SARS-CoV-2 infection.

The advanced stages of HIV infected people (AIDS)—if co-infected with SARS-CoV-2, shows prolonged shedding of virus in all body fluids. Therefore, continuous weekly monitoring of virus in all body fluids accompanied with cytokine profile to predict the "cytokine storm," will be helpful in administration of corticosteroids (antiinflammatory) for managing the window of risk and also the B-cell and T-cell function should be monitored to mark the disease course which will help to treat added infection of SARS-CoV-2 and HIV together. Antiinflammatory corticosteroids, especially dexamethasone treatment for 1–2 weeks should be fruitful to alleviate cytokine storm and thereby limit the cytotoxic effects on lung tissue and delay or cease the induction of fibrosis, which will be beneficial to maintain the capacity of lung function. Anticoagulant is also administered in PLWH under observation to inhibit thrombosis/coagulation effects predicted due to SARS-CoV-2.

The observation of T-cell count in PLWH is an essential parameter, as the maximum benefit of vaccination depends on the number of primed T-cells, which can cross-talk with B-cells to induce them for maturation and differentiation (plasma and memory B cells) to generate long-term memory cells and thereby leading to the protection. Therefore, the timing of the COVID-19 vaccination for PLWH can be chosen for each patient depending on the their total CD4+ T-cell count- which will ensure the optimum signaling between T and B cells.

4 Effect of COVID-19 and current treatment or management strategies for mentally ill patients

In this section, we discuss epidemiology and treatment options for mentally ill patients affected by COVID-19.

The global pandemic caused by SARS-COV2 has not only affected physical health but has severely impacted global market, economy, agriculture, health care, etc. Despite employing all resources to mitigate the aftermath of this pandemic, the failures and uncertainty involved have caused a lot of mental distress among people. In this era of heavy social media users, exposure to un authentic and misleading information about the pandemic has caused spread of conflict, rumors and negative social behaviors. Most impacted are the infected and sick patients, healthcare workers and their family members since they are directly on the receiving end of the pandemic's consequences. Mental health problems like anxiety, depression, insomnia, and emotional outbursts often interfere with decision making capacity of health workers (Kang et al., 2020). Further, isolation strategies to break the transmission chain has created panic, fear, and acute physiological stress within people. As WHO speculated, isolation has led to an increased use of alcohol, drugs, insomnia, loneliness, anxiety, abusive behavior, and depression (World Health Organization, 2020b). A massive change in regular activities and routine has played a role in increasing stress about workplace factors, livelihood factors making this pandemic a psychological pandemic as well. Apart from acute emotional effects, chronic mental disorders like posttraumatic stress due to loss of a colleague/family and obsessive-compulsive disorders like maladaptive behavior of sanitization are rising. Increasing financial losses, shortage of resources, irregular and conflicting information from authorities, trial and error public health measures and looming uncertainty increases the risk of mental illness, unhealthy behavior like suicidal thoughts and noncompliance with public health directives.

4.1 Impact of COVID-19 on mentally ill patients

The distress, uncertainty, and the unpredictability of the pandemic with no treatment in sight has led to relapse of anxiety, depression, panic, psychosis, delirium, and suicidality in mentally ill patients. Patients with limited access to treatment will experience a further depletion in attention due to unavailability of resources for care and therapy which may increase their anguish. Patients with serious psychiatric conditions like schizophrenia are already socioeconomically disadvantaged and with the lockdown, isolation, stay at home orders with subsequent reduced access to employment can only aggravate their distress economically as well as socially stressing the patient caregivers as well (Gautam et al., 2020).

Patients with severe mental illness who need treatment and rehabilitation consistently are finding it difficult due to lockdowns as well as limited access to healthcare in psychiatric hospitals and also there is always the risk of exposure with regular hospital visits (Lima et al., 2020; Muruganandam et al., 2020), reported in their study that 72% of the patients with severe mental illness did not know about symptoms and about 64% were not aware of the precautionary measures about COVID-19. 8.3% of the patients were ignorant or not aware of the transmission mode of the SARS-CoV-2. With home isolation being mandatory all over the country, the hardships and burden on the caregivers was higher in this patient category which manifests in the form of very or no social support, increased negative expressed emotions (Nirmala et al., 2011), domestic violence toward patients (Afe et al., 2016) thereby raising the risk of relapse significantly (Altman et al., 2006). Other factors like social isolation, financial strain, negative social interactions, low emotional support, and psychological distress enhances the burden of the caregiver.

Deterioration of the patients who were stable before lockdown was seen in around 30% of them. The cause could be high liability to stress in home isolation, (Altman et al., 2006), major life events (Sam et al., 2019), poor access to psychiatric hospitals and poor treatment compliance (Xiao et al., 2015), disturbed biological rhythm (Karatsoreos, 2014), and upsurge of caregiver burden (Nirmala et al., 2011). Psychiatric doctors who were in regular consultations with the mentally ill patients exhibited more awareness of the recent situation suggesting that regular access to treatment is directly proportional in improving the condition of the patients as well as appraising them to the current ongoing pandemic. Novel set of psychiatric symptoms related to COVID-19 or exacerbation of preexisting psychopathology in patients with SMI can be seen in such pandemic (Fischer et al., 2020). This sector of population with relapse translates to poor hygienic conditions, inability to practice social distancing, delay in seeking and reporting medical attention, aggression, suicidal behavior, increased substance use, poor compliance for their psychiatric treatment and comorbid medical illness will have a major social impact during the pandemic (Gunnell et al., 2020).

4.2 Treatment of mentally ill patients during COVID-19

The consequence of the pandemic on mental health is considered less important than its physical one. The flood of patients and their immediate dismissal on recovery to facilitate admission of more patients often causes neglect in proper psychiatric care. Attention from mental health professionals is required to avoid the psychological risks that occur due to confinement of patients. Facilities like regular follow-up with telemedicine to monitor suicide risk, PTSD risk could be helpful (Chevance et al., 2020). Further, experienced psychiatrists should help governments in framing management plans and create awareness among public like the development of a psychological support plan in France. Self-help manual to deal with stress by the disease are proposed for better management (Zhou, 2020). Health policy makers should show an inclusive approach to accommodate therapeutic needs of different effected groups. Telepsychiatry via online means is an appropriate alternative to deal with the challenges of this pandemic. It has an advantage of providing accessibility to underserved, rural areas, greater flexibility and availability of appointments and reduced costs.

Providing general guidelines to public along with a free 24-h helpline in collaboration with mental health volunteers and coordinated supervision of psychological consultants would be an ideal strategy to support people. To reduce the risk of increasing mental disorders from continuous exposure to temporary symptoms like anxiety, depression, loneliness; communication with family, colleagues and use of professional helplines must be encouraged (Fiorillo and Gorwood, 2020). The sources of stress must be limited, spread of unverified information must be monitored. Asking for professional help to seek emotional aid, dealing with significant repetitive symptoms, such as panic attacks, persistent insomnia must be easily accessible. Health care systems and policymaking should focus on prevention and interventions related to the public mental health to deal with pandemic associated mental health challenges. Regional factors and other parameters should be taken into account to meet the mental health needs of the population. A strong collaborative network for effective therapeutic strategies accessible to public easily could help alleviate the ongoing and to come mental health challenges.

The ongoing pandemic has affected millions of people across the globe mentally, physically, and emotionally. The losses of loved ones, enforced isolation and reduced healthcare system have seen to be the case in almost every country. We, humans are social animals by nature and due to the contagious nature of the disease we are unable to isolate ourselves for long periods of time and this is having a negative effect on our mental wellbeing. All age groups across the continents have been having adverse effects due to lesser social interactions. Mentally ill patients who already have stress are having an extremely difficult time coping up with the new norms. Regular access to hospital care as well as medication due to lockdowns and fear of spread of the outbreak of COVID-19 has seen to have a relapse of their conditions. The only way moving forward is to have regular telephonic counseling by the doctors.

5 COVID-19 and Ayurveda's holistic lifestyle approach

Here, we elaborate the relevance of Ayurveda and Yoga for treating COVID-19 patients.

Much of the human history is littered with epidemics and pandemics apart from history course changing social events. It is been well described about epidemics, pandemics in the ancient book of medicine Charaka samhitha pertaining to Ayurveda branch of medicine. While epidemics are sudden out breaks and confine to particular area, pandemics are global in nature. Epidemics are described as aupasargika roga and pandemics asjanapadodhvansa roga (Murthy, 2010) in Ayurveda. Janapadodhvansa means annihilation of populations.

Due to the hegemony of COVID-19 pandemic, some preventive measure has to be in place until an effective cure is found. Recently the AYUSH ministry of the Indian Government had an initiative to receive proposals from Ayurvedic and homeopathic medicine researchers and received more than 2000 proposals and are under active consideration for funding. As per Ayurveda experts, medicinal plants such as giloy, amla, shilajit, and neem are suggested to be helpful in enhancing the immune systems (Rajput, 2020). As per Dr. Chauhan, director, Jiva ayurveda, a tablespoonful of Chywanprash daily intake boosts the immune system and may prevent the spread of the virus. Many traditional Ayurvedic medicinal such as guduchi/glioy (*Tinospora cordifolia*), kutki (*Picrorhiza kurroa*), Amalaki or amla (*Emblica officinalis*), neem (*Azadirachta indica*), tulsi (basil) are suggested to for daily intake for enhancing the immune system (Mondal et al., 2011; Jamshidi and Cohen, 2017; Girija and Sivan, 2020; Roy and Bhattacharyya, 2020; Mishra et al., 2021). Good digestion plays an important role in fighting diseases and a regular intake of ginger tea or mint tea or fennel tea are recommended for better digestion. Recent reports indicate that there is 15% hike in the demand of turmeric powder, shilajith, aswagandha in India as people are looking for alternative measures to manage COVID-19 (Jagetia and Aggarwal, 2007). "Nasya," a therapeutic intervention for cold, head ache, sour throat, can be alleviated by giving oils such as anu oil and shadabindu oil (Kar et al., 2020; Tomooka et al., 2000; Mittal and Chand, 2020; Rajput, 2020). As per, Baba Ram dev, a famous yoga guru, giloy and tulsi are suggested to be effective for treating COVID-19 (Ozah, 2020; Tillu et al., 2020). Yoga exercises such as pranayama, kapalabhati and anulom vilom are recommended for boosting immunity (Eda et al., 2013). Abhyagna (self-massage) as per Ayurveda, stabilizes nervous system, relieves stress, and supports immune system (Majumdar et al., 2020). Sesame oil can be used to do the massage. In addition, oil pulling and nasya can be tried to boost the immunity (Nagendra, 2020).

Some yoga poses such as Utaanasana (standing forward bend) or sarvanga asana helps the lymphatic system to drain pathogens and waste products (Fulambarker et al., 2012; Infante et al., 2014; Lim and Cheong, 2015; Raghuram et al., 2008). Warm bath with Epsom salts, ginger oil, cardamom, rosemary, eucalyptus, cedar, pine, cinnamon, basil, poine helps in keeping the virus at bay. A quality sleep helps in production of cytokines that helps immune system to fight pathogens (Fulambarker et al., 2012; Liu et al., 2014; Lim and Cheong, 2015). Meditation not calms down the mind but also helps in keeping sound mental status so that proper messages can be transmitted through the brain during the vital periods of infections and diseases, reduces oxidative stress there by helping immune system (Donesky-Cuenco et al., 2009; Gupta et al., 2014; Guleria et al., 2015; Kusnanto et al., 2018; Bushell et al., 2020).

It has been found that the general treatments including the Ayurveda and holistic practices are very important to enhance host immune response against RNA viral infection. The AYUSH Ministry of Indian government is actively seeking proposals and boosting funding for establishing the validity of some Ayurveda medicines as viral drugs and improves the immune system. It is highly being encouraged by the government of India for all Ayurveda physicians to collaborate and follow scientific guide lines to support Ayurveda claims. So as of now the best available remedy to combat the Covid-19 is the effective utilization of Ayurveda therapy and holistic management with the adoption of yoga practice, proper diet regimen, and detoxification procedures to bring back the energies (doshas) to balance.

The health care systems were challenged by COVID-19 pandemic across the globe, which in turn has brought the world attention to body's immune system against the pathogenic organisms. COVID-19 pandemic has brought serious psychological and mental distress among the people as the diseased are more vulnerable viral infections in the respiratory tract. As per *Charaka Samhita, the ancient Ayurveda text*, immunity plays a significant role in the prevention and progression of the disease and maintenance of homeostasis in the body. The Ayurveda primarily focuses on building the strong immunity in addition to strengthening the mind by getting rid of stress. Several treatments in Ayurveda including herbal decoctions and immunomodulators (Rasayana) are known to enhance the immune system against the respiratory diseases. As per the Ayurvedic prescription, which are routinely practiced in many households, consumption of hot water and Ayurvedic herb infused water in addition to steam inhalation and gargling with medicated water do wonders in preventing respiratory illness caused by COVID-19. Yoga and Pranayama have positive effect on strengthening the immune system and the respiratory system to maximize the efficient oxygen intake.

In the next section, we present various digital platforms used for contract tracing and managing COVID-19–related information.

6 Softwares/web tools/digital platforms used for COVID-19 management

Unprecedented levels of COVID-19 pandemic necessitated urgent development/usage digital platforms through web tools, social media platforms such as WhatsApp and Facebook. WHO and various health organizations have developed various digital tools for dissemination of COVID-19–related information. GoData (WHO GoData, 2021) is a web and mobile based digital platform, which is used by World Health organization (WHO). It is used for collecting COVID-19 data from sources like labs, hospitals, etc. It is also used for tracing the contacts of COVID-19–infected persons. It also provides data visualization and a dashboard to have an overall glimpse of the COVID-19 information. Maldives used this software to manage COVID-19 outbreak.

In India, CoWIN portal is used for registration of COVID-19 vaccination (CoWin, 2021). Using this portal, the citizens can register for COVID-19 vaccination and schedule it at various hospitals. Those who vaccinated can download the vaccination certificate from the portal. For contact tracing, "Arogya Setu" (meaning-"Health Bridge") mobile-Bluetooth enabled app is used to know the information of infected people in the vicinity in real-time mode. It alerts if a person using the app comes in contact with the infected person which enables for timely medical treatment. It assesses the possibility of infection through the self-assessment test. It enables the regulatory bodies of the Government of India to identify COVID-19 hotspots and enforce predictive localized lockdown or restricted movement so that the spread of virus can be reduced or quarantined. The Arogya Setu app is primarily used for COVID-19 contact tracing. In other countries, there are many such digital tools are used. Similar contact tracing apps are used in many other countries world-wide with exhaustive list of them available on Wikipedia (Wikipedia, 2021).

7 Concluding remarks

The devastating effects of COVID-19 pandemic created a situation requiring an urgent and war footing efforts to contain the disease. Perhaps, it is for the first time in medical history that a causative agent for the disease and development of vaccines from bench to bed happened within a couple years which itself is a remarkable achievement of human efforts. However the availability and administration of vaccines for billions of people is proving to be a daunting task due to the production and logistics. As the information related to the COVID-19 is still pouring in, researchers and administrations are constantly adopting various strategies to contain the disease. It is anticipated that, as the time progresses, the virus gets weak and probably COVID-19 becomes a short illness like a flu and could be contained with periodic vaccination. It is reassuring that the many vaccines that are available now could work effectively against several variants of the SARS-CoV-2 barring few strains. In future, the management of the COVID-19 would become a routine and well standardized procedure giving a scope for better management of patients suffering from other diseases like cancer, HIV, and mental illness.

Acknowledgments

This work is supported by a grant from Department of Science and Technology, Government of India [ECR/2016/001685] to Dr. Divijendra Natha Reddy S. Teesta Katte is supported by the fellowship from this grant.

References

Afe, T.O., et al., 2016. Intimate partner violence, psychopathology and the women with schizophrenia in an outpatient clinic South-South, Nigeria. BMC Psychiatry 16 (1). https://doi.org/10.1186/s12888-016-0898-2.

Alrubayyi, A., et al., 2021. Characterization of humoral and SARS-CoV-2 specific T cell responses in people living with HIV. Res. Square. https://doi.org/10.21203/rs.3.rs-309746/v1.

Altman, S., et al., 2006. Predictors of relapse in bipolar disorder: a review. J. Psychiatr. Pract. 12 (5), 269–282. https://doi.org/10.1097/00131746-200609000-00002.

Arber, D.A., et al., 2016. The 2016 revision to the World Health Organization classification of myeloid neoplasms and acute leukemia. Blood 127 (20), 2391–2405. https://doi.org/10.1182/blood-2016-03-643544.

Arends, C.M., et al., 2018. Hematopoietic lineage distribution and evolutionary dynamics of clonal hematopoiesis. Leukemia 32 (9), 1908–1919. https://doi.org/10.1038/s41375-018-0047-7.

Atyeo, C., et al., 2020. Distinct early serological signatures track with SARS-CoV-2 survival. Immunity 53 (3), 524–532. e4 https://doi.org/10.1016/j.immuni.2020.07.020.

Australian Bureau of Statistics, 2009. National Health Survey: Summary of Results, 2007–2008. ABS, Canberra. Available from: https://www.abs.gov.au/ausstats/abs@.nsf/mf/4364.0. (Accessed 4 June 2021).

Australian Bureau of Statistics, 2013. Profiles of Health, Australia, 2011–13. ABS, Canberra. Available from: https://www.abs.gov.au/ausstats/abs@.nsf/lookup/4338.0main+features12011-13. (Accessed 4 June 2021).

Australian Institute of Health and Welfare, 2012. Breast Cancer in Australia: An Overview. Cancer Series no. AIHW, Canberra, p. 71.

Avanzato, V.A., et al., 2020. Case study: prolonged infectious SARS-CoV-2 shedding from an asymptomatic immunocompromised individual with cancer. Cell 183 (7), 1901–1912. e9 https://doi.org/10.1016/j.cell.2020.10.049.

Aydillo, T., et al., 2020. Shedding of viable SARS-CoV-2 after immunosuppressive therapy for cancer. N. Engl. J. Med. 383 (26), 2586–2588. https://doi.org/10.1056/nejmc2031670.

Ayerdi, O., et al., 2020. Preventive efficacy of tenofovir/emtricitabine against severe acute respiratory syndrome coronavirus 2 among pre-exposure prophylaxis users. Open Forum Infect. Dis. 7 (11). https://doi.org/10.1093/ofid/ofaa455.

Baden, L.R., El Sahly, H.M., et al., 2021. Efficacy and safety of the mRNA-1273 SARS-CoV-2 vaccine. N. Engl. J. Med. 384 (5), 403–416. https://doi.org/10.1056/NEJMoa2035389.

Barbui, T., et al., 2021. High mortality rate in COVID-19 patients with myeloproliferative neoplasms after abrupt withdrawal of ruxolitinib. Leukemia 35 (2), 485–493. https://doi.org/10.1038/s41375-020-01107-y.

Baselga, J., 2001. Clinical trials of Herceptin(R) (trastuzumab). Eur. J. Cancer 37 (Suppl. 1), 18–24. Available from: http://www.ncbi.nlm.nih.gov/pubmed/11342196. (Accessed 21 August 2021).

Bastard, P., Rosen, L.B., et al., 2020. Autoantibodies against type I IFNs in patients with life-threatening COVID-19. Science 370 (6515). https://doi.org/10.1126/science.abd4585, eabd4585.

Baud, D., et al., 2020. Real estimates of mortality following COVID-19 infection. Lancet Infect. Dis. 20 (7), 773. https://doi.org/10.1016/S1473-3099(20)30195-X.

Beigel, J.H., et al., 2020. Remdesivir for the treatment of covid-19—final report. N. Engl. J. Med. 383 (19), 1813–1826. https://doi.org/10.1056/nejmoa2007764.

Beke, A., et al., 2020. Multilayer intraclonal heterogeneity in chronic myelomonocytic leukemia. Haematologica 105 (1), 112–123. https://doi.org/10.3324/haematol.2018.208488.

Bernitz, J.M., et al., 2016. Hematopoietic stem cells count and remember self-renewal divisions. Cell 167 (5), 1296–1309. e10 https://doi.org/10.1016/j.cell.2016.10.022.
Bhaskaran, K., et al., 2021. HIV infection and COVID-19 death: a population-based cohort analysis of UK primary care data and linked national death registrations within the OpenSAFELY platform. Lancet HIV 8 (1), e24–e32. https://doi.org/10.1016/S2352-3018(20)30305-2.
Blanco, J.L., et al., 2020. COVID-19 in patients with HIV: clinical case series. Lancet HIV 7 (5), e314–e316. https://doi.org/10.1016/S2352-3018(20)30111-9.
Blomberg, B., et al., 2021. Long COVID in a prospective cohort of home-isolated patients. Nat. Med., 1–7. https://doi.org/10.1038/s41591-021-01433-3.
Boehm, T., 2011. Design principles of adaptive immune systems. Nat. Rev. Immunol. 11 (5), 307–317. https://doi.org/10.1038/nri2944.
Boulle, A., et al., 2020. Risk factors for coronavirus disease 2019 (COVID-19) death in a population cohort study from the Western Cape Province, South Africa. Clin. Infect. Dis. https://doi.org/10.1093/cid/ciaa1198.
Braunstein, S.L., et al., 2021. Coronavirus disease 2019 (COVID-19) infection among people with human immunodeficiency virus in New York city: a population-level analysis of linked surveillance data. Clin. Infect. Dis. 72 (12), E1021–E1029. https://doi.org/10.1093/cid/ciaa1793.
Bray, F., et al., 2018. Global cancer statistics 2018: GLOBOCAN estimates of incidence and mortality worldwide for 36 cancers in 185 countries. CA Cancer J. Clin. 68 (6), 394–424. https://doi.org/10.3322/caac.21492.
Breccia, M., et al., 2020. Chronic myeloid leukemia management at the time of the COVID-19 pandemic in Italy. A campus CML survey. Leukemia 34 (8), 2260–2261. https://doi.org/10.1038/s41375-020-0904-z.
Bushell, W., et al., 2020. Meditation and yoga practices as potential adjunctive treatment of SARS-CoV-2 infection and COVID-19: a brief overview of key subjects. J. Altern. Complement. Med. 26 (7), 547–556. https://doi.org/10.1089/acm.2020.0177.
Cattaneo, C., et al., 2020. Clinical characteristics and risk factors for mortality in hematologic patients affected by COVID-19. Cancer 126 (23), 5069–5076. https://doi.org/10.1002/cncr.33160.
Cavallo, F., et al., 2011. 2011: the immune hallmarks of cancer. Cancer Immunol. Immunother. 60 (3), 319–326. https://doi.org/10.1007/s00262-010-0968-0.
Cengiz Seval, G., Topçuoğlu, P., Demirer, T., 2021. Treatment approaches for managing patients with hematological malignancies in the time of COVID-19 pandemic. Turk. J. Med. Sci. https://doi.org/10.3906/sag-2101-276.
Center for Disease Control and Prevention, 2021. Available from: https://www.cdc.gov/. (Accessed 5 May 2021).
Ceravolo, A., Orsi, A., Parodi, V., Ansaldi, F., 2013. Influenza vaccination in HIV-positive subjects: latest evidence and future perspective. J. Prev. Med. Hyg. 54 (1), 1–10.
Chai, P., et al., 2020. Genetic alteration, RNA expression, and DNA methylation profiling of coronavirus disease 2019 (COVID-19) receptor ACE2 in malignancies: a pan-cancer analysis. J. Hematol. Oncol. 13 (1). https://doi.org/10.1186/s13045-020-00883-5.
Chen, P., et al., 2021. SARS-CoV-2 neutralizing antibody LY-CoV555 in outpatients with Covid-19. N. Engl. J. Med. 384 (3), 229–237. https://doi.org/10.1056/nejmoa2029849.
Chevance, A., et al., 2020. Ensuring mental health care during the SARS-CoV-2 epidemic in France: a narrative review. L'Encéphale, 193–201. https://doi.org/10.1016/j.encep.2020.04.005.
Childs, K., et al., 2020. Hospitalized patients with COVID-19 and human immunodeficiency virus: a case series. Clin. Infect. Dis. 71 (8), 2021–2022. https://doi.org/10.1093/cid/ciaa657.
Cooper, T.J., et al., 2020. Coronavirus disease 2019 (COVID-19) outcomes in HIV/AIDS patients: a systematic review. HIV Med. 21 (9), 567–577. https://doi.org/10.1111/hiv.12911.

CoWin, 2021. Cowin Vaccine Portal. Available from: https://selfregistration.cowin.gov.in/. (Accessed 5 May 2021).

Dandachi, D., et al., 2020. Characteristics, comorbidities, and outcomes in a multicenter registry of patients with human immunodeficiency virus and coronavirus disease 2019. Clin. Infect. Dis. https://doi.org/10.1093/cid/ciaa1339.

Davies, M.-A., 2020. HIV and risk of COVID-19 death: a population cohort study from the Western Cape Province, South Africa. medRxiv. https://doi.org/10.1101/2020.07.02.20145185.

Dawa, N., Narain, J., 2021. COVID-19 & HIV/AIDS pandemics: parallels & lessons. Indian J. Med. Res. 153 (1), 214–218. https://doi.org/10.4103/ijmr.IJMR_2598_20.

Del Amo, J., et al., 2020. Incidence and severity of COVID-19 in HIV-positive persons receiving antiretroviral therapy: a cohort study. Ann. Intern. Med. 173 (7), 536–541. https://doi.org/10.7326/M20-3689.

Dietz, J.R., et al., 2020. Recommendations for prioritization, treatment, and triage of breast cancer patients during the COVID-19 pandemic. The COVID-19 pandemic breast cancer consortium. Breast Cancer Res. Treat. 181 (3), 487–497. https://doi.org/10.1007/s10549-020-05644-z.

Díez-Fuertes, F., De La Torre-Tarazona, H.E., Calonge, E., et al., 2019. Transcriptome sequencing of peripheral blood mononuclear cells from elite controller-long term non progressors. Sci. Rep. 9, 14265. https://doi.org/10.1038/s41598-019-50642-x.

do Nascimento, R.G., Otoni, K.M., 2020. Histological and molecular classification of breast cancer: what do we know? Mastology 30, 20200024. https://doi.org/10.29289/259453942020202000024.

Dobbs, L.G., 1989. Pulmonary surfactant. Annu. Rev. Med. 40, 431–446. https://doi.org/10.1146/annurev.me.40.020189.002243.

Dombret, H., Gardin, C., 2016. An update of current treatments for adult acute myeloid leukemia. Blood 127 (1), 53–61. https://doi.org/10.1182/blood-2015-08-604520.

Donesky-Cuenco, D.A., et al., 2009. Yoga therapy decreases dyspnea-related distress and improves functional performance in people with chronic obstructive pulmonary disease: a pilot study. J. Altern. Complement. Med. 15 (3), 225–234. https://doi.org/10.1089/acm.2008.0389.

Doulatov, S., et al., 2012. Hematopoiesis: a human perspective. Cell Stem Cell 10 (2), 120–136. https://doi.org/10.1016/j.stem.2012.01.006.

Doyle, T., Goujon, C., Malim, M.H., 2015. HIV-1 and interferons: who's interfering with whom? Nat. Rev. Microbiol. 13 (7), 403–413. https://doi.org/10.1038/nrmicro3449.

Dzierzak, E., Bigas, A., 2018. Blood development: hematopoietic stem cell dependence and independence. Cell Stem Cell 22 (5), 639–651. https://doi.org/10.1016/j.stem.2018.04.015.

Eaves, C.J., 2015. Hematopoietic stem cells: concepts, definitions, and the new reality. Blood 125 (17), 2605–2613. https://doi.org/10.1182/blood-2014-12-570200.

Ector, G.I.C.G., et al., 2020. Prevalence of COVID-19 diagnosis in Dutch CML patients during the 2020 SARS-CoV2 pandemic. A prospective cohort study. Leukemia 34 (9), 2533–2535. https://doi.org/10.1038/s41375-020-0964-0.

Eda, N., et al., 2013. Effects of yoga exercise on salivary beta-defensin 2. Eur. J. Appl. Physiol. 113 (10), 2621–2627. https://doi.org/10.1007/s00421-013-2703-y.

Elfiky, A.A., 2020. Ribavirin, Remdesivir, Sofosbuvir, Galidesivir, and Tenofovir against SARS-CoV-2 RNA dependent RNA polymerase (RdRp): a molecular docking study. Life Sci. 253. https://doi.org/10.1016/j.lfs.2020.117592.

Engebraaten, O., Vollan, H.K.M., Børresen-Dale, A.L., 2013. Triple-negative breast cancer and the need for new therapeutic targets. Am. J. Pathol. 183 (4), 1064–1074. https://doi.org/10.1016/j.ajpath.2013.05.033.

Fenwick, C., et al., 2019. T-cell exhaustion in HIV infection. Immunol. Rev. 292 (1), 149–163. https://doi.org/10.1111/imr.12823.

Ferlay, J., et al., 2015. Cancer incidence and mortality worldwide: sources, methods and major patterns in GLOBOCAN 2012. Int. J. Cancer 136 (5), E359–E386. https://doi.org/10.1002/ijc.29210.

Ferrara, F., et al., 2020. Impact of Covid-19 on the treatment of acute myeloid leukemia. Leukemia 34 (8), 2254–2256. https://doi.org/10.1038/s41375-020-0925-7.

Fiorillo, A., Gorwood, P., 2020. The consequences of the COVID-19 pandemic on mental health and implications for clinical practice. Eur. Psychiatry 63 (1). https://doi.org/10.1192/j.eurpsy.2020.35.

Fischer, M., et al., 2020. COVID-19 paranoia in a patient suffering from schizophrenic psychosis – a case report. Psychiatry Res. 288. https://doi.org/10.1016/j.psychres.2020.113001.

Fouad, Y.A., Aanei, C., 2017. Revisiting the hallmarks of cancer. Am. J. Cancer Res. 7 (5), 1016–1036.

Fulambarker, A., et al., 2012. Effect of yoga in chronic obstructive pulmonary disease. Am. J. Ther. 19 (2), 96–100. https://doi.org/10.1097/MJT.0b013e3181f2ab86.

Galimberti, S., et al., 2020. Tyrosine kinase inhibitors play an antiviral action in patients affected by chronic myeloid leukemia: a possible model supporting their use in the fight against SARS-CoV-2. Front. Oncol. 10. https://doi.org/10.3389/fonc.2020.01428.

Gautam, M., et al., 2020. Current and future challenges in the delivery of mental healthcare during COVID-19. SN Compr. Clin. Med. 2 (7), 865–870. https://doi.org/10.1007/s42399-020-00348-3.

Geretti, A.M., et al., 2020. Outcomes of coronavirus disease 2019 (COVID-19) related hospitalization among people with human immunodeficiency virus (HIV) in the ISARIC World Health Organization (WHO) Clinical Characterization Protocol (UK): a prospective observational study. Clin. Infect. Dis. https://doi.org/10.1093/cid/ciaa1605.

Gervasoni, C., et al., 2020. Clinical features and outcomes of patients with human immunodeficiency virus with COVID-19. Clin. Infect. Dis. 71 (16), 2276–2278. https://doi.org/10.1093/cid/ciaa579.

Girija, P.L.T., Sivan, N., 2020. Ayurvedic treatment of COVID-19/SARS-CoV-2: a case report. J. Ayurveda Integr. Med. https://doi.org/10.1016/j.jaim.2020.06.001.

Gorbalenya, A.E., et al., 2020. The species severe acute respiratory syndrome-related coronavirus: classifying 2019-nCoV and naming it SARS-CoV-2. Nat. Microbiol., 536–544. https://doi.org/10.1038/s41564-020-0695-z.

Gordon, D.E., et al., 2020. A SARS-CoV-2 protein interaction map reveals targets for drug repurposing. Nature 583 (7816), 459–468. https://doi.org/10.1038/s41586-020-2286-9.

Guleria, R., et al., 2015. Yoga is as effective as standard pulmonary rehabilitation in improving dyspnea, inflammatory markers, and quality of life in patients with COPD. Chest 148 (4), 907A. https://doi.org/10.1378/chest.2266469.

Gunnell, D., et al., 2020. Suicide risk and prevention during the COVID-19 pandemic. Lancet Psychiatry 7 (6), 468–471. https://doi.org/10.1016/S2215-0366(20)30171-1.

Gupta, A., et al., 2014. Pranayam for treatment of chronic obstructive pulmonary disease: results from a randomized, controlled trial. Integr. Med. 13 (1), 26–31. Available from: https://europepmc.org/articles/PMC4684118. (Accessed 22 August 2021).

Hadi, Y.B., Naqvi, S.F.Z., et al., 2020. Characteristics and outcomes of COVID-19 in patients with HIV: a multicentre research network study. AIDS 34 (13), F3–F8. https://doi.org/10.1097/QAD.0000000000002666.

Hamming, I., et al., 2004. Tissue distribution of ACE2 protein, the functional receptor for SARS coronavirus. A first step in understanding SARS pathogenesis. J. Pathol. 203 (2), 631–637. https://doi.org/10.1002/path.1570.

Hanahan, D., Weinberg, R.A., 2000. The hallmarks of cancer. Cell 100 (1), 57–70. https://doi.org/10.1016/S0092-8674(00)81683-9.

Hanahan, D., Weinberg, R.A., 2011. Hallmarks of cancer: the next generation. Cell 144 (5), 646–674. https://doi.org/10.1016/j.cell.2011.02.013.

Hanson, K.E., et al., 2020. Infectious Diseases Society of America guidelines on the diagnosis of coronavirus disease 2019. Clin. Infect. Dis. https://doi.org/10.1093/cid/ciaa760.
Härter, G., et al., 2020. COVID-19 in people living with human immunodeficiency virus: a case series of 33 patients. Infection 48 (5), 681–686. https://doi.org/10.1007/s15010-020-01438-z.
Hoffmann, M., et al., 2020. SARS-CoV-2 cell entry depends on ACE2 and TMPRSS2 and is blocked by a clinically proven protease inhibitor. Cell 181 (2), 271–280. e8 https://doi.org/10.1016/j.cell.2020.02.052.
Hoffmann, C., et al., 2021. Immune deficiency is a risk factor for severe COVID-19 in people living with HIV. HIV Med. 22 (5), 372–378. https://doi.org/10.1111/hiv.13037.
Horby, P.W., et al., 2020. Lopinavir–ritonavir in patients admitted to hospital with COVID-19 (RECOVERY): a randomised, controlled, open-label, platform trial. Lancet 396 (10259), 1345–1352. https://doi.org/10.1016/S0140-6736(20)32013-4.
Hu, B., et al., 2021a. Characteristics of SARS-CoV-2 and COVID-19. Nat. Rev. Microbiol. 19 (3), 141–154. https://doi.org/10.1038/s41579-020-00459-7.
Hu, B., Huang, S., Yin, L., 2021b. The cytokine storm and COVID-19. J. Med. Virol., 250–256. https://doi.org/10.1002/jmv.26232.
Hu, R., et al., 2021c. Brief report: virologic and immunologic outcomes for HIV patients with coronavirus disease 2019. J. Acquir. Immune Defic. Syndr. 86 (2), 213–218. https://doi.org/10.1097/QAI.0000000000002540.
Huang, C., et al., 2020. Clinical features of patients infected with 2019 novel coronavirus in Wuhan, China. Lancet 395 (10223), 497–506. https://doi.org/10.1016/S0140-6736(20)30183-5.
Hus, I., et al., 2021. The management of hematologic malignancies during the COVID-19 pandemic. Expert. Opin. Pharmacother. 22 (5), 565–582. https://doi.org/10.1080/14656566.2020.1849143.
Infante, J., et al., 2014. Levels of immune cells in transcendental meditation practitioners. Int. J. Yoga 7 (2), 147. https://doi.org/10.4103/0973-6131.133899.
Jagetia, G.C., Aggarwal, B.B., 2007. "Spicing up" of the immune system by curcumin. J. Clin. Immunol. 27 (1), 19–35. https://doi.org/10.1007/s10875-006-9066-7.
Jain, A., et al., 2020. How to use a prioritised approach for treating hematological disorders during the COVID-19 pandemic in India? Indian J. Hematol. Blood Transfus., 605–615. https://doi.org/10.1007/s12288-020-01300-0.
Jamshidi, N., Cohen, M.M., 2017. The clinical efficacy and safety of tulsi in humans: a systematic review of the literature. Evid. Based Complement. Alternat. Med. 2017. https://doi.org/10.1155/2017/9217567.
Jia, H.P., et al., 2005. ACE2 receptor expression and severe acute respiratory syndrome coronavirus infection depend on differentiation of human airway epithelia. J. Virol. 79 (23), 14614–14621. https://doi.org/10.1128/jvi.79.23.14614-14621.2005.
Kalichman, S.C., et al., 2020. Intersecting pandemics: impact of SARS-CoV-2 (COVID-19) protective behaviors on people living with HIV, Atlanta, Georgia. J. Acquir. Immune Defic. Syndr. 85 (1), 66–72. https://doi.org/10.1097/qai.0000000000002414.
Kalil, A.C., et al., 2021. Baricitinib plus remdesivir for hospitalized adults with Covid-19. N. Engl. J. Med. 384 (9), 795–807. https://doi.org/10.1056/nejmoa2031994.
Kang, L., et al., 2020. The mental health of medical workers in Wuhan, China dealing with the 2019 novel coronavirus. Lancet Psychiatry 7 (3). https://doi.org/10.1016/S2215-0366(20)30047-X, e14.
Kar, S., et al., 2020. Ayurvedic preventive and curative protocol for Covid 19-a proposal. J. Ayurveda Integr. Med. 5 (2). Available from: https://www.jaims.in/jaims/article/view/869. (Accessed 22 August 2021).
Karatsoreos, I.N., 2014. Links between circadian rhythms and psychiatric disease. Front. Behav. Neurosci. 8 (May). https://doi.org/10.3389/fnbeh.2014.00162.

Karmen-Tuohy, S., et al., 2020. Outcomes among HIV-positive patients hospitalized with COVID-19. J. Acquir. Immune Defic. Syndr. 85 (1), 6–10. https://doi.org/10.1097/QAI.0000000000002423.

Katopodis, P., et al., 2020. Pan-cancer analysis of transmembrane protease serine 2 and cathepsin L that mediate cellular SARS-CoV-2 infection leading to COVID-19. Int. J. Oncol. 57 (2), 533–539. https://doi.org/10.3892/ijo.2020.5071.

Katopodis, P., et al., 2021. COVID-19 and SARS-CoV-2 host cell entry mediators: expression profiling of TMRSS4 in health and disease. Int. J. Mol. Med. 47 (4). https://doi.org/10.3892/ijmm.2021.4897.

Kong, Q., et al., 2020. Analysis of the susceptibility of lung cancer patients to SARS-CoV-2 infection. Mol. Cancer 19 (1). https://doi.org/10.1186/s12943-020-01209-2.

Kotsopoulos, J., et al., 2012. Breastfeeding and the risk of breast cancer in BRCA1 and BRCA2 mutation carriers. Breast Cancer Res. 14 (2). https://doi.org/10.1186/bcr3138.

Krammer, F., 2020. SARS-CoV-2 vaccines in development. Nature 586 (7830), 516–527. https://doi.org/10.1038/s41586-020-2798-3.

Kuba, K., et al., 2005. A crucial role of angiotensin converting enzyme 2 (ACE2) in SARS coronavirus-induced lung injury. Nat. Med. 11 (8), 875–879. https://doi.org/10.1038/nm1267.

Kusnanto, K., et al., 2018. The effectiveness of spiritual emotional breathing towards respiratory function and immune response of tuberculosis patients. J. Ners 13 (1), 93. https://doi.org/10.20473/jn.v13i1.8373.

Leclerc, M., et al., 2021. Allogeneic haematopoietic stem cell transplantation from SARS-CoV-2 positive donors. Lancet Haematol. 8 (3), e167–e169. https://doi.org/10.1016/S2352-3026(21)00025-9.

Lee, J.S., Shin, E.C., 2020. The type I interferon response in COVID-19: implications for treatment. Nat. Rev. Immunol. 20 (10), 585–586. https://doi.org/10.1038/s41577-020-00429-3. 32788708.

Li, G., et al., 2020a. Coronavirus infections and immune responses. J. Med. Virol. 92 (4), 424–432. https://doi.org/10.1002/jmv.25685.

Li, L., et al., 2020b. Effect of convalescent plasma therapy on time to clinical improvement in patients with severe and life-threatening COVID-19: a randomized clinical trial. JAMA 324 (5), 460–470. https://doi.org/10.1001/jama.2020.10044.

Liang, W., et al., 2020. Cancer patients in SARS-CoV-2 infection: a nationwide analysis in China. Lancet Oncol. 21 (3), 335–337. https://doi.org/10.1016/S1470-2045(20)30096-6.

Libster, R., et al., 2021. Early high-titer plasma therapy to prevent severe Covid-19 in older adults. N. Engl. J. Med. 384 (7), 610–618. https://doi.org/10.1056/nejmoa2033700.

Lim, S.A., Cheong, K.J., 2015. Regular yoga practice improves antioxidant status, immune function, and stress hormone releases in young healthy people: a randomized, double-blind, controlled pilot study. J. Altern. Complement. Med. 21 (9), 530–538. https://doi.org/10.1089/acm.2014.0044.

Lima, C.K.T., et al., 2020. The emotional impact of Coronavirus 2019-nCoV (new Coronavirus disease). Psychiatry Res. 287. https://doi.org/10.1016/j.psychres.2020.112915.

Lippi, G., Plebani, M., 2020. Laboratory abnormalities in patients with COVID-2019 infection. Clin. Chem. Lab. Med. 58 (7), 1131–1134. https://doi.org/10.1515/cclm-2020-0198.

Liu, X.C., et al., 2014. Effects of yoga training in patients with chronic obstructive pulmonary disease: a systematic review and meta-analysis. J. Thorac. Dis. 6 (6), 795–802. https://doi.org/10.3978/j.issn.2072-1439.2014.06.05.

Lo-Coco, F., et al., 2013. Retinoic acid and arsenic trioxide for acute promyelocytic leukemia. N. Engl. J. Med. 369 (2), 111–121. https://doi.org/10.1056/nejmoa1300874.

Lu, R., et al., 2020. Genomic characterisation and epidemiology of 2019 novel coronavirus: implications for virus origins and receptor binding. Lancet 395 (10224), 565–574. https://doi.org/10.1016/S0140-6736(20)30251-8.
Mahmood, T.B., et al., 2021. Evaluation of the susceptibility and fatality of lung cancer patients towards the COVID-19 infection: a systemic approach through analyzing the ACE2, CXCL10 and their co-expressed genes. Curr. Res. Microb. Sci. 2. https://doi.org/10.1016/j.crmicr.2021.100022, 100022.
Majumdar, A.D., Soni, V.M., Munjal, N., 2020. Ayurveda and yoga: an immunity booster at the time of COVID-19 pandemic. Int. J. Res. Eng. Sci. Manage. 3 (6), 678–680.
Mao, Y., et al., 2016. Epidemiology of lung cancer. Surg. Oncol. Clin. N. Am. 25 (3), 439–445. https://doi.org/10.1016/j.soc.2016.02.001.
Meyerowitz, E.A., et al., 2020. Disproportionate burden of coronavirus disease 2019 among racial minorities and those in congregate settings among a large cohort of people with HIV. AIDS 34 (12), 1781–1787. https://doi.org/10.1097/QAD.0000000000002607.
Mirzaei, H., et al., 2021. COVID-19 among people living with hiv: a systematic review. AIDS Behav. 25 (1), 85–92. https://doi.org/10.1007/s10461-020-02983-2.
Mishra, A., et al., 2021. The use of integrative therapy based on Yoga and Ayurveda in the treatment of a high-risk case of COVID-19/SARS-CoV-2 with multiple comorbidities: a case report. J. Med. Case Rep. 15 (1). https://doi.org/10.1186/s13256-020-02624-1.
Mittal, B., Chand, T., 2020. Global care through ayurveda in pandemic of COVID-19. Int. J. Health Sci. Res. 10 (6), 165. Available from: www.ijhsr.org. (Accessed 23 August 2021).
Moir, S., Fauci, A.S., 2017. B-cell responses to HIV infection. Immunol. Rev. 275 (1), 33–48. https://doi.org/10.1111/imr.12502.
Mondal, S., et al., 2011. Double-blinded randomized controlled trial for immunomodulatory effects of Tulsi (*Ocimum sanctum* Linn.) leaf extract on healthy volunteers. J. Ethnopharmacol. 136 (3), 452–456. https://doi.org/10.1016/j.jep.2011.05.012.
Morales-Ortega, A., et al., 2020. Imatinib for COVID-19: a case report. Clin. Immunol. 218. https://doi.org/10.1016/j.clim.2020.108518, 108518.
Murthy, K.R.S., 2010. Sushruta Samhita. Chaukhambha orientalia, Varanasi, India, p. 430. Kalpasthan.
Muruganandam, P., et al., 2020. COVID-19 and severe mental illness: impact on patients and its relation with their awareness about COVID-19. Psychiatry Res. 291. https://doi.org/10.1016/j.psychres.2020.113265.
Nadkarni, G.N., Lala, A., Bagiella, E., et al., 2020. Anticoagulation, bleeding, mortality, and pathology in hospitalized patients with COVID-19. J. Am. Coll. Cardiol. 76 (16), 1815–1826. https://doi.org/10.1016/j.jacc.2020.08.041.
Nagendra, H., 2020. Yoga for COVID-19. Int. J. Yoga 13 (2), 87. https://doi.org/10.4103/ijoy.ijoy_27_20.
Nirmala, B.P., Vranda, M.N., Reddy, S., 2011. Expressed emotion and caregiver burden in patients with schizophrenia. Indian J. Psychol. Med. 33 (2), 119–122. https://doi.org/10.4103/0253-7176.92052.
O'Connell, D.A., et al., 2020. Recommendations from the Canadian Association of Head and Neck Surgical Oncology for the Management of Head and Neck Cancers during the COVID-19 pandemic. J. Otolaryngol. Head Neck Surg. 49 (1). https://doi.org/10.1186/s40463-020-00448-z.
Okoh, A.K., et al., 2020. Coronavirus disease 19 in minority populations of Newark, New Jersey. Int. J. Equity Health 19 (1). https://doi.org/10.1186/s12939-020-01208-1.
Ozah, B., 2020. Triphala: a useful therapeutic supplement during COVID-19 pandemic. J. Drug Deliv. Ther. 10 (4), 219–220. https://doi.org/10.22270/jddt.v10i4.4153.
Pal, M., et al., 2020. Severe acute respiratory syndrome coronavirus-2 (SARS-CoV-2): an update. Cureus 12 (3). https://doi.org/10.7759/cureus.7423.

Pallikkuth, S., et al., 2021. Persistence of SARS-CoV-2-specific AB response in HIV+ individuals on art. Top. Antiviral Med. 29 (1), 88. Available from: https://120qrk11gh163n79gg1cg656-wpengine.netdna-ssl.com/wp-content/uploads/2021/03/march-2021.pdf%0Ahttp://ovidsp.ovid.com/ovidweb.cgi?T=JS&PAGE=reference&D=emexb&NEWS=N&AN=635068176. (Accessed 23 August 2021).
Park, A., Iwasaki, A., 2020. Type I and Type III interferons – induction, signaling, evasion, and application to combat COVID-19. Cell Host Microbe 27, 870–878.
Park, L.S., Rentsch, C.T., Sigel, K., et al., 2020. COVID-19 in the largest U.S. HIV cohort. In: Presented at AIDS 2020 23rd International AIDS Conference, Abstract LBPEC23.
Patel, V.V., et al., 2020. Clinical outcomes by HIV serostatus, CD4 count, and viral suppression among people hospitalized with COVID-19 in the Bronx, New York. J. Int. AIDS Soc. 23 (Suppl. 4), 171–172. Available from: http://ovidsp.ovid.com/ovidweb.cgi?T=JS&PAGE=reference&D=emexa&NEWS=N&AN=634079965. (Accessed 20 August 2021).
Patnaik, M.M., et al., 2020. Special considerations in the management of patients with myelodysplastic myndrome/myeloproliferative neoplasm overlap syndromes during the SARS-CoV-2 pandemic. Am. J. Hematol. 95 (8), E203–E208. https://doi.org/10.1002/ajh.25853.
Paul, S., et al., 2021. Treating leukemia in the time of COVID-19. Acta Haematol. 144 (2), 132–144. https://doi.org/10.1159/000508199.
Pelland-Marcotte, M.C., et al., 2020. Infections as a potential long-term risk following childhood leukemia. Med. Hypotheses 137. https://doi.org/10.1016/j.mehy.2020.109554.
Pelosi, G., Sonzogni, A., Viale, G., 2010. The classification of lung carcinoma: time to change the morphology-based approach? Int. J. Surg. Pathol. 18 (3), 161–172. https://doi.org/10.1177/1066896910361736.
Peluso, M.J., et al., 2020. A high percentage of people with human immunodeficiency virus (HIV) on antiretroviral therapy experience detectable low-level plasma HIV-1 RNA following coronavirus disease 2019 (COVID-19). Clin. Infect. Dis. https://doi.org/10.1093/cid/ciaa1754.
Perlman, S., Netland, J., 2009. Coronaviruses post-SARS: update on replication and pathogenesis. Nat. Rev. Microbiol. 7 (6), 439–450. https://doi.org/10.1038/nrmicro2147.
Perou, C.M., et al., 2000. Molecular portraits of human breast tumours. Nature 406 (6797), 747–752. https://doi.org/10.1038/35021093.
Piccolomo, A., et al., 2020. Immunomodulatory drugs in acute myeloid leukemia treatment. Cancers, 1–14. https://doi.org/10.3390/cancers12092528.
Pišlar, A., et al., 2020. The role of cysteine peptidases in coronavirus cell entry and replication: the therapeutic potential of cathepsin inhibitors. PLoS Pathog. https://doi.org/10.1371/journal.ppat.1009013.
Prabhu, S., Poongulali, S., Kumarasamy, N., 2020. Impact of COVID-19 on people living with HIV: a review. J. Virus Erad. 6 (4). https://doi.org/10.1016/j.jve.2020.100019.
Prensner, J.R., Chinnaiyan, A.M., 2011. Metabolism unhinged: IDH mutations in cancer. Nat. Med. 17 (3), 291–293. https://doi.org/10.1038/nm0311-291.
Pruss, D., et al., 2014. Development and validation of a new algorithm for the reclassification of genetic variants identified in the BRCA1 and BRCA2 genes. Breast Cancer Res. Treat. 147 (1), 119–132. https://doi.org/10.1007/s10549-014-3065-9.
Qian, Y.R., et al., 2013. Angiotensin-converting enzyme 2 attenuates the metastasis of non-small cell lung cancer through inhibition of epithelial-mesenchymal transition. Oncol. Rep. 29 (6), 2408–2414. https://doi.org/10.3892/or.2013.2370.
Qin, C., et al., 2020. Dysregulation of immune response in patients with coronavirus 2019 (COVID-19) in Wuhan, China. Clin. Infect. Dis. 71 (15), 762–768. https://doi.org/10.1093/cid/ciaa248.

Radice, P., Pierotti, M., 1997. Molecular genetics of breast cancer. Q. J. Nucl. Med. 41, 189–199.

Raghuram, N., et al., 2008. Influence of yoga on mood states, distress, quality of life and immune outcomes in early stage breast cancer patients undergoing surgery. Int. J. Yoga 1 (1), 11. https://doi.org/10.4103/0973-6131.36789.

Rajput, D.S., 2020. Evolution, ayurveda, immunity, and preventive aspects for emerging infectious diseases such as COVID-19. Int. J. Res. Pharm. Sci. 11 (special issue 1), 86–93. https://doi.org/10.26452/ijrps.v11iSPL1.2227.

Rojas, K., Stuckey, A., 2016. Breast cancer epidemiology and risk factors. Clin. Obstet. Gynecol. 59 (4), 651–672. https://doi.org/10.1097/GRF.0000000000000239.

Roy, S., Bhattacharyya, P., 2020. Possible role of traditional medicinal plant neem (*Azadirachta indica*) for the management of COVID-19 infection. Int. J. Res. Pharm. Sci. 11 (special issue 1), 122–125. https://doi.org/10.26452/IJRPS.V11ISPL1.2256.

Sam, S.P., Nisha, A., Varghese, P.J., 2019. Stressful life events and relapse in bipolar affective disorder: a cross-sectional study from a tertiary care center of southern India. Indian J. Psychol. Med. 41 (1), 61–67. https://doi.org/10.4103/ijpsym.ijpsym_113_18.

Samad, A., Jafar, T., Rafi, J.H., 2020. Identification of angiotensin-converting enzyme 2 (ACE2) protein as the potential biomarker in SARS-CoV-2 infection-related lung cancer using computational analyses. Genomics 112 (6), 4912–4923. https://doi.org/10.1016/j.ygeno.2020.09.002.

Sanyaolu, A., et al., 2020. Comorbidity and its impact on patients with COVID-19. SN Compr. Clin. Med. 2 (8), 1069–1076. https://doi.org/10.1007/s42399-020-00363-4.

Shalev, N., et al., 2020. Clinical characteristics and outcomes in people living with human immunodeficiency virus hospitalized for coronavirus disease 2019. Clin. Infect. Dis. 71 (16), 2294–2297. https://doi.org/10.1093/cid/ciaa635.

Sheng, J.Y., et al., 2020. Management of breast cancer during the COVID-19 pandemic: a stage- and subtype-specific approach. JCO Oncol. Pract. 16 (10), 665–674. https://doi.org/10.1200/op.20.00364.

Sigel, K., et al., 2020. Coronavirus 2019 and people living with human immunodeficiency virus: outcomes for hospitalized patients in New York City. Clin. Infect. Dis. 71 (11), 2933–2938. https://doi.org/10.1093/cid/ciaa880.

Sikov, W.M., et al., 2015. Impact of the addition of carboplatin and/or bevacizumab to neoadjuvant once-per-week paclitaxel followed by dose-dense doxorubicin and cyclophosphamide on pathologic complete response rates in stage II to III triple-negative breast cancer: CALGB 40603. J. Clin. Oncol. 33 (1), 13–21. https://doi.org/10.1200/JCO.2014.57.0572.

Singh, A.P., et al., 2020. Management of lung cancer during the COVID-19 pandemic. JCO Oncol. Pract. 16 (9), 579–586. https://doi.org/10.1200/op.20.00286.

Snijder, E.J., et al., 2006. Ultrastructure and origin of membrane vesicles associated with the severe acute respiratory syndrome coronavirus replication complex. J. Virol. 80 (12), 5927–5940. https://doi.org/10.1128/jvi.02501-05.

Spinelli, M., et al., 2021. Sars-cov-2 seroprevalence and igg levels are lower among people living with hiv. Top. Antiviral Med. 29 (1), 242. Available from: https://120qrk11gh163n79gg1cg656-wpengine.netdna-ssl.com/wp-content/uploads/2021/03/march-2021.pdf%0Ahttp://ovidsp.ovid.com/ovidweb.cgi?T=JS&PAGE=reference&D=emexb&NEWS=N&AN=635068812. (Accessed 23 August 2021).

Spinner, C.D., et al., 2020. Effect of remdesivir vs standard care on clinical status at 11 days in patients with moderate COVID-19: a randomized clinical trial. JAMA 324 (11), 1048–1057. https://doi.org/10.1001/jama.2020.16349.

Spiro, S.C., Silvestri, G.A., 2005. One hundred years of lung cancer. Am. J. Respir. Crit. Care Med. 172 (5), 523–529. https://doi.org/10.1164/rccm.200504-531OE.

Stacey, A.R., et al., 2009. Induction of a striking systemic cytokine cascade prior to peak viremia in acute human immunodeficiency virus type 1 infection, in contrast to more modest and delayed responses in acute hepatitis B and C virus infections. J. Virol. 83 (8), 3719–3733. https://doi.org/10.1128/jvi.01844-08.

Stebbing, J., et al., 2020. COVID-19: combining antiviral and anti-inflammatory treatments. Lancet Infect. Dis. 20 (4), 400–402. https://doi.org/10.1016/S1473-3099(20)30132-8.

Stiehl, T., Lutz, C., Marciniak-Czochra, A., 2016. Emergence of heterogeneity in acute leukemias. Biol. Direct 11 (1). https://doi.org/10.1186/s13062-016-0154-1.

Stoeckle, K., et al., 2020. COVID-19 in hospitalized adults with HIV. Open Forum Infect. Dis. 7 (8). https://doi.org/10.1093/ofid/ofaa327.

Suwanwongse, K., Shabarek, N., 2020. Clinical features and outcome of HIV/SARS-CoV-2 coinfected patients in The Bronx, New York city. J. Med. Virol. 92 (11), 2387–2389. https://doi.org/10.1002/jmv.26077.

Swerdlow, S.H., et al., 2016. The 2016 revision of the World Health Organization classification of lymphoid neoplasms. Blood 127 (20), 2375–2390. https://doi.org/10.1182/blood-2016-01-643569.

Tang, B., et al., 2020. The landscape of coronavirus disease 2019 (COVID-19) and integrated analysis SARS-CoV-2 receptors and potential inhibitors in lung adenocarcinoma patients. Front. Cell Dev. Biol. 8. https://doi.org/10.3389/fcell.2020.577032.

Tennant, D.A., et al., 2009. Metabolic transformation in cancer. Carcinogenesis. https://doi.org/10.1093/carcin/bgp070.

Tesoriero, J.M., et al., 2021. COVID-19 outcomes among persons living with or without diagnosed HIV infection in New York State. JAMA Netw. Open 4 (2). https://doi.org/10.1001/jamanetworkopen.2020.37069.

Testa, U., Castelli, G., Pelosi, E., 2020. Breast cancer: a molecularly heterogenous disease needing subtype-specific treatments. Med. Sci. 8 (1), 18. https://doi.org/10.3390/medsci8010018.

Tillu, G., et al., 2020. Public health approach of ayurveda and yoga for COVID-19 prophylaxis. J. Altern. Complement. Med. 26 (5), 360–364. https://doi.org/10.1089/acm.2020.0129.

Tomooka, L.T., Murphy, C., Davidson, T.M., 2000. Clinical study and literature review of nasal irrigation. Laryngoscope 110 (7), 1189–1193. https://doi.org/10.1097/00005537-200007000-00023.

Truong, T.T., et al., 2021. Increased viral variants in children and young adults with impaired humoral immunity and persistent SARS-CoV-2 infection: a consecutive case series. EBioMedicine 67. https://doi.org/10.1016/j.ebiom.2021.103355.

UniProt, 2021. Uniprot Proteomics Database. Available from: https://www.uniprot.org/uniprot/P00519. (Accessed 5 May 2021).

Vardhana, S.A., Wolchok, J.D., 2020. The many faces of the anti-COVID immune response. J. Exp. Med. 217 (6). https://doi.org/10.1084/jem.20200678, e20200678.

Venkatesan, P., 2021. NICE guideline on long COVID. Lancet Respir. Med. 9 (2), 129. https://doi.org/10.1016/s2213-2600(21)00031-x.

Visentin, A., et al., 2017. Major infections, secondary cancers and autoimmune diseases occur in different clinical subsets of chronic lymphocytic leukaemia patients. Eur. J. Cancer 72, 103. https://doi.org/10.1016/j.ejca.2016.11.020.

Vizcarra, P., et al., 2020. Description of COVID-19 in HIV-infected individuals: a single-centre, prospective cohort. Lancet HIV 7 (8), e554–e564. https://doi.org/10.1016/S2352-3018(20)30164-8.

von Minckwitz, G., et al., 2019. Trastuzumab emtansine for residual invasive HER2-positive breast cancer. N. Engl. J. Med. 380 (7), 617–628. https://doi.org/10.1056/nejmoa1814017.

Wan, H., et al., 2010. The angiotensin-converting enzyme 2 in tumor growth and tumor-associated angiogenesis in non-small cell lung cancer. Oncol. Rep. 23 (4). https://doi.org/10.3892/or_00000718.
Wang, W., et al., 2020a. Detection of SARS-CoV-2 in different types of clinical specimens. JAMA 323 (18), 1843–1844. https://doi.org/10.1001/jama.2020.3786.
Wang, Y., et al., 2020b. Remdesivir in adults with severe COVID-19: a randomised, double-blind, placebo-controlled, multicentre trial. Lancet 395 (10236), 1569–1578. https://doi.org/10.1016/S0140-6736(20)31022-9.
Weinkove, R., et al., 2020. Managing haematology and oncology patients during the COVID-19 pandemic: interim consensus guidance. Med. J. Aust. 212 (10), 481–489. https://doi.org/10.5694/mja2.50607.
Weinreich, D.M., et al., 2021. REGN-COV2, a neutralizing antibody cocktail, in outpatients with Covid-19. N. Engl. J. Med. 384 (3), 238–251. https://doi.org/10.1056/nejmoa2035002.
WHO, 2021. World Health Organisation Coronavirus (COVID-19) Dashboard. Available from: https://covid19.who.int/. (Accessed 5 May 2021).
WHO GoData, 2021. WHO Data About Transmission and Contact. Available from: https://openwho.org/courses/godata-en. (Accessed 5 May 2021).
WHO HIV/AIDS, 2021. WHO HIV/AIDS Fact Sheet. Available from: https://www.who.int/news-room/fact-sheets/detail/hiv-aids. (Accessed 5 May 2021).
WHO Solidarity Trial Consortium, 2021. Repurposed antiviral drugs for Covid-19—interim WHO Solidarity trial results. N. Engl. J. Med. 384 (6), 497–511. https://doi.org/10.1056/nejmoa2023184.
Wikipedia, 2021. Wikipedia Covid-19 Apps List. Available from: https://en.wikipedia.org/wiki/COVID-19_apps. (Accessed 5 May 2021).
Winichakoon, P., et al., 2020. Negative nasopharyngeal and oropharyngeal swabs do not rule out COVID-19. J. Clin. Microbiol. 58 (5). https://doi.org/10.1128/JCM.00297-20.
Winters, S., et al., 2017. Breast cancer epidemiology, prevention, and screening. Prog. Mol. Biol. Transl. Sci. 151, 1–32. https://doi.org/10.1016/bs.pmbts.2017.07.002.
World Health Organization, 2020b. Mental Health and Psychosocial Considerations During the COVID-19 Outbreak. WHO Reference Number: WHO/2019-nCoV/MentalHealth/2020.1. https://www.who.int/docs/default-source/coronaviruse/mental-health-considerations.pdf. (Accessed June 2021).
Xiao, J., et al., 2015. High relapse rate and poor medication adherence in the Chinese population with schizophrenia: results from an observational survey in the People's Republic of China. Neuropsychiatr. Dis. Treat. 11, 1161–1167. https://doi.org/10.2147/NDT.S72367.
Xu, Z., et al., 2020. Pathological findings of COVID-19 associated with acute respiratory distress syndrome. Lancet Respir. Med. 8 (4), 420–422. https://doi.org/10.1016/S2213-2600(20)30076-X.
Yang, Y., et al., 2020. Exuberant elevation of IP-10, MCP-3 and IL-1ra during SARS-CoV-2 infection is associated with disease severity and fatal outcome. medRxiv. https://doi.org/10.1101/2020.03.02.20029975. 2020.03.02.20029975.
Zang, R., et al., 2020. TMPRSS2 and TMPRSS4 promote SARS-CoV-2 infection of human small intestinal enterocytes. Sci. Immunol. 5 (47). https://doi.org/10.1126/sciimmunol.abc3582.
Zhang, L., Guo, H., 2020. Biomarkers of COVID-19 and technologies to combat SARS-CoV-2. Adv. Biomarker Sci. Technol. 2, 1–23. https://doi.org/10.1016/j.abst.2020.08.001.
Zhang, Y.Z., Holmes, E.C., 2020. A genomic perspective on the origin and emergence of SARS-CoV-2. Cell 181 (2), 223–227. https://doi.org/10.1016/j.cell.2020.03.035.

Zhang, Y., et al., 2018. Hematopoietic hierarchy – an updated roadmap. Trends Cell Biol. 28 (12), 976–986. https://doi.org/10.1016/j.tcb.2018.06.001.
Zhang, H., et al., 2020. Expression of the SAR2-Cov-2 receptor ACE2 reveals the susceptibility of COVID-19 in non-small cell lung cancer. J. Cancer 11 (18), 5289–5292. https://doi.org/10.7150/jca.49462.
Zhao, H., Mendenhall, M., Deininger, M.W., 2020. Imatinib is not a potent anti-SARS-CoV-2 drug. Leukemia 34 (11), 3085–3087. https://doi.org/10.1038/s41375-020-01045-9.
Zheng, M., 2016. Classification and pathology of lung cancer. Surg. Oncol. Clin. N. Am. 25 (3), 447–468. https://doi.org/10.1016/j.soc.2016.02.003.
Zhou, X., 2020. Psychological crisis interventions in Sichuan Province during the 2019 novel coronavirus outbreak. Psychiatry Res. 286. https://doi.org/10.1016/j.psychres.2020.112895.
Zhou, P., et al., 2020. A pneumonia outbreak associated with a new coronavirus of probable bat origin. Nature 579 (7798), 270–273. https://doi.org/10.1038/s41586-020-2012-7.
Zhu, J., Emerson, S.G., 2002. Hematopoietic cytokines, transcription factors and lineage commitment. Oncogene 21 (21 rev. iss. 2), 3295–3313. https://doi.org/10.1038/sj.onc.1205318.
Zhu, Z., et al., 2020. From SARS and MERS to COVID-19: a brief summary and comparison of severe acute respiratory infections caused by three highly pathogenic human coronaviruses. Respir. Res. 21 (1). https://doi.org/10.1186/s12931-020-01479-w.
Ziegler, C.G.K., et al., 2020. SARS-CoV-2 receptor ACE2 is an interferon-stimulated gene in human airway epithelial cells and is detected in specific cell subsets across tissues. Cell 181 (5), 1016–1035. e19 https://doi.org/10.1016/j.cell.2020.04.035.

CHAPTER SIX

Revisiting the efficacy of policies in the Indian primary healthcare sector: Interventions and approaches during the COVID-19 pandemic

Rashmi Rai[a] and Priyanka Singh[b]
[a]School of Business and Management, CHRIST University, Bengaluru, Karnataka, India
[b]School of Management and Commerce, Poornima University, Jaipur, Rajasthan, India

Abbreviations

CHCs	Community Health Centers
CHWs	community health workers
DBT	Department of Biotechnology
eVIN	Electronic Vaccine Intelligence Network
IRDAI	The Insurance Regulatory and Development Authority of India
MoH&FW	The Ministry of Health and Family Welfare in India
SHS GmbH	Siemens Healthineers Holding I Gmb
UIP	universal immunization program
VHGs	Village Health Guides

1 Introduction

When the very first patient was reported with pneumonia-like symptoms in China, nobody on this earth had the slightest idea of how things would change after this. This, invisible with naked eyes, opponent, has taken the entire world under its shock waves. On January 30, 2020, the World Health Organization classified the global COVID-19 outbreak as an immediate public health emergency for the whole world to be concerned about. On March 11, 2020, it was declared a pandemic. On a worldwide scale, as of May 29, 2021, there have been 169,118,995 confirmed cases and 3,519,175 fatalities (Covid19.who.int, 2021). Since then, every individual present on

Lessons from COVID-19
https://doi.org/10.1016/B978-0-323-99878-9.00009-1

this earth has been putting all their efforts into staying safe and survive this crisis. The healthcare industry has emerged as a critical player in this war against the novel coronavirus.

The healthcare industry or medical industry is much bigger than usual, one knows. This sector provides all possible products and services to help patients cure, prevention, rehabilitation, or palliative care. There are many subdivisions in the modern healthcare sector. To meet the health requirements of individuals and the whole population, this sector is dependent on interdisciplinary teams of paraprofessionals and trained professionals. This industry holds the key to provide good quality and healthy life to the people in any country. The significant players or participants in this entire process of delivering healthcare to the communities and individuals have been depicted in Fig. 1 as follows.

Before going ahead on the road of understanding this novel virus and its impact on the healthcare industry and its workers, the history of pandemics has to be understood. This is not the first time that humanity is facing something like this. With the evolution of civilizations, these epidemics and pandemics have always been a part of our lives. Table 1 enlists the top 10 worst hitting pandemics in world history in the recent past.

India, too, has its share of such epidemics. Table 2 lists the most recent Indian pandemics/epidemics that have brought humanity to its knees. During the 19th century, India mostly had close encounters with epidemics like

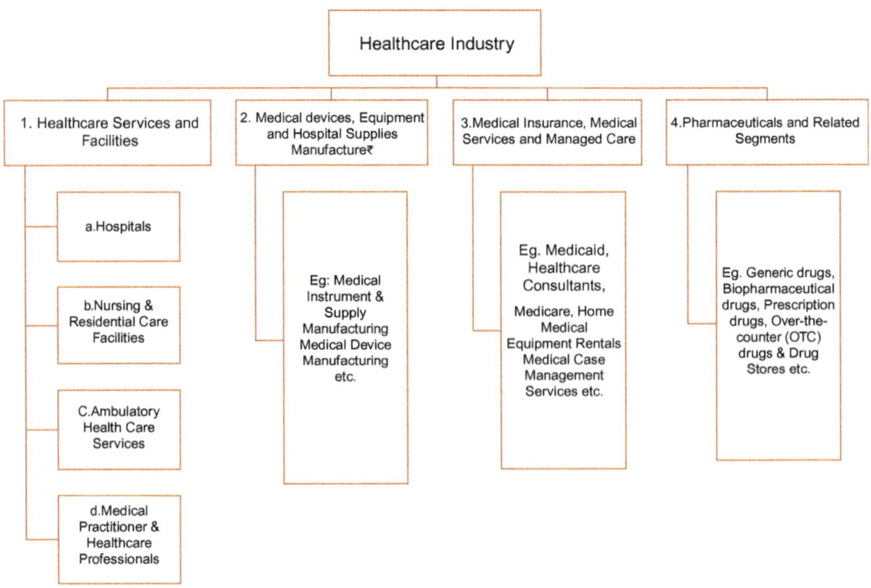

Fig. 1 Healthcare industry structure (TechnoFunc, 2021).

Table 1 Most fatal pandemics in the world history.

Pandemic	Duration	Death toll	Causes
HIV/AIDS pandemic	2005–12	36,000,000	HIV/AIDS
Flu pandemic	1968	1,000,000	Influenza
Asian flu	1956–58	2,000,000	Influenza
Flu pandemic	1918–20	20–50,000,000	Influenza
Sixth cholera pandemic	1910–11	More than 800,000	Cholera
Russian flu pandemic	1889–90	1,000,000	Influenza
Third cholera pandemic	1852–60	1,000,000	Cholera
The Black Death	1346–53	75–200,000,000	Bubonic plague
Plague of Justinian	541–542 AD	25,000,000	Bubonic plague
Antonine Plague	165 AD	5,000,000	Unknown

Source: Earth5R, 2021. Covid 19 (Coronavirus) and 10 Worst Pandemics in History. [Online] https://earth5r.org/covid-19-coronavirus-and-other-pandemics/ (Accessed 20 May 2021).

Table 2 Major epidemics in the 20th century in India.

Pandemic/epidemic	Duration
Nipah outbreak	2018
Indian swine flu outbreak	2015
Odisha jaundice epidemic	2014
H1N1 flu pandemic	2009
Gujarat jaundice epidemic	2009
Dengue outbreak	2006
Chikungunya outbreak	2006
Meningococcal meningitis epidemic	2005
SARS epidemic	2003
Dengue epidemic	2003
Plague of Northern India	2002
Surat plague epidemic	1994
Small pox epidemic	1974
Polio epidemic	1970–90
Influenza pandemic	1918

Source: Swetha, G., Eashwar, V., Gopalakrishnan, S., 2019. Epidemics and pandemics in India throughout history: a review article. Indian J. Public Health Res. Devel. 10(8), 1570.

Cholera and Plague. The primary reasons behind these infections were caused by poor hygiene factors and practices, poor living conditions, illiteracy, overcrowded slums, heavy rainfall, and floods.

1.1 COVID-19 and the world

Wuhan Municipal Health Commission, Wuhan, Hubei Province, China, reported some patients with symptoms like pneumonia on December 31, 2019. Eventually, a novel coronavirus was identified. Soon, in January 2021, the first corona patient was detected outside China in Thailand. This was just the beginning. In the same month, the United States of America (USA), Nepal, Vietnam, France, Malaysia, Russia, Italy, United Kingdom, India, Philippines, UAE reported their first case of the novel coronavirus. In response to this speedy spread of the virus, many countries closed their borders to foreign tourists. All the flights to China originating from many countries were canceled for an indefinite time duration. In the meanwhile, the number of cases in China was exploding. This novel coronavirus got its name COVID-19 by WHO on February 11, 2020. Most countries adopted emergency lockdown as an immediate measure to control the spread of this disease in their country, including India, in March 2020. In the next 9 months, the world saw the spread of this virus, and the count rose to 82 million, and the death count was more than 1.8 million (News, 2021). The United Kingdom started administrating a thoroughly trialed and tested COVID-19 vaccine on its people and became the first nation in the world to do so on December 8, 2020 (Kantis et al., 2021) (Graph 1).

Mahajan and Kaushal (2020) mentioned in their article that as of March 11, 2020, COVID-19 had spread to 114 countries, with 118,326 active cases and 4292 deaths, and was declared a pandemic by the World Health Organization (WHO). This viral outbreak had an impact on India as well. The situation worsened within a week of the pandemic's announcement. After China, Italy had become the second most affected country. While the virus spread like wildfire, scientists put in all their efforts, and they started

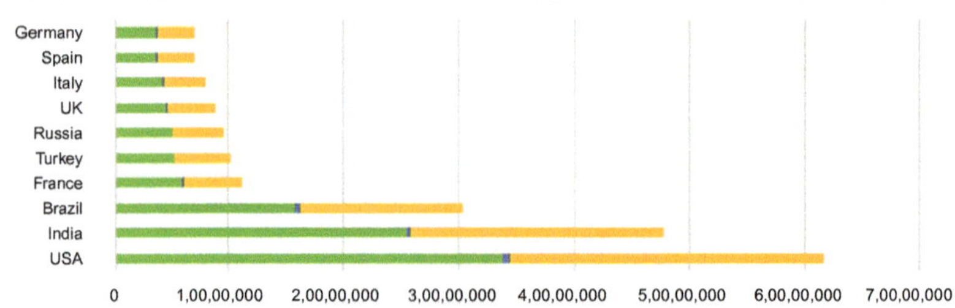

	USA	India	Brazil	France	Turkey	Russia	UK	Italy	Spain	Germany
Total Cases	3,37,74,94	2,54,96,33	1,57,35,48	58,98,347	51,39,485	49,57,756	44,50,392	41,67,025	36,19,848	36,15,896
Total Deaths	6,01,330	2,83,276	4,39,379	1,08,040	45,186	1,16,575	1,27,691	1,24,497	79,502	87,148
Total Recovered	2,72,53,32	2,19,86,36	1,42,47,60	51,81,486	49,71,245	45,72,226	42,81,947	37,27,220	33,42,024	33,40,400

Total Cases Total Deaths Total Recovered

Graph 1 Statistical reference to the total number of cases of coronavirus in the most affected countries in the world. *(Source: Worldometers.info, 2021. COVID Live Update: 171,010,903 Cases and 3,556,329 Deaths From the Coronavirus – Worldometer. [Online] https://www.worldometers.info/coronavirus/#countries (Accessed 19 May 2021).)*

understanding more about it. In this process, using a mask, social distancing, and washing hands were discovered as the essential means of reducing the chances of getting infected with this virus. The governments declared emergencies and immediately completed lockdown to break the chain of infection. This did help in controlling the spread of this disease even though it affected the world economy very adversely. Once the spread of infection got under control and the countries decided to lift the restrictions and let the economy open to revival, this virus came back with much more threatening effects. This is usually called the second wave of COVID-19. Since last year, sooner or later, almost all the countries on the world map have been or are presently facing this second wave of coronavirus. Countries like Kyrgyzstan, Australia, South Korea, Israel, New Zealand, United States, Southeast Asia, India, Nepal, Laos, Thailand, United Kingdom, Germany, Japan, and Spain have either suffered or are suffering or are on the verge of suffering the second wave of coronavirus (WION, 2021; Standard, 2021).

The second wave of coronavirus marked its re-entry in India in mid-March 2021, almost a year after it appeared for the first time here. Moreover, this time, it has been much faster in infecting people. This time, new mutations have been observed in the virus by scientists. India's top virologists had confirmed that when in September 2020, the UK-variant was first found in India, it should have been considered an alarm for India (Priyamvatha, 2021). Because of these mutants of coronavirus, India has registered 2,720,716 active cases and 303,720 deaths, as reported by the Ministry of Health and Family Welfare on May 24, 2021 (MoHFW, 2021a,b). This rising number of infected individuals has been putting extreme pressure on the Indian healthcare system. The demand and supply equation of major medical facilities like hospital beds, emergency medicines, oxygen supplies, ICU beds, ventilators, etc., is in jeopardy. All this has further led to add to the severity of the situation and worsen the whole scenario. India began its vaccination phase in January 2021 (Correspondent, S, 2021). Vaccination has been considered a solid intervention to take control of this crippling situation. However, the shortage of vaccination supplies has further just added to the trouble. Getting the entire Indian population vaccinated anywhere nearby to stop this pandemic seems a mammoth task for the Indian Government. Some of the significant trends of this second wave that has been a point of concern for India (Varma, 2021) are as follows:

(a) As per the Union Health Ministry, what was initially confined to 3–5 states in India has spread to 10 states. Furthermore, these 10 states of India account for 73% of the new cases registered (The Economic

Times, 2021). Andhra Pradesh, Delhi, Haryana, Uttar Pradesh, Tamil Nadu, Karnataka, Kerala, West Bengal, Rajasthan, and Maharashtra flag bearers.

(b) Indian railway enjoys the reputation of employing one of the most significant numbers of employees in the world. During the pandemic, it has continued serving as an essential service. Indian railway has played an important role and the transportation of essentials of COVID-19 like drugs, equipment, and oxygen. However, all this has put the Indian railway employees in a vulnerable situation. As per the senior officials of Indian railways, 1000 employees are getting infected daily (Press Trust of India, 2021).

(c) To control the second wave COVID-19 situation, many Indian states and union territories have announced night curfews with Section 144, stringent restrictions on weekends, or partial lockdown. This restriction poses extreme challenges for the lower-income and daily wage workers whose livelihood is in great danger.

(d) Unlike the first wave of COVID-19, rural India reports a 1.39 times higher number of cases than urban India (Jha, 2021). This is a great matter of concern for the governing bodies. This is being considered as an upcoming terror. When urban India faces such a hike in the COVID-19 massacre despite the availability of good healthcare facilities, the upcoming picture of rural India seems unimaginable. There are limitations of these facilities in the rural parts of India.

(e) Trouble for India does not seem to be ending here. A new health problem called Mucormycosis, the Black fungus has emerged as an epidemic (Ray, 2021). This disease is being associated with coronavirus. Various clinical reasons are being discussed behind the cause of this trouble.

(f) Recently, IIT Kanpur, in their study, the third wave of COVID-19 has been predicted. No time frame has been disclosed as such, but it is being said that this third wave would probably put the children and newborns in a threatening position.

This COVID-19 pandemic has brought a revolutionary shift in the healthcare industry. In India, the change in the pre- and postscenario is remarkable. Because of this, pandemic is visible through the overall outlook of the country's seriousness and investment toward human health. In the financial year of 2017, the healthcare industry of India was approximately 160 billion USD. Moreover, it was worth over 140 billion US dollars as of 2016. This has been estimated to go up to 370 billion USD by 4 (Bajaj, 2021). The public health expenditure value for the financial year 2018 for India was recorded at approximately ₹1.58 trillion (Statista Research Department, 2021). This accounted for 1.28% of the GDP of India. The per capita health expenditure in India was calculated around ₹1600. However, there was not an equal distribution of this amount in all the parts of India. The Indian Government introduced the "Ayushman Bharat National Health Protection Mission" in August 2018 (National Portal of India, n.d.). This plan covers secondary and tertiary care hospitalization for a family of five for $5000 per year (on a family floater basis).

Other schemes like "Mission Indradhanush" aimed at achieving 90% immunization in India (Rastogi, 2019).

Business in the healthcare sector is considered giants of the industry had taken over several established multispecialty healthcare groups and hospitals. This sector has appeared attractive for inviting FDI and huge investments from other countries (ETHealthWorld, 2021).

The tide of digitalization has pushed telemedicine in the Indian healthcare industry. This technology is viewed as a beautiful opportunity to reach out to the most unreachable in the country. Various leading industries of India have also started pouring in liquidity in the upcoming field of telemedicine. The Indian Government had also been too active to make the best of these opportunities. As a result, according to the NITI Aayog report (2018), the Indian Government plans to increase public healthcare spending from 1.1% to 2.5% of GDP over the next 4 years. This was further planned to go up to 5% in 5 years (Mishra, 2019).

The trend of single-specialty hospitals and specialty clinics has been like hot selling cake in India. This trend has helped in penetrating the untapped market. There has been a new success mantra called the "Bouquet hospital" model.

All this has made humankind put on their thinking hats. All the nations are all set with their arms and ammunition to counter any war conditions. Still, nobody was ready to handle a world crisis where the opponent is so minute that it is not even visible by the naked eyes. This was something nobody was prepared to take. As soon as COVID-19 struck the world, it compelled all the countries to introspect themselves rather than pointing fingers at others. This pandemic has highlighted the weak links of all the countries, whether developed or developing nations. For example, it has been too complicated for countries like the United States and United Kingdom to control the mortality rate in 2020. Similarly, the situation is getting horrible in India in 2021.

COVID-19 has brought the healthcare industry into the limelight in India because earlier, this was not enjoying much attention by the nation. On one end, India's healthcare industry has done a commendable job of treating and curing COVID-19 patients, which is a humongous task because of the population. However, on the other end, it has to face many hardships similar to many other sectors. The most critical pillars in combating the COVID-19 pandemic are frontline healthcare staff. Also, the best logistics would be insufficient if our frontline staff are not safe and well supported. Given the magnitude of the epidemic, it is critical to protect the health of these individuals as a public health measure. To this end, determining the prevalence of psychological manifestations in healthcare personnel is vital. Evidence-based assessments and mental health interventions for this group, on the other hand, are rare globally and nearly nonexistent in India. There are some data from India on mental health manifestations among frontline healthcare providers (Chew et al., 2020).

The virus causes debility, morbidity, and death, but it also causes massive physical and psychological fatigue to a large degree. As a result of this breakdown, health departments and ministries are contacting retired medical personnel and others who spend more time researching to encourage them to return to clinical practice to alleviate the mounting stresses on the health system. Indeed, many healthcare workers accept that a vaccine is necessary to stop the virus's spread, particularly in light of recent mutations that are thought to make it more contagious.

In the pre-COVID-19 era, India was planning to stretch its expenditure on public healthcare, but during the COVID-19, India has spent much higher than what it would have ever targeted. Because of this pandemic, other health-related issues of India, like the crisis of malnutrition, infant healthcare, etc., have been amplified. The 15th Finance Commission has raised a projection of ₹5.38 lakh crores for the Ministry of Health between 2020 and 2025 for primary healthcare and conducting immunization, testing, screening, and treating COVID-19. This amount would grow much higher when the non-COVID-19 conditions are accounted for (Kurian, 2021).

To achieve Universal Health Coverage, India needs to improve its healthcare services from the bottom to rural India. This COVID-19 pandemic exposed the structural weaknesses of the Indian healthcare industry right from inadequate equipment, supplies, medicines, insufficient and overloaded healthcare workers, unethical practices, black marketing of lifesaving drugs, ambiguity in immunization drive, etc. Proper and accurate government intervention would only be able to ensure an improvement in these areas. The Indian Government has already started attending to these issues one by one.

The Indian pharmaceutical industry is the largest provider of generic medicines in the world. It stands at third rank in the world by volume and 14th place by pharmaceutical production value. It accounts for 20% of the medical supplies (India Brand Equity Foundation, 2021). By 2030, this industry is expected to go up to $130 billion. India successfully developed its COVID-19 vaccination called Covaxin by the pharmaceutical company named Bharat Biotech. Post-COVID-19, India can be more focused on getting health insurance, as this has gained momentum. The proof is the growth of 17.16% Y-O-Y to ₹51,637.84 crores (US$ 7.39 billion) in the gross direct premium income that was underwritten in FY20 (India Brand Equity Foundation, 2021).

1.2 India's measures to fight COVID-19

- Steps for precaution: To control the viral infection spread, the Indian Government has strict screenings and compulsory quarantine rules for all incoming travelers from international destinations. It has also canceled all the international flights. Even traveling within the country has been restricted and under strict scrutiny. Along with all this, the Indian Government made all possible arrangements for the emergency evacuation of its expatriates from various parts of the world. Further, restrictions like complete lockdown have been implemented. Under this rule, other than few essential services, all the rest of the movements were suspended. Special passes and permissions are issued for special urgent situations.
- Steps related to medical facilities: The government has designated 1264 government laboratories and 1326 private laboratory centers to diagnose COVID-19 (Indian Council for Medical Research, 2021). The government is putting in many efforts to meet the rising demand for beds, ICU beds, ventilators, oxygen, etc. Meanwhile, the government is all dedicated to the mission vaccination for India. Covaxin is all developed and made in India vaccination. From no production to the second-largest manufacturer of PPE kits, the Indian Government is putting all efforts into fighting back coronavirus.
- Steps related to financial assistance: Looking at the turbulent times, the Indian Government has already announced various relief packages, funds, and plans for low-income groups, daily wage earners, laborers,

farmers, hawkers, etc. They are also being supported by direct benefits transferred from the government. Various healthcare-related insurance schemes have been announced. Moreover, many more relief plans and support functions are being rendered by the Indian Government. The investment in public healthcare has been expanded in the Union Budget 2021 to 137% YoY. This brings the total healthcare allocation for the financial year 4 to ₹223,846 crores (US$ 30.70 billion). The Government of India announced ₹64,180 crores (US$ 8.80 billion) for strengthening the National Health Mission in the union budget 2021–22 (The Hindu, 2021). This amount would be used to develop primary, secondary, and tertiary care. The healthcare institutions and infrastructure are aimed to be improved and upgraded to international standards and capacities to detect and cure new & emerging diseases. Other initiatives take in India to strengthen the healthcare industry during recent times:

- More than 5.84 crores doses of COVID-19 vaccines have been exported to 70 countries, including Morocco, South Africa, Brazil (Mukherjee, 2021).
- The National Backward Classes Finance and Development Corporation (NBCFDC) and Apollo Medskills Pvt. Ltd. have signed a Memorandum of Understanding Ltd. will co-fund COVID-19 vaccination administration training workshops for NBCFDC target community nurses, medical & nursing students, and pharmacists (Press Information Bureau, 2021).
- The procurement of Varian Medical Systems, Inc. by Siemens Healthineers Holding I Gmb (SHS GmbH) has been agreed upon by the Competition Commission of India (CCI) (Orissadiary.com, 2021).
- Under the vaccination drive of India, on May 27, 2021, as per the Ministry of Health and Welfare dashboard, 20,26,95,874 Indian citizens have been vaccinated successfully (MoHFW, 2021a,b).
- Under the scheme of Pradhan Mantri Garib Kalyan Yojana, the Union Minister of Finance & Corporate Affairs Nirmala Sitharaman, under Pradhan Mantri Garib Kalyan Yojana, announced Rs 1.70 lakh crore relief package for people with poverty to combating coronavirus (Pib.gov.in, 2021).
- In Pradhan Mantri Kisan Samman Nidhi (PMKSN) that the Indian Government entirely funds, all farmer households receive annual income support of Rs. 6000/- in three equal installments of Rs. 2000/- every 4 months under the scheme.

- Since lockdown was imposed, the MNREGA, an essential aspect of the Central Government's response to the COVID-19 issue, has been seen with cautious optimism. MNREGA provides a rural home with 100 days of pay employment per year if all adult members are prepared to conduct unskilled manual labor at the minimum wage (Megsres.nic.in, 2021).

India has taken the initial steps to cross-learning between various states and administrated the best practices in the healthcare industry. A lot is still to be done. This COVID-19 pandemic has brought an economic crisis in the country, which would, in turn, push millions of people below the poverty line. To ensure the health and well-being of this new and larger group of the poor, all local governments, state governments, the Central Government, and citizens must work together.

During this time, India's broad coverage of over 25,000 primary healthcare centers (PHCs), which are the first and lowest health tiers and delivers critical preventative, and remedial health services such as vaccinations and immunizations, has proven to be a lifesaver. Essential medications, maternity and child health, and health education are difficult to manage in rural, suburban, and underprivileged areas.

Be it in rural or urban areas, the entire system is linked to primary healthcare centers. As a result, PHCs' ability to provide safe, patient-centered care to meet the population's current health demands, as well as strengthening and including PHCs in this pandemic response, could play a critical role in breaking the virus's chain of transmission through early detection, service variations, management of mild-to-moderate types of cases at the periphery and could help in assisting the vast population. This could prove to be a cost-effective technique of reducing the number of lives lost and suffering in the short and long term.

1.3 India fights COVID-19 with computer science and software engineering

Like the many other countries around the world, India, too, has turned all the stones to fight against the unknown enemy called the novel coronavirus. Computer science and software engineering has been some of the most effective weapons in this war. Indian Government, both at the central and state level, nonprofit organizations, private players, hospitals, etc., have taken help from IT and ITES companies to develop various software and smartphone-based applications (World, 2020).

Some of the major software and apps developed in India during COVID-19 to manage and control the pandemic and help people handle their health are as follows:

(a) **Aarogya Setu**: This is the primary contact tracing application widely used by India. The National Informatics Centre under the Ministry of Electronics & Information Technology has developed this smartphone-based application. This application keeps track of contact with other people who are using the app. This app uses the phone's GPS capabilities and Bluetooth features and alerts users to contact a COVID-19 positive person (The Hindu, 2020).

(b) **COVID-19 Feedback**: The Indian Ministry of Electronics and Information Technology has developed this survey as a tool by gathering information from the users regarding their recent COVID-19 tests/treatments (Budd et al., 2020). This app has proved to be very helpful to the government to identify the coronavirus effect in various areas and improve the medical facilities in those areas.

(c) **MyGov**: This is a Government of India app that is a platform for the engagement of Indians where they share their opinions, creative ideas, comments, and suggestions directly to the Government of India.

(d) **SAHYOG**: This app compliments Aarogya Setu in the process of contact tracing and creating public awareness and deliveries of essential items to the needy (Dst.gov.in, 2021).

(e) **Lyfas COVID score**: Developed by Acculi Labs of Bangalore, an application-based score shows one's propensity to COVID-19 infection. This plays a significant role in the early detection of disease and the assessment of the infection. Lyfas is a "proper medical screening test" that depends on test results (Sahay, 2020).

(f) **COVID Severity Score**: Recently, the software has been developed which uses an algorithm to calculate a COVID Severity Score, eventually identifying the COVID-19 patients who require ventilation. The Foundation has developed this software for Innovation in Health, Kolkata, with biotechnology and IIT Guwahati (Ghosh, 2021a,b).

(g) **The Central Bed Allotment system software**: This software has been developed to manage the shortage of hospital beds for COVID-19 patients in Karnataka by the Bruhat Bengaluru Mahanagara Palike, the Bangaluru's civic body (Poovanna, 2020).

(h) **The Delhi Corona app**: This mobile phone-based application helps update people about vacant hospital beds for COVID-19 patients in Delhi (Chaturvedi, 2020).

(i) NCDIR e-Mortality Software (NCDIR e-Mor): To meet the requirement of reporting COVID-19 deaths more appropriately, the National Centre for Disease Informatics and Research under the Indian Council of Medical Research has developed this software (Kaul, 2020).

(j) The Vee + Svasa mobile app: With the support from Johns Hopkins University, United States, software developers have developed a smartphone-based mobile app, which guides COVID-19 patients isolating at home. This app provides vital information on reaching out to local medical facilities and various informative and educational videos (IANS, 2021).

(k) CoWIN: COVID Vaccine Intelligence Network (CoWIN) system has emerged as the backbone of the biggest vaccination drive in this world against coronavirus. This system benefits everyone involved in the process, including government employees in India. It is a cloud-based IT solution for planning, administering, monitoring, and assessing COVID-19 vaccination (Ghosh, 2021a,b).

2 Methodology

The approach for performing a review and synthesis of the literature addresses the contentious and complex research question to address how there has been a remarkable change in India's healthcare industry due to the pandemic in the last one and a half years and the role of primary healthcare. There are several methods for performing a literature review of research studies and reports; however, a desk research methodology was chosen as the best tool for interpreting and critiquing existential studies on the role of primary healthcare during the pandemic. In this research, various literature published between 2020 and 2021 were reviewed. The period selected is justifiable since there is an onset of coronavirus during specific in addition. The body of literature for review depends on relevant studies that address the subject of interest. All possibly available secondary data from reputed databases like Scopus, WOS, and Google Scholar search engines, newspapers, government websites, etc., have been being excavated to meet this purpose; secondary sources have been used to analyze the data (Prisma Diagram below). This chapter also examines how COVID-19 has impacted Indian health workers. This chapter aims to critically explore the role of PHC's and the government's policies and processes to deal with COVID-19 and any other unforeseen situations that the country may encounter in the future.

The Prisma diagram of systematic review is mentioned below

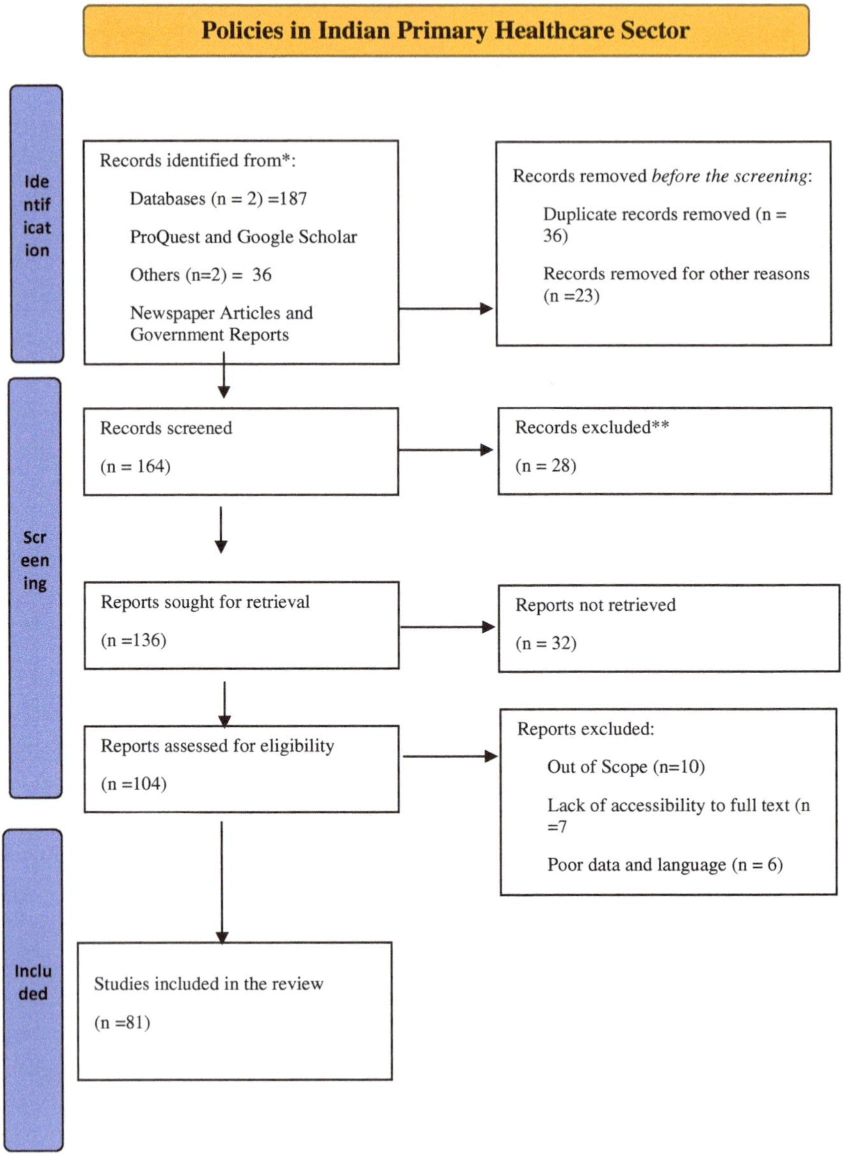

3 Journey of PHC from conceptualization to the reality

In the Indian context, the concept of primary healthcare (PHC) is not new. Its evolution dates to 1946; the Bhore Committee proposed a primary healthcare center (PHC). As per this committee, PHC would be responsible for combining preventive and curative healthcare as the most basic health unit in rural India. The first few primary healthcare centers (PHCs) in India were set up under the Community Development (Ranga Rao, 1993) Program in 1952. This set the base to create a three-tier healthcare system (M/o Statistics & Programme Implementation, GOI – MOSPI, 2016). For the first four decades, successive government bodies continued to build the network of PHCs, with one to three PHCs being constructed per decade, with the help of various committees (Table 3).

Governments worldwide were looking to improve their healthcare systems' efficiency, efficacy, and responsiveness. The importance of primary healthcare in accomplishing these goals cannot be overstated. India's National Health Policy (NHP) 2017 advocated for boosting primary healthcare systems and allocating two-thirds or more of government health spending to primary care, and increasing the overall government health budget to 2.5% of GDP by 2025, up from 1.18% in 2015–16 (Ministry of Health and Welfare, Government of India, 2017). According to the Government's Rural Health Statistics Report (2018–10), the government has continually endeavored, as shown in the Table 4.

3.1 Challenges faced by PHC during COVID-19

Rural India has a strong subcenter, Primary Health Centre (PHC), and Community Health Center (CHC). While a robust plan was being made to strengthen the PHC, that's when the pandemic has hit hard and also impacted the primary healthcare survival in emerging economies, and so in India too; currently, there is a vast population of rural India which are deprived of primary healthcare due to shortfall of these centers, the number is quite alarming like 18% shortfall at the subcenter level, 22% at the primary healthcare center, and 30% at the community level. Though India has been trying hard to increase the number of facilities, the workers working in this area of healthcare have been substantially low as recommended by WHO. Looking at the statistics, rural India has only 3.2 government hospitals bed

Table 3 Timeline of evolution of Primary Health Centre in India.

Timeline	Recommendations
1946—Bhore Committee	All administrative levels' preventative and curative services will be integrated, and the Primary Health Centre is developed in two stages: short term and long term
1952—Mudaliar Committee	Strengthen of PHC before opening new ones, and All India Health service should replace Indian Medical service
1967—Jungalwalla	Integration of health organizations at all levels in the country by taking few steps like special pay for particular work, equal pay for equal work, common seniority, improvement in service conditions
1973—Kartar Singh Committee	A single cadre of versatile workers should be formed by combining many groupings of peripheral workers. A single Primary Health Centre must serve a 50,000-people community PHC established three cadres of health workers between community-level workers and doctors, notably multipurpose health workers and health assistants
1975—Shrivastava Committee	For planning, a "Referral Services Complex" and a Medical and Health Education Commission were established
1977—Rural Health Scheme	It was constructed on the principles of "placing people's health in people's hands"
1977—Village Health Guide Scheme	Village Health Guides (VHGs) assist rural communities with preventative, promotive, and primary curative care
1978—Alma-Ata Conference (PHC)	As a result of the declaration, primary healthcare (PHC) became the official health policy of all member countries

per 10,000. First, India imposed a lockdown on March 23, 2020, which shut down all public transportation. Then, as things began to recover, India was hit by a second wave of the virus, making healthcare services even more inaccessible.

Medical personnel, particularly doctors and nurses, were diverted to take COVID-19 patients. At the same time, many frontline workers and social activists were involved in contact tracing, which caused absenteeism of community deployment of women healthcare workers and caregivers to continue the immunization program (Ministry of Health & Family Welfare, 2021).

Table 4 Number of PHC, CHC, and subcenter in India.

	The average number of villages covered in a rural area	2005 (Rural)	2019 (Urban + rural)	Increase in the number
Subcenter	4	146,026	160,713 (3302 + 157,411)	11,385
Primary Health Centre (PHC)	26	23,236	30,045 (5190 + 24,855)	1619
Community Health Centre (CHC)	120	3346	5685 (350 + 5335)	1989

Source: Government of India Ministry of Health and Family Welfare Statistics Division, 2019. Rural Health Statistics. Government of India.

Social distancing norms suggested by WHO further put a question mark on the feasibility of separating waiting rooms for immunization, and curative services became a challenge.

One of the other challenges faced was that the primary healthcare workers were at an increased risk of contracting the virus while handling the patient and had to go into isolation when they felt they had been exposed to this virus.

The acute shortage of PPE kits in the first wave was severe (Kumar, 2020), because of which the production of PPE kits all over the world was increased to tackle the second wave, which hit hard in India. PHC requires support and boost to strengthen themselves at many ends. This pandemic has necessitated us to do much restructuring so that they are well prepared to handle this pandemic and its variations of the second and third wave, small measures like separate space to treat COVID-19 patients while ensuring social distancing and proper usage of the mask. Despite various initiatives by the government, like the National Health Mission, adequate and reasonable healthcare is still an illusion. Rural Indians face an acute shortage of medical representatives which will have a long-lasting negative impact on the healthcare system in rural India, especially regarding the quality of care available to them. Many states were not prepared to handle COVID-19 and their transmission due to the issues mentioned above (Rekha, 2020). The rural Indian health system is divided into three tiers: primary, secondary, and tertiary care. The subcenter is the primary point of contact between the primary healthcare system and the community (Rai et al., 2021). In rural India, a substantial network of subcenters, Primary Health Centres (PHCs), and Community Health Centers were built (CHC). Due to preexisting vulnerability caused by a lack of health infrastructure in rural areas and a diversion of essential medical resources for providing care, many secondary and tertiary care clinics in low and lower-middle-income countries face significant challenges in managing the COVID-19 pandemic. Several secondary and tertiary care clinics that previously handled outpatient cases have been repurposed to provide medical care and supervision for COVID-19 clients (Garg et al., 2020).

3.2 Role of PHC to mitigate the crisis

PHC in India has a complex structure of government services and private sectors pharmacies and small clinics. In contrast, this system has always been backfired with criticisms for leading to fragmentation and poor quality of care due to dependence on each other. At this moment of the pandemic, the variety of primary care offered cannot be overlooked. They can play a good role in mitigating this crisis in several ways.

- Testing centers: Using the PHC, pharmacies, and health and wellness centers as testing locations. This will help make the testing quicker, reduce the waiting time, and reduce the patient volume at the critical health centers.
- Telehealth: The transition from hospital-based services to telemedicine and virtual treatment and increased demand for portable point-of-care solutions are two of the most critical impacts on the healthcare industry. Demand for digital health and drive-through clinics has also increased. Although there is no denying the importance of human contact in emergency treatment and that it cannot be entirely replaced by technology, long term, a strategic transition toward automation and digital transformation is on the horizon. In the short term, this involves tasks including contact tracing and AI-based solutions for detecting early infections and controlling and suppressing the spread. As a result of the crisis, major healthcare companies collaborate on open-source ventilator prototypes, vaccine testing, drug development, and essential equipment manufacturing. It is inspiring to see first-of-their-kind humanitarian collaborations that go beyond and beyond the call of duty (Sachan, 2021).

  In India, the telemedicine market has enormous potential in the eHealth segment. According to a recent Inc42 Plus report titled India's eHealth Market Opportunity Report, 2021, it is expected to expand at a

31% compound annual growth rate to $5.4 billion by 2025 (CAGR) 2021 (Dayalani et al., 2021).

The Indian Government has already released telemedicine practice guidelines, but adoption has been restricted or reserved for more extensive facilities. Telehealth can be used by primary care providers for remote triaging, ensuring critical health services, and monitoring tools to find possible COVID-19 hotspots (Graph 2).

- Safe care: Improving facility operations necessitates new ideas, such as deciding the order of treatment of the incoming patients before arriving at a clinic and providing staff with adequate personal protective equipment (PPE). Guidelines for proper PPE use and establishing a safe environment for infection protection and control are available from India's Ministry of Health and Family Welfare. At the PHC stage, supply chain shortages for PPE can be partially resolved by encouraging at-home treatment and telehealth when necessary.
- Deployment of community health workers (CHWs): CHWs can provide community-based care and address COVID-19 infection in hard-to-reach and remote areas when adequately resourced and compensated. Other countries' CHWs have been able to provide uninterrupted treatment through the pandemic's most challenging moments. The present crisis is a brilliant opportunity to increase the capacity of Accredited Social Health Activists (ASHAs) to provide preventative and effective curative care during the pandemic and beyond by educating and equipping them with appropriate PPE and payment (Abdel-All et al., 2019). To quickly build up the expertise and skills of physicians, nurses, and other health professionals, a mix of various approaches—written

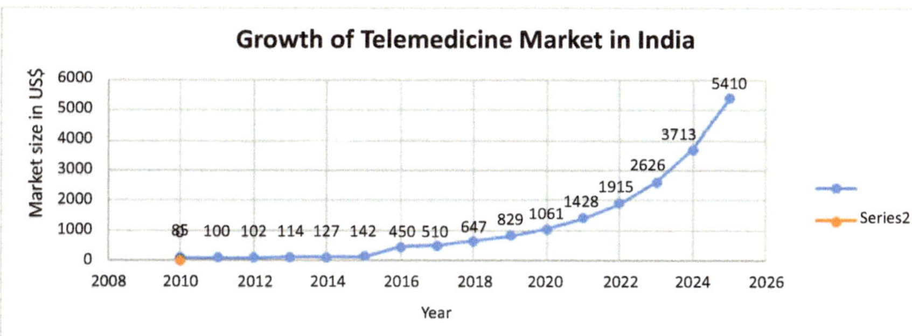

Graph 2 Telemedicine market in India. *(Source: Dayalani, V., Dayalani, V., Staff, I., 2021. Telemedicine: A Post-COVID Reality in India. [Online] Inc42 Media. Available from: https://inc42.com/datalab/telemedicine-a-post-covid-reality-in-india.)*

protocols, web sessions, on-the-job training and support, and telephonic one-on-one conversations—works well. This awareness is essential for them to feel empowered and confident when they deal with the situation. A balanced combination of accountability and power has to be introduced and executed at the grass-root level. A regular audit and the community's feedback would help ensure transparency in the entire flow of action.

- Home care: We may prevent unnecessary visits to health facilities by arming patients and their families with more knowledge of maintaining their home health. Enabling self-management at home would be beneficial both in terms of infection prevention and in terms of operations. Especially in light of how overburdened healthcare facilities are at the moment. This online platform, for example, can be used to provide COVID-19 risk information to a patient and is available in various languages. These widely disseminated infographics can aid patients in determining when hospitalization is required versus when at-home treatment is appropriate.
- Clear Health Messages: A clear and compelling risk communication stream must be established to avoid mixed signals at the local and national levels. Consistent messaging through private and public primary care clinics can help reach a large audience across several contact points with the health system. ASHAs may rely on links with local communities in more remote areas to provide consistent information (Saprii et al., 2015).
- Safe community practices: Most rural inhabitants live far from tertiary hospitals, and the same strategy used in large hospitals is likely to be unsuccessful in the long run. The relevance of individual and group behavior in pandemic control becomes vital in these circumstances. Putting boundaries in place would not be enough to encourage good behavior.

There is fear that coronavirus care will hinder care for persons with other conditions in public health circles, resulting in higher mortality. This anxiety is not illogical. People with life-threatening illnesses have less access to medicines, treatments, and diagnostics. Tuberculosis (T.B.), which kills over 1200 people every day in India, has been demonstrated in prior epidemics to increase fatalities from these underlying illnesses (Mohan Nachiket Mor, 2020).

3.3 Vaccination drive and PHC's role

Having a widespread urban and rural India's Vaccination Program universal immunization program (UIP), it is one of the world's most well-known kinds, targeting over 2.67 crore babies and 2.9 crore pregnant women each year. India lacks adequate resources and preparation for the present COVID-19 outbreak, including vaccine supply, shipping, manufacturing, and availability. The Department of Biotechnology (DBT), according to the government, has backed 10 vaccine proposals, 7 of which are in clinical trials. To streamline COVID-19 vaccine logistics, India built the Electronic Vaccine Intelligence Network (eVIN). It automates vaccine stock management, cold chain monitoring, and logistics at all levels of vaccine storage across the country.

The massive immunization campaign in India started on January 16, 2021. The health ministry planned to vaccinate four target categories: healthcare employees, people over 50, public workers, and people under 50 with comorbidities, with the first two groups receiving vaccinations first in a 30-million-person launch, but COVID-19's second wave was a cause for worry, and the government opened the immunization for above 18 years to combat the virus. The status of immunization program is stated below (Graph 3).

In their recent announcement dated June 7, 2021, the Central Government has rolled out a new policy of vaccinating the country free of cost, wherein private hospitals can procure 25% vaccine from the manufacturer directly and the rest the Central Government will use 75% to vaccinate

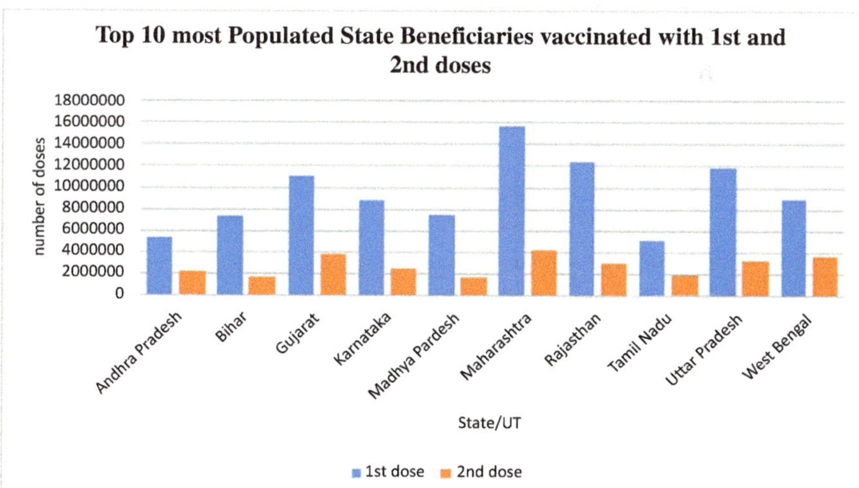

Graph 3 Top 10 most populated beneficiaries vaccinated with a first and second dose of coronavirus. *(Source: https://www.mohfw.gov.in/pdf/CumulativeCovidVaccinationCovergeReport as of May 28, 2021.)*

the people of India. This is indeed a landmark announcement during these crucial times.

State governments and hospitals will now buy vaccinations directly from manufacturers under the Central Government's revised vaccination program.

Because India is the world's largest vaccine producer, it appears that vaccines are in short supply. Experts estimate that vaccinating India's entire population would take years at this pace (BBC News, 2021).

The ability to operate cold chains that keep vaccines is dependent on the availability of electricity. Nearly 5% of rural PHCs in India, which serve over 2.8 million people, do not have access to electricity. As the government prepares for the COVID-19 immunization campaign, there is an opportunity to improve the energy efficiency of rural hospitals by designing better structures and investing in renewable energy sources such as solar. To accelerate a vaccination drive, the government has plans to seek associated healthcare professionals such as pharmacists and public health officials as pharmacists know cold chain storage that might help maintain the doses of the vaccine safe (Kumar et al., 2021).

3.4 How the present crisis can be an opportunity for change in the healthcare industry

Recent memory's most significant health crises have revealed our healthcare system's many flaws and imbalances and the importance of investing in "well-being" personally and systemic. It has brought in a new era of digital and technological advancements that will assist communities in meeting their requirements much more promptly. The question is what can be done in the future with the knowledge gained from this situation. Here are a few things that can be made to prevent similar crises in the future.

- Potential for job creation in the healthcare sector: India's healthcare sector has experienced a rapid and sustained expansion in recent years, resulting in many job openings. According to research conducted by KPMG and the FICCI, the healthcare business grew to become the fifth-largest employer in 2015; according to the National Sustainable Development Commission, the health sector will directly employ over 7.5 million people by 4, with around 2.7 million new employments created between 2017 and 4—an average of over 500,000 new positions per year. The health industry can employ many women employees. According to the WHO study, economic growth is boosted by USD

0.77 due to indirect and induced impacts for every dollar spent in the health sector.

- National Digital Health Mission (NDHM): Our honorable Prime Minister Narendra Modi announced the launch of the NDHM in his address to the nation on India's 74th Independence Day. The mission's goals include creating databases of public and private hospitals, health service providers, laboratories, and pharmacies, improving clinical decision-making, and delivering Telemedicine services (Sarwal et al., 2021).
- Medical manufacturing adoption: Nontraditional businesses like the auto and defense industries are experimenting with producing ventilators and lifesaving equipment. N95 masks, for example, are made by Honeywell, while ventilators are made by Tesla and Mahindra Auto. However, their long-term ability to work in the medical device industry is unknown. Still, such companies may think of diversifying in these areas as they have massive potential in the future.
- Greater Focus on Digital Technology: Digital interfaces for remote patient monitoring and teleconsultations for nonemergency or elective physician consultations will become more common in the sector. Digital tools are already in use for contact tracing and some of the most notable technological advancements.

4 Discussion

When the first case of COVID-19 was reported in India on January 27, 2020, nobody knew that this monster would engulf 37,04,099 Indians (Ministry of Health and Family Welfare, 2021) within 15 months. Telemedicine services are gaining popularity, and the government has introduced new regulations to make it a lawful business in India. The Ministry of Health and Family Welfare (MoH&FW) has announced new rules in collaboration with NITI Aayog to allow medical practitioners to work from home. In addition, the government has launched the NDHM to address the country's health issues (National Digital Health Mission). Health I.D.s, Telemedicine, health records, e-pharmacy, and Digi-doctor services are all part of this goal.

PHC is critical for ensuring global health security and accelerating progress toward universal health coverage. Strengthening PHC now will protect communities from future COVID-19 variants and other disease threats, aid in the recovery of social and economic activities by ensuring people's health, and contribute to long-term global health goals.

More money should be put into primary healthcare, particularly in low- and middle-income nations, so that individuals may obtain inexpensive, accessible, and high-quality treatment regardless of where they reside or their circumstances.

- More and better data should be produced and used to aid leaders in identifying significant deficiencies in health systems far before the next crisis comes.
- Protect and support PHC workers as the backbone of robust health systems. They provide the tools they need to effectively combat COVID-19, prevent future disease outbreaks, and offer access to critical services.
- As part of the Ayushman Bharat National Health Protection Scheme, the Indian Government wants to refurbish and build 150,000 primary care centers (Gopichandran and Subramaniam, 2020).
- Nonetheless, to strengthen PHC in India and drastically boost their capacity and functions during a pandemic, a significant focus on infrastructural upgrades like ordering more ventilators, etc.
- Governments must make the most of these expenditures by stressing primary healthcare as the foundation for a healthier, more equitable future (Ministry of Health and Family Welfare 2021a). The key to this achievement is the availability of quality and competitive medical facilities and skilled doctors at reasonable pricing and supportive immigration and insurance coverage, further investments in innovation, and growth by the Indian Government.

It is a wake-up call for us, and what is most important thing right now is to take the lessons learned from this pandemic and apply them in various Indian states where healthcare systems can be improved. We need to invest in and prepare healthcare workers for this epidemic; launch a massive public-education campaign, and establish a robust surveillance system to help reduce the spread and fatalities.

5 Conclusion

Coronavirus took the world by storm, and we have not recovered from it yet. To fight this monstrous virus, the government raised its budget allocation from 52,800 crores for health in 2018–19 (Business Today on May 13, 2021) to over ₹2.2 lakh crores in 2021–22. More than 15 types of health insurance schemes and policies are available for Indian citizens by the Government of India. The Indian pharmaceutical industry, which stands as the third-largest producer globally, has been growing exponentially. All this and many more are happening in the Indian healthcare industry. The healthcare sector was also significantly impacted and underwent various changes. This pandemic has affected almost one-sixth population as India being the second-most populous country globally, with a population of 1.35 billion. Both the business and public sectors were involved in the overall response to the pandemic. Private Indian healthcare organizations stepped up and provided the government with all of the resources needed, including testing COVID cases, quarantine facilities, medical professionals, and requisite equipment at government COVID-19 hospitals and home care. India's healthcare market is predicted to grow to USD 372 billion by 4, thanks to improved healthcare knowledge, increased income, and easier access to insurance. The Indian Government wants healthcare spending to reach 2.5% of GDP (gross domestic product) by 2025 (Sarwal et al., 2021).

Therefore, a study of its trends and forecasts is essential to formulate effective strategies.

India, specifically, has a long way to go in this race. India has to take essential measures to increase the number of investments and resources in this sector. The quality of health services, the access to health facilities for everyone, and the preparedness for handling any such emergencies in the future have to be looked at. Gaining self-dependency in research and development, technology, raw materials, and production cannot be overlooked.

Glossary

ASHA Accredited Social Health Activists is a community of health workers governed by the Ministry of Health and Family Welfare in India, in 2005.

FICCI Federation of Indian Chambers of Commerce and Industry (FICCI) is an association of Indian business organizations established in 1927 and is dedicated to promoting the growth and global competitiveness of Indian businesses.

Ministry of AYUSH The Ministry of Ayurveda, Yoga, Naturopathy, Unani, Siddha, Sowa-Rigpa, and Homeopathy is purposed with developing education, research, and propagation of indigenous alternative medicine systems in India.

NBCFDC National Backward Classes Finance and Development Corporation was established in 1992 by the Government of India to improve and develop the economic activities for the members of Backward Classes who live below double the poverty line.

NDHM The National Digital Health Mission aims to develop the backbone necessary to support the integrated digital health infrastructure of the country. It will bridge the existing gap among different stakeholders of the Healthcare ecosystem through digital highways.

NHM The National Health Mission was launched by the Indian Government in 2013 by combining National Rural Health Mission and National Urban Health Mission, which aims to provide universal access to quality healthcare, affordable and equitable.

NHP National Health Policy is the decisions, plans, and actions undertaken by the Indian Government to achieve specific healthcare goals in India.

NITI Aayog This is a public policy think tank of the Government of India, established to achieve sustainable development goals with cooperative federalism by fostering the involvement of State Governments of India in the economic policy-making process using a bottom-up approach.

NSDC National Skill Development Corporation is a not-for-profit public limited company incorporated on July 31, 2008, under section 25 of the Companies Act, 1956, as a Public-Private Partnership model by the Ministry of Finance in India.

PHC Primary Health Centre, sometimes referred to as public health centers, are state-owned rural healthcare facilities in India.

PM-JAY Pradhan Mantri Jan Arogya Yojana is the most significant health assurance scheme in the world, which aims at providing a health cover of Rs. 5 lakhs per family per year for secondary and tertiary care hospitalization to over 10.74 crores poor and vulnerable families (approximately 50 crore beneficiaries) that form the bottom 40% of the Indian population.

Pradhan Mantri Garib Kalyan Anna Yojana It is a food security welfare scheme announced by the Government of India in March 2020 during the COVID-19 Pandemic in India.

Primary healthcare State-owned rural healthcare facilities in India.

Secondary healthcare District hospitals and Community Health Caters at the block level.

Tertiary healthcare Third level of the health system in which specialized consultative care is provided, usually on primary and secondary healthcare referral.

References

Abdel-All, M., Abimbola, S., Praveen, D., Joshi, R., 2019. What do Accredited Social Health Activists need to provide comprehensive care that incorporates non-communicable diseases? Findings from a qualitative study in Andhra Pradesh, India. Hum. Resour. Health 17 (1), 73.

Bajaj, A., 2021. Healthcare Industry in India Is Projected to Reach $372 bn by 2022. https://www.investindia.gov.in/sector/healthcare. (Accessed 25 May 2021).

BBC News, 2021. India Coronavirus: Over-18s Vaccination Drive Hit by Shortages (Online) https://www.bbc.com/news/world-asia-india-56345591. (Accessed 4 June 2021).

Budd, J., Miller, B., Manning, E., Lampos, V., Zhuang, M., Edelstein, M., Rees, G., Emery, V., Stevens, M., Keegan, N., Short, M., Pillay, D., Manley, E., Cox, I., Heymann, D., Johnson, A., McKendry, R., 2020. Digital technologies in the public-health response to COVID-19. Nat. Med. 26 (8), 1183–1192.

Chaturvedi, A., 2020. Delhi Launches an App to Help Track Hospital Beds for Covid-19 Patients (Online). Hindustan Times. https://www.hindustantimes.com/india-news/delhi-launches-app-to-help-track-hospital-beds-for-covid-19-patients/story-hXqAkjGqze28mQIVPcGZTM.html. (Accessed 25 July 2021).

Chew, N., Lee, G., Tan, B., Jing, M., Goh, Y., Ngiam, N., Yeo, L., Ahmad, A., Ahmed Khan, F., Napolean Shanmugam, G., Sharma, A., Komalkumar, R., Meenakshi, P., Shah, K., Patel, B., Chan, B., Sunny, S., Chandra, B., Ong, J., Paliwal, P., Wong, L., Sagayanathan, R., Chen, J., Ying Ng, A., Teoh, H., Tsivgoulis, G., Ho, C., Ho, R., Sharma, V., 2020. A multinational, multicentre study on the psychological outcomes and associated physical symptoms amongst healthcare workers during COVID-19 outbreak. Brain Behav. Immun. 88, 559–565.

Correspondent, S, 2021. Coronavirus | World's Largest Vaccination Programme Begins in India on January 16 (Online). The Hindu. https://www.thehindu.com/news/national/coronavirus-worlds-largest-vaccination-programme-begins-in-india-on-january-16/article33582069.ece. (Accessed 25 May 2021).

Covid19.who.int, 2021. WHO Coronavirus (COVID-19) Dashboard (Online) https://covid19.who.int/. (Accessed 30 May 2021).

Dayalani, V., Dayalani, V., Staff, I., 2021. Telemedicine: A Post-Covid Reality in India (Online). Inc42 Media. https://inc42.com/datalab/telemedicine-a-post-covid-reality-in-india/. (Accessed 4 June 2021).

Dst.gov.in, 2021. Integrated Geospatial Platform to Help Area-Specific Strategies & Decisions in COVID-19 Outbreak | Department of Science & Technology. [Online]. Available from: https://dst.gov.in/integrated-geospatial-platform-help-area-specific-strategies-decisions-covid-19-outbreak>. (Accessed 17 September 2021).

ETHealthWorld, 2021. Indian Healthcare Industry in 2018 and Forecast for 2019. ET HealthWorld. [Online]. ETHealthworld.com https://health.economictimes.indiatimes.com/news/industry/indian-healthcare-industry-in-2018-and-forecast-for-2019/67286959. (Accessed 25 May 2021).

Garg, S., Basu, S., Rustagi, R., Borle, A., 2020. Primary health care facility preparedness for outpatient service provision during the COVID-19 pandemic in India: cross-sectional study. JMIR Public Health Surveill. 6 (2), e19927. https://publichealth.jmir.org/2020/2/e19927. (Accessed 28 May 2021).

Ghosh, A., 2021a. What Is CoWIN, and What You Need to Register on the App for Covid Vaccine Shot. The Print (Online) https://theprint.in/health/what-is-cowin-and-what-you-need-to-register-on-the-app-for-covid-vaccine-shot/579307/. (Accessed 28 July 2021).

Ghosh, P., 2021b. What Is Covid Severity Score? Govt's New Software for Better Covid-19 Management (Online). Hindustan Times. https://www.hindustantimes.com/india-news/what-is-covid-severity-score-govt-s-new-software-for-better-covid-19-management-101624103804398.html. (Accessed 25 July 2021).

Gopichandran, V., Subramaniam, S., 2020. Response to Covid-19: an ethical imperative to build a resilient health system in India. Indian J. Med. Ethics 05 (02), 89–92. https://doi.org/10.20529/ijme.2020.026.

IANS, 2021. Johns Hopkins-Supported App to Guide Covid Patients at Home in India (Online). News18. https://www.news18.com/news/india/johns-hopkins-supported-app-to-guide-covid-patients-at-home-in-india-3885473.html. (Accessed 24 July 2021).

India Brand Equity Foundation, 2021. Indian Pharmaceuticals Industry Report (Online). India Brand Equity Foundation.

Indian Council for Medical Research, 2021. Total Operational (Initiated Independent Testing) Laboratories Reporting to ICMR (Online) https://www.icmr.gov.in/pdf/covid/labs/archive/COVID_Testing_Labs_30052021.pdf. (Accessed 1 June 2021).

Jha, A., 2021. Second Wave Spreading Much Faster in Rural India Than First. https://www.hindustantimes.com/india-news/second-wave-spreading-much-faster-in-rural-India-than-first-101620416984127.html. (Accessed 25 May 2021).

Kantis, C., Kiernan, S., Bardi, J., 2021. UPDATED: Timeline of the Coronavirus | Think Global Health (Online). Council on Foreign Relations. https://www.thinkglobalhealth.org/article/updated-timeline-coronavirus. (Accessed 20 May 2021).

Kaul, R., 2020. Covid-19: New Software in Focus for Registry of Deaths (Online). Hindustan Times. https://www.hindustantimes.com/india-news/new-software-in-focus-for-registry-of-deaths/story-vkI73C8ZLNqUTPlMom20KI.html. (Accessed 26 July 2021).

Kumar, R., 2020. Fever, flu, and family physicians during COVID 19 pandemic 2020 in India. J. Fam. Med. Prim. Care 9 (4), 1781 (Online) https://www.jfmpc.com/article.asp?issn=2249-4863;year=2020;volume=9;issue=4;spage=1781;epage=1783;aulast=Kumar. (Accessed 28 May 2021).

Kumar, V.M., Pandi-Perumal, S.R., Trakht, I., et al., 2021. Strategy for COVID-19 vaccination in India: the country with the second-highest population and number of cases. npj Vaccines 6, 60. https://doi.org/10.1038/s41541-021-00327-2.

Kurian, O.C., 2021. Running to Stand Still: Healthcare in India in 2021. https://www.orfonline.org/expert-speak/running-stand-still-healthcare-india-in-2021/. (Accessed 27 May 2021).

M/o Statistics & Programme Implementation, GOI – MOSPI, 2016. India – Social Consumption - Health Survey: NSS 71st Round, Schedule 25, January–June 2014. National Sample Survey Office.

Mahajan, P., Kaushal, J., 2020. Epidemic trend of COVID-19 transmission in India during lockdown-1 phase. J. Community Health 45 (6), 1291–1300.

Megsres.nic.in, 2021. Salient Features of MGNREGA | Official Website of State Rural Employment Society, Government of Meghalaya, India. [Online]. Available from: https://megsres.nic.in/salient-features-mgnrega. (Accessed 17 September 2021).

Ministry of Health & Family Welfare, 2021a. Containment Plan: Novel Coronavirus Disease 2019 (COVID 19): Version 2 (Online). Ministry of Health & Family Welfare. https://www.mohfw.gov.in/pdf/Containmentplan16052020.pdf. (Accessed 4 June 2021).

Ministry of Health and Welfare, Government of India, 2017. National Health Policy (Online). Ministry of Health and Welfare, Government of India, p. 28. https://www.nhp.gov.in/nhpfiles/national_health_policy_2017.pdf. (Accessed 25 May 2021).

Mishra, A., 2019. Healthcare Industry 2018 Recap 2019 Forecast. https://www.medicalmagazine.in/healthcare-industry-2018-recap-2019-forecast/. (Accessed 26 May 2021).

Mohan Nachiket Mor, P., 2020. Covid-19 Crisis: Shift Focus From Hospitals to Primary Care. BusinessLine by Times of India (Online) https://www.thehindubusinessline.com/opinion/covid-19-crisis-shift-focus-from-hospitals-to-primary-care/article31278485.ece. (Accessed 3 June 2021).

MoHFW, 2021a. Micro Plan for Containing Local Transmission of Coronavirus Disease (COVID-19) (eBook). Ministry of health and Welfare, Government of India, pp. 1–26. https://www.mohfw.gov.in/pdf/ModelMicroplanforcontainmentoflocaltransmissionofCOVID19.pdf. (Accessed 28 May 2021).

MoHFW, 2021b. MoHFW. [Online] Mohfw.gov.in https://www.mohfw.gov.in/. (Accessed 27 May 2021).

Mukherjee, I., 2021. Covid Vaccine Export: India Exports over Twice the Number of Doses Used at Home. India News – Times of India. [Online] The Times of India https://timesofindia.indiatimes.com/india/india-exports-over-twice-the-number-of-doses-used-at-home/articleshow/81540812.cms. (Accessed 2 June 2021).

National Portal of India, n.d. https://www.india.gov.in/spotlight/ayushman-bharat-national-health-protection-mission. Ayushman Bharat. National Health Protection Mission. National Portal of India.

News, W., 2021. Significant Undercount of Covid-19 Deaths Globally, Real Number About 2 Times Higher Than Official Stats. WHO – Times of India. [Online] The Times of India https://timesofindia.indiatimes.com/world/us/significant-undercount-of-covid-19-deaths-globally-real-number-about-2-times-higher-than-official-stats-who/articleshow/82848634.cms. (Accessed 22 May 2021).

Orissadiary.com, 2021. CCI Approves Acquisition by Siemens Healthineers Holding I Gmb (SHS GmbH) of Varian Medical Systems, Inc. (Varian). [Online] orissadiary.com

https://orissadiary.com/cci-approves-acquisition-by-siemens-healthineers-holding-i-gmb-shs-gmbh-of-varian-medical-systems-inc-varian/. (Accessed 2 June 2021).
Pib.gov.in, 2021. Finance Minister Announces Rs 1.70 Lakh Crore Relief Package Under Pradhan Mantri Garib Kalyan Yojana for the Poor to Help Them Fight the Battle Against Corona Virus. [Online] Available from: https://pib.gov.in/PressReleasePage.aspx?PRID=1608345. (Accessed 14 September 2021).
Poovanna, S., 2020. Covid-19: Karnataka govt Develops Software to Manage Shortage of Hospital Beds. [Online] mint https://www.livemint.com/news/india/covid-19-karnataka-govt-develops-software-to-manage-shortage-of-hospital-beds-11593930441365.html. (Accessed 26 July 2021).
Press Information Bureau, 2021. COVID Vaccination Administration Training Programme for Health Care Workers Belonging to Target Group of NBCFDC (Online) https://pib.gov.in/Press Release Detail.aspx?PRID=1694468. (Accessed 2 June 2021).
Press Trust of India, 2021. Covid Effect: 1,952 Employees Dead, 1,000 Infected Daily, Says Railways. https://www.business-standard.com/article/indian-railways/covid-effect-1-952-employees-dead-1-000-infected-daily-says-railways-121051000958_1.html. (Accessed 25 May 2021).
Priyamvatha, P., 2021. How India's Second Covid Wave Started, What Went Wrong, and What Can Be Done: top Virologist Answers (Online). India Today. https://www.indiatoday.in/coronavirus-outbreak/story/india-second-covid-wave-start-went-wrong-top-virologist-answers-details-1795743-2021-04-28. (Accessed 24 May 2021).
Rai, R., Tripathi, S., de Lange, A.H., 2021. Healthy healthcare systems in India: a prognosis. In: Tevik Løvseth, L., de Lange, A.H. (Eds.), Integrating the Organization of Health Services, Worker Wellbeing and Quality of Care Towards Healthy Healthcare. Springer Nature Switzerland AG, https://doi.org/10.1007/978-3-030-59467-1 (Accessed 28 May 2021).
Ranga Rao, S., 1993. Administration of Primary Health Centres in India. Mittal Publications, New Delhi, India.
Rastogi, A., 2019. Mission Indradhanush. https://www.nhp.gov.in/mission-indradhanush1_pg. (Accessed 25 May 2021).
Ray, S., 2021. India Declares 'Black Fungus' Epidemic as Infections Rise Among Covid-19 Patients. https://www.forbes.com/sites/siladityaray/2021/05/20/india-declares-black-fungus-epidemic-as-infections-rise-among-covid-19-patients/?sh=38fe3f7110af. (Accessed 25 May 2021).
Rekha, M., 2020. COVID-19: Health Care System in India. Health Care: Curr. Rev. (S1), 262. https://doi.org/10.35248/2375-4273.20. S1.262.
Sachan, D., 2021. How Will COVID-19 Shape the Future of the Healthcare Industry? [Online] Cyient.com https://www.cyient.com/blog/medical-technology-healthcare/how-will-covid-19-shape-the-future-of-the-healthcare-industry. (Accessed 4 June 2021).
Sahay, A., 2020. Indian Startup Develops Covid 19 Detecting Mobile App, Takes 5 Minutes. Hindustan Times. https://www.hindustantimes.com/india-news/indian-startup-develops-covid-19-detecting-mobile-app-takes-5-minutes/story-pB69DtRslPDJkx3tF1gOdN.html (Accessed 25 July 2021).
Saprii, L., Richards, E., Kokho, P., Theobald, S., 2015. Community health workers in rural India: analysing the opportunities and challenges Accredited Social Health Activists (ASHAs) face in realising their multiple roles. Hum. Resour. Health 13 (1), 95.
Sarwal, R., Prasad, U., Madangopal, K., Kalal, S., Kaur, D., Kumar, A., Regy, P., Sharma, J., 2021. Investment Opportunities in India's Healthcare Sector (Online). NITI Aayog. https://niti.gov.in/sites/default/files/2021-03/InvestmentOpportunities_HealthcareSector_0.pdf. (Accessed 22 May 2021).

Standard, B., 2021. International News: World News Headlines, World Breaking News, Global News. [Online] Business-standard.com https://www.business-standard.com/international?time=1622423456. (Accessed 20 May 2021).

Statista Research Department, 2021. Estimated Value of Public Health Expenditure in India From Financial Year 2017 to 2020. https://www.statista.com/statistics/684924/india-public-health-expenditure/#:~:text=In%20fiscal%20year%202018%2C%20the,percent%20of%20the%20country's%20GDP. (Accessed 26 May 2021).

TechnoFunc, 2021. Sectors of Healthcare Industry. Technofunc.com. https://www.technofunc.com/index.php/domain-knowledge/healthcare-industry/item/sectors-of-healthcare-industry. (Accessed 23 May 2021).

The Economic Times, 2021. Ten States Account for Over 73 Per cent of New COVID-19 Cases in India. Read more at https://economictimes.indiatimes.com//news/india/ten-states-account-for-over-73-per-cent-of-new-covid-19-cases/articleshow/82516130.cms?utm_source=contentofinterest&utm_medium=text&utm_campaign=cppst. (Accessed 30 May 2021).

The Hindu, 2020. How Does the Aarogya Setu App Work? (Online) https://www.thehindu.com/news/national/how-does-the-aarogya-setu-app-work/article31532073.ece. (Accessed 27 July 2021).

The Hindu, 2021. Healthcare Industry Welcomes Increased Budget Allocation. [Online]. Available from: https://www.thehindu.com/business/budget/healthcare-industry-welcomes-increased-budget-allocation-for-health-well-being/article33717111.ece. (Accessed 17 September 2021).

Varma, A., 2021. Second COVID-19 Wave in India: Here Are Some Challenges & Points of Concern (Online) https://www.republicworld.com/india-news/general-news/second-covid-19-wave-in-india-here-are-some-challenges-and-points-of-concern.html. (Accessed 25 May 2021).

WION, 2021. Coronavirus Second Wave Hits Countries as Lockdown Ends (Online) https://www.wionews.com/photos/coronavirus-second-wave-hits-countries-as-lockdown-ends-308495. (Accessed 20 May 2021).

World, G, 2020. Top Indian Apps to Fight COVID-19 (Online). Geospatial World. https://www.geospatialworld.net/blogs/top-indian-apps-to-fight-covid-19/. (Accessed 25 July 2021).

Further reading

Associates, D, 2021. COVID-19 in India: Updates Till December 31, 2020 – India Briefing News (Online). India Briefing News. https://www.india-briefing.com/news/covid-19-india-december-31-2020-20585.html/. (Accessed 22 May 2021).

Chathukulam, J., John, M.S., 2000. Empowerment of women panchayat members: learning from Kerala (India). Asian J. Women's Stud. 6, 66–101.

Declaration of Alma-Ata, n.d. International Conference on Primary Health Care, Alma-Ata, USSR, 6–12 September 1978. https://www.who.int/publications/almaata_declaration_en.pdf?ua=1 (Accessed 7 January 2021).

Government of India, 2021. Indian Public Health Standards (IPHS) Guidelines for Primary Health Centers. Revised 2012. [Online] Clinicalestablishments.gov.in. http://clinicalestablishments.gov.in/WriteReadData/360.pdf. (Accessed 25 May 2021).

Independence Day 2018, PM Narendra Modi May Announce National Healthcare Policy on August 15; Ayushman Bharat Cover for 10 Crore Poor Families. https://www.india.com/business/indepedence-day-2018-pm-narendra-modi-may-announce-national-healthcare-policy-on-august-15-ayushman-bharat-to-offer-rs-5-lakh-cover-to-10-crore-poor-families-3222173/. (Accessed 26 May 2021).

Khazir, M., Abdullah, S., Tangade, P., Jain, A., Gupta, A., 2018. How Primary Health Care was originated in India. TMU J. Dent. 5 (3), 10–12 (Online) http://www.tmujdent.co.in/pdf/vol5issue3/vol%205%20issue%203_04.pdf. (Accessed 28 May 2021).

Mahajan, P.B., 2010. ROME scheme: from reorientation to research-oriented medical education, a new beginning. Indian J. Med. Res. 132, 110 (Medline: 20693602).

Ministry of Health & Family Welfare, 2020. Containment Plan: Novel Coronavirus Disease 2019 (COVID 19): Version 2. https://www.mohfw.gov.in/pdf/Containmentplan16052020.pdf. (Accessed 23 May 2021).

Ministry of Health & Family Welfare, 2021b. Micro plan for containing local transmission of coronavirus disease (COVID-19).

Mohfw.gov.in, 2021. MoHFW. Home (Online) https://www.mohfw.gov.in/. (Accessed 24 May 2021).

Organization, W. and (UNICEF), U, 2021. Immunization in the Context of COVID-19 Pandemic: Frequently Asked Questions (FAQ). 16 April 2020. [Online] Apps.who.int https://apps.who.int/iris/handle/10665/331818. (Accessed 28 May 2021).

PM Office, 2021. Cabinet Approves the Allocation of Additional Food Grain to NFSA Beneficiaries Under Pradhan Mantri Garib Kalyan Anna Yojana (Phase III) for Another Period of Two Months, May and June 2021. [Online] Pmindia.gov.in https://www.pmindia.gov.in/en/news_updates/cabinet-approves-allocation-of-additional-foodgrain-to-nfsa-beneficiaries-under-pradhan-mantri-garib-kalyan-anna-yojana-phase-iii-for-another-period-of-two-months-may-and-june-2021/?comment=disable. (Accessed 27 May 2021).

Pmkisan.gov.in, 2021. Home. [Online] Available from: https://pmkisan.gov.in/. (Accessed 17 September 2021).

Press Information Bureau Delhi, 2021. Key Highlights of Union Budget 2021–22 (Online) https://pib.gov.in/PressReleasePage.aspx?PRID=1693907. (Accessed 1 June 2021).

Royal, A., Mali, M.A., Kumar, V., Wagh, I.A., Bhushan, S., Mokal, A.N., Mehta, K., Bhattacharya, S., 2021. Harnessing the potential of the primary healthcare facilities in India to respond COVID-19 Pandemic: a scoping evidence-based research synthesis. J. Fam. Med. Prim. Care 10, 116–121 (Online) https://www.jfmpc.com/text.asp?2021/10/1/116/307936. (Accessed 31 May 2021).

Social Consumption, 2014. In: Health Survey: NSS 71st Round, Schedule 25, January–June 2014, India (pdf). http://www.icssrdataservice.in/datarepository/index.php/catalog/107,DDI-IND-MOSPI-NSSO-71Rnd-Sch25pt0-Jan-June-2014. (Accessed 25 May 2021).

Tatacapitalblog, 2020. What Are the Steps Taken by the Government to Fight Coronavirus in India? https://www.tatacapital.com/blog/trends/what-are-the-steps-taken-by-the-government-to-fight-coronavirus-in-India/. (Accessed 25 May 2021).

Ved, R., Gupta, G., Singh, S., 2019. India's health and wellness centres: realizing universal health coverage through comprehensive primary health care. WHO South East Asia J. Public Health 8 (1), 18–20. https://doi.org/10.4103/2224-3151.255344. Medline: 30950425.

World Health Organization, 1978. Primary Health Care: Report of the International Conference on Primary Health Care Alma Ata, USSR, 6–12 September 1978. Geneva, Switzerland. (Google Scholar).

World Health Organization, 2020. Coronavirus Disease 2019 (COVID-19): Situation Report-51. World Health Organization. https://www.who.int/docs/default-source/coronaviruse/situation-reports/20200311-sitrep-51-covid-19.pdf?sfvrs n=1ba62e57_10. (Accessed 2 April 2020).

Worldometers.info, 2021. COVID Live Update: 171,010,903 Cases and 3,556,329 Deaths From the Coronavirus. Worldometer (Online) https://www.worldometers.info/coronavirus/#countries. (Accessed 19 May 2021).

CHAPTER SEVEN

Benefits and use of blockchain technology to support supply chain during COVID-19

Giuseppe Ciaburro
Department of Architecture and Industrial Design, Università degli Studi della Campania Luigi Vanvitelli, Borgo San Lorenzo, Aversa, Italy

1. Introduction

Blockchain is a decentralized distributed database consisting of a chain of blocks, containing chronologically correlated transactions validated by a system of cryptographic algorithms and rules. The data, once entered within the blocks, can no longer be modified without the consent of the majority of the system (Nofer et al., 2017). Each record is stored in such a way as to contain a portion of data referable to previous transactions: This connection makes alteration virtually impossible without it being immediately visible to the entire network. In turn, the blocks to become part of the chain are subjected to a validation process based on the principle of distributed consent, a consent that makes superfluous the figure of a supervisor to ensure its legitimacy. The blockchain is therefore a decentralized ledger based on the principle of distributed trust which, thanks to its innovative configuration, does not require a third party who guarantees its incorruptibility because it is its very nature that protects it (Zheng et al., 2018).

Our company is facing an important challenge that no technology has been able to solve so far. This is the so-called trust gap which defines the degree of trust on the part of users in making a transaction. Today, in fact, it is not possible to execute a transaction without the intermediation of a third party in which the contracting parties place their trust (Wüst and Gervais, 2018). But according to some scholars this model, due to its inefficiencies, is doomed to fail. In this regard, there have been numerous crises that have hit the economic system in recent decades, most recently the financial crisis of 2008 which originated from the collapse of the US banking giant Lehman and Brothers. These critical issues have brought user confidence levels to an all-time low in regard to institutions (Li et al., 2020).

Lessons from COVID-19
https://doi.org/10.1016/B978-0-323-99878-9.00003-0

The Internet that once promised to be a strength for democratic information has divided public opinion, facilitated the spread of fake news, and allowed populists to foment contempt for journalists, scientists, and real facts. Until then, the only way to carry out digital transactions of any kind was entrusted to the validation by an intermediary, who confirmed the identity of the contracting parties and the consistency of the declared assets (Klems et al., 2017). Intermediaries such as banks and large social media have thus become the guarantors of trust and consequently the guarantors of the operation. This system has obvious limitations, is senselessly slow, expensive and can suffer cyber-attacks. In addition, the profit created by the digital revolution has been distributed asymmetrically to large intermediaries (Dinh et al., 2018).

Before the birth of the blockchain, any digital asset was infinitely copyable. There was no technological mechanism capable of confirming or not, without the control of an intermediary, that a certain amount of money had not already been spent. To date, when information is exchanged on the Internet, using the http protocol, an exact copy of the data to be transmitted is sent to the recipient (Pilkington, 2016). Obviously, if the transaction or exchange of information has money as its object, this mechanism cannot be adopted unless an intermediary comes into play. This is because, when a transaction is made, it is the single entity, the single information that must be sent and not a copy of it. Thanks to the contribution offered by the distributed database, it is in fact possible to avoid that a given sum of money is the subject of more than a single transaction, thus solving the problem of double spending. Thanks to blockchain technology, a new system has been established in which trust is not in the hands of intermediaries but is established through cryptography and intelligent code: Trust is the basis of this new medium of exchange (Yli-Huumo et al., 2016). A blockchain allows to eliminate the intermediary allowing the parties to trust the system through the mechanism of consent. Consensus is the foundation on which distributed systems are structured. The blockchain is a tool that allows to reach consensus in the execution of a collective activity that involves entities that do not necessarily trust each other, but that have a common goal (Risius and Spohrer, 2017).

A Supply Chain is a network of individuals, organizations, resources, activities, and technologies involved in the processes of creating and selling products or services, from raw materials to the final product (Mentzer et al., 2001). The primary objective of a supply chain is to satisfy demand in the quantities, time and place required with the lowest possible cost, bringing added value to the end customer (Beamon, 1998). Within the supply networks there are a certain number of entities, which have a common interest, but which, at the same time, are separate and therefore do not necessarily trust each other. Supply Chain Management (SCM) is the management of this supply network, which aims to integrate the organizational units along the supply chain and coordinate material, information, and financial flows to satisfy customer requests, improving the competitiveness of the supply chain (Min and Zhou, 2002). The supply chain must be conceived as a value system to which all the players in the chain contribute. The success of the entire system depends on the ability of the individual players to interact with each other. The continuous connection between all the nodes of the network and at the same time between the companies and the final customers becomes an essential element and the basis of a new business model in which the physical and information flows must be extended beyond the boundaries of the company. Blockchain technology has the potential to fundamentally change supply chain management (Casado-Vara et al., 2018). The use of smart contracts to manage supply relationships, the tracking of products and information at every level of the supply chain, the birth of decentralized marketplaces are just some of the applications of this technology (Amr et al., 2019).

In this chapter we will first introduce the basic concepts of blockchain technology, and then move on to the analysis of the essential characteristics of the supply chain. Finally, the applications based on blockchain technology adopted to address the difficult emergency due to COVID-19 will be analyzed, focusing attention on Blockchain-based solutions for the management of the anti-COVID-19 vaccination campaign.

The chapter is organized as follows: In Section 2, Blockchain technologies are described in detail. Fundamental topics such as consent, transaction, smart contract, and proof of work are addressed. Section 3 introduces the essential concepts of the supply chain, analyzing the applications of these concepts in different fields. Section 4 explores examples of applications of Blockchain technology in the management of the COVID-19 pandemic with reference to the administration of vaccines. Finally, Section 5 summarizes the essential points of the work.

2. Introducing blockchain basic concepts

A blockchain is essentially a transactional ledger distributed between nodes connected in a peer-to-peer communications network. To record a transaction, an agreement must be reached between the participants through a consent mechanism: No one will be able to modify the data without the permission of the other participants (Cachin, 2016). By sharing the database across multiple nodes, the blockchain eliminates the need for intermediaries, which were previously required to verify, coordinate and record transactions. Despite its recent history, the blockchain is evolving toward multiple applications and declinations, even moving away from the original concept of Bitcoin, developed by Nakamoto. The birth of Blockchain technology coincides precisely with the appearance of Bitcoin, which constitutes its first historical application. Everything, therefore, begins in November 2008, when the mysterious Satoshi Nakamoto publishes a paper (Nakamoto and Bitcoin, 2008), which illustrates the operation of the Blockchain technology as originally conceived. Bitcoin was born as a tool for the realization of a well-defined project: Creating a virtual payment system independent of institutions. Compared to other virtual currencies, Bitcoin has achieved relatively wide circulation since it was the first to solve the double-spending problem. This consists of making a digital transaction while maintaining the original copy of the exchanged currency (Badertscher et al., 2017). To solve this risk, Bitcoin has exploited distributed ledger technology, which replaces the centralized intermediary in its role of recording each transaction. But since anyone can read and write to the ledger, security issues could arise if any actor attempts to tamper with the ledger. Bitcoin offers a solution to this problem by creating an incentive to behave correctly (Garay et al., 2015). Some actors, called miners, group transactions into blocks by solving a computational problem, called proof of work, which requires hardware with a high computing capacity. Miners who successfully create a block are rewarded with Bitcoin, thus creating a strong incentive to act correctly. In fact, the mining process, in addition to being expensive from a computational point of view, requires an enormous amount of electricity, thus discouraging any hackers to act incorrectly (Calvão, 2019).

A blockchain network is made up of nodes, defined as computational entities that communicate and work jointly with other nodes to complete a transaction: A node can operate on both physical and virtual hardware. In most blockchain networks, each node performs a certain action, such as generating and propagating blocks. In these networks one or more nodes will temporarily assume the role of leader, however, in some networks the nodes play multiple roles instead (Zheng et al., 2017). In a centralized network, all resources, hardware, and software, are stored in a single point. All other systems must connect to this node to have access to resources whenever they need them. While this system offers more control, it is not transparent and furthermore, if you pass this single point of access, you will have access to all data. A decentralized system allocates hardware, software, and computational resources in different workstations. The resources are then divided between the nodes and each node requests the resource it needs to use from the other (Belotti et al., 2019). This structure attributes effective features to the chain (Fig. 1).

The blockchain is therefore a distributed ledger of blocks that holds valid transactions that have been performed on the peer-to-peer network. Each block contains a timestamp of creation and a hash, or pointer, that links each block to the previous one: This continuous link forms a chain. The distributed structure is the key feature concerning the blockchain. A distributed network, unlike centralized and decentralized networks, is a system where data and resources are replicated on various nodes. Each node keeps a record of the transactions between the various nodes on the network. The nodes identify themselves with each other via the IP (Internet Protocol) address, while each node can send a transaction to any other node on the network if it knows the recipient's public key, without any central authority involved in the transaction. The absence of a central server therefore strengthens the security of the system (Aste et al., 2017).

In a peer-to-peer network, nodes can communicate directly with each other without the need for a central authority. There are no hierarchies as each node is at the same level but, depending on the type of blockchain, the nodes can however perform different functions, such as miner, validator, database, etc.

2.1 Distributed databases

Information systems architectures have developed and evolved over the years, passing from centralized schemes to distributed and widespread

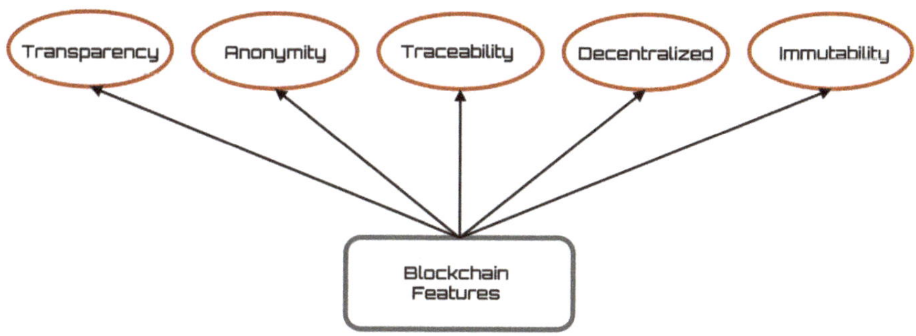

Fig. 1 Blockchain features.

models, more responsive to the decentralization and cooperation needs of modern organizations (Ceri, 2017).

A centralized computer system is therefore characterized by the fact that the data and applications reside in a single processing node, while a distributed computer system is characterized by at least one of the following two conditions:

1. The applications, cooperating with each other, reside on several processing nodes (distributed processing)
2. The unitary information assets are hosted on several processing nodes (distributed database)

When an organization is geographically distributed, it can choose to store its database on a central server or to distribute it to several local servers. A distributed database is a single logical database physically spread over several computers connected to each other by a telematic network. We emphasize that a distributed database is truly a database, not a series of files. The distributed database is still centrally managed as a business asset, providing local flexibility and customization capabilities. The network must allow users to share data, so a user in location A must be able to access the data stored in location B. Sites in a distributed system can be spread over a large area or a small area. Computers can range from PCs to large servers or even supercomputers (Muzammal et al., 2019).

A distributed database requires multiple instances of a Database Management System (DBMS), running on each remote site. The degree to which these different DBMS instances collaborate or work in partnership characterizes the different types of distributed database environments. It is important to distinguish between distributed and decentralized databases. A decentralized database is similarly stored on computers in multiple locations; however, the computers are not linked together by a network to make the data appear to be stored in a single logical database (Fig. 2). Thus, users located at the various sites cannot share data. A decentralized database can be thought of as a collection of independent databases, rather than having the geographic distribution of a single database (Halaburda, 2018).

A distributed system is therefore made up of a set of spatially separated autonomous entities that communicate and coordinate their respective actions with each other through the exchange of messages. The reasons that push an organization to choose to distribute data across multiple sites may be different, and we will analyze some of them below. Modern organizations are often geographically distributed, sometimes even across national borders. In some cases, each unit has the power to create its own information systems,

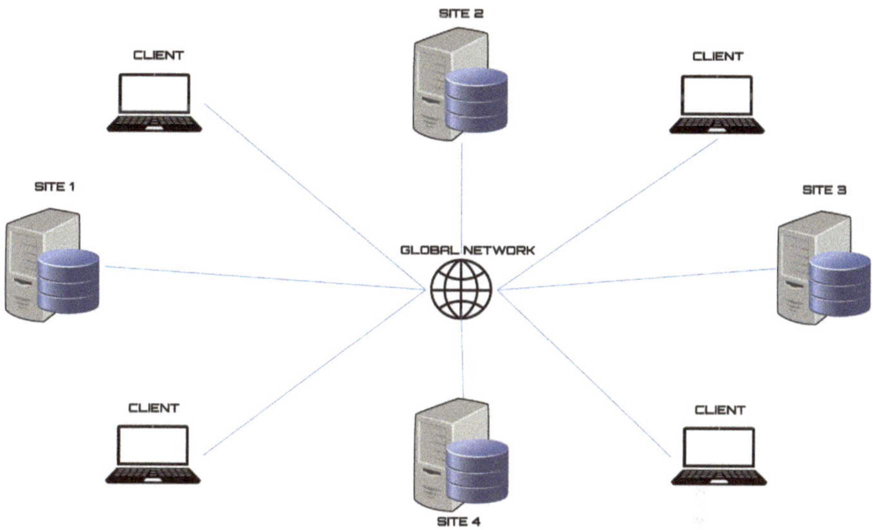

Fig. 2 Distributed database architecture.

and these units process local data over which they cannot have control. Corporate mergers and acquisitions frequently create such conditions (Chowdhury et al., 2018). Another reason is that of the need to share data; decisions in moderately complex business environments require sharing of data between different work units, so it is necessary to consolidate data through local databases accessible on demand. To all this are added economic reasons related to the costs and reliability of the system. The costs of managing large amounts of data across a communications network or managing a large volume of transactions from remote sources can still be high, even though they have dropped significantly recently. So much so that in many cases it can be cheaper to store data and applications where they are needed. Furthermore, the dependence on communication systems by the database always involves an element of risk, which determines the need to have local copies or fragments of data to guarantee the reliability of the system and rapid access to data throughout the organization (Lo et al., 2017).

Today, many organizations purchase packaged application software from various vendors. Each package is designed to work with its own database, and possibly with different database management systems. A distributed database can, in this case, be particularly useful for providing functionality to applications.

Replicating data from distributed databases across several separate computers is a strategy to ensure that a damaged database can be quickly recovered, and users can have access to the data while the primary site is being restored. Replicating data across multiple sites is a natural form of a distributed database. Replication is a typical property of the distributed DBMS that allows you to allocate the same portions of the database on different nodes. Replication is considered useful to reduce the transfer of information between the different nodes within the same transaction or query. The use of replication increases the locality of the data used by each application but introduces the problem of multiple transactions, that is, transactions to be performed on multiple nodes simultaneously (Tapscott and Tapscott, 2017).

2.2 Distributed database security

In recent years, the storage, retrieval, and sorting of information have become increasingly important in many sectors of society, this has led to growing attention to issues related to database security. As regards some fields of use of databases, we can even say that data security is to be considered a priority aspect over others, in fact, while an incorrect design, which provides a very slow but safe database, could also be accepted by a banking institution, a well-optimized database that allows anyone to modify its data would be clearly unacceptable for any company (Rhee et al., 2005).

Data security generally includes two aspects:

1. data protection using encryption techniques
2. control over access to data.

While the problems related to cryptography to secure the storage or sending of data are common to many IT sectors, the problem of controlling access to data, which we will deal with, is more specific to traditional and distributed databases.

We can enumerate three basic security stages for each database:

1. user authentication
2. control authorization to view the data
3. prevention or reduction of attacks through inference channels

The first two points can be shown with a common situation for a database. When a user requests access to the system, the first task of the DBMS is to positively authenticate it, usually via the user-id/password pair; once connected to the system, the user will presumably submit queries to the database, before replying it is again the task of the DBMS to ensure that the user is authorized, by the database administrator, to view the requested data (Bertino and Sandhu, 2005).

The last point is a problem specific to relational databases and is based on the possibility, by unauthorized users, of obtaining confidential information through logical procedures without accessing the protected data.

Generally, we can assert that the problems related to the three stages presented can be solved in traditional databases with common sense, experience and above all with careful planning. As far as distributed databases are concerned, however, the scenario is considerably complicated. In fact, the possibility of designing and implementing a distributed database in various ways means that the resolution of security problems raises conceptual questions even before implementation (Maurya et al., 2020).

Returning to the security stages of a database, user authentication is a prerequisite for each system, correct identification allows, in fact, to determine the user's privileges and group. During the design phase of a distributed database, the first question to ask, regarding security, is who will be responsible for authenticating users.

2.3 Elements of a blockchain

Blockchain technology is characterized by its constituent elements which, through a synergistic process, create a complex system capable of returning an automatic system of transactions (Sherman et al., 2019). The constituent elements of a Blockchain are listed and described in the following list (Fig. 3):

- Transaction: The transaction is that good, value or information that is exchanged between two or more subjects on a blockchain platform and that needs to be approved and verified and archived. It consists of information regarding the transaction and a Cryptographic Key, which is a set of public key cryptographs that allow the verification of users' identity (Durach et al., 2021).
- Cryptography: Cryptography is the discipline that studies how to make information secure, that is, confidential and intact, by taking a plaintext and transforming it into ciphertext, which is incomprehensible to those who do not know the details of the transformation. Confidentiality is a concept like privacy but is only one component of it: it refers to the ability to protect data from those who are not authorized to read it. Integrity, on the other hand, refers to the ability to protect data from unauthorized changes (Fernández-Caramés and Fraga-Lamas, 2020). To protect information with encryption, it must be transformed into something equivalent but not decipherable and not easily traceable to the original: this is

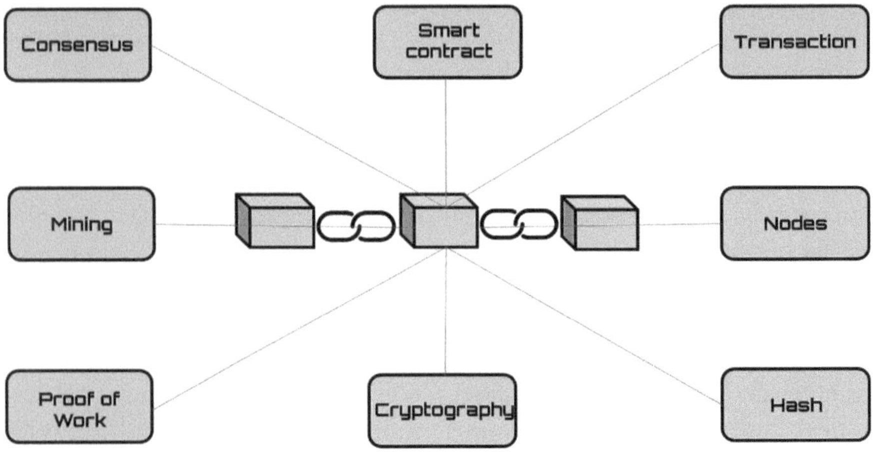

Fig. 3 Key elements of a blockchain.

the act of encryption. Deciphering, on the other hand, is the reverse operation: from an encrypted communication its original, clear, and intelligible form is obtained again. A well-defined procedure for encrypting and decrypting data is called a cryptographic algorithm and, to work, it may require the use of one, no or more keys, conceptually like the passwords we are used to using. A system based on public key cryptography is reliable and secure since it does not require the seller to use the buyer's private information, such as his credit card number. Transactions take place through the exchange of signed information.

- Mining: Mining is the process that creates new blocks, validated, and adds them to the Blockchain; the nodes that carry out the mining process are called miners. Each miner goes through a series of steps that lead to the production of a new block: It collects and decides which information, gathered from the peer-to-peer network, to include in a new block. Verify that all transactions it included in the block are valid. It selects the most recent block in the longest branch of the block chain and inserts a hash of that block into the new block it is creating. He tries to solve the proof of work for the new block and at the same time observes what other new blocks are created by other nodes. If it finds a solution to the proof of work problem, the new block is added to the chosen chain and shared on the network. If another node solves the proof-of-work problem first, its block is subjected to validity checks. If it is valid, it is added to a local copy of the Block Chain and shared on the network, otherwise it is discarded. As miners try to create new blocks simultaneously, with most of their time spent solving the proof of work problem, it happens that there are different versions of the Blockchain at a given time (Wang et al., 2019). This happens because new blocks are created regularly every 10 min, so during this time all nodes try to solve the proof of work. When a node finds a valid solution, it earns a certain number of bitcoins as a reward, provided for by the protocol, shares the block on the network and the nodes that receive the new block, after verifying it, add it to their chain, starting to work on a new block. In this way the nodes synchronize approximately every 10 min.

- Nodes: A node is any hardware device capable of communicating with other devices belonging to the same network. The various nodes are connected to each other and each of them also acts as a server for the management of transactions within the network.
- Consent: Consensus protocols are essential as they allow the proper functioning of any blockchain system. In practice, these are the algorithms that regulate the transaction validation mechanism and establish the rules by which such transactions are transcribed on the latter to form blocks. It is precisely these consensus mechanisms that break the paradigm of the more classic centralized consensus in favor of institutions around the world (Benchoufi et al., 2017). The consensus mechanisms guarantee that the information aggregated to the blocks is true and reliable, two of the most used mechanisms are the proof of work (PoW) and the proof of stake (PoS).
- Proof of work: It plans to put the miners of the network in competition, offering compensation in cryptocurrency for the resolution of a series of very complex computational problems to validate and add a block of transactions within a chain. This approach is characterized at the same time by an almost perfect security, to the detriment of what are perceived as the main limitations of proof of work, that is, slowness and high energy expenditure (Kumar et al., 2019).
- Smart contracts: Indicates computerized contracts programmed to be executed automatically, when preset conditions are fulfilled. Although the smart contract can also be conceived independently of the blockchain, only the characteristics of the latter guarantee that the smart contract cannot be modified and the automatic execution of the computer code that is its essence. In other words, smart contracts do not necessarily have to exist in a blockchain, but only blockchain technology and its platform are, at present, capable of providing them with the security

and reliability that allow them to overcome the need for recourse to a third-party authority and intermediaries. The smart contract, in essence, represents one of the possible applications of the blockchain, among the most advanced and interesting, and it is therefore necessary to treat the two institutions as intimately connected and connected (Singh et al., 2020).

- Hash: The hash code of a block represents its authentication code. It can be considered as the digital signature that determines its uniqueness and ensures the inviolability of the entire block. The hash of the reference block records all the information relating to, while the hash with the information relating to the previous block allows you to create the chain and link one block to another. In practice, it starts from a variable-length data string (input) which is then processed by the hash function, transforming the string to a predefined length (Ren et al., 2020).

2.4 Blockchain architecture

Every single block of a Blockchain is a structure that records transactions that will then be included in the register. A transaction is a change of state that changes blockchain data from one value to another. A block includes the block header, a list of valid transactions, the hash of the previous block and its hash: A single block can contain many transactions. If a block is tampered with, the hash changes and the corresponding hashes of all subsequent blocks in the chain will also need to change for the chain to still be recognized as valid: This waterfall pattern ensures that a block cannot be changed without forcing a change in at least 80% of the blocks of the chain (Syed et al., 2019) (Fig. 4).

The enormous computational and energy power required to carry out this operation makes the blockchain practically immutable: The greater the number of blocks that have been added to the chain, the greater the security of the system. The block header contains three sets of data: the pointer to the previous block (hash), a series of information such as timestamp and proof of work and finally a report of all the transactions contained in the block. The first block in a chain is called the genesis block and each new block is added on top of the previous one. Therefore, each block can be identified in two ways: through its cryptographic hash or through its position in the chain identified by the block height, which defines the number of blocks that precede it in the blockchain (Vincent et al., 2020). The position of a block in the chain or its distance from the genesis block can be used to

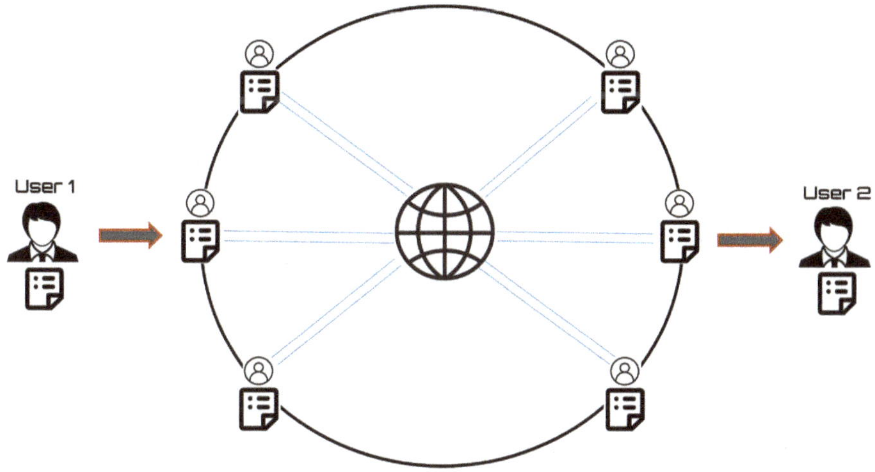

Fig. 4 The Blockchain architecture.

identify the block. However, this position may not be unique due to the presence of bifurcations in the chain (fork). A hard fork occurs when updates are made to the programming language or technology underlying the blockchain. In the context of cryptocurrencies, if the fork were not resolved, it would lead to two different versions of the coin, which could compromise its value. The number of confirmed blocks in the entire Blockchain is called Block Height.

2.5 Blockchain operation

Each node on the network has a set of keys: one private and one public. The private one is used to encrypt the transaction before it is sent. To send a transaction, the sender needs his private key and the recipient's public key. Before being registered on the Blockchain, the transaction must undergo two phases: one for signature and one for verification (Fu and Zhu, 2019). The data encryption by the sender through the private key is defined as the signing phase. The verification phase, on the other hand, consists in the solution of a computational problem (proof of work), which ensures that the same transaction does not occur twice. Proof-of-work involves looking for a value that, once hashed. In this phase, the time stamp of the block also takes place, which further strengthens the security of the chain by associating the block with a legally valid date and time (Niranjanamurthy et al., 2019). The transaction mechanism can be divided into five stages (Fig. 5):

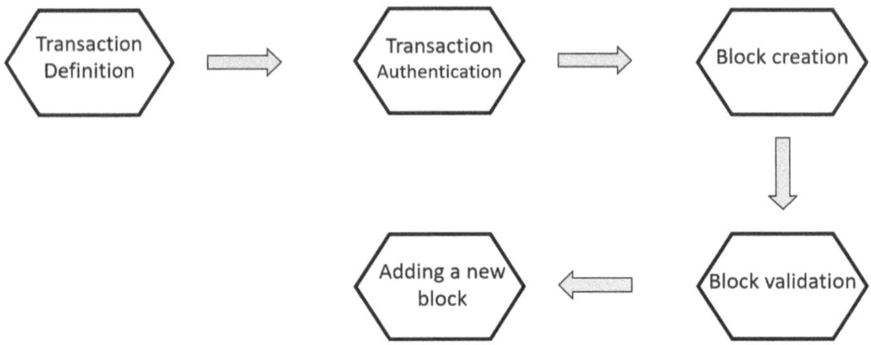

Fig. 5 Transaction mechanism.

1. Transaction definition: The sender generates the transaction by specifying the recipient's public key details and the transaction value. Additionally, this transaction must be authorized with the sender's cryptographic digital signature, which verifies that the transaction is valid and secure.
2. Transaction authentication: Once sent to the network, the transaction is received by the nodes, which authenticate it by decrypting the digital signature. This transaction waits in a pool of pending transactions until a block is created.
3. Block creation: Each node of the network takes charge of the transaction combining it with other pending transactions and creating a block. Subsequently, each node works to solve the proof of work related to its block and, once solved, they transmit it to all the other nodes.
4. Block validation: The nodes in charge of validating the received block accept it only if all the transactions in it are valid and have not already been spent.
5. Block chain: After each transaction recorded in a block has been accepted, the new block is connected to the last block in the chain. The updated version of the chain is then sent to the network, which accepts it as the updated version on which future blocks will be recorded. The nodes express acceptance of the block by attempting to create the next block in the chain, using the hash of the block accepted as the previous hash.

The blockchain is a system that uses cryptography to secure transactions. This concept leads to a redefinition of the intermediary's role as guarantor of the validity of the system. Trust is now based on the consensus mechanism, a process in which most validators in the network come to an agreement regarding the state of the registry (Dogru et al., 2018).

The main elements of a consensus mechanism are:

- Decentralized structure: No central authority can finalize processes or transactions
- Quorum: Nodes exchange messages through a predefined set of steps
- Authentication: This protocol is used to verify the identity of the participants
- Integrity: Strengthens the validation and verification of the integrity of the process
- Nonrepudiation: Used to verify that the sender has sent the message
- Privacy: This protocol ensures that only the actual recipients of a message have access to it
- Error tolerance: Network configuration that ensures that the efficiency and speed of operations are not compromised by the failure of individual nodes or servers.

For example, the consensus mechanism exploited in Bitcoin cryptocurrency is based on the longest chain mechanism, where the chain with the greatest proof of work is defined as the valid one. However, some limitations of the original Blockchain technology have facilitated the exploration of new consensus mechanisms. New platforms have tried to create more scalable and more energy efficient mechanisms to reach consensus among the network nodes. The "proof of work" (PoW) mechanism consists in solving a mathematical computational problem to link the hash related to the transaction with that of the last block registered on the blockchain. However, this computational process must be supported by very powerful hardware, which therefore will require a substantial supply of energy (Dhillon et al., 2017). By multiplying the energy consumed for a single transaction by the total of transactions required per second, there will be a large demand for both electrical and computing energy. To compensate for the increase in hardware speed over time, the difficulty of proof-of-work is determined by a moving average that aims to create an average number of blocks per hour. If the blocks are generated too fast, the difficulty increases. The "proof of stake" (PoS) mechanism represents a valid alternative to the PoW scheme, as it is based on a more efficient computational procedure. Even though the blocks are generated in a similar way to the PoW, the hashing procedure takes place in a limited search space, instead of the unlimited space of the PoW. In this way the transaction can be processed in less time and the system will be faster and require less energy (Kim and Deka, 2020). However, this system is not without risks, in fact, the probability that a miner is chosen for the creation of a block depends on the quantity of "coins" it possesses and not on the computational power.

3. Supply chain explained

A Supply Chain is a network of individuals, organizations, resources, activities, and technologies involved in the processes of creating and selling products or services, from raw materials to the final product (Stevens, 1989). The primary objective of a supply chain is to satisfy demand in the quantities, time and place required with the lowest possible cost, bringing added value to the end customer. Supply Chain Management (SCM) is the management of this supply network, which aims to integrate the organizational units along the supply chain and coordinate materials, information, and financial flows to meet customer requests by improving the competitiveness of the supply chain (Lambert and Cooper, 2000).

Supply Chain Management is a network of distribution facilities and means whose function is to obtain materials, the transformation of these materials into intermediate products and finished products, and the distribution of these finished products to the end user (Fig. 6). Use synchronized and efficient processes that generate value for the company. A supply chain consists of three parts: procurement, production, and distribution (Mentzer et al., 2001). The supply part focuses on how, where and when the raw materials for production and the different services required are purchased and supplied. Supply Chain Management becomes a management model that integrates human capital, processes, and technology. The goal is to synchronize and integrate the flow of materials and services, the flow of information and the flow of money of an organization. Currently, supply chain management is a vital issue in business and is taking on a prominent place

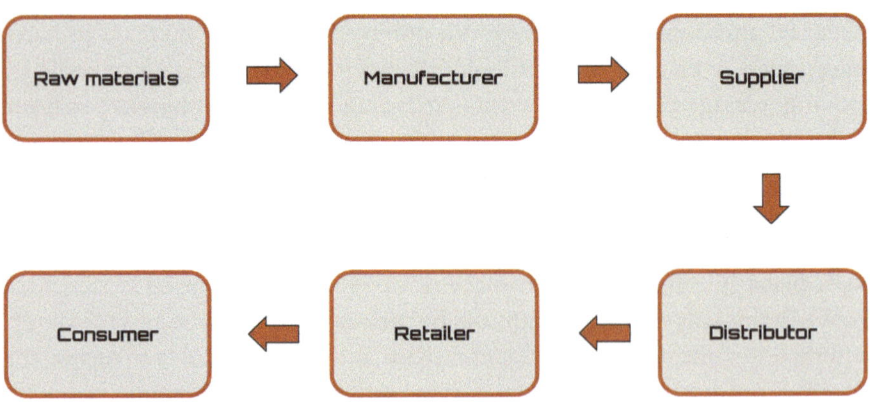

Fig. 6 Supply Chain Management flow.

around the world. With increasingly competitive markets, we need to have a very efficient use of resources. We live in a highly globalized world, where corporate supply chains have improved exponentially. In the past it was believed that the logistics area did not generate value for the company, but today all successful international companies have improved their supply chain through its implementation and, consequently, reduce costs and optimize processes to obtain a worldwide advantage (Davis, 1993).

Crucial in the management of the supply chain is the correct management of the supply chain, which represents a chain in which each node must function and return a product that meets expectations. A problem in the chain gear leads to low product quality that generates a bad reputation of the company, no customer loyalty, poor product acquisition or in the worst-case total rejection by the customer (Beamon, 1998).

It therefore becomes essential to associate the planned activities with a control system of the effectiveness of each step of the process. For this control to be fully effective, it must be carried out by an independent body acting as guarantor. Only in this way will the trust of all components of the supply chain be ensured. In this context, Blockchain-based technologies can provide that added value to ensure technological progress imposed by the new paradigms of Industry 4.0 (Min and Zhou, 2002).

3.1 Supply chain basic concepts

A supply chain is made up of all parties involved, directly or indirectly, in satisfying a customer request. It includes not only the manufacturer and suppliers, but also transport, warehouses, retailers and even the customers themselves. Within each organization, the supply chain includes all the functions necessary to receive and satisfy a customer request. These functions include, but are not limited to, new product development, marketing, operations, distribution, finance, and customer service. All these functions can be summarized in a matrix that highlights the various steps and planning activities necessary for each organization area (Croxton et al., 2001).

This definition highlights two contexts: intraorganizational context and interorganizational context. In the intraorganizational context, decisions are made regarding sales order processes, demand forecasting and planning, distribution, procurement, and production planning. In the interorganizational context, on the other hand, a company is involved in a network of customers and suppliers who exchange flows of materials and information with each other (Hugos, 2018).

The network of a supply chain consists of facilities, transportation resources, storage resources, human capital, and inventory. Its complexity is determined by the fact that each independent organization can have one or more suppliers and customers who in turn could have as many suppliers and as many customers. In addition, logistical third parties may be involved, which can provide goods or services to the company and send them back to the company itself or directly to the customer. Within this network, material, information, and money are exchanged between the various levels. It is precisely because of this high complexity that the complete management of every constituent element of the chain is essential, which also includes cost reduction among the objectives. The supply chain must efficiently integrate all its actors in such a way as to minimize costs at the system level and satisfy high service targets. Regardless of the type of production, industrial sector or size, every company needs to control the flow of materials from the supplier to the end customer as an essential step to achieve a good level of service. Therefore, as a key block in the supplier-customer chain, product distribution and procurement need to be managed properly within companies, without underestimating their importance (Ellram, 1991).

The operations in the modern supply chain are very complex and consist of some phases ranging from the receipt of raw materials to the delivery of the final product to the consumer. The process consists mainly of the following stages:

- Determination of the availability of raw materials and costs. Before the product can begin to be made, it is important to plan where and how the raw materials can be purchased, the time needed to receive them and the quantities available.
- Transformation of raw materials into finished products. This phase varies from company to company, depending on the structure and organization.
- Finished products are shipped to the distribution center through a distribution network planning.
- The distribution facility uses the products to supply a retail store on time.
- The products are delivered into the hands of the consumer with the aim of fully satisfying his needs.

From the procurement of raw materials to the final delivery of goods, companies rely on the supply chain to manage the procedure quickly and efficiently. Supply chains determine when the product must be made, delivered to the warehouse and storage centers, and finally delivered to a retail store or shipped (Simatupang and Sridharan, 2002).

It is a rather complex procedure which, being widely variable, is based on past experiences and future forecasts that try to consider delays and other volatilities. Today's supply chains are under pressure from many points of view, trying to keep up with an increasingly demanding environment. Phenomena such as Industry 4.0, globalization and digitization translate into an increasingly complex, hyperconnected business context, in which data and information are the masters. In today's world, customer service needs, working capital and operating costs are set to rise, and supply chain leaders in many industries are reporting increasing chain complexity. The supply chain landscape is changing faster than ever, leading many companies to reduce investment to survive (Thomas and Griffin, 1996).

Since traditional supply chains are fragmented and operate through independent organizations that focus primarily on local optimization, most of today's supply chains appear as analog machines attempting to solve the problems of a digital world. They appear as decentralized structures, which are unable to survive in the new business environment. The major operational challenges that must be faced are:

- Response times: The current supply chain structure, built on independent silos, ensures that the decision-making process is linear. The passage of information from one functional structure to another is therefore long and laborious, creating wasted time and delays that result in response times to the market that are too high for the current context.
- Lack of visibility: Traditional supply chain processes and the technologies used do not allow for end-to-end visibility along the chain. This lack of visibility is evident at the ordering, production, and shipping level. It therefore results in imprecise and not always consistent planning, which causes an increase in unnecessary costs, as well as a difficulty and inability to detect specific problems that could spread throughout the entire network.
- Conflicts of priorities: Independent organizations in a supply chain are characterized by their metrics, their Key performance indicators (KPIs) and their priorities. Each of these elements is aligned with the business needs of the organization itself. It is complicated within a fragmented global network to coordinate all the priorities of individual independent organizations; this can easily lead to delays, conflicts of interest and inefficiency along the supply chain.
- Inefficient supply model: The new multichannel world is very complex and consequently difficult to manage by the static structure of traditional fragmented supply chains. They were built based on the concept of large volumes and limited number of items. Today's world is instead

characterized by high customization, punctual and rapid orders, which require greater organizational and planning efficiency following a common line from upstream to downstream.
- Inflexible technology: Existing technological platforms for managing supply chains appear to be static and inflexible, too expensive, and complicated. Not agile enough to address the growing demands of todays and future supply chains.
- Lack of advanced transversal skills: In current conditions, there seem to be numerous operational gaps regarding transversal skills between one element of the supply chain and another. The competencies present among supply chain organizations are often too specific and not broad enough to understand end-to-end dependencies.

The extent of the changes required to readjust a company to the new world is significant and requires efforts on the part of individual organizations that must readjust to the complex system situation, forgetting the traditional linear system. The key steps in moving to the next generation of the supply chain, such as, a collaborative digital supply chain, involve the decomposition of functional silos that need to be reorganized into a more efficient structure, the redefinition of priorities and the exchange of data in real time, aimed at to the creation of schedules and synchronized realizations (Bozarth et al., 2008).

The entire Supply Chain sector must necessarily transition from a linear system to a complex system: In the modern industrial sector, the evolution of demand and the increase in competition are pushing producers and distribution to reformulate strategic choices and reorganize processes, operational. To achieve ambitious goals of efficiency and effectiveness in response to market demand, companies are led to seek greater levels of integration between activities. The traditional logic of Supply Chain Thinking and the management rules consolidated up to now are based on the erroneous assumption that supply chains are linear systems. Considering this vision, it would be possible to divide the supply chain into its individual components, optimize the performance of each of them, and obtain an optimized overall system. With a linear view of the supply chain, in which the output is a linear function of the individual inputs, it should be stable and simple to manage and optimize. The reality, however, is different; Complex Adaptive Systems (CAS) science provides a new description of supply chains, according to which the supply chain is a complex and nonlinear system (Chan, 2001). Adaptive complex systems are characterized by groups of agents linked in a process of co-adaptation, in which the adaptation moves of each have consequences for the entire group of individuals. The supply chain must therefore be a nonlinear system, whose behavior is not equal to the sum of the individual parts that compose it, but rather is due to the interactions between them. According to this concept, a small change in initial conditions can lead to large shifts elsewhere. It is essential that the value chain has an efficient organization, because all the links contribute to giving value. The first step necessary to enable the desired progress in the supply chain is to understand this new reality and then apply more efficient solutions and be able to optimize processes. Unfortunately, most supply chains still follow the old style: fragmentation and little flexibility. If previously the focus was on the optimization of some logistic functions within the same company, for example transport and the distribution structure, now the attention must be shifted to the whole of the supply chain processes, functions that in the traditional approach were not so close they must now be strongly linked together.

The integration of the supply chain into a complex ecosystem can take place not only intracompany but also intercompany. In fact, due to the greater dependence on the network, it is now impossible to think of a single company's supply chain strategy. Each of the members of the chain is influenced by the objectives and decisions of all the actors; it is not enough to focus attention only on internal activities, but it is necessary to extend the integration also to all the actors outside the company boundaries who contribute with varying intensity to the achievement of the objectives.

3.2 Blockchain in supply chain management

The importance of distribution, in a world where international trade multiplies and electronic commerce generates an exponentially increasing number of orders, means that many transactions related to transactions are digitized to connect the physical world of the circulation of goods. The supply chain can be made up of many stages and locations, making it increasingly difficult to track each stage in the chain as a result. Furthermore, the lack of transparency on the part of the supply chain hinders the trust between the parties involved in the process, making it impossible for the final consumer to be sure of the true value of the product or service he is purchasing. A series of bad practices occur around the supply chain, such as counterfeiting, the black market, forced labor or poor working conditions, the responsibility of which is very difficult to investigate. Blockchain technology can provide transparency and security to this entire process, thus strengthening the supply chain management (SCM). Even the simplest blockchain application, such as recording all transactions in a distributed ledger, could reveal new data that benefits the supply chain enormously (Francisco and Swanson, 2018).

The technological advances that have characterized the economic and industrial landscape in the last 20 years have led to the end of linear supply chains, giving rise to dynamically connected Digital Supply Networks (DSNs), able to better respond to market dynamics. The introduction of these new configurations has substantially transformed the way in which companies exchange and share information, leading to the birth of complex ecosystems in which processes are integrated with each other. In any case, the management of information and the control of interactions between products and supply chain actors remains a very complex activity. In fact, it requires careful collection of data and their secure archiving to guarantee a continuous and reliable flow of information between the various players involved in the chain. In this regard, although digital technologies have favored and simplified the sharing of information and made it possible to address some of the major problems that characterize the supply chain at various levels, their implementation is not without challenges. In fact, in relation to digital transformation, among the difficulties that businesses must face, there is precisely the understanding of which technologies to invest and at what time. This choice can dictate both the rapid progress of the firm and its differentiation and its collapse and/or exit from the market (Korpela et al., 2017).

Despite the continuous innovations and improvements introduced by digital technologies, there are still many challenges that characterize the current supply networks: paper-based processes are still very widespread, and decision making among the various players in the supply chain is becoming increasingly complex. Due to the presence of separate information systems that provide limited visibility on the individual business functions. These difficulties are affecting all industrial sectors across the board and are leading to the emergence of complex ecosystems that are difficult to manage and coordinate.

But many of the challenges that characterize the SCM cannot be faced with current technologies. In fact, there is currently a lack of solutions that allow to support collaboration and cooperation between the different entities involved. In fact, it is precisely from cooperation that the sharing of information arises. This remains the key element in the supply chain to mark the transition from linear structures to integrated ecosystems in which companies collaborate with each other to optimize the management of flows and intercompany processes. Within this context, it seems clear how the blockchain can play a leading role (Saberi et al., 2019).

Let's see now why blockchain is so important and what deeply distinguishes it from the technologies that preceded it. To date, centralized systems have proved to be the most practical tool for obtaining data security and guaranteeing transparency within the Supply Chains. From a strictly operational point of view, blockchain is not a more efficient technology than current centralized data management platforms. In fact, the distributed database requires greater computational power and consequently a greater energy requirement for the operation of the system. Nevertheless, the advantages that derive from its implementation are innumerable and lie precisely in its infrastructure and in the assumptions that constitute its foundations. The blockchain is a tool that allows to reach consensus in the execution of a collective activity that involves entities that do not necessarily trust each other, but that have a common goal. Trust, which is the essential tool to which companies use, when making an exchange or a transaction, up to the birth of the blockchain, was achieved thanks to the involvement of a centralized intermediary: that is, a central authority in which parties placed their trust and that they assumed the burden and responsibility of verifying the integrity and truthfulness of the transactions. In other words, the blockchain is trustless and, thanks to its distributed nature and consensus mechanisms, it allows the participants of a community to trust each other without resorting to a middleman. In fact, it is not necessary that the individual participants trust a particular node but, it is sufficient, that they place their trust in the system (Schmidt and Wagner, 2019).

The above integrates very well with the supply chain: In fact, within the supply networks there are a certain number of entities, which have a common goal and interest, but which, at the same time, are separate and therefore do not trust necessarily of each other. And it is precisely from trust and the communion of intent that the sharing of information between the players in the supply chain can be achieved. Sharing information in an exchange allows, among other things, to reduce the information asymmetry and the transaction costs associated with it. The reduction of costs that companies must face in resorting to the market can bring business models to a stage in which each company is highly specialized and acquires on the market all the goods and services complementary to the creation of products or the provision of services. The blockchain also allows you to establish trust in all those intercompany relationships characterized by the absence of an intermediary. In fact, in such contexts, the companies involved in an exchange rather than in a transaction do not trust each other and there is information asymmetry, they rely on bargaining. In this regard, to date, when two companies share data, financial information, and intellectual property with each other, the trust they develop in each other in relation to integrity and performance is governed by contracts (Abeyratne and Monfared, 2016).

Contracts make it possible to avoid continuous checks, provide guarantees but, above all, reduce risk. Having said that, defining and structuring a contract that offers complete guarantees and protections to companies, as well as being theoretically impossible, is very complex due to the lack of visibility and sharing of information. In fact, today, due to the elongation that characterizes the productive ecosystems, the participants do not know each other and consequently have no visibility on the activities and data that flow within the system. This causes trust to be built in another way. The blockchain acts as an intermediary or provides the infrastructure on which the parties can build trust and carry out exchanges. To date, digital technologies have removed the physical limits that exist in data transfer. For now, the only barrier that still exists and that does not allow the optimization of the information flow is the lack of trust. Blockchain technology can remove this limit, finally allowing us to exploit the real benefits of this hyperconnected era. Before the blockchain, in fact, the great technological innovations starting from the Internet made it possible to solve some of the great challenges that characterized the corporate and social landscape such as digitization, cloud computing, digital data management. But no technology to date has made it possible to solve the problem of lack of trust. That is, no technology has made it possible to guarantee that the information shared between different partners could be used for one's own advantage rather than for the benefit of one's competitors. The blockchain itself has not introduced any technical innovation. In fact, this is based on the combination of already existing technologies which, however, linked together, allow to create an ecosystem that defines a new concept of trust. And within the supply chains there is no lack of digitalization, there is no lack of data management, there is no lack of distributed systems, but there is no lack of trust (Treiblmaier, 2018). The big challenge lies in understanding when to capitalize on blockchain and how to combine it with other digital technologies to generate important benefits within supply networks.

4. Blockchain-based model for vaccine supply chain

Blockchain technology has already been proposed by several studies as a possible solution to the criticalities connected with the management of problems in the health sector.

4.1 Applications of Blockchain technology in healthcare

Below we will analyze some possible application solutions of Blockchain technology to deal with real cases.

- Patient Medical Records (PHR): There are currently numerous medical records in which patients can store the results of various tests (Ivan, 2016; Dimitrov, 2019). Some of these examples are Apple Health or Microsoft HealthVault, which use centralized systems. Using a Blockchain-based system, the data could be stored in a distributed way, allowing the patient to control which data to share and with whom. The rest of traditional health systems, as well as devices, can be connected to this system to perform any type of test and store the result in the Blockchain. Patients will have full control of their data, as well as having an immutable track that shows when which data was accessed and who accessed it (Esposito et al., 2018).
- Data exchange between traditional care and telemedicine: Telemedicine is gaining popularity among patients who need minor but urgent care and, for whatever reason, must avoid long waits in a traditional medical consultation. The data collected and the treatment delivered through this type of system may be inaccessible to primary care physicians, which in turn will result in an incomplete medical history of the patient. This in turn will generally result in a decrease in the quality of future diagnoses and treatments. Using Blockchain it is possible to eliminate the intermediaries that hinder the exchange of medical data and allow direct relationships between telemedicine and general practitioners. A smart contract can be used to organize exchanges between the various health systems (Ahmad et al., 2021).
- Shared patient data management: Most patients diagnosed with some type of disease want to have a second medical opinion on treatment or diagnosis. At present, this process actively involves the patient, as she must obtain all her medical data and hand it over to the second doctor. This process is by no means recommended considering the patient's situation. A possible solution to this problem would be a

Blockchain-based system that acts as an intermediary between patients and multiple healthcare providers around the world (Tian et al., 2019). This system will give the patient total freedom to decide which medical data to share and with whom.

- Addressing opioid substance abuse: There is a health crisis in the United States due to opioid substance abuse. Currently there is abuse both by health professionals, with unnecessary prescriptions, and by the patient who undergoes a real improvement in the short term at the cost of increasing his dependence on these substances. One possible solution would be to create a trust network consisting of hospitals and pharmacies to store opioid-related transactions (Raghavendra, 2019). For hospitals and pharmacies, the existing incentive would be to be able to compile a data set on opioids and their consumers. Likewise, patients could gain an increase in the quality of their medical care thanks to this large dataset and its possible applications, and they could also be better informed about the risks of these substances.
- Shared registry of a disease: Another interesting use case would be the creation of a distributed and shared registry of the medical data of patients with some type of severely disabling disease. Sharing data on these diseases is critical as treatments are complex and highly personalized. The idea is to build a learning ecosystem that using Blockchain allows to share predictive models, built using shared data and that allow medical professionals to obtain prognosis and improve diagnosis and final treatment (Piccininni et al., 2020).
- Health Insurance Management: Clients of health insurance companies who have an accident that results in permanent disability or even death require a monthly income from their insurance or compensation in the latter case. While it is true that there is a certain percentage of fraud, in most cases it is resolved automatically. To expand and ensure said automation, the use of smart contracts is proposed to orchestrate this process (Radanović and Likić, 2018). The entire award process will be transparent to both the insurer and the client, showing possible errors and fraud that could be investigated in a timely manner. These smart agreements could also be used to ensure awareness and updating of current company policies.
- Pharmaceutical Product Safety: According to the World Health Organization, it is estimated that counterfeit pharmaceuticals worth up to US $ 200 billion are sold globally each year and 50% of these drugs are purchased over the Internet. Counterfeiting, in general, occurs when a

manufacturer or distributor takes back a portion of the manufactured drugs and resells them, or introduces counterfeit drugs into the original batches. The problem is that the technological solutions that are being adopted are unable to dispel these illicit acts. Product traceability refers to the tracking of items at the unit level, from start to finish as they move through the supply chain. Thanks to the Blockchain application, all participants in the exchange can access the origin and location, authenticate the elements that make it up and verify compliance with the requirements and agreements (Nørfeldt et al., 2019).

There are numerous authors who have studied possible solutions of Blockchain technology in the health sector to improve current systems by exploiting its intrinsic characteristics. A first application concerned the management of Electronic Health Records (EHR): Chenthara et al. (2020) proposed a framework based on Blockchain technology for the management of Electronic Health Records (EHR). The framework uses the distributed ledger platform Hyperledger. It is a distributed ledger that is a source of replicated, shared, and synchronized digital data geographically distributed across multiple sites, countries, or institutions. The framework created by the authors then uses InterPlanetary File System (IPFS) to store the EHRs. For transaction security, the framework uses a unique cryptographic public key cryptographic algorithm. Hylock and Zeng (2019) have exploited Blockchains to process patient health data. This is sensitive data that must be treated with great caution, which is why the authors have proposed a new blockchain-based framework called HealthChain. To guarantee the exchange of data, the Health Level-7 Fast Healthcare Interoperability Resources was used, which represents a framework for the electronic exchange of health information. Encryption is guaranteed thanks to the generation of a pair of public and private keys. Public keys are stored in the blockchain and are suitable for securing and verifying transactions. Dubovitskaya et al. (2020) have developed an authorized blockchain-based EHR management system. With the use of this system, the patient will be able to manage their health data also referring to multiple hospitals. The protection of the patient's privacy will be guaranteed, as well as the security of health data management, and it will be possible to control access to the patient so that the latter can know who has had access to her data. Xia et al. (2017) proposed a new system for sharing health data based on Blockchain. The system was called MeDShare and ensures data auditing and control, through continuous monitoring of access to data and the adoption of smart contracts. Other applications of Blockchain technology have concerned the personal health record exchange (Lee et al., 2020), the medical data access and permission management (Azaria et al., 2016), the validation of the patient's identity (Mettler, 2016), a secure supply of drugs (Baunm, 2017).

Since about the end of 2019 the world has been affected by the largest pandemic ever recorded so far due to the uncontrolled spread of the virus called COVID-19. The spread of COVID-19 has caught the world off guard. There are still many questions that do not have an answer and perhaps will not have it for a long period of time. Many of the issues that stakeholders intend to analyze concern the future and are because the main world economies, the ones most involved in global value chains, have suffered. The spread of the pandemic was fast and devastating, catching most of the Western states unprepared that had never had to deal with such an emergency, at least in the last century. Nonexistent or at least outdated pandemic plans did the rest. The inability to contain the spread of the epidemic has prompted many states to impose rigorous lockdown policies that have had very heavy repercussions on economies. The evident need for an effective experimentation to produce an anti-COVID-19 vaccine was immediately understood (Van Bavel et al., 2020).

Research centers around the world immediately took steps to identify the gene of the virus and subsequently some of these centers began an experimentation to produce the vaccine. The use of modern technologies also based on the use of artificial intelligence has made it possible to prepare a vaccine in record time and subject it to an experimental campaign to verify its effects first on animals and then on humans. At the end of this phase, the largest vaccine administration campaign ever carried out in the world was carried out with the use of enormous financial and logistical resources. Given the short duration of the experimentation and given the widespread use of the vaccine on a world scale, some criticalities connected with its use only came to the surface during the administration phase, undermining the confidence of the population on the effective efficacy of the vaccines and the severity of the side effects. To overcome these difficulties, a Blockchain-based technology could have made an important contribution to the effectiveness of the vaccine administration campaign.

4.2 Vaccine characteristics

Some diseases caused by viruses, bacteria or fungi can reach humans due to close contact with various animal species. The passage of microbial agents from one species to another can be the main cause of the spread of new epidemics and pandemics. The diseases that result from this close contact between humans and animals are called zoonoses, or diseases that can be naturally transmitted from vertebrate animals to humans and vice versa. Precisely this animal-human transmission would represent the cause of the outbreak of the COVID-19 pandemic, which since the end of 2019 has caused millions of victims around the world (Le et al., 2020).

Coronaviruses belong to a large family of viruses that can be found both within animals and within humans. They are viruses known for their ability to cause diseases ranging from the more well-known cold to more serious diseases such as SARS and MERS. It defines itself as "new coronavirus," that virus that had never been found inside a human organism, exactly what happened in Wuhan, China, in December 2019. Coronaviruses are so called because they present a particular structure that seems to recall that of a crown, an image due to the tips present on their surface (Corey et al., 2020).

A pandemic can be fought through various forms of prevention:

- Primary prevention, whose task is to prevent the disease from manifesting itself. The restrictive measures of the government, social distancing, hand washing, personal protective equipment (PPE), and disinfection of environments are part of primary prevention.
- Secondary prevention, the task of which is to identify a disease early to limit its evolution as much as possible and limit the damage related to it. This category includes screening with molecular and antigenic swabs and contact tracing systems with COVID-19–positive patients.
- Tertiary prevention, the purpose of which is the earliest possible treatment to limit the impact of complications. This category includes pharmacological and nonpharmacological therapies.

It was immediately evident that there is no therapy that has proven to be certainly effective in the treatment of COVID-19 infection. Vaccines are the most effective tools to prevent, control and eliminate infectious diseases and to minimize their impact on humans. Once administered, the vaccines simulate the first contact with the infectious agent, evoking an immunological response like that caused by natural infection, without however causing the disease and its complications. The principle behind this mechanism is immunological memory: the ability of the immune system to remember which foreign microorganisms have attacked our body in the past and to respond quickly. Without vaccinations, our body can take up to 2 weeks to produce enough antibodies to counter the invader. A time interval during which the microorganism can cause damage to our body (Graham, 2020).

Vaccines are biological preparations consisting of killed or attenuated microorganisms, or by some of their constituents (antigens), or by substances produced by microorganisms and made safe (such as tetanus toxoid which derives from the treatment of tetanus toxin) or, again, from proteins obtained with genetic engineering techniques. Vaccines generally also contain sterile water (or a saline-based physiological solution) and some may also contain, in small quantities, an adjuvant to improve the immune system response, a preservative (or an antibiotic) to prevent contamination of the vaccine by part of bacteria, some stabilizers to keep the properties of the vaccine unaltered during storage (Jeyanathan et al., 2020).

Vaccines are drugs, and as with all drugs there are benefits—which consist in the prevention of a disease—and risks of occurrence of adverse events. As with all drugs, a vaccine only enters the market when international regulatory authorities, such as the European Medicine Agency (EMA) in Europe and the Food and Drug Administration (FDA) in the United States, have verified that the benefits outweigh the risks. Naturally, as for all drugs, the surveillance of the benefit-risk profile continues even after placing on the market, first to check if there are any rare adverse events that cannot be highlighted in the premarketing phase, due to their relative limitation. The number of subjects involved in the studies. Over time, the margins of uncertainty still present at the time of registration also reduce (Knoll and Wonodi, 2021).

4.3 Vaccine trust and the limits of information

Vaccine surveillance is part of drug surveillance activities which, according to the WHO definition, is the set of actions undertaken to collect, archive, identify, analyze, evaluate, and inform about the risks and benefits of medicines, to maintain, modify, suspend, or revoke their marketing authorization or any other regulatory action. Vaccine surveillance allows us to analyze the benefit/risk ratio of each vaccine and ascertain that this ratio remains favorable over time. In the presence of an adverse event that occurred after vaccination this is analyzed because the appearance of an adverse event after the vaccine does not necessarily imply that the cause is the vaccine itself (Malik et al., 2020).

Trust in vaccines is trust in the efficacy and safety of vaccines and in the healthcare system that provides them. Trust in vaccines refers to the belief that vaccination serves the best health interests of the public and its members. Public confidence in vaccination is essential to ensure a high prevalence of vaccination. Over the years, researchers have been involved in combating fake news on vaccines and autism, contesting news stories, and providing references in the literature on the subject.

The benefits of vaccination can be difficult to explain to the public. Healthy people may not recognize the role of vaccines in preventing disease and reducing its spread, because vaccinations prevent infectious diseases rather than treat or control their symptoms in nature and therefore have no visible effect on already ill individuals. Vaccines undergo rigorous scientific evaluation by regulatory authorities. Each vaccine is rigorously evaluated for safety, quality, and efficacy to determine if it can be licensed, using all available scientific evidence from animal data, human clinical studies and manufacturing information to assess its benefits and risks.

The perception of the benefits of vaccinations has weakened precisely because of the successes achieved by vaccination policies: it is said that vaccines are the main victims of their successes. As the frequency of prevented diseases decreases, the perception of their danger is lost, and many are led to think that the vaccine is useless. At the same time, doubts about the safety of vaccines, and therefore about their risk/benefit ratio, increase. Healthy people would, in theory, be willing to undergo prevention only if it has zero risk. Several factors have been identified that undermine trust in vaccines and the propensity to undergo vaccination:

1. Complacency: Perceived risks for vaccine-preventable diseases are low and the vaccine is therefore considered unnecessary. Complacency is the result of the success of vaccines. This barrier breaks down by informing about the still existing risks of pathologies.
2. Confidence: includes confidence in the efficacy and safety of vaccines, but also in the institutions that offer it, in the institutions that produce it, in doctors and health personnel. It is also influenced by political and religious ideologies.
3. Convenience: is understood as the accessibility to vaccines (clinic hours, remoteness of the same, any costs to be borne by the user).

4.4 Blockchain solutions for vaccine administration

The development of a vaccine is a very long process, which takes from 7 to 10 years, during which research is conducted in successive stages that include quality tests, preclinical trials, and stages of clinical trials in humans. The clinical trial includes three phases of studies:

- Phase 1: Studies conducted on healthy volunteers for the identification of the optimal dose and the evaluation of safety in humans.

- Phase 2: Exploratory studies conducted on small groups of people, generally fewer than 100.
- Phase 3: Confirmatory studies conducted on thousands or tens of thousands of people.

The development of vaccines to stop the spread of the COVID-19 virus has highlighted the importance of information data in its digital dimension. To significantly reduce the time needed to develop a vaccine, an extremely complex information management was required. The distributed management of data within a certain community, provided for by the blockchain model, allows for a parallel development of the various phases, guaranteeing a significant reduction in time. But this aspect is only one of the many advantages offered by Blockchain technology, we can highlight the problems connected with respecting the privacy of patients who undergo testing protocols, and those who are subsequently vaccinated. Platforms based on Blockchain technology can be regulated in such a way as to provide for decentralized information management with respect for the principle of privacy by design (Ramirez Lopez and Beltrán Álvarez, 2020).

The development of vaccines against COVID-19 has highlighted the importance of digital data, indissolubly tying the development of a vaccine to the information necessary to produce it: The vaccine contains all the information necessary to design it, to produce it and finally to distribute it. The search for a vaccine against COVID-19 required, in fact, to acquire, sift and correct a huge amount of information quickly and efficiently to forge ahead for its distribution. These are genetic information on the virus, biological and genetic information on how the human body reacts to the virus, health information relating to patients who undergo testing protocols first and then once vaccinated must be considered to identify any effects, long-term vaccine. Information relating to the storage conditions of the vaccine, some vaccines, in fact, must be stored at prohibitive temperatures ranging between −90°C and −60°C. Finally, there is also information relating to logistics to be processed once it must be distributed, because you need to know exactly where each vial is and at what temperature it is in order not to frustrate the vaccination campaign (Antal et al., 2021).

The management of this gigantic amount of information that must be collected, stored safely, quickly, and effectively screened to identify any errors and correct them immediately by identifying the right solutions as soon as possible, requires a radical change of approach and use of innovative technologies. Blockchain technology makes it possible to move from centralized management of information data to decentralized management to ensure transparency, speed, and greater efficiency in the use of information needed for vaccine development. Without this support it is not possible to arrive at a ready response to a pandemic that has developed very quickly, hitting hard every corner of the globe. In fact, if on the one hand the production of vaccines was characterized by short times, the distribution of the same took different times depending on the management policy undertaken by the different countries. Difficulty in procurement, and the complex administration procedure required a long time which often slowed down the effectiveness of the vaccination campaign (Yong et al., 2020).

Also, for the administration of vaccines it is necessary to have a third-party guarantor acting as a central bank to guarantee the value of the securities held; this validation process is assured in an equally secure manner by the entire community. The same goes for information regarding vaccines with blockchain technology. These are no longer managed centrally by a single person who first collects all the information, then processes them and searches for errors and, finally, transmits them all to the relevant agency to request authorization according to a linear time. Instead, this information is immediately made available to the community and the same authority to proceed simultaneously with their validation so as to identify and correct errors and then forward them without delay to the relevant agency so that they can issue the authorization. In other words, all the different phases are merged here and in fact carried out simultaneously, guaranteeing transparency and efficiency (Musamih et al., 2021).

The vaccine development process takes years to go from its conception to the operational phase of commercialization. This is because, for obvious safety reasons, the process for its development is particularly complex and divided into phases, some of which are in turn divided into further sub-phases. From the comparison of the data collected in the different phases, the level of effectiveness of the vaccine is obtained: After verifying the compliance of all the results produced by the tests with the required standards, the manufacturer then proceeds to send a dossier to the competent authorities to request registration and, obtained official clearance, marketing authorization. But once the authorization is obtained, a further period of control begins, with which the secondary effects on vaccinated people are carefully monitored to test the safety of the vaccine over the years on a growing number of the population. At this point you have a safe vaccine. However, the length of the experimentation process also leads to an exponential increase in costs that not all countries are able to face. The articulation of the process that leads the vaccine to be developed, tested, and then administered is particularly complex, although necessary to have a safe product, it can appear particularly cumbersome. For this reason, also in the scientific field, it was requested to be able to skip the last phase to put countries in competition, thus opening to a sort of mass experimentation, which happened on time for the Russian and Chinese vaccines. Blockchain technology, on the other hand, makes this conceptual leap unnecessary, which simultaneously implies the assumption of an unsustainable series of risks. Because the unification of the phases leads, following a substantially transparent process, to reach a level of efficiency and safety that is far from comparable to any shortcut you plan to take (Omar et al., 2021).

This is because managing billions of information requires a truly radical change of strategy. The blockchain already intervenes in the exploratory phase in which the study of the genetic characteristics of the virus is started to identify the antigen necessary to inhibit its action and thus provoke the response of the immune system. There are hundreds of genetic sequences that need to be compared at this stage and this can be done much more quickly and effectively if a considerable number of scientists all over the world take part in this operation, sharing materials through the blockchain that in this way result in evidence of tampering.

In the next, preclinical phase, in which the possible candidate is tested in vitro and in vivo on guinea pigs, with blockchain technology the information collected is made available to the community of scientists to check all the data, identify any errors and contextually find the most appropriate solutions. This allows biotech companies, among other things, not to lose their intellectual property rights and their competitive advantage over their main competitors.

In the third and last clinical phase, information relating to the trial on thousands and thousands of patients, in particular data on their immune response, adverse effects, clinical conditions etc. These data must be managed in a coordinated and secure manner to be well understood before the authorization process is initiated with the authorities of the various countries. However, patient information must obviously be collected based on an informed consent that must be managed anonymously so as not to be associated with any information leading to their reidentification and this is precisely possible through blockchain platforms which, if managed in a manner safe, they can encourage people to take part in vaccine testing protocols (Hernández-Ramos et al., 2021).

In the authorization phase, data must be shared between the parties in real time to shorten the vaccine approval and marketing process as much as possible. And here, once again, blockchain platforms prove indispensable.

In the vaccine distribution phase, blockchain platforms contribute significantly to the success of the procedure. In fact, it is estimated that up to 30% of the vaccine stocks are lost during the storage phase, because the characteristics of the vaccines require an extremely effective system for controlling the storage conditions of the vaccines. This system requires a precise location of each batch and even of each vial to reconstruct each step up to the moment of its administration. A monitoring system is needed to accompany this very delicate phase on which the success of the vaccination campaign depends. And this not only to optimize the distribution of the vaccine at the level of a single country, but also to allow its distribution all over the world, especially in developing countries so as not to penalize them to avoid, among other things, that they may then constitute a potential site of resurgence of the virus which would risk nullifying the effectiveness of the vaccination campaign (Tsoi et al., 2021).

Ultimately, blockchain technologies allow a truly radical paradigm shift in the field of vaccines whose potential has been tapped by various actors internationally. Given the potential of this technological breakthrough, a conversion of current procedures into truly responsible forms of research and innovation is necessary for its success. Blockchain technology, in fact, with its structural instance of transparency, sharing and control of fully digitized information raises no small questions regarding the respect of privacy.

In general, the idea is to develop tools for implementing the protection of personal data on blockchain platforms, whatever the object. In the mechanisms of collection and data computing of genetic data these cannot be stored in in-house servers and for this reason we often proceed to put all the data on cloud managed by third parties. However, there are several examples of data encryption tools that have been developed for genetic data as an alternative to mechanisms focused instead on the mere compensation of the owners of the personal data. The possibility of implementing certain "privacy enhancing tools" within cloud-based modules and blockchain platforms makes it clear how it is completely feasible to create tools capable of increasing the level of protection of personal data even within distributed systems and based on the transparency of data with respect to a certain community. Provided that these tools are developed by design, that is, at the same time as the design of a platform to be applied to the field of vaccines.

Almost 2 years after the WHO declaration of a COVID-19 pandemic, the inequality between rich and poor countries in access to vaccines is more acute and dramatic than ever. The wealthiest nations have vaccinated most of the population, while most developing countries still have not been able to vaccinate at least 10% of the population, with a structural shortage of medical supplies and oxygen supplies. This is the alarm raised by the World Health Organization. To overcome this criticality, the proposal to overcome the current monopoly held by pharmaceutical companies on vaccine patents has come from many parts of the world. A proposal, which if approved, would allow to increase world production, and start distribution in all poor countries that need it immediately.

5. Conclusion

In this chapter we first introduced the basic concepts of blockchain technology, and then we moved on to the analysis of the essential characteristics of the supply chain. Finally, the applications based on blockchain technology adopted to address the difficult emergency due to COVID-19 were analyzed, focusing attention on Blockchain-based solutions for the management of the anti-COVID-19 vaccination campaign.

We have seen that Blockchain technology proves to be particularly effective in managing the delicate phases of the Supply Chain. Blockchain technology therefore allows you to monitor the process of distribution, storage, and administration of vaccines for COVID-19. The approach is not so different from those already adopted, for example, in the automotive industry to certify the origin of raw materials or in the healthcare sector in the fight against counterfeit drugs. For example, it guarantees to optimize the control of the cold chain necessary to keep the vials of the vaccine required by messenger vaccines at extremely low temperatures. The technological evolution in this case comes to the aid of the world community to face one of the most difficult tests of the modern era.

References

Abeyratne, S.A., Monfared, R.P., 2016. Blockchain ready manufacturing supply chain using distributed ledger. Int. J. Res. Eng. Technol. 5 (9), 1–10.

Ahmad, R.W., Salah, K., Jayaraman, R., Yaqoob, I., Ellahham, S., Omar, M., 2021. The role of blockchain technology in telehealth and telemedicine. Int. J. Med. Inform. 148, 104399.

Amr, M.A., Eljazzar, M.M., Kassem, S.S., Ezzat, M., 2019. Merging supply chain and blockchain technologies. In: The 28th International Conference for the International Association of Management of Technology (IAMOT).

Antal, C.D., Cioara, T., Antal, M., Anghel, I., 2021. Blockchain platform for COVID-19 vaccine supply management. arXiv preprint arXiv:2101.00983.

Aste, T., Tasca, P., Di Matteo, T., 2017. Blockchain technologies: the foreseeable impact on society and industry. Computer 50 (9), 18–28.

Azaria, A., Ekblaw, A., Vieira, T., Lippman, A., 2016. Medrec: using blockchain for medical data access and permission management. In: 2016 2nd International Conference on Open and Big Data (OBD). IEEE, pp. 25–30.

Badertscher, C., Maurer, U., Tschudi, D., Zikas, V., 2017. Bitcoin as a transaction ledger: a composable treatment. In: Annual International Cryptology Conference. Springer, Cham, pp. 324–356.

Baunm, S., 2017. Health IT Startups Working to Secure Pharma Supply Chains? Medcity News. [Online]. Available from: https://medcitynews.com/2017/01/drug-supply-chain-security-and-technology/. (Accessed 12 May 2021).

Beamon, B.M., 1998. Supply chain design and analysis: models and methods. Int. J. Prod. Econ. 55 (3), 281–294.

Belotti, M., Božić, N., Pujolle, G., Secci, S., 2019. A vademecum on blockchain technologies: when, which, and how. IEEE Commun. Surv. Tutorials 21 (4), 3796–3838.

Benchoufi, M., Porcher, R., Ravaud, P., 2017. Blockchain protocols in clinical trials: transparency and traceability of consent. F1000Res. 6, 66.

Bertino, E., Sandhu, R., 2005. Database security-concepts, approaches, and challenges. IEEE Trans. Dependable Secure Comput. 2 (1), 2–19.

Bozarth, C.C., Handfield, R.B., Weiss, H.J., 2008. Introduction to Operations and Supply Chain Management. Pearson Prentice Hall, Upper Saddle River, NJ.

Cachin, C., 2016. Architecture of the hyperledger blockchain fabric. In: Workshop on Distributed Cryptocurrencies and Consensus Ledgers. vol. 310. No. 4.

Calvão, F., 2019. Crypto-miners: digital labor and the power of blockchain technology. Econ. Anthropol. 6 (1), 123–134.

Casado-Vara, R., Prieto, J., De la Prieta, F., Corchado, J.M., 2018. How blockchain improves the supply chain: case study alimentary supply chain. Procedia Comput. Sci. 134, 393–398.

Ceri, S., 2017. Distributed Databases. Tata McGraw-Hill Education.

Chan, S., 2001. Complex adaptive systems. In: ESD. 83 Research Seminar in Engineering Systems. vol. 31, pp. 1–19.

Chenthara, S., Ahmed, K., Wang, H., Whittaker, F., Chen, Z., 2020. Healthchain: a novel framework on privacy preservation of electronic health records using blockchain technology. PLoS One 15 (12), e0243043.

Chowdhury, M.J.M., Colman, A., Kabir, M.A., Han, J., Sarda, P., 2018. Blockchain versus database: a critical analysis. In: 2018 17th IEEE International Conference on Trust, Security and Privacy in Computing and Communications/12th IEEE International Conference on Big Data Science and Engineering (TrustCom/BigDataSE). IEEE, pp. 1348–1353.

Corey, L., Mascola, J.R., Fauci, A.S., Collins, F.S., 2020. A strategic approach to COVID-19 vaccine R&D. Science 368 (6494), 948–950.

Croxton, K.L., Garcia-Dastugue, S.J., Lambert, D.M., Rogers, D.S., 2001. The supply chain management processes. Int. J. Logist. Manage. 12 (2), 13–36.

Davis, T., 1993. Effective supply chain management. Sloan Manage. Rev. 34, 35.

Dhillon, V., Metcalf, D., Hooper, M., 2017. Blockchain Enabled Applications. Apress, Berkeley, CA, p. 72.

Dimitrov, D.V., 2019. Blockchain applications for healthcare data management. Healthc. Inform. Res. 25 (1), 51.

Dinh, T.T.A., Liu, R., Zhang, M., Chen, G., Ooi, B.C., Wang, J., 2018. Untangling blockchain: a data processing view of blockchain systems. IEEE Trans. Knowl. Data Eng. 30 (7), 1366–1385.

Dogru, T., Mody, M., Leonardi, C., 2018. Blockchain Technology & Its Implications for the Hospitality Industry. Boston University.

Dubovitskaya, A., Baig, F., Xu, Z., Shukla, R., Zambani, P.S., Swaminathan, A., et al., 2020. ACTION-EHR: patient-centric blockchain-based electronic health record data management for cancer care. J. Med. Internet Res. 22 (8), e13598.

Durach, C.F., Blesik, T., von Düring, M., Bick, M., 2021. Blockchain applications in supply chain transactions. J. Bus. Logist. 42 (1), 7–24.

Ellram, L.M., 1991. Supply-chain management: the industrial organisation perspective. Int. J. Phys. Distrib. Logist. Manage. 21 (1), 13–22. https://doi.org/10.1108/09600039110137082.

Esposito, C., De Santis, A., Tortora, G., Chang, H., Choo, K.K.R., 2018. Blockchain: a panacea for healthcare cloud-based data security and privacy? IEEE Cloud Comput. 5 (1), 31–37.

Fernández-Caramés, T.M., Fraga-Lamas, P., 2020. Towards post-quantum blockchain: a review on blockchain cryptography resistant to quantum computing attacks. IEEE Access 8, 21091–21116.

Francisco, K., Swanson, D., 2018. The supply chain has no clothes: technology adoption of blockchain for supply chain transparency. Logistics 2 (1), 2.

Fu, Y., Zhu, J., 2019. Operation mechanisms for intelligent logistics system: a blockchain perspective. IEEE Access 7, 144202–144213.

Garay, J., Kiayias, A., Leonardos, N., 2015. The bitcoin backbone protocol: analysis and applications. In: Annual International Conference on the Theory and Applications of Cryptographic Techniques. Springer, Berlin, Heidelberg, pp. 281–310.

Graham, B.S., 2020. Rapid COVID-19 vaccine development. Science 368 (6494), 945–946.

Halaburda, H., 2018. Blockchain revolution without the blockchain? Commun. ACM 61 (7), 27–29.

Hernández-Ramos, J.L., Karopoulos, G., Geneiatakis, D., Martin, T., Kambourakis, G., Fovino, I.N., 2021. Sharing pandemic vaccination certificates through blockchain: case study and performance evaluation. arXiv preprint arXiv:2101.04575.

Hugos, M.H., 2018. Essentials of Supply Chain Management. John Wiley & Sons.

Hylock, R.H., Zeng, X., 2019. A blockchain framework for patient-centered health records and exchange (HealthChain): evaluation and proof-of-concept study. J. Med. Internet Res. 21 (8), e13592.

Ivan, D., 2016. Moving toward a blockchain-based method for the secure storage of patient records. In: ONC/NIST Use of Blockchain for Healthcare and Research Workshop. ONC/NIST, Gaithersburg, Maryland, United States, pp. 1–11.

Jeyanathan, M., Afkhami, S., Smaill, F., Miller, M.S., Lichty, B.D., Xing, Z., 2020. Immunological considerations for COVID-19 vaccine strategies. Nat. Rev. Immunol. 20 (10), 615–632.

Kim, S., Deka, G.C. (Eds.), 2020. Advanced Applications of Blockchain Technology. Springer.

Klems, M., Eberhardt, J., Tai, S., Härtlein, S., Buchholz, S., Tidjani, A., 2017. Trustless intermediation in blockchain-based decentralized service marketplaces. In: International Conference on Service-Oriented Computing. Springer, Cham, pp. 731–739.

Knoll, M.D., Wonodi, C., 2021. Oxford–AstraZeneca COVID-19 vaccine efficacy. Lancet 397 (10269), 72–74.

Korpela, K., Hallikas, J., Dahlberg, T., 2017. Digital supply chain transformation toward blockchain integration. In: Proceedings of the 50th Hawaii International Conference on System Sciences.

Kumar, G., Saha, R., Rai, M.K., Thomas, R., Kim, T.H., 2019. Proof-of-work consensus approach in blockchain technology for cloud and fog computing using maximization-factorization statistics. IEEE Internet Things J. 6 (4), 6835–6842.

Lambert, D.M., Cooper, M.C., 2000. Issues in supply chain management. Ind. Mark. Manage. 29 (1), 65–83.

Le, T.T., Andreadakis, Z., Kumar, A., Román, R.G., Tollefsen, S., Saville, M., Mayhew, S., 2020. The COVID-19 vaccine development landscape. Nat. Rev. Drug Discov. 19 (5), 305–306.

Lee, H.A., Kung, H.H., Udayasankaran, J.G., Kijsanayotin, B., Marcelo, A.B., Chao, L.R., Hsu, C.Y., 2020. An architecture and management platform for blockchain-based personal health record exchange: development and usability study. J. Med. Internet Res. 22 (6), e16748.

Li, X., Jiang, P., Chen, T., Luo, X., Wen, Q., 2020. A survey on the security of blockchain systems. Futur. Gener. Comput. Syst. 107, 841–853.

Lo, S.K., Xu, X., Chiam, Y.K., Lu, Q., 2017. Evaluating suitability of applying blockchain. In: 2017 22nd International Conference on Engineering of Complex Computer Systems (ICECCS). IEEE, pp. 158–161.

Malik, A.A., McFadden, S.M., Elharake, J., Omer, S.B., 2020. Determinants of COVID-19 vaccine acceptance in the US. EClinicalMedicine 26, 100495.

Maurya, A.K., Singh, A., Tripathi, U.N., Pandey, S., Singh, D., 2020. Security in distributed database system: a survey. J. Comput. Math. Sci. 11 (7), 43–51.

Mentzer, J.T., DeWitt, W., Keebler, J.S., Min, S., Nix, N.W., Smith, C.D., Zacharia, Z.G., 2001. Defining supply chain management. J. Bus. Logist. 22 (2), 1–25.

Mettler, M., 2016. Blockchain technology in healthcare: the revolution starts here. In: 2016 IEEE 18th International Conference on E-Health Networking, Applications and Services (Healthcom). IEEE, pp. 1–3.

Min, H., Zhou, G., 2002. Supply chain modeling: past, present and future. Comput. Ind. Eng. 43 (1–2), 231–249.

Musamih, A., Jayaraman, R., Salah, K., Hasan, H., Yaqoob, I., Al-Hammadi, Y., 2021. Blockchain-based solution for distribution and delivery of COVID-19 vaccines. IEEE Access 9, 71372–71387.

Muzammal, M., Qu, Q., Nasrulin, B., 2019. Renovating blockchain with distributed databases: an open source system. Futur. Gener. Comput. Syst. 90, 105–117.

Nakamoto, S., Bitcoin, A., 2008. Bitcoin: A Peer-to-Peer Electronic Cash System. Available from: https://bitcoin.org/bitcoin.pdf. (Accessed 25 May 2021).

Niranjanamurthy, M., Nithya, B.N., Jagannatha, S., 2019. Analysis of Blockchain technology: pros, cons and SWOT. Clust. Comput. 22 (6), 14743–14757.

Nofer, M., Gomber, P., Hinz, O., Schiereck, D., 2017. Blockchain. Business & information. Syst. Eng. 59 (3), 183–187.

Nørfeldt, L., Bøtker, J., Edinger, M., Genina, N., Rantanen, J., 2019. Cryptopharmaceuticals: increasing the safety of medication by a blockchain of pharmaceutical products. J. Pharm. Sci. 108 (9), 2838–2841.

Omar, I.A., Jayaraman, R., Debe, M.S., Salah, K., Yaqoob, I., Omar, M., 2021. Automating procurement contracts in the healthcare supply chain using blockchain smart contracts. IEEE Access 9, 37397–37409.

Piccininni, M., Rohmann, J.L., Logroscino, G., Kurth, T., 2020. Blockchain-based innovations for population-based registries for rare neurodegenerative diseases. Front. Blockchain 3, 20. https://doi.org/10.3389/fbloc.2020.00020.

Pilkington, M., 2016. Blockchain technology: principles and applications. In: Research Handbook on Digital Transformations. Edward Elgar Publishing.

Radanović, I., Likić, R., 2018. Opportunities for use of blockchain technology in medicine. Appl. Health Econ. Health Policy 16 (5), 583–590.

Raghavendra, M., 2019. Can blockchain technologies help tackle the opioid epidemic: a narrative review. Pain Med. 20 (10), 1884–1889.

Ramirez Lopez, L.J., Beltrán Álvarez, N., 2020. Blockchain application in the distribution chain of the COVID-19 vaccine: a designing understudy. Advance (preprint).

Ren, Y., Zhu, F., Sharma, P.K., Wang, T., Wang, J., Alfarraj, O., Tolba, A., 2020. Data query mechanism based on hash computing power of blockchain in internet of things. Sensors 20 (1), 207.

Rhee, K., Kwak, J., Kim, S., Won, D., 2005. Challenge-response based RFID authentication protocol for distributed database environment. In: International Conference on Security in Pervasive Computing. Springer, Berlin, Heidelberg, pp. 70–84.

Risius, M., Spohrer, K., 2017. A blockchain research framework. Bus. Inform. Syst. Eng. 59 (6), 385–409.

Saberi, S., Kouhizadeh, M., Sarkis, J., Shen, L., 2019. Blockchain technology and its relationships to sustainable supply chain management. Int. J. Prod. Res. 57 (7), 2117–2135.

Schmidt, C.G., Wagner, S.M., 2019. Blockchain and supply chain relations: a transaction cost theory perspective. J. Purch. Supply Manage. 25 (4), 100552.

Sherman, A.T., Javani, F., Zhang, H., Golaszewski, E., 2019. On the origins and variations of Blockchain technologies. IEEE Secur. Priv. 17 (1), 72–77.

Simatupang, T.M., Sridharan, R., 2002. The collaborative supply chain. Int. J. Logist. Manage. 13 (1), 15–30.

Singh, A., Parizi, R.M., Zhang, Q., Choo, K.K.R., Dehghantanha, A., 2020. Blockchain smart contracts formalization: approaches and challenges to address vulnerabilities. Comput. Secur. 88, 101654.

Stevens, G.C., 1989. Integrating the supply chain. Int. J. Phys. Distrib. Mater. Manage. 19 (8), 3–8. https://doi.org/10.12691/ijefm-2-2-2.

Syed, T.A., Alzahrani, A., Jan, S., Siddiqui, M.S., Nadeem, A., Alghamdi, T., 2019. A comparative analysis of blockchain architecture and its applications: problems and recommendations. IEEE Access 7, 176838–176869.

Tapscott, A., Tapscott, D., 2017. How blockchain is changing finance. Harv. Bus. Rev. 1 (9), 2–5.

Thomas, D.J., Griffin, P.M., 1996. Coordinated supply chain management. Eur. J. Oper. Res. 94 (1), 1–15.

Tian, H., He, J., Ding, Y., 2019. Medical data management on blockchain with privacy. J. Med. Syst. 43 (2), 26.

Treiblmaier, H., 2018. The impact of the blockchain on the supply chain: a theory-based research framework and a call for action. Supply Chain Manage. 23 (6), 545–559.

Tsoi, K.K., Sung, J.J., Lee, H.W., Yiu, K.K., Fung, H., Wong, S.Y., 2021. The way forward after COVID-19 vaccination: vaccine passports with blockchain to protect personal privacy. BMJ Innov. 7 (2), 337–341.

Van Bavel, J.J., Baicker, K., Boggio, P.S., Capraro, V., Cichocka, A., Cikara, M., et al., 2020. Using social and behavioural science to support COVID-19 pandemic response. Nat. Hum. Behav. 4 (5), 460–471.

Vincent, N.E., Skjellum, A., Medury, S., 2020. Blockchain architecture: a design that helps CPA firms leverage the technology. Int. J. Account. Inform. Syst. 38, 100466.

Wang, W., Hoang, D.T., Hu, P., Xiong, Z., Niyato, D., Wang, P., et al., 2019. A survey on consensus mechanisms and mining strategy management in blockchain networks. IEEE Access 7, 22328–22370.

Wüst, K., Gervais, A., 2018, June. Do you need a blockchain? In: 2018 Crypto Valley Conference on Blockchain Technology (CVCBT). IEEE, pp. 45–54.

Xia, Q.I., Sifah, E.B., Asamoah, K.O., Gao, J., Du, X., Guizani, M., 2017. MeDShare: trustless medical data sharing among cloud service providers via blockchain. IEEE Access 5, 14757–14767.

Yli-Huumo, J., Ko, D., Choi, S., Park, S., Smolander, K., 2016. Where is current research on blockchain technology?—a systematic review. PLoS One 11 (10), e0163477.

Yong, B., Shen, J., Liu, X., Li, F., Chen, H., Zhou, Q., 2020. An intelligent blockchain-based system for safe vaccine supply and supervision. Int. J. Inform. Manage. 52, 102024.

Zheng, Z., Xie, S., Dai, H., Chen, X., Wang, H., 2017. An overview of blockchain technology: architecture, consensus, and future trends. In: 2017 IEEE International Congress on Big Data (BigData Congress). IEEE, pp. 557–564.

Zheng, Z., Xie, S., Dai, H.N., Chen, X., Wang, H., 2018. Blockchain challenges and opportunities: a survey. Int. J. Web Grid Serv. 14 (4), 352–375.

CHAPTER EIGHT

Novel coronavirus disease (COVID-19): Emergence, early infection rate, and deployment strategies for preventive solutions

Mohona Munshi[a], Saptashish Deb[b], Santanu Malakar[c], K.R. Jolvis Pou[d], and Sourav Chakraborty[e]

[a]Department of Chemical Engineering, Vignan Foundation for Science, Technology, and Research, Vadlamudi, Guntur, Andhra Pradesh, India
[b]Center for Rural Development and Technology, Indian Institute of Technology Delhi, New Delhi, India
[c]Department of Food Engineering, National Institute of Food Technology Entrepreneurship and Management, Sonipat, Haryana, India
[d]Department of Bioresource Engineering, McGill University, Sainte-Anne-de Bellevue, Montreal, QC, Canada
[e]Department of Food Engineering and Technology, Tezpur University, Tezpur, Assam, India

1 Introduction

Novel coronavirus marked as coronavirus disease 19 (COVID-19) first showed its symptoms in Wuhan, China, and got identified in December 2019 (Zhou et al., 2020). The People's Republic of China was the first to report to the World Health Organization (WHO) that from December 31, 2019 to January 3, 2020, 44 cases of pneumonia with some unknown etiologies have been registered in different hospitals (Tandon, 2020). On January 7, 2020, the virus was first identified, and the scientists found it as coronavirus having 95% similar homology with the bats (Singhal, 2020). The International Committee on Taxonomy of Virus (ICTV) called it severe acute respiratory syndrome coronavirus 2 (SARS-CoV-2) and found it similar to severe acute respiratory syndrome (SARS). SARS-CoV-2 has spread quickly throughout the world and caused serious concern about this disease. As it is a newly emerged virus, during the first wave, there was no known medicine or vaccine to treat the disease. However, every possible effort is being applied with all the available facilities and knowledge to safeguard people from this emerging infectious disease.

It has been found that the virus can cause common colds, coughs, breathing difficulties, and loss of taste and smell. At the very beginning, one-sixth

Lessons from COVID-19
https://doi.org/10.1016/B978-0-323-99878-9.00017-0

of individuals infected by novel coronavirus developed breathing difficulty and become extremely infected. People having severe diseases like diabetes, heart disease, blood pressure, and blood cancer are found more probability of severe condition. World Health Organization recommended some precautionary measures to stop the spreading of COVID-19 like; wash hands frequently, wear a face mask, avoid contact with sick people, practice good hygiene, and maintain social distance. Simultaneously, various drugs and other remedial therapies and foods (used for other similar kinds of diseases) have been applied to reduce the severity. Researchers around the globe immediately started an investigation to develop new and effective treatment methods and vaccines to overcome this deadly challenge.

Studies on past pandemics exhibited large-scale outbreaks over a wide geographical area and caused morbidity and mortality, and significantly disrupted economic, political, and social well-being. It is also observed in the current COVID-19 pandemic; the effect has created a worldwide devastating situation. This study focuses on the historical perspective of novel coronavirus, transmissibility, and incubation period, spreading behavior of COVID-19 by principal component analysis (PCA), various awareness and preventive measures, and potential application of allopathic therapy, dietary remedy, and herbal medicines to fight against the COVID-19 virus mainly during the first wave and until the development of the vaccine. This chapter can be used as an edifying approach for forestalling and strategy making against any COVID-19 like pandemics in the ensuing times.

2 Various epidemics and pandemics in the history of human civilization

Presently, COVID-19 is an overwhelming challenge faced by the public health system of the entire world. It can be called "History repeating itself" while harking back to the different history of pandemics and how the world combated with these widespread diseases.

2.1 Spanish flu

When peeped into history, one of the oldest and the worst pandemics faced were in 1918, toward the end of World War 1. The influenza disease also called the Spanish flu which was spreading rapidly. It was estimated that it hits the world in spring 1918 and ended in early summer 1919. It had affected around 200–700 million people worldwide and there was a death of 50–100 million, and 21 million in India alone. This pandemic mainly affected young people, mostly the infants and young people of 20–40 age groups. This led to the closures of schools, businesses, colleges, etc. (Reid, 2005). This flu was highly contagious and spread through cough, sneezes, talks, respiratory droplets, and transmitted through the air. Symptoms observed were the fever with shivers, sore throat, headache, tiredness, cough, and sometimes nosebleeds. In some cases, patients were facing some worst complications, especially in the respiratory system. The postmortem report of the dead bodies caused by Spanish flu showed grossly oversized spleens, swollen lungs, necrotic tissue, and pulmonary alveoli overflowing with albuminous exudate (Tognotti, 2003). It was a very challenging task to control the mortality rate owing to the fewer numbers of hospitals and intensive care units at that time. The areas harshly affected by the disease had a persistent and severe decline in the economy. Altogether the pandemic had a spike in mortality and gave an economic shock (Correia et al., 2020). Thus far, very limited economic data are available for post-1918 influenza. However, the economic problem caused by the 1918 pandemic was short term (Garrett, 2008).

2.2 Plague

There were continuous three plague pandemics that hit the world, first in the 6th century in Byzantium, it swept from Central Asia and killed 40% of the population in Constantinople in 541–542 AD. Second in the 14th century in Europe also called the black death which killed millions in Asia and near Europe East in 1347 to early 1400s and lastly in the 19th century, this plague reappeared in Hong Kong in 1894 (Butler, 2009; Khan, 1995). At that time, the worst affected was India which killed nearly 12 million people between 1896 and 1936. The plague was caused by the bacteria called *Yersinia pestis*. It was a highly infectious and fatal disease characterized by high fever, inflammation of lymphatic glands forming buboes, and pneumonia. It was spread through the urban and densely populated localities transmitted by rats and the sporadic cases through the epizootic infection of several animals. The prevention taken was prompt isolation of the infection suffering from the plague into infectious disease. Later, it was found that streptomycin was the drug of choice for the treatment. Sulfadiazine and sulfamerazine were used during the large outbreaks. In the first week of September 1994, there were 325 suspected cases of plague in 23 states of India. By September last week, the pneumonic plague had spread rapidly in Surat, Gujarat (752 cases and 44 deaths), and by October, it crossed more than 4000 suspected cases countrywide. Surat was the worst affected center of the epidemic. The report indicated that the mortality rate of pneumonic plague in India was found to be 7% (Butler, 2009). The economic losses were suffered around 300–500 million *per annum* and the worst victims were the industries in and around Surat (Gujarat) and Bombay (Maharashtra) (Khan, 1995). Altogether, India suffered a huge economic breakdown during this pandemic.

2.3 Cholera

In 1849, there was the first outbreak of cholera in London, British due to the contaminated water. Since 1817, the world has already faced six epidemics of cholera, and the seventh one began in 1961, came into India and is still in progress. Kolkata city of West Bengal, India was the homeland for this waterborne disease located in the Ganges Delta (Mandal, 2011). The seventh outbreak (El Tor cholera) was first reported in the island of Java. It is the seventh pandemic that spread all over the world. Celebes Island witnessed 29 deaths and 109 cases in 1961. In Macau, 72 cases with first death in 1962. Its way of spreading was found in poor persons having diet deficiency and living in unsanitary conditions. Cholera was generally caused by the bacteria *Vibrio cholerae*. Water was one of the important vectors of infection not because of the possible survival of *Vibrios* but due to the stagnant contaminated water. The isolation of contacts and carriers was necessary for numerous areas, but it was not enforced. Sulfa drugs were used for the treatment. Hong Kong used streptomycin and chloramphenicol and was found to be effective for the treatment. Environmental sanitation was one of the prevention measures that were taken, and public health education and vaccination were developed all over the world in the later period. Proper nutrition intake of Vitamin A and C also protein intakes were made higher in amounts (Felsenfeld, 1969). Symptoms observed were watery and lose bloody mucus in diarrhea and dehydration, fever, and abdominal pain (Dutta et al., 2013).

2.4 Smallpox

Smallpox is one of the most contagious diseases, a frequently fatal feared in the centuries. In the 20th century, because of vaccination, it was reduced in Europe and North America. But in the 1960s, it was endemic in Africa and Asia. In 1905–44, there were 1916 deaths out of 17,510 affected cases. The disease was common, it has characteristic symptoms and distinct seasonality, and it mainly affected small children. Vaccination introduced in 1802 was an effective measure of prevention. This disease was caused by the *Variola* virus and spread through direct contact. The symptoms observed were headache, backache, fever, and enanthema in the tongue, mouth, and oropharynx. The rash begins with small reddish macules which papules in 2–3 days. The lesion first appeared on the face and gradually covers the whole body, and the rash remains for 5–8 days. Relatively, lesions on palms remain for a longer time. After severe smallpox, pitted lesions are seen in 65%–80% of survivors (Breman and Henderson, 2002).

2.5 Severe acute respiratory syndrome

SARS is an epidemic caused in humans and suspected to be present in animal reservoirs as the host probably civet cats which is still uncertain. The outbreak of SARS was first observed in November 2002 and caused a lot of panic in China and the world at large (Qiu et al., 2018). The first symptom observed was high fever with chill, cough and breathing difficulty, malaise, and headache were some of the other primary symptoms. High and prolonged fever with diarrhea was the confirmed symptoms for SARS. Exposures such as close contact with a person with SARS caused transmission. The study of transmission dynamics of this infection was based on a simple mathematical framework in which different interventions of approaches could be assessed during the epidemic. The researchers attempted to calculate R_0 known as the reproduction number to keep control over the spreading of the infection. Progressive estimation of the effective reproductive number R_t (the secondary cases generation average rate) delivers a quantitative evaluation of success or failure. Guangdong, where the major outbreak took place, had infected more than 8000 people and 774 died. A higher mortality rate was found in people with an age of more than 60 years and lesser mortality in young people. SARS has low transmissibility and effective measures were taken by World Health Organization to keep the spreading of the virus under control. SARS epidemic was under control by taking into account certain preventive measures such as the closing of schools, colleges, and businesses and restricting the movement within the country, isolation of the suspected cases and encouragement of rapid reporting to the health care centers (Anderson et al., 2004). The economic impact triggered by SARS in China and Hong Kong suggested a huge economic loss. The economic effect gave a persistent shock as the epidemic lasted longer than anyone imagined of it. So, the more persistent it was in the core country the larger economic impact was faced by the country (Lee and McKibbin, 2004).

2.6 H1N1 influenza

H1N1 influenza is also known as swine flu named because the genes in the virus showed similarity with the influenza viruses occurring in North American pigs (CDCP, 2019). The outbreak of H1N1 came into notice in 2009 and spread across the globe. Subsequently, the infected persons were hospitalized, and antiviral treatment was given, and all the suspected cases were isolated for further screening. The most death rates were found in people below 30 years of age (Mishra et al., 2010). Its transmission was through cough, sneeze, and respiratory droplets (CDCP, 2019). Symptoms reported were asthma, shortness of breath, pneumonia, fever and cough, chest pain, low blood pressure, drowsiness, hemoptysis, and cyanosis for age 65 years and above. In children, persistent fever, convulsions, dyspnea, and respiratory distress were detected in most of the cases. The diagnosis was performed with the help of reverse transcription-polymerase chain reaction (RT-PCR). H1N1 influenza caused a severe influence on the economic framework and morbidity of our society. The shutdown of schools, offices, and industries resulted in an economic breakdown. The economic flow has been disturbed and earning members were bound to miss work which caused a huge financial loss and burdened with hospitalization expenditure. The mean age which affected the most was found to be 41.5 years from 3 months to 85 years of age (Kumar et al., 2015). However, it was less devastating than the 1918 pandemic.

All these diseases have swept the communities and killed many people as it is now observed in the COVID-19 impact which has already created a devastating effect in the United States, India, Brazil, Spain, and other parts of the world. These diseases have greatly affected the whole world in the past both in terms of economy and mortality rates. Comparatively, the past pandemics were less virulent than COVID-19 as they spread through direct transmission as well as they were less contagious. Therefore, there was a need for necessary precautionary measures and information particularly during the initial stage of COVID-19 to minimize and control the impacts of the pandemic.

3 Transmissibility and severity of COVID-19

Coronavirus is a single nanosegmented, single-stranded, encompassed ribonucleic acid. Coronavirus is named because of its crown type appearance with 9–12 nm long spikes which is similar to solar corona (Zu et al., 2020).

It is a group of viruses belong to the family coronaviridiae and mostly affects humans through zoonotic transmission. In the year 1966, scientists Tyrell and Bynoe first discovered coronavirus from the patients of common colds (Velavan and Meyer, 2020). There are seven subtypes of coronavirus present in nature and out of these seven subtypes; β coronavirus has the potential to cause severe disease. COVID-19 virus belongs to B lineage of the β coronavirus (Zhou et al., 2020) and it is a new strain that has not been identified earlier in human beings and also the first strain of COVID-19 among various other strains identified till date and that is the reason it is called novel coronavirus (nCoV).

Once a person is infected by nCoV, then it has been noticed that clinical manifestation starts within a week in most of the cases consisting of dry cough, fever, fatigue, breathing problem, loss of taste and smell, and pneumonia in most severe cases (Guarner, 2020). Though the COVID-19 virus or SARS-CoV-2 is categorized in the family of severe acute respiratory syndrome coronavirus (SARS-CoV) and Middle East respiratory syndrome coronavirus (MERS-CoV) family, SARS-CoV-2 is completely different in behavior as compared to MERS-CoV and SARS-CoV. The main difference of the COVID-19 virus is that it spreads faster than MERS-CoV and SARS-CoV. The incubation period of this virus is around 2–14 days and symptoms start appearing a minimum after 3–4 days, thus the virus is unknowingly spread to other people by the infected person and increases the spreading rate. A survey showed that the COVID-19 pandemic getting double in number within a week and each infected person infecting 2.2 other people on average (Chan et al., 2020).

Initially, the COVID-19 virus shows the possible transmission from animal to human. But further studies confirmed the transmission of this disease from human to human, either through direct contact or droplets (Chan et al., 2020; Wang et al., 2020; Chang et al., 2020). During the initial days of spreading, the unavailability of testing kits and medical equipment created the worst situation to diagnose the infected patients. Thin slice chest computed tomography (CT) did a significant job in batting this irresistible sickness, and then real-time PCR came into picture to diagnose this disease at the clinical level (Zu et al., 2020). Wooden shaft is not recommended while collecting the swabs sample as it may contain substances that may destroy some viruses subsequently which will destroy the real-time PCR result. At the same time for better sample collection, deep cough sputum should be collected for testing after the mouth of the patient is rinsed properly with water (Islam et al., 2020).

The number of deaths from COVID-19 is much more than its predecessors. At the time of SARS-CoV, the fatality rate was 10% (774 deaths out of 8098 cases) and during the MERS-CoV, the fatality rate was 34% (858 deaths out of 2494 cases) (Mahase, 2020). Whereas the COVID-19 has reported many more deaths and confirmed cases than SARS-CoV and MERS-CoV (3,751,988 deaths out of 174,376,256 cases) up to June 8, 2021 (Worldometer, 2021). The United States is leading both in the number of cases and deaths from COVID-19 (Worldometer, 2021). Aged people (age more than 60 years) with past medical history (like lung disease and diabetes), pregnant women, and health professionals are at high risk of this disease. Moreover, high population densities, less diagnosis capacity, and poor hygiene maintenance are some of the key points for the speedy spreading of this virus.

Gathering a large number of people is considered to be the key reason behind this epidemic becoming pandemic (Dharmshaktu, 2020). The mass gathering includes cultural and spiritual events, festivals, sporting events, performances, conferences, shopping malls, cinema halls, public spaces (parks, beaches), public transport, etc. Mass gathering that draws participants from other affected regions or countries would increase the spreading of this disease. Local transmission is also one of the factors of the severity and the spreading rate of this virus in highly populated countries such as China, India, and other parts of the world.

4 Incubation period of COVID-19 virus

Research has reported that the COVID-19 virus incubation period based on 138 cases found that the average duration of appearance of the first symptoms to dyspnea, admitting in the hospital to acute severe respiratory syndrome, was observed as 5 days (range 1–10), 7 days (range 4–8), and 8 days (range 6–12), respectively (Wang et al., 2020; Wu et al., 2020). In another report covering 425 cases, the average was 5.2 days (95% CI, 4.1–7.0 days) and the median incubation period was 3 days (range 0–24) based on the study of 1324 cases (Guan et al., 2020; Li et al., 2020). It might be in some cases symptoms were visible as early as the first range and a single case might have shown late symptoms as of the last range mentioned. On the other hand, SARS, MERS, and swine flu were found to be 2–7 days (Docherty et al., 2020), 2–14 days (CDCP, 2020), and 1–4 days (Jilani et al., 2019), respectively. This estimation showed a lot of variation based on the sample size and the medical history of the infected persons. As of now, the COVID-19 virus incubation period is found varying and as more information and data will be available, higher precise estimations will emerge (Chatterjee et al., 2020).

5 Symptoms of COVID-19

According to data from the World Health Organization, this CoV falls into one of the major viruses responsible for the illness. This type of virus can cause common cold, cough, and pneumonia. The major common symptoms are dry cough (60%), high fever (99%), sore throat or difficulty in breathing, myalgia (44%), and dyspnea. Other mild symptoms seen in the patient are chest pain, headache, runny nose, nasal congestion, diarrhea, dizziness, and vomiting which instigate gradually (Wang et al., 2020; Chang et al., 2020). In addition to respiratory symptoms, 36.4% (78 out of 214) patients appeared with COVID-19 symptoms which affect the central nervous system of the body and gives birth to above-mentioned neurological diseases along with disturbed consciousness and paresthesia (Wu et al., 2020). Patients suffering from severe infections have acute symptoms such as abdominal pain, pharyngeal pain, dyspnea, and anorexia (Chen et al., 2020). Also, the elderly person having comorbidities have more risks especially people suffering from hypertension, diabetes, cardiovascular diseases, and cerebrovascular diseases have the most adverse outcomes.

Symptoms such as lymponia, prolonged prothrombine time, elevated lactase dehydrogenase, and elevated D-dimer were also observed in COVID-19–infected persons. The most common complications found were acute respiratory distress syndrome, acute cardiac injury shock, arrhythmias, and acute kidney problems. These abnormalities were very similar to that of symptoms found in SARS-CoV and MERS-CoV (Chatterjee et al., 2020). It can cause pneumonia, even seizure pneumonia, and also severe diseases like MERS and SARS. Research indicated that olfactory dysfunction or anosmia is now recognized as one of the symptoms of COVID-19. COVID-19 virus infects and damages the epithelium nasal cells by interacting with the spike(s) protein and angiotensin-converting enzyme 2 (ACE-2) proteins on the target cell which leads to the olfactory dysfunction of the patients (Brann et al., 2020). This infection can be as severe as admitting people to the intensive care unit (ICU) and may require ventilator support and can be as mild as having a short-term illness. Acute pancreatic, the elevation of alanine aminotransferase (ALT) to more than fivefold upper normal limit and anaphylaxis are also the outcomes of

COVID-19 (Bhatnagar et al., 2020). To tackle this infection, it is needed to reduce the symptoms which can only be possible by constructing multidisciplinary care and isolation wards, which would empower the health system. Scientists, researchers, and health experts are working together to get more evidence about the transmissibility and severity of COVID-19.

6 Spreading behavior of COVID-19 by PCA during the initial phase

Principal component analysis was implemented for analyzing the COVID-19 spreading behavior in the whole world during the first wave. The application of PCA is an innovative approach for significantly interpreting the spreading behavior of the virus. A total of four components namely the number of confirmed cases, number of recovered cases, number of active cases, and number of deceased cases were considered for the mapping of PCA within different countries (Worldometer, 2020). Results demonstrated in Fig. 1 showed the COVID-19 spreading behavior within different countries. Total cases, total recovered, total deaths, and active cases

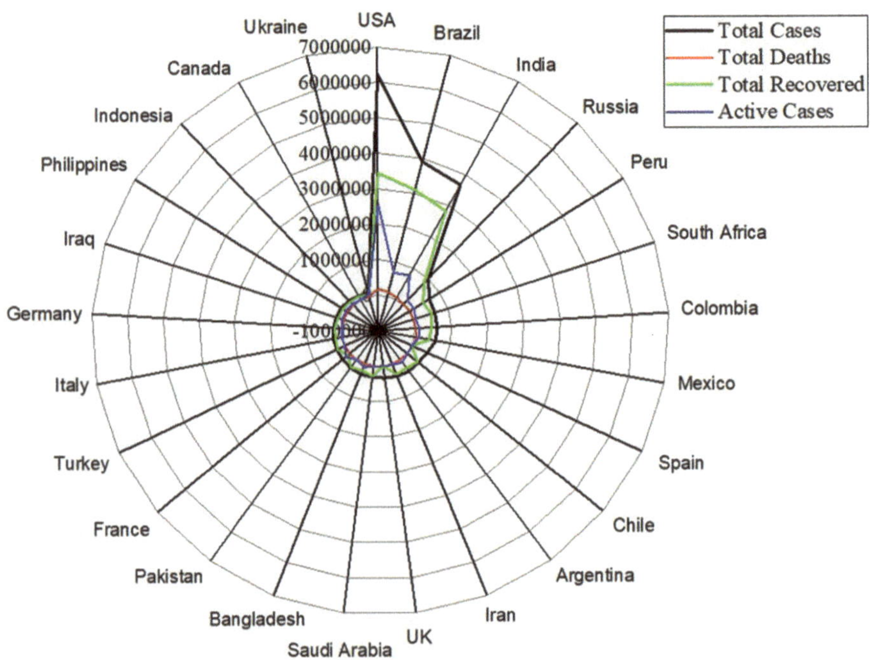

Fig. 1 The scenario of COVID-19 spreading across the whole world.

Table 1 Extracted eigen vectors of the PCA for COVID-19 spreading rate in the world.

Types of cases	Coefficients of PC-1	Coefficients of PC-2
Total cases	0.51506	−0.22024
Total deaths	0.49506	0.39401
Total recovered	0.4954	−0.70737
Active cases	0.49417	0.54395

were considered as the components for PCA. A total of 25 countries were considered for the PCA-based interpretation. Based on the results of Table 1, total and active cases were selected as PC-1 and PC-2, respectively. From the scores represented in Table 2, the highest ranking of the United States can be observed. Fig. 2 shows the position of different countries based

Table 2 PCA scores for the COVID-19 spreading rate in the world.

Country	Principal component 1	Principal component 2
United States	7.35991	1.02625
Brazil	3.83766	−0.93391
India	3.0631	−1.1328
Russia	−0.05745	−0.33435
Peru	−0.2299	0.07801
South Africa	−0.4496	−0.21125
Colombia	−0.37968	−0.02601
Mexico	0.1028	0.40101
Spain	−0.67603	0.27283
Chile	−0.69056	−0.14815
Argentina	−0.68968	−0.02866
Iran	−0.60114	0.01152
United Kingdom	−0.57545	0.40732
Saudi Arabia	−0.85394	−0.13002
Bangladesh	−0.81685	0.02188
Pakistan	−0.84948	−0.10992
France	−0.52413	0.42022
Turkey	−0.86654	−0.06902
Italy	−0.53869	0.23671
Germany	−0.85536	−0.01885
Iraq	−0.87554	0.02578
Philippines	−0.92308	0.01802
Indonesia	−0.92733	0.06505
Canada	−0.96378	0.05953
Ukraine	−1.01927	0.09879

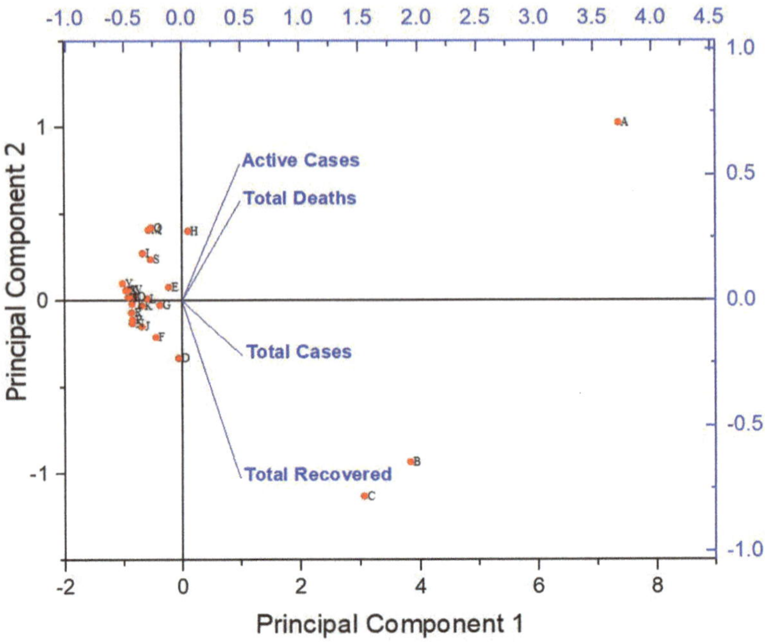

Fig. 2 Results of PCA for the COVID-19 spreading within the whole world. A: USA; B: Brazil; C: India; D: Russia; E: Peru; F: South Africa; G: Colombia; H: Mexico; I: Spain; J: Chile; K: Argentina; L: Iran; M: UK; N: Saudi Arabia; O: Bangladesh; P: Pakistan; Q: France; R: Turkey; S: Italy; T: Germany; U: Iraq; V: Philippines; W: Indonesia; X: Canada; Y: Ukraine.

on PCA ranking. The United States shows its position in between PC-1 and PC-2. On the other hand, from Fig. 2, it can also be revealed that India and Brazil hang around total recovered cases.

7 Preventive measures taken by the top most affected countries to combat the COVID-19 during the first wave

7.1 Screening to find suspected cases

Initially when the number of cases started increasing during early January 2020 in Wuhan, China, and other regions of China, immediately various countries started screening all the passengers coming from China. As soon as it was found that the spreading rate of COVID-19 increases in Wuhan and Hubei province of China, countries around the world started airlifting their citizens from China as well as from other affected countries. Different countries have set the number of symptoms for proper screening to ascertain the suspected cases. Symptoms like fever, sore throat, running nose, coughing, etc. were taken into consideration while screening the suspected cases (Gupta et al., 2020). Later, several countries have initiated screening people showing the symptoms of COVID-19 even though they have no foreign travel history or close contact history with the person suffering from COVID-19.

7.2 Detecting and monitoring the rate of spreading

Countries throughout the world have started incorporating various laboratory testing criteria after observing an increased number of COVID-19 cases worldwide (Chan et al., 2020). Testing of samples collected from different suspected cases was initiated in various countries with immediate effect. Oropharyngeal and nasopharyngeal sample collection and transferring for further laboratory testing at 4°C temperature within 24 h of the collection were started from suspected cases. As it is a new virus, the initial diagnosis was difficult, so to get the final confirmation, collection of stool, blood, and urine samples was begun for examination. Further, a real-time PCR kit was employed to detect the suspected cases and increase the testing rate (Gupta et al., 2020). For accurate detection, better monitoring and to reduce the rate of spreading, once a confirmed case is known, police and local administrative bodies started finding all the persons who came in contact with the infected person for testing and quarantining as per the symptoms.

7.3 Other preventive measures

Starting from the beginning of COVID-19, governments of various countries and their respective administrative departments have started close monitoring of the situation. Constant review of different emergency issues such as hospital preparedness, diagnostics, infection prevention and control, logistics, and risk management have been initiated with immediate effect. A country like India (National Centre for Disease Control) introduced a helpline number to address public concerns (World Health Organization, 2020a). Apart from screening foreign return passengers, governments of various countries around the world began issuing different travel advisories regarding foreign travel (Gössling et al., 2020). In a highly populated country like India, both the central government and all the states' governments commenced working together to provide additional manpower and logistics support for better and smooth screening (World Health Organization, 2020b). The Ministry of Tourism, Government of India instigated communication with the hotels association in India to embolden travelers visiting in different identified states to come forward for voluntary screening and help the government to stop the spreading of COVID-19 (World Health Organization, 2020c). Governments around the world along with WHO started appealing to all the citizens to stay at home and follow COVID-19 appropriate behavior such as wearing a mask, social distancing, frequent hand washing or hand sanitization, etc. Children below 10 years of age and people over 65 years of age (excluding medical professionals, public representatives, and government servants) were strictly instructed to stay at home and to avoid any kind of mass gathering. Mask and hand sanitizers were considered essential commodities in various countries. Almost every country has started imposing restrictions on international flights in order to break the transmission chain of COVID-19. A country like India has experienced the world's biggest nationwide "lock down" to halt the transmission chain. On March 24, 2020 when confirmed cases in India starts increasing, the Government of India declared a nationwide lockdown for 21 days with effect from March 25, 2020, to April 14, 2020, under section 6(2) (i) of the Disaster Management Act, 2015. Further, international and domestic flight services, railway services, and interstate passenger connectivity were suspended till April 14, 2020 (World Health Organization, 2020d). To assess the risk of COVID-19 infection of the citizens of India, the Government of India launched a mobile-based app named, "Aarogya Setu" on April 2, 2020. The Ministry of Health and Family Welfare (MoHFW) provided a guiding document on the appropriate management strategy as represented in Fig. 3 (Ministry of Health and Family Welfare, 2020).

8 Potential dietary remedies, herbal medicines, and allopathic therapy for COVID-19

Foods and herbs have always been a potential supplement for the prevention and treatment of several diseases like influenza, SARS-CoV-1, and MERS for decades. Foods such as *Aloe vera, Astragalus membranaceous, Angelica gigas, Ganoderma sucidum, Panax ginseng,* and *Scutellaria baicalensis* (Chinese skull cap) exhibit various immunomodulatory properties. They stimulate cytokines and activate lymphocytes, which enhances macrophage actions and increases killer cell counts (Tan and Vanitha, 2004). Rice bran, *Lawsonia alba* (Henna), wheat bran, *Echinacea purpurea* (Eastern purple cornflower), *Cisampelos pareira* Linn (Velvetleaf), and *Plumbago zeylanica* (Ceylon leadwort) stimulate phagocytosis. Eucalyptus oil has been reported to give

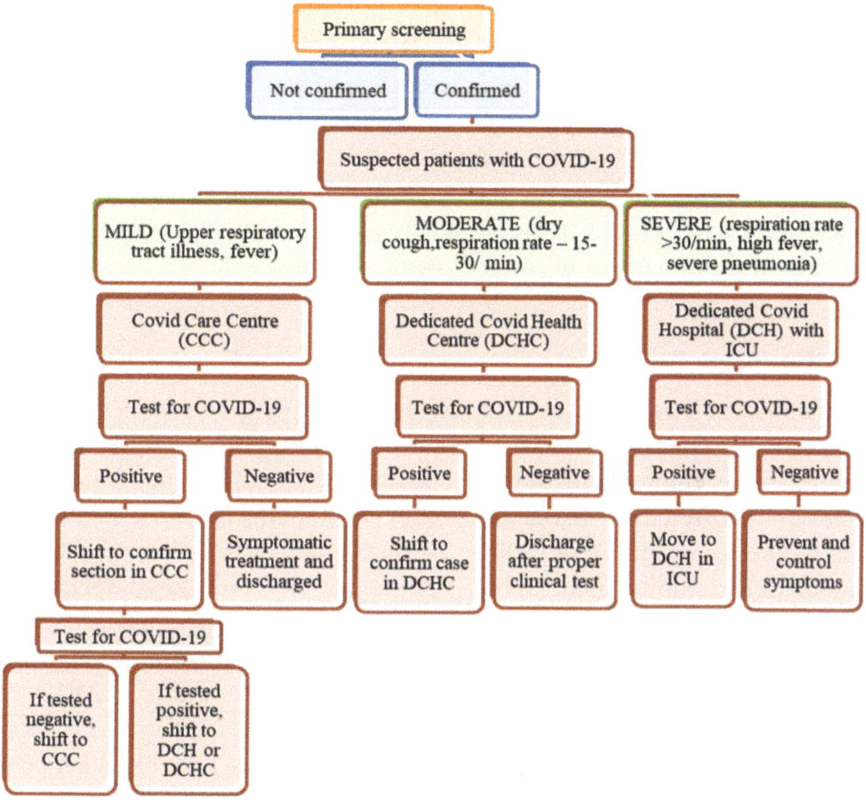

Fig. 3 Appropriate management strategy laid down by the Ministry of Health and Family Welfare, Government of India.

immunoregulatory effects against infectious diseases (Sadlon and Lamson, 2010; Serafino et al., 2008). It can be said that the collective use of these foods and herbs can help to increase the immune system to combat COVID-19. However, their applications must be verified through proper scientific studies (Panyod et al., 2020). During the first wave of COVID-19, there was not a single approved vaccine or treatment for this infectious disease and different possible approaches were applied to fight against the virus.

Studies revealed that various bioactive compounds present in foods and herbs can serve as a dietary therapy against COVID-19. The authors believe that foods and herbs can be helpful for four potential approaches: (a) to boost the immune system and prevent infection, (b) it can be used as an antiviral agent by coating them over masks, (c) essential oil can be used as a disinfectant to stop air transmission, and (d) can be used as surface sanitizers to provide a disinfected environment. Reaerosolization of masks is a good method to disinfect the masks. So, the coating of essential oil or any antiviral compound can reduce infection chances (Panyod et al., 2020). The phytochemicals, bioactive compounds in foods, and various supplements employed during the first wave of COVID-19 which may be still useful as a therapeutic option for the prevention and treatment of the COVID-19 virus are summarized in the following sections.

8.1 Vitamins

B vitamins are water soluble, and they function as coenzymes. Vitamin B2 serves for the energy metabolism of all cells, and it has been found that the United States elder groups suffer from its deficiency (Powers, 2003). The research indicated that MERS CoV was reduced in the human plasma products by the consumption of vitamin B2 (Keil et al., 2016). Vitamin B3 (nicotinamide) inhibits neutrophil infiltration in the lungs with an antiinflammatory effect due to ventilator-induced lung injuries (Jones et al., 2015). Vitamin B6 has a vital role in defining human immune function. Therefore, B vitamins were on the list of an alternative to COVID-19 treatment (Zhang and Liu, 2020).

Vitamin C also called ascorbic acid is a water-soluble vitamin. It has been seen that vitamin C enhanced the chick embryo trachean organ cultures resistance against avian coronavirus infection. It also acts as an antihistamine agent to give relief from flu-like symptoms such as swollen sinuses, runny nose, and sneezing. Human-controlled trials have also supported these findings. Vitamin C-supplemented herbs reduce or lower the incidence of pneumonia COVID which causes respiratory tract infection which can be sustained by the help of vitamin C (Field et al., 2002; Hemilä, 1997; Atherton et al., 1978).

Vitamin D helps in stimulating the maturation of cells known as immune cells, also maintains bone integrity in calves which give rise to bovine coronavirus (Nonnecke et al., 2014). Researchers have described the promising results of vitamin D related to the supplementation for respiratory tract infections, pulmonary fibrosis, and autoimmune diseases (Panfili et al., 2020). Normal to high blood levels of vitamin D have also shown a synergistic effect with tocilizumab patients by suppressing interleukin 6 (IL-6) improved osteocyte-mediated osteoclastogenesis and decreasing disease activity. Nevertheless, the data and information on COVID-19 survivors are lacking; vitamin D supplements before and after the injection may produce an antifibrotic role. Based on these direct and indirect productions, there can be a possible influence of this vitamin reaction to the virus and may provide a modulating result on the drug being administered (Panfili et al., 2020).

8.2 Omega (Ω) 3 fatty acids

Ω-3 fatty acids consist of a long chain of polyunsaturated fatty acids (PUFA) which are mediators of inflammation and adaptive responses. Ω-3 and Ω-6 PUFA present in food provide anti- and proinflammatory effects. Protectin D1 Ω-3 PUFA-derived lipid mediator attenuates influenza virus replication by RNA export machinery. Application of protectin D1 with peramivir may save mice from mortality against flu (Morita et al., 2013). Therefore, Ω-3 along with D1 was also on the list to serve as an antiviral drug against COVID-19 (Zhang and Liu, 2020).

8.3 Selenium

Selenium is found in trace amounts and is one of the essential elements in the body which provides defense against diseases. Selenium deficiency can cause oxidative stress in the host which can bring alteration in the genome of the virus making it more virulent (Guillin et al., 2019). It is because selenium assists a group of an enzyme in accordance with vitamin E in order to avoid the oxidative damage and free radicals formation (Harthill, 2011). It was found that selenium along with ginseng leaf saponins has a synergistic effect to give an immune response to the live virulent infectious bronchitis COVID in chicks (Ma et al., 2019) and that is the reason selenium is considered as an alternative treatment for COVID-19.

8.4 Zinc

Zinc is a dietary mineral that is necessary for the improvement of the adaptive and inherent immune system. A deficiency of this mineral in the system can cause susceptibility to infections. Zinc supplement reduces the mortality rate caused due to lower respiratory tract infections (Awotiwon et al., 2017). It has been seen that zinc along with zinc ionospheres pyrithione can impair a range of RNA viruses, and these at low concentrations impede replication of SARS corona (TeVelthuis et al., 2010). So, zinc is effective not only on symptoms like low respiratory infection and diarrhea, but also for COVID treatment (Zhang and Liu, 2020).

8.5 Curcumin

It is a natural polyphenolic compound that can be used as a potential treatment for COVID-19 patients. The preliminary for COVID infection is interaction with the human cell and viral spike protein. Angiotensin-converting enzyme 2 (ACE-2) presents in the human respiratory tract which acts as the receptor is identified by the SARS-CoV-2 spike protein. Then the viral genome RNA is released in the cytoplasm which follows membrane fusion and the RNA codes for instant replication of proteins and transcription complex (Jia et al., 2005). After entering the cell, the CoV enables the expression of gene and encoding of genome ensues. This will again in turn encode the accessory protein which allows the adaption of CoV to the human host. This curcumin can restrain the virus entry to the cell, prevent the virus encapsulation and viral protease, and modulate different cell signaling pathways. Curcumin has various antiviral activities and is a therapeutic choice for the management of COVID-19 infection. Curcumin can modulate several molecular targets that get attachment and internalization of SARS-CoV-2 in various organs including the kidney and liver. Curcumin can modulate cellular signals such as apoptosis, inflammation, and RNA replication. It also suppresses pulmonary edema and fibrosis associated with the pathway of COVID-19 infection. But the bioavailability of curcumin is less which can only be mitigated by the administration of nontoxic limits. Overall, the immunomodulatory and antiinflammatory effects show evidence of the antifibrotic and pulmonary protective nature of this phytochemical on lung tissue making it a potential way of COVID-19 treatment (Zahedipour et al., 2020).

8.6 Probiotics

Probiotic actions like the influence on cytokine production by intestinal epithelial cells. Immunoglobulin A (IgA) secretion and stimulation increase mucosal immunity and activate phagocytosis and macrophage production. Its principal effect on innate and adaptive immunity makes it a possible inhibitor. But all probiotics do not possess the same characteristics, thus a more potential targeted approach is required through characterization of properties by the development of potential COVID-19 application. The virus of COVID-19 has shown influences on intestinal microbiota dysbiosis, and probiotics have demonstrated efficacy for the respiratory tract viral infections management. The postmortem of many COVID-19 patients has revealed that severe respiratory syndrome and severe lung, heart, and liver tissue damage. Some exhibited intestinal microbial dysbiosis with reduced probiotics such as bifidobacterium and lactobacillus which indicate the need for the gastrointestinal function of all the infected persons (Xu et al., 2020). This dysbiosis is linked with various other infections of the respiratory tract through the gut lung axis. Application of prebiotic or probiotic and nutritional support are recommended for COVID-19–infected persons to control the intestinal microbiota and decrease secondary infection owing to translocation of bacteria. As there was no effective treatment for COVID-19 infection during the first wave due to a lack of evidence and trait, so the urgent need for prevention using probiotics against COVID-19 related to gut microbiota was one of the alternative methods (Bottari et al., 2020). Further research is required to address the probiotic role in attenuating COVID-19 either by the immunomodulatory actions on systematic inflammation or by direct interaction with the lungs.

8.7 Chinese medicines

Rhizoma Polygonati is an herbal food grown in Mount Tai whose rhizome is commonly used as herbal medicine and it belongs to the family *Liliaceae polygonatum*. It consists of polysaccharides and has been used to treat symptoms having a deficiency of lungs, spleen, and weakness of qi. Various clinical applications and recommendation evidence, and different potential compounds were observed in Rhizoma Polygonati for anti-COVID-19. Rhizoma Polygonati can also eliminate the cytokine of COVID-19 by treatment of lung inflammation enhancing the immune system response in mice. Furthermore, polygonatum polysaccharide from rhizome and sulfation Radix Codonopsis (Dangshen) composition polysaccharide were observed to have an effect against the new castle disease virus. This can be a promising feature of Rhizoma Polygonati to combat viruses. Further investigation and more trials are required to develop the drugs (Mu et al., 2021). Glycyrrhizin present in licorice root can prevent the SARS virus replication in vitro and also serve as an alternative approach for the treatment of SARS. Baicalin, another Chinese herb shows the potential to inhibit SARS-CoV. Ginseng stem leaf saponins could be used for the significant enhancement of specific antibody responses to the infectious bronchitis virus. Therefore, researchers suggested that these can also be used to enhance immunity against COVID-19 (Zhang and Liu, 2020).

8.8 *Nigella sativa* (*N. sativa*) compounds

N. sativa, a black seed globally used as medicine in the plant as for its oil and seeds in food systems. It consists of potential natural antiviral agents against COVID-19. Nigellone has a high affinity toward COVID as the ACE-2 interface interacts with various hydrophilic and hydrophobic bonding. *N. sativa* possesses gut absorption ability and high solubility which makes it suitable for future optimization of potent derivatives. ACE-2 is a highly stable interface that can bind free energy assay by acquiring a low level of energy. It was found to have a higher binding affinity (8.2 kcal/mol) compared to chloroquine against SARS-CoV2:ACE2 which can be an acceptable inhibitor to interrupt the interaction of viral host. So, these findings suggested that nigellone, a carbonyl polymer of thymoquinone has the potential to act as the inhibitor (Ahmad et al., 2020).

8.9 Application of allopathic therapy

During the initial phase, there was not a single effective treatment available for COVID-19 (Wu and McGoogan, 2020). Throughout the world, various drugs have been applied to treat COVID-19 patients. It has been found that more than a dozen of allopathic drugs have been applied and many of them showed their potentiality at different levels although the clinical affectivity was under observation. As there was no specific drug or vaccine available for this disease and the world was desperately waiting for a vaccine or effective medicine against this pandemic. Doctors were trying to apply all possible drugs based on their previous track record against other similar kinds of diseases to save as much as possible lives (Singh et al., 2020). Chloroquine, hydroxychloroquine (HCQ)- the derivative of chloroquine, and remdesivir were at the top of the list among all the drugs applied to treat COVID-19 patients. Chloroquine is an old drug and medically used worldwide for more than the last 70 years. Chloroquine is cheap, approved for malaria, and WHO recommended it as an essential drug. HCQ is used in India for treating type II diabetes patients since 2004 (Singh et al., 2020; Cortegiani et al., 2020). Similarly, remdesivir showed effective results against MERS and SARS. A study on remdesivir in mice showed that remdesivir improved lung function by reducing the viral load (Cortegiani et al., 2020). Methylprednisolone was also used for the treatment of COVID-19. Thymosin α-1 has been used as an immune enhancer for SARS patients to control the spreading. As methylprednisolone has side effects related to corticoid-induced death of thymocytes, therefore, researchers and scientists have recommended using thymosin α-1 before methylprednisolone (Zhang and Liu, 2020). Similarly, cyclophilin has also played a vital part in inhibiting virus replication. So, it was expected to inhibit cyclophilus and halt the coronavirus genomes replication including SARS-CoV and avian infections such as bronchitis virus. So, this may act as a COVID-19 inhibitor and therefore, scientists and doctors were expecting positive results from these medicines while treating COVID-19 patients, especially HCQ for COVID-19 patients with diabetes and in many cases positive results were observed after using all these drugs. However, the efficiency of these drugs for COVID-19 is still not clear. Apart from chloroquine, hydroxychloroquine, and remdesivir drugs like; ribavirin plus interferon, camostat mesilate, lopinavir or ritonavir, darunavir or cobicistat, nelfinavir, favipiravir, umifenovir, etc., were the other drugs that have been applied for COVID-19 treatment around the world (Singh et al., 2020; Lai et al., 2020). Ribavirin plus interferon (showed mixed result against MERS-CoV), camostat mesilate (found efficiently blocked COVID-19 virus in lung cells during in vitro study), and lopinavir or ritonavir (found efficient against SARS-CoV-1 both in human and in vitro studies) were the other promising drugs after chloroquine, hydroxychloroquine, and remdesivir and applied to manage COVID-19–infected persons in various places. Some drugs like darunavir, cobicistat, and nelfinavir were used for COVID-19 patients because of their anti-HIV ability. However, darunavir or cobicistat was never approved against coronavirus or other respiratory viruses. Similarly, medicine having a previous track record as an antiviral medicine such as favipiravir for filovirus, arenavirus, bunyavirus, etc., and umifenovir for coronaviruses were also in the trial and have been applied to treat many COVID-19 patients (Singh et al., 2020).

Patients with comorbidity are at higher risk of COVID-19 than patients with a strong immune system. Therefore, drugs that are effective for other diseases and drugs with antiviral, antioxidant, antiinflammatory, and immunomodulation ability can be practiced for the treatment of COVID-19 patients to lessen the severity of other diseases as well as to boost up the body immune system to fight against COVID-19. Infected persons having mild symptoms such as cough, fever, throat pain, etc. can also take these drugs depending on the condition of the symptoms after consulting with the medical practitioner and they can stay in home isolation so that severe patients will get a bed in hospitals (Lai et al., 2020). However, the application of antiviral drugs for patients with comorbidity is risky and the probability of mortality rates is high (Pascarella et al., 2020).

Depending on the severity of the patient apart from medicine, saving the failure of the respiratory system is an effective technique to save the life from COVID-19 (Pascarella et al., 2020). In the case of hypoxia or respiratory distress, oxygen therapy is especially required to save the respiratory system. But to avoid any kind of lung injury, level of arterial $SatO_2$ must be monitored carefully at the time of oxygen therapy and the level of $SatO_2$ must be within the range of 93%–96%.

Apart from all these practices, it has been found that some specific antibodies developed in the bodies of patients get recovered from COVID-19 and these antibodies have the potential to treat other active COVID-19 patients through plasma therapy. Initially, it was found that five out of five patients in critical condition with acute respiratory distress syndrome showed clinical improvement after the application of plasma therapy. States like Delhi (capital of India) officially applied plasma therapy to treat COVID-19–infested persons and achieved several positive outcomes. Similarly, other countries also applied this technique and get several positive outputs, and countries like the United States adopted this technique to treat COVID-19 patients during the initial phase of COVID-19. However, a significant level of scientific studies is still required to get clarity about the adoptability of plasma therapy against COVID-19. Moreover, enhancement of the immune response of the host body is the main concern during the initial days and before the discovery of vaccines to fight against the SARS-CoV-2 virus. Therefore, particularly until there was not a specific vaccine or medicine for COVID-19, doctors and scientists around the world were applying all these allopathic treatments along with other remedies to reduce the worst scenario of this pandemic.

9 Conclusions

Lessons from the various historical pandemics and epidemics, COVID-19 transmissibility, severity, incubation period, spreading behavior using PCA application of allopathic therapy, dietary remedy and herbal medicine, and precautionary measures taken by the various countries to combat COVID-19 pandemic particularly during the first wave were deciphered in this chapter. PCA showed the spreading behavior of COVID-19 within different countries. The analysis within the 25 most severely affected countries during the first wave showed the United States at a higher position in between PC-1 and PC-2. It was observed that India and Brazil were around total recovered cases. Foods and herb-based products were employed in different approaches: improve the immune system, prevent infection, use as an antiviral agent by coating them over the mask, and the essential oil as a disinfectant to stop air transmission and as a surface sanitizer to provide a disinfected environment. During the initial phase, chloroquine, hydroxychloroquine, and remdesivir were the most commonly used drugs to treat COVID-19 patients in terms of allopathic therapy along with some dietary remedies and medicinal herbs as an immunity booster. Although there was no such strong scientifically and experimentally verified evidence regarding the application of allopathic therapy, dietary remedy, and medicinal herbs for the treatment of COVID-19–infected persons, these techniques were commonly applied to fight this deadly pandemic, particularly during the initial phase when there was no known vaccine.

Acknowledgment

The second and fourth authors express their gratitude to the Indian Institute of Technology Delhi for providing research fellowship and the Government of India for providing the National Overseas Scholarship, respectively.

References

Ahmad, S., Abbasi, H.W., Shahid, S., Gul, S., Abbasi, S.W., 2020. Molecular docking, simulation and MM-PBSA studies of Nigella sativa compounds: a computational quest to identify potential natural antiviral for COVID-19 treatment. J. Biomol. Struct. Dyn. 12, 1–16. https://doi.org/10.1080/07391102.2020.1775129.

Anderson, R.M., Fraser, C., Ghani, A.C., Donnelly, C.A., Riley, S., Ferguson, N.M., Gabriel, M.L., Lam, T.H., Anthony, J.H., 2004. Epidemiology, transmission dynamics and control of SARS: the 2002–2003 epidemic. Philos. Trans. R. Soc. B Biol. Sci. 359, 1091–1105.

Atherton, J.G., Kratzing, C.C., Fisher, A., 1978. The effect of ascorbic acid on infection chick-embryo ciliated tracheal organ cultures by coronavirus. Arch. Virol. 56, 195–199. https://doi.org/10.1007/BF01317848.

Awotiwon, A.A., Oduwole, O., Sinha, A., Okwundu, C.I., 2017. Zinc supplementation for the treatment of measles in children. Cochrane Database Syst. Rev. 6, 1–17. https://doi.org/10.1002/14651858.CD011177.pub3.

Bhatnagar, T., Murhekar, M.V., Soneja, M., Gupta, N., Giri, S., Wig, N., Gangakhedkar, R., 2020. Lopinavir/ritonavir combination therapy amongst symptomatic coronavirus disease 2019 patients in India: protocol for restricted public health emergency use. Indian J. Med. Res. 151, 184–189. http://www.ncbi.nlm.nih.gov/pubmed/23144490.

Bottari, B., Castellone, V., Neviani, E., 2020. Probiotics and Covid-19. Int. J. Food Sci. Nutr. 72 (3), 293–299. https://doi.org/10.1080/09637486.2020.1807475.

Brann, D., Tsukahara, T., Weinreb, C., Logan, D.W., Datta, S.R., 2020. Non-neuronal expression of SARS-CoV-2 entry genes in the olfactory system suggests mechanisms underlying COVID-19-associated anosmia. BioRxiv. https://doi.org/10.1101/2020.03.25.009084. The Preprint Server for Biology.

Breman, J.G., Henderson, D.A., 2002. Diagnosis and management of smallpox. N. Engl. J. Med. 346, 1300–1308.

Butler, T., 2009. Plague into the 21st century. Clin. Infect. Dis. 49, 736–742.
CDCP, 2019. H1N1 Flu. Centers for Disease Control and Prevention, pp. 1–9.
CDCP, 2020. Middle East Respiratory Syndrome (MERS). Centers for Disease Control and Prevention.
Chan, J.F.W., Yuan, S., Kok, K.H., To, K.K.W., Chu, H., Yang, J., Xing, F., Liu, J., Yip, C. C.Y., Poon, R.W.S., Tsoi, H.W., 2020. A familial cluster of pneumonia associated with the 2019 novel coronavirus indicating person-to-person transmission: a study of a family cluster. Lancet 395 (10223), 514–523. https://doi.org/10.1016/S0140-6736(20)30154-9.
Chang, D., Lin, M., Wei, L., Xie, L., Zhu, G., Cruz, C.S.D., Sharma, L., 2020. Epidemiologic and clinical characteristics of novel coronavirus infections involving 13 patients outside Wuhan, China. JAMA 323 (11), 1092–1093. http://jamanetwork.com/article.aspx?doi=10.1001/jama.2020.1623.
Chatterjee, P., Nagi, N., Agarwal, A., Das, B., Banerjee, S., Sarkar, S., Gupta, N., Gangakhedkar, R.R., 2020. The 2019 novel coronavirus disease (COVID-19) pandemic: a review of the current evidence. Indian J. Med. Res. 151 (2–3), 147–159. https://doi.org/10.4103/ijmr.ijmr_519_20.
Chen, N., Zhou, M., Dong, X., Qu, J., Gong, F., Han, Y., Qiu, Y., Wang, J., Liu, Y., Wei, Y., Yu, T., 2020. Epidemiological and clinical characteristics of 99 cases of 2019 novel coronavirus pneumonia in Wuhan, China: a descriptive study. Lancet 395 (10223), 507–513. https://doi.org/10.1016/S0140-6736(20)30211-7.
Correia, S., Luck, S., Verner, E., 2020. Pandemics depress the economy, public health interventions do not: evidence from the 1918 flu. SSRN Electron. J. https://ssrn.com/abstract=3561560.
Cortegiani, A., Ingoglia, G., Ippolito, M., Giarratano, A., Einav, S., 2020. A systematic review on the efficacy and safety of chloroquine for the treatment of COVID-19. J. Crit. Care 57, 279–283. https://doi.org/10.1016/j.jcrc.2020.03.005.
Dharmshaktu, N.S., 2020. The lessons learned from current ongoing pandemic public health crisis of COVID 19 and its management in India from various different angles, perspectives and way forward. Epidemiol. Int. 5 (1), 1–4. https://orcid.org/0000-0002-4520-079X.
Docherty, A.B., et al., 2020. Features of 20 133 UK patients in hospital with Covid-19 using the ISARIC WHO Clinical Characterisation Protocol: prospective observational cohort study. BMJ. https://doi.org/10.1136/bmj.m1985.
Dutta, D., Chowdhury, G., Pazhani, G.P., Guin, S., Dutta, S., Ghosh, S., Rajendran, K., Nandy, R.K., Mukhopadhyay, A.K., Bhattacharya, M.K., Mitra, U., 2013. Vibrio cholerae non-O1, non-O139 serogroups and cholera-like diarrhea, Kolkata, India. Emerg. Infect. Dis. 19 (3), 464–467.
Felsenfeld, O., 1969. Some observations on the cholera (E1 Tor) epidemic in 1961–62. Bull. World Health Organ. 28, 289–296.
Field, C.J., Johnson, I.R., Schley, P.D., 2002. Nutrients and their role in host resistance to infection. J. Leukoc. Biol. 71 (1), 16–32. https://doi.org/10.1189/jlb.71.1.16.
Garrett, T.A., 2008. Pandemic economics: the 1918 influenza and its modern-day implications. Fed. Reserve Bank St. Louis Rev. 90, 75–93.
Gössling, S., Scott, D., Hall, C.M., 2020. Pandemics, tourism and global change: a rapid assessment of COVID-19. J. Sustain. Tour. 29 (1), 1–20. https://doi.org/10.1080/09669582.2020.1758708.
Guan, W.J., Ni, Z.Y., Hu, Y., Liang, W.H., Ou, C.Q., He, J.X., Liu, L., Shan, H., Lei, C.L., Hui, D.S., Du, B., 2020. Clinical characteristics of coronavirus disease 2019 in China. N. Engl. J. Med. 382 (18), 1708–1720. https://doi.org/10.1016/S0140-6736(20)30211-7.

Guarner, J.M.D., 2020. Three emerging coronaviruses in two decades: the story of SARS, MERS, and now COVID-19. Am. J. Clin. Pathol. 153 (4), 420–421. https://doi.org/10.1093/ajcp/aqaa029.

Guillin, O.M., Vindry, C., Ohlmann, T., Chavatte, L., 2019. Selenium, selenoproteins and viral infection. Nutrients 11 (9), 2101. https://doi.org/10.3390/nu11092101.

Gupta, N., Potdar, V., Praharaj, I., Giri, S., Sapkal, G., Yadav, P., Choudhary, M.L., Dar, L., Sugunan, A.P., Kaur, H., Munivenkatappa, A., 2020. Laboratory preparedness for SARS-CoV-2 testing in India: harnessing a network of virus research & diagnostic laboratories. Indian J. Med. Res. 151 (2–3), 216–225. https://doi.org/10.4103/ijmr.IJMR_594_20.

Harthill, M., 2011. Micronutrient selenium deficiency influences evolution of some viral infectious diseases. Biol. Trace Elem. Res. 143 (3), 1325–1336. https://doi.org/10.1007/s12011-011-8977-1.

Hemilä, H., 1997. Vitamin C intake and susceptibility to pneumonia. Pediatr. Infect. Dis. J. 16 (9), 836–837. https://doi.org/10.1097/00006454-199709000-00003.

Islam, A., Ahmed, A., Naqvi, I.H., Parveen, S., 2020. Emergence of deadly severe acute respiratory syndrome coronavirus-2 during 2019–2020. Virusdisease 31 (2), 128–136. http://link.springer.com/10.1007/s13337-020-00575-1.

Jia, H.P., Look, D.C., Shi, L., Hickey, M., Pewe, L., Netland, J., Farzan, M., Wohlford-Lenane, C., Perlman, S., McCray Jr., P.B., 2005. ACE2 receptor expression and severe acute respiratory syndrome coronavirus infection depend on differentiation of human airway epithelia. J. Virol. 79 (23), 14614–14621. https://doi.org/10.1128/JVI.79.23.14614-14621.2005.

Jilani, T.N, Jamil, R.T., Siddiqui, A.H., 2019. H1N1 Influenza. StatPearls.

Jones, H.D., Yoo, J., Crother, T.R., Kyme, P., Ben-Shlomo, A., Khalafi, R., Tseng, C.W., Parks, W.C., Arditi, M., Liu, G.Y., Shimada, K., 2015. Nicotinamide exacerbates hypoxemia in ventilator-induced lung injury independent of neutrophil infiltration. PLoS One 10 (4). https://doi.org/10.1371/journal.pone.0123460, e0123460.

Keil, S.D., Bowen, R., Marschner, S., 2016. Inactivation of Middle East respiratory syndrome coronavirus (MERS-CoV) in plasma products using a riboflavin-based and ultraviolet light-based photochemical treatment. Transfusion 56 (12), 2948–2952. https://doi.org/10.1111/trf.13860.

Khan, S.I., 1995. Plague in India. Aligarh Muslim University, Aligarh, India.

Kumar, P., Sachan, A., Kakar, A., Gogia, A., 2015. Socioeconomic impact of the recent outbreak of H1N1. Curr. Med. Res. Pract. 5 (4), 163–167. https://doi.org/10.1016/j.cmrp.2015.06.007.

Lai, C.C., Liu, Y.H., Wang, C.Y., Wang, Y.H., Hsueh, S.C., Yen, M.Y., Ko, W.C., Hsueh, P.R., 2020. Asymptomatic carrier state, acute respiratory disease, and pneumonia due to severe acute respiratory syndrome coronavirus 2 (SARS-CoV-2): facts and myths. J. Microbiol. Immunol. Infect. 53 (3), 404–412. https://doi.org/10.1016/j.jmii.2020.02.012.

Lee, J.W., McKibbin, W.J., 2004. Globalization and disease: the case of SARS. Asian Econ. Pap. 3 (1), 113–131.

Li, Q., Guan, X., Wu, P., Wang, X., Zhou, L., Tong, Y., Ren, R., Leung, K.S., Lau, E.H., Wong, J.Y., Xing, X., 2020. Early transmission dynamics in Wuhan, China, of novel coronavirus–infected pneumonia. N. Engl. J. Med. 382, 1199–1207. https://doi.org/10.1056/nejmoa2001316.

Ma, X., Bi, S., Wang, Y., Chi, X., Hu, S., 2019. Combined adjuvant effect of ginseng stem-leaf saponins and selenium on immune responses to a live bivalent vaccine of Newcastle disease virus and infectious bronchitis virus in chickens. Poult. Sci. 98 (9), 3548–3556. https://doi.org/10.3382/ps/pez207.

Mahase, E., 2020. Coronavirus: covid-19 has killed more people than SARS and MERS combined, despite lower case fatality rate. BMJ 368. https://doi.org/10.1136/bmj.m641, m64.

Mandal, S., 2011. Cholera epidemic in and around Kolkata, India: endemicity and management. Oman Med. J. 26 (4), 288–289.

Ministry of Health and Family Welfare, 2020. Guidance Document on Appropriate Management of Suspect/Confirmed Cases of COVID-19. https://www.mohfw.gov.in/. (Accessed 21 May 2020).

Mishra, A.C., Chadha, M.S., Choudhary, M.L., Potdar, V.A., 2010. Pandemic influenza (H1N1) 2009 is associated with severe disease in India. PLoS One 5 (5), e10540.

Morita, M., Kuba, K., Ichikawa, A., Nakayama, M., Katahira, J., Iwamoto, R., Watanebe, T., Sakabe, S., Daidoji, T., Nakamura, S., Kadowaki, A., 2013. The lipid mediator protectin D1 inhibits influenza virus replication and improves severe influenza. Cell 153 (1), 112–125. https://doi.org/10.1016/j.cell.2013.02.027.

Mu, C., Sheng, Y., Wang, Q., Amin, A., Li, X., Xie, Y., 2021. Potential compound from herbal food of *Rhizomapolygonati* for treatment of COVID-19 analyzed by network pharmacology: viral and cancer signaling mechanisms. J. Funct. Foods 77. https://doi.org/10.1016/j.jff.2020.104149, 104149.

Nonnecke, B.J., McGill, J.L., Ridpath, J.F., Sacco, R.E., Lippolis, J.D., Reinhardt, T.A., 2014. Acute phase response elicited by experimental bovine diarrhea virus (BVDV) infection is associated with decreased vitamin D and E status of vitamin-replete preruminant calves. J. Dairy Sci. 97 (9), 5566–5579. https://doi.org/10.3168/jds.2014-8293.

Panfili, F.M., Roversi, M., D'Argenio, P., Rossi, P., Cappa, M., Fintini, D., 2020. Possible role of vitamin D in Covid-19 infection in pediatric population. J. Endocrinol. Investig., 1–9. https://doi.org/10.1007/s40618-020-01327-0.

Panyod, S., Ho, C.T., Sheen, L.Y., 2020. Dietary therapy and herbal medicine for COVID-19 prevention: a review and perspective. J. Tradit. Complement. Med. 10, 420–427. https://doi.org/10.1016/j.jtcme.2020.05.004.

Pascarella, G., Strumia, A., Piliego, C., Bruno, F., Del Buono, R., Costa, F., Scarlata, S., Agrò, F.E., 2020. COVID-19 diagnosis and management: a comprehensive review. J. Intern. Med. 288 (2), 192–206. https://doi.org/10.1093/ajcn/77.6.1352.

Powers, H.J., 2003. Riboflavin (vitamin B-2) and health. Am. J. Clin. Nutr. 77 (6), 1352–1360. https://doi.org/10.1093/ajcn/77.6.1352.

Qiu, W., Chu, C., Mao, A., Wu, J., 2018. The impacts on health, society, and economy of SARS and H7N9 outbreaks in China: a case comparison study. J. Environ. Public Health, 1–8. https://doi.org/10.1155/2018/2710185.

Reid, A., 2005. The effects of the 1918–1919 influenza pandemic on infant and child health in Derbyshire. Med. Hist. 49 (1), 29–54.

Sadlon, A.E., Lamson, D.W., 2010. Immune-modifying and antimicrobial effects of Eucalyptus oil and simple inhalation devices. Altern. Med. Rev. 15 (1), 33–43.

Serafino, A., Vallebona, P.S., Andreola, F., Zonfrillo, M., Mercuri, L., Federici, M., Rasi, G., Garaci, E., Pierimarchi, P., 2008. Stimulatory effect of Eucalyptus essential oil on innate cell-mediated immune response. BMC Immunol. 9 (1), 1–16. https://doi.org/10.1186/1471-2172-9-17.

Singh, A.K., Singh, A., Shaikh, A., Singh, R., Misra, A., 2020. Chloroquine and hydroxychloroquine in the treatment of COVID-19 with or without diabetes: a systematic search and a narrative review with a special reference to India and other developing countries. Diabetes Metab. Syndr. Clin. Res. Rev. 14 (3), 241–246. https://doi.org/10.1016/j.dsx.2020.03.011.

Singhal, T., 2020. A review of coronavirus disease-2019 (COVID-19). Indian J. Pediatr. 87 (4), 281–286. https://doi.org/10.1007/s12098-020-03263-6.

Tan, B.K., Vanitha, J., 2004. Immunomodulatory and antimicrobial effects of some traditional Chinese medicinal herbs: a review. Curr. Med. Chem. 11 (11), 1423–1430. https://doi.org/10.2174/0929867043365161.
Tandon, P.N., 2020. COVID-19: impact on health of people & wealth of nations. Indian J. Med. Res. 151 (2–3), 121–123. http://www.ncbi.nlm.nih.gov/pubmed/23144490.
TeVelthuis, A.J., van den Worm, S.H., Sims, A.C., Baric, R.S., Snijder, E.J., van Hemert, M.J., 2010. Zn^{2+} inhibits coronavirus and arterivirus RNA polymerase activity in vitro and zinc ionophores block the replication of these viruses in cell culture. PLoS Pathog. 6 (11). https://doi.org/10.1371/journal.ppat.1001176, e1001176.
Tognotti, E., 2003. Scientific triumphalism and learning from facts: bacteriology and the 'Spanish flu' challenge of 1918. Soc. Hist. Med. 16 (1), 97–110.
Velavan, T.P, Meyer, C.G, 2020. The COVID-19 epidemic. Trop. Med. Int. Health 25 (3), 278–280. https://doi.org/10.1111/tmi.13383.
Wang, D., Hu, B., Hu, C., Zhu, F., Liu, X., Zhang, J., Wang, B., Xiang, H., Cheng, Z., Xiong, Y., Zhao, Y., 2020. Clinical characteristics of 138 hospitalized patients with 2019 novel coronavirus–infected pneumonia in Wuhan, China. JAMA 323 (11), 1061–1069. https://doi.org/10.1001/jama.2020.1585.
World Health Organization, 2020a. Novel Coronavirus (2019-nCov): Situation Report-1. https://www.who.int/docs/default-source/wrindia/india-situation-report 1.pdf?sfvrsn=5ca2a672_0. (Accessed 3 July 2020).
World Health Organization, 2020b. Novel Coronavirus (2019-nCov): Situation Report-4. https://www.who.int/docs/default-source/coronaviruse/situation-reports/2020a0124-sitrep-4-2019-ncov.pdf?sfvrsn=9272d086_8. (Accessed 3 July 2020).
World Health Organization, 2020c. Novel Coronavirus (2019-nCov): Situation Update Report-6. https://www.who.int/docs/default-source/wrindia/situation-report/india-situation-report-6606711da860b4d38b266c91265952977.pdf?sfvrsn=2f6c5c95_2. (Accessed 15 July 2020).
World Health Organization, 2020d. Novel Coronavirus (2019-nCov): Situation Update Report-10. https://www.who.int/docs/default-source/wrindia/situation-report/india-situation-report-10.pdf?sfvrsn=48298da5_2. (Accessed 15 July 2020).
Worldometer, 2020. Coronavirus Cases. https://www.worldometers.info/coronavirus/?fbclid=IwAR35ZFiRZJ8tyBCwazX2N-k7yJjZOLDQiZSA_MsJAfdK74s8f2a_Dgx4iVk. (Accessed 31 August 2020).
Worldometer, 2021. Coronavirus Cases. https://www.worldometers.info/coronavirus/?fbclid=IwAR35ZFiRZJ8tyBCwazX2N-k7yJjZOLDQiZSA_MsJAfdK74s8f2a_Dgx4iVk. (Accessed 8 June 2021).
Wu, Z., McGoogan, J.M., 2020. Characteristics of and important lessons from the coronavirus disease 2019 (COVID-19) outbreak in China: summary of a report of 72 314 cases from the Chinese Center for Disease Control and Prevention. JAMA 323 (13), 1239–1242. https://doi.org/10.1001/jama.2020.2648.
Wu, D., Wu, T., Liu, Q., Yang, Z., 2020. The SARS-CoV-2 outbreak: what we know. Int. J. Infect. Dis. 94, 44–48. https://doi.org/10.1016/j.ijid.2020.03.004.
Xu, Z., Shi, L., Wang, Y., Zhang, J., Huang, L., Zhang, C., Liu, S., Zhao, P., Liu, H., Zhu, L., Tai, Y., 2020. Pathological findings of COVID-19 associated with acute respiratory distress syndrome. Lancet Respir. Med. 8 (4), 420–422. https://doi.org/10.1016/S2213-2600(20)30076-X.
Zahedipour, F., Hosseini, S.A., Sathyapalan, T., Majeed, M., Jamialahmadi, T., Al-Rasadi, K., Banach, M., Sahebkar, A., 2020. Potential effects of curcumin in the treatment of COVID-19 infection. Phytother. Res. 34 (11), 2911–2920. https://doi.org/10.1002/ptr.6738.
Zhang, L., Liu, Y., 2020. Potential interventions for novel coronavirus in China: a systematic review. J. Med. Virol. 92 (5), 479–490. https://doi.org/10.1002/jmv.25707.

Zhou, P., Yang, X.L., Wang, X.G., Hu, B., Zhang, L., Zhang, W., Si, H.R., Zhu, Y., Li, B., Huang, C.L., Chen, H.D., 2020. A pneumonia outbreak associated with a new coronavirus of probable bat origin. Nature 579 (7798), 270–273. https://doi.org/10.1038/s41586-020-2012-7.

Zu, Z.Y., Jiang, M.D., Xu, P.P., Chen, W., Ni, Q.Q., Lu, G.M., Zhang, L.J., 2020. Coronavirus disease 2019 (COVID-19): a perspective from China. Radiology 296 (2), E15–E25. https://doi.org/10.1148/radiol.2020200490.

CHAPTER NINE

Challenges and opportunities in the provision of mental health care services during the COVID-19 pandemic and beyond

Magnolia B. Ngcobo-Sithole and Thabisa E. Mabusela
Department of Psychology, Nelson Mandela University, Gqeberha, South Africa

1 Introduction

The COVID-19 pandemic is unlike any other pandemic, and it has led to a revolution in mental health care services. This revolution occurred following the World Health Organization's (WHO) declaration of COVID-19 as a pandemic on January 30, 2020 (Lavah, 2020). As of May 2021, 1,637,848 active cases of COVID-19 had been identified in South Africa (Media Statement, 24 May 2021) and this number is expected to grow considering the third wave projections and the ease of transmission of the virus.

When WHO issued recommendations for physical distancing to curb the spread of the virus, governments imposed various strategies to guide populations on quarantine requirements and the need to stay at home. According to Lavah (2020) in Israel, social gatherings were canceled, schools were closed, institutions of higher learning were closed, and public transportation was minimized. Similarly, the South African government acted rapidly imposing a strict "national lockdown" policy on March 26, 2020 which essentially required citizens to stay at home as much as possible, except to get essentials such as food or medications.

When people are prevented to move, there will be adjustment problems. Consequently, populations worldwide presented with psycho-social problems. Some difficulties that they experienced in coping manifested themselves in depression, anxiety, substance use, somatization, and in many other ways (Lavah, 2020; Qiu et al., 2020; Wang et al., 2020). People with certain health conditions and comorbidities were identified as particularly at risk and there was a concern that if they get infected, they faced the

Lessons from COVID-19
https://doi.org/10.1016/B978-0-323-99878-9.00008-X

possibility of presenting with more severe symptoms. World Health Organisation (2020) identified comorbidities associated with the respiratory or the circulatory system or compromised immune systems as more vulnerable. We argue that the mental health consequences of such unprecedented societal changes from the lockdown were severe in South Africa given considerable psychiatric morbidity associated with an already challenged health system, a high unemployment rate, and poverty.

The effect of COVID-19 on mental health and well-being was felt at the individual level, interpersonal level, community level, nationally, and internationally. This perspective was adopted from the ecological model. It ensures that we view not only the impact of COVID-19 comprehensively, but we also view benefits, risks, and opportunities related to telehealth in a parallel way. At the individual level, routines were disrupted due to working from home, home-schooling, restricted movements, anxiety, and fear of being infected or even dying was heightened, whether someone was exposed to the virus or not (Maldonato et al., 2020).

At the interpersonal level, it is noted that people are by nature social beings and need to interact and work cooperatively with one another in order to survive and flourish in an effective manner (Nature Human Behaviour, 2020). Social life is made up of various relationships with several people who may be family, friends, work colleagues, and so on (Psychology Today, 2020). COVID-19 has had a severe impact on the amount of social contact that can occur between individuals, including putting severe limitations on physical interactions between individuals. Citizens were not able to provide even the kind of social support they would have otherwise provided to affected friends and colleagues. This lack of contact and usual interactions with friends, family, and colleagues, as mentioned earlier, has impacted negatively on the mental well-being of citizens throughout the world.

Inchausti et al. (2020) distinguish at least three different groups likely to be psychologically impacted by the pandemic. The first group that we identify consists of frontline health care professionals. In some countries, the health care system, including both institutions and frontline workers, has been severely burdened, resulting into high numbers of health care and frontline workers experiencing more severe signs of mental health problems. The literature indicates that increased workload and frequent exposure to the virus, coupled with insufficient access to personal protective equipment resulted in high levels of anxiety, depression, and insomnia. Stress, anxiety, and symptoms of depression were consistently reported in a review of literature by Shreffler et al. (2020), on the impact of COVID-19 on health care workers. In response to an increased demand for services and the need to use telepsychology, psychologists in South Africa reported experiences of both physical and emotional fatigue (Goldschmidt et al., 2020).

The second group at high risk includes individuals who, because of the pandemic, had experienced adverse events such as death in the family, threats to their health due to the pandemic, being unable to work, and even losing their jobs. Already, substantial research papers are addressing the devastating impact of bereavement during COVID-19, which has been complicated by the protocols that need to be observed following the death of someone with suspected or confirmed COVID-19 (Aguiar et al., 2020; Das et al., 2021; Maddrell, 2020; Santos et al., 2021).

A third group of people also at high risk for mental health challenges includes individuals who, prior to the pandemic, already had a history of psychiatric disorders (Inchausti et al., 2020). Those with severe or complex disorders would even be more vulnerable, due to low resilience and depleted coping mechanisms. Moreover, the lack of social support due to social distancing, as well as the isolation that may be required if one contracts the virus, are some of the additional factors that are likely to exacerbate existing psychiatric disorders.

2 WHO guidelines on mental health response during COVID-19 pandemic

In recognition of the likely increase in mental health conditions, not only with regard to worsening of already existing conditions, but also the likely increase in the number of people suffering from mental health difficulties, the WHO Secretariat, working together with other United Nations (UN) agencies, outlined a policy brief with the following recommendations directed at minimizing the impact of the COVID-19 pandemic on mental health (United Nations, 2020):

> *Apply a whole-of-society approach to promote, protect and care for mental health.*
> ***(United Nations, 2020, p. 3)***

In essence, this is an urge to governments to make mental health and psychosocial support services and interventions an integrated part of their COVID-19 response. This is an encouragement toward an adoption of a proactive approach toward prevention by promoting literacy and awareness, in particular with regard to adversities that are generally known to impact mental health, which are likely to increase during this time, including domestic violence and poverty. The policy also highlights the importance of sensitive communication that acknowledges and empathizes with the distress that people feel at this time.

> *Ensure widespread availability of emergency mental health and psychosocial support*
>
> ***(United Nations, 2020, p. 3)***

Among other things, this encourages nations to invest in technology to facilitate tele-counseling services for both frontline health workers and community members that may require urgent interventions. This is in the context of already existing mental health services to persons who are already diagnosed with mental conditions which should continue uninterruptedly despite the pandemic. Nations are urged to recognize the need for extra effort to reach people at high risk and those in vulnerable situations, as well as the promotion of equal access to telehealth and other essential and affordable technologies (World Health Organisation, 2021). This is an area that cannot be overemphasized considering the impact of isolation and social distancing, which has found a lot of people living alone, and not able to attend any social gatherings they may have used in the past as a form of social and emotional support.

> *Support recovery from Covid-19 by building mental health services for the future.*
>
> ***(United Nations, 2020, p. 3)***

This is in recognition of the fact that the impact of COVID-19 for many societies is likely to be a long-term process. If one also considers the economic impact of COVID-19, not only to countries but to individuals—the loss of income, the resultant family impact, etc.—mental health services are likely to continue to be even more crucial and in demand beyond COVID-19. The UN urges nations to actually take advantage of the current interest in mental health, subsequent to COVID-19, and reinvest in strategies that will assist in reorganizing their mental health and psychosocial support services; in the process bring in more community-based services and capacitate community members and community organizations to provide support, protect, and promote human rights at large and further assist governments in the planning, execution, and overseeing of these services.

Despite the best of efforts, in a survey undertaken by WHO from June to August 2020, among 130 countries, 93% of them had experienced disrupted or halted critical mental health services during the COVID-19 pandemic. Significant disparities were also quite evident: while over 80% of high-income countries were able to switch to telemedicine and teletherapy services, less than 50% of low-income countries were able to achieve this (World Health Organisation, 5 October 2020).

China, being the first country to experience COVID-19, with its previous experience with the 2003 SARS outbreak, was, as early as January 2020, able to provide some guidelines for psychological crisis interventions to minimize the psychosocial effects of the COVID-19 outbreak. These guidelines, in line with the UN and WHO recommendations, specified that psychological crisis intervention should be part of the public health response to the COVID-19 outbreak, organized by the joint prevention and control mechanism at the city, municipal, and provincial levels (Dong and Bouey, 2020). Although criticized for lack of clarity when it comes to the actual implementation of the principles, it does show forward thinking and ability to learn from previous experiences. Other countries such as South Africa have been criticized for only prioritizing biological approaches to responses to the pandemic, while putting mental health services on the back seat (Nguse and Wassenaar, 2021). The appointment of a Socio-Behavioral Ministerial Advisory Committee on COVID-19, which became effective in October 2020 (Nguse and Wassenaar, 2021) gives promise and hope to not only the recognition of the psychosocial impact of the pandemic but also hope for an increase in resources toward the management of the mental health outcomes of COVID-19.

3 The delivery of psychological services through online channels

The requirements for citizens to socially distance has led to an increase in the use of digital technologies in the provision of mental health care. Different types of digital services have been introduced with a variety of concepts in circulation. World Health Organization (2016) uses the term e-health to describe the use of technologies to support health and health-related fields including the provision of health care services. The "e" prefix indicates electronic means. One concept that is relevant to psychology is telepsychology.

Telehealth, on the other hand, encompasses a broad scope of technological tools that are used to engage with clients remotely for clinical purposes. In a commentary, Blandford et al. (2020, p. 1364) suggest that "Telehealth is the provision and management of health care in which individuals (often working with family members) manage aspects of their care with remote support from health-care professionals." Prior to COVID-19, the Health Professions Council of South Africa (HPCSA) had practice guidelines for telemedicine (Health Professions Council of South Africa, 2014). The concept "telehealth" was introduced as an umbrella for telemedicine and other health care services provided remotely, such as telepsychology. The above definition for telehealth is closely aligned to an earlier definition used by Dart and colleagues where it was indicated that telehealth is "the use of electronic information and telecommunications technologies to support long-distance clinical health care, patient and professional health-related education, public health and health administration" (Dart et al., 2016, p. 339).

We draw from the available literature, synthesize and summarize the most relevant information to add to the available knowledge on telehealth. The intention is to guide mental health care providers and trainees. The chapter proved to be of importance to the authors, as telehealth remains a relatively new and largely unexplored domain. The chapter provides brief background on telehealth before COVID-19, telehealth during the pandemic and post the pandemic. Opportunities and challenges are identified.

3.1 Methodology

We decided upon a review method which allowed us to conduct a scientific study without being extremely formal. While a quantitative review is often desirable, we used a phenomenological literature review method sourced from Randolph (2009). A phenomenological approach enabled us to capture rich descriptions of the challenges and opportunities encountered in the provision of telehealth services during the pandemic. In compiling this chapter, we observed five steps to ensure that the obtained data were comprehensive and nonjudgmental. These were bracketing, data collection, the identification of meaningful statements, and assign meaning to what we obtained. We are psychologists who have lived and worked through the COVID-19 pandemic. The pandemic has changed our personal lives and working lives. We have experienced the lockdown and shifted from working in the office to work from home. This is an experience worth reporting. However, through bracketing, we placed our experiences of telepsychology aside and engaged deeply with what we found in the literature. Therefore, by focusing on what came out of the literature, our reporting was guaranteed to be unbiased.

We also observed the general guidelines for conducting literature reviews. We conducted an initial selection of potential articles through the screening of the title and abstract. Where the title and abstract did not provide sufficient information to determine eligibility, we continued to download the full-text publications of all potentially relevant citations. We searched both the gray literature and academic literature. The reference lists of all full-text publications were also retrieved and scanned to determine articles that are relevant to this review. Research studies written in English that also met the following criteria were included: (1) studies that presented qualitative data, commentaries or reviews on the use of telehealth interventions pre and during the COVID-19 pandemic; (2) studies that reported findings for South Africa were of special interest. We structured the literature search and discussion of the findings by identifying the following themes: (1) progress in telehealth, (2) challenges in telehealth services, (3) opportunities in telehealth services, and (4) lessons for the future. In the next paragraph, we provide a brief overview of the method.

3.2 Progress in telehealth

Globally, telehealth has advanced at a rapid pace in most health care specialties and specifically in the practices of psychological assessment, psychotherapy, and rehabilitation. By simply browsing the internet, it is easy to see that the self-help crusade has also benefited from telehealth as there are many health care professionals who now offer internet-based interventions.

In the South African context, telehealth was identified as an intervention that could significantly contribute to improvement of primary health and medical care services in rural areas. Katchienga (2008) reports on a study conducted on 12 sites (hospitals and clinics) in the Eastern Cape Province. In this study, institutional managers, technical support staff, and medical staff were interviewed. The objective was to identify the challenges associated with the introduction and sustainability of telehealth services in rural areas of South Africa. Consequently, budgetary constraints, frequent power cuts, unavailability of technicians, and lack of bandwidth were identified (Katchienga, 2008).

Both the Health Professions Act (Department of Health, 1974) and the Mental Health Care Act Number 17 of 2002 (Department of Health, 2002) make provision for different categories of health professionals to provide a wide range of health services to individuals and communities. Mental health care services in South Africa are provided by some of the following: nurses, psychiatrists, psychologists, social workers, occupational therapists, traditional healers, and, in some instances, nongovernmental organizations. This list is not exhaustive but provides an idea of the vital role players in mental health care who had to adapt their services to telehealth where possible.

When looking at the literature on the provision of psychological services, we discovered that, prior to the pandemic, despite the availability of adequate technology (e.g., advanced computers), face-to-face psychological interventions were the preferred mode of intervention. Telepsychology was only used when people wanted to avoid the perceived stigma of being seen going to a psychologist or when there were geographical barriers related to distance, or lack of services, transportation, and time to travel to appointments.

During the pandemic, an increased use of telepsychology to provide psychological assessment, diagnosis, and therapy was observed. Keeping in mind that there was no formal training offered in telehealth, generally, psychologists had to upskill themselves rapidly in telepsychology, yet this approach to psychological services brings with it benefits and risks (Goldschmidt et al., 2020). Telehealth involves the use of technological devices ranging from telephones, cell phones to internet, or wi-fi–supported interactive audio and videoconferencing techniques, including but not limited to directing clients to self-help websites, blogs, and social media pages all aimed at eliminating psychological distress (Goldschmidt et al., 2020). It is beyond the scope of this chapter to look in detail at all the modalities that have been used in telehealth; however, an attempt will be made to look at some of the recent trends in this area.

Chou et al. (2016) describe videoconferencing as the use of secure videoconference hardware and software that allows for synchronous and interactive meetings, incorporating both audio and visual streaming between client and service provider regardless of them being at different sites. There has also been significant growth in the area of software to support these virtual interactions. G2 (2021) lists several of these tools, including *Zoom, Microsoft Teams, Skype, Webex Meetings,* and *GotoMeeting* in the top five. The impact of cost of hardware and software, existing infrastructure (or lack thereof), requirements for software updates that may need to be considered (Chou et al., 2016), licensing issues, is likely to be an obstacle especially in medium to low-income countries such as South Africa. The emerging proliferation of these platforms also brings about many other challenges for practitioners who deal with confidential patient information. Issues of privacy and security, compliance with regulatory bodies—professional boards, health insurances—ethical practice, are concerns that need to be high in the minds of health professionals when considering which platforms to use. A number of countries such as the United States and Europe have put in place some regulatory policies and bodies to facilitate best practices (Crico et al., 2018) on issues of compliance, privacy, and security. The *Protection of Personal Information Act* which recently came into effect in South Africa is also likely to contribute to increased recognition of the importance of protection of client information.

While videoconferencing offers the advantage of synchronous meetings between client and mental health provider, there are also computerized interventions and web-based interventions that provide for asynchronous access. Many therapists have websites in which they put educational and therapeutic information for their clients, as well as for the general public. Even before the widespread use of the internet, certain intervention tools such as *cognitive behavior therapy (CBT)* have been available through specifically designed software programs, *cCBT*, allowing the client to self-diagnose, personalize their treatment goals and make use of the therapy tools the program provides, allowing for both therapist involvement and noninvolvement (Aboujaoude et al., 2015). A recent review on computerized and web-based *CBT* programs has been undertaken by Wright et al. (2019) and provides more information on these and other programs. Other examples in this regard include interventions such as *Computer-Aided Vicarious Exposure* (Clark et al., 1998), *OC-Check* (Baer et al., 1987) which have been used in the treatment of obsessive-compulsive disorders (Herbst et al., 2012). Some of these computer programs are actually internet-mediated programs, examples of which include programs such as *Drinker's Check-up (DCU)*, *Moderate Drinking*, *Alcohol Use Disorders Identification Test* in the area of addiction self-assessment and relapse prevention (Molfenter et al., 2015), to mention but a few. Research suggests that emails have been used largely for brief exchanges with patients rather than as a modality for intervention; however, some web-based programs use emails to support the asynchronous therapy experience.

Another area that seems to be getting more interest is virtual reality exposure therapy (VRET), a new tool for conducting exposure therapy with the help of computer-generated virtual environments, that mimic real-life situations, thus allowing systematic exposure to the feared situation without actually being physically in that situation (Opris et al., 2012; Aboujaoude et al., 2015). In a review on the use of VRET in anxiety disorders, Meyerbroker and Emmelkamp (2010) concluded that it could be a viable alternative to in vivo therapy, which exposes the client to the actual anxiety provoking situation. Efficacy studies reviewed by Aboujaoude et al. (2015) suggest that VRET appears to have considerable potential in the treatment of psychiatric conditions such as phobias, posttraumatic stress disorder, obsessive compulsive disorders, and substance use disorders.

Mobile devices are increasingly being used in telehealth programs, through various software applications, which have been enabled by the advent of smartphones. These are capable of more than just making a call or texting but enable users to engage virtually and interactively through both the visual and audio streams. The role of mobile phones in tele-mental health is discussed extensively by Chan et al. (2014) and Price et al. (2014). Mobile devices have been found to be quite useful for a number of activities in the telehealth field, including treatment monitoring and compliance through regular reminders to clients, health education, health surveys, as well as for delivery of services such as counseling and therapy through audio and visual systems (Chan et al., 2014). According to the American Psychological Association (2020), there are up to 20,000 mental health apps on the market. Some of these target specific psychological disorders, as evident in a review of literature by Lui et al. (2017) and in the Psyberguide Website (Psyberguide.org, n.d. (http://psyberguide.org)). For "stress and anxiety" alone, Psyberguide gives you information on up to 176 apps with regards to its credibility and whether it has received any professional reviews or not. Psyberguide lists and rate mental health apps on scientific credibility, user experience, and transparency on data handling (American Psychological Association, 2020) and is one of the sites that can be consulted for information on available apps.

Some common features are evident in mobile apps, as evident in those included in Lui et al.'s (2017) review. Some apps are designed as stand-alone interventions in place of patient—therapist interactions, e.g., *PTSD Coach* (Miner et al., 2016), *SuperBetter* (Roepke et al., 2015) which targets depressives, while others are designed to support therapeutic processes, e.g., *The Stress Manager* (Newman et al., 2014), which targets Generalized Anxiety Disorder posttreatment, and *FOCUS* (Ben-Zeev et al., 2014), which targets schizophrenic disorders. Apps may include symptom monitoring, offer therapeutic skills, or psychoeducation; some are interactive and recommend specific therapeutic skills as feedback to the user's self-assessment, as the examples given above.

An area of progress is also evident within the South African context. The South African Depression and Anxiety Group (SADAG) website lists some mental health apps addressing various areas including symptom monitoring, stress, anxiety and sleep management, and many more (www.sadag.org). Collaboration between government, mobile network operators, and technology companies has assisted in facilitating services such as the logging of referrals and contact tracing of COVID-19 patients. The Vula mobile application, for example, was instrumental not only in contact tracing but also in actually facilitating psychological support for frontline health care workers (https://www.vulamobile.com/newsmedia).

Only one-third of the population in South Africa makes use of smartphones (https://statista.com), meaning that access to some of these mental health services will still be a challenge for the majority of the population. Short Message Service (SMS) or text messaging, which does not require a smartphone, has also been used successfully in telehealth. In a review of literature, Aguilera and Munoz (2011) noted that text-messaging has been used to send appointment reminders, medication reminders, to share health information and to monitor symptoms and behavior after treatment. From their own study, Aguilera and Munoz (2011) concluded that SMS may have an advantage as an adjunct to psychotherapy because of regular therapist contact, which encourages the client to continue participating and applying therapeutic interventions posttreatment.

The emergence of a greater number of technologies and software applications has certainly contributed significantly in new ways of not only interacting but also treating clients, with the advantage of making clients also to be in control of their treatment. All this though has not come without challenges, as it will be apparent in our next discussion.

3.3 Challenges in telehealth services

From a lay person's perception, the provision of psychological services through emails, SMS's, Skype, Zoom or MS Teams, etc. seems uncomplicated than the provision of medical services; however, from a legal-ethical perspective, this is a complex process. The following discussion highlights some of the challenges. These are presented in terms of the themes identified in the literature.

3.3.1 Therapeutic alliance

Rees and Stone (2005) observed that when working through the internet, the therapeutic alliance is seriously impacted and it is difficult to achieve a deep connection with a client. This observation was confirmed by psychologists that they interviewed. While the interviews were conducted in 2005, there is recent evidence suggesting that concerns about the therapeutic alliance continue to be raised by practitioners (Sammons et al., 2020).

According to Carl Rogers, a therapist must be nonjudgmental, warm, display respect and a willingness to help. Clients must feel that the therapist is authentic and cares unconditionally (Rogers, 1951). These are conditions for therapy that are difficult to transmit through emails or SMS's yet they are crucial determinants for adherence, treatment progress, and outcome. Additionally, one of the biggest challenges that psychologists face when working online is the absence of nonverbal cues. In technology-mediated communication, there is an increased risk of misinterpretation.

3.3.2 Treatment approaches

Psychologists offer a range of treatment modalities. These include assessing and treating individuals or groups; the provision of short-term or long-term interventions as well as in-hospital or out-of-hospital services. Research indicates that a number of treatment modalities lend themselves fairly well to telehealth interventions (Cooper et al., 2019). However, some clinicians may be more comfortable with one specific modality and duration than others, when they practice face to face, but experience adjustment challenges when they practice virtually. For example, Goldschmidt et al. (2020) note that practitioners in their study tended to use short-term interventions that largely focused on strengthening their clients' coping skills, containment, and or psychoeducation, rather than addressing deep-seated intrapsychic conflicts, which practitioners experience as more amenable to face to face than telehealth settings. This suggests that practitioners may find themselves shifting from one therapeutic modality and duration to another when they provide telehealth interventions, which may not necessarily be well received by some of their existing clients, who are used to or have preference for specific treatment approaches.

3.3.3 Access

Access to efficient mental health care and psychological services has long been considered a human rights issue. However, a proportion of the South African population is technologically illiterate, they have limited economic resources, and some are too old to understand how telehealth works. Despite good intentions of certain practitioners and organizations to make some time available to provide telehealth services, the uptake of these services at times has not been optimum. Second, a wide variety of online platforms can be overwhelming to inexperienced users (both clients and practitioners). Third, sudden lockdown measures could have averted putting into place adequate technical support (Maldonato et al., 2020), which might have contributed to easier and improved access.

3.3.4 Connectivity, data, hardware, and software

Telehealth requires connectivity and data. There are a variety of factors that affect connectivity. The most common technological problems that have been encountered are related to audio transmission or video transmission. These problems happen as a result of poor connectivity, hardware, software, or a combination of these three computer systems.

Data costs in the South African context have been identified as extremely high (Goldschmidt et al., 2020). The pandemic has brought with it increased rates of unemployment. This means that a majority of the population cannot afford data. Second, recurrent power cuts mentioned previously also contribute to the challenges related to connectivity. Third, lack of suitable technological devices prevents access to telehealth.

3.3.5 Blurred boundaries

Under normal circumstances, clients and psychologists must respect each other's boundaries. This relates to times when they can contact each other and the mode of contact. Psychologists are expected to have policies about when and where they will be available for clients. During the pandemic, it was noted that boundaries were blurred. At times clients found it difficult to keep to the time of the sessions as well as practitioners finding it difficult to keep to 50-/60-min sessions due to clients needing more time to feel contained (Goldschmidt et al., 2020). While earlier studies showed that telehealth services lower the utilization of health care services and the workload of health care professionals, the opposite was observed during the pandemic. Due to anxiety, clients were calling psychologists frequently and expected psychologists to meet their expectations. On the other hand, the frequent contact might have been initiated by psychologists. Psychologists might have felt isolated due to the mandated quarantine requirements and end up boundary crossing consciously or unconsciously through asynchronous communications such as emails, in a bid to reassure their clients of their availability. Such communications could be interpreted by clients as indication that the practitioner is available 24 h of the day, in which case if the practitioner does not respond to client communication after hours, this could be interpreted as neglect (Cooper et al., 2019).

3.3.6 *Privacy and confidentiality*

The psychology profession holds privacy and confidentiality high on the list of ethical priorities. Cooper and colleagues argue that "the risk of a confidentiality breach is much greater through electronic transmission" (Cooper et al., 2019, p. 1080) than in face-to-face meetings. During the pandemic, privacy and confidentiality was not guaranteed from the increased and numerous technological devices and platforms used to provide psychological services (Goldschmidt et al., 2020). Moreover, due to lockdown regulations and many people working from home, privacy for the clients also became an issue, where one would have to be in session, while other family members are also at home, which heightens the risk of being overhead. Included here are general distractions that may be created within the home environment, which may impact on client not being fully "present" in the session (Scharff et al., 2020).

3.3.7 *Multiple relationships*

Contact through social media platforms became the norm during the pandemic and this can have a negative impact on professional relationships. As early as 2011, Goss, in Drum and Littleton (2014) had observed that, in telepsychology, communication between the client and the clinician uses modalities that are often used for social interactions with family and friends (emails, video-conferencing, etc.), and can occur at any hour of the day or even at night. As a result, both parties can now virtually enter each other's homes, which raises the risk for an increased sense of intimacy between client and therapist. Conducting sessions in casual spaces may also risk the practitioner being seen as just another "buddy" or friend the client talks to online (Drum and Littleton, 2014).

3.3.8 *Clothing and grooming*

The manner in which people dress communicates more information about someone than verbal communication and it plays a significant role in creating the first impression (Forsythe et al., 1985). Generally, psychologists are expected to dress neatly and conservatively. Working from home has made people feel there is no need to dress professionally and this might offend clients, or even reduce the psychologist to the status of just another friend the client is chatting to online (Drum and Littleton, 2014).

3.3.9 *Competencies*

A major challenge for sustainable telehealth programs is related to competencies. There is a misperception that telehealth is easy to use. Despite considerable access to technology many psychologists lack skills necessary to practice telepsychology effectively and provide safe services to clients. They are then expected to acquire the technical knowledge and skills that will allow them to offer telepsychology services.

4 Opportunities in telehealth services

4.1 Opportunities in patient care

Access is a double-edged sword. Telehealth creates an opportunity for more convenient ways of accessing mental health services. For both client and clinician, this may result in reduced need to travel and saving on associated expenses as such, less time away from families, and a lowered rate of missed appointments. Counseling sessions for individual clients or couples or families or support groups can be carried out without the limitations posed by geographical location or transport needs.

Telehealth facilitates disclosure. In a pilot study conducted by Saberi et al. (2013), 57% of participants reported feeling more at ease to disclose sensitive issues they would ordinarily have had difficulty discussing mainly because they were not face to face with someone. In support of this, during the COVID-19 pandemic, it was observed that domestic violence reporting increased globally (Mittal and Singh, 2020). The findings were based on the calls for help made to women's organizations and hotlines through telephone, emails, SMS's, and apps.

Telehealth promotes compliance with treatment and prevents premature termination from therapy. In Traube et al. (2020), over 90% of parents participating in a telehealth parenting program reported having a strong relationship with their educator, which made it easier for the parents to be willing to engage in new activities and parenting strategies the educators advised them to try. Furthermore, reporting on their experience of using a telehealth-based modality, the parents felt that this was similar or better than a face-to-face experience; they also indicated that in fact they had specifically chosen the telehealth experience because of its convenience and the privacy it offered.

As a response to the urgent need of psychological services during the pandemic, rapid psychological first aid was identified as highly effective. Psychological first aid is a first-line response intended to minimize the effect of acute stress and trauma and assist people to cope effectively with difficult life events (Maldonato et al., 2020, p. 284). Two objectives were the focus of this intervention: (1) controlling distress and fear of the disease and (2) reducing adjustment difficulties.

In Maldonato et al. (2020), it is conveyed that telehealth has direct and indirect roles in reducing the spread of infections. During the outbreak, technology proved to be very efficient in allowing users to:

(a) receive the correct information and prevent the spreading of fake news;
(b) report their symptoms despite the fear of disease;
(c) encourage activities and strategies directed at prevention; and
(d) decrease or prevent psychological outcomes due to pandemic regulations.

These opportunities can be observed in future pandemics.

One other opportunity observed from the frequent use of self-monitoring apps for COVID-19 symptoms is the positive impact this process has on enhancing patient self-management. Patient self-management is a vital process in chronic disease management. This can be transferred to the management of chronic mental health problems going forward.

Telehealth also helps to expedite epidemiological research that is needed to inform decisions for future health care delivery as well as to support policy makers to predict society's needs and make appropriate decisions and prompt interventions (Blandford et al., 2020). During the pandemic, the command council relied extensively on data obtained through telehealth research to make decisions related to COVID-19. There is still a great need to enhance the evidence for technology applications within the health sector as clinicians and consumers expand their use in numerous areas.

Another advantage for the use of telepsychology relates to information management. Psychologists obtain information primarily from clients through interviews, psychometric assessments, and through interviews with family members and work colleagues or educators where necessary. They may receive reports from referral sources or other professionals involved in the care of their clients. They are expected to take reasonable steps to keep this information safe and secure. Technology has made this process easier to manage. Audio-recordings and other files are now kept safely protected with passwords.

4.2 Opportunities in the education and training of psychologists

The COVID-19 pandemic necessitated a transformation in the delivery of education and training by institutions of higher learning all over the world.

The education and training of psychologists had to be facilitated through telehealth, including the clinical supervision of interns. Interns are expected by the regulating bodies to have weekly individual supervision and group supervision. Due to COVID-19, the supervision sessions are facilitated securely by technological services. Similar to group face-to-face supervision, interns share cases and are able to learn about a broader spectrum of disorders than they are currently exposed to in their settings. The experiences reported by Scharff et al. (2020) specifically speak to similar changes that many training institutions within the field had to adopt to still be able to continue to fulfill their training requirements. The flexibility and innovation that telehealth can provide cannot be overstated.

5 Lessons for the future

In the light of the contributions and opportunities highlighted above, telehealth services continued to be effective in the promotion of mental health, even at a time of crisis when COVID-19 regulations of social distancing made it difficult for citizens to consult their service providers for psychosocial support. The urgent nature of the interventions and the critical points raised in this chapter shed light on the need to optimize mental health services and telehealth interventions with intelligent systems.

This crisis showed that all health care services should set up new protocols and systems that are capable of managing a wide scale of remote interventions. Governments need to make significant investments and commitments to establish the necessary infrastructure that will make telehealth modalities available to patients living in rural areas and the most vulnerable. Medical aids have increasingly reimbursed telehealth services which can fast-track its adoption going forward.

Through positive outcomes in the use of telehealth services, some encouraging evidence can be highlighted in research. Previously, it was mentioned how telehealth increases self-disclosure in situations where fears of negative evaluation may be prominent with human partners (Blandford et al., 2020). We need comparative studies on the diversity of telehealth platforms.

To facilitate more inclusion in the digital space, telehealth solutions must be easy to use, and be affordable for individuals and health care organizations. Funding models may need to be revisited to cater more for vulnerable citizens and organizations. Governments need to benchmark and learn from each other what works well. Just as COVID-19 has accelerated digital literacy, so too telehealth can accelerate health literacy.

Access to the latest data security and encryption systems will become more and more important to protect patient privacy. Patients need to be educated continuously so that they are aware of the privacy choices they are making when they select telehealth. This knowledge will promote data security and avoid disclosure of sensitive personal information. Privacy and security issues are likely to become more complex, as the use of different telehealth modalities expands.

Finally, telehealth is technology driven. It is crucial for developing countries like South Africa to invest in a basic communication infrastructure capable of linking the remote areas with the metropolitan areas and medical facilities. With partnerships between government and telecommunications entities, combined with the current advances in digital communications, substantial progress can be achieved in improving service delivery in remote areas and enhance health management of citizens regardless of their geographical location.

6 Conclusions

The primary objective of the chapter was to provide a brief overview of the developments in telehealth services, as well as to identify challenges and opportunities in telehealth services. Consequently, it was noted that there has been progress in the use of telehealth services. Telehealth is a rapidly growing exciting practice with numerous possibilities. Several challenges were also identified. These included the impact on the therapeutic alliance, treatment approaches, access, connectivity, blurred boundaries, privacy and confidentiality, multiple relationships, clothing and grooming,and competencies. These challenges are not in any way the only ones observed in the use of telehealth. We are highlighting them because of their ethical implications for the practice of the professionals involved.

We have also identified opportunities and grouped them into two broad themes. The themes are opportunities in health care and opportunities in the education and training of psychologists. A possible way forward was highlighted. We conclude by highlighting that as telehealth clinical tools proliferate (with supportive evidence-based research on their effectiveness), they can be incorporated into the education and training of psychologists and other health care professionals, as well as assist in public health management. Indeed, studies in the efficacy of telepsychology also continue to provide substantial evidence in support for its effectiveness either in short-term interventions or in long-term interventions and in individual or group settings. We acknowledge that we have not included discussions of policy developments related to technology-mediated services. This is an important area to be covered in future.

References

Aboujaoude, E., Salame, W., Naim, L., 2015. Telemental health: a status update. World Psychiatry 14 (2), 223–230. https://doi.org/10.1002/wps.20218.

Aguiar, A., Pinto, M., Duarte, R., 2020. Grief and mourning during the COVID-19 pandemic in Portugal. Acta Med. Port. 33 (9), 543–545. https://doi.org/10.20344/amp.14345.

Aguilera, A., Munoz, R., 2011. Text messaging as an adjunct to CBT in low-income populations: a usability and feasibility pilot study. Prof. Psychol. Res. Pract. 42 (Dec), 472–478. https://doi.org/10.1037/a0025499.

American Psychological Association, 2020. Providing care in innovative ways: as more people get mental health services via apps and tele-heath, psychologists are working to ensure their quality. Trend Mental Health 51, 1.

Baer, L., Minichiello, W.E., Jenike, M.A., 1987. Use of a portable-computer program in behavioral treatment of obsessive–compulsive disorder. Am. J. Psychiatry 144 (8), 1101. https://doi.org/10.1176/ajp.144.8.1101b.

Ben-Zeev, D., Brenner, C.J., Begale, M., Duffecy, J., Mohr, D.C., Mueser, K.T., 2014. Feasibility, acceptability, and preliminary efficacy of a smartphone intervention for schizophrenia. Schizophr. Bull. 40, 1244–1253. https://doi.org/10.1093/schbul/sbu033.

Blandford, A., Wesson, J., Amalberti, R., AlHazme, R., Allwihan, R., 2020. Opportunities and challenges for telehealth within, and beyond, a pandemic. Lancet Digit. Health. https://doi.org/10.1016/S2589-7500(20)30196-5. Published online August 10.

Chan, S.R., Torous, J., Hinton, L., Yellowlees, P., 2014. Mobile tele-mental health: increasing applications and a move to hybrid models of care. Healthcare 2, 220–233. https://doi.org/10.3390/healthcare2020220.

Chou, T., Comer, J.S., Turvey, C.L., Karr, A., Spargo, G., 2016. Technological considerations for the delivery of real-time child telemental healthcare. J. Child Adolesc. Psychopharmacol. 26 (3), 192–197. https://doi.org/10.1089/cap.2015.0043.

Clark, A., Kirkby, K.C., Daniels, B.A., Marks, I.M., 1998. A pilot study of computer-aided vicarious exposure for obsessive–compulsive disorder. Aust. N. Z. J. Psychiatry 32 (2), 268–275. https://doi.org/10.3109/00048679809062738.

Cooper, S.E., Campbell, L.F., Barnwell, S.S., 2019. Telepsychology: a primer for counselling psychologists. Couns. Psychol. 47 (8), 1074–1114. https://doi.org/10.1177/0011000019895276.

Crico, C., Renzi, C., Graf, N., Buyx, A., Kondylakis, H., Koumakis, L., Pravettoni, G., 2018. mHealth and telemedicine apps: in search of a common regulation. Ecancer 12, 853. https://doi.org/10.3332/ecancer.2018.853.

Dart, E.H., Whipple, H.M., Pasqua, J.L., Furlow, C.M., 2016. Legal, regulatory, and ethical issues in telehealth technology. In: Computer-Assisted and Web-Based Innovations in Psychology, Special Education, and Health. Elsevier Inc, https://doi.org/10.1016/B978-0-12-802075-3.00013-9.

Das, A., Singh, T., Varma, R., Arya, K.Y., 2021. Death and mourning in the frontline health care professional and their families during COVID-19. Front. Psychiatry 12. https://doi.org/10.3389/fpsyt.2021.624428, 624428.

Department of Health, 1974. Health Professions Act 56 of 1974. https://www.hpcsa.co.za/Uploads/Legal/legislation/health_professions_ct_56_1974.pdf.

Department of Health, 2002. Mental Health Care Act 17 of 2002. https://www.gov.za/sites/default/files/gcis_document/201409/a17-02.pdf.

Dong, L., Bouey, J., 2020. Public mental health crisis during Covid-19 pandemic, China. Emerg. Infect. Dis. 26 (7), 1616–1618. https://doi.org/10.3201/eid2607.200407.

Drum, K.B., Littleton, H.L., 2014. Therapeutic boundaries in telepsychology: unique issues and best practice recommendations. Prof. Psychol. Res. Pract. 45 (5), 309–315. https://doi.org/10.1037/a0036127.

Forsythe, S.M., Drake, M.F., Hogan, J.H., 1985. Influence of clothing attributes on the perception of personal characteristics. In: Solomon, M.R. (Ed.), The Psychology of Fashion. D.C. Heath, Lexington, pp. 267–278.

G2, 2021. Best Video Conferencing Software in 2021a. http://www.g2.com/categories/viode-conferencing. (Accessed 30 July 2021).

Goldschmidt, L., Langa, M., Masilela, B., Ndhlovu, L.M., Mncina, B., Maubane, B., Bujela, K., 2020. Telepsychology and the COVID-19 pandemic: the experiences of psychologists in South Africa. S. Afr. J. Psychol., 1–11. https://doi.org/10.1177/0081246321993281.

Health Professions Council of South Africa, 2014. General Ethical Guidelines for Good Practice in Telemedicine. Booklet 10. HPCSA, Pretoria.

Herbst, N., Voderholzer, U., Stelzer, N., Knaevelsrud, C., Hertenstein, E., Schlegl, S., Nissen, C., et al., 2012. The potential of telemental health applications for obsessive-compulsive disorder. Clin. Psychol. Rev. 32, 454–466. https://doi.org/10.1016/j.cpr.2012.04.005.

Inchausti, F., Macbeth, A., Hasson-Ohayon, I., Dimaggio, G., 2020. Telepsychotherapy in the age of COVID-19: a commentary. J. Psychother. Integr. 30 (2), 394–405. https://doi.org/10.1037/int0000222.

Katchienga, M.O., 2008. Technological innovations in health care: challenges of managing telehealth technology in South Africa. In: IEEE International Engineering Management Conference., https://doi.org/10.1109/IEMCE.2008.4617976.

Lavah, Y., 2020. Psychological distress related to COVID-19 – the contribution of continuous traumatic stress. J. Affect. Disord. 277, 129–137. https://doi.org/10.1016/j.jad.2020.07.141.

Lui, J.H.L., Marcus, D.K., Barry, C.T., 2017. Evidence-based apps? A review of mental health mobile applications in a psychotherapy context. Prof. Psychol. Res. Pract. https://doi.org/10.1037/pro0000122. Advance online publication.

Maddrell, A., 2020. Bereavement, grief, and consolation: emotional-affective geographies of loss during COVID-19. Dialogues Hum. Geogr. 10 (2), 107–111. https://doi.org/10.1177/2043820620934947.

Maldonato, N.M., Scandura, C., Lipardi, A., Chiodi, A., De Lucia, S., Continisio, G.I., et al., 2020. Psychological first aid models during the COVID-19 outbreak. The role of InfoCommunication Technologies. In: 11th IEEE International Conference on Cognitive Infocommunications – CogInfoCom, September 23–25. Online on MaxWhere 3D Web.

Media Statement, 24 May 2021. Update on Covid-19. From: https://sacoronavirus.co.za/2020/10/22/mental-health-and-covid-19/. (Accessed 28 May 2021).
Meyerbroker, K., Emmelkamp, P.M.G., 2010. Virtual reality exposure therapy in anxiety disorders: a systematic review of process-and-outcome studies. Depress. Anxiety 27 (10), 933–944. https://doi.org/10.1002/da.20734.
Miner, A., Kuhn, E., Hoffman, J.E., Owen, J.E., Ruzek, J.I., Taylor, C.B., 2016. Feasibility, acceptability, and potential efficacy of the PTSD Coach app: a pilot randomized controlled trial with community trauma survivors. Psychol. Trauma Theory Res. Pract. Policy 8, 384–392. https://doi.org/10.1037/tra0000092.
Mittal, S., Singh, T., 2020. Gender-based violence during Covid-19 pandemic: a mini-review. Front. Glob. Womens Health 08. https://doi.org/10.3389/fgwh.2020.00004.
Molfenter, T., Boyle, M., Holloway, D., Zwick, J., 2015. Trends in telemedicine use in addiction treatment. Addict. Sci. Clin. Pract. 10, 14. https://doi.org/10.1186/s13722-015-0035-4.
Nature Human Behaviour, 2020. The cooperative human. Nat. Hum. Behav. 2, 427–428. https://doi.org/10.1038/s41562-018-0389-1.
Newman, M.G., Przeworski, A., Consoli, A.J., Taylor, C.B., 2014. A randomized controlled trial of ecological momentary intervention plus brief group therapy for generalized anxiety disorder. Psychotherapy 51, 198–206. https://doi.org/10.1037/a0032519.
Nguse, S., Wassenaar, D., 2021. Mental health and Covid-19 in South Africa. S. Afr. J. Psychol. 51 (2), 304–313. https://doi.org/10.1177/00812463211001543 journals.sagepub.com/home/sap.
Opris, D., Pintea, S., Garcia-Palacios, A., Botella, C., Szamoskozi, S., David, D., 2012. Virtual reality exposure therapy in anxiety disorders: a quantitative meta-analysis. Depress. Anxiety 29, 85–93. https://doi.org/10.1002/da.20910.
Price, M., Yuen, E.K., Goetter, E.M., Herbert, J.D., Forman, E.M., Acierno, R., Ruggiero, K.J., 2014. mHealth: a mechanism to deliver more accessible, more effective mental health care. Clin. Psychol. Psychother. 21 (5), 427–436. https://doi.org/10.1002/cpp.1855.
Psyberguide.org. http://psyberguide.org. (Accessed 30 July 2021).
Psychology Today, 2020. Social Life. https://www.psychologytoday.com/za/basics/social-life.
Qiu, J., Shen, B., Zhao, M., Wang, Z., Xie, B., Xu, Y., 2020. A nationwide survey of psychological distress among Chinese people in the COVID-19 epidemic: implications and policy recommendations. Gen. Psychiatry 33, 100213. https://doi.org/10.1136/gpsych-2020-100213.
Randolph, J.J., 2009. A guide to writing the dissertation literature review. Pract. Assess. Res. Eval. 14 (13). https://doi.org/10.7275/b0az-8t74.
Rees, S., Stone, S., 2005. Therapeutic alliance in face-to-face versus video-conferenced psychotherapy. Prof. Psychol. Res. Pract. 36 (6), 649–653.
Roepke, A.M., Jaffee, S.R., Riffle, O.M., McGonigal, J., Broome, R., Maxwell, B., 2015. Randomized controlled trial of SuperBetter, a smartphone-based/internet-based self-help tool to reduce depressive symptoms. Games Health J. 4 (3), 235–246. https://doi.org/10.1089/g4h.2014.0046.
Rogers, C.R., 1951. Client-Centred Therapy. Constable, London.
Saberi, P., Yuan, P., John, M., Sheon, N., Johnson, M., 2013. A pilot study to engage and counsel HIV-positive African American youth via telehealth technology. AIDS Patient Care STDs 27 (9), 529–532. https://doi.org/10.1089/apc.2013.0185.
Sammons, M.T., VandenBos, G.R., Martin, J.N., 2020. Psychological practice and the COVID-19 crisis: a rapid response survey. J. Health Serv. Psychol. 46, 51–57. https://doi.org/10.1007/s42843-020-00013-2 (PMC free article] [PubMed] [CrossRef] [Google Scholar).

Santos, S., Sa, T., Aguiar, I., Cardoso, I., Correia, Z., Correia, T., 2021. Case report: parental loss and childhood grief during COVID-19 pandemic. Front. Psychiatry 12, 626940. https://doi.org/10.3389/fpsyt.2021.626940.

Scharff, A., Breiner, C.E., Ueno, L.F., Underwood, S.B., Merrit, C.E., Welch, L.M., et al., 2020. Shifting a training clinic to teletherapy during the COVID-19 pandemic: a trainee perspective. Couns. Psychol. Q. https://doi.org/10.1080/09515070.2020.1786668.

Shreffler, J., Petrey, J., Huecker, M., 2020. The impact of COVID-19 on healthcare worker wellness: a scoping review. West. J. Emerg. Med. 21 (5), 1059–1066. https://doi.org/10.5811/westjem.2020.7.48684.

Traube, D.E., Hsiao, H., Rau, A., Hunt-O'Brien, D., Lu, L., Islam, N., 2020. Advancing home based parenting programs through the use of telehealth technology. J. Child Fam. Stud. 29, 44–53. https://doi.org/10.1007/s10826-019-01458-w.

United Nations, 2020. Policy Brief: Covid-19 and the Need for Action on Mental Health. https://unsdg.un.org/resources. (Accessed 29 July 2021).

Wang, C., Pan, R., Wan, X., Tan, Y., Xu, L., Ho, C.S., Ho, R.C., 2020. Immediate psychological responses and associated factors during the initial stage of the 2019 coronavirus disease (COVID-19) epidemic among the general population in China. Int. J. Environ. Res. Public Health 17 (5), 1729. https://doi.org/10.3390/ijerph17051729.

World Health Organisation, 2020. World Health Organisation Situation Report – 90. WHO. https://www.who.int/docs/default-source/coronaviruse/situation-reports/20200419-sitrep-90-covid-19.pdf?sfvrsn=551d47fd_4. (Accessed 8 June 2021).

World Health Organisation, 5 October 2020. Covid-19 Disrupting Mental Health Services in Most Countries, WHO Survey. WHO News release https://www.who.int/news/item/05-10-2020-covid-19-disrupting-mental-health-services-in-most-countries-who-survey. (Accessed 29 July 2021).

World Health Organisation, 2021. Promoting Mental Health Preparedness and Response for Public Health Emergencies. WHO. https://apps.who.int/gb/ebwha/pdf_files/EB148/B148_CONF5-en.pdf.

World Health Organization, 2016. Global Diffusion of eHealth: Making Universal Health Coverage Achievable. Report of the third global survey on eHealth, WHO. https://www.who.int/goe/publications/global_diffusion/en/.

Wright, J.H., Mishkind, M., Eels, T.D., Chan, S.R., 2019. Computer-assisted cognitive-behaviour therapy and mobile apps for depression and anxiety. Curr. Psychiatry Rep. 21 (7), 62. https://doi.org/10.1007/s11920-019-1031-2.

CHAPTER TEN

Applications of machine learning approaches to combat COVID-19: A survey

Sanju Tiwari[a], Onur Dogan[b,c], M.A. Jabbar[d], Shishir Kumar Shandilya[e], Fernando Ortiz-Rodriguez[a], Sailesh Bajpai[f], and Sourav Banerjee[g]

[a]Universidad Autonoma de Tamaulipas, Ciudad Victoria, Mexico
[b]Department of Industrial Engineering, Izmir Bakircay University, Izmir, Turkey
[c]Research Center for Data Analytics and Spatial Data Modeling (RC-DAS), Izmir Bakircay University, Izmir, Turkey
[d]Vardhaman College of Engineering, Hyderabad, India
[e]School of Computing Science and Engineering, VIT Bhopal University, Bhopal, India
[f]Regional Center for Biotechnology, Faridabad, India
[g]Kalyani Government Engineering College, Kalyani, India

1 Introduction

Artificial intelligence (AI) is presented as a technology that automates computers to integrate the intelligence like human to execute tasks, along with machine learning (ML), natural language processing, virtual reality, knowledge graphs, biometrics, computer vision, and augmented reality (Szegedy et al., 2017). ML is considered as a subset of AI for making the decision and prediction (Yue et al., 2020; Yan et al., 2020a, b) and deep learning (DL) is presented as a subset of ML. There are different ML methods such as logistic regression, decision tree, Adaboost, K-nearest neighbor (KNN), support vector machine, K-means clustering, Naïve Bayes, Hidden Markov Models, density clustering, etc. (Breiman, 2001; Ong et al., 2020; van der Maaten and Hinton, 2008) and also several DL methods such as recurrent neural networks, convolutional neural networks, deep belief networks, restricted Boltzmann machines (Greff et al., 2016; Skalic et al., 2019).

AI is significant to automate the task (Li et al., 2007; Martin, 2007; Singh et al., 2014, 2017) by diagnosing the gestures of the diseased person from the collected information by visual sensors such as time-of-flight pressure imaging (Casas et al., 2019), RGB, or thermal cameras. AI-based methods have been successfully applied in different situations and automated treatment and diagnoses in clinical trials. Deep neural networks are applied for COVID-19 treatment using medical images to provide

https://doi.org/10.1016/B978-0-323-99878-9.00014-5

challenging results (Dogan et al., 2021; Huang et al., 2020a; Ng et al., 2020; Ozturk et al., 2020; Tabik et al., 2020; Wang et al., 2020). These techniques are based on DL (Oh et al., 2020; Toğaçar et al., 2020; Ucar and Korkmaz, 2020), while the applications of DL model are a challenging topic in the AI field in medical image processing and analysis (Kermany et al., 2018; Lakhani and Sundaram, 2017). In this COVID-19 crisis (Tiwari et al., 2020), the medical fraternity is seeking for technologies to track and monitor the infection status of COVID-19 disease. Due to the rapid spread of this pandemic, many researchers are working to get the solution to help mankind (Jin et al., 2020; Kaye et al., 2020; Lawand and Al Tabbah, 2020; Velavan and Meyer, 2020). AI has been identified as decisive technology to tackle the pandemic. This pandemic poses several challenges to the AI community. AI works as an evidence-based tool and can be used to fight against the Corona virus. AI will help the physicians to identify the symptoms of a patient. The significant use of AI to cope up with COVID-19 is

(1) monitoring and prediction of disease;
(2) early detection of the disease and prognosis;
(3) drug and vaccine;
(4) social control or contact tracing of the individuals who affected with the disease;
(5) helping health-care workers to fight against COVID-19; and
(6) projection of cases and mortality.

AI has the potential and can improve decision making to fight against COVID-19 by developing valuable and advanced algorithms such as DL. In this study, AI applications in a pandemic are considered in three groups: molecular, clinical, and social scales (Bullock et al., 2020). The molecular scale includes molecular modeling to diagnose the proteins found in SARS-CoV-2 infection and identify potential treatment. AI applications of molecular scale comprise predicting protein structure, repurposing the drug, discovering the drug, discovering the vaccine, improving viral nucleic acid testing, and better understanding infection. Most AI tools in the clinical scale are applied to diagnose and treat using medical imaging, such as X-ray scans and computational tomography (CT). AI supports predicting the evolution of the disease and monitoring and measurement processes. AI applications of clinical scale cover diagnosis with medical imaging, disease tracking with noninvasive measurement, and prediction of patient outcome. The social scale is further categorized into two: infodemiology and epidemiology.

This study aims to present different aspects of AI technology to fight against pandemics with various measures for facing the pandemic. Therefore, it is organized as follows. Section 2 gives a comprehensive background of the study. It involves two main parts: related works about pandemic and COVID-19, and applications of AI/ML in emerging diseases. Section 3 presents the AI/ML applications related to COVID-19. Detection, diagnosis monitoring, prediction of disease and mortality, drugs and vaccines preparation, drug repurposing, social awareness, and control by the Internet are discussed in this section. Section 4 gives both challenges and future directions. Section 5 represents the conclusion of the study.

2 Background

2.1 Pandemic and COVID-19

Any disease infection is pretended to occur as a susceptible person creating contact with an infectious person in a community or workplace area. If infection appeared, it spread to the other person and continues to the community in an asymptomatic state. Various infectious diseases caused several lives and led to severe conditions that took enough time to control the disease. The pandemic and epidemic have been applied to explain the nature of disease that appears with a period. If the disease cases are overgrowing than usual and cause the lives in a particular area, then it is declared as an epidemic (Orbann et al., 2017). In other term, pandemic is an infectious disease outbreak that indefinitely raises the morbidity and mortality over a huge geographical area. Epidemic has been increased over the past century due to several factors such as increasing worldwide travel, exploitation of land, and harming the natural resources (Morse, 2001). According to the previous studies, smallpox infection caused 500 million lives in the whole world in the past 100 years (Henderson, 2009). In 1918, the Spanish influenza outbreak caused 17–100 million lives, as an estimation (Spreeuwenberg et al., 2018). Different kinds of pandemics have been reported for the last 20 years such as H1N1 influenza in 2009, Middle East respiratory syndrome coronavirus (MERSCoV) in 2012, and acute respiratory syndrome coronavirus (SARS-CoV) in 2002–03. We have discussed several pandemics with their period and the death toll in Table 1 (Swapnarekha, 2020; Swapnarekha et al., 2020).

COVID-19 outbreak was reported in Wuhan, China as a pandemic, in December 2019 as a cluster of deadly respiratory infections and grows rapidly as an epidemic all over the world. Coronaviruses are found zoonotic and

Table 1 List of pandemics.

Name	Time period	Fatalities
Russian flu	1889–90	1M
Spanish flu	1918–19	40–50M
Asian flu	1957–58	1.1M
Hong Kong flu	1968–70	1M
HIV/AIDS	1981–present	25–35M
Swine flu	2009–10	200,000
SARS	2002–03	770
Ebola	2014–16	11,000
MERS	2015–present	850
COVID-19	2019–present	34,252 (writing time)

easily transmitted among people and animals. It is still under investigation to explore how it is transmitted into animal reservoirs and others. As there was no vaccine and fixed treatment for COVID-19 pandemic, hence social distancing has been declared the most accepted strategy for its control and prevention. It is necessary to isolate the person who has a travel history and contact with the infected patient. Social distancing, quarantine, and isolation play an important role in controlling and prevent the infection of COVID-19 deadly disease.

2.2 Applications of AI and ML in emerging diseases

Science and technology considering AI and ML toward several pandemics as well as COVID-19. The health-care sector needs urgent support of new technologies such as IoT, AI, Big Data, and ML to tackle with the new diseases. AI and ML models are significant for practical analysis in the biomedical fields. These tools are significantly effective to combat with various diseases (dengue, flu, zika, ebola, cholera, H1N1, influenza, and swine fever) with other methods such as classification, preprocessing of data, forecasting, prediction, pattern recognition, and monitoring. These methods are significant to identify, treat, and predict pandemic infections. Since the outbreak of COVID-19, AI and ML tools are playing a significant role to combat with the deadly disease (Hollister, 2020). ML is considered as a subset of AI and helps machines to understand "training samples" or patterns in data preprocessing to make or predict intelligent decisions. There are four primary areas of AI (tracking and prediction, treatment and cure, early warning, data dashboard, and alert) to contribute against COVID-19.

Tracking and predicting COVID-19 transmission are prominent data inputs for tackling the pandemic by planning, preparation, and management with the health authorities (Naudé, 2020). It also identifies the epidemiological curve and attending pandemic situation and predicts future projections for taking possible control measures to reduce transmission. Recently, a tracking app "Aarogya Setu" (Aarogya Setu App, 2020) is launched in India to track newly infected cases by using smartphones and Bluetooth to determine any person nearby infected person.

Early warning and alerts help control the disease outbreak, such as COVID-19. AI-based alert models help diagnose the patterns by mining online content, news, and other sources to predict early warnings for preparedness measures such as "Bluedot" (BlueDot, 2020), a Canadian mode, and WHO Early Warning System. These models help take preventive actions such as quarantine, isolation, hotspot mapping, intelligent contact tracing, cluster prediction, and containment.

Treatment and cures. AI advances to find new drug discoveries and repurpose existing drugs for COVID-19 patients. In COVID-19, several data centers and research labs use AI technologies for treatment and vaccine diagnosis. ML techniques are significant to control, check, trail, and approve new drugs.

Data dashboard. Several institutions such as the Johns Hopkins University and the OECD (oecd.ai) have presented attractive dashboards to trace the virus transmission and showing the current status of confirmed, recovered, and diseased cases. COVID-19 tracker is a notable dashboard for several countries to present the country wise data analysis.

Bullock et al. (2020) have presented a survey with AI applications to show how AI can efficiently reduce the diagnosis and perform cheaper and faster COVID-19 tests. Authors have categorized the applications of AI in several ways: molecular scale, clinical scale, and social scale. A hierarchical representation of AI applications has shown in Fig. 1.

2.2.1 AI applications at molecular scale

Molecular scale covers molecular modeling to diagnose the proteins involved in SARS-CoV-2 and identify potential treatment. There are some structural proteins such as envelope proteins (E), nucleocapsid proteins (N), spike proteins (S), and membrane proteins (M), and nonstructural proteins such as 3-chymotrypsin-like, protease, and the papain-like protease (Liu et al., 2020; Zhavoronkov et al., 2020).

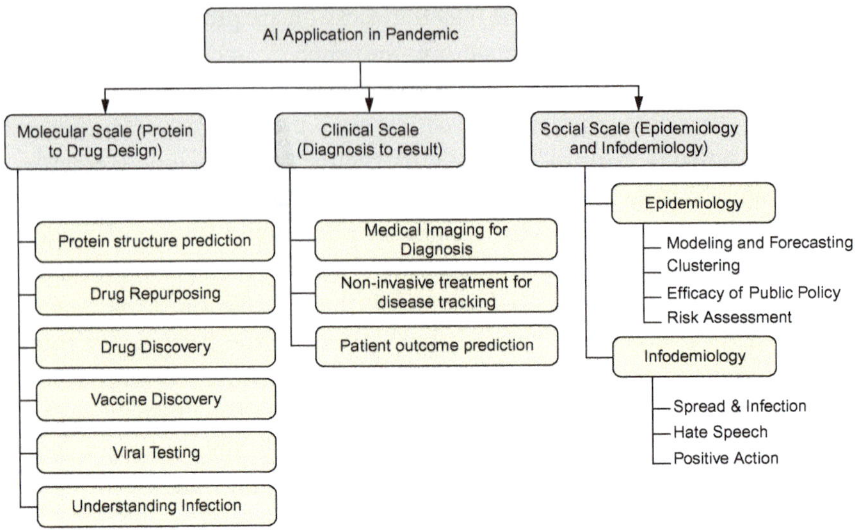

Fig. 1 AI applications in pandemic (Bullock et al., 2020).

AI application of molecular scale comprises prediction of associated proteins structure, diagnosing drugs that can effectively target these proteins, and new compounds to make the further test as a possible treatment (Naudé, 2020). Several molecular scales have been discussed in this section.

Prediction of protein structure. Experimental approaches such as X-ray crystallography generally describe protein structure, but sometimes they are expensive and time consuming, so computational models are applied to predict the structure of proteins. There are two primary approaches, template modeling to predict structure as a template-free modeling and template sequence for unknown related systems.

Repurposing of drug. Several studies have been focused on detecting known elements that can be useful in lessening infections along with approved drugs. For repurposing the drug, four different approaches can be managed by AI, such as the forecasting of protein-ligand binding affinities, the construction of biomedical knowledge graphs, molecular docking simulations, and gene expression signatures analysis.

Discovery of drug. Some studies offer to explore utterly new aggregate to target SARS-CoV-2. Tang et al. (2020) have applied a reinforcement learning approach to explore the aggregates constrain the 3C-like protease. They have designed a novel "deep Q-learning network along with the fragment-based drug design" (ADQN-FBDD) to generate the lead elements that targets SARS-CoV-2 3CLpro. This work resulted the derivatives series from extracted lead elements by the structure-based optimization policy. Finally, they have extracted 47 lead compounds from their AI model and derivatives. Nguyen et al. (2020) have used a generative network complex for finding the drug. They have designed a structural-based drug repositioning model that is based on mathematics and learning to explore 1465 drugs in the DrugBank that is approved by the Food and Drug Administration and it is found that these drugs are deeply effective to 2019-nCoV. Bung et al. (2021) designed a generative model for SMILES input strings. This model is proposed as a classifier to predict the next character of strings.

Discovery of vaccine. Vaccine discovery is a different area as drug discovery. Antibodies are developed for virus neutralizing with the help of B-cells and the body needs T-cells to kill the virus precisely. Generally, vaccine design aims two significant objectives: (a) diagnosing proper epitopes for achieving and (b) assuring that these epitopes can be described by major histocompatibility protein that are generated by human leukocyte antigen allele.

Improving viral nucleic acid testing. ML techniques are applying to enhance the virus nucleic acid diagnosing test. Metsky et al. (2020) associated ML with CRISPR tool to design assay samples for diagnosing 67 respiratory viruses along with SARS-CoV-2. ML models have been constructed to create assays that are predicted specifically, quickly, and sensitively. They have experimentally explored four SARS-CoV-2 develops with a CRISPR-Cas13 identification system and then tested the performance of SARS-CoV-2. They also describe the speed and sensitivity of this assay by applying synthetic targets along with fluorescent as well as lateral flow detection. Lopez-Rincon et al. (2020) follow convolutional neural network model for nucleic acid sequences to categorize where it is linked to SARS-CoV-2. This work has proposed a deep convolutional neural network that can design features automatically by the virus's genome sequence. This work has proposed a state-of-the-art deep convolutional neural network that is able to create features automatically by the virus's genome sequence. Results has shown that proposed method is suitable to categorize SARS-CoV-2 and differentiating by other strains of coronavirus such as HCoV-OC43, MERS-CoV, HCoV-229E, HCoV-HKU1, etc.

Better infection understanding. ML is used to pay more attention for better understanding of SARS-CoV-2 infectivity and infection severity such as support vector machines (Cortes and Vapnik, 1995) and KNNs, along with decision trees, to predict the hierarchical viruses classifications (Randhawa et al., 2020) based on their genomic sequence.

2.2.2 AI applications at clinical scale

Most AI and ML techniques are used to diagnose and treat medical imaging, such as X-ray scans and CT. AI supports to predict the evolution of the disease and for monitoring and measurement process.

Diagnosing with medical imaging. AI techniques are widely applied in diagnostic methodologies such as screening, medical imaging, and diagnosing of COVID-19 patients (Ai et al., 2020). Medical imaging (Fang et al., 2020; Kanne et al., 2020) can observe image patterns and radiological signatures for COVID-19 cases. ML approaches can help promote the analysis of scanning by using different architecture such as Inception (Szegedy et al., 2015), ResNet (He et al., 2016; Zhou et al., 2018) that can train directly.

Disease tracking with noninvasive measurement. Several approaches not required medical imaging equipment for tracking and diagnosing COVID-19 disease. Various efforts have been done to use mobile apps for identifying COVID-19 with the help of embedded sensors to diagnose COVID-19 symptoms (Maghdid et al., 2020) and identify high-risk patients through phone-based surveys.

Prediction of patient outcome. It is difficult to predict outcomes of patient about planning, preparation, and optimization in health systems for COVID-19 epidemic. It is important to diagnose the aspects that cause patients at risk, developing respiratory syndrome, and fatalities due to respiratory failure. Some approaches such as support vector machines (Cortes and Vapnik, 1995) and XGBoost algorithm (Chen and Guestrin, 2016) are used to detect important measurable factors to predict death risk. Medical imagery is also applied in several areas for predicting patient outcome.

2.2.3 Social scale: Infodemiology and epidemiology

The social scale is further categorized into two: infodemiology and epidemiology. This section will further discuss it.

Infodemiology. Online web sources and social media are the key channels for disseminating the virus information and explaining its dynamics. Although AI and ML carried enough research but still need a better understanding of social dynamics in pandemics. Several factors are discussed to disseminate information related to the pandemic, such as spread and infection, hate speech, and positive action. Singh et al. (2020) use Twitter for the dissemination of spread and infection. They have analyzed a huge volume of tweets related to coronavirus queries. They have explored that an important spatiotemporal relationship available among new cases and information flow of COVID-19. It is also noticed that this research has taken first step to understand the conversation of social media about COVID-19. Gallotti et al. (2020) also examined twitter social media posts across 64 languages. They have designed an Infodemic Risk Index to measure the magnitude of risk to irrelevant news across the globe. This study explored that measurable waves of unreliable news anticipated the growth of COVID-19 contagion and these fake news can cause a critical threat to public health. Mejova and Kalimeri (2020) have analyzed the Facebook advertisements to explore the spread and infection information. An incremental growth has been observed in hate speech and verbal abuses that can cause physical violence in any country during the pandemic. Several efforts are going on for curating the particular news data about the virus and conduct fact checking to analyze the relevancy. Pandey et al. (2022) have presented a method for analyzing the similarity among the World Health Organization (WHO) recommendations and regular headlines of news. They have explored that a multipronged device learning application conveying vernacular bite-sized audios and also revealed that conversational AI is an impressive approach to lessen the unreliable information.

Epidemiology. SARS-CoV-2 virus transmission received much attention to forecast models and new information. The epidemiological research area is vast and resulted in several modeling efforts. Most of the models build on well-designed classical models such as SIR and SEIR models with ML techniques for modeling tasks such as forecasting and modeling statistics, clustering, Bayesian analysis, and risk assessment. Several AI applications have been designed for forecasting local and national data, such as total confirmed cases, recovery rates, and fatality cases. Several models have been offered to examine the model structure and optimal approaches for forecasting data daily. They have applied different modeling techniques such as LSTM-GRU architecture (Cho et al., 2014; Hochreiter and Schmidhuber, 1997) for time-series prediction and analysis (Dutta and Bandyopadhyay, 2020) and CNN-based approaches (LeCun et al., 2015), where integer facts have been merged and reframed into "images" (Huang et al., 2020b). Clustering is another ML technique that aims to create groups considering similarities among clusters. Carrillo-Larco and Castillo-Cara (2020) have implemented the ML techniques for detecting general public health-care aptitude and interest associated with COVID-19. Hu et al. (2020) proposed AI-based methods for the forecasting of real-time COVID-19 data to measure the length, size, and controlling duration of pandemic in China. Bayesian analysis techniques also presented significant insights to handle the uncertainty and small datasets.

Table 2 ML techniques in diseases prediction.

Disease	ML technique	Country	References
Dengue	Classification and regression tree	Bangladesh	Muurlink et al. (2018)
Oyster norovirus	Genetic programming	The United States	Chenar and Deng (2018)
Dengue	Multiregression and Naïve Bayes	India	Agarwal et al. (2018)
H1N1 flu	Neural network	Japan	Koike and Morimoto (2018)
Influenza	Random forest	Iran	Tapak et al. (2019)
Dengue fever	Neural network	Japan	Anno et al. (2019)
Swine fever	Random forest	China	Liang et al. (2020)

Table 2 discusses how ML techniques are applied in different emerging diseases and played an important role in tackling the diseases.

3 Applications of AI and ML in COVID-19

Practitioners encounter critical issues in the diagnosis of nCov-2019 because SAR-CoV-2 viruses spread quickly. As the approved system employed for diagnosing COVID-19, the RT-PCR approach is not useful due to few barriers (Singh et al., 2018). The limitations of RT-PCR can be anticipated analyzing medical images because growing digital methods help to control pandemic by employing statistics, ML/AI methods (Swapnarekha, 2020). The capability of these models has been presented in a different form of usage, from disease detection and forecasting to social control. Various applications include real-time data study for detecting disease, treatment monitoring, drug/vaccines development, and forecasting of infection and death (Patel et al., 2019).

3.1 Detection and diagnosis

COVID-19 outbreak is not only appeared as a medical contagious but also it is an economic contagious (Baldwin, 2020). Early detection of the infection is critical for personalized patient care, satisfactory patient quarantine, and diagnosis. Since the first, the false-negative test may delay treatment and boost the danger of viral transmission to healthy people; fast detection of infected people with COVID-19 is essential. AI techniques are equipped to expand the early detection of disease infection. Mei et al. (2020) aimed to create an AI-based early detection model that can recognize coronavirus infection by considering chest CT scans. They have integrated AI algorithms to assimilate chest CT results with clinical systems, laboratory testing, and exposure history to speedily identify infected patients.

3.2 Treatment monitoring

Epidemiological research at the population and individual level should be procured at a specified period, with infection-oriented data gathered longitudinally. Diagnosis and treatment ways are minimal because of the limited knowledge of novel viruses at the beginning of an epidemic. Moreover, infectious diseases can be spread rapidly from one person to the other. Therefore, unknown aspects of the virus, symptoms' severity, and critical fatality rates cause the prediction problem's seriousness, especially the pandemic size and location (Agrebi and Larbi, 2020). Various forecasting models based on ML methods can be applied to forecast the infection by using different variables such as age, sex, underlying diseases, and preexisting immunity. Postnikov (2020) asserts a simple ML model can represent the epidemic parameters qualitatively. He has proposed an appropriate model to reproduce the pandemic dynamics qualitatively as well as quantitatively along with high degree of correlation that helps to estimate predictions. This model is a three-compartmental SIR (susceptible-infectious-recovered-removed) model to the logistic regression with the primary characteristics of the epidemic process. Wu et al. (2020) measured COVID-19 pandemic size and predicted the scope of public health risks locally and globally using the SEIR (susceptible-exposed infectious-recovered) model. Shao and Shan (2020) explained using some critical estimation to smoother the infection of the pandemic. They have designed a SEIRD model to simulate the control measures and pandemic prevention.

3.3 Prediction of disease and mortality

Creating pandemic prediction models with high accuracy is required to reveal insights about the spread and outcomes of the outbreak. These models are critical for governments and lawmakers to recommend effective strategies and evaluate the implemented strategies' results (Remuzzi and Remuzzi, 2020). SEIR models consider the considerable incubation time when people are infected and increase the accuracy of the prediction model for the Varicella and Zika outbreaks (Pan et al., 2012; Zha et al., 2020). The incubation time is a random variable in SEIR and SIR models, and there is a balance without thinking about the disease (Dantas et al., 2018). However, traditional SIR and SEIR models do not consider variables such as social distance and quarantines (Imran et al., 2017). Another common technique mainly applied to a contagious disease is that the R0 calculates the number of individuals who can infect another infected person. In the R0 model, additional weight is used for individuals who were not infected with the disease or were not protected by a vaccine (Chimmula and Zhang, 2020). It can also be applied to detect a novel virus's infection rate (Zhang et al., 2020). In such techniques, however, it is hard to determine the initial point of the contagious disease and the interaction with others during the incubation time.

Many well-known and undiscovered variables included in the outbreak, the confusion of community response in different areas, and differentiation in avoiding tactics had strikingly extended model difficulty (Chimmula and Zhang, 2020; Darwish et al., 2020). Eventually, conventional pandemic prediction models encounter unusual difficulties in delivering more stronger effects. Therefore, various new models have developed, including some assumptions such as social distancing and quarantines (Rypdal and Sugihara, 2019; Scarpino and Petri, 2019; Zhan et al., 2019).

Some ML-based methods have been proposed to predict the spread and results of the outbreak to master the limitations of these kinds of statistical methods (Chimmula and Zhang, 2020; Ucar and Korkmaz, 2020). Long short-term memory (LSTM) networks based on DL were applied in some studies to forecast coronavirus infections (Dutta and Bandyopadhyay, 2020; Huang et al., 2020b; Tomar and Gupta, 2020). The LSTM models employed in the networks cannot describe the spatiotemporal elements together in these studies. Chimmula and Zhang (2020) presented an LSTM model by adjusting alternative internal connections between the input and output cells. Ardabili et al. (2020) applied multilayered perceptron and adaptive network-based fuzzy inference system methods to the extremely complicated nature of COVID-19 and behavioral differences in several countries (Italy, China, Iran, Germany, and the United States).

Table 3 gives the various ML techniques that used to predict COVID-19 outbreak.

3.4 Drugs and vaccines preparation

Drug and vaccine improvement is a critical responsibility in fighting a pandemic. AI can reduce drug discovery duration and improve performance, although it is highly costly and time consuming (Mamoshina et al., 2016). A scientific team at the MIT built a model to prevent the coronavirus

Table 3 ML techniques for COVID-19.

References	ML approach	Explanation
Tuli et al. (2020)	Robust Weibull fitting model	Levenberg–Marquardt algorithm
Pourghasemi et al. (2020)	Random forest	Provides risk maps to manage and control the pandemic in Iran
Chimmula and Zhang (2020)	Long short-term memory networks	Considers the fundamental characteristics of COVID-19 to predict the trends and possible stopping time in Canada and around the world
Alzahrani et al. (2020)	ARIMA	Predicts the anticipated everyday count of COVID-19 infected cases in Saudi Arabia
Ribeiro et al. (2020)	More than one	Compares short-term prediction methods in Brazilian
Ahamad et al. (2020)	More than one	Analyzes patient symptoms to predict the pandemic diagnoses
Zhu et al. (2020)	Deep learning	Predicts the possible hosts of coronaviruses
Fong et al. (2020)	Polynomial neural network	Proposes three ML techniques that can work with scarse data

that conduces toward COVID-19 by creating a "decoy" receptor that might be considered as a vaccination. Coronaviruses bind ACE2 receptors in the body and induce sickness. The MIT professionals have applied an AI method to affect the link between the bats and the virus (Busse et al., 2020). Some studies concentrate on discovering novel composites for practice in centering on SARS-Cov2 by using a particular method to identify inhibitors for the 3Clike protease (Zhavoronkov et al., 2020). Such techniques employ three kinds of information: the protein structure, the cocrystalized ligands, and the homology form of the protein. Several approaches, such as Generative Auto-encoders and Generative Adversarial Networks, are applied for each type of information (Makhzani et al., 2015). The experts examine possible candidates applying a reinforcement learning method with a prize capacity that combines determinants, such as medication measurements, similarity, newness, and variety. AI balances to not dramatically change the whole pharmaceutical life cycle, from regulative procedures to pharmacovigilance. In summary, AI and ML speed up drug testing in real time and recognize beneficial drugs for the treatment of patients with COVID-19.

Moreover, AI can support screening prepared drugs and speeding up antiviral progress to treat COVID-19. CORD-19 dataset can be used to train AI and ML algorithms. The resulting prototype can be practiced to monitor for current drugs that probably show effectiveness in the treatment of patients with COVID-19 (Ahuja et al., 2020).

3.5 Drugs repurposing

With no vaccine or potential treatment recently available, the coronavirus has outbreak speedily across the globe and affected the world's economy and an ever-increasing amount of fatalities. It is an initial task to search for any existing drug repurposed to save the human population.

Drug discovery is a complex process, needing several validation layers before the drug may come into use. Considering the present scenario of the pandemic, a dual approach is required to protect the human from this deadly disease (Zhou et al., 2020):

- Repurposed drugs—diagnose the opportunities in the available set of known drugs; and
- Drug screening—work on new optimized molecules.

Drug repurposing, identifying effective drugs from available drugs, will lessen the time and cost compared to the new drug discovery. Though drug repurposing is sometimes based on chance observations, target-based repurposing depends on a prior understanding of the specific molecular or cellular element that the proposed drug recognizes (Pizzorno et al., 2019). The focus could be on already approved marketed drugs or those under clinical trials against the CoVs in general, and the SARS-CoV-2 in particular.

For repurposed drugs, it is essential to compare the genome of several coronaviruses, which infects humans. The target does not need to have the exact mechanism of action in both the diseased states. So, the drug could be an antivirals agent that will target the viral proteins essential tool of the viral life cycle, such as virus-host cell interactions, replication, assembly, etc., would belong to this class. Several drugs have been repurposed as anti-HCoV, using network proximity analysis (Cheng et al., 2018) and "complementary exposure" pattern (Cheng et al., 2019) of drugs and HCoV-host interactions in the human genome.

Besides drug repurposing, a virtual screening based on molecular docking appears as an essential tool for gaining new antiviral molecules. Researchers and physicians can apply this tool as a complementary method to synthesize new compounds or assign the repositioning of drugs (Marinho et al., 2020; Milite et al., 2019).

One aspect of proposing a new drug is to find the drug pockets in the structure of the viral proteins. Since the quaternary structure of COVID-19 spike (S) glycoprotein is resolved (Wrapp et al., 2020), and can be downloaded from the Protein Data Bank opens to Structural Biology new aspects to find new drugs specific to spike protein. The S glycoprotein plays the main role in COVID-19 infection by mediating attachment of viral particles to the host cell receptor, it is also involved in cell-to-cell fusion and activates neutralizing antibodies, addressing also virulence determinants (Spaan et al., 1988). The quaternary structure is important for the virus's virulent property. By using databases such as PockDrug-Server (Hussein et al., 2015), it is believed that analysis of protomer-protomer COVID-19 interfaces S glycoprotein could be a proper initial or beginning point for the prediction of new ligands and that by intervening with quaternary structure assembly of COVID-19 S glycoprotein may present therapeutic process against viral life cycle (Bongini et al., 2020).

3.6 Social awareness and control by the Internet

Social media platforms present many opportunities at both individual and enterprise levels, such as targeting marketing, personalized campaigns, valuable insights about the business, and fast communication. However, they cause a crisis over people. Populaces are exposed to misinformation that may lead to propagation. The WHO's response to challenging this problem based on wrong information in social media is practicing its Information Network for Epidemics (EPIWIN) platform for presenting the correct data to principal partners (Zarocostas, 2020). Besides, the Facebook Ad Library (Facebook, 2020) investigated all advertisements using the keywords "COVID-19" and "coronavirus" from 34 countries. Maddah and Beigzadeh (2020) have introduced a scheme for COVID-19 detection by using the data collected from individuals' smartphones and sensors. In another study, a smartphone's sound taken from a microphone was processed to identify the cough type (Nemati et al., 2019). AI and ML algorithms can learn and predict the threat contamination that can signify early detection of a jeopardous case for quarantine purposes. Therefore, an AI-based application can decrease the spread of the virus to weak populations (Allam and Jones, 2020).

4 Challenges and future directions

AI, as an effective method, has been generally used in health care. Among the existing analytical techniques, AI has been explored as the most promising tool for humankind. AI is used in various medical sectors such as medical data analysis, disease identification and diagnosis, drug manufacturing and discovery, vaccine development, robotic surgery, monitoring the patient's condition, tracking, and forecasting the nature of the virus.

4.1 Challenges

AI has a significant role on the health-care industry and great potential to solve health-care problems. Even though widespread applications of AI in health care are emerging, but enormous challenges lie hard. Some of the challenges of AI in health-care:

AI tools, that are adopted by health-care industries, are not matured and entirely sophisticated (Panch et al., 2019). Premature use of AI tools will record inefficient output and harm the users.

Regularity body. Even though the exponential growth of AI applications continues, there is no regularity body to deal with emerging algorithms.

Lack of Big Data. Many organizations do not have big data to enable AI in their organizations. AI methods need a huge quantity of data for training of the model.

Adoptability. Many health-care professionals lack the capabilities to use/adopt AI in health-care. Human barriers to the adoption of AI are substantial. The health-care industry is lagging in adopting (Wiljer and Hakim, 2019).

Data ownership, control, and consent are also a challenge for implementing AI in health-care.

Standard policy. Organizations must adopt procedures and policies for data privacy. Organizations that adopt AI must safeguard the data with all stakeholders.

Lack of regulation. Regulations to adopt AI in medical research lack standard. One main regulatory issue in choosing AI in health care is archaic regulatory infrastructure. Traditional regulations for health-care cannot be applied to AI-based health-care systems (Analytics India Magazine, 2020a).

Metrics, used in AI for measuring the performance of the algorithm, often do not reflect the clinical applicability. Parameters such as accuracy and area under the curve do not necessarily represent clinical efficacy (Keane and Topol, 2018; Saito and Rehmsmeier, 2015).

Data exchanging is another challenge in adopting AI in health-care. The sharing of health-care data is critical in the operationalization of AI. AI systems require data from various clinical studies. All the parties in the health-care ecosystem should exchange data considering privacy (Jiang et al., 2017).

Risk of adversarial attack. AI algorithms are susceptible to the risk of adversarial attack (Finlayson et al., 2019).

Algorithmic bias. Another challenge in adopting AI in health-care systems is algorithm bias. There are three types of bias namely, (i) model bias, (ii) model variance, and (iii) outcome noise (Kelly et al., 2019).

Interoperability. AI systems are having a lack of interoperability with other health-care platforms (Analytics India Magazine, 2020b). One of the significant challenges in adopting AI in health-care is inconsistency in health-care records, which cause inaccurate analysis (MindFields, 2020).

Uncertainty and mixed data. Due to uncertain and mixed health-care data, standard models record lower accuracy for predicting pandemic diseases.

4.2 Future directions

Even though AI has solved some of the health-care sector's complex challenges, the implementation of AI in health-care is still at the nascent stage, and the extent of AI to the health-care sector should be increased.

AI should be integrated with susceptible-exposed-infectious-recovered (SEIR) model to enhance the prediction of epidemic diseases in terms of accuracy. There should be some benchmark framework to assess the current AI techniques. Transfer learning methods and computational efficiency can be adopted, and inference using pretrained networks can be adopted along with AI for new applications (Panayides et al., 2020).

Novel algorithms must be developed to provide a more accurate diagnosis and prediction of diseases with a reduced response. In the future, AI will become more advanced and can carry a wide range of tasks. AI should be more ethical and should make more ethical decisions, and AI will not substitute the doctors for three reasons: responsibility, credibility, and accuracy. Public-private partnerships will help the progress of AI in health-care. Testing AI/ML algorithms will increase trust in AI/ML.

5 Conclusions

AI and ML are advanced analytical techniques having great potential to deal with uncertainties, incompleteness, and inconsistencies in data. These techniques are promising and, therefore, used by many researchers focused on COVID-19. Researchers and scientists are exploring all possible efforts to fight COVID-19 pandemic. This chapter presents a thorough review of the pandemic and COVID-19, applications of AI/ML in emerging diseases, and applications in AI/ML COVID-19, such as detection and diagnosis, treatment monitoring, prediction of disease, and mortality, drugs and vaccines preparations, and drugs repurposing. Several challenges have been presented to make an impact on the health-care industry and have great potential to solve health-care problems. Finally, the chapter has concluded with the future directions that will help researchers, academicians, practitioners, and physician for finding the details about AI/ML techniques in pandemic.

References

Aarogya Setu App, 2020. Accessed 6 June 2020 https://www.npci.org.in/aarogya-setu-app.

Agarwal, N., Koti, S.R., Saran, S., Kumar, A.S., 2018. Data mining techniques for predicting dengue outbreak in geospatial domain using weather parameters for New Delhi, India. Curr. Sci. 114 (11), 2281–2291.

Agrebi, S., Larbi, A., 2020. Use of artificial intelligence in infectious diseases. In: Artificial Intelligence in Precision Health, Elsevier, pp. 415–438.

Ahamad, M.M., Aktar, S., Rashed-Al-Mahfuz, M., Uddin, S., Lio, P., Xu, H., Summers, M. A., Quinng, J.M.W., Moni, M.A., 2020. A machine learning model to identify early stage symptoms of SARS-CoV-2 infected patients. Expert Syst. Appl. 160, 113661.

Ahuja, A.S., Reddy, V.P., Marques, O., 2020. Artificial intelligence and COVID-19: a multidisciplinary approach. Integr. Med. Res. 9 (3), 100434.

Ai, T., Yang, Z., Hou, H., Zhan, C., Chen, C., Lv, W., Tao, Q., Sun, Z., Xia, L., 2020. Correlation of chest CT and RT-PCR testing in coronavirus disease 2019 (COVID-19) in China: a report of 1014 cases. Radiology 296 (2), E32–E40.

Allam, Z., Jones, D.S., 2020. On the coronavirus (COVID-19) outbreak and the smart city network: universal data sharing standards coupled with artificial intelligence (AI) to benefit urban health monitoring and management. In: Healthcare, vol. 8, p. 46.

Alzahrani, S.I., Aljamaan, I.A., Al-Fakih, E.A., 2020. Forecasting the spread of the COVID-19 pandemic in Saudi Arabia using ARIMA prediction model under current public health interventions. J. Infect. Pub. Health 13, 914–919.

Analytics India Magazine, 2020a. What regulatory challenges holding back the adoption of AI in healthcare in 2020. Accessed 23 June 2020 https://analyticsindiamag.com/what-regulatory-challenges-holding-back-the-adoption-of-ai-in-healthcare-in-2020/.

Analytics India Magazine, 2020b. InsightBrief. AI in health care, benefits challenges and risks. Accessed 23 June 2020 https://analyticsindiamag.com/what-regulatory-challenges-holding-back-the-adoption-of-ai-in-healthcare-in-2020/.

Anno, S., Hara, T., Kai, H., Lee, M.-A., Chang, Y., Oyoshi, K., Mizukami, Y., Tadono, T., 2019. Spatiotemporal dengue fever hotspots associated with climatic factors in Taiwan including outbreak predictions based on machine-learning. Geospat. Health 14 (2), 183–194.

Ardabili, S.F., Mosavi, A., Ghamisi, P., Ferdinand, F., Varkonyi-Koczy, A.R., Reuter, U., Rabczuk, T., Atkinson, P.M., 2020. Covid-19 outbreak prediction with machine learning. Algorithms 13 (10), 249.

Baldwin, R., 2020. Accessed 30 May 2020 https://foreignpolicy.com/2020/03/09/coronavirus-economic-pandemic-impact-recession/.

BlueDot, 2020. BlueDot: outbreak risk software. Accessed 6 June 2020 https://bluedot.global/.

Bongini, P., Trezza, A., Bianchini, M., Spiga, O., Niccolai, N., 2020. A possible strategy to fight COVID-19: interfering with spike glycoprotein trimerization. Biochem. Biophys. Res. Commun. 528, 35–38.

Breiman, L., 2001. Random forests. Mach. Learn. 45 (1), 5–32.

Bullock, J., Luccioni, A., Pham, K.H., Lam, C.S.N., Luengo-Oroz, M., 2020. Mapping the landscape of artificial intelligence applications against COVID-19. J. Artif. Intell. Res. 69, 807–845.

Bung, N., Krishnan, S.R., Bulusu, G., Roy, A., 2021. De novo design of new chemical entities for SARS-CoV-2 using artificial intelligence. Future Med. Chem. 13 (6), 575–585.

Busse, L.W., Chow, J.H., McCurdy, M.T., Khanna, A.K., 2020. COVID-19 and the RAAS—a potential role for angiotensin II? Crit Care 24, 136.

Carrillo-Larco, R.M., Castillo-Cara, M., 2020. Using country-level variables to classify countries according to the number of confirmed COVID-19 cases: an unsupervised machine learning approach. Wellcome Open Res. 5, 56.

Casas, L., Navab, N., Demirci, S., 2019. Patient 3D body pose estimation from pressure imaging. Int. J. Comput. Assist. Radiol. Surg. 14 (3), 517–524.

Chen, T., Guestrin, C., 2016. XGBoost: a scalable tree boosting system. In: Proceedings of the 22nd ACM SIGKDD International Conference on Knowledge Discovery and Data Mining, pp. 785–794.

Chenar, S.S., Deng, Z., 2018. Development of genetic programming-based model for predicting oyster norovirus outbreak risks. Water Res. 128, 20–37.

Cheng, F., Desai, R.J., Handy, D.E., Wang, R., Schneeweiss, S., Barabasi, A.-L., Loscalzo, J., 2018. Network-based approach to prediction and population-based validation of in silico drug repurposing. Nat. Commun. 9 (1), 1–12.

Cheng, F., Kovács, I.A., Barabási, A.-L., 2019. Network-based prediction of drug combinations. Nat. Commun. 10 (1), 1–11.

Chimmula, V.K.R., Zhang, L., 2020. Time series forecasting of COVID-19 transmission in Canada using LSTM networks. Chaos Solit. Fractals 135, 109864.

Cho, K., Van Merriënboer, B., Gulcehre, C., Bahdanau, D., Bougares, F., Schwenk, H., Bengio, Y., 2014. Learning phrase representations using RNN encoder–decoder for statistical machine translation. In: Proceedings of the 2014 Conference on Empirical Methods in Natural Language Processing (EMNLP). Association for Computational Linguistics, Doha, Qatar, pp. 1724–1734.

Cortes, C., Vapnik, V., 1995. Support-vector networks. Mach. Learn. 20 (3), 273–297.

Dantas, E., Tosin, M., Cunha Jr, A., 2018. Calibration of a SEIR-SEI epidemic model to describe the Zika virus outbreak in Brazil. Appl. Math. Comput. 338, 249–259.

Darwish, A., Rahhal, Y., Jafar, A., 2020. A comparative study on predicting influenza outbreaks using different feature spaces: application of influenza-like illness data from Early Warning Alert and Response System in Syria. BMC Res. Notes 13 (1), 1–8.

Dogan, O., Tiwari, S., Jabbar, M.A., Guggari, S., 2021. A systematic review on AI/ML approaches against COVID-19 outbreak. Complex Intell. Syst. 7, 1–24.

Dutta, S., Bandyopadhyay, S.K., 2020. Machine learning approach for confirmation of covid-19 cases: positive, negative, death and release. Iberoam. J. Med. 2 (3), 172–177.

Facebook, 2020. Facebook Ad Library. Accessed 30 May 2020 https://www.facebook.com/ads/library/?active_status=all&ad_type=all&country=GB&impression_search_field=has_impressions_lifetime.

Fang, Y., Zhang, H., Xie, J., Lin, M., Ying, L., Pang, P., Ji, W., 2020. Sensitivity of chest CT for COVID-19: comparison to RT-PCR. Radiology 296 (2), E115–E117.

Finlayson, S.G., Bowers, J.D., Ito, J., Zittrain, J.L., Beam, A.L., Kohane, I.S., 2019. Adversarial attacks on medical machine learning. Science 363 (6433), 1287–1289.

Fong, S.J., Li, G., Dey, N., Crespo, R.G., Herrera-Viedma, E., 2020. Finding an accurate early forecasting model from small dataset: a case of 2019-nCoV novel coronavirus outbreak. arXiv preprint arXiv:2003.10776.

Gallotti, R., Valle, F., Castaldo, N., Sacco, P., De Domenico, M., 2020. Assessing the risks of "infodemics" in response to COVID-19 epidemics. Nat. Hum. Behav. 4 (12), 1285–1293.

Greff, K., Srivastava, R.K., Koutník, J., Steunebrink, B.R., Schmidhuber, J., 2016. LSTM: a search space odyssey. IEEE Trans. Neural Netw. Learn. Syst. 28 (10), 2222–2232.

He, K., Zhang, X., Ren, S., Sun, J., 2016. Deep residual learning for image recognition. In: Proceedings of the IEEE Conference on Computer Vision and Pattern Recognition, pp. 770–778.

Henderson, D.A., 2009. Smallpox: The Death of a Disease: The Inside Story of Eradicating a Worldwide Killer. Prometheus Books.

Hochreiter, S., Schmidhuber, J., 1997. Long short-term memory. Neural Comput. 9, 1735–1780.

Hollister, M., 2020. AI can help with the COVID-19 crisis-but the right human input is key. Accessed 7 June 2020 Available at: https://www.weforum.org/agenda/2020/03/covid-19-crisis-artificial-intelligence-creativity/.

Hu, Z., Ge, Q., Jin, L., Xiong, M., 2020. Artificial intelligence forecasting of COVID-19 in China. arXiv preprint arXiv:2002.07112.

Huang, C., Wang, Y., Li, X., Ren, L., Zhao, J., Hu, Y., Zhang, L., Fan, G., Xu, J., Gu, X., et al., 2020a. Clinical features of patients infected with 2019 novel coronavirus in Wuhan, China. Lancet 395 (10223), 497–506.

Huang, C.-J., Chen, Y.-H., Ma, Y., Kuo, P.-H., 2020b. Multiple-input deep convolutional neural network model for COVID-19 forecasting in China. medRxiv.

Hussein, H.A., Borrel, A., Geneix, C., Petitjean, M., Regad, L., Camproux, A.-C., 2015. PockDrug-Server: a new web server for predicting pocket druggability on holo and apo proteins. Nucleic Acids Res. 43 (W1), W436–W442.

Imran, M., Usman, M., Dur-e-Ahmad, M., Khan, A., 2017. Transmission dynamics of Zika fever: a SEIR based model. Differ. Equ. Dyn. Syst. 29 (3), 463–486.

Jiang, F., Jiang, Y., Zhi, H., Dong, Y., Li, H., Ma, S., Wang, Y., Dong, Q., Shen, H., Wang, Y., 2017. Artificial intelligence in healthcare: past, present and future. Stroke Vasc. Neurol. 2 (4), 230–243.

Jin, Y.-H., Cai, L., Cheng, Z.-S., Cheng, H., Deng, T., Fan, Y.-P., Fang, C., Huang, D., Huang, L.-Q., Huang, Q., et al., 2020. A rapid advice guideline for the diagnosis and treatment of 2019 novel coronavirus (2019-nCoV) infected pneumonia (standard version). Mil. Med. Res. 7 (1), 4.

Kanne, J.P., Little, B.P., Chung, J.H., Elicker, B.M., Ketai, L.H., 2020. Essentials for Radiologists on COVID-19: An Update—Radiology Scientific Expert Panel. Radiological Society of North America.

Kaye, R., Chang, C.D., Kazahaya, K., Brereton, J., Denneny III, J.C., 2020. COVID-19 anosmia reporting tool: initial findings. Otolaryngol. Head Neck Surg. 163 (1), 132–134. 0194599820922992.

Keane, P.A., Topol, E.J., 2018. With an eye to AI and autonomous diagnosis. J. Med. Imaging Radiat. Sci. 40 (1), 1–3.

Kelly, C.J., Karthikesalingam, A., Suleyman, M., Corrado, G., King, D., 2019. Key challenges for delivering clinical impact with artificial intelligence. BMC Med. 17 (1), 195.

Kermany, D.S., Goldbaum, M., Cai, W., Valentim, C.C.S., Liang, H., Baxter, S.L., McKeown, A., Yang, G., Wu, X., Yan, F., et al., 2018. Identifying medical diagnoses and treatable diseases by image-based deep learning. Cell 172 (5), 1122–1131.

Koike, F., Morimoto, N., 2018. Supervised forecasting of the range expansion of novel non-indigenous organisms: Alien pest organisms and the 2009 H1N1 flu pandemic. Glob. Ecol. Biogeogr. 27 (8), 991–1000.

Lakhani, P., Sundaram, B., 2017. Deep learning at chest radiography: automated classification of pulmonary tuberculosis by using convolutional neural networks. Radiology 284 (2), 574–582.

Lawand, N., Al Tabbah, S., 2020. Coronavirus disease 2019 (COVID-19): prevention and disinfection. Int. J. Biol. Med. 2, 10–14.

LeCun, Y., Bengio, Y., Hinton, G., 2015. Deep learning. Nature 521 (7553), 436–444.

Li, J., Udayasankar, U.K., Toth, T.L., Seamans, J., Small, W.C., Kalra, M.K., 2007. Automatic patient centering for MDCT: effect on radiation dose. Am. J. Roentgenol. 188 (2), 547–552.

Liang, R., Lu, Y., Qu, X., Su, Q., Li, C., Xia, S., Liu, Y., Zhang, Q., Cao, X., Chen, Q., et al., 2020. Prediction for global African swine fever outbreaks based on a combination of random forest algorithms and meteorological data. Transbound. Emerg. Dis. 67 (2), 935–946.

Liu, C., Zhou, Q., Li, Y., Garner, L.V., Watkins, S.P., Carter, L.J., Smoot, J., Gregg, A.C., Daniels, A.D., Jervey, S., et al., 2020. Research and Development on Therapeutic Agents and Vaccines for COVID-19 and Related Human Coronavirus Diseases. ACS Publications.

Lopez-Rincon, A., Tonda, A., Mendoza-Maldonado, L., Claassen, E., Garssen, J., Kraneveld, A.D., 2020. Accurate identification of SARS-CoV-2 from viral genome sequences using deep learning. bioRxiv. https://pesquisa.bvsalud.org/global-literature-on-novel-coronavirus-2019-ncov/resource/en/ppbiorxiv-990242.

Maddah, E., Beigzadeh, B., 2020. Use of a smartphone thermometer to monitor thermal conductivity changes in diabetic foot ulcers: a pilot study. J. Wound Care 29 (1), 61–66.

Maghded, H., et al., 2020. A novel AI-enabled framework to diagnose coronavirus COVID-19 using smartphone embedded sensors: design study. In: 2020 IEEE 21st International Conference on Information Reuse and Integration for Data Science (IRI), Las Vegas, NV, USA, 2020, pp. 180–187.

Makhzani, A., Shlens, J., Jaitly, N., Goodfellow, I., Frey, B., 2015. Adversarial autoencoders. arXiv:1511.05644.

Mamoshina, P., Vieira, A., Putin, E., Zhavoronkov, A., 2016. Applications of deep learning in biomedicine. Mol. Pharm. 13 (5), 1445–1454.

Marinho, E.M., de Andrade Neto, J.B., Silva, J., da Silva, C.R., Cavalcanti, B.C., Marinho, E.S., Júnior, H.V.N., 2020. Virtual screening based on molecular docking of possible inhibitors of COVID-19 main protease. Microb. Pathog. 148, 104365.

Martin, C.J., 2007. Optimisation in general radiography. Biomed. Imaging Interv. J. 3 (2), e18.

Mei, X., Lee, H.C., Diao, K.Y., Huang, M., Lin, B., Liu, C., Xie, Z., Ma, Y., Robson, P.M., Chung, M., et al., 2020. Artificial intelligence-enabled rapid diagnosis of patients with COVID-19. Nat. Med. 26 (8), 1224–1228.

Mejova, Y., Kalimeri, K., 2020. Advertisers jump on coronavirus bandwagon: politics, news, and business. arXiv preprint arXiv:2003.00923.

Metsky, H.C., Freije, C.A., Kosoko-Thoroddsen, T.-S.F., Sabeti, P.C., Myhrvold, C., 2020. CRISPR-based surveillance for COVID-19 using genomically-comprehensive machine learning design. BioRxiv.

Milite, C., Amendola, G., Nocentini, A., Bua, S., Cipriano, A., Barresi, E., Feoli, A., Novellino, E., Da Settimo, F., Supuran, C.T., et al., 2019. Novel 2-substituted-benzimidazole-6-sulfonamides as carbonic anhydrase inhibitors: synthesis, biological evaluation against isoforms I, II, IX and XII and molecular docking studies. J. Enzyme Inhib. Med. Chem. 34 (1), 1697–1710.

MindFields, 2020. Artificial intelligence in healthcare. Accessed 23 June 2020 https://www.mindfieldsglobal.com/ai-in-healthcare-report.

Morse, S.S., 2001. Factors in the emergence of infectious diseases. In: Plagues and Politics, Springer, pp. 8–26.

Muurlink, O.T., Stephenson, P., Islam, M.Z., Taylor-Robinson, A.W., 2018. Long-term predictors of dengue outbreaks in Bangladesh: a data mining approach. Infect. Dis. Model. 3, 322–330.

Naudé, W., 2020. Artificial intelligence against COVID-19: an early review. IZA Discussion Paper.

Nemati, E., Rahman, M.M., Nathan, V., Vatanparvar, K., Kuang, J., 2019. A comprehensive approach for cough type detection. In: 2019 IEEE/ACM International Conference on Connected Health: Applications, Systems and Engineering Technologies (CHASE), pp. 15–16.

Ng, M.-Y., Lee, E.Y.P., Yang, J., Yang, F., Li, X., Wang, H., Lui, M.M.-S., Lo, C.S.-Y., Leung, B., Khong, P.-L., et al., 2020. Imaging profile of the COVID-19 infection: radiologic findings and literature review. Radiology 2 (1), e200034.

Nguyen, D., Gao, K., Chen, J., Wang, R., Wei, G., 2020. Potentially highly potent drugs for 2019-nCoV. bioRxiv.

Oh, Y., Park, S., Ye, J.C., 2020. Deep learning COVID-19 features on CXR using limited training data sets. IEEE Trans. Med. Imaging 39 (8), 2688–2700. https://doi.org/10.1109/TMI.2020.2993291.

Ong, E., Wang, H., Wong, M.U., Seetharaman, M., Valdez, N., He, Y., 2020. Vaxign-ML: supervised machine learning reverse vaccinology model for improved prediction of bacterial protective antigens. Bioinformatics 36 (10), 3185–3191.

Orbann, C., Sattenspiel, L., Miller, E., Dimka, J., 2017. Defining epidemics in computer simulation models: how do definitions influence conclusions? Epidemics 19, 24–32.

Ozturk, T., Talo, M., Yildirim, E.A., Baloglu, U.B., Yildirim, O., Acharya, U.R., 2020. Automated detection of COVID-19 cases using deep neural networks with X-ray images. Comput. Biol. Med. 121, 103792.

Pan, J.R., Huang, Z.Q., Chen, K., 2012. Evaluation of the effect of varicella outbreak control measures through a discrete time delay SEIR model. Chinese J. Prev. Med. 46 (4), 343–347.

Panayides, A.S., Amini, A., Filipovic, N.D., Sharma, A., Tsaftaris, S.A., Young, A., Foran, D.J., Do, N., Golemati, S., Kurc, T., et al., 2020. AI and medical imaging informatics: current challenges and future directions. IEEE J. Biomed. Health Inf. 24 (7), 1837–1857.

Panch, T., Mattie, H., Celi, L.A., 2019. The "inconvenient truth" about AI in healthcare. NPJ Digit. Med. 2 (1), 1–3.

Pandey, R., Gautam, V., Pal, R., Bandhey, H., Dhingra, L.S., Misra, V., et al., 2022. A machine learning application for raising wash awareness in the times of covid-19 pandemic. Sci. Rep. 12 (1), 1–10.

Patel, B.N., Rosenberg, L., Willcox, G., Baltaxe, D., Lyons, M., Irvin, J., Rajpurkar, P., Amrhein, T., Gupta, R., Halabi, S., et al., 2019. Human-machine partnership with artificial intelligence for chest radiograph diagnosis. NPJ Digit. Med. 2 (1), 1–10.

Pizzorno, A., Padey, B., Terrier, O., Rosa-Calatrava, M., 2019. Drug repurposing approaches for the treatment of influenza viral infection: reviving old drugs to fight against a long-lived enemy. Front. Immunol. 10, 531.
Postnikov, E.B., 2020. Estimation of COVID-19 dynamics "on a back-of-envelope": does the simplest SIR model provide quantitative parameters and predictions? Chaos Solit. Fractals 135, 109841.
Pourghasemi, H.R., Pouyan, S., Heidari, B., Farajzadeh, Z., Shamsi, S.R.F., Babaei, S., Khosravi, R., Etemadi, M., Ghanbarian, G., Farhadi, A., Safaeian, R., Heidari, Z., Tarazkar, M.H., Tiefenbacher, J.P., Azmi, A., Sadeghian, F., 2020. Spatial modelling, risk mapping, change detection, and outbreak trend analysis of coronavirus (COVID-19) in Iran (days between 19 February to 14 June 2020). Int. J. Infect. Dis. 98, 90–108.
Randhawa, G.S., Soltysiak, M.P.M., El Roz, H., de Souza, C.P.E., Hill, K.A., Kari, L., 2020. Machine learning using intrinsic genomic signatures for rapid classification of novel pathogens: COVID-19 case study. PLoS One 15 (4), e0232391.
Remuzzi, A., Remuzzi, G., 2020. COVID-19 and Italy: what next? Lancet 395 (10231), 1225–1228.
Ribeiro, M.H.D.M., da Silva, R.G., Mariani, V.C., dos Santos Coelho, L., 2020. Short-term forecasting COVID-19 cumulative confirmed cases: perspectives for Brazil. Chaos Solit. Fractals 135, 109853.
Rypdal, M., Sugihara, G., 2019. Inter-outbreak stability reflects the size of the susceptible pool and forecasts magnitudes of seasonal epidemics. Nat. Commun. 10 (1), 1–8.
Saito, T., Rehmsmeier, M., 2015. The precision-recall plot is more informative than the ROC plot when evaluating binary classifiers on imbalanced datasets. PLoS One 10 (3), e0118432.
Scarpino, S.V., Petri, G., 2019. On the predictability of infectious disease outbreaks. Nat. Commun. 10 (1), 1–8.
Shao, P., Shan, Y., 2020. Beware of asymptomatic transmission: study on 2019-nCoV prevention and control measures based on extended SEIR model. BioRxiv. https://doi.org/10.1101/2020.01.28.923169.
Singh, V., Chang, Y.-J., Ma, K., Wels, M., Soza, G., Chen, T., 2014. Estimating a patient surface model for optimizing the medical scanning workflow. In: International Conference on Medical Image Computing and Computer-Assisted Intervention, pp. 472–479.
Singh, V., Ma, K., Tamersoy, B., Chang, Y.-J., Wimmer, A., O'Donnell, T., Chen, T., 2017. Darwin: deformable patient avatar representation with deep image network. In: International Conference on Medical Image Computing and Computer-Assisted Intervention, pp. 497–504.
Singh, R., Singh, R., Bhatia, A., 2018. Sentiment analysis using machine learning technique to predict outbreaks and epidemics. Int. J. Adv. Sci. Res. 3 (2), 19–24.
Singh, L., Bansal, S., Bode, L., Budak, C., Chi, G., Kawintiranon, K., Padden, C., Vanarsdall, R., Vraga, E., Wang, Y., 2020. A first look at COVID-19 information and misinformation sharing on Twitter. arXiv preprint arXiv:2003.13907.
Skalic, M., Jiménez, J., Sabbadin, D., De Fabritiis, G., 2019. Shape-based generative modeling for de novo drug design. J. Chem. Inf. Model. 59 (3), 1205–1214.
Spaan, W., Cavanagh, D., Horzinek, M.C., 1988. Coronaviruses: structure and genome expression. J. Gen. Virol. 69 (12), 2939–2952.
Spreeuwenberg, P., Kroneman, M., Paget, J., 2018. Reassessing the global mortality burden of the 1918 influenza pandemic. Am. J. Epidemiol. 187 (12), 2561–2567.
Swapnarekha, H., 2020. Role of intelligent computing in COVID-19 prognosis: a state-of-the-art review. Chaos Solit. Fractals 138, 109947.
Swapnarekha, H., Behera, H.S., Nayak, J., Naik, B., 2020. Role of intelligent computing in COVID-19 prognosis: a state-of-the-art review. Chaos Solit. Fractals 138, 109947.

Szegedy, C., Ioffe, S., Vanhoucke, V., Alemi, A.A., 2017. Inception-v4, inception-resnet and the impact of residual connections on learning. In: Thirty-First AAAI Conference on Artificial Intelligence.

Szegedy, C., Liu, W., Jia, Y., Sermanet, P., Reed, S., Anguelov, D., Erhan, D., Vanhoucke, V., Rabinovich, A., 2015. Going deeper with convolutions. In: Proceedings of the IEEE Conference on Computer Vision and Pattern Recognition, pp. 1–9.

Tabik, S., Gómez-Ríos, A., Martín-Rodríguez, J.L., Sevillano-García, I., Rey-Area, M., Charte, D., Guirado, E., Suárez, J.L., Luengo, J., Valero-González, M.A., et al., 2020. COVIDGR dataset and COVID-SDNet methodology for predicting COVID-19 based on Chest X-Ray images. IEEE J. Biomed. Health Inform. 24 (12), 3595–3605. https://doi.org/10.1109/JBHI.2020.3037127.

Tang, B., He, F., Liu, D., Fang, M., Wu, Z., Xu, D., 2020. AI-aided design of novel targeted covalent inhibitors against SARS-CoV-2. bioRxiv.

Tapak, L., Hamidi, O., Fathian, M., Karami, M., 2019. Comparative evaluation of time series models for predicting influenza outbreaks: application of influenza-like illness data from sentinel sites of healthcare centers in Iran. BMC Res. Notes 12 (1), 353.

Tiwari, S.M., Gaurav, D., Abraham, A., 2020. COVID-19 outbreak in India: an early stage analysis. Int. J. Sci. Rep. 6 (8), 332–339.

Toğaçar, M., Ergen, B., Cömert, Z., 2020. COVID-19 detection using deep learning models to exploit Social Mimic Optimization and structured chest X-ray images using fuzzy color and stacking approaches. Comput. Biol. Med. 121, 103805.

Tomar, A., Gupta, N., 2020. Prediction for the spread of COVID-19 in India and effectiveness of preventive measures. Sci. Total Environ. 728, 138762.

Tuli, S., Tuli, S., Tuli, R., Gill, S.S., 2020. Predicting the growth and trend of COVID-19 pandemic using machine learning and cloud computing. Internet Things 11, 100222.

Ucar, F., Korkmaz, D., 2020. COVIDiagnosis-Net: deep Bayes-SqueezeNet based diagnostic of the coronavirus disease 2019 (COVID-19) from X-ray images. Med. Hypotheses 140, 109761.

van der Maaten, L., Hinton, G., 2008. Visualizing data using t-SNE. J. Mach. Learn. Res. 9 (Nov), 2579–2605.

Velavan, T.P., Meyer, C.G., 2020. The COVID-19 epidemic. Trop. Med. Int. Health 25 (3), 278.

Wang, L., Lin, Z.Q., Wong, A., 2020. Covid-net: a tailored deep convolutional neural network design for detection of covid-19 cases from chest x-ray images. Sci. Rep. 10 (1), 1–12.

Wiljer, D., Hakim, Z., 2019. Developing an artificial intelligence-enabled health care practice: rewiring health care professions for better care. J. Med. Imaging Radiat. Sci. 50 (4), S8–S14.

Wrapp, D., Wang, N., Corbett, K.S., Goldsmith, J.A., Hsieh, C.-L., Abiona, O., Graham, B. S., McLellan, J.S., 2020. Cryo-EM structure of the 2019-nCoV spike in the prefusion conformation. Science 367 (6483), 1260–1263.

Wu, J.T., Leung, K., Leung, G.M., 2020. Nowcasting and forecasting the potential domestic and international spread of the 2019-nCoV outbreak originating in Wuhan, China: a modelling study. Lancet 395 (10225), 689–697.

Yan, L., Zhang, H.-T., Goncalves, J., Xiao, Y., Wang, M., Guo, Y., Sun, C., Tang, X., Jin, L., Zhang, M., et al., 2020a. A machine learning-based model for survival prediction in patients with severe COVID-19 infection. medRxiv.

Yan, L., Zhang, H.-T., Xiao, Y., Wang, M., Sun, C., Liang, J., Li, S., Zhang, M., Guo, Y., Xiao, Y., et al., 2020b. Prediction of criticality in patients with severe Covid-19 infection using three clinical features: a machine learning-based prognostic model with clinical data in Wuhan. MedRxiv, 27.

Yue, H., Yu, Q., Liu, C., Huang, Y., Jiang, Z., Shao, C., et al., 2020. Machine learning-based CT radiomics method for predicting hospital stay in patients with pneumonia associated with SARS-CoV-2 infection: a multicenter study. Ann. Transl. Med. 8 (14), 859.
Zarocostas, J., 2020. How to fight an infodemic. Lancet 395 (10225), 676.
Zha, W.-T., Pang, F.-R., Zhou, N., Wu, B., Liu, Y., Du, Y.-B., Hong, X.-Q., Lv, Y., 2020. Research about the optimal strategies for prevention and control of varicella outbreak in a school in a central city of China: based on an SEIR dynamic model. Epidemiol. Infect. 148, e56.
Zhan, Z., Dong, W., Lu, Y., Yang, P., Wang, Q., Jia, P., 2019. Real-time forecasting of hand-foot-and-mouth disease outbreaks using the integrating compartment model and assimilation filtering. Sci. Rep. 9 (1), 1–9.
Zhang, S., Diao, M., Yu, W., Pei, L., Lin, Z., Chen, D., 2020. Estimation of the reproductive number of novel coronavirus (COVID-19) and the probable outbreak size on the Diamond Princess cruise ship: a data-driven analysis. Int. J. Infect. Dis. 93, 201–204.
Zhavoronkov, A., Zagribelnyy, B., Zhebrak, A., Aladinskiy, V., Terentiev, V., Vanhaelen, Q., Bezrukov, D.S., Polykovskiy, D., Shayakhmetov, R., Filimonov, A., et al., 2020. Potential non-covalent SARS-CoV-2 3C-like protease inhibitors designed using generative deep learning approaches and reviewed by human medicinal chemist in virtual reality., https://doi.org/10.26434/chemrxiv.11829102.v1.
Zhou, Z., Siddiquee, M.M.R., Tajbakhsh, N., Liang, J., 2018. UNet++: a nested U-Net architecture for medical image segmentation. In: Deep Learning in Medical Image Analysis and Multimodal Learning for Clinical Decision Support, Springer, pp. 3–11.
Zhou, Y., Hou, Y., Shen, J., Huang, Y., Martin, W., Cheng, F., 2020. Network-based drug repurposing for novel coronavirus 2019-nCoV/SARS-CoV-2. Cell Discov. 6 (1), 1–18.
Zhu, H., Guo, Q., Li, M., Wang, C., Fang, Z., Wang, P., Tan, J., Wu, S., Xiao, Y., 2020. Host and infectivity prediction of Wuhan 2019 novel coronavirus using deep learning algorithm. BioRxiv.

CHAPTER ELEVEN

Machine learning modeling techniques and statistical projections to predict the outbreak of COVID-19 with implication to India

W. Regis Anne[a] **and S. Carolin Jeeva**[b]
[a]PSG College of Technology, Coimbatore, India
[b]Karunya Institute of Technology and Sciences, Coimbatore, India

1 Introduction

The global pandemic, COVID-19, is a human development crisis and the number of deaths due to this virus is increasing rapidly. According to the World Health Organization (2021), due to the spread of COVID-19, countries around the world have implemented many nonpharmaceutical interventions to control the virus. The study by Human Development Group infers that due to the pandemic, the countries have announced lockdown, school closures, and movement restrictions. The World Health Organization during March 2020 announced COVID-19 as a pandemic and it has affected different parts of the globe. This virus easily affects the persons who have less immunity and other health disorders. The people who are affected with this virus suffer from severe cough, cold, fever, tastelessness, and odorlessness. Although this virus originated in Wuhan, China, it has affected the whole world. According to the survey by Worldometer (2021), the coronavirus cases throughout the globe are found to be 222,839,277 and the death rate about 4,601,398 as on September 2021. Also in India, the cases have been steadily rising since March 8, 2020. India has reached 33,096,718 cases and stands in second place out of 223 countries. In order to diminish the spread, lockdown was announced after March 24, 2020 throughout India. Due to the pandemic, the economic growth of countries has dropped due to loss of jobs and nonfunctioning of many industries.

Lessons from COVID-19
https://doi.org/10.1016/B978-0-323-99878-9.00011-X

Regression techniques by data modeling are the techniques to solve prediction problems in machine learning. Regression analysis in supervised learning is used for prediction of time series data. This predictive modeling approach explores the relation among the target and independent variable in a dataset and best fit the input and the target variable. The regression approach determines the predictor strength and forecasts the trend of the time series analysis. In this chapter, machine learning regression models such as Lasso, Linear Regression, Ridge, Elastic-Net, Random Forest Regressor, AdaBoost Regressor, LGBM Regressor, and XGBoost Regressor are considered in this study to predict the exponential increase of the mortality rate, number of confirmed cases, and recovery rate. Also the Facebook Prophet Model was used to predict the outbreak and compared with machine learning regression models. For building the models, the real-time dataset was extracted from Johns Hopkins University which includes the number of confirmed cases, death, and recovered daily cases of COVID-19. The models are trained, tested, and compared for their performances based on the parameters *R*-squared value, *R*-squared modified score, Mean Squared deviation, and Root Mean Square Error. The results are tabulated to observe the best model for pandemic outbreak prediction. Based on the results of predictions from these models, the concerned officials take necessary steps to control the outbreak of COVID-19 pandemic.

2 Literature survey

Francesca et al. (2021) conducted a study on patients hospitalized due to COVID-19 based on geographical area of origin was presented and the results found that there was no difference in the death rate of COVID-19 patients between Europeans and non-European countries. However, the ICU admission rate of patients was found to be high in non-European countries compared to European countries. Williamson et al. (2020) developed a health analytics platform OpenSAFELY that determines the factors resulting in increased mortality rate due to COVID-19 in England. It was found that the death rate of male is higher than females, increase in age, and patients with diabetes, severe asthma, and other medical problems also contribute to the death rate. The study by Balaji et al. (2020) presents the impact of COVID-19 in India. The features considered are gender, age, travel history, and nationality of patients based on the statistical significance. It was found that the age of the person has an association with COVID-19 in India. Yadav et al. (2020) in their study proposed machine learning regression algorithms by using the tasks namely prediction of COVID-19 based on a particular region, different types of mitigation, the end stage of pandemic, spread rate of COVID-19, and correlation between the virus and the climatic condition. Dharun et al. (2021) in their work proposed machine learning approach to find the relationship between health care, lockdown policies, and the signs of early containment of COVID-19. Vatsal et al. (2020) proposed Prophet model for decision-making based on time series data. The study was carried out to analyze the cases before and after lock down. Yuri et al. (2020) in their study present the measures taken by countries to face the pandemic situation. The study reports when implementing voluntary, enforceable steps, the COVID cases are reduced. Shaikh et al. (2021) considered machine learning–based model to determine the optimal regression model considering linear and polynomial regression based on India COVID-19 data set. The time series forecasting is used to forecast the COVID-19 cases that occur in future. Nazrul et al. (2021) in their study present the direct and indirect causes for COVID-19. Mohammad et al. (2021) study reports during the COVID-19 how the lockdown has changed health care. The COVID patients are affected with chronic obstructive pulmonary disease. Punn et al. (2020) in their study used various approach in order to develop a mathematical model by learning the daily analysis of COVID-19 cases and thereby predicting the future. Anne and Jeeva (2020) in their study use ARIMA model and Ramanathan and Dhanwant (2020) presented susceptible Infected Recovered model for time series analysis. Kınacı et al. (2021) use a time series analysis and efficiency measurement approach to analyze the pandemic situation due to COVID-19. Namasudra et al. (2021) presented neural network approach in predicting COVID-19 cases and thereby help the health consultants to carry out proper measures to control the COVID-19 outbreak.

3 Predicting and analyzing COVID-19 outbreak

The COVID-19 dataset by Philips (2020) has become essential in order to take necessary action to curb the infection. COVID-19 has caused havoc in the lives of people all over the world.

The second wave has caused more damage in certain countries irrespective of the strict social distancing, hand washing, lockdowns, and vaccination. The time frame for this study is from April 2020 to August 2021. The number of reported confirmed cases for few top affected countries is represented in Fig. 1. From Fig. 1 we understand that in the United

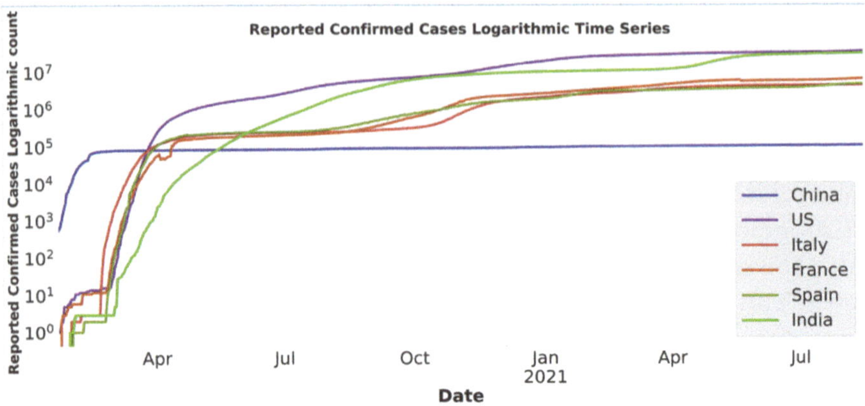

Fig. 1 Number of reported cases in top affected countries.

States and India, the number of reporting cases is increasing next only to Spain, France, and Italy.

The number of reported, confirmed, recovered, and deaths in India is displayed in Fig. 2. It depicts that in a particular time period, the number of confirmed cases has crossed many lakhs and this calls for the immediate need for analysis and controlling measures in India. The average growth factor, in the case of India, is 1.04252508 that is calculated by the ratio of the sum of growth difference and the length of growth difference. Since the value is above 1, it infers that the new cases are steadily rising. This reflects the collapse of the public health care system in India.

In this chapter, the outbreak is predicted by (1) Machine learning regression models and (2) Facebook Prophet Model. The machine learning regression models were selected for prediction because the models can predict accurately for large dataset and also can learn automatically and predict without any interventions from human side. The COVID-19 dataset generates large amount of time series data on daily basis leading to accurate predictions by these models. Also, the models are able to learn and modify the errors for an optimum cost function. Though the machine learning models predict accurately, the effect of lockdown on the infection rate is explored using Prophet model. The Prophet model works well with daily data and has options for seasonality and lockdown (holidays) that can be explored.

The overall architecture of the model is given in Fig. 3. The COVID-19 dataset was acquired, cleaned, and explored. The dataset was split into the training and the testing dataset. The independent feature Y is predicted from the dependent features x_1, $x_2 \ldots x_n$ using function $f(x)$. Then the logistic

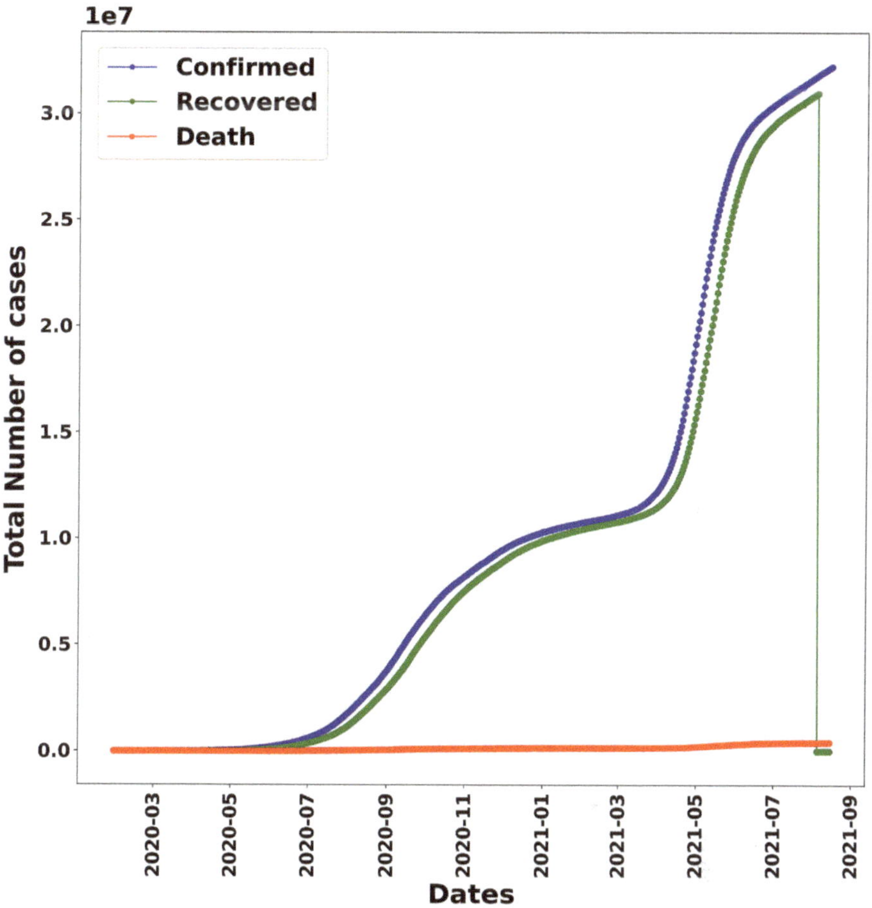

Fig. 2 Number of reported confirmed, recovered, and death in India.

models are built and trained according to their learning methodology. The logistic models are trained to minimize the bias and variance. Since the bias and variance trade-off is met, high bias and high variance will not affect the performance of the algorithm. After training, the logistic models are evaluated on the test data and various performance metrics are measured. The best logistic models are considered based on the performance metrics to predict the outbreak. Also, the Prophet model was trained with the COVID-19 dataset. The model was trained and cross-validated to tune the hyper parameters. The evaluation metrics are compared with the previously obtained output parameters from the best logistic models. The best optimized model for prediction is selected based on the evaluation metrics.

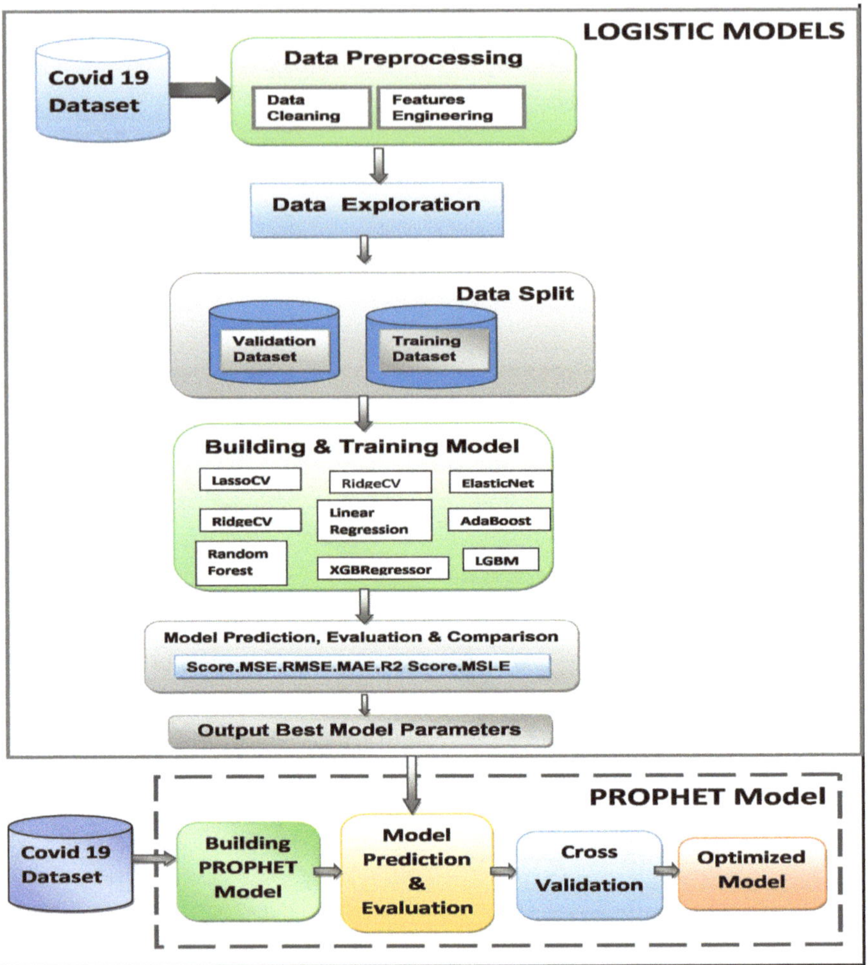

Fig. 3 Architecture of the machine learning and Prophet model.

3.1 Machine learning regression models to predict the outbreak of COVID-19

In this chapter, we are considering the dataset from John Hopkins University which is updated every day at 6 am UTC that contain the cases of COVID-19 (Coronavirus Research Center, 2020). First, decomposition is performed on the dataset to find out the trend and seasonal components in order to predict the time series data with greater accuracy. The time series data show seasonal variation, so additive decomposition is performed which classifies the data of confirmed cases into four components of observed, trend, seasonal, and residual. The data clearly show a trend in the data with no seasonal components and the residuals show variation with high variability toward the end.

Machine learning regression models are used to predict the continuous independent variable based on one or more dependent variables. Various machine learning regression models such as Lasso, Linear Regression, Ridge, Elastic-Net, Random Forest, AdaBoost Regressor, LGBM Regressor, and XGBoost Regressor are used to predict the confirmed, death rate, and recovery rate from the COVID-19 dataset.

3.1.1 Linear regression model

The main advantage of linear regression is to find the linear regression between the variables. The linear regression is given in Eq. (1).

$$Y = a + bX \tag{1}$$

where X is the independent variable, Y the dependent variable, b represents the slope of the line, and a is a constant.

3.1.2 Least absolute shrinkage and selection operator model

Lasso is a regression algorithm that is used when two or more parameters are highly correlated. Regularization is the concept used to avoid overfitting. The Lasso algorithm uses a shrinkage technique where the coefficients of determination are shrunk to zero. The main advantages of using Lasso regression is it reduces overfitting, works well on different data sets, selects the features, and regularizes the model. When the data set is large with high correlation, then this algorithm is used. In Lasso, the tuning parameter that controls the amount of shrinkage is determined by cross-validation. The cross-validation represents the number of folds considered; in our work, the cross-validation is set to threefolds to fivefolds. The mathematical form of Lasso regression is given in Eq. (2).

$$\sum_{i=1}^{N}\left(y_i - \sum_{j=1}^{p} x_{ij}\beta_j\right)^2 + \lambda \sum_{j=1}^{p} |\beta_j| \tag{2}$$

where λ represents the quantity of shrinkage. The value $\lambda = 0$ considers all parameters, $\lambda = \infty$ eliminates the features, bias increases when there is an increase in λ and variance increases when there is a decrease in λ. β_j is the true parameter that has to be estimated from the sample.

3.1.3 Ridge model

Ridge Regression is a regression model and is used when multicollinearity is found in the dataset. In this regression model, L2 regularization method is used which has the outcome of shrinking the coefficients for the input parameters which does not contribute much in the predicting process. The feature weights are updated as the loss function contains another additional squared term. Ridge Regression avoids overfitting. The mathematical form of Ridge is given in Eq. (3).

$$\sum_{i=1}^{N}\left(y_i - \sum_{j=1}^{p} x_{ij}\beta_j\right)^2 + \lambda \sum_{j=1}^{p} w_j\beta_j^2) \tag{3}$$

where w_j is the weights used, and ordinary Least Squares is achieved when lambda is zero.

3.1.4 Elastic-Net model

Elastic-Net overcomes the limitations of both Lasso and Ridge Regression. This algorithm is the mixture of Lasso and Ridge Regression which comprises of L1 and L2 penalties. In this algorithm, variable selection and regularization are done simultaneously and are used when the dimensional data are greater than the samples. The Elastic-Net is given in Eq. (4).

$$\frac{\sum_{i=1}^{n}\left(y_i - x_i^J\beta\right)^2}{2n} + \lambda\left(\frac{1-\alpha}{2}\sum_{j=1}^{m}\beta_j^2 + \alpha\sum_{j=1}^{m}\left|\beta_j\right|\right) \tag{4}$$

where $\alpha=0$ corresponds to the ridge and $\alpha=1$ to the Lasso.

3.1.5 Random Forest model

Random Forest is a metaestimator that creates multiple decision trees on different samples of the dataset. The Gini index or Entropy is used to branch on a node to create the tree. This is done by calculation of impurity on classification due to randomness of selection of samples. The Gini index is used to conclude how the nodes are added to the branch of the decision tree and is given in Eq. (5). Then finally voting is done to combine all the trees to do final prediction by improving accuracy and to prevent overfitting.

$$\text{Gini} = 1 - \sum_{i=1}^{C}(P_i)^2 \tag{5}$$

where P_i denotes the relative frequency of the class and C denotes the total number of classes. The entropy is given in Eq. (6).

$$\text{Entropy} = \sum_{i=1}^{C} - P_i * \log_2(p_i) \tag{6}$$

where P_i denotes the relative frequency of the class and C denotes the total number of classes.

3.1.6 Adaptive Boosting model

The AdaBoost Regressor is an adaptive regressor where the data are fit and then the weights are adjusted to minimize the error. Many weak classifiers are generated and are ensembled to form a strong classifier. This model is able to capture the nonlinearity in the real world. First, the data are made to learn with the set weight value and weak classifiers are built. Then the weights are modified to build a strong classifier. The learning rate and the number of weak learners can be controlled to define the model accuracy. The model can be cross-validated to optimize the correctness and accuracy. The growth function $H(x)$ that bounds the generalization error is given in Eq. (7).

$$H(x) = \text{sign}\left(\sum_{t=1}^{T} \propto_t h_t(x)\right) \tag{7}$$

where x is equal to sign of the weighted sum of the outputs $h_t(x)$ of T weak classifiers with the weights equal to $(\propto_t)$.

3.1.7 Light Gradient Boosted Machine model

The Light Gradient Boosted Machine (LGBM) Regressor selects the features automatically and boosts examples with larger gradients resulting in faster training and accurate predictions. In the architecture of LGBM Regressor, the tree grows leaf wise and chooses the leaf whose delta loss is maximum. The modeling rate controls the growth of selecting the gradients according to the learning graph. The learning rate is 0.15. The accuracy can be augmented by increasing the number of leaves and building deeper trees. The only disadvantage of this method is it leads to overfitting.

3.1.8 Extreme Gradient Boosting model

The algorithm eXtreme Gradient Boosting (XGBoost) is derived from Gradient boosting model. The gradient of the loss function is computed using the Eq. (8).

$$r_{im} = -\alpha \left[\frac{\delta L(y_i, F(x_i))}{\delta F(x_i)} \right]_{F(x)=F_{m-1}(x)} \tag{8}$$

where r_{im} is the pseudo residuals, L is the loss function, m is the iteration number, α denotes the learning rate, and $F(x)$ gives the predictions from the model.

The machine learning algorithms are validated using the COVID-19 dataset and are used for predicting the outbreak. Fig. 4 gives the predicted and observed data for various machine learning algorithms on the COVID-19 dataset. The performance metrics for these algorithms are given in Table 1. The Regression accuracy metrics determine the prediction error rates and the performance of the model.

3.2 Performance metrics

The performance metrics used are Mean Squared Error, Mean Absolute Error, Root Mean Squared Error, Root Mean Squared Log Error, Max Error, and R-squared to validate the model.

The Mean Squared Error (MSE) compares the original and the predicted values and obtains the squared variance over the dataset. This metric is given in Eq. (9).

$$\text{MSE} = \frac{1}{N} \sum_{i=1}^{N} (y_i - \widehat{y})^2 \tag{9}$$

where y_i is the observed value of the ith attribute, $\widehat{y}$ is the predicted value of the ith observation, and N denotes the number of samples in the dataset.

The Mean Absolute Error (MAE) is determined by considering the comparison between the original and the predicted values and is obtained by the averaged absolute difference over the dataset. The metrics is given in Eq. (10).

$$\text{MAE} = \frac{1}{N} \sum_{i=1}^{N} |y_i - \widehat{y}| \tag{10}$$

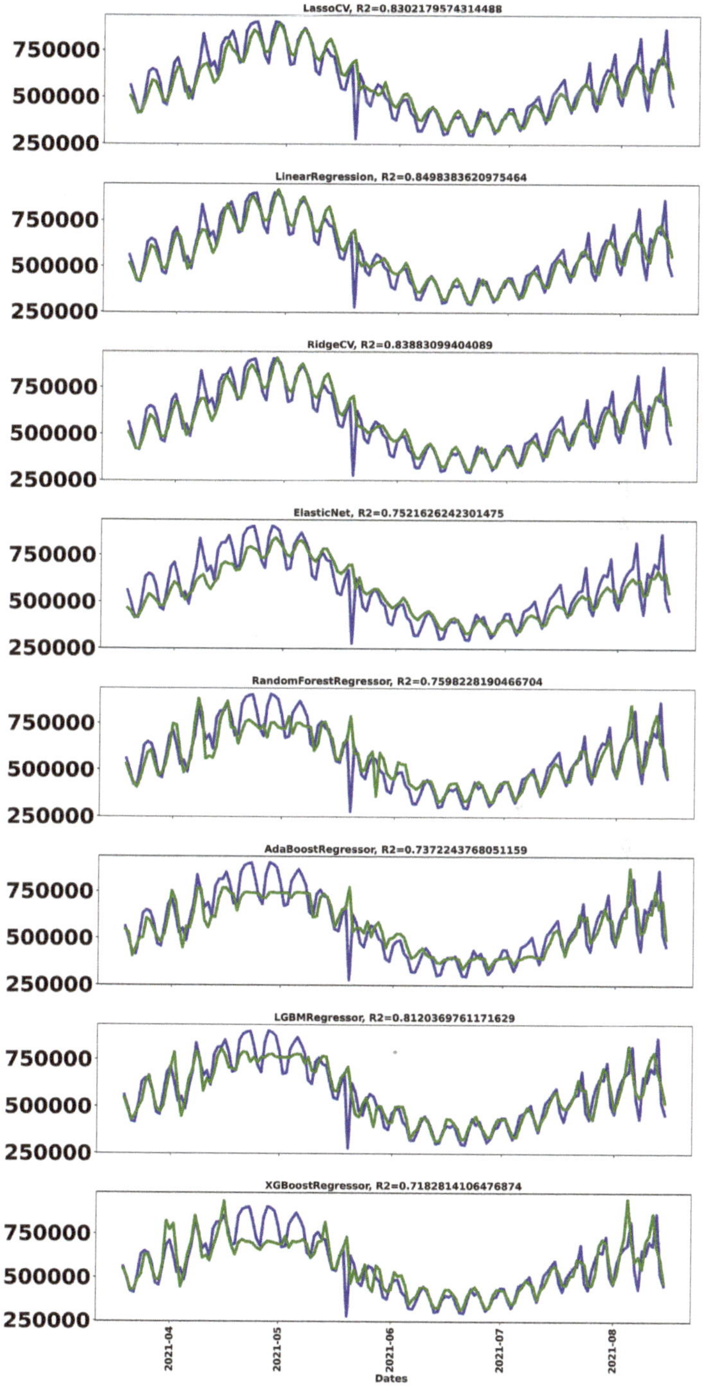

Fig. 4 Predicted vs observed Graph.

Table 1 Parameters of the different machine learning regression models.

Model/metrics	Score	MSE	MAE	RMSE	MSLE	Max error	R^2 error
Lasso Model	0.9424	67,824	47,874	67,824	0.01725	419,619	0.830217
Linear Regression	0.9466	63,785	42,956	63,785	0.01521	419,016	0.849838
Ridge Model	0.9449	66,082	44,925	66,082	0.01683	425,594	0.83883
Elastic-Net	0.9294	81,945	61,696	81,945	0.02391	419,554	0.752162
Random Forest Regressor	0.9918	84,180	57,346	84,180	0.03077	541,365	0.738463
AdaBoost Regressor	0.9767	718,760,288	65,593	89,428	0.04089	472,286	0.704833
LGBM Regressor	0.9785	71,363	50,532	71,363	0.02726	432,701	0.812036
XGBoost Regressor	0.9969	87,367	59,759	87,367	0.01952	453,285	0.718281

where y_i is the observed value of the ith attribute, $\hat{y}$ is the predicted value of the ith observation, and N denotes the quantity of dataset.

The Root Mean Square Error (RMSE) is determined by the square root of MSE. The metrics is given in Eq. (11).

$$\text{RMSE} = \sqrt{\frac{1}{N}\sum_{i=1}^{N}(y_i - \hat{y})^2} \tag{11}$$

where y_i is the actual observation of the ith attribute, $\hat{y}$ is the estimated value of the ith observation, and N denotes the number of samples in the dataset.

The Mean Square Log Error (MSLE) is proportional measure of true and predicted values in logarithmic scale. The formula is given in Eq. (12).

$$\text{MSLE} = \frac{1}{N}\sum_{i=1}^{N}(\log(y_i + 1) - \log(\hat{y} + 1))^2 \tag{12}$$

where N denotes the number of observations in the dataset, y_i is the actual observation of the ith attribute, $\hat{y}$ is the estimated value, and log(x) is the natural logarithm of x($\log_e x$).

The Max Error denotes the maximum residual error that captures the worst case error between the predicted value and the true value.

R-Squared Error (R^2) denotes the coefficient of values that are fit when compared with the original value. The formula is given in Eq. (13).

$$R^2 = 1 - \frac{\sum(y_i - \hat{y})^2}{\sum(y_i - \bar{y})^2} \tag{13}$$

where y_i denotes the experimental value of the dependent variable and $\bar{y}$ denotes the mean value of y and $\hat{y}$ is the estimated time series.

Table 1 specifies the different parameters and it is inferred that the AdaBoost Regressor and LGBM Regressor perform second best to the other algorithms. XGBoost and Random Forest Regressor perform the best and surpass all the algorithms. Though the machine learning regression models provide high accuracy on prediction of high dimensional data, these methods can be compared with Prophet model for better performance.

4 Prophet model to predict confirmed cases of COVID-19 with implication to India

Facebook developed the Prophet model in the year 2017. The forecasting can be done for the future specified number of days. The Prophet model by Taylor et al. (2018) is constructed on the supervised regression technique given in Eq. (14).

$$y(t) = g(t) + h(t) + s(t) + e(t) \tag{14}$$

where $g(t)$ denotes the trend function which is used to model the non-periodic differences in time series values that is represented using Fourier series, $s(t)$ denotes the periodic changes the daily or weekly or monthly or quarterly or yearly COVID confirmed cases, $h(t)$ denotes the lockdown that affects the pandemic, and $e(t)$ the error term which is any unconditional changes in a particular situation. The logistic growth model with respect to the time series COVID-19 dataset is given in Eq. (15).

$$g(t) = \frac{C}{1 + e^{-k(t-m)}} \tag{15}$$

where C is the carrying capacity which represents the maximum number of people affected with the virus at time t, k is the rate of growth of the virus, and m is the offset parameter. The linear piece-wise growth model with respect to the time series COVID data is given in Eq. (16).

$$g(t) = \frac{c(t)}{1 + e^{\left(-\left(k+a(t)^{t}\delta\right)\left(t-\left(m+a(t)^{t}\gamma\right)\right)\right)}} \tag{16}$$

where δ, γ, $a(t)$ are rate adjustments and t is a series of history points. Internally, the model parameters use Stan (2018) to optimize the model using maximum a priori optimization. The parameters can also be computed using Nonlinear Least Squares Estimation method by using Scipy Curve fit optimization library of python. The COVID-19 dataset is given as input to the Prophet model and the values of the confirmed cases are calculated. The timestamp *ds* and the number of confirmed cases y that is to be predicted is the input data frame to the model. The dataset is used to fit to the model. Later, future data frame, a function of the Prophet model predicts the total confirmed cases for future referenced dates. The parameters β, δ, k, m, *trend*, Y and sigma_obs are displayed using the function model.params() from the fbprophet package. Now with these parameters, the forecasting is done. The model parameters are listed below,

Prophet Model Parameters:

{'beta': array([[-0.00021026, -0.00038018, -0.0001145, 0.00028692, 0.00022041, -0.00010876]]),
'delta': array([[3.19732253e-07, -2.37462250e-08, 4.51080641e-09, 7.04436707e-08, 6.38785132e-03, 1.29831752e-04, 2.67351316e-02, 1.92588740e-01, 3.81474053e-01, 4.02797917e-01, 1.18428021e-01, 2.71412175e-04, -6.21269821e-09, -5.56374804e-08, -8.55928785e-06, -3.05403869e-01, -3.40221280e-01, -1.72022445e-01, -7779656e-04, -1.40185075e-07, -3.31293438e-09, 2.01034969e-07, 1.07461156e+00, 1.65596694e+00, 2.17609675e-08]]),
'k': array([[0.04070934]]),
'm': array([[-0.00405455]]), 'sigma_obs': array([[0.03471788]]),
'trend': array ([[-4.05455451e-03, -3.98133627e-03,3.90811804e03, 1.11838091e+00,1.12392322e+00]])}

The Prophet model shows very good results for linear and nonlinear trends of data. The dataset after the exploratory data analysis is fed to the Prophet model and the configured Prophet object is fitted on to the data. Then the testing data can be given to the configured model to make predictions and it can be visualized and evaluated. The data for prediction are considered for the confirmation cases pertaining to India. The data for India are extracted from the dataset, and the data consist of time series of dates and its number of persons confirmed with COVID-19 for each date. Fig. 5 shows a steep increase in number of positive cases in India.

The Mean Average Percentage Error (MAPE) measures the forecast error by the average number of times the forecast was predicted incorrectly. The Median Average Percentage Error (MDAPE) is the distance between the predicted and actual values. The error diagnostics is presented in Table 2. The minimum error is reported on the sixth day so the future values can be predicted by looking into the past 6 days' data.

Fig. 6 shows the forecasted values with true cases and the confidence travel. Though the model has predicted accurately, its performance can still be increased by incorporating the other features like lockdown, social distancing, and vaccination.

4.1 Fine tuning lock down in India on Prophet model

The increasing trend of COVID-19 in India and the alarming death rates forced the government to initiate lockdown in various states of India. In this analysis, we have considered a standard lockdown of 21 days and the general

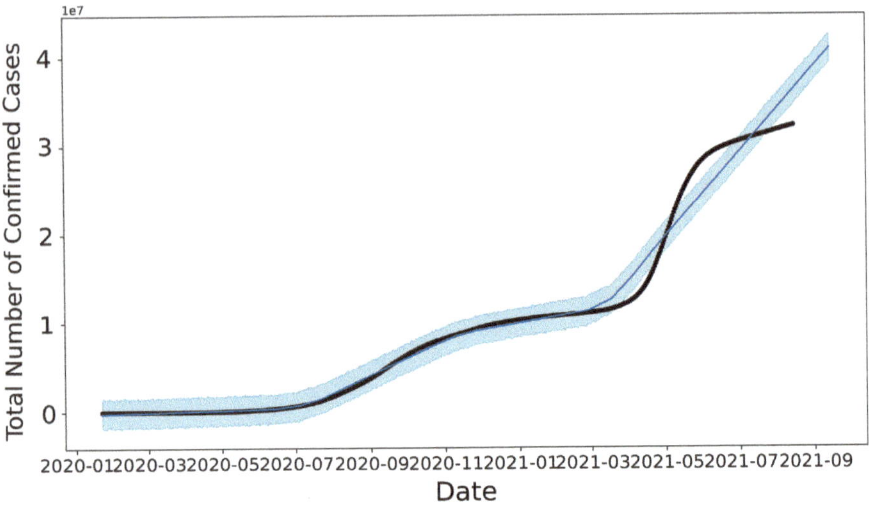

Fig. 5 Predictions by Prophet model.

Table 2 Performance metrics of the Prophet model without lockdown.

S. no	Horizon (days)	MSE	RMSE	MAE	MAPE	MDAPE
0	3	8.72E+12	2,953,283	1,605,713	0.11791	0.08859
1	4	9.54E+12	3,089,469	1,683,991	0.12526	0.09808
2	5	1.04E+13	3,224,369	1,762,106	0.13278	0.10551
3	6	1.13E+13	3,359,880	1,840,509	0.14032	0.1175
4	7	1.22E+13	3,490,687	1,917,196	0.14814	0.12911
5	8	1.32E+13	3,627,296	1,998,473	0.15665	0.13876
6	9	1.41E+13	3,753,757	2,075,367	0.16552	0.15286
7	10	1.50E+13	3,871,026	2,147,617	0.17382	0.1658
8	11	1.58E+13	3,968,933	2,208,384	0.18112	0.17724
9	12	1.65E+13	4,064,855	2,266,841	0.18792	0.18793
10	13	1.73E+13	4,158,632	2,323,585	0.19396	0.19803

holidays into account. The time period of lockdown considered was from April 1, 2021 to April 21, 2021. The effect of lockdown has certainly reduced the confirmed cases, and the predicted number of cases from the Prophet model accurately captures the lockdown. The number of new cases reached nearly 3 lakhs during the month of May, but the lockdown efforts reduced the cases to 1 lakh from the month of June. This reduction of cases from 3 lakhs to 1 lakh due to lockdown is very well reflected in the model. The Prophet model predicts accurately the decline of positive cases after lockdown as displayed in Fig. 7.

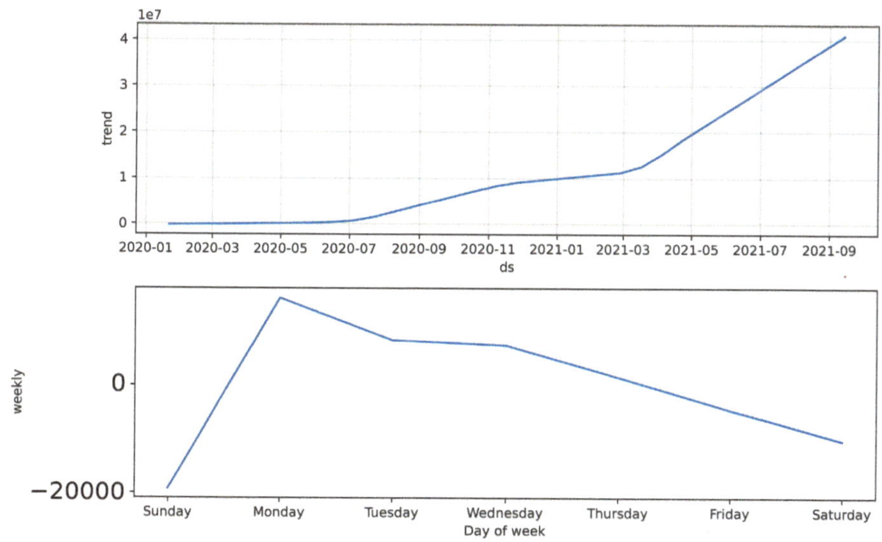

Fig. 6 Trend and weekly components of Prophet model.

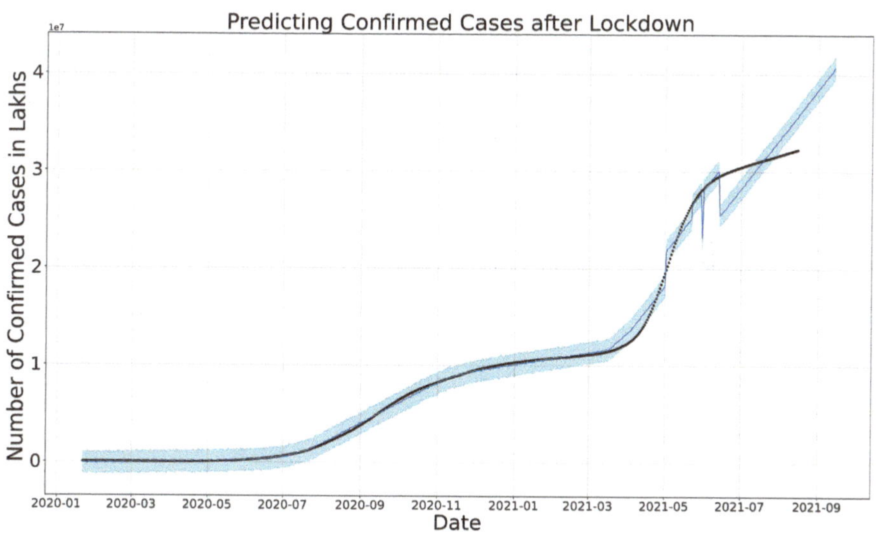

Fig. 7 Predictions after lockdown for India on the Prophet model.

The effects of holidays and the different components of weekly, seasonal, and monthly trends are depicted in Fig. 8. The model's performance can be validated by cross-validation provided by the Prophet model. The cross-validation divides the data into training and testing data and validates the model for the data.

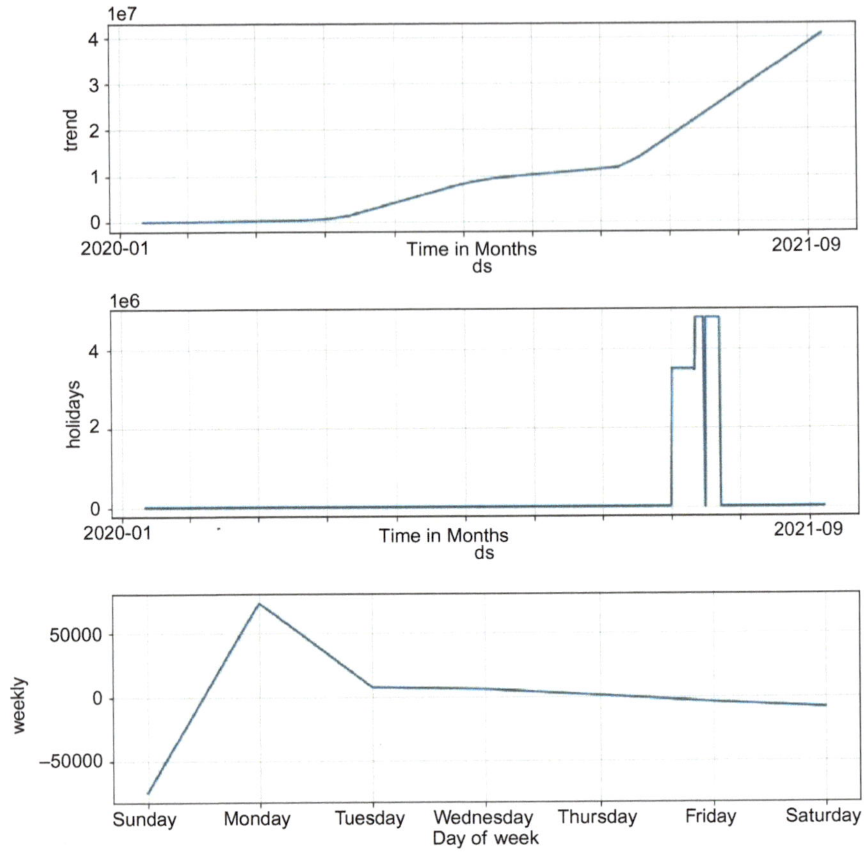

Fig. 8 Components of the Prophet model after lockdown.

The error diagnostics with induced lockdown is presented in Table 3. The average of MSE of the model is 1.63584e+13, RMSE is 3.54115e+06, MAE is 2.05495e+06, MAPE is 0.194318, and MDAPE is 0.175774. Though the model metrics are higher at the beginning, after the training of the model, the metrics shows considerable performance after tuning.

4.2 Training hyper parameters in the Prophet model

The hyper parameters are adjustable parameters in the fbprophet package that can be tuned for optimized models and thereby make accurate predictions. The tuneable parameters in this package are,

Table 3 Performance metrics of the Prophet model with induced lockdown.

S. no	Horizon (days)	MSE	RMSE	MAE	MAPE	MDAPE
0	3	6.27E+11	791,735	523,706	0.06732	0.063846
1	4	8.67E+11	931,006	606,786	0.07712	0.068728
2	5	1.14E+12	1,068,044	687,181	0.08583	0.075562
3	6	1.49E+12	1,220,729	773,787	0.094408	0.082972
4	7	1.89E+12	1,375,043	862,597	0.103471	0.090085
5	8	2.3E+12	1,517,478	948,903	0.113134	0.099895
6	9	2.67E+12	1,632,800	1,020,493	0.122923	0.106873
7	10	3.01E+12	1,736,261	1,085,523	0.13209	0.11212
8	11	3.37E+12	1,835,882	1,146,395	0.140436	0.115872
9	12	3.75E+12	1,937,323	1,206,764	0.148252	0.119255

changepoint_prior_scale: This effective parameter establishes the trend at various trend change points. The prior scale value is normalized so the most probable value is 0.1. The default of 0.05 works for many time series, but this could be tuned to the range of [0.001, 0.5].

seasonality_prior_scale: This parameter regulates the seasonal pattern of the rise and fall of confirmed cases. The possible values for tuning would probably be [0.01, 10].

holidays_prior_scale: This controls the flexibility to include lockdown effects. This default value can be set to 10. The probable values are tuned on a range of [0.01, 10].

seasonality_mode: Options are ['additive', 'multiplicative']. Default is "additive," but many business time series will have multiplicative seasonality.

These parameters are tuned using cross-validation to get the best parameter values. The Prophet model has a function cross_validation( ) to find out the best hyper parameter values for the tunable parameters. For this, a parameter grid of values is formed with the possible values. Then a new model is trained for all the possible combination of values and the best hyper parameter values are selected. These best values can be used to train the model for predictions. Table 4 gives the possible hyper parameter values.

The best fit values for the hyper parameters by cross-validation are: changepoint_prior_scale is 0.5, seasonality_prior_scale is 0.01, and holidays_prior_scale is 0.01. The RMSE error that resulted after the model was trained with the best fit parameters is 1.3186e+13. This proves that

Table 4 Hyper parameters for the Prophet model.

S. no	Hyper parameters	Values
1.	changepoint_prior_scale	0.001, 0.01, 0.1, 0.5
2.	seasonality_prior_scale	0.01, 0.1, 1.0,5.0, 10.0
3.	holidays_prior_scale	0.01, 0.1, 1.0, 5.0, 10.0

cross-validation of best fit parameters reduces the MSE by 18%. The code and dataset for this chapter is provided in Anne and Jeeva (2021a,b).

4.3 Execution time complexity of the machine learning models and the Prophet model

The model complexity of machine learning algorithms for prediction can depend on many criteria like the number of features considered, size of the training and testing data, parameters used for optimization, the depth the model achieves, the execution time of the algorithm based on the processing capabilities, the language used to implement the algorithm, and the operating software. The execution time complexities of the models used for prediction are given in Table 5. It is observed that Elastic-Net, LGBM Regressor, and Prophet Model need more execution time than other regressors because of the high prediction accuracy. Techniques like Dimensionality reduction, Principal Component Analysis, and Multiprocessing can be used to reduce the execution time.

Table 5 Execution time complexity of the prediction models.

S. no	Models	Execution time complexity (s)
1.	Lasso Regressor	0.060781
2.	Linear Regression	0.001045
3.	Ridge Regressor	0.00145
4.	Elastic-Net Regressor	0.163782
5.	Random Forest Regressor	0.073406
6.	AdaBoost Regressor	0.033182
7.	LGBM Regressor	0.183558
8.	XGBoost Regressor	0.011524
9.	Prophet Model	0.10627

5 Discussion and implications

COVID-19 is an evolving contagious infection that causes a significant mortality rates in many parts of the world. India stands in second position next to the United States. Initially in the absence of vaccines, public adherence to the control measures failed poorly in India which was a result of the attitude and practices of the people. The number of positive cases numbered to 33,096,718 and the number of deaths to 441,443. This exponential growth due to lack of control measures are predicted accurately by the machine learning regression models and Facebook Prophet Model. The Prophet model has given the predictions on weekly and monthly basis with high consistency. This alarming infection rate and mortality rate resulted in Government of India to intervene in imposing lockdown to control the spread. Other efforts include suspension of domestic and international flights, awareness campaigns, guidelines, and national curfew on the citizens. This impact caused the reduction of infection rate and mortality rate and is well captured by the Facebook Prophet Model. In India, as on September 8, 2021, 707,543,018 have been vaccinated and the number of new cases has reduced drastically. The effect of vaccination can also be included as input parameter and prediction model can be explored. These study findings can be used by policy makers and health care industry to predict in advance the infection ratio and to further take appropriate action for hospital preparedness and relief health care facilities. Tuning the hyper parameter for accurate prediction requires prior knowledge and skills but using Facebook provides easy to use tuneable parameters. In this chapter, the tuned parameters using cross-validation predict the infection rate and mortality rate more accurately and can be extended for other business scenarios. This pandemic has caused financial crisis, work loss, and psychological effects. By the predictions made, people can intuitively expect the nature and length of lockdowns and appropriately plan their work and activities. Implications of lessons learnt from the first wave and second wave can be applied for any other infectious diseases.

6 Conclusion

In this chapter, first, we have analyzed the COVID-19 dataset from the John Hopkins University and have analyzed the top countries affected by COVID-19 during the first and second waves. Second, we have used machine learning regression models to predict the outbreak. Out of all the models, Random Forest Regressor, AdaBoost Regressor, and LGBM perform better than the other regression algorithms. Third, the Facebook Prophet Model is used to predict the outbreak, and the performance is better than the regression models. Also, the effect of lockdown is simulated in the Prophet model and the model has correctly predicted the current data with minimum error. The growth of confirmed cases has been predicted as stable after lockdown as predicted accurately by the Prophet model.

References

Anne, W.R., Jeeva, S.C., 2020. ARIMA modelling of predicting COVID-19 infections. medRxiv, 1–4. https://doi.org/10.1101/2020.04.18.20070631. Accessed 4 January 2021.

Anne, W.R., Jeeva, S.C., 2021a. Statistical Analysis of COVID-19. Google Colab. 22 April. Available from: https://colab.research.google.com/drive/1dEzTxFmjTdhISnsxuFCx2u-Z1PqxBs2t. (Accessed 10 August 2021).

Anne, W.R., Jeeva, S.C., 2021b. Machine Learning and Prophet Model for COVID-19 Prediction. Google Colab. 22 April. Available from: https://colab.research.google.com/drive/1uwXHPUeirfYlejb7xpPQRT4Q0v9o8o7t. (Accessed 10 August 2021).

Balaji, M.K., Sankararaman, G., Suresh, S., 2020. A study on impact of Covid-19 in India. Test Eng. Manage. 83, 16056–16062. Available from: https://www.academia.edu/43352226/A_Study_on_Impact_of_Covid_19_in_India. (Accessed 5 February 2021).

Coronavirus Research Center, 2020. COVID-19 Data in Motion. Coronavirus Research Center, John Hopkins University, Maryland. Available from: https://covidinfo.jhu.edu/diagnostic-testing/testing-dashboard/. (Accessed 4 June 2021).

Dharun, K., et al., 2021. Exploring the growth of Covid-19 cases using exponential modelling across 42 countries and predicting signs of early containment using machine learning. Transbound. Emerg. Dis. 68, 1001–1018. https://doi.org/10.1111/tbed.13764 (Accessed 4 March 2021).

Francesca, F., et al., 2021. COVID-19 and geographical area of origin. Clin. Microbiol. Infect. 27, 632.e1–632.e5. Available from: https://www.clinicalmicrobiologyandinfection.com/article/S1198-743X(20)30707-2/fulltext. (Accessed 4 March 2021).

Kınacı, H., Unsal, M.G., Kaap, R., 2021. A close look at 2019 novel coronavirus (COVID-19) infections in Turkey using time series analysis & efficiency analysis. Chaos Solitons Fractals 143. https://doi.org/10.1016/j.chaos.2020.110583 (Accessed 23 April 2021).

Mohammad, A., Shanya, S., Kennedy, S., Davies, G.A, 2021. Impact of COVID-19 lockdown on the incidence and mortality of acute exacerbations of chronic obstructive pulmonary disease: national interrupted time series analyses for Scotland and Wales. BMC Med. 19 (1). https://doi.org/10.1186/s12916-021-02000-w.

Namasudra, S., Dhamodharavadhani, S., Rathipriya, R., 2021. Nonlinear neural network based forecasting model for predicting COVID-19 cases. Neural. Process. Lett., 1–21. Available from: https://link.springer.com/article/10.1007%2Fs11063-021-10495-w. (Accessed 5 June 2021).

Nazrul, et al., 2021. Excess Deaths Associated With Covid-19 Pandemic in 2020: Age and Sex Disaggregated Time Series Analysis in 29 High Income Countries. 373. Available from: https://www.bmj.com/content/373/bmj.n1137. (Accessed 24 April 2021).

Philips, T., 2020. Oxford Covid-19 Government Response Tracker. Github. 8 April. Available from: https://github.com/OxCGRT/covid-policy-tracker/blob/master/data/OxCGRT_latest.csv. (Accessed 4 June 2021).

Punn, N., Sonbhadra, S., Agarwal, S.K., S., 2020. COVID-19 epidemic analysis using machine learning and deep learning algorithms. medRxiv, 1–9. https://doi.org/10.1101/2020.04.08.20057679 (Accessed 5 June 2021).
Ramanathan, V., Dhanwant, J., 2020. Forecasting COVID-19 Growth in India Using Susceptible-Infected-Recovered (SIR) Model. 2004.00696. Available from: https://arxiv.org/abs/2004.00696. (Accessed 5 March 2021).
Shaikh, S., et al., 2021. Analysis and prediction of COVID-19 using regression models and time series forecasting. In: Proceedings of the Eleventh International Conference on Cloud Computing, Data Science & Engineering, pp. 989–995, https://doi.org/10.1109/Confluence51648.2021.9377137 (Accessed 5 May 2021).
Stan, 2018. Open-Source Software. 18 September. Available from: https://mc-stan.org/. (Accessed 4 April 2021).
Taylor, S.J., et al., 2018. Forecasting at scale. Am. Stat. 72 (1), 37–45. https://doi.org/10.1080/00031305.2017.1380080 (Accessed 5 May 2021).
Vatsal, T., Dolly, S., Mamta, M., 2020. An eye on the future of COVID-19: prediction of likely positive cases and fatality in India over a 30-day horizon using the prophet model. Disaster Med. Public Health Prep., 1–7. Available from: https://pubmed.ncbi.nlm.nih.gov/33203489/. (Accessed 24 April 2021).
Williamson, E.J., et al., 2020. Factors associated with COVID-19 related death using OpenSAFELY. Nature 584 (7821), 430–436. Available from: https://pubmed.ncbi.nlm.nih.gov/32640463/. (Accessed 5 May 2021).
World Health Organization, 2021. Coronavirus Disease (COVID-19) Pandemic. World Health Organization. 20 March. Available from: https://www.who.int/emergencies/diseases/novel-coronavirus-2019. (Accessed 2 April 2021).
Worldometer, 2021. COVID Live - Coronavirus Statistics. Available from: https://www.worldometers.info›coronavirus. (Accessed 5 May 2021).
Yadav, M., Perumal, M., Srinivas, M., 2020. Analysis on novel coronavirus (COVID-19) using machine learning methods. Chaos Solitons Fractals 139, 110050. https://doi.org/10.1016/j.chaos.2020.110050 (Accessed 6 May 2021).
Yuri, B., Anne-Sophie, L., McCourt, J., 2020. Initial impact of global risk mitigation measures taken during the combating of the COVID-19 pandemic. Saf. Sci. 128. https://doi.org/10.1016/j.ssci.2020.104773 (Accessed 4 May 2021).

CHAPTER TWELVE

Lexical modeling and weighted matrices for analyses of COVID-19 outbreak

V. Kakulapati[a], Sheri Mahender Reddy[b], and Nitesh Kumar[c]
[a]Sreenidhi Institute of Science and Technology, Hyderabad, Telangana, India
[b]Otto-Friedrich University of Bamberg, IsoSySc, Bamberg, Germany
[c]Centurion University of Technology and Management, R. Sitapur, Odisha, India

1. Introduction

COVID-19 is transmitting to all people, even newborns who are at risk. People with severe health debilities such as hypertension, diabetes, chronic kidney disease, respiratory problems, and cardiovascular illness are at higher risk of contracting the infection and developing severe complications. Medical professionals and WHO recommend that the population at any age group the appropriate measures against the virus, such as hand washing, protecting the nose mouth, proper exercise hygiene, and decontaminating conditions. The significant probability of the transmissible virus for senior persons with disabilities with persistent disorders is considerable. The aging of human immunity steadily decreases its ability to respond to the disease owing to other health problems.

Pulmonary infection caused by a new Coronavirus, the 2019 Coronavirus, has spread globally across 222 countries. Since April 26, 2021, 148,145,493 COVID-19 recognized cases and more than 31,271,098 mortality worldwide, based on the current World Health Organization (World Meters Statistics).

In order to interpret immunological test cases of infections, computational formulating of diagnostic biomarkers is immensely useful and allows us to make efforts to prevent disease spread by reducing the threats of global health. In addition, computational analysis and biotechnological investigation mostly need to cooperate and significantly eliminate the outbreak of COVID-19. The prediction of the outbreak and termination time of the disease is completed by numerical techniques. It allows us to decide correctly on the actions needed to limit communicable diseases. Unfortunately,

Lessons from COVID-19
https://doi.org/10.1016/B978-0-323-99878-9.00005-4

COVID-19 spread rapidly around the world in 2019. Then it is a serious predicament since the prevalence of SARS-COV-2 is high (World Health Organization, 2019). Therefore, infectious statistical data are essential to increase awareness and inform engagement (Rivers et al., 2019).

In diagnosing the disease, determining its epidemiological, patient treatment, and reducing propagation, the screening test of the COVID-19 is essential. Standardized policies and methodologies harmonize existing medical tests regarding efficient diagnostic methods in the worldwide battle against the disease outbreak. Furthermore, the specification of even more severe acute respiratory variants is entrusting scholars, practitioners, and biologists to enhance the cluster-based precision and accuracy of antibodies and diagnostic testing. Easy, scalable, fast, and cost-effective diagnostic procedures for COVID-19 can substantially assist in creating high sensitivities, which provide efficient screening capabilities in the outbreak on-demand. It is a fundamental scientific reference for precise estimation of the diagnosis difficulties of COVID-19 and enhanced illness fight techniques (Kevadiya et al., 2021).

Topic modeling tools are beneficial when a community combines to realize the contamination activities and calculate its removal or survival conditions. Scientific research, government, and civilians are now very anxious about the high transmission rate of the infection and the significant mortality rate. Coronavirus is an infectious ailment first recognized in December 2019 by a Coronavirus in Wuhan. When a patient coughs or sneezes excessively, the COVID-19 virus spreads through droplets. These droplets rapidly spread in the air and also settle on the surfaces.

Proposing a new framework and system that uses ML approaches to retrieve significant and relevant characteristics from the COVID-19, including nonnegative matrix factoring for NLP. Linguistic approaches have been influenced by computational linguistics for an extended period. Over 100 years, probabilistic reasoning influenced linguistics (Frege, 1967), and a prominent origin in the computational modeling of languages is conceptual grammar, and among the most commonly recognized language models (Levelt, 2008).

The SVM is a nonlinear method of machine learning for the classification of entities using analysis methods. SVM intends to find the best hyperplane which identifies all input variables with one category from the observations in another (Cortes and Vapnik, 1995).

In order to achieve optimum precision, the SVM method to forecast an occurrence of COVID-19 is developing. COVID-19 estimation SVM classification analyses a numerous cases dataset that enables particular capabilities for every collection. The objective was to establish an SVM-based model to predict epidemics that could analyze the COVID-19 virus and provide a testing process before this analysis. The SVM approach is used to produce the central perspective of a small training set, particularly in the context of the outbreak assessment. The SVM model is also being used to ensure the highest precision to anticipate a new Coronavirus pandemic.

The AUC-ROC curve is a classification problem, which requires continuous improvement at different thresholds. ROC is the probabilistic progression, while AUC is the entropy measure of the extent or measurement. It indicates whether the classifier can differentiate among classes. The increased the AUC, the better the classifier. The higher the AUC, the better the model determines among patients and no disease.

The semantic technique builds the concept of sentiment on the analysis of individual words or expressions; emotional lexicons are typically using: they provide an accessible emotional vocabulary from the dictionary, estimate sentiment weights, and use a combined weight function.

LDA topic modeling is a popular sampling technique for allocating enormous datasets into semantically relevant subgroups. Files are arbitrarily chosen variations of subjects in the dataset that constitute the reasoning between topics special for a given subject. The President of the United States, for instance, has published a news story about healthcare. The issues in the news would be suitable for the president of the US, health insurance, and political beliefs. However, they convey LDA medicine in language that might exist in more than one topic and maybe joint into issues.

The model addresses the issue by analyzing a document on topics and identifying that concept is closer to the content laterally on all subject variations. It helps the keywords to understand which documents are the topics. PLSA is equivalent to LDA, excluding the subject; allocation should be SDP. SDPs detect if papers cover a few subjects; just a few words are used often in these areas. The consequences are a word pattern and then the identical problem formalities. The findings contained the LDA generalization of the PLSA model (Kakulapati and Reddy, 2020).

Statistical models used to anticipate infections can discuss the severity and preventability of the diagnosis. It is utilizing to guide and assist pick the proper health decisions. The proposed method has important implications. First, the classifier precisely analyzes disease patterns and impacts to enhance diagnosing and assessing physicians' therapeutic urgencies. Second, the process utilized to estimate the many factors disturbing the transmission of the ailment is prognostic and determines the efficacy.

This work intends to build and validate a precisely predicted machine learning model

- The model is predicting the Coronavirus patients and older people with underlying diseases by using SVM with AUC.
- The model proposed is a framework of recognition based on the lexicon. It integrates awareness with the intensity of emotional lexicons to accurately recognize the substance of feelings in words and accumulate exact feeling knowledge.
- The proposed model understands the interactions less noisy than existing treatment approaches, using classification techniques. Therefore, the words in the SVM model are summarizing and analyzed.
- The model organizes the latest advanced techniques for the assessment of words in datasets. The impact of integrating lexicons of perception and LDA with word cloud was visualizing.

The clinical evaluation facilitates the diagnosis of COVID-19. Severe acute respiratory syndrome Coronavirus 2 viruses can be anticipating more correctly based on the kind and mix of symptoms. It can allow for a fast diagnostic evaluation of the illness in a high prevalence environment. Cough, myalgia, smell/goodness loss, and fiver over 37.5°C have a high positive preview rate for infection with SARS-CoV-2 (Mardian et al., 2021).

The remaining sections of this chapter are explaining effectively. Section 2 discusses past studies addressing the lexical interpretation techniques and the LDA modeling of linguistics. Section 3 elaborates on some diagnostic measures of COVID-19. Then discuss detailed methodology and its training processes, including the system architecture in Section 4. Section 5 offers experimental findings for several language pairings utilizing the proposed lexical interpretation model of learning applications. Section 6 discusses our model assessment methods. Section 7 concludes. Finally, Section 8 explains our future updations.

2. Related work

Developing a suitable computerized screening test for medical professionals might facilitate immediate diagnosis assessment, for example, formalized legitimate examination of relevant signs for COVID-19. To reduce further transmission at the initial stage of the virus, this is essential to have an early warning system considering a diagnosis of different numerous medical factors (Van Loon et al., 2021).

Blood samples are taken from patients to identify the Coronavirus with the RT-PCR method (Chan et al., 2020). Patients tested the impact of (RdRp)/Hel) and found that COVID-19 identification (RdRp)/Hel) inpatient cases also do not interfere with other bacterial pathogens and biological Coronaviruses. The author stated the potential to affect public welfare via strengthening the COVID-19 lab diagnosis and treatment in this thorough diagnostic screening.

Predict the probability of patients with underlying issues having influenced Coronavirus applying an ML algorithm to estimate the disease prevalence and serious complications. Simulation of outbreaks with this forecasting technique includes a massive range of possible conditions. Forecasting can elevate the interpretation of demographic changes and unpredictable age structure and recommendations for pandemic avoidance. Although COVID-19 causes minor infections among the majority of the patients, it does require special attention for the mortality risk of patients with preexisting diseases (Kakulapati et al., 2020).

The RT-PCR recommended validating diagnoses for COVID-19, which can supplement a diagnosing medical analysis and antibodies and antibodies tests. Although antimicrobial testing mainly suggests antigen detection because of the slow onset of symptoms, antigenic testing can quickly identify severely contagious patients in the illness trajectory that can considerably limit spread (Mardian et al., 2021).

Linguistic approaches, directive approaches, ML techniques, hybrid techniques, and multilabel techniques are inherent in different human classifiers. In Al-A'abed and Al-Ayyoub (2016), a lexicon-based Twitter and Facebook emotional language evaluation method has been establishing. They revealed that 89.7% of the lexicon-based strategy is operative and attain an accurateness of 90%. In another investigation, sentimental reagents were evaluating in the Coronavirus epidemic by analyzing tweets (Kaila and Prasad, 2020). The eight sentiments were studying together with a subsample of tweets. The consequences enable the identification of optimistic and pessimistic beliefs that are almost equal. The patients' anxiety was the leading emotion, followed by governments' optimism, which influenced the tweets.

Twitter messages were evaluated in linguistics (Abd-Alrazaq et al., 2020) during February 2, 2020, and March 15, 2020, and assessed the tweets were retrieved in single (uni-gram) or dual (bi-gram) keyword occurrences. Twelve topics have been recognized and classified into four major topics: the origin of the epidemic, potential effects on individuals, regions, the financial system, and measures of minimizing infection risk. Emotion recognition, identity verification, sentiment classification, etc. are different applications for text summarization. In addition, opinions of Indian government policies using a Lexicon Vocabulary were investigating (Verma et al., 2019).

A methodology is known as a dynamic analysis of NLP. It aims to recognize and remove the polarization of feelings from information by establishing whether the test is positive, negative, or neutral (García-Díaz et al., 2020). Two sentiment analyzing methodologies exist: machine learning and lexical-based analysis. Machine training employs algorithms to detect feelings, but the approach to lexicons is positive and negative (Drus and Khalid, 2019).

Many investigations have been carried out in sentiment classification, utilizing a computational intelligence approach by (Zhang et al., 2018), described in (Jelodar et al., 2020), employing a computational intelligence model to classify emotions. The NLP is used to analyze topics to determine the underlying issues associated with COVID-19 on social sites. Objects are organizing by utilizing the LSTM RNN model.

The n-gram-derived method (Acebal et al., 2006) provides a valid approximation of the Integrated Probability of origin and destination text from the maximum likelihood of a specific n-gram combination. The basics of a conventional linguistic string of words or n-gram models are mathematical concepts such as topic modeling and thinning methods. However, mathematical models have increasingly been enough to learn simple models in which nonlinear linguistic interactions and contextual word classification occur (Mikolov et al., 2013). The n-gram interpretation method (Hai Son et al., 2012) describes the model as a consequence of a bidirectional phrase paired sequence with a perceptron, the probabilities of a word sequence. Rebuild the bilateral technique (Devlin et al., 2014) as an alternative to the KNN rescoring module in the n-gram decoder instead of using the KNN scorer. The maximum likelihood (Schwenk, 2012) is then adapted to the word sequence in a source sequence.

In the epidemic COVID-19 in China, a statistical model was developed by Yang et al. (2020). The pandemic's intensity and frequency and the maximum epidermal aspect are predicted by a simplified deterministic concept of susceptible eroded infectious recovered. This is a significant consequence for investigating the propagation and spreading of COVID-19 utilizing computational mathematics methods.

Modeling topics analyzed massive datasets of geotagged tweets (Dahal et al., 2019), including global warming using topic modelization and text analytics. In retrieving the topics in the text, LDA uses feature selection and VAD (Valence Aware Dictionary and Sentiment Reasoner) to assess fundamental emotional reactions. Emotion recognition illustrated that if users respond to government or weather patterns incidents, most conversation is unfavorable. In contrast, topic modeling showed that numerous such topics of climate change discussions are broad but more significant.

The LDA approach used to analyze new COVID-19 epidemics using facts acquired indicates that people are scared of new Coronaviruses' worldwide epidemics (Kaila and Prasad, 2020). Muthusami et al. (2020) established the COVID-19 epidemic to evaluate emotions utilizing various ML algorithms. Bakshi et al. (2016) used the NLTK library to clean and text to analyze tweets for categorization of public opinion. Several organizations expressed their opinions on Twitter.

Analytical methods have for many decades generated probabilistic insights and perspectives for epidemic decision-making and policy incorporation in the epidemic (Wu et al., 2020a). Several experiments conducted for COVID-19 specifically are performed. For example, COVID-19's description model is produced by transmission changing aspects in China and anticipates global and regional disease transmission data reported in China. Read et al. (2020) discussed the initial outbreaks' effective atomic rate, utilizing a hypothesis of regular incremental Poisson's latency for information transformation.

The sentiment evaluates a particular segment of the text's emotions, feelings, opinions, and attitudes (Medhat et al., 2014). A fundamental objective for emotional investigation is to examine if a term in a specific aspect is favorable or unfavorable (Ravi and Ravi, 2015).

Researchers use consistent weights (Nurhayati et al., 2012), binary weights (Mukhaiyar and Pasaribu, 2012), distance-based weights. This methodology of identifying weight persists qualitatively. The specified weight matrix infers better correlations among areas. This matrix is a hybrid of the reasonable inverse distance weight (IDW) matrix with the patient ratios among provinces, and the IDW matrix changed.

3. About COVID-19 diagnostic methods

In diverse hosts like animals and people, Coronavirus causes moderate-to-severe infectious respiratory illness, transfers, and survives in various hosts. The virus is detected in patients with high temperatures, intense muscle aches, lung congestion, sputum production, respiratory distress, dyspnea, hemoptysis, and diarrhea. In addition, anosmia and ageusia have been documented.

It is recommended to take a throat swab to assess and evaluate the infection in the initial evaluation of COVID-19. In order to prevent tongue injury, the rear of the pharynx should be swabbed. On the contrary, pulmonary lowering samples are recommended for use in saliva, low respiration aspirates, and bronchial washing (Pan et al., 2020). Thus, to increase the sensitivity of the testing and save access to a good combination of NP and OP swabs and repetitive sampling.Consequently, between samples, the accuracy of the NP swab may not be consistent. Physicians may also be susceptible to infection in the procedure of testing due to aerosols production (Guo et al., 2020).

Additionally, the requirement to separate COVID-19 from seasonal influenza instances may delay emergencies, facilities' slow care and treatment for persistent with coronavirus, and constitute a significant source of apprehension (Liu and Pan, 2020). Such problems affect the scientific method of whether diagnostic procedures are best for combating the impending growth of COVID-19 infections effectively and identifying difference between COVID-19 illnesses and seasonal influenza.

3.1 Different diagnostic tests

Diagnostic procedures can show that you may have an infectious disease with COVID-19 and respond appropriately to quarantine or detach yourself. The diagnoses are types that can be determining whether you have an autoimmune disorder of COVID-19. Diagnosis specimens are often collected by spitting into tubes with a nasal or mouth swab or saliva taken.

In antibody diagnostics, the SARS-CoV-2 virus that further stimulates COVID-19 is used to detect antibodies in the human immune system. However, the analysis of persistent COVID-19 contagion is not completed by antibody analysis. Once infected, immunoglobulins can be taken several days or even weeks and can last many weeks or more in human blood after recovering. Medical professionals collect blood samples from the patients for the detection of antibodies.

Worldwide, government agencies have authorized numerous diagnostic procedures; nevertheless, the right policies are still unclear, dependent on the health status or the objectives of the research of the patient (Sanyaolu et al., 2020). For example, in Europe, the CE-IVD and FDA authorized or utilized for data analysis 365 different commercialized tools. Some are immunological investigations, polymerase chain reaction procedures, NGS-based procedures, and two marketed instruments depending on other technologies (European Commission, 2020). And, therefore, it is transparent that it can be challenging to select accurate therapeutic testing. The test result may be positive or negative for COVID-19.

3.1.1 COVID-19 positive

In other words, people are currently suffering from an infectious illness with the COVID-19 virus. Taking immediate action to protect themselves and prevent the spread of infection to others. People have to isolate themselves until the symptoms disappear and they have to have an average temperature for 24 h and at least 10 days after the first appearance of signs or are proven positive, whichever is later. The patient recommends staying in social exclusion extended if they have symptoms associated with COVID-19 or have a health status that affects their illness control. If the result is positive, and no signs or symptoms have developed, isolation 1 week after the testing.

3.1.2 COVID-19 negative

The COVID-19 virus probably didn't contaminate. Depending on the test sample's efficiency and effectiveness, a fake negative test result may occur. If the patient is already tested negative and may get contaminated in perspective, it is essential to recognize isolation rules, masks, and washing hands to prevent possible spreading. If the patient continues to have signs, the doctor may prescribe repetitive tests.

3.1.3 Polymerase chain reaction test

This COVID-19 test is also known as a molecular test and examines the virus's genes to use a scientific technique known as PCR. A fluids spectrum is collected with insertion into the patient nose of a nasopharyngeal swab and fluid from the patient nasal or a mediate turbine swab to test for the presence. An oropharyngeal swab is deposited in a test tube, saliva in the mouth, or split into a tube in rare instances. If investigated on the spot, or some few consecutive days—or more in regions with testing delays—findings may be received in minutes when transmitted to individuals impacted. PCR testing is quite precise if appropriately performed by a healthcare provider, although specific instances may miss a quick test.

3.1.4 Antigen test

In the COVID-19 test, various proteins in the virus are detected. Specific antigen testing can deliver findings in minutes to use a long nose swab for a fluid sample. These are sent for analysis to a laboratory. However, if the guidelines are executed precisely, a positive antigen testing procedure is recognized accurately, and there is a rise in the possibility of wrongly negated results. That is, the infection is contaminated, but the outcome is negative. Therefore, a PCR test to validate negative antigen testing may be recommended (Mayo Clinic).

It enables precise control of synthesized antibodies, a profound understanding of antibodies generated by various tissue contexts, and may cause false negatives if the development of gene products is limited.

3.1.5 RT-PCR-based molecular tests

The molecular RT-PCR procedures are the golden standards utilized worldwide to determine COVID-19 infection in a confirmed manner. Investigators had already completely sequenced the SARS-CoV-2 genome (Wu et al., 2020b), initiated the structure of biological primers and samples precise to the SARS-CoV-2 RNA molecules to analyze COVID-19 infectious disease and some other similar symptoms, including regular influenza or contagious bacterial infections. The entire SARS-CoV-2 genomic sequencing has a frequency of 29,903 bp. It contains the specific functionality: A 50 base Poly-A cap, 1/ab opening with genome polymerization RNA, spike proteins, membrane receptor, molecule and nucleocapsid protein, and 35-bp polyA tail synthesis. Time required for the test; qualified professionals and adequate infrastructure for data interpretation.

3.1.6 Chest computed tomography

The scan results are noninvasive and comprise several X-ray observations of the chest to collect cross-sectional images (Whiting et al., 2015). Primary care physicians investigate the images to identify abnormalities that can result in diagnosis. The radiological features of the Coronavirus vary from stage to stage and depend on the severity of the infection. For instance, in the initial phases of the disease (0–2 days), more prevalent standard CT results with significant respiratory infiltration rise 10 days after symptoms. The general characteristics of COVID-19 consist mainly of the bilaterally symmetrical and peripheral opacity zone in the lower lobes and pulmonary congestion (Bernheim et al., 2020). Numerous retrospective investigations showed that CT scans are much more precise and had enhanced undesirable result proportions than RT-PCR, depending on those scanning features.

Loop-mediated isothermal amplification: By relying on certain SARS-CoV-2 genomes, the possibility of active infection exists. It is analytical and uses reagents that are precisely framed to construct new sequence structures for replication. It is quick and needs no extra safety equipment.

However, the limit of detection of 125 viruses/mL is extremely low. The development of the appropriate reagents might be complicated, and the reactivity of waste can intervene. The consequences can also really be a measured level of viral infection.

3.1.7 Robotic process automation

It is used to handle particular difficulties arising from the epidemic. COVID-19 analysis involves many repeated administrators, including system identification and registration of patients, accurately designated test kits, and recording test findings into national databases with millions of other entries in certain situations. In addition, a great demand for testing in many nations has resulted in shortages, although social separation provisions for employees remain valid.

These are COVID-19 diagnostic procedures, and several other ways are available, such as CRISPR, RT-LAMP, Droplet Digital PCR, Serological techniques, etc.

4. Framework

Creating a lexical framework to define how medications, diagnostics, and related information coexist in coronavirus health data. E-enhanced the accuracy of the data to analyze proportional medicines depending on the current proposed approach. Diagnostic tests may be cooperatively acceptable. To get the fundamental features and prediction models, use a lexical framework for weight matrices.

The elements of the framework (Fig. 1) are discussed below:

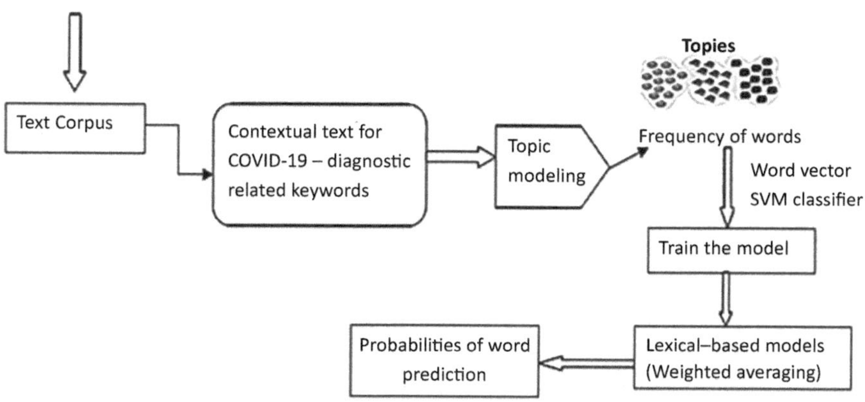

Fig. 1 The framework of the proposed method.

4.1 SVM

It is a technique to categorize texts into distinct groups. SVM is a supervised learning classification. For the particular text, the label takes the "n" number of characteristics. It is an effective regression-classifier and significantly correlated with the dataset supporting the significant stake of efficient data (Mayo Clinic). Therefore, analyzing the model's performance becomes one of the essential priorities after data analysis. SVM is a supervised vector theory learning method. The data are classified in vectors in the area to categorize the data using this methodology. Hyperplanes are utilized for the decision-making and classification of data points by keeping the various categories from one another as far as feasible.

4.2 Lexicon intelligence

Lexicons imply accumulated perspective data that provide a foundation for conceptualization. While lexicon data are commonly assumed to play a function in analyzing linguistic (Falkum and Vicente, 2015), it is unknown in the context of every phrase. For instance, it can be set aside uniquely in the lexicon or the frequency of the interpretation affecting the lexical entries and its method—lexicons in a feature vector utilized distributed word form or incorporating. Term integrations are observed as a lexicon module that performs as a lexicon. The more identical the variations of two words are, the exact equivalent the phrase interpretations are optimized.

Possible descriptions (Boleda, 2020) are demographic semantic models of the word weight, especially LSA (Landauer and Dumais, 1997), suitable for patients using different word modeling methodologies. This is probably because (a) the observational effectiveness of the model is to describe lexicons via word embedding in a variety of tasks, and (b) that the same allow us interoperable continue providing linguistic and historical data because that can also investigate every parameter impact in isolation and permutation. Thus, in specific terms, the utilization of linguistic information is a selection of modeling.

There are various methods for creating topics based on documents. Modeling is one of the most useful. This chapter built an LDA model that can be used in multiple processes to allocate subjects. To better understand modeling topics, models are assigned to determine an issue in datasets. The topic modeling technique is important as theme models make it possible to decide on a matter in datasets.

A key issue is to provide an approach to determine similarities between crucial phrases and emotive linguistic concepts. With this goal, we computed a massive data word similarity. Especially in obtaining the linear word vectors, representation and syntax applied a derivative from LSA. Through an SVD, T1 term cooccurrences in corpus documents (Deerwester et al., 1990) are acquired utilizing the decrease in the word by document matrix.

4.3 Feature extraction

The high-dimensional data (Ahmed et al., 2017) are one of the summarization concerns. The valuable advice of morphing words into matrices (or vectors) of features is to use specific extraction process methods. It utilized two of the most influential methodologies for retrieving attributes: n-gram and TF-IDF, utilizing chronological tweets. The n-gram model is a popular method in text mining and NLP for testing and validation.

An n-gram is utilized to process correlative phrases in a prescribed period as per linguistic, statistical analyses. In this analysis, the n-gram process such as $n=1$ to $n=4$ was working to recognize the data context (i.e., unigram, bigram, trigram, and quat-gram). The concept TF-IDF is an effective method of evaluating the importance of a word or phrase that extracts data and utilizes NLP. The weighted text frequency is employed. In an extensive collection of documents, TF-IDF aims to identify the linguistic features inside the text. The TF-IDF methodology uses the degree of the relative frequency across the corpus of the documents, which is quite effective.

4.4 Tokenization

Preprocessing tokenization refers to the splitting of long feature vectors into tokens. These tokens may be phrases that are further dividing into small terms then subdivided into words. For example, the phrase: "hard effort pays off before the tokenization."

4.5 Normalization

The normalization process in data preparation transforms a word into a simple form for elevated linguistic consistency. It contains the transformation to the upper or lower case of all text.

4.6 Stemming

This is subsequent step in the tokenization phase. The next step is to alter parent words to reduce keyword types or categories.

4.7 Word vectors

These express words significantly more efficiently and have a significantly lower space than a smooth validity, encode vector, and contain semantic word information. These are the primary features of word vectors. Prior to proceeding into determining word vectors mystified, it is necessary to recognize the critical aspect behind the concept of word vectors (Deep Learning Demystified, 2021).

Lexical items become more frequent than different word combining.

- When a word is around, it does not always signify that it has a comparable significance.
- Words with similar meanings are regularly using when we evaluate the frequency of terms found closer together.
- Utilize a single phrase, say the nth term, only effect the nth row in the weight matrix, as all other rows are 0.
- The nth row of the weight matrix has all the learned information about the nth word, and for the nth term, this row is the trained word vector.

NMF is frequently employing for high dimension data such as summarization. Since it consistently generates sparse, significant features from a set of primary input vectors (Xu et al., 2003). It uses nonnegative weights, which are common approaches including Term Frequency – Inverse Document Frequency.

1. Matrix A = Matrix W * Matrix H
2. A = DTM for m and n words of textual data (m X n)
3. As an input, NMF takes A and factorizes it into two nonnegative matrices, W and H, with dimensions k, i.e., several topics.
4. W = In the matrix (m × k) for K-topics, the W rows weigh many of those values reveal the importance of the link between documents and subjects in the test document.
5. The topic (k × n) matrix column is H, which offers weights for phrases (columns) concerning the subjects (rows). By picking the data in a particular column and selecting the terms at the top, we may create a description (topic) of the subject.
6. The document-topic matrix is proportionally scaled: Measure the document-topic matrix so that the topic values associated with every document add up to one to evaluate and illustrate components of NMF comparable to LDA's topic proportions.
7. Measure the topic matrix correspondingly: Measure the topic matrix so that the term values for each subject are one.

5. Implementation result

Text corpus consists of the verbal information from elderly persons as well as doctors. It also includes the data from the COVID-recovered patients.

All of the information gathered is modeled using TM, and probable topics-terms are extracted. These show us the pertinent information regarding the terms frequently used around the COVID patients. Using SVM for the vectors obtained from topic modeling, we classify the vectors for precise information from the recovered patients, doctors, and others with respective probabilities.

The infection of COVID-19 can vary from mild to acute with indications such as temperature, cold, coughing, shortness of breath, exhaustion, anxiety, tasting or smell loss, chest infection, mucus, sneezing, nausea, and severe dehydration. Acute diseases, increased morbidity, and death may result.

This information may be helpful in decision-making during the spread of COVID.

Data: Coronavirus pandemic classified as a health emergency by WHO investigators, and healthcare facilities openly access the pandemic data. Two datasets have been collected and incorporated from the Kaggle open-source data repository. The dataset contains the patient information showing pre-existing diseases and age.

5.1 Prepossessing

The gathered data are prepared to create the subsequent stage during this stage. This process consists of three major phases. First, remove duplicated characters, corrective text, normalization, elimination of words, and linguistic recognition in a cleaning step. A further objective of the tokenization approach is to transform the text into tokens once it generates vectors—lastly, linguistic patterns and extracting features.

During lexicon definition, the actual case documents are preprocessing to apply topic modeling to describe individual patients in a vector format such as analogous to vector documentation. The word "vector" reflects the numerous times a subject occurs in a patient file. Repetitive conditions repeat in a file; for example, chronic conditions generally signify a significantly greater intensity, leading to increased weights. The condition that only occurs occasionally in the patients' information, such as sometimes coughing or headache, is lowered and less influenced by the topic profiles.

There are five main steps in implementation: text cleaning, tokenization, stop word removal, lemmatization, and persistence. Retrieving certain features from the text data should be an input for classification algorithms in a precisely considered form. In the retrieval, numerous approaches are used. TF-IDF is applied to estimate a bag of words that separates text into words for a vector (Sethi et al., 2020). If there is one word, the approach discusses it as a unigram, the two-word as bigram, and the three-word as trigram (Chakraborty et al., 2020). The vector is extracted from this model using "unigram" approach. While executing the LDA model, several parameters need to be defined. Essential factors that should be adequately choosing include the number of topics (k) and the number of iterations that affect several times LDA executed through every text. In addition, it is also essential to develop the sample size according to the given dataset. Thus, this procedure is carried when the model executes, and K values are changed until the optimum outcome is obtained.

5.2 Evaluating metrics

The classifiers' performance evaluates with precision, sensitivity, and specificity. In each cross-validation fold, the three metrics were estimated. The correlation coefficients were gradually aggregated—assess the classification accuracy utilized for the ROC (receivers operating characteristic) analysis. Thus, a measure of classification effectiveness is the AUC (area under the curve) measured from the ROC curve.

5.2.1 Precision

It's the performance measure. Precision offers the fractional value for the total samples in a dataset of the properly predicted samples. Precision measurements correctly recognized the fraction of real positive.

5.2.2 ROC curve

The efficiency of the classification model is calculated using a measure. AUC represents the area under the ROC curve. AUC underlines how effective it is that the optimistic categories are isolated from the pessimistic.

5.2.3 N-gram

An n-gram model of language given the word sequence w,

$$P\left(wi|wi-1, wi-2, \ldots, wi-n+1\right)$$

where wi is the ith word of the sequence.

Quantify matrices of similarities in combinations such that associated words achieve strong effects of similarity. Then, based on the input text, employ lexical similarity. F or all word combinations, the correlation method returns a value between 0, which shows a few words are not correlated, and 1, which implies that they are pretty similar.

5.2.4 Semantic extraction

The topic modeling LDA, the sampling of Gibbs (Sethi et al., 2020; Blei et al., 2003), and the COVID-19-related analysis utilize lexical extraction and hidden topic discoveries. Furthermore, COVID-19 observations may vary on various topics. Recognize such significant topics and reveal them in this step. The collected documents, such as COVID-19, relevant notes, and words, were considered topics (K) based on the LDA model. Asymmetric Dirichlet distribution is generated from the distinct topic distributions. A COVID-19-related statement in a dataset has been used to measure the likelihood of observed values D.

ML methods assist the medical diagnosis of suspected COVID-19 for studying language indicators from the verbal expressions of older adults. Emphasize here that the optimal trained model for the illness group prediction includes strong lexical and high n-gram morphological characteristics (Figs. 2–4).

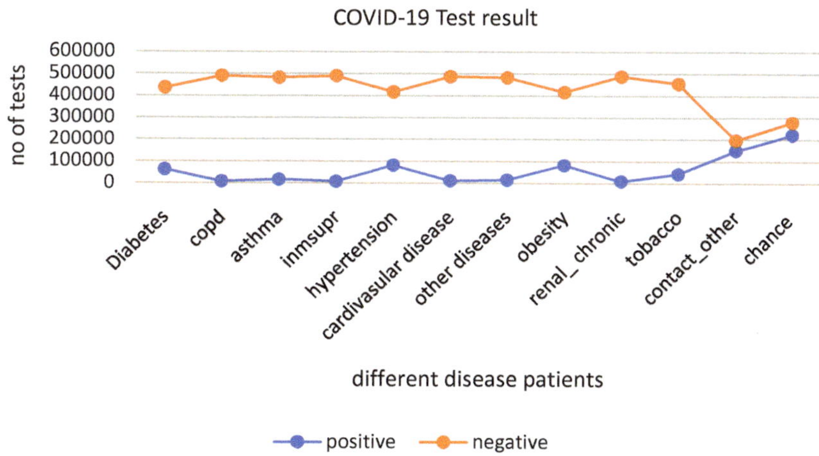

Fig. 2 Chance of COVID-19 test result of a patient with pre-existing diseases.

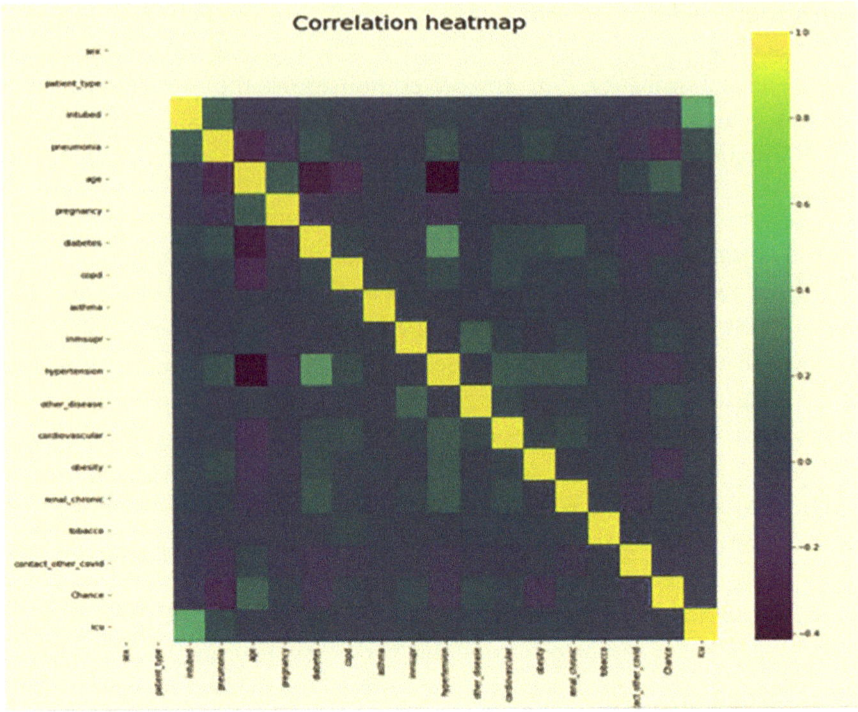

Fig. 3 Correlation heatmap.

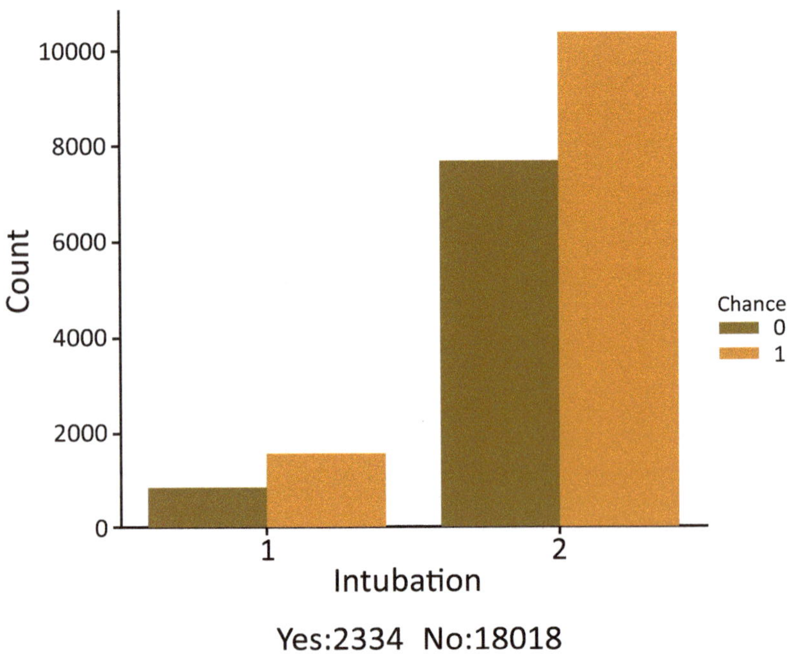

Fig. 4 Intubation COVID-19 patients. SVM classification accuracy: 64%.

Table 1 The COVID-19 patients with preexisting diseases.

	Sex	Patient_ type	Intubed	Pneumonia	Age	Pregnancy	Diabetes	Copd	Asthma	Inmsupr
0	2	1	97	2	27	97	2	2	2	2
1	2	1	97	2	24	97	2	2	2	2
2	1	2	2	2	54	2	2	2	2	2
3	2	2	2	1	30	97	2	2	2	2
4	1	2	2	2	60	2	1	2	2	2

Table 2 COVID-19 result with other chronic diseases.

S. No.	COVID-19 result	Positive	Negative
1	Diabetes	62,349	435,702
2	Copd	8276	489,970
3	Asthma	16,214	482,036
4	Inmsupr	8071	489,959
5	Hypertension	81,340	416,863
6	Cardiovascular disease	11,419	486,764
7	Other diseases	15,392	482,107
8	Obesity	81,929	416,293
9	Renal_ chronic	10,019	488,197
10	Tobacco	42,955	455,158
11	Contact_other	149,051	196,966
12	Chance	220,657	279,035

The following observations were completed by Tables 1 and 2. Topics 85 and 18 shared comparable notions of patients. Topic 85 included words referring to people, such as "people," "virus,", "day," "bad," "stop," "news," "worse," "sick," "spread," and "family." This topic is the first-ranked topic discovered from the generated latent topics, in which most users express their opinion and comment on this issue. Based on Table 1 and Fig. 5 in this topic, the terms people and virus were the most highlighted words, with word-weights of 0.1295% and 0.0301%, respectively. Also, we can see the importance of the term "family" from this topic. In addition, Topic 18 contains the telling words "virus," "people," "symptoms," "infection," "cases," "disease," "pneumonia," "coronavirus," and" treatment." Other revealing words in Topic 18 included "people," "infection," and "treatment." These terms initially suggest a set of user comments about treatment issues. Moreover, the sentiment analysis of the terms suggests that negative words were more highlighted than positive words (Tables 3 and 4).

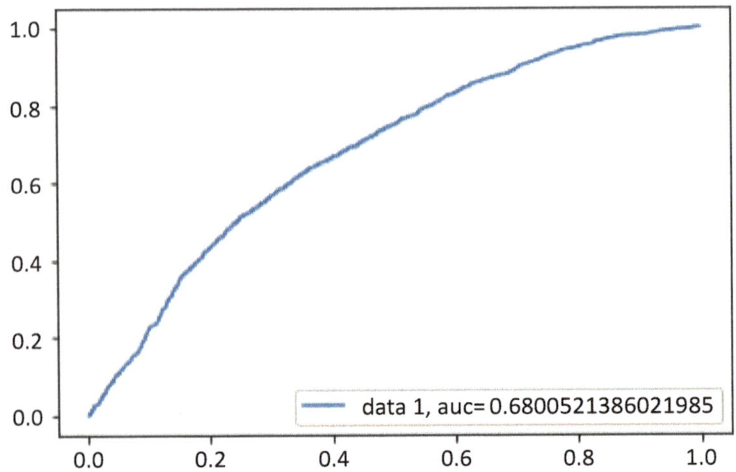

Fig. 5 Performance of COVID-19 tests receiver under area curve.

LM is trained to output a probability distribution over the vocabulary V given a context. Generically, p(V | c) = LM(c). Each word is typically encoding as a vector—a word embedding—learned as training and static across contexts. These word embeddings are stored in an input matrix Wi (n × |V|, where n is the embedding size (Figs. 6 and 7).

COVID-19 results

2—279,035, 1—220,657, 3—66,910

Where 2 represents COVID-19 negative, 1 represents COVID-19 positive, 3 represents COVID-19 waiting.

Now here we are replacing 1 with 1, 2 with 0, and 3 with 2.

This work is focusing on giving the chances of being affected by Coronavirus. So, the main focus is either chance is positive or negative, hence neglect awaiting cases.

6. Discussion

In this chapter, A COVID-19 pandemic model passed from humans to humans was designed and analyzed. To date, the suspected cases of COVID-19 continue to increase worldwide every day. Considering health risks, then, the forecast of infected people is especially notable. SVM classifies infected people as positive, negative, and waiting and predicting risk analysis those are suffering from underlying chronic diseases, such as diabetes, malignancy, and overweight. LDA models require the input parameters used, and it is challenging to choose this number since the correct number depends on the continuous measurement.

Table 3 LDA Gibbs 8 PD topic probabilities.

S. No.	V1	V2	V3	V4	V5	V6	V7	V8
1	0.115625	0.128125	0.140625	0.140625	0.103125	0.103125	0.140625	0.128125
2	0.135246	0.135246	0.118852	0.151639	0.118852	0.118852	0.102459	0.118852
3	0.128472	0.114583	0.142361	0.114583	0.086806	0.170139	0.128472	0.114583
4	0.090659	0.101648	0.123626	0.156593	0.090659	0.145604	0.156593	0.134615
5	0.109043	0.140957	0.119681	0.119681	0.119681	0.109043	0.119681	0.162234
6	0.204128	0.075688	0.094037	0.084862	0.12156	0.158257	0.167431	0.094037
7	0.144231	0.092949	0.105769	0.182692	0.080128	0.13141	0.13141	0.13141
8	0.11	0.136667	0.096667	0.136667	0.176667	0.15	0.11	0.083333
9	0.132143	0.103571	0.117857	0.146429	0.146429	0.117857	0.117857	0.117857
10	0.117188	0.127604	0.169271	0.075521	0.117188	0.117188	0.179688	0.096354
11	0.085616	0.167808	0.113014	0.126712	0.126712	0.099315	0.15411	0.126712
12	0.198052	0.107143	0.107143	0.12013	0.172078	0.107143	0.094156	0.094156
13	0.160714	0.089286	0.160714	0.089286	0.117857	0.103571	0.132143	0.146429
14	0.16358	0.175926	0.138889	0.101852	0.07716	0.114198	0.114198	0.114198
15	0.129747	0.129747	0.129747	0.117089	0.091772	0.167722	0.117089	0.117089
16	0.090625	0.115625	0.278125	0.090625	0.090625	0.090625	0.103125	0.140625
17	0.085294	0.144118	0.132353	0.108824	0.120588	0.167647	0.120588	0.120588
18	0.103125	0.128125	0.103125	0.178125	0.090625	0.090625	0.090625	0.215625
19	0.117089	0.129747	0.10443	0.155063	0.129747	0.167722	0.091772	0.10443
20	0.107558	0.130814	0.177326	0.177326	0.107558	0.130814	0.072674	0.09593

Table 4 LDA Gibbs 8 PD topics to terms.

S. No.	Topic 1	Topic 2	Topic 3	Topic 4	Topic 5	Topic 6	Topic 7	Topic 8
1	Breathing	Increase	COVID	Start	Recover	Exercises	Patients	Rest
2	Stress	Needs	Care	Health	Taken	Body	Physical	Best
3	Loved	Recovery	Health	Treatment	Pulmonary	People	Stay	Sore
4	Throat	Activity	Strong	Mental	Fear	Rehabilitation	Foods	Heart
5	Scared	Follow	Conditions	Keep	Importance	Drinking	Getting	Exercising
6	Back	Overcome	Advice	Fluids	Panic	Muscle	Negative	Isolation

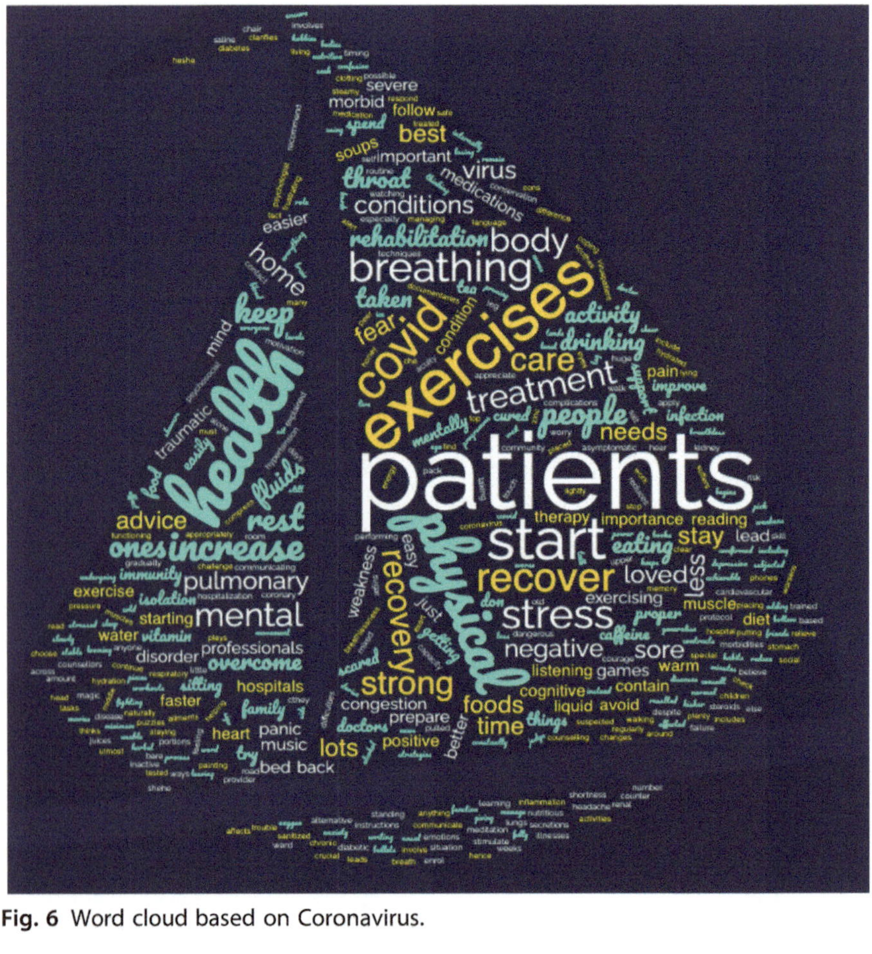

Fig. 6 Word cloud based on Coronavirus.

Fig. 7 Word cloud based on Coronavirus.

The main issue of employing LDA models is an unsupervised training method; inadequate monitoring is often acceptable and expanded the test to examine if the semantic characteristics of diagnostic tests may depend on the different COVID-19-related concerns. In this context, an existing dataset considered significant Latin subjects of COVID-19 keywords was linked to numerous difficulties. LDA is a probabilistic model that implies that every word in a dataset creates a mixture of (latent) unnoticed subjects applied to documents. A topic is described as a categorical word distribution. Therefore, it is concluded that there are prospects of quality management if more information is collected with these machine learning algorithms. As we have a significant issue in addressing the deadly virus, the work benefits the population in a certain sense by analyzing diagnostic tests and necessary action. Also, it was examined that people with preexisting diseases with COVID-19 have predicted risk analysis.

7. Conclusion

The COVID-19 pandemic highlighted the significance of managing a medical crisis in diagnostic procedures that significantly affect the global social, financial, and healthcare. In this work, the diagnosis of COVID-19 using SVM has three limitations: selecting a feature vector, an effective SVM input feature subset, and establishing the best kernel parameters. These limitations are significant, since choosing the subset feature influences the kernel parameters and likewise. The number of samples in developing assessment methods is an important aspect. Along with the strategic evaluation of an uncertainties associated lexicon, the word vector was designing. In addition, a sample of feelings senses is considering. The added annotation makes it possible to differentiate emotional sensations with intensity and multifactorial. Lexical Semantically Analysis depicted the vector illustration emotions classifications and realized a practical weight function wherein a generic phrase's compelling and valuable meaning was defined. The vocabulary of feeling in investigations is of enormous importance. A good quality lexicon guarantees the efficiency of the process supervised.

8. Future work

Fuzzy methods will be used in the future to effectively analyze the content of pharmaceutical assessments using phrase vectors and dynamic classification algorithms. These subsequent tests are supporting for intensive reasons. It is necessary to identify the generative models that create theoretical and realistic knowledge for COVID-19 diagnostic analyses. Predicting preclinical diseases, pandemic trends, and precise analyses of human-to-human spread in medical personnel and serosurveys. Though subsequent diagnoses are necessary for managing and controlling outbreaks, fast, scalable, and high-precision research has the most significant cost-efficient multiplexing diagnostics that identify several diseases at once.

References

Abd-Alrazaq, A., Alhuwail, D., Househ, M., Hamdi, M., Shah, Z., 2020. Top concerns of tweeters during the COVID-19 pandemic: infoveillance study. J. Med. Internet Res. 22 (4), e19016.

Acebal, J., Banchs, R., Crego, J., Brosa, A., Lambert, P., Fonollosa, J., Costa-Jussa, M., 2006. N-gram-based machine translation. Comput. Linguist. 32 (4), 527–549. https://doi.org/10.1162/coli.2006.32.4.527.

Ahmed, H., Traore, I., Saad, S., 2017. Detection of Online Fake News Using N-Gram Analysis and Machine Learning Techniques. pp. 127–138.

Al-A'abed, M., Al-Ayyoub, M., 2016. A lexicon-based approach for emotion analysis of arabic social media content. In: Proceedings of the International Computer Sciences and Informatics Conference (ICSIC 2016), Amman, Jordan.

Bakshi, R.K., Kaur, N., Kaur, R., Kaur, G., 2016. Opinion mining and sentiment analysis. In: 2016 3rd International Conference on Computing for Sustainable Global Development (INDIACom), IEEE, pp. 452–455.

Bernheim, A., Mei, X., Huang, M., Yang, Y., Fayad, Z.A., Zhang, N., Diao, K., Lin, B., Zhu, X., Li, K., Li, S., Shan, H., Jacobi, A., Chung, M., 2020. Chest CT findings in coronavirus disease-19 (COVID-19): relationship to duration of infection. Radiology 70. https://doi.org/10.1148/radiol.2020200463, 200463.

Blei, D.M., Ng, A.Y., Jordan, M.I., 2003. Latent dirichlet allocation. J. Mach. Learn. Res. 3, 993–1022.

Boleda, G., 2020. Distributional semantics and linguistic theory. Annu. Rev. Linguist. 6, 213–234.

Chakraborty, K., Bhatia, S., Bhattacharyya, S., Platos, J., Bag, R., Hassanien, A.E., 2020. Sentiment analysis of COVID-19 tweets by deep learning classifiers-a study to show how popularity is affecting accuracy in social media. Appl. Soft Comput. 97, 106754.

Chan, J.F.-W., Yip, C.C.-Y., Tang, T.H.-C., Wong, S.C.-Y., Leung, K.-H., Fung, A. Y.-F., Ng, A.C.-K., Zou, Z., Tsoi, H.-W., Choi, G.K.-Y., Tam, A.R., Cheng, V. C.-C., Chan, K.-H., Tsang, O.T.-Y., Yuen, K.-Y., 2020. Improved molecular diagnosis of COVID-19 by the novel, highly sensitive, and specific COVID-19-RdRp/Hel real-time reverse transcription-PCR assay validated in vitro and with clinical specimens. J. Clin. Microbiol. 58 (5).

Cortes, C., Vapnik, V., 1995. Support-vector networks. Mach. Learn. 20, 273–297.

Dahal, B., Kumar, S.A.P., Li, Z., 2019. Topic modeling and sentiment analysis of global climate change tweets. Social Network. Anal. Min., 1–20. https://doi.org/10.1007/s13278-019-0568-8.

Deep Learning Demystified, 2021. https://deeplearningdemystified.com/article/nlp-1. (Accessed 18 May 2021).

Deerwester, S., Dumais, S.T., Furnas, G.W., Landauer, T.K., Harshman, R., 1990. Indexing by latent semantic analysis. J. Am. Soc. Inf. Sci. 41 (6), 391–407.

Devlin, J., Zbib, R., Huang, Z., Lamar, T., Schwartz, R., Makhoul, J., 2014. Fast and robust neural network joint models for statistical machine translation. In: Proceedings of the

Association for Computational Linguistics (ACL), Baltimore, pp. 1370–1380, https://doi.org/10.3115/v1/P14-1129.
Drus, Z., Khalid, H., 2019. Sentiment analysis in social media and its application: systematic literature review. Prog. Comput. Sci. 161, 707–714.
European Commission, 2020. Current Performance of COVID-19 Test Methods and Devices and Proposed Performance Criteria. EC, Brussels. https://www.mayoclinic.org/tests-procedures/covid-19-diagnostic-test/about/pac-20488900. (Accessed 12 May 2021).
Falkum, I., Vicente, A., 2015. Polysemy: current perspectives and approaches. Lingua 157, 1–172. https://doi.org/10.1016/j.lingua.2015.02.002.
Frege, G., 1967. Begrifsschrif, a formula language, modelled upon that of arithmetic, for pure thought. In: From Frege to Godel: A Source Book in Mathematical Logic, 1879–1931, pp. 1–82.
García-Díaz, J.A., Cánovas-García, M., Valencia-García, R., 2020. Ontology-driven aspect-based sentiment analysis classification: an infodemiological case study regarding infectious diseases in Latin America. Futur. Gener. Comput. Syst. 112, 641–657.
Guo, W.L., Jiang, Q., Ye, F., Li, S.Q., Hong, C., Chen, L.Y., Li, S.Y., 2020. Effect of throat washings on detection of 2019 novel coronavirus. Clin. Infect. Dis. 71 (8), 1980–1981. https://doi.org/10.1093/CID/ciaa416. 32271374.
Hai Son, L., Allauzen, A., Yvon, F., 2012. Continuous space translation models with neural networks. In: Proceedings of the 2012 Conference of the North American Chapter of the Association for Computational Linguistics. Human Language Technologies, pp. 39–48.
Jelodar, H., Wang, Y., Orji, R., Huang, H., 2020. Deep sentiment classification and topic discovery on novel Coronavirus or covid-19 online discussions: NLP using LSTM recurrent neural network approach. IEEE J. Biomed. Health Inform. 24, 2733–2742.
Kaila, R.P., Prasad, A.V.K., 2020. Informational flow on twitter – coronavirus outbreak – topic modeling approach. Int. J. Adv. Res. Eng. Technol. 11 (3), 128–134.
Kakulapati, V., Reddy, S.M., 2020. Risk analysis of coronavirus caused death by the probability of patients suffering from chronic diseases – a machine learning perspective. JCR 7 (14), 2626–2633.
Kakulapati, V., Reddy, S.M., Deepthi, B.S.S., Tavares, J.M.R.S., 2020. Machine learning analysis of topic modeling re-ranking of clinical records. In: Advances in Ubiquitous Sensing Applications for Healthcare, Smart Biosensors in Medical Care. Academic Press, ISBN: 9780128207819, pp. 153–177. ISSN 25891014.
Kevadiya, B.D., Machhi, J., Herskovitz, J., et al., 2021. Diagnostics for SARS-CoV-2 infections. Nat. Mater. 20, 593–605.
Landauer, T.K., Dumais, S.T., 1997. A solution to Plato's problem: the latent semantic analysis theory of acquisition, induction, and representation of knowledge. Psychol. Rev. 104 (2), 211–240.
Levelt, W.J.M., 2008. Formal Grammars in Linguistics and Psycholinguistics: Volume 1: An Introduction to the Theory of Formal Languages and Automata, Volume 2: Applications in Linguistic Theory; Volume 3: Psycholinguistic Applications. John Benjamins Publishing.
Liu, S., Pan, C., 2020. Differentiating diagnosis of COVID-19 or influenza in patients based on laboratory data during flu season. EClinicalMedicine 26, 100511.
Mardian, Y., Kosasih, H., Karyana, M., Neal, A., Lau, C.Y., 2021. Review of current COVID-19 diagnostics and opportunities for further development. Front. Med. 8, 615099.
Medhat, W., Hassan, A., Korashy, H., 2014. Sentiment analysis algorithms and applications: a survey. Ain Shams Eng. J. 5 (4), 1093–1113.

Mikolov, T., Yih, W.-t., Zweig, G., 2013. Linguistic regularities in continuous space word representations. In: Proceedings of HLT-NAACL, pp. 746–751.
Mukhaiyar, U., Pasaribu, U., 2012. A new procedure for generalized STAR modeling using the IAcM approach. ITB J. Sci. 44, 179–192. https://doi.org/10.5614/itbj.sci.2012.44.2.7.
Muthusami, R., Bharathi, A., Saritha, K., 2020. COVID-19 outbreak: tweet-based analysis and visualization towards the influence of coronavirus in the world. Gedrag Organ. Rev. 33, 534–549.
Nurhayati, N., Pasaribu, U., Neswan, O., 2012. Application of generalized space-time autoregressive model on GDP data in West European countries. J. Prob. Stat., 1–16. https://doi.org/10.1155/2012/867056.
Pan, Y., Zhang, D., Yang, P., Poon, L.L.M., 2020. Viral load of SARS-CoV-2 in clinical samples. Lancet Infect. Dis. 20 (4), 411–412.
Ravi, K., Ravi, V., 2015. A survey on opinion mining and sentiment analysis: tasks, approaches and applications. Knowl.-Based Syst. 89, 14–46.
Read, J.M., Bridgen, J.R.E., Cummings, D.A.T., Ho, A., Jewell, C.P., 2020. Novel coronavirus 2019-nCoV: early estimation of epidemiological parameters and epidemic predictions. medRxiv 2020. https://doi.org/10.1101/2020.01.23.20018549, 20018549.
Rivers, C., Chretien, J.P., Riley, S., et al., 2019. Using "outbreak science" to strengthen the use of models during epidemics. Nat. Commun. 10, 3102.
Sanyaolu, A., Okorie, C., Marinkovic, A., Ayodele, O., Abbasi, A.F., Prakash, S., Ahmed, M., Kayode, D., Jaferi, U., Haider, N., 2020. Navigating the diagnostics of COVID-19. SN Compr. Clin. Med., 1–8.
Schwenk, H., 2012. Continuous space translation models for phrase-based statistical machine translation. In: COLING (Posters), pp. 1071–1080.
Sethi, M., Pandey, S., Trar, P., Soni, P., 2020. Sentiment Identification in COVID-19 Specific Tweets. pp. 509–516.
Van Loon, N., Verbrugghe, M., Cartuyvels, R., Ramaekers, D., 2021. Diagnosis of COVID-19 based on symptomatic analysis of hospital healthcare Workers in Belgium: observational study in a large Belgian tertiary care center during early COVID-19 outbreak. J. Occup. Environ. Med. 63 (1), 27–31.
Verma, P., Khanday, A., Rabani, S., Mir, M., Jamwal, S., 2019. Twitter sentiment analysis on Indian government project using R. Int. J Recent Technol. Eng. 8, 8338–8341. https://doi.org/10.35940/ijrte.C6612.098319.
Whiting, P., Singatullina, N., Rosser, J.H., 2015. Computed tomography of the chest: I. basic principles. Contin. Educ. Anaesth. Crit. Care Pain 15 (6), 299–304. https://doi.org/10.1093/bjaceaccp/mku063.
World Health Organization, 2019. https://www.who.int/. (Accessed 26 April 2021).
Wu, F., Zhao, S., Yu, B., et al., 2020a. A new coronavirus associated with human respiratory disease in China. Nature 579, 265–269.
Wu, J.T., Leung, K., Leung, G.M., 2020b. Nowcasting and forecasting the potential domestic and international spread of the 2019-nCoV outbreak originating in Wuhan, China: a modelling study. Lancet 395 (10225), 689–697. Epub 2020 Jan 31. Erratum in: lancet.
Xu, W., Liu, X., Gong, Y., 2003. Document Clustering Based On Non-negative Matrix Factorization. SIGIR Forum (ACM Special Interest Group on Information Retrieval), pp. 267–273, https://doi.org/10.1145/860435.860485.
Yang, Z., Zeng, Z., Wang, K., Wong, S.S., Liang, W., Zanin, M., Liu, P., Cao, X., Gao, Z., Mai, Z., Liang, J., Liu, X., Li, S., Li, Y., Ye, F., Guan, W., Yang, Y., Li, F., Luo, S., Xie, Y., Liu, B., Wang, Z., Zhang, S., Wang, Y., Zhong, N., He, J., 2020. Modified SEIR and AI prediction of the epidemics trend of COVID-19 in China under public health interventions. J. Thorac. Dis. 12 (3), 165–174.

Zhang, L., Wang, S., Liu, B., 2018. Deep learning for sentiment analysis: a survey. Wiley Interdiscip. Rev. Data Min. Knowl. Discov. 8 (4), e1253.

Further reading

Corman, V.M., Landt, O., Kaiser, M., Molenkamp, R., Meijer, A., Chu, D.K., Bleicker, T., Brünink, S., Schneider, J., Schmidt, M.L., Mulders, D.G., Haagmans, B.L., van der Veer, B., van den Brink, S., Wijsman, L., Goderski, G., Romette, J.L., Ellis, J., Zambon, M., Peiris, M., et al., 2020. Detection of 2019 novel coronavirus (2019-nCoV) by real-time RT-PCR. Euro. Surveill. 25 (3), 2000045.

Jelodar, H., Wang, Y., Yuan, C., et al., 2019. Latent Dirichlet allocation (LDA) and topic modeling: models, applications, a survey. Multimed. Tools Appl. 78, 15169–15211.

Loeffelholz, M.J., Tang, Y.W., 2020. Laboratory diagnosis of emerging human coronavirus infections – state of the art. Emerg. Microbes Infect. 9 (1), 747–756.

Mimno, D., Wallach, H.M., McCallum, A., 2008. Gibbs sampling for logistic normal topic models with graph-based priors. In: NIPS Workshop on Analyzing Graphs. vol. 61.

Prabhakar Kaila, D., Prasad, D.A., et al., 2020. Informational flow on twitter-corona virus outbreak-topic modelling approach. Int. J. Adv. Res. Eng. Technol. 11 (3), 128–134.

Streiner, D.L., Cairney, J., 2007. What's under the ROC? An introduction to receiver operating characteristics curves. Can. J. Psychiatr. 52 (2), 121–128.

CHAPTER THIRTEEN

Design of IoT-enabled, scalable mobile application for ASHA workers in COVID-19 data management

Joshi Manisha S.[a], Umadevi V.[b], Shankru Guggari[c], Ravi Kumar[b], Anusha Sonar[a], and Neha Sreedharala[a]
[a]Department of Medical Electronics Engineering, B.M.S. College of Engineering, Bengaluru, India
[b]Department of Computer Science and Engineering, B.M.S. College of Engineering, Bengaluru, India
[c]Machine Intelligence Research Labs, Auburn, WA, United States

1 Introduction

The infectious coronavirus has spread in the entire world. World Health Organization (WHO) has declared it as a pandemic. Its onset is in China at the end of 2019, and the number of active cases is increasing in the entire world (Cucinotta and Vanelli, 2020). In India, the first case of coronavirus pandemic was reported on 30 January, 2020 (Alansari et al., 2018). If tested positive for coronavirus, people were either advised for two weeks home quarantine or hospitalization depending on the severity. During this epi- demic, in rural and urban India, ASHA (Accredited Social Health Activists) workers are frontline warriors. The ASHA program is a key component of National Health Mission (NHM) of India, launched in 2006. The main objective of NHM is to improve the availability of quality health care for people, particularly, rural India with main focus on women and children (Masuda and Viswanathan, 2019). According to NHM guidelines, any woman in the age group of 25–45 years, educated up to eighth class and residing in the village can be selected as ASHA. After selection, ASHAs undergo formal training. Their job is to create health awareness, conduct immunization drives, and facilitate reproductive and child healthcare, and promoting other healthcare initiatives in their respective state. ASHAs receive performance based incentives for community level health interventions. There are around 10.61 lakh ASHAs across the country, who act as a

Lessons from COVID-19
https://doi.org/10.1016/B978-0-323-99878-9.00004-2

link between the community and the public health system (Rahul et al., 2021).

During COVID-19 epidemic, coronavirus disease was rapidly spreading in India. To control spread of the disease, community mass screening was indispensable. There was immediate necessity of capturing the data related to public health, resources available in hospitals and quarantine camps, contact tracing, information-sharing and further decision-making, etc., for prevention, management, treatment and follow-up of COVID-19.

As a part of NHM of India, ASHAs were trained to check the health parameters and conduct health surveys. Everyday ASHAs were going door to door to check fever, SpO_2 and conduct survey. If any health issues were noticed, ASHAs took the patient to the nearest health centres for further treatment. Each ASHA worker notes down the data about number of infected people in home quarantine, their contact tracing information. They also captured information on elderly people staying alone, existing ailments of people surveyed. Further, they also noted down health data of pregnant women. In doing this exercise, they were also collecting information about availability of beds, doctors, nurses, number of ventilators and oxygen cylinders in the hospital, data on quarantine camps, containment zones, etc. In survey field work, ASHA workers were able to cover average 30 houses, sometimes 40 in a day. They gave this collected information to authority in public health centres. Later, this collected data was passed on to Zonal Admin to take further actions and avoid spread of the disease.

After reading the published news related to field work of ASHA workers, we realized that the process was time-consuming and not well organized (Health and Department, 2020), Kulkarni (2021). If it becomes automated, ASHAs can give service to more people in their respective wards and surveys could be conducted swiftly. To address above-mentioned issues and make process efficient, we designed an IoT enabled mobile app to capture two vital parameters and facilitate fast data collection by ASHA. This will be helpful in COVID-19 data management to treat more infected patients with available resources in the hospitals.

The structure of the chapter is as follows: Related works are described in Section 2. Various application softwares are presented in Section 3. Proposed design model is introduced in Section 4. Description about the Android package kit is given in Section 5. Visualization of the proposed app, view of the details and softwares and services used to develop the application are explained in Sections 6, 7, and 8 respectively. Finally, concluding remarks are given in Section 9.

2 Related works

Technical papers enlisted here, rightly helpful in the development of our IoT-enabled medical system and a mobile app. Design of health monitoring system based on Internet of Things (IoT) has been presented in (Kannan et al., 2019). Sensors collect patients' body parameters such as temperature, motion, etc. This data was transferred to the microcontroller and further to cloud server. Medical history can be stored in the cloud for easy access and future analysis. Utility computing and wireless sensor networks for proof-of-concept design have been discussed (Rolim et al., 2010). Currently available mobile applications to address COVID-19 have been explained in (Noronha et al., 2020).

Low-cost, scalable, rapid, and effective device design for fever screening proposed in the studies of Kaplan et al. (2011) could be useful in many situations. The various features of COVID-19 mobile health applications were evaluated in (Ming et al., 2020). Authors have presented comparative analysis based on basic features on which various apps have been developed. The functionality of the apps was assessed according to information available on important parameters of COVID-19 useful for public and health authority. In (Singh et al., 2020), the applications IoT useful for health monitoring and hospital management system have been explored. The work proposed in (Xie et al., 2020) have focused on conditions related to difficulty in breathing and oxygenation provided as potential prognostic biomarkers. This study reported that oxygen saturation values greater than 90% are indicative of high likelihood of patient survival and such patients must receive maximum supportive care. Further, this study also mentioned, the patients with oxygen saturation values less than 90% and breathing difficulty despite oxygen supplementation, are at high mortality risk, may be more likely to benefit from investigational drugs and antibody drug therapy.

3 Application software developed by various other countries

In this section, we discuss various mobile Apps and websites developed towards coronavirus health monitoring which is useful for general public. Coronavirus health monitoring mobile Apps can be categorized as Symptoms Apps, Contact tracing Apps, Health monitoring Apps and prevalence Apps.

1. Coronavirus symptoms apps: The applications developed in this category will ask various questions to the users to check whether health symptoms are towards coronavirus disease. Accordingly, based on answers to queries, it guides users to see the doctor or not. The COVID Symptom Tracker, is an epidemiological research mobile application developed in the United Kingdom that runs on Android and iOS. It is a team work amongst Kings College London, Guys and St Thomas' Hospitals and ZOE Global Limited (ZOE, 2021). There are applications like Symptomate—Symptom Checker Infermedica (2021), Data4Life (Data4file, 2021) that deal only with COVID-19 symptoms questionnaires to assist people regarding what the symptoms mean and suggest them what next steps they should be taking.
2. Coronavirus Contact Tracing Apps: Asymptomatic carriers spread the virus and individuals are at potential risk of fatal infections. The globe grapples with the COVID-19 pandemic by deploying contact tracing applications to trace the movement of COVID-19-infected population (Chen et al., 2020). Many nations developed smartphone applications to trace contacts of infected people and infected areas. Based on this information, it is possible to identify infected zones region wise. This information is very useful to public and NGOs, and government to take necessary steps and precautions to fight against the corona virus. Digital contact tracing applications use mobile technologies like GPS, Bluetooth, and Quick Response (QR) codes for digital tracking and update users about their encounters with infected population. Compared to traditional contact tracking, this automated and digital technique provides government bodies a cost-effective and scalable solution (Amann et al., 2021).

   COVID-19 digital contact tracking applications are being developed by most of the nations. Asian nations with past SARS experience, particularly China and Singapore, were pioneers in deploying contact tracking applications and other digital disease surveillance technologies using well-developed digital infrastructures. Europeans with the Pan-European Privacy-Preserving Proximity Tracing (PEPP-PT) co-operative, is one of the earliest to build contact tracing apps. Austrian Red Cross was the first in Europe to develop "Stop Corona" digital contact-tracing App. Subsequently, Germany's "Corona-Warn-App" and Switzerland's "Swiss Covid-App" were created jointly by the two federal technical schools in Switzerland (Troncoso et al., 2020).

   The "GoCoronaGo" app (Rambha and Simmhan, 2021) developed by the professors of Indian Institute of Science, India, helps to find the people who have come in contact with COVID-19 positive public, using the GPS and Bluetooth technology. In the backend, temporal network analytics is being used for handling distant contacts. Maharashtra Government of India introduced MahaKavach App to Track Suspected COVID-19 Cases. This App helps public to contribute and help in tracing the contacts with potential risk of COVID-19, thereby helping Health officials (State innovation society, 2020). List of few contact tracing Apps developed by various countries is shown in Table 1. The source (Wikipedia, 2021) provides various COVID-19 Apps developed by other countries.

Few concerns that need to be addressed during the development phase of contact tracing applications are as follows (Akinbi et al., 2021):

- User data privacy concerns
- Lack of Trust
- Ethical issues
- Security vulnerabilities
- Technical constraints
- User behavior and participation

3. Coronavirus Health Monitoring Apps: 'Aarogya Setu' App developed by Government of India helps public to join essential health services, in the combined fight against COVID-19 (National Informatics Centre, 2021; Gupta et al., 2020). Indian Institute of Technology Bombay professors and students, from India, have developed 'Corontine' (Sukumar, 2021), a scalable platform, for the government bodies and private

Table 1 List of contact tracing Apps developed by various countries.

Country	Contact tracing Apps
Brazil	VirusMapBR
Canada	COVID Alert
China	Health Code
France	TousAntiCovid
Germany	Corona-Warn-App
India	Aarogya Setu
Italy	SM-COVID-19
Malaysia	SELangkah
Russia	Social Monitoring
United Kingdom	Protect Scotland
United States	PathCheck
New Zealand	NZ COVID

enterprises. The Geo-fencing feature incorporated herein helps the administrator to get alerts when a person having COVID-19 symptoms breaks the quarantine.

4. Coronavirus Prevalence Apps: This category of Apps give the user the updated news and health information on Coronavirus. The World Health Organization (WHO) dashboard provides the region wise data on amount of confirmed cases and deaths in various parts of the world Dashboard (2021).

4 Design of proposed IoT enabled device

We have developed an IoT enabled portable device and a mobile App for ASHA workers. It consisted of a non-contact Infrared sensor (MLX90614) and SpO_2 sensor (MAX30100) for measuring fever and SpO_2 respectively, during mass screening. These sensors were interfaced with node MCUESP32, using I2C communication. ESP32 was programmed to get digital values of the recorded vitals. These readings were displayed and stored on cloud platforms using its Wi-Fi module. Further, this device was interfaced with mobile App "ASHA BOT", to assist ASHA workers during the field work.

Fig. 1 shows the pictorial representation of IoT enabled device and a mobile app to aid ASHA workers during COVID-19 pandemic. During mass screening, when ASHA workers use this device, it captures revealed health parameters on ASHA Bot, in the respective fields and further data is stored on the sever. This server data is password protected by zonal officer who will be Admin for COVID-19 data management system.

5 Android package kit development

5.1 Design flow for the mobile app development

The mobile app starts with a Login page. The user has two options, either to login as Admin or as Asha worker. In either of the login options, the user has to provide the username and password. On successful login, the user is taken to the respective home page, Admin Home page or Asha Worker page. Fig. 2 shows the flow of operations during login.

Admin, on logging in, is provided with the following options: View Registered Asha worker, Patients Details, Hospital Details, Containment Zone Details, Quarantine camp data, ASHA Workers Details, Public

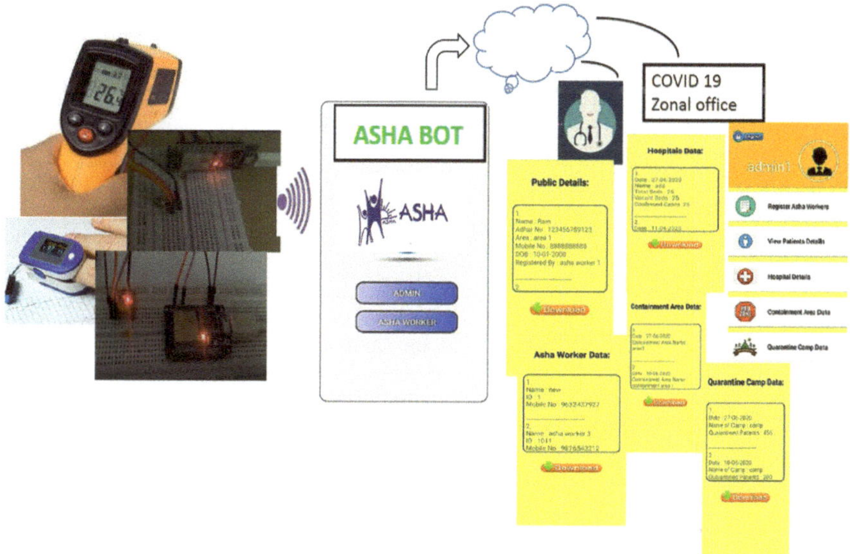

Fig. 1 Design of IoT enabled system and mobile app ASHA Bot for ASHA workers.

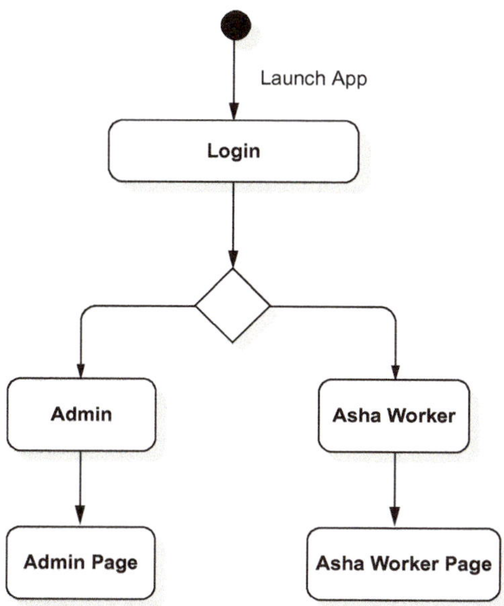

Fig. 2 Login process flow.

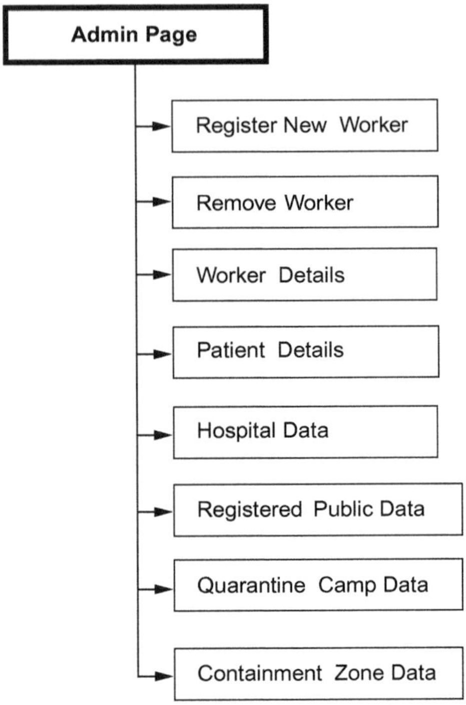

Fig. 3 Design of admin page.

Details. If ASHA worker is currently not on roll Admin can also Remove ASHA Worker. Fig. 3 illustrates various selections under Admin page.

Various handles provided for Asha worker include, Register public, Conduct Survey, Collect Hospital data, Collect Containment data and Collect quarantine camp data. Fig. 4 represents various entities provided to Asha worker on successful login.

5.2 Design of admin and ASHA worker page

This section describes various options provided to Admin. Admin is a zonal officer on duty during COVID-19 pandemic and has access to perceive the information's in various handles provided shown in Fig. 4. Admin will also register ASHA workers in his area for COVID-19 duty. ASHA worker logs in with her phone number and ID to use this application.

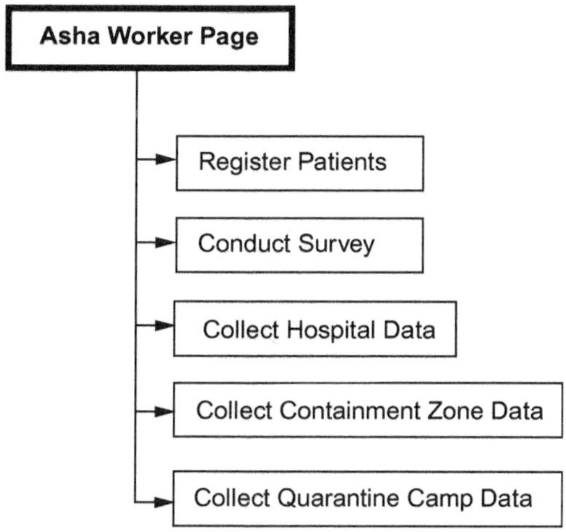

Fig. 4 Design of ASHA workers page.

5.2.1 Register ASHA worker

Under this handle, the Admin needs to enter all the details of new Asha Worker to register her. Upon valid entry of data, the worker gets registered. Fig. 5 shows the process of new Asha Worker registration.

5.2.2 View patients details

The Admin can view the health-related details of the public which were collected by the Asha Worker and apply various filters on the result.

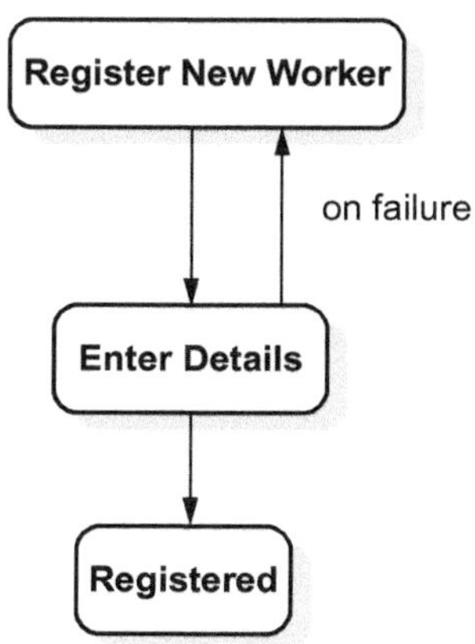

Fig. 5 Registering new Asha worker.

5.2.3 View hospital details

This option provides the options to view all the hospital details such as hospital name, number of beds available, number of test samples collected, number of positive test cases and the location of the hospital, which have been collected by the workers.

5.2.4 Containment zone details

All details related to containment zone such as name of the zone, its location and related images are provided under this option.

5.2.5 Quarantine camp data

Information related to quarantine camps such as name of the camp, number of patients quarantined, location and related images are available here.

5.2.6 View workers details

All the registered ASHA workers details such as name, mobile number and ID are available here.

5.2.7 View details of people who participated in door to door survey

The basic details about their name, date of birth, mobile number, address and ADHAR (Unique identification number given to public) number are available here.

5.2.8 Remove ASHA workers

The Admin has the choice to delete any ASHA worker account if she is not on the roll. Fig. 6 shows the steps in deleting an ASHA worker account.

5.3 Description of the various fields under ASHA worker page

This section introduces various stages which need to be performed under the ASHA worker page are as follows:

5.3.1 Register people during survey

This is a one-time process. The parameters include: Name, Mobile Number, Address, Age and Aadhar Number. Details are collected and stored. Fig. 7 shows the process of registering public.

5.3.2 Conduct survey

The health-related information of the community is collected here from time to time.

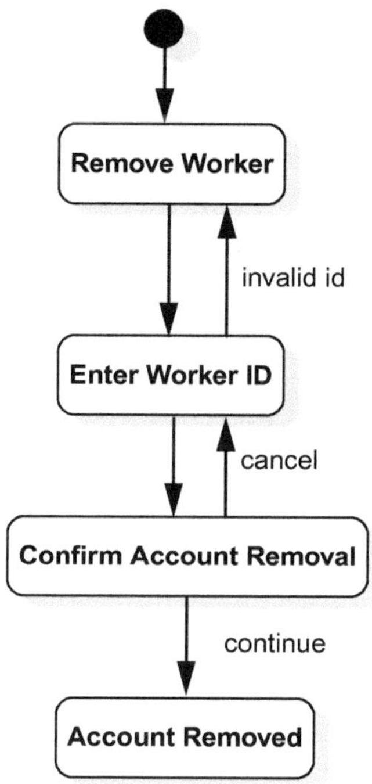

Fig. 6 Delete ASHA worker account.

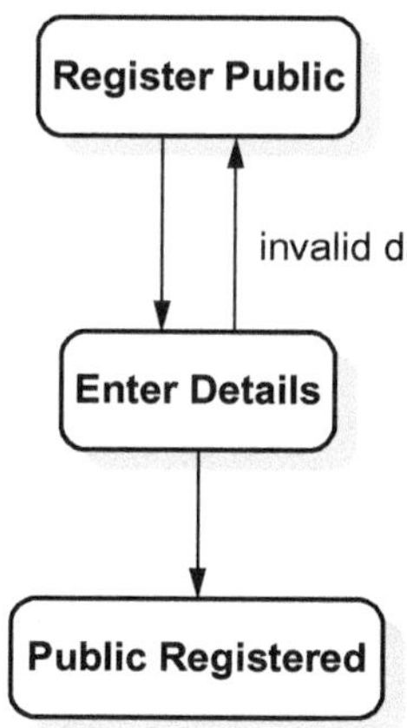

Fig. 7 Registering new subjects for survey.

- Step 1: Enter the Aadhar number (unique public ID) of subject/participant and click on load to fetch the details. If found not registered, then the subject is needed to be registered in "Register Public" option.
- Step 2: Enter the health-related data of the subject/participant.
- Step 3: Click on "Submit" to save the details.

Fig. 8 illustrates the steps involved in conducting survey.

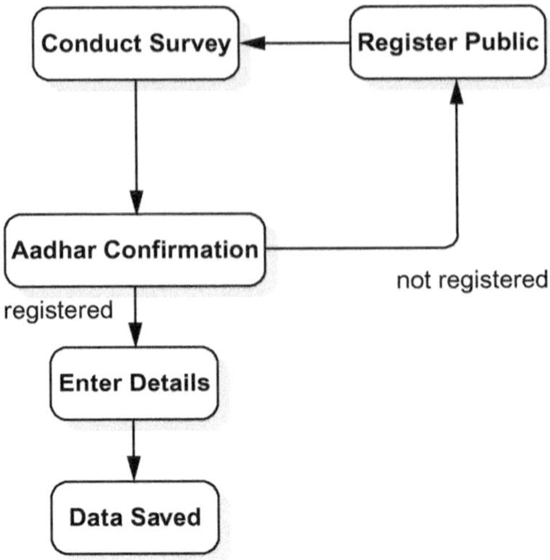

Fig. 8 Conduction of survey.

5.3.3 Hospital data

ASHA worker can also approach hospitals in the community to gather the data along with on-site pictures. In details of hospital ASHA collects data like: Name of the hospital, total beds available, vacant beds available, samples collected on date, samples tested, samples confirmed and images if necessary. At present, three images can be uploaded per hospital and can be increased as well. Fig. 9 illustrates the steps involved in collecting hospital details.

5.3.4 Containment zone data

Details such as name of the zone, its location and related images are collected here. Images from each containment zone can be uploaded. Fig. 10 illustrates various steps involved in collecting containment zone details.

Quarantine Camp Data: Under this handle, details such as name of the Quarantine Camp, number of patients quarantined, its location and related images are collected here. Images from containment zone can also be

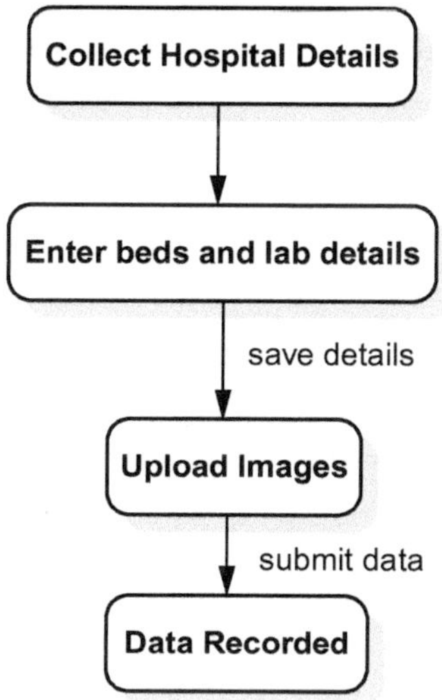

Fig. 9 Collecting hospital data.

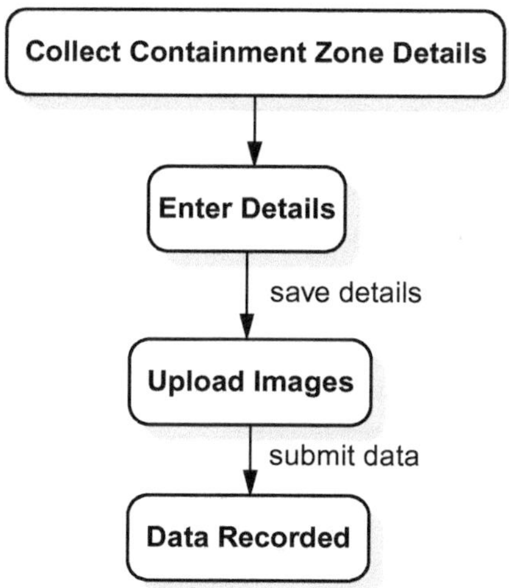

Fig. 10 Collect containment zone details.

uploaded. Figs. 11 and 12 illustrate various steps involved in collecting quarantine camp details.

Real time data storage: Data which are collected stored in real-time at two places, such as Google Firestore database and Google sheets. The authorized user has access to all the data.

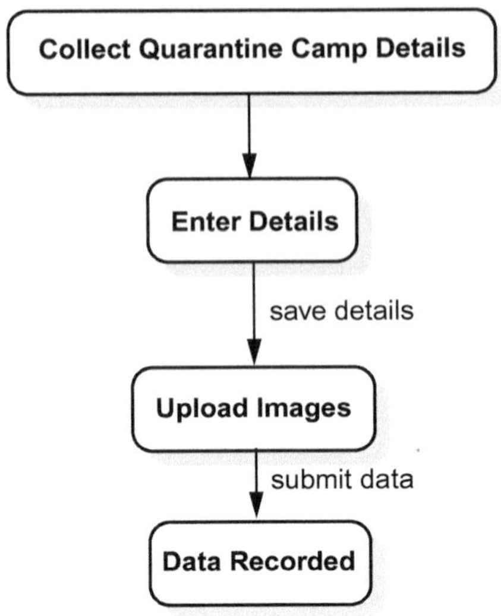

Fig. 11 Collecting Quarantine Camp details.

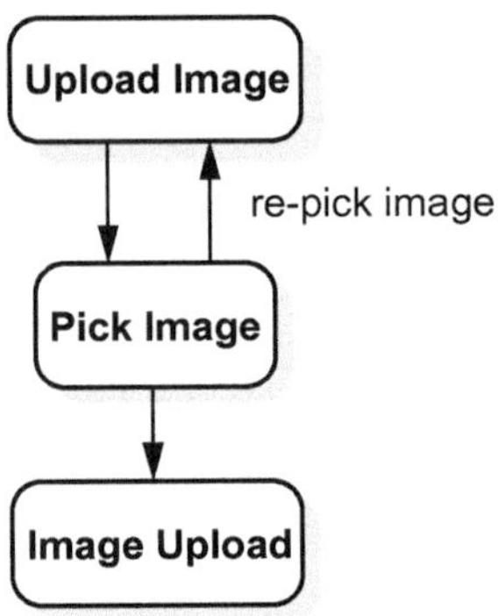

Fig. 12 Upload picture of the site.

6 Visualization of utility of the ASHA bot app

In this section, various entities of ASHA Bot mobile app are introduced. These sample results represent utility of the app and not the actual data collected.

6.1 Login page

Login the main page where the user needs to add her credentials like username and password as indicated in Fig. 13.

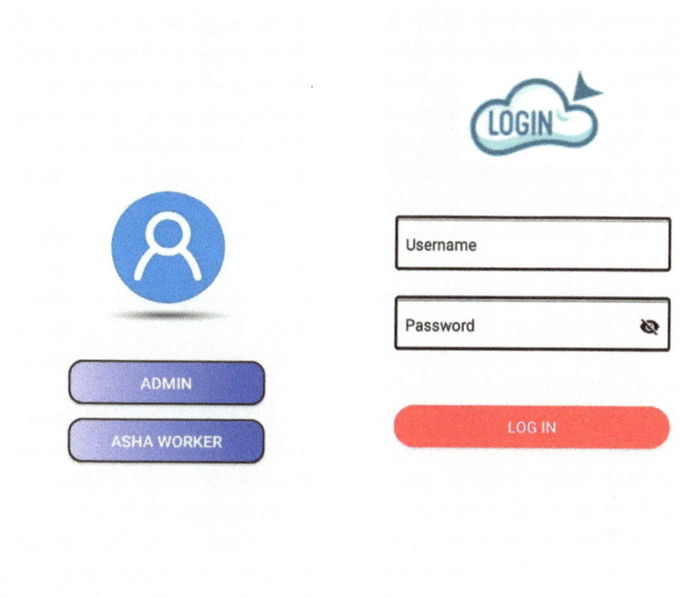

Fig. 13 Login page for Admin and ASHA worker.

6.2 Design of admin page

Explores attributes which are available in the admin page are discussed in detail.

6.2.1 Entities in admin home page

Various entities considered in the design of Admin page have been considered based on first hand from ASHA workers and information availed from the COVID-19 information portal for public Fig. 14.

6.2.2 Register ASHA worker

Fig. 15 shows registration of ASHA worker by Admin. ASHA worker unique ID, mobile number and name are all essential fields

7 View public details

Every day in door-to-door visit, before starting survey, ASHA logs in and after registration of public she captures temperature with non-contact method and SpO_2 level. This is represented in Fig. 16. Once registered,

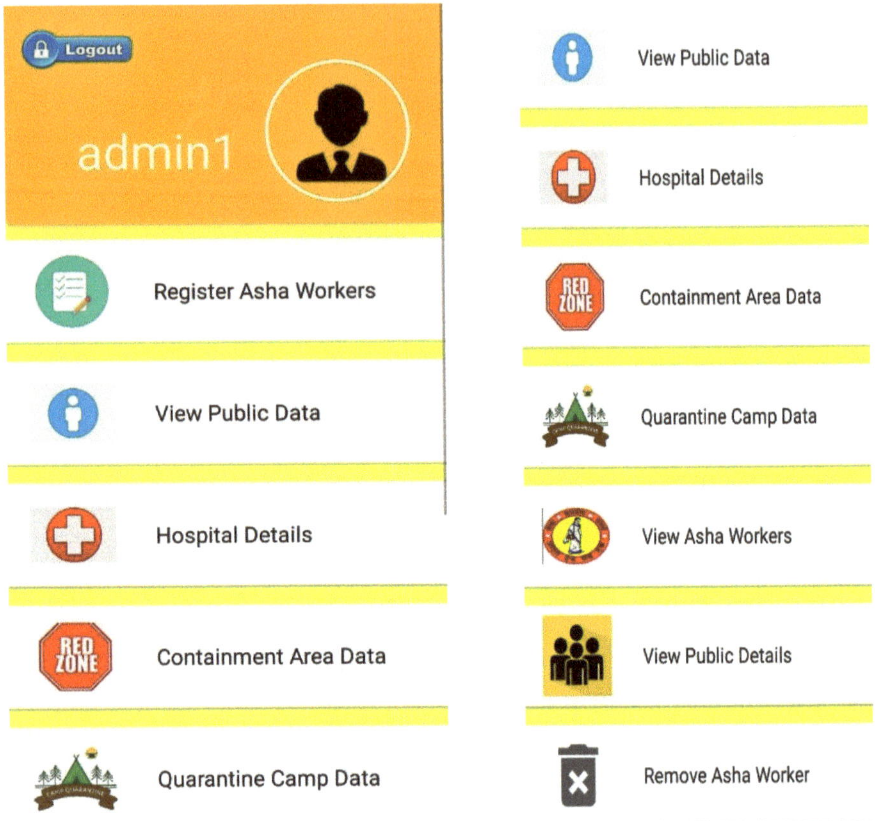

Fig. 14 Admin Home Page.

in the next visit based on previously entered details ASHA can continue with direct information collection.

In the statistics, longitude and latitude details are accessed which gives location of the public mobile number. Fig. 17 indicates various fields that would be useful in contact tracing operation and for analysis. During analysis details such as mobile number, AADHAR number (Identification number given by the Indian government for its citizen), Longitude and Latitude information help in contact tracing.

7.1 View hospital details

Figs. 18 and 19 indicate the data collected by ASHA from hospital and Admin can access it for the analysis. Various fields include Date, Name of Hospital, Number of beds available, Location of the Hospital and other Lab related data and link for the images captured on site.

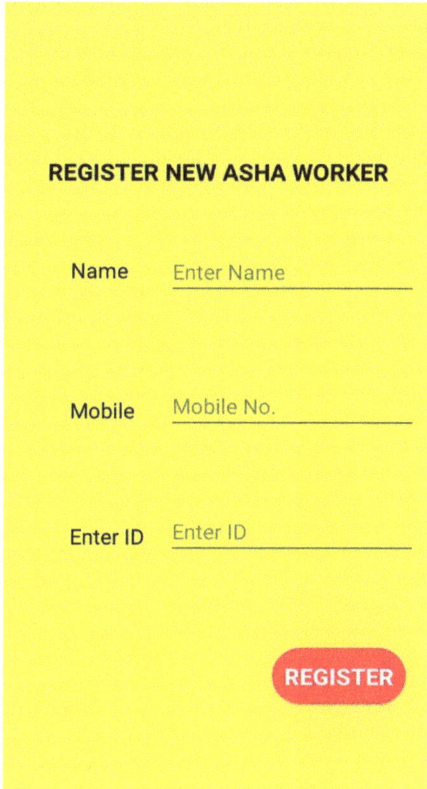

Fig. 15 Register Asha Worker.

Fig. 16 Sample of patient details.

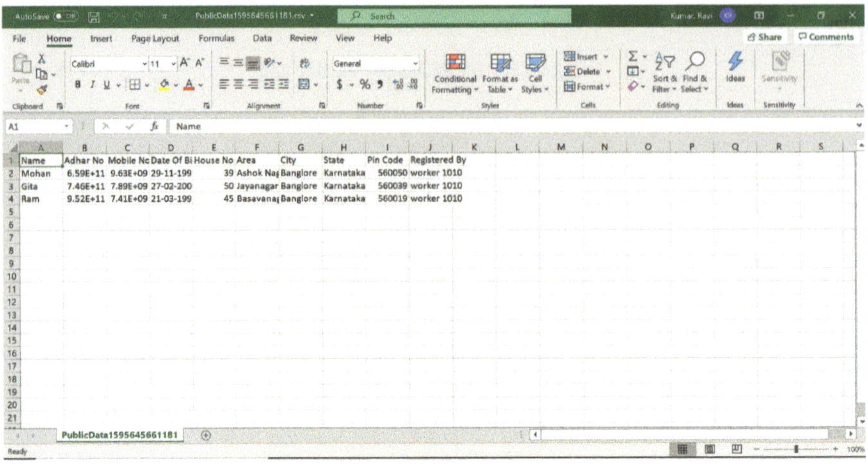

Fig. 17 Accessing public data for analysis.

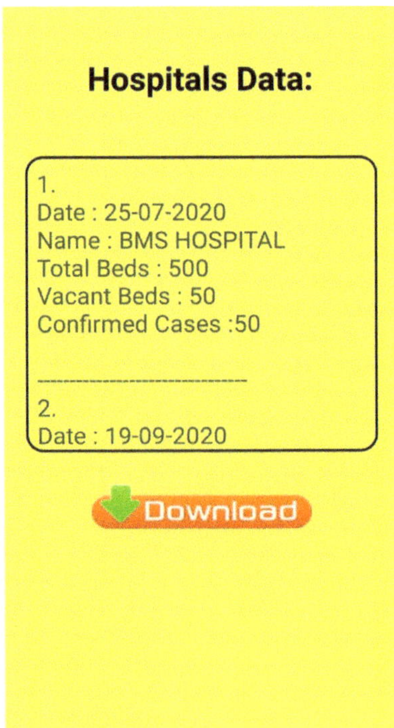

Fig. 18 Sample data collected from Hospital about vacant beds and confirmed cases in hospital.

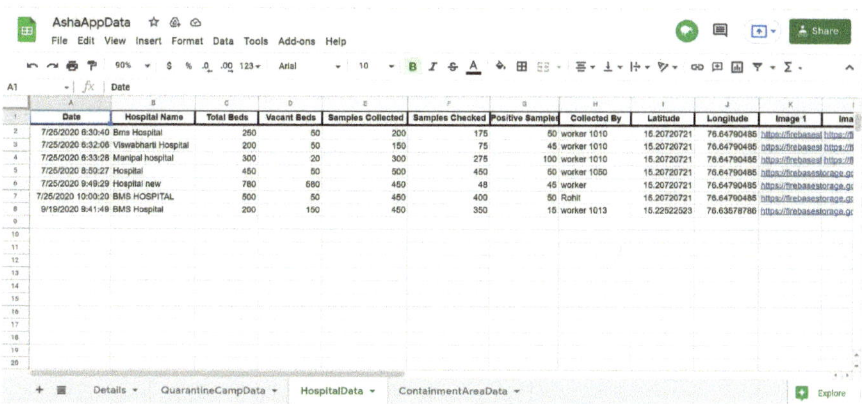

Fig. 19 Hospital data for analysis data downloaded by admin.

7.2 Containment zone details

Fig. 20 exemplifies the data collected by ASHA workers who are working in particular Ward and Containment Zone. This data can be accessed by Admin after down load depicted in Fig. 21. Various fields such as Date, Name and location of the Containment Zone and related images.

Fig. 20 Sample data of containment zone.

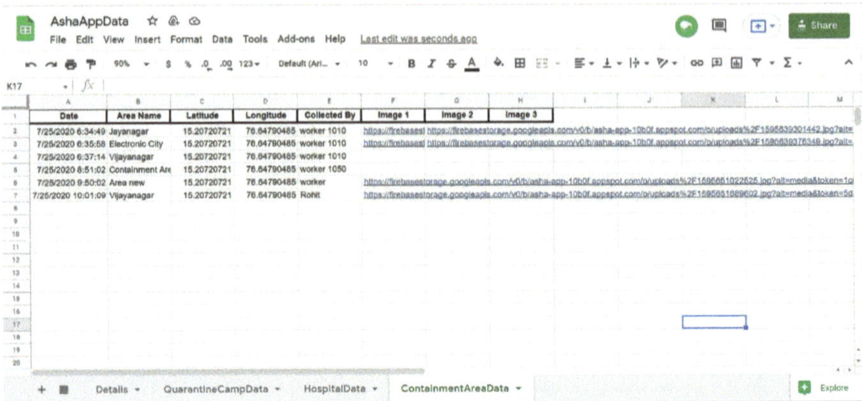

Fig. 21 Containment zone data for analysis.

7.3 Quarantine camp data

Fig. 22 shows statistics collected by ASHA at Quarantine Camp and pictorial representation of statistics available to Admin for further analysis. Fig. 23 shows various sub entities which include Date, Name of the Camp, Number of people quarantined, Location of the Quarantine Camp and supporting images.

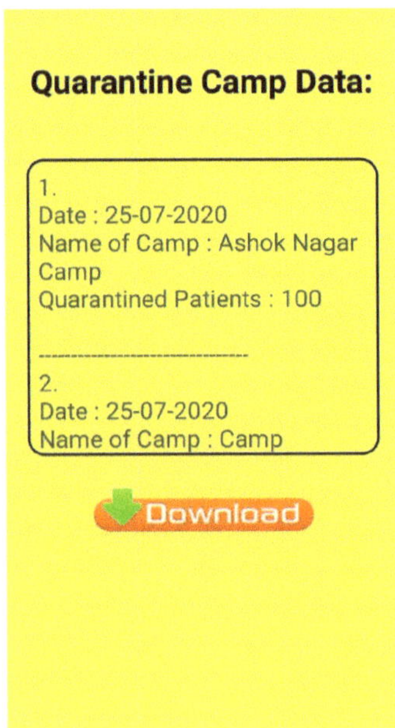

Fig. 22 Sample data on Quarantine camp.

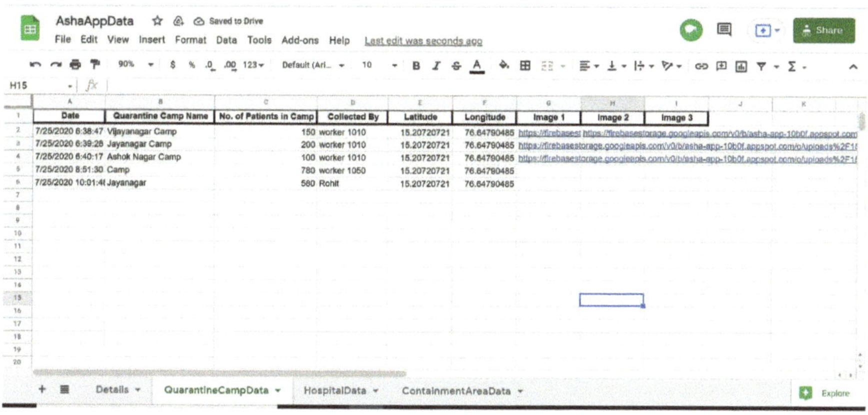

Fig. 23 Quarantine camp data for analysis.

7.4 Subpage to view ASHA worker details

Admin can track the number of ASHA workers currently on COVID-19 duty. Fig. 24 shows the page for Admin and statistics in Fig. 25.

7.5 View public details

Admin can get the details about the subjects in public survey and ASHA worker responsible for the task, shown in Figs. 26 and 27. Various entities

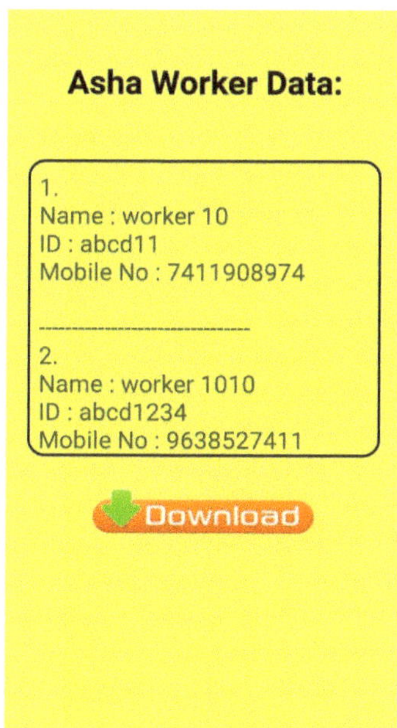

Fig. 24 Sample Registered ASHA worker details.

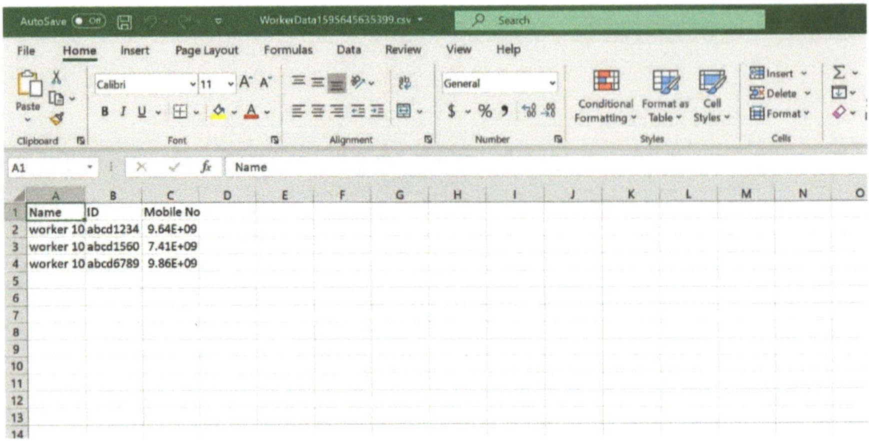

Fig. 25 ASHA worker statistics.

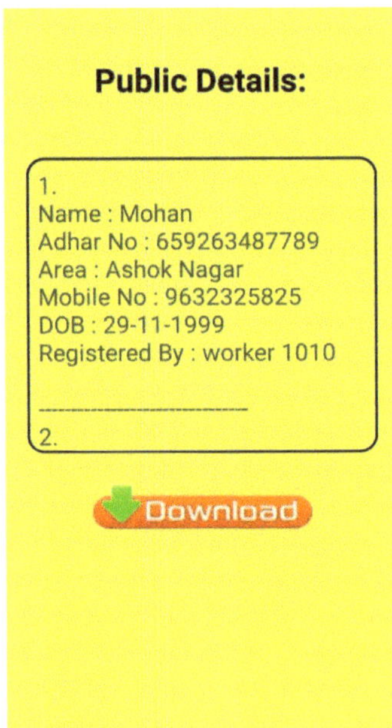

Fig. 26 Sample public details collected by ASHA.

include Name, ADHAR Number, and Mobile number, Date of Birth, House Number, Area, City, State and Pin Code of survey participants.

7.6 Remove ASHA workers

Admin can remove ASHA workers who are not on roll as indicated in Fig. 28.

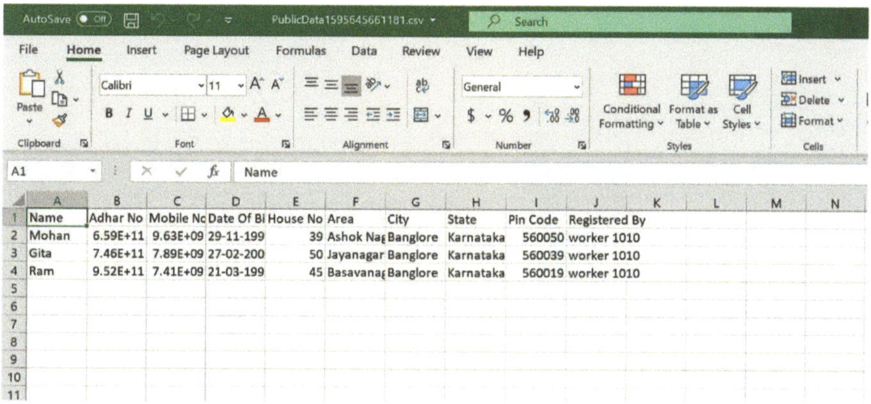

Fig. 27 Public details for analysis.

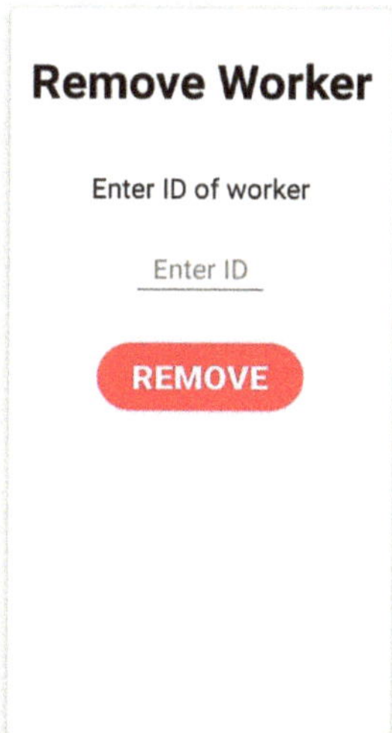

Fig. 28 Remove ASHA worker.

7.7 ASHA worker page

This is an important page for ASHA worker for their activity. The detailed explanation of the about these pages are as follows:

7.7.1 Home page

Fig. 29 represents various fields for which ASHA worker has to collect the data.

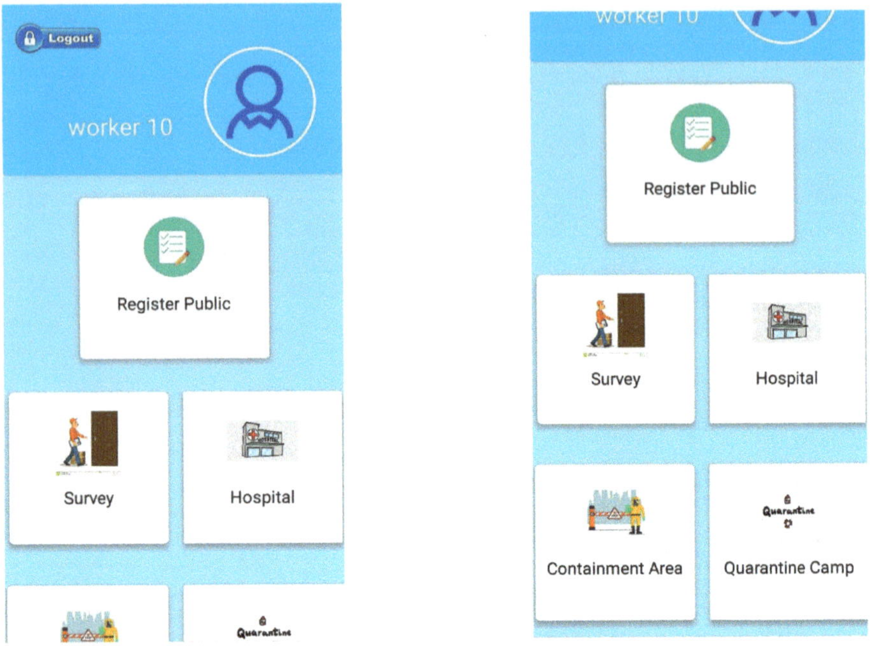

Fig. 29 ASHA worker home page.

7.7.2 Register subject

ASHA registers new subject for the survey. She need to enter the information in respective field. She will use the IoT enabled hand held device to capture body temperature and Spo2 level with click on load tab. This is exemplified in the Figs. 30 and 31.

7.7.3 Conducting survey

ASHA worker ask a few more polar questions of Yes/No type to a person so that she can enter the status. These questions are related to health alignment of organs like heart or kidney or COVID-19 cases in the family or their travel history. This is as indicated in Fig. 32.

ASHA worker needs to ask questions about indicators which are available on the page as indicated in Fig. 32.

7.7.4 Assemble hospital data

ASHA visits to hospitals lab to collect the spot pictures and data about number of beds available in the hospital, vacant beds, number of COVID swab samples collected, tested and how many samples are tested positive. ASHA enters figures in respective fields to get data on Hospital and Quarantine camps as represented in Figs. 33 and 34, respectively.

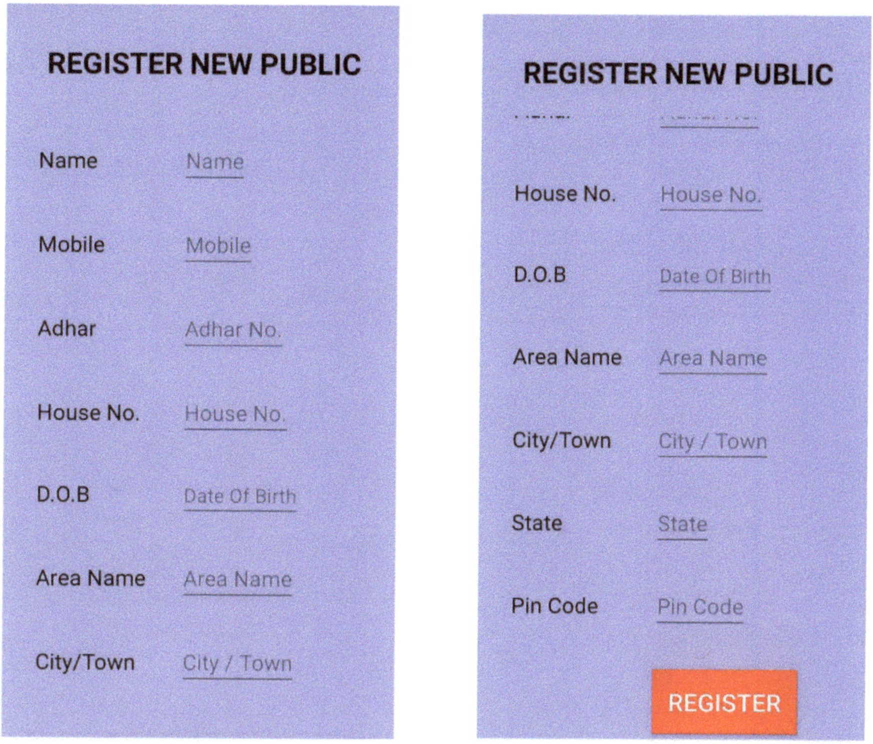

Fig. 30 Register Subjects.

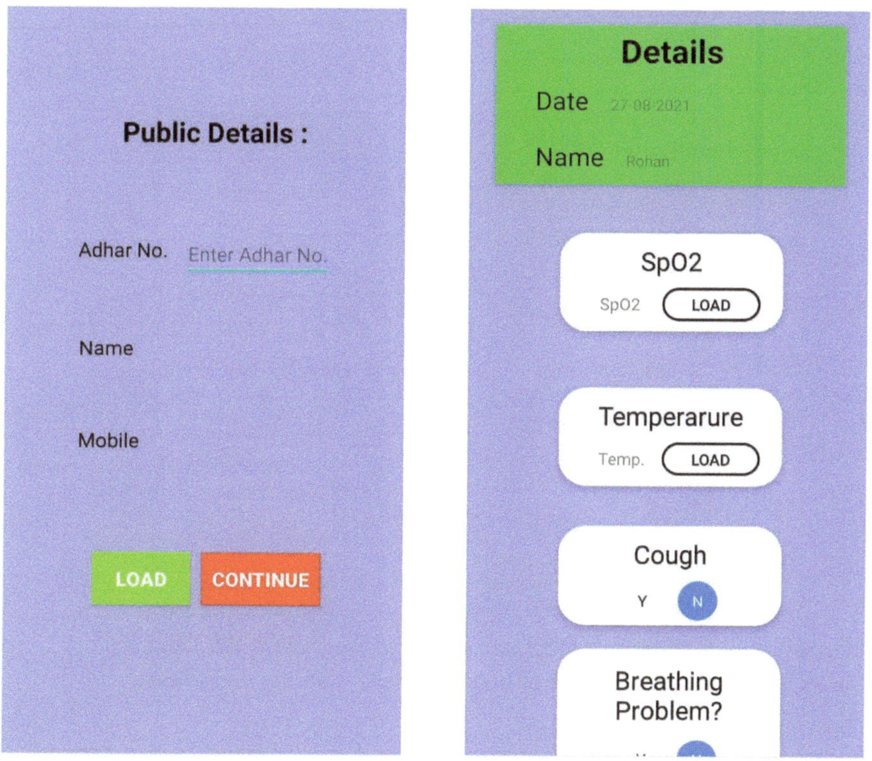

Fig. 31 ASHA worker registers a subject and captures body temperature and SpO_2.

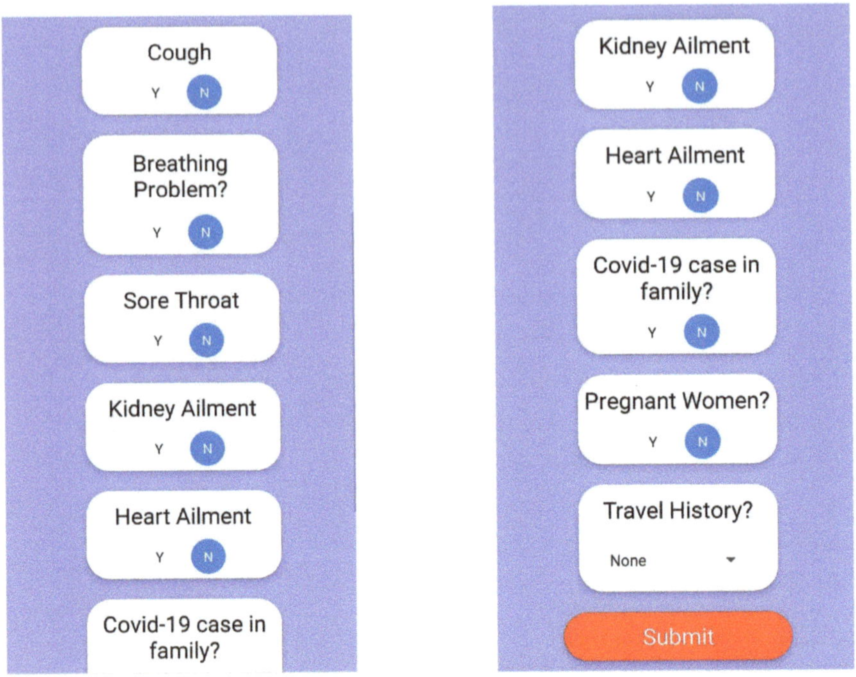

Fig. 32 Questionnaire with yes/no on health symptoms.

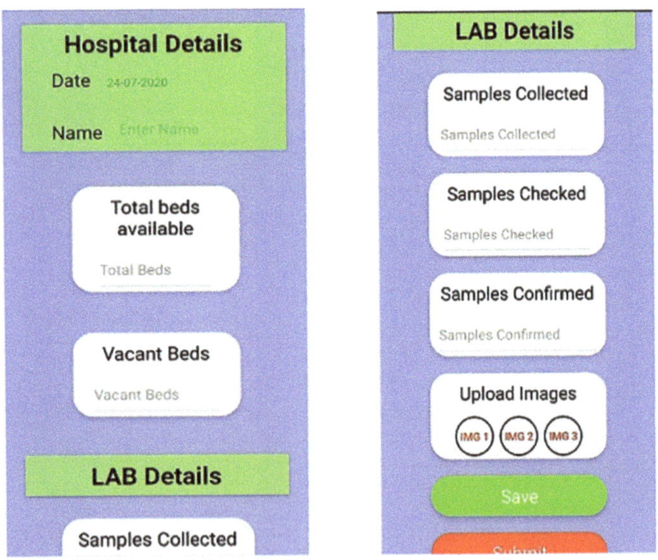

Fig. 33 Hospital data—number of bed availability, statistics on samples.

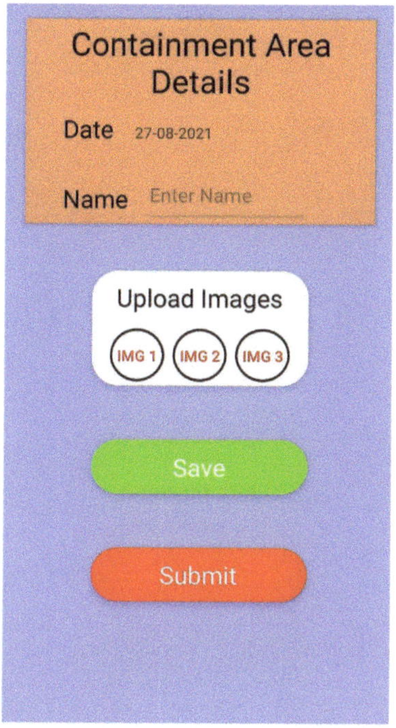

Fig. 34 Containment zone data.

7.7.5 Contentment zone data

ASHA worker visits to Containment Zones in their ward to get the latest statistics. She will do listing of contacts if person is found COVID-19 positive, along with their tracking, identification, quarantine follow up contacts. She will take live photos about supply of Essentials and medicines to the people in Containment Zone etc. This will give an idea to authority about how well the facility is reaching to the people as demonstrated in Fig. 34.

7.7.6 Quarantine camp data

During Covid 19 pandemic, in various wards Quarantine camps were formed for the people who are not COVID-19 positive but who are believed to have been exposed to the infection. Such people were kept separated and their movement was restricted for the purpose of preventing transmission of disease.

Persons were quarantined in their homes, and in community-based facilities. ASHA will visit quarantine camps, to collect the live pictures about the

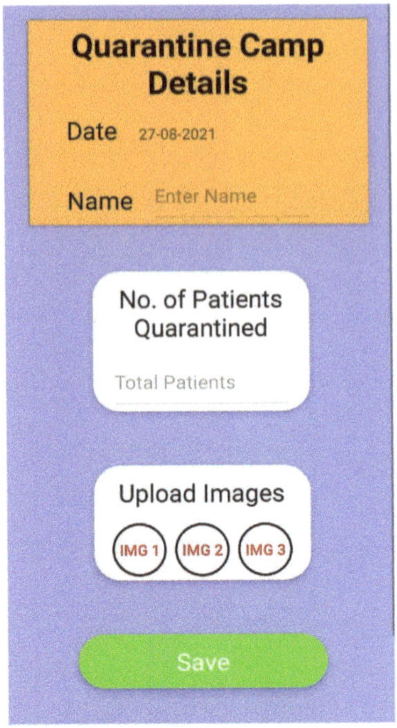

Fig. 35 Quarantine Camp Data and facility available.

physical infrastructure and functional Service requirement at quarantine facilities. Quarantine camp information is shown in Fig. 35.

8 Software and services used

Softwares used in the development of this mobile application are as follows:

- Android Studio: Android Studio has been used to develop the whole interface. The language chosen in Android Studio for this app development is Java.
- Google Firestore Database: Google Firestore database has been used to store data in real time.
- Google Sheets: Google sheets has been used to collect and store data in real time.
- Google Auth: Google Auth has been used for authentication purpose.
- Google Storage: Google Storage has been used to store media files.

App usage: Currently this device and app is in testing stage. Android application package (Apk) has been provided to authorities to download it and further give access to ASHA workers to test it on field.

9 Conclusions

In this chapter, we have explained and exemplified utility of our designed IoT enabled mobile app ASHA Bot, developed particularly for ASHA workers to collect on filed data and zonal officers can utilize this to realize day to day statistics of COVID-19. The proposed app is further scalable for other statistical needs. ASHA workers can use this application later with addition of necessary handles, as they primarily work as health workers for ladies and children.

Acknowledgment

The work presented here is funded by Visvesvaraya Technological University (VTU) under the scheme COVID-19 related innovative ideas and research, under TEQIP III. Authors are thankful to ASHA workers who gave valuable inputs during the development process. Authors are also thankful to physicians from B.M.S. Hospital trust for providing valuable suggestions.

Conflict of interest

The authors declare that there is no conflict of interests regarding the publication of this paper.

References

Akinbi, A., Forshaw, M., Blinkhorn, V., 2021. Contact tracing apps for the covid-19 pandemic: a systematic literature review of challenges and future directions for neo-liberal societies. Health Inf. Sci. Syst. 9 (1), 1–15.

Alansari, Z., Soomro, S., Belgaum, M.R., Shamshirband, S., 2018. The rise of internet of things (IoT) in big healthcare data: review and open research issues. In: Progress in Advanced Computing and Intelligent Engineering. Springer Singapore, Singapore, pp. 675–685.

Amann, J., Sleigh, J., Vayena, E., 2021. Digital contact-tracing during the covid-19 pandemic: an analysis of newspaper coverage in Germany, Austria, and Switzerland. PLoS One 16 (2), e0246524.

Chen, S., Yang, J., Yang, W., Wang, C., Barnighausen, T., 2020. Covid-19 control in China during mass population movements at new year. Lancet 395 (10226), 764–766.

Cucinotta, D., Vanelli, M., 2020. Who declares covid-19 a pandemic. Acta Biomed. 91 (1), 157.

Dashboard, W.H.E., 2021. Who Coronavirus (Covid-19) Dashboard. https://covid19.who.int/.

Data4file, 2021. Coronavirus: Track your Symptoms with the data4life App. https://www.data4life.care/en/data4life-app/.

Gupta, R., Bedi, M., Goyal, P., Wadhera, S., Verma, V., 2020. Analysis of covid-19 tracking tool in India: case study of aarogya setu mobile application. Digit. Gov. Res. Pract. 1 (4), 1–8.

Health and Department, F. W, 2020. Asha Worker—Covid-19 Information Portal. https://covid19.karnataka.gov.in/page/Capacity+Building/Health/ASHA+WORKER/en.

Infermedica, 2021. Symptomate. https://symptomate.com/.

Kannan, P., Nandhini, S., Nasrine, J., Naveena, V.R., 2019. Implementation of cloud based health care monitoring system using IoT. Int. Res. J. Eng. Technol. 6 (3), 3979.

Kaplan, R.B., Johnson, T.M., Schneider, R.O., Krishnan, S.M., 2011. A design for low cost and scalable non-contact fever screening system. In: 2011 ASEE Annual Conference & Exposition, pp. 22–34.

Kulkarni, T., 2021. Asha Workers in Karnataka Spend Hours Tracing Covid-19 Contacts Daily. https://www.thehindu.com/news/cities/bangalore/they-go-where-others-fear-to-tread/article31428115.ece.

Masuda, Y., Viswanathan, M., 2019. Future Direction—Open Healthcare Platform 2030 and IoT Healthcare Platform. Springer Singapore, Singapore, pp. 147–151.

Ming, L.C., Untong, N., Aliudin, N.A., Osili, N., Kifli, N., Tan, C.S., Goh, K.W., Ng, P. W., Al- Worafi, Y.M., Lee, K.S., et al., 2020. Mobile health apps on covid-19 launched in the early days of the pandemic: content analysis and review. JMIR mHealth uHealth 8 (9), e19796.

National Informatics Centre, G. o. I, 2021. Aarogyasetu app. https://www.mygov.in/aarogya-setu-app/.

Noronha, N., D'Elia, A., Coletta, G., Wagner, N., Archer, N., Navarro, T., Lokker, C., 2020. Mobile Applications for Covid-19: A Scoping Review.

Rahul, P., Chander, K.R., Murugesan, M., Anjappa, A.A., Parthasarathy, R., Manjunatha, N., Kumar, C.N., Math, S.B., 2021. Accredited social health activist (asha) and her role in district mental health program: learnings from the covid 19 pandemic. Community Ment. Health J. 57 (3), 442–445.

Rambha, T., Simmhan, Y., 2021. Gocoronago—Contact Tracing App and Network Analytics. https://covid19.iisc.ac.in/gocoronago-contact-tracing-app-and-network-analytics/.

Rolim, C.O., Koch, F.L., Westphall, C.B., Werner, J., Fracalossi, A., Salvador, G.S., 2010. A cloud computing solution for patient's data collection in health care institutions. In: 2010 Second International Conference on eHealth, Telemedicine, and Social Medicine. IEEE, pp. 95–99.

Singh, R.P., Javaid, M., Haleem, A., Suman, R., 2020. Internet of things (IoT) applications to fight against covid-19 pandemic. Diabetes Metab. Syndr. Clin. Res. Rev. 14 (4), 521–524.

State innovation society, M, 2020. Mahakavach. https://www.indiascienceandtechnology.gov.in/hi/technologies/mahakavach?field$_a$rea$_i$d=2457.

Sukumar, R., 2021. Coronavirus: Iit bombay's 'Corontine' App to Track the Quarantined. https://news.careers360.com/coronovirus-iit-bombays-corontine-app-track-quarantined.

Troncoso, C., Payer, M., Hubaux, J.-P., Salath'e, M., Larus, J., Bugnion, E., Lueks, W., Stadler, T., Pyrgelis, A., Antonioli, D., et al., 2020. Decentralized Privacy-Preserving Proximity Tracing. arXiv preprint arXiv:2005.12273.

Wikipedia, 2021. Covid-19 Apps. https://en.wikipedia.org/wiki/COVID-19$_a$pps.

Xie, J., Covassin, N., Fan, Z., Singh, P., Gao, W., Li, G., Kara, T., Somers, V.K., 2020. Association between hypoxemia and mortality in patients with covid-19. In: Mayo Clinic Proceedings. vol. 95. Elsevier, pp. 1138–1147.

ZOE, 2021. Zoe Covid Study. https://covid.joinzoe.com/.

CHAPTER FOURTEEN

Reflecting on the impact of COVID-19 on healthcare and IT sector with special emphasis on India: A collection of multifarious cases with few empirical evidences

Samuel S. Mitra, Peter A. Arockiam, Joseph Kulandai, Milton Costa, and Ruby Mary Notts
St. Xavier's College (Autonomous), Kolkata, West Bengal, India

1. Introduction

The ever-growing concern to curtail the blood-thirsty pandemic of COVID-19 has been strongly felt since the death rates started to surge worldwide. After claiming several lives across countries, doctors, scientists and other potential hotshots are relentlessly mulling over strategies to unshackle the world from the hovering shadow of the deadly disease. The adverse effects triggered by COVID-19 are unprecedented and rather uncanny. Jettisoning the global deaths, the pandemic itself has given a lot of headache in terms of plummeting economy, derailing employments, creating personal stresses and blighting several other dimensions of life. Truth to be told, the impact left by COVID-19 will be strongly felt even after its ultimate exit. In spite of a plethora of measures has been taken to neutralize the adverse effects of COVID-19, still the impact has overshadowed and overpowered the measures as the think-tank of scientists, doctors and potential stakeholders still seems befuddled of unshackling the world from the global pandemic and its ill effects. Although the impact of COVID-19 has been thwarted across several dimensions of the economy, the healthcare and technology sectors have witnessed wholesome metamorphosis in its very nature, let alone, functioning. In fact, these two sectors have also been lauded for its impeccable role in shaping up appropriate measures to blunt the adverse

Lessons from COVID-19
https://doi.org/10.1016/B978-0-323-99878-9.00007-8

effects of COVID-19 by myriad head-turning innovations in spite of being severely affected by the deadly virus. This is the very essence of the present case where the objective of lies in discussing the effects of COVID-19 on various subsectors of such two major sectors as well as highlighting the several changes experienced by the subsectors.

Although this has been a much talked about topic which has garnered prodigious attention and intrigue in the past few years, there lay several myths regarding the characteristic of the virus itself, let alone, its aftermath. In this light, it is imperative to discuss about the present issues at hand for greater awareness among the masses.

The current case probes into how the different subsectors within the two major sectors of healthcare and technology has been affected by COVID-19. The case is a pioneering effort attempted at deliberating upon such impact in India.

The cascading impact generated by COVID-19 has been felt at every corners of the world. The disease is making broad headlines every day, especially in India and is still claiming numerous lives. The impact of COVID-19 has been enormous in all sectors of the economy in India. But, there is a need to first and foremost reflect on the impact upon healthcare systems and information technology. The reason behind this is that since the virus is a menacing pandemic, its first effect would be on the health of an individual and since the pandemic has compelled government of all countries to enforce lockdowns, the only solace during these testing times lies in the development and innovation of various technologies which can help people out of this despairing hole and keeping the society running and upbeat which otherwise would have come to a complete standstill.

Before getting headway with the principal aspects of the case, it is important to establish the rationale behind undertaking such a case study in India. India is considered to be one of the leading nations of the world and the aura swirling the sacrosanct nation gives the country an enamoring identity and a competitive edge. In a developing country, where hunger and poverty, under-developments and employment crisis has long been a persistent issue to deal with, the outbreak of COVID-19 in the country has given the nation yet another headache. India has been reeling under pressure from the large scale impacts triggered by COVID-19, whether be it, death cases, shrinking economy, poverty and hunger hitting rock bottom, etc. In this context, it is also admirable to think upon the fact that India in spite of a mammoth 130 billion population is managing COVID-19 with aplomb and the some of its technological innovations during this time of pandemic has been head turning (Wikipedia, 2021a,b,c). To further reflect upon such issues, the present case is a pioneering effort to reflect upon the impact left by COVID-19 on the two major sectors of India which are healthcare and technology. To serve this purpose, a random choice of eighteen subtopics has been made, ten from healthcare sector and eight from the IT sector. Each subtopic consists of a moderately long description of the present scenario and concludes stating the current situations, challenges, adverse effects and benefits.

1.1 Impact of COVID-19 on Healthcare Sector

- ***History of COVID-19***

Covid-19 novel Coronavirus is a global pandemic first identified in Wuhan region of China around November 2019 (Liu, et al., 2020). Since its first emergence in China, it later spread to all other countries of the world and by the middle of March' 2020, it was declared as a pandemic by the "World Health Organization" (WHO). Before being declared as a global pandemic, it initially came into existence as an epidemic which was first noticed in mainland China (Bhargava, 2021). Although the emergence of Coronavirus remains a confidential topic of discussion, the topic has gathered a lot of steam in recent times. China's continuous denial of the fact that the virus did not originate from their laboratories or "Huanan South China Seafood Market" and the other few countries persistently accusing China for the origination and spread of virus has created a gargantuan controversy. COVID-19 novel Coronavirus (SARS-CoV-2) is deemed as the next big pandemic after the 100 year old pandemic "Spanish Flu" (Influenza) during the period 1918–1920 (Chaplin, 2020). The virus is like a flu which is highly contagious and blood-thirsty as witnessed by the overall deaths of people all across the world and the existence of active cases globally.

Initially the virus was said to spread by droplets of saliva or discharge out of the nose of a person who is already infected through cough or sneeze. After some time, it was observed that even without cough or sneeze, the virus was spreading from person to person via close contact which made the virus deemed highly contagious. Most people contaminated by the virus will observe mild to moderate respiratory illness in themselves and would not be able to recover with special treatment. Coronavirus is particularly dangerous for those children who fall under the age of 14 years and elderly people above 55 years of age. People who already have medical and health issues like diabetes, cardio syndromes and respiratory problems are prone to develop more serious effects by the disease which also makes them vulnerable to death. COVID-19 has wreaked havoc ever since its outbreak disrupting economies of all countries and halting the lives and physical as well as mental health of people. One of the striking revelations of COVID-19 has been the myths and facts that has surrounded the disease and generated mixed perceptions among people. One such strong myth was the initial perception of several people who shared a common thought that the disease could be destroyed in hot and humid conditions unlike the cold conditions in which the virus was unstoppable, a manifestation of the people of European and American countries which have a cold climate where several people lost their lives unlike the South Asian countries which have a rather hot and humid climate where the death rates has been low and recovery rate high. However, this perception did not hold true as time passed by, even the people in South Asian countries, particularly, in India, Pakistan and Indonesia fell prey to the virus and thereafter the juggernaut of the disease has been unstoppable.

To curtail the menacing blood-thirsty pandemic of COVID-19, the government of each and every country enforced lockdowns. As a result, it became mandatory that the people would strictly follow certain protocols of COVID-19 and norms of social distancing. Some precautionary measures included wearing of face masks, use of hand-sanitizers, maintaining a safe distance of 2 m or more from each other, restricted gatherings and many more. After the lockdowns were lifted up and the government of all countries slowly relaxed the COVID-19 protocols by allowing gatherings in public places, there has been a rather passive attitude displayed among the people regarding adhering to precautionary measures. Slowly the spread of the virus started picking up pace and cases escalated again, with few countries going into a re-lockdown mode. This is the same case with India after losing close to 3 lakh people.

- ***Problems and challenges in manufacturing and supplying vaccines for COVID-19***

Ever since the potential outbreak of COVID-19 novel Coronavirus, the scientists, doctors and other associated medical experts have been mulling over manufacturing appropriate vaccines to blunt and fight the blood thirsty disease and ultimately help the world to get rid of the deadly virus. However, there has been a stiff challenge in the process of identification of COVID-19 vaccines as several problems and challenges have come to the surface. In the backdrop of the current bedlam, there has been a monumental rise in the interest around manufacturing and distribution of effective vaccines for COVID-19. Although few vaccines have been developed, its overall impact and effectiveness still remains a myth to many. While some people have lauded over its effectiveness while the others have been wary of taking it, as they see it as a potential threat to their immune system.

Several first generation vaccines need "ultra-cold chain" technology and are quite expensive, thereby posing hurdles to global vaccination campaign and in countries that have low and middle level income generation, access to such vaccines remains a big question mark coupled with uncertainty of the effectiveness of vaccines in people of such country. Also, the upsurge in new variants continues to pose major concern over mutating effect. This calls on the part of the government to consistently develop new vaccines and look after the safety, efficacy and quality aspects. Four primary challenges explored in this context are the maintenance of strong "research and development" incentives, conducting "coordinated clinical trials," efficient and transparent authorization of "safe and effective vaccines" and continuous monitoring their impacts (Santos, 2020).

One of the biggest challenge for any government of a country is the proper development, authorization and distribution of COVID-19 vaccines not only in their native country but also to other countries, which implies that COVID-19 vaccines need to be developed continuously, supplied and disseminated across the globe and successfully deployed within the country (Forman et al., 2021). In this light, a major headache lies with the Government of India, to manufacture and distribute as many as 130 billion COVID-19 vaccines taking into consideration its mammoth population which ranks second in the world after China. In this context, it is expected that the government scales up manufacturing capacities and reduce and eliminate hindrances to meet the quantity and timeline of delivery. This calls for large scale faster production of vaccines and efficient supply chain to foster the process. In India, the manufacturing and daily dosage has been slow but is expected to gradually pick up the pace as the laboratories together with its scientists, medical experts and doctors brace up for an excruciating challenge. In India, currently two types of COVID-19 vaccines are being used which are "Covaxin" and "Covishield." India has also line up for Russia's "Sputnik V" which is expected to help its cause in giving large scale doses to its people and on 1st May' 2021, 1.5 lakh doses of "Sputnik V" has already arrived in India (Kumar, 2021).

- ***Changes of legislation on clinical trials and re-purposing of licensed drugs for the treatment of COVID-19***

The clinical trial research has been severely affected by COVID-19 pandemic in safe and effective manner. This holds true by looking that trials frequently deal with populations who are vulnerable to risk of COVID-19. In this light, thousands of trials have already been suspended or completely stopped due to hardships faced during COVID-19 lockdowns. The method of clinical trials is regarded as a premier method for testing and validation of new drugs and therapies. Based on successful trials, new drugs are said to be approved. In fact, it is extremely daunting to look at the number of people involved in a clinical trial. In this context, few adjustments have been made to clinical trials which have simplified the very process and are expected to benefit COVID-19-affected patients in the long haul. Some of the adjustments include the utilization of remote consents, conducting visits of telehealth study and shipment of oral study treatment to the house of the affected patients (Awasthi, 2020). According to the survey of "The University of Texas Southwestern Medical Center" (UTSW), the professionals of clinical research found that the coordinators, managers and nurses of clinical trials experienced positive feelings. Similarly, 90% of respondents witnessed changes which had a positive impact on the safety, treatment procedures and experience of staff and patients. The staff and patients also supported positive COVID-19 clinical research adjustments in the postpandemic era.

There has been much hype and anticipation in the identification of drugs which potentially could be repurposed to wield and cure COVID-19. Drug repurposing refers to a process "by which new therapeutic uses for existing drugs are identified" (Knight, 2021). The process is also referred to as "Repositioning" or "Re-profiling." Currently, there are two categories of drugs that are being investigated for the purpose of repurposing which are drugs that have the capacity to inhibit the Coronavirus lifecycle and drugs that have the ability to blunt the impact of COVID-19 infection (Balfour, 2020). The first category of drugs are antivirals and currently only one such antiviral has been in use for the treatment of COVID-19 and has been proven effective in faster recovery time from COVID-19-affected patients as observed. The name of the antiviral drug is "Remdesivir" which was first developed in the year 2009 to cure Hepatitis C.

Apart from this, a study revealed a panel of 100 molecules having 21 existing drugs which were effective in blunting COVID-19. Two such have already been approved by the US "Food and Drug Administration" (FDA), "Astemizole" and "Clofazimine," which were initially licensed for the treatment of allergies and leprosy. Four of such are working with "Remdesivir" which also includes "Tetrandrine" which was initially licensed for the treatment of malaria. Thirteen of such has been clinically tested and show favorable ability in fighting COVID-19. The second category of are those which have the ability to blunt the effects of COVID-19 infection. One such category of drugs includes "Glucocorticoids" which is a very powerful antiinflammatory drug that inhibits the generation and existence of T cells and macrophages. However, its benefit in counteracting COVID-19 has come under the scanner as a meta-analysis revealed that it might be detrimental to nonsevere patients, increasing mortality and delay of viral clearance. However, "Drug Safety Research Unit" has opined that the repurposed drug for COVID-19 still needs to undergo a lot of testing to prove its safety and effectiveness. The reviews from their team provided with an overview of the 50 drugs that could inhibit one or more than one steps of the COVID-19 lifecycle and many more that could counteract the deadly infection of COVID-19.

- ***Effects of COVID-19 on primary health care***

Primary Health Care forms the backbone of essentials health catering globally as it meets over 80% of the health needs of an individual. It plays a pivotal role in tracking responses to the identification and triaging cases of COVID-19, diagnosis, helps people cope up with anxiety and reduces demand services of hospitals. During the initial outbreak of the pandemic, WHO emphasized on the role and significance of primary health care and provided interim guidelines for appropriate response by primary health care to COVID-19. The guidelines consisted of 6 principles which are deliverance of necessary health services, identification and management of potential COVID-19 cases, averting the risk of spread of infection, ameliorating existing surveillance, strengthen risk communication and engagement of community and provisions related to services of COVID-19.

The providers and facilities of primary health care play an instrumental role in the tough tussle with COVID-19. The cognizance of the GOI along with the governments of various states has been witnessed and they have responded by issuing necessary guidelines to manage both COVID-19 as well as other health cases (Kumar and Kumar, 2021). Such guidelines are in complete parlance with that issued by the WHO. Such guidelines provide a transparent direction to the apparatus of entire primary health care service. Largely because of this, several health care systems have been able to display solidity in the stiff battle against COVID-19. But, some states have struggled in maintaining an appropriate primary health care service largely due to scarce skilled manpower, poor infrastructure and faulty equipment and facilities. In India, that of late COVID-19 cases have escalated and unfolding an uncanny humanitarian crisis which does not augur well. This has triggered an immediate need for a better "primary health care system."

In India, primary health care system is delivered via a complex blend of government setups along with pharmacies and clinics belonging to the private sector. This has been criticized because of poor coordination and fragmentation but an effective coordination between private and public sector could help leverage the existent assets into an efficient COVID-19 plan. These would include improved access to COVID-19 testing, expansion of tele-health, utilization of community health workers, helping people care for themselves at home and providing messages related to clear health. The ultimate aim of primary health care system is to help the world get rid of COVID-19. In India, about 130 million doses being supplied compared to its humungous population of 130 billion, including first and second doses of vaccination, only 10% of the total population have received at least one dose. According to Economist (2020), "with this current pace India is not expected to vaccinate even 70% of its population until the end of 2022." India is one of the largest global vaccine manufacturers, however, due to the disruptions in its supply chain and conundrum in acquiring raw materials are leading to shortages at sites of vaccination and production delays.

To make inroads to this malaise, primary health care is expected to play a key role. Desai et al. (2021) in their study have suggested certain implications in the landscape of primary health care service. Primary health care staff could be trained to administer vaccines safely and responsibly. They can help reduce the hesitation and build trust in both vaccines and health system. Such staff could also monitor for adverse outcomes and ensure that the second doses are powered by data tracking in properly coordinated information system. The increase in donor and funding from the government in supporting vaccine drives provides ample of opportunity to prioritize on quick wins but simultaneously fine-tunes the delivery and underlying capacity of primary health care in India. Stronger primary health care system will help mitigate the load of morbidity as well as mortality from delayed essential care, foster continuance of COVID-19 vaccination, improve baseline population status of health and strengthen health system. Some of the opportunities to strengthen primary health care via COVID-19 response are promoting trust by getting proximate, building better information system and supporting reeling health workforce.

- ***Effects of COVID-19 on doctors, medical professionals, nurses and supporting staffs of hospitals***

It is a fact well-documented that during COVID-19, the doctors, nurses, medical professionals and all the associated staff of health sector has been the frontline warriors. They have been relentless when talking in terms of service to the nation, a strong testimony of myriad such doctors, nurses, medical experts and healthcare staff who have died as they eventually succumbed to the blood-thirsty disease trying to save the common man. Amidst, the unparalleled crisis, the doctors, nurses, medical experts and other staff of healthcare services have faced several challenges in helping reduce the contamination rate, developing strategies, formulating appropriate long-term plans and obviously, continuous quest with scientists aiming to bring out vaccines for treating the disease (Xu et al., 2021). In addition to this, such group of people have also been exposed to tremendous psychological stress, burnout and levels of fatigue and some such medical professionals have committed suicide while the other have also died due to COVID-19 (Shreffler et al., 2020).

In fact, healthcare workers are more susceptible to the risk of COVID-19 than the common people as they are tasked with a herculean challenge involved in treating the COVID-19 affected people as well as travails of managing their own health. Health professionals during these testing times are required to do their work under extreme stressful conditions even without appropriate protective equipment and have been placed with an uphill task of getting involved in tough decision making related to ethical implications.

The boisterous situation has been excruciatingly challenging in the context of humanitarian, vulnerable and low-income nations, who do not have good health systems. Besides, myriad health services related to sexual and reproductive cases have been side-lined which has also resulted in increased maternal mortality and morbidity. It is noteworthy to mention that the impact of COVID-19 on women health care workers have been monumental. Globally, women accounts for 70% of workers in health as well as social sector. They have been placed with a prodigious challenge of leading from the front, whether, at hospitals, at old age homes or at community mobilizing places. In fact, COVID-19 contaminations among female health care workers are twice than that of their male counterparts (UN Women Data Hub, 2020). At least more than 55% of women catering to health care sector have reported more psychological stress levels and burnout when juxtaposed to male workers (UN Women Data Hub, 2020).

- ***Socio-Economic Effects of COVID-19 on Migrant Workers***

Talking in the Indian context, where Coronavirus is making major headlines every day and where the GDP has seen a sharp spiral, the lives of low income groups especially the migrant workers has hit a nadir. The enforcement of lockdowns has seen the closure of factories which has posed prodigious challenges for the migrant workers. There are major socio-economic issues looming over the future of such workers who stay away from their native places and work to earn their livelihood. Migrant workers working in industrial units have been severely affected by their loss of jobs which has snatched their means of livelihood for them and their family, resulting in poverty, hunger, dislocation and death (Yadav, 2020). The COVID-19 lockdown has really hit the manufacturing industries very hard and the effects have been catastrophic indeed, taking into consideration its relevance in contributing to the Indian GDP which is a nifty 20%.

After the announcement of nationwide lockdown in India, India's 40 million migrants had to cope up with new types of challenges (BBC, 2020). Even before the lockdown, the manufacturing industries were not performing well. The impact on the informal sector of manufacturing industries has been more devastating. According to Interact Analysis COVID-19 Insight Service "Global Manufacturing would shrink by −7.5% in 2020 wherein Global Industrial Production will be losing value of almost 2.8 trillion and Global Machinery Production will collapse by more than 11% due to the impact of COVID-19."

In a developing country like India, where the modus vivendi of industrial migrants has not been great, COVID-19 on the socio-economic lives of these workers has had a rather abysmal impact. In this light, when we see the actual picture of migrant workers in India it reveals a whopping 139 million migrants as per the data released by World Economic Forum. As per Wikipedia, most of the migrants predominantly originate from the states of Madhya Pradesh, Uttar Pradesh, Bihar and Rajasthan, while the capital of India, Delhi and the commercial capital of India, Mumbai allure the highest number of migrants according to the 2011 Census of India. Majority of the migrant workers make up for a predominant chunk of laborers who are paid wages on a regular basis, who work in tough conditions of procuring, construction, textiles and various other units (Gopalan-Hema and Misra, 2020).

Truth to be told, myriad workers especially from the regions from Orissa, Jharkhand and Chhattisgarh are also subjected to unfair wages. Most of the migrants are rural natives living in cities as a means to support their livelihood and family. In fact, migrant workers often lack freedom of movement because of their status of immigration and therefore are more vulnerable to exploitation. These workers are so desperate for work that they might even accept basic amenities of life like food, clothing and shelter instead of minimum wages to survive. According to World Bank, "India's 40 million migrants are facing the major brunt of the situation." The multiple hardships faced by the migrant workers in India have been one of the most ignominious scenarios ever witnessed in the socio-economic life of Indian workers. Their pathetic condition after being unemployed and dislocated has been a major talked about issue, which resulted in poverty, hunger, starvation, exodus from workplace-to-home, physical exhaustion, accidents, brutal assaults by the policemen, refusal of timely medical attention, suicides and deaths.

The global pandemic left the world reeling and its menacing aftermath is still being experienced by the migrant workers. The lockdowns meant shutdown of industrial units which resulted in massive unemployment crisis among the migrants. It leads to food shortages. While ration was distributed to the poor people, the migrants were deprived of food largely due to the norm of area specific ration cards or other government documents like Aadhaar Card. The scenarios were quite devastating as workers were clearly starving out of hunger. It resulted in the migrants taking a walk from their workplaces to their native regions. Complete lockdowns meant no means of transportation of any kind as a result the migrants had to walk thousand kilometers. Many of them did it while remaining hungry and thus there were massive violations in the rules of social distancing as they were traveling in large groups. The results of such exodus were mostly physical exhaustion and rapid spread of the menacing virus. Furthermore, to add to the woes of such workers, many such workers were arrested by the police for violation of laws, some were brutally beaten up by the police, some died out of physical exhaustion and many workers died to due accidents faced during their journey back home (Aravind, 2020).

Finally, the government came to the forefront to tackle the challenging issues of these stranded migrants of various states. Over 45 lakh people were provided facilities of being ferried back home through the arrangement of over 4000 "Special Shramik Trains" which started on 9th May 2020. However the poor management of the government resulted in the delay of such train and also inadequate providence of food and water to the migrants. In fact, one of the reasons in the surge of COVID-19 cases in India was largely due to the implementation of the initiative of "Special Shramik Trains." Likewise, bus facilities were also arranged to help the migrant workers travel to their home. This initiative was greatly adopted and implemented with great conviction by Bollywood actor Sonu Sood who provided food, water and help travel thousands of migrants from cities to home. The migrants were also provided facilities like food and shelter from the National Disaster Relief Fund (NDRF) as per the directives of Home Ministry given to all states. Thousands of relief camps had also been set up by the government of different states in collaboration with the NGOs, which provided food and shelter to lakhs of migrant workers as well as adequate quarantine measures (Londhe, 2020).

The Central Government had earlier released a whopping "Rs. 11,092 Crore to states and UTs under NDRF," to provide facilities like food and appropriate shelter for migrants. For providing employment opportunities and wages to workers, the "average daily wages under the MGNREGA" were increased to Rs. 202 from previously Rs. 182 to help the providence of job and wages to such migrant workers ably backed and supported by Rs. 1000 Crore from "PM CARES Fund." The Finance Minister, Mrs. Sitharaman also announced free ration for 80 million migrant workers by spending an eye-twitching ₹35 billion. In addition to this, the GOI had also launched the "Garib Kalyan Rojgar Abhiyaan" endeavor to blight the menacing effect of COVID-19 on migrant workers. This endeavor is actually a rural public works scheme launched with an initial funding of Rs. 50,000 Crore for a mammoth 116 districts in 6 states.

- ***Psychological Stress effects of COVID-19 on human beings—Empirical Analysis***

It is a no-brainer that the COVID-19 has taken a prodigious toll on the mental health of human beings. It all started with the initial COVID-19 lockdowns in 2020, where people were instructed to adhere to strict quarantine policy of being forced to stay at home and prohibited visiting outdoors. After the lockdowns were lifted up, people have been instructed to adhere to the COVID-19 protocols of safety rules and social distancing. To add to the extra unaccustomed burden on people, further restrictions were placed in the operations of businesses and manpower at work.

Moreover, the COVID-19 lockdowns has been a nightmare for every individual and a devastating force for disrupting businesses, economies, health and mental well-being. People belonging to the low-income groups and middle-aged income groups have been given a lot of food for thought as their ways of income has been snatched or otherwise shrinked. Even for rich businessmen, dealing with psychological stress has been a major issue. In addition to this, people belonging to other professions like teaching, medical service, entrepreneurship, service, etc. all have experienced psychological stress to some extent (Singh et al., 2020). Many people have also committed suicide since they were not able to deal with psychological stress that came their way. Therefore, it becomes utmost essential to discuss about the topic of psychological stress effects of COVID-19 on human beings.

To serve this purpose, 250 people belonging to the state of West Bengal, living in various districts like Kolkata, Burdwan, Birbhum, Howrah, Hooghly, North 24 Parganas, and South 24 Parganas have been surveyed, and the most dominant factors of psychological stress have been explored with the help of Exploratory Factor Analysis by the use of IBMs SPSS version 23. The respondents are employed at various professions and belonging to various age categories. We have analyzed the data in the forthcoming paragraphs as well as the key factors of psychological stress have been highlighted.

From Table 1, we observe the demographic statistics which is distributed across gender, age, occupation and income.

Conducting an exploratory factor analysis is crucial to explore the relevant factors that reflect the various determinants of psychological stress and social stress. However, before, that the "KMO and Bartlett's Test of Sphericity" has been conducted for checking whether that the sample size is adequate, which will further indicate if it is worthwhile to run a Factor Analysis (Frost, 2020) (Table 2).

Table 1 Demographic statistics.

Demographic construct	Classification	Population statistics	Percentage
Gender	Male	140	0.56
	Female	110	0.44
	Total	**250**	**1.00**
Age	Below 18	16	0.06
	18–24	70	0.28
	25–34	82	0.33
	35–44	44	0.18
	45–54	28	0.11
	Above 55	10	0.04
	Total	**250**	**1.00**
Current Occupation	Student	79	0.32
	Service	85	0.34
	Business	38	0.15
	Others	48	0.19
	Total	**250**	**1.00**
Monthly Income	Less than 10,000	36	0.14
	10,001–25,000	96	0.38
	25,001–50,000	89	0.36
	50,001–100,000	24	0.10
	Above 100,000	5	0.02
	Total	**250**	**1.00**

Authors' own calculations.

Table 2 KMO and Bartlett's test of sphericity.

Kaiser-Meyer-Olkin Measure of Sample Adequacy	0.804
Bartlett's Test of Sphericity Approx. Chi-Square	784.369
df.	9
Sig.	.000

The "KMO Bartlett's Test of Sphericity" gives confirmation to the fact that running the Factor Analysis test was appropriate. The ideal values should exceed 0.6, which is explained by the "KMO Test Statistic" reporting figure of 0.804 (>0.6). The significance shows a value of 0 ($P = .000$, $P < .05$). This is a confirmation to the fact that Factor Analysis can be performed.

The above table (Table 3) shows us Factor Analysis conducted obtaining a TVE (Total Variance Explained). According to the TVE, results highlight the number of factors obtained with the condition that their Eigen values are greater than 1 (Eigen value >1). As we move down the table (Table 3), it is observed that Eigen value decreases. Hence, the Eigen values falling below 1 are not reported and taken into consideration (Sevincer et al., 2017). It is proved by the Component 1 and Component 2 accounting for and of the total variance explained respectively. Principal Component Analysis helped to extract the variables according to the requisite of the Eigen values are greater than 1 (Eigen values > 1).

Table 3 Factor analysis.

	Initial eigenvalues			Extraction sums of squared loadings		
Component	**Total**	**% of variance**	**Cumulative %**	**Total**	**% of variance**	**Cumulative %**
1	4.214	46.820	46.820	3.105	34.500	34.500
2	1.100	12.220	59.040	2.319	25.766	60.026
3	0.876	9.733	68.733			
4	0.749	8.322	77.095			
5	0.610	6.777	83.872			
6	0.531	5.900	89.772			
7	0.407	4.522	94.324			
8	0.321	3.566	97.890			
9	0.192	2.110	100.00			

Extraction Method: Principal Component Analysis.
Based on authors' own calculations.

Table 4 Rotated component matrix.
Rotated component matrix[a]

	Component	
	1	2
Frustration	0.728	0.156
Job Security	0.749	0.178
Financial Security	0.547	0.319
Emotional Drain	0.595	0.371
Lack of Self-Esteem	0.497	0.492
Extreme Alertness at Workplace	0.593	0.47
Lack of Leisure Activities	0.272	0.735
Relationship with Family Members	0.432	0.618
Lack of Outdoor Activities	0.816	0.168

[a]Rotation converged in 3 iterations.
Extraction Method: Principal Component Analysis.
Rotation Method: Varimax with Kaiser Normalization.
Authors' own calculations.

Table 4 shows the Rotated Component Matrix according to which the variables would get accommodated in the factor loadings, thereby showing the final results. The component may be arranged in the following manner (Table 5).

The 9 variables are disintegrated into 2 factors which we have renamed as Component I and Component II. Component I has been renamed as Psychological Stress and Component II as Social Stress.

There were an aggregate of 9 key dominant factors of psychological stress that have been identified which are frustration, job security, financial security, emotional drain, lack of self-esteem, extreme alertness at workplace, lack of leisure activities, relationship with family members and lack of outdoor activities.

Table 5 Arrangements of components.

Component I	Component II
Frustration	Lack of Leisure Activities
Job Security	Relationship with Family Members
Financial Security	Lack of Outdoor Activities
Emotional Drain	
Lack of Self-Esteem	
Extreme Alertness at Workplace	

Authors' own calculations.

- ***Effects of COVID-19 on kids and youth***

The pandemic of COVID-19 has taken a serious toll on both physical as well as mental health of people. The kids have been jettisoned from an otherwise a very jolly and playful environments of the yesteryears. Given their active modus vivendi of rush hours during school time, tiffin time or the playground and parks accommodated with them, since the outbreak of the pandemic the kids have been deprived of such pleasures which has made their lives quite monotonous and their personality close to being an introvert. According to Human Rights, 2020, due to COVID-19 pandemic, kids are getting schooled at home by online classes which itself is quite tough on them. Many kids who belong to weaker sections of the society have suffered because of this noticeable change in conducting studies through online mode. Particularly, those kids who stay in remote villages and receive education from local schools and private schools have severely suffered the wrath of the pandemic. Adding to their woes, the quarantines and precautionary measures like following norms of social distancing, wearing of masks, frequent sanitization of hands and outdoor activities being snatched away have been quite ruthless.

The impact of the COVID-19 pandemic has also severely hit the youth. Given the hectic modus operandi of the young people, whether be it hitting the gym early morning, or going to college, or going for work, either indulging in outdoor activities or hanging out with friends in the late evening, everything has been snatched away by the pandemic. Although people are working from home and even undertaking online classes to keep afloat their desire for learning and getting educated, they have clearly struggled to keep themselves upbeat in outdoor activities which are seen as a potent part of the schedule of the present day youths. Lack of outdoor activities or leisure time is having an inexorable impact on the physical and mental health of the young people (Bahl et al., 2021).

- ***Health and safety best practices for use in public spaces during and after COVID-19***

The health and safety of people during COVID-19 era and even in the post-COVID-19 period is utmost essential and cannot be compromised on any way. The government of all countries has established certain rules to be followed by their citizens at public places. Wearing of masks/double-masks, sanitization of hands, maintaining of 2 m or more distance from each other, etc. are some of the precautionary measures are being relentlessly practiced by the people in public places. Besides, governments have imposed certain restrictions on travel ban from country to country and a quarantine period of

14 day or more for people who visit their territories from another country. The governments have also imposed restrictions on gatherings both social and political. The places of worship like temples, churches, mosques and other have observed a temporal close and religious gatherings have been strictly prohibited. In countries, where COVID-19 cases are minimal and manageable, the religious gatherings have been restricted to a certain limit. Tournaments like cricket, football and others continue to take place but there are restrictions in crowd capacity in stadiums. The rules are particularly harsh for the players as they are required to train only in few numbers and in batches. Strict quarantine protocols are being practiced by them especially remaining fully inside their respective hotel rooms which is mentally tough for any athlete. Restaurants, hotels, clubs and other places of visit have been temporarily shut or are running with very low crowd capacity. Strict safety protocols of COVID-19 are being followed there which involves wearing of masks, thermal testing before entering and sanitization of hands (World Health Organization, 2020).

- ***How COVID-19 pandemic has affected global healthcare and its implications for future of healthcare***

The emergence of novel Coronavirus has changed the trajectory of the whole world. The wrath of the pandemic has got reeling all major sectors of an economy. The jolts triggered by the pandemic has been felt severely all across the globe, especially in the ambit of healthcare sector. It is quite astounding to notice the changes in global healthcare sector because of a contagious life threatening disease. The pandemic has changed the very roots of functioning of a healthcare sector and even poses a plethora of dimensions by which such changes could stay even after the pandemic gets over. Governments and investors are now openly encouraging healthcare spending and exploring new multilevel delivery strategies. The gap between healthcare delivery and public health is now getting bridged. Healthcare institutions are leading the bandwagon for battle against COVID-19. Business models are being reshuffled, supply chain are being fine-tuned, exquisite attention is being given to training and development, etc. Strategic alignment between healthcare systems and clients has been a blessing in disguise as partners are moving in different trajectories but eventually arriving in a same common place. Healthcare system is going largely "digital" which is another feather in the cap for the sector taking into consideration even the small players who are providing robust healthcare services by proper digitalization of their contents (Hassoun, 2021).

The COVID-19 era is a new dawn and a learning curve for the global healthcare sector. As there has been an exponential increase in the healthcare spending for COVID-19, companies that are conducting research, producing test kits, developing vaccines and supplying medical equipment. A key reason to this is that the government would not invest only in damage control but also aim to prevent the resurgence of the COVID-19 pandemic. In this light, it becomes vital to deliberate on the short-term, medium-term and long-term implications of COVID-19 on healthcare sector (Infosys BPM, 2021).

Short-term Implications: The next six months would be crucial for managing this pandemic. There will be huge pressure on the infrastructure of hospitals and clinics. Non-immediate surgeries will see a decline and business should be prepared for delays in payments largely because of the inconsistencies in the proportion of demand and supply.

Medium-term Implications: The only standout points for healthcare system lies in the upsurge in investments in primary and intensive care. Financing pressure is going to be humongous for healthcare providers and other public players. However, things are expected to be back to terms once the outbreak flattens.

Long-term Implications: The governments together with the organizations are required to reprioritize the plans of long term healthcare at a macro level. The post-COVID-19 era is likely to witness the healthcare sector adopt new concepts like telehealth, remote care, and other myriad digital solutions for enhanced patient care.

1.2 Impact of COVID-19 on Computer and Informatics

- ***Role and impact of digital technologies during COVID-19***

The global crisis triggered by the COVID-19 pandemic is a multifaceted one, which has seen uncountable deaths and devastating socio-economic dimensions. The most severe setback witnessed during the COVID-19 pandemic has been the lockdowns which has plummeted all major sectors of the economy. To cope up with this malaise and keep abreast during these testing times, most of the sectors are switching to "digital" way of doing business. Digital solutions are playing a pivotal role not only in the landscape of scientific research but also helping continue the economic endeavors and delivery of important services which also includes healthcare and education. New tools like "COVID-19 information portals," hackathons, e-services, virtual consultations regards to medicine and self-diagnosis applications and many other digital technologies have been put in place to cope up with the challenging times. It has been observed that the adoption of digital technologies during COVID-19 pandemic has accelerated and escalated compared to the past years and that many of such changes are here to stay for long term (LaBerge et al., 2020). Investments in digital initiatives has also increased. The quantum leap taken by the adoption of digital technologies at both organizational as well as industrial level has been phenomenal. Consumers have been witnessed to switch on to online channels. Most notably, the adoption of digital technologies have been twice as much in sectors like healthcare and pharmacies, professional and financial services. Similar escalations have also been observed in the digitization of core internal operations and of interactions in supply chain management. The largest changes are most likely to stay for a long term. A primary reason for this is seen the heavy investments made in digital technologies which has eviscerated some of the bottlenecks of the virtual world. Some other reasons are cost-effectiveness and meeting customer needs quickly (Zhenmin, 2020). Besides, investments in data security and artificial intelligence are also being made to help organizations be in a better place compared to the past days. E-learning, e-healthcare services, e-business, e-marketing, e-commerce, e-banking, etc. are some of the most impeccable methods in which digital technologies have played a gargantuan role.

- ***E-learning during COVID-19—Empirical Investigation***

One of the spectacular advancements in the landscape of technology has been the successful integration of information and communication technology in the teaching-learning process which has established itself as an important medium of instruction delivery. Institutions worldwide are now blending information and communication technology with traditional modes of instruction delivery in order to ameliorate the teaching-learning process. Such innovation in technology has made an inexorable impact on the landscape of education where institutions at the present era are witnessed to have a penchant toward e-learning.

Undoubtedly E-learning is fast gaining the upper hand and is being embraced prodigiously during this time of this ongoing COVID-19 pandemic. E-learning is commonly known as online learning or open learning and has its association with advanced learning technology (ALT), which deals with both technologies as well as learning methodologies using multimedia technologies. Truth to be told, the advent of distance education marked the turning point in the milieu of education as it paved the way for e-learning. E-learning overcomes certain barriers like attendance, traveling and costs. It also allows higher participation and better interaction. E-learning is facilitated completely online via multimedia technologies like video-conferencing, chat rooms, computer based communication, e-mail, electronic forums, etc. E-learning also supports a plethora of e-resources that can be accessed at any time by the students, teachers and other professionals, thereby, strengthening the teaching-learning process. The urgent need and ineluctable relevance of e-learning has been strongly felt in recent times after the emergence and potential outbreak of COVID-19 pandemic wreaked havoc. The government of all countries enforced lockdowns to curtail the deadly virus and as a result is stymied the ever smooth trajectory of education. India was no different as the lockdowns enforced from the middle of March 2020 brought the whole country and all external activities to a standstill. This proved to be a deadly blow for the students and their future keeping them at bay from their education and thus a cloud of uncertainty was hovering around. Soon after, the institutions in India resorted to e-learning and granted permission to all schools, colleges and universities to conduct online classes for their students to keep the sacrosanct element of education afloat. It has been witnessed that both the students as well as the teachers have embraced the concept of e-learning with mirth during these testing times (Mitra et al., 2021).

The attitudes and behavior of students toward e-learning seems to be an intriguing domain of study and research. To serve this purpose, a total of 352 respondents studying in different colleges and universities in the state of West Bengal have been surveyed. The survey areas include Kolkata, Burdwan, Howrah, Hooghly and South 24 Parganas. The theoretical model of "Technology Acceptance Model" (TAM) developed by Fred Davis (1989) has been adopted to address the present issue (Fig. 1).

The following hypothesis has been framed:

H_1. **There is a significant relationship between Perceived Ease of Use and Perceived Usefulness**

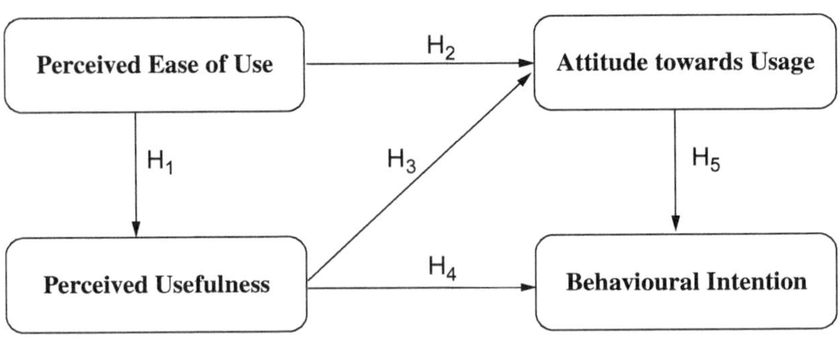

Fig. 1 Research model. *(Self-developed by authors.)*

H_2. **There is a significant relationship between Perceived Ease of Use and Attitude towards Usage**

H_3. **There is a significant relationship between Perceived Usefulness and Attitude towards Usage**

H_4. **There is a significant relationship between Perceived Usefulness and Behavioural Intention**

H_5. **There is a significant relationship between Attitude towards Usage and Behavioral Intention**

The questionnaire which has been administered online to the students consist of questions which are based on the constructs of TAM which are "Perceived Ease of Use, Perceived Usefulness, Attitude towards Usage and Behavioural Intention." For the purpose of data analysis, IBM's SPSS version 23 has been used. The results of the findings has been represented below, one by one.

1.2.1 Reliability analysis

A reliability test has been conducted to check if the variables of the research model, viz., "Perceived Ease of Use," "Perceived Usefulness," "Attitude towards Usage," and "Behavioral Intention," fit perfectly in the questionnaire by the use of Cronbach's Alpha score. Accordingly, the threshold limit should be greater than 0.6 (Bravo and Potvin, 1991), it is observed that in this case, the figure report 0.763, indicating that all the variables fit perfectly in the questionnaire (Table 6).

1.2.2 Correlation analysis

After conducting the reliability analysis, it is vital to find out the relationship between the 6 factors as well as to examine the hypotheses of our proposed research model. To serve this purpose, we have conducted a correlation test by using SPSS version 23. Table 7 shows that the correlation between PEOU, PU, ATU, and BI is positive and significant, thereby confirming that our original hypotheses made in the literature are related to TAM. The correlation statistics has been presented below.

Table 6 Cronbach's alpha.

Cronbach's alpha	Cronbach's alpha based on standardized items	N of items
0.763	0.763	17

Table 7 Correlation test.

Factor	PEOU	PU	ATU	BI
PEOU				
Pearson Correlation		0.628[a]	0.705[a]	0.712[a]
Sig. (2-tailed)	1	0.000	0.000	0.000
N		352	352	352
PU				
Pearson Correlation	0.628[a]		0.654[a]	0.728[a]
Sig. (2-tailed)	0.000	1	0.000	0.000
N	352		352	352
ATU				
Pearson Correlation	0.705[a]	0.654[a]		0.749[a]
Sig. (2-tailed)	0.000	0.000	1	0.000
N	352	352		352
BI				
Pearson Correlation	0.712[a]	0.728[a]	0.749[a]	
Sig. (2-tailed)	0.000	0.000	0.000	1
N	352	352	352	

[a]Correlation significant at the 0.01 level (2-tailed).
Authors' own calculations.

1.2.3 Regression analysis

To further strengthen our research findings, we have also conducted a regression statistics to test the different proposed hypothesis.

First, we examine the relationship between H_2 and H_3.

As we can see from Table 8, the value of R square indicates that the two predictors (PU, PEOU) explains 71.7% variations in ATU. It explains the rationality of this model, although there might be other oblivious factors having an impact on the respondents' ATU. The standardized coefficients (β) shows that PU (β=0.553) have a larger impact than PEOU (β=0.381). Also, the Sig. indicates that both of the predictors have a significant and positive impact on ATU scores being less than 0.001 level.

From Table 9 it is confirmed that all the two predictors namely PU and ATU had a significant and positive influence on BI, with (β=0.594) and (β=0.603) respectively for each predictor. Each of the four predictors have Sig=0.

Finally, we conduct a regression analysis to examine H_1.

Finally, one more determination of a regression model was done to test our fourth hypothesis, i.e. influence of PEOU on PU. As evidenced from

Table 8 Regression test.
Predictors: PEOU, PU → Dependent variable: ATU

Model summary				
Model	**R**	**R square**	**Adjusted R square**	**Std. error of estimate**
1	.876[a]	.717	.713	.60436

Coefficients[b]					
	Unstandardized coefficients		**Standard coefficients**		
Model	**B**	**Std. error**	**Beta**	**t**	**Sig.**
1 (Constant)	.378	.193		1.534	.143
PEOU	.363	.050	0.381	6.826	.000
PU	.587	.057	0.553	10.342	.000

[a]Predictors (constant), PEOU, PU.
[b]Dependent variable: ATU.
Authors' own calculations.

Table 10, the value of R Square is 0.687 which represents that PEOU explains 68.7% variations in PU. We also notice that Standard Coefficient value is ($\beta = 0.381$), PEOU had a significant and positive impact on PU.

Hence, our proposed research model along with the hypotheses are rightly proven correct as evidenced by the robust examination and analysis.

Table 9 Regression test.
Predictors: PU, ATU → Dependent variable: BI

Model summary				
Model	**R**	**R square**	**Adjusted R square**	**Std. error of estimate**
1	.895[a]	.724	.707	.57964

Coefficients[b]					
	Unstandardized coefficients		**Standard coefficients**		
Model	**B**	**Std. error**	**Beta**	**t**	**Sig.**
1 (Constant)	.456	.177		1.749	.092
PU	.483	.068	0.594	6.554	.000
ATU	.599	.072	0.603	8.688	.000

[a]Predictors (constant), PU, ATU.
[b]Dependent variable: BI.
Authors' own calculations.

Table 10 Regression test.
Predictors: PEOU → Dependent variable: PU

Model summary				
Model	**R**	**R square**	**Adjusted R square**	**Std. error of estimate**
1	.809[a]	.687	.690	.56438

Coefficients[b]					
	Unstandardized coefficient		**Standard coefficients**		
Model	**B**	**Std. error**	**Beta**	**t**	**Sig.**
1 (Constant)	.378	.193		1.534	.143
PEOU	.363	.050	0.381	6.826	.000

[a]Predictors (constant), PEOU.
[b]Dependent variable: PU.
Authors' own calculations.

According to our research findings, Perceived Usefulness (PU) had a significant impact on Attitude toward Usage (ATU). It was also observed that PU was significantly related to Behavioral Intention (BI). The reason behind this could be that students are willing to adopt a beneficial technology that could make learning more convenient during the pandemic situation. Perceived Ease of Use (PEOU) was significantly related to ATU of online teaching. The findings of the present research study also proved that PEOU had a strong influence on PU, suggesting that providing adequate user training is vital for fine-tuning the students' perception about the usefulness of a technology which is quite unique. Ultimately, we comprehend that ATU has been prodigious in shaping up the BI of students toward e-learning as both psychological and physiological faculties are a nifty driving force in the development of perceived likelihood of students.

- ***Digital transformation of the healthcare sector triggered by the COVID-19 pandemic***

The greatest exemplification of digital transformation in the healthcare sector during COVID-19 is the operations of telemedicine or contactless healthcare services (Jason, 2020). The various technological innovations resulting from the COVID-19 is using the existing tools or standards and repurposing them. The influx of patients in hospitals had earlier exposed the loopholes in the current healthcare system. This primarily ushered an astounding digital transformation of the healthcare system aiming at improved care, reduction of operational cost and time saving treatments.

Tele-consultation became a norm as it allowed physicians to attend more patients via virtual platforms and even connect to physicians in foreign countries. There was a steep rise witnessed in the adoption of various tele-consultation start-ups like Practo, Teladoc Health, MeMD, Doctordemand, Kry, and accuRx. This also boosted the rise in adoption of video-conferencing software like Zoom, Microsoft Teams and Google Duo. Tele-consultation has also minimized the medical expenses for patients. A consumer survey was conducted by American Well which reported that 61% of those people who were willing to switch to tele-consultation would actually do it as they saw it as more convenient option and quicker service. In comparison, 54% would adopt it to save money. Slowly and steadily, there were various e-health apps most notably "Aarogya Setu" app of India which provided services of detecting COVID-19 contamination. It was a special "syndromic mapping and self-assessment" digital service which was developed by the National Informatics Centre. The app witnessed installations of more than 100 million per day. It was lauded by the WHO. Now, the healthcare sector seems to be improvising further as digital transformations are speaking heavily for it. The treatment of COVID-19, reservation of beds for COVID-19-contaminated patients, and vaccination drives are all taking place by primarily by the use of digital services, either by visiting the website or app and filling in the required information (Bijlani, 2021). It is also noteworthy to mention about the impeccable role played by Artificial Intelligence (AI) during this pandemic. A detailed study about the use and benefits of AI to provide the required IT infrastructure amidst COVID-19 pandemic has been explained in the next subsection of the study.

- ***Benefits and use of AI to provide IT infrastructure during COVID-19***

While the role of tele-consultation largely bridged the gap between the patients and the doctors, a major conundrum existed in dealing with non-COVID patients as most of the doctors were seen dedicating their entire time dealing with COVID-19 patients. The integration of AI with medical systems brought a seismic shift in the IT infrastructure and the overall healthcare system during COVID-19. One of the strongest benefit obtained by the use of AI is that it can analyze medical data very fast and produce an output that can help doctors in the final decision. This is very crucial as many errors would otherwise be attributed to oversights in a rush. AI is also being used for risk prediction, diagnosis, treatment planning, exploring and manufacture of drugs and study of various diseases. One of the most significant role of AI in the IT infrastructure during this pandemic is its impregnable help provided by auto-learning from the data available to make accurate predictions. Start-ups and educational organizations like DarwinAI, Qure.ai, 1Qbit, and COVIDSWIFT made AI-rooted solutions within reach of doctors. Besides, AI also accelerated the process of drug development and vaccination. It also helped the researchers to understand the anatomy of the virus and predict the determinants which would generate an immune response (Toews, 2020).

Start-ups consider two trajectories for swift vaccine development: the first, repurposing of existing drugs and second, the development of new vaccines. The start-ups involved with the former are BenevolentAI, Cyclica, Innoplexus, and Deargen, while Iktos, Exscientia, Insilico Medicine, and SRI International. Pharmaceutical companies like Pfizer, Sanofi, AstraZeneca and GSK have also collaborated with these start-ups to accelerate the development of vaccine, which is considered to be one of the swiftest feats in the history of medicine. Start-ups like Soporis Health, Artelus, and Sensely are using AI to monitor and study the medical history of the patients and symptoms for providing predictive feedback about a person's health (Toews, 2020). Such head turning solutions are showing the picture of the future of telemedicine and access to health that are capable of reaching out to patients before they themselves find the urgency for medical help.

- ***Benefits and use of Cloud Computing to provide IT infrastructure during COVID-19***

The pandemic of COVID-19 has widely metamorphosed the operations of business. Major organizations are relying on cloud applications and cloud services has become a "new normal." A study by CommVault revealed that 93% of business leaders opined that they are moving some portions of their infrastructure to cloud services. The ineluctable importance of Cloud Computing during COVID-19 are flexibility, reduced operational costs and quicker deployment. Cloud Computing offers flexibility which is needed to adjust to fluctuating business environments. During these times of slow growth and low profits, companies have been able to remove storage spaces, applications and unwanted features, hence, paying only for the resources that has been used. Cloud Computing has helped several companies eliminate extreme expense of hardware, cost of IT resources, strengthened maintenance of internal systems of data and modernizations of IT infrastructures and automation of processes. Companies have been able to save substantial costs of capital and witness higher returns on investments. With the use of cloud computing, companies got the advantages of better deployment and launching of programs and applications seamlessly and faster. In fact, flexible, cost-effective solutions and scalable have been the keys to thrive during a horrendous time of a global pandemic (Nguyen, 2020).

- ***Benefits and use of Big Data Management and Machine Learning Techniques to provide IT infrastructure during COVID-19***

Amidst COVID-19 pandemic, big data analytics have played an instrumental role in tracking and reducing health disparities among patient populations. With the tools of big data analytics, providers have delivered the required care to the required patients at the required time. The clinics have used big data to navigate the initial phase of the pandemic which has given them essential information to treat patients (Marr, 2020). Surveillance infrastructure has been used to track contaminated people. This was the case in China, where thermal scanners were installed in train stations. This helped in detecting COVID-19 cases. The presence of cameras also helped the governments of all countries to spot if quarantine protocols were followed. Much like the "Aarogya Setu App" of India, China's "Close Contact Detector" app was also used to detect contamination.

In continents like Europe and America, where contamination rates were high and myriad people lost their lives during the initial outbreak of the pandemic, a mobile app to provide data in order to control the virus with an integrated strategy was being planned via the development of a mobile app by "Oxford University's Big Data Institute" along with the government officials. A similar app called "FluPhone" was developed in 2011, but it was not largely adopted. In USA, the government is planning along with technological behemoths like Facebook, Google and many others for using location data from the smartphone users of the country to track movements and understanding patterns. Besides, dashboards from WHO has been providing real-time statistics, which has been imperative to see the progress of contagion and to inform models about the extent to which the virus could invade. The dashboards pull data from across the world to reveal confirmed COVID-19 cases and deaths. This data is then used for creation of models and prediction of hotspots, thus, enabling decisions (Kent, 2020). Big data has provided an enormous amount of data to the scientists and doctors to frame informed decisions in order to combat the COVID-19 fight. In a nutshell, the benefits of Big Data has been seen in being used as an antecedent and potent tool for analyzing the transmission of COVID-19 virus, movement, monitoring of health and prevention of spread of COVID-19 (Godfried, 2020).

Outbreak analytics takes all the data which is available and then processes it through machine learning to create disease models. These models are a representation of the predictions related to the peak contamination rates and outcomes. Machine Learning Tools (MLT) have been classified into 3 themes which are "Computational Epidemiology theme, Early Detection and Diagnosis theme and Disease Progression theme" (Syeda et al., 2020).

- ***Modeling techniques and statistical projections that are used to predict the spread of the COVID-19 virus and decision making***

The disease of COVID-19 has affected more than 170 countries and the accelerating pace of cases and mortality has been quite high. In this light, forecasting techniques has been assisting to design strategies and productive decision-making. These techniques helps in assessing the past situations which will enable robust predictions about situations to occur in future. Forecasting techniques are playing a pivotal role in yielding accurate predictions. Besides, collection of data from various platforms also play an instrumental role in the process of forecasting. Forecasting the spread of COVID-19 disease can be done on the basis of parameters like impact of environmental factors, impact of quarantine, period of incubation, demographics, daily death counts, availability of medical facilities, mobility, strategic policies, awareness about COVID-19 and many more. Mishra et al. (2020) in their study analyzed certain prediction algorithm and metrics of model accuracy. The various prediction models considered in their study include ARIMA, SARIMA, GARCH, Prophet, and LSTM. Model accuracy metrics were used to make a comparison between the fitness and performance of prediction of the ARIMA, SARIMA and Prophet models. These criteria are the "Schwarz Criterion" (SC), "Akaike Information Criterion" (AIC), "Mean Absolute Error" (MEA), "Mean Absolute Percentage Error" (MAPE), "Root Mean Square Error" (RMSE) and "Theil Inequality Coefficient" (Theil's U). Their study was based on India which should guide future researches and their findings would be of extreme importance to the users of models and statistical techniques.

- ***Effects of COVID-19 on virtual healthcare with usage of IoT technology***

The jolts triggered by the pandemic sent shockwaves all across the world which ultimately resulted in the healthcare services being conducted virtually. Prior to this, healthcare sector of India has been modernizing at a breakneck pace which had carried out medical activities with accuracy. After the outbreak of Coronavirus, technology has been hailed as a talisman and a much needed tonic to help the world cope up with myriad challenges that existed. It has been noticed that medical professionals have been adopting new methods of treating patients, simultaneously avoiding in-person treatments, unless absolutely vital (Mehta, 2021).

Several companies have come to the forefront to assist society during these testing times. One such company is Loterra, which is a marketplace which helps businesses to find appropriate IoT service providers. It also extended its services by partnering with several other companies to provide medical devices and products. A common example would be the monitoring of a patient's temperature to detect whether he has been affected or not. Wearable IoT devices such as smartwatches has been providing required information about a patient's heart rate, blood oxygen level, blood sugar level, etc. The integration of IoT gadgets with smart-sensors and algorithms in the milieu of medicine, which are connected to an application by cloud and other computing devices, has really been extremely helpful in fighting this ongoing pandemic of COVID-19 (D'mello, 2021). Some of the significant services offered by IoT in healthcare include telemedicine, robotic sanitization, contact tracing and privatization and protection of data. As per the Vodafone IoT Spotlight Report (2020), 84% of businesses claimed that IoT was essential for their survival during COVID-19. IoT has also been used in cold supply chain to monitor the vials of COVID-19 vaccines in real time and identify the loopholes in the logistics.

Escalation in the use of smartphones, smart bracelets and patches has been witnessed which has helped in the detection, regulation and management of COVID-19 cases and symptoms. "Corona-combat" drones equipped with thermal scanner, disinfectant tanks, spotlights, night vision cameras and durable medical boxes were installed in New Delhi, India with the intention of curbing the spread of the virus. The drones approached people of New Delhi in their respective balconies to check their temperatures and even provided medical supplies. The potential of robotics has been prodigiously hailed during COVID-19. A Japanese COVID-19 testing robot was established that has conducted around 2000 independent PCR tests per day without the help of clinicians, except for collecting the samples. This has large scale implications as it would increase the global COVID-19 testing capacity. In hospitals, nonsurgical robots have been used to disinfect reusable products such as medical equipment, PPE, and hospital beds. Besides, IoT sensors have also been installed in office spaces for monitoring and reporting on air-quality and detection of COVID-19 particles in the air. The high traffic areas also witnessed the installation of IoT sensors and thermal detectors for identification of people with high temperatures. The role played by IoT during COVID-19 in the milieu of virtual healthcare has been impeccable and augurs outstandingly well for the coming days in the tussle against the deadly disease (Wessing, 2021).

2. Conclusion

The present endeavor is a case-based study which highlights and describes the impact of COVID-19 pandemic on healthcare and IT sectors. Although most of the study has been developed on the basis of existing literatures in the form of available e-resources, blogs, posts, e-newspapers, etc., the study is a pivotal find in the light of the given situation dealing with the bedlam triggered by COVID-19, the challenges faced by various sectors, and the myriad innovations and changes that have been witnessed. In a nutshell, both the disadvantages and advantages have been highlighted. The current ongoing pandemic of COVID-19 novel Coronavirus is an unprecedented global crisis which is enforcing major changes in almost all sectors. Although the challenges poised at the face of each and every sector have been immense, the focus especially gets on healthcare and IT sector. Healthcare sector is now the main sector of any country that is being hailed as the talisman and answer to the global pandemic, while the IT sector is the antecedent and the nifty driving force for any changes, particularly the bewildering metamorphosis of the eye-twitching percolations of technological innovations in the landscape of healthcare sector. Truth to be told, the complete evisceration of the COVID-19 pandemic will not happen overnight and is to take some time. Nevertheless, many hotshots and stakeholders have opined that the emergence of the pandemic was a blessing in disguise especially for the healthcare and IT sectors as major weaklings of such sectors has been exposed and has given their leaders much food for thought. It is during these head-scratching challenges, that the sectors has been able to step up with the best of agile solutions which is slowly but steadily making giant strides in proving vital in the context of the present times. In fact, most of the changes are here to stay for the long haul even in the postpandemic era.

References

Aravind, E., 2020. Covid-19 will have unprecedented effect on migrant economy. The Economic Times. Available at http://economictimes.indiatimes.com. (Accessed 5 June 2021).

Awasthi, P., 2020. Revised clinical trial rules due to Covid-19 may benefit patients in long run: Survey. BusinessLine. Available at http://www.thehindubusinessline.com. (Accessed 3 June 2021).

Bahl, D., Bassi, S., Arora, M., 2021. The Impact of COVID-19 on Children and Adolescents: Early Evidence in India. ORF. Available at http://www.orfonline.org. (Accessed 6 June 2021).

Balfour, H., 2020. Drug Safety Research Unit says repurposed drugs for COVID-19 still require a lot of testing. European Pharmaceutical Review. Available at http://www.europeanpharmaceuticalreview.com. (Accessed 3 June 2021).

Bhargava, H.D., 2021. Coronavirus History. WebMD. Available at http://www.webmd.com. (Accessed 1 June 2021).

Bijlani, V., 2021. Digital transformation of healthcare: Beyond COVID-19. CDO TRENDS. Available at http://www.cdotrends.com. (Accessed 8 June 2021).

Bravo, G., Potvin, L., 1991. Estimating the reliability of continuous measures with Cronbach's alpha or the intraclass correlation coefficient: toward the integration of two traditions. J. Clin. Epidemiol. 44 (4–5), 381–390.

Chaplin, S., 2020. COVID-19: a brief history and treatments in development. Prescriber 31 (5), 23–28.

D'mello, A., 2021. The role of IoT in healthcare during Covid-19. IoTNOW. Available at http://www.iot-now.com. (Accessed 10 June 2021).

Davis, F.D., 1989. Perceived usefulness, perceived ease of use, and user acceptance of information technology. MIS Q. 13 (3), 319–340.

Desai, E., Ratcliffe, H., Bitton, A., Schwarz, D., 2021. COVID-19 and primary health care: How can India leverage a current crisis to build a stronger future? Ariadne Labs. Available at http://www.ariadnelabs.medium.com. (Accessed 4 June 2021).

Economist, 2020. An effective covid-19 vaccine is a turning point in the pandemic. Available at http://www.economist.com. (Accessed 5 June 2021).

Forman, R., Shah, S., Jeurissen, P., Jit, M., Mossialos, E., 2021. COVID-19 vaccine challenges: what have we learned so far and what remains to be done? Health Policy 125 (5), 553–567.

Frost, H.R., 2020. Eigenvectors from Eigenvalues Sparse Principal Component Analysis (EESPCA).

Godfried, I., 2020. Machine Learning Methods to Aid in Coronavirus Response. Towards Data Science. Available at http://www.towardsdatascience.com. (Accessed 9 June 2021).

Gopalan-Hema, S., Misra, A., 2020. COVID-19 pandemic and challenges for socio-economic issues, healthcare and National Health Programs in India. Retrieved from http://www.ncbi.nlm.nih.gov.

Hassoun, H.T., 2021. The Impact of COVID-19 on Global Healthcare. Cedars Sinai. Available at http://www.cedars-sinai.org. (Accessed 8 June 2021).

Infosys BPM, 2021. The COVID-19 era: A new learning curve for global healthcare. Available at http://www.infosysbpm.com. (Accessed 8 June 2021).

Jason, C., 2020. How COVID-19 Accelerated the Digital Transformation of Healthcare. EHRIntelligence. Available online at http://www.ehrintelligence.com. (Accessed 8 June 2021).

Kent, J., 2020. How Big Data Analytics Can Mitigate COVID-19 Health Disparities. HealthITAnalytics. Available at http://www.healthitanalytics.com. (Accessed 9 June 2021).

Knight, C., 2021. Repurposing Drugs for COVID-19. News Medical. Available at http://www.news-medical.net. (Accessed 3 June 2021).

Kumar, N.R., 2021. 1.5 lakh doses of sputnik V land in India. The Hindu. Available at http://www.thehindu.com. (Accessed 3 June 2021).

Kumar, S., Kumar, A., 2021. Understanding the role of primary Care in Covid 19 response in India. PLOS. Available at http://www.yoursay.plos.org. (Accessed 4 June 2021).

LaBerge, L., O'Toole, C., Schneider, J., Smaje, K., 2020. How COVID-19 has pushed companies over the technology tipping point – and transformed business forever. McKinsey & Company. Available at http://www.mckinsey.com. (Accessed 8 June 2021).
Liu, Y.-C., Kuo, R.-L., Shih, S.-R., 2020. COVID-19: the first documented coronavirus pandemic in history. Biom. J. 4 (4), 328–333.
Londhe, V., 2020. The impact of COVID-19 on India's migrant workers. Sedex. Available at http://www.sedex.com. (Accessed 5 June 2021).
Marr, B., 2020. The Vital Role of Big Data In the Fight Against COVID-19 (Coronavirus). Linkedin. Available at http://www.linkedin.com. (Accessed 9 June 2021).
Mehta, Y., 2021. The role of IoT in healthcare during Covid-19. IoTNOW. Available at http://www.iot-now.com. (Accessed 10 June 2021).
Mishra, P., Al Khatib, A.M.G., Sardar, I., Mohammed, J., Ray, M., Kumar, M., Rawat, D., Pandey, S.A., Dubey, A., Feys, J., Rono, K., 2020. Modelling and forecasting of COVID-19 in India. J. Infect. Dis. Epidemiol. 6, 162.
Mitra, S.S., Banerjee, S.A., Arockiam-Peter Hembrom, A., Rasquinha, P., 2021. Perception of post graduate students towards E-learning in the 'new normal': an empirical investigation. Int. J. Adv. Innov. Res. 8, 83–87.
Nguyen, K., 2020. Cloud Computing During COVID-19 and Beyond. Experian. Available at http://www.experian.com. (Accessed 9 June 2021).
Santos, W.G., 2020. Natural history of COVID-19 and current knowledge on treatment therapeutic options. Biomed. Pharmacother. 129, 110493. Retrieved from http://www.ncbi.nlm.nih.gov.
Sevincer, G.M., Kaya, A., Bozkurt, S., Akin, E., Kose, S., 2017. Reliability, validity and factorial structure of the Turkish version of the weight self-stigma questionnaire (Turkish WSSQ). Psychiatry Clin. Psychopharmacol. 27 (4), 386–392.
Shreffler, J., Petrey, J., Huecker, M., 2020. The impact of COVID-19 on healthcare worker wellness: A scoping review. West. J. Emerg. Med. 21 (5), 1059–1066. Retrieved from http://www.ncbi.nlm.nih.gov.
Singh, S., Roy, D., Joshi, G., 2020. Impact of COVID-19 and lockdown on mental health of children and adolescents: a narrative review with recommendations. Psychiatry Res. 293, 113429. Retrieved from http://www.ncbi.nlm.nih.gov.
Syeda, H.B., Mahanazuddin, S., Feliciano, Y.J., 2020. Role of machine learning techniques to tackle the COVID-19 crisis: systematic review. JMIR Med. Inform. 9, e23811. Retrieved from http://www.ncbi.nlm.nih.gov.
Toews, R., 2020. These Are The Startups Applying AI To Transform Healthcare. Available at http://www.forbes.com. (Accessed 9 June 2021).
UN Women Data Hub, 2020. COVID-19: Emerging gender data and why it matters. Available at http://www.data.unwomen.org. (Accessed 6 June 2021).
Wessing, T., 2021. Surge in IoT during COVID-19 pandemic helps pave the way for new IoT laws. LEXOLOGY. Available at http://www.lexology.com. (Accessed 10 June 2021).
Wikipedia, 2021a. Impact of COVID-19 on female staff. Available at http://www.en.m.wikipedia.org. (Accessed 5 June 2021).
Wikipedia, 2021b. Impact of the COVID-19 pandemic on healthcare workers. Available at http://www.en.m.wikipedia.org. (Accessed 6 June 2021).
Wikipedia, 2021c. Impact of COVID-19 in India. Available at http://www.en.m.wikipedia.org. (Accessed 10 June 2021).
World Health Organization, 2020. Coronavirus disease (COVID-19): Health and safety in the workplace. Available at http://www.who.int. (Accessed 6 June 2021).
Xu, Z., Fan, J., Ding, J., Feng, X., Tao, S., Zhou, J., Qian, L., Tao, K., Hambly, B.D., Bao, S., 2021. The impact of COVID-19 on primary care general practice consultations in a teaching hospital in Shanghai, China. Front. Med.

Yadav, R., 2020. Impact of COVID-19 on Indian Migrant Workers. Critical Edges. Available at http://www.criticaledges.com. (Accessed 5 June 2021).

Zhenmin, L., 2020. COVID-19 and the role of digital technologies for achieving SDGs. UNCTAD. Available at http://www.unctad.org. (Accessed 8 June 2021).

Further reading

Australian Human Rights Commission, 2020. Impacts of COVID-19 on children and young people who contact Kids Helpline. Available at http://www.humanrights.gov.au. (Accessed 6 June 2021).

Dorn, A., 2020. COVID-19 and readjusting clinical trials. World Report 396 (10250), 523–524.

CHAPTER FIFTEEN

Modeling of cyber threat analysis and vulnerability in IoT-based healthcare systems during COVID

Romil Rawat[a], Vinod Mahor[b], Bhagwati Garg[c], Mukesh Chouhan[d], Kiran Pachlasiya[e], and Shrikant Telang[f]

[a]Department of Computer Science Engineering, Shri Vaishnav Vidyapeeth Vishwavidyalaya, Indore, India
[b]Department of Computer Science Engineering, IPS College of Technology and Management, Gwalior, India
[c]Union Bank of India, Branch, Gwalior, India
[d]Department of Computer Science and Engineering, Government Polytechnic College, Sheopur, India
[e]Department of Computer Science Engineering, NRI Institute of Science and Technology, Bhopal, India
[f]Department of Information Technology, Shri Vaishnav Vidyapeeth Vishwavidyalaya, Indore, India

1 Introduction

IoT refers to smart gadgets that enable real-world objects to communicate and think. It is a communication paradigm in which a variety of heterogeneous objects will connect and share details. These communication gadgets will become increasingly important in people's lives and will have a revolutionary influence on the world of technology as well as on people's social lives. IoT devices are outgrowing their capacity over time. According to current data, there were 30 billion IoT devices linked worldwide in 2020 (Hussain et al., 2021).

Furthermore, it is predicted that by 2025, 75.44 billion IoT devices will be connected globally. Manufacturing, agriculture, transportation, the electric grid, and healthcare, among other areas, have all recognized IoT footprints (Ghazanfar et al., 2020). Because the data are directly connected to humans in an IoT-based healthcare system, security is the key concern. An intensive care unit (ICU) is a unique and crucially operating section of a hospital where patients who require urgent medical care receive specialized treatment. Patients who are critically ill or wounded and require constant medical care are usually admitted to the ICU. The ICU's equipment and technologies serve a critical role in keeping the patient alive and well. Any communication breakdown caused by a cyber-security attack or vulnerability injection in this situation might have serious consequences for a patient's life, even death in some cases. As a result, an attack-proof IoT-based

Lessons from COVID-19
https://doi.org/10.1016/B978-0-323-99878-9.00016-9

(Lacerda and Fernandes, 2016) healthcare system is an urgent requirement with a safe and reliable data transfer environment between medical sensors and actuators.

There has been a lot of effort done so far to automate patient monitoring and aid medical professionals in remotely analyzing the patient's health condition. Some techniques depend on fog computing to execute some of the computation on the edge, rather than sending identifiable information to the cloud, to protect patients' privacy. Cyber-attacks against IoT healthcare (Hussain et al., 2020a,b) systems, on the other hand, have become the major target of intruders. More than 90% of healthcare systems have been targeted by cyber-attacks, according to reports. The healthcare industry has grown increasingly appealing to cyber-criminals, according to White House intelligence. Furthermore, throughout the COVID-19 era, cyber-attacks increased dramatically as COVID-19 (Hussain et al., 2020a,b) expanded. Cyber-criminals have begun to actively attack IoT healthcare services and systems.

In IoT healthcare contexts, the security and integrity of data are critical. Any data breach or manipulation in healthcare systems might expose patients to significant health risks. Similarly, if a modification to a patient's medical record is undetected by a professional physician, it might result in an unintentional death. Furthermore, cyber-attacks (Alrashdi et al., 2019a,b) on IoT healthcare systems might interrupt medical treatments significantly. For instance, suppose a hacker obtains access to an infusion pump and modifies its settings so that it begins delivering a significant amount of insulin to a patient, resulting in severe hypoglycemia. Consider what happens if a cyber-criminal obtains access to a pacemaker and either slows or speeds up the heartbeat. In that situation, the patient may experience severe bradycardia or tachycardia, which might result in death. As a result, the security of healthcare systems has become the most pressing and vital issue of system design requirements.

Because of their limited memory, processing capability, and power, IoT devices are resource constrained. Because of the unique characteristics of IoT devices, standard security solutions are ineffective at detecting malicious threats in the IoT environment. As a result, designing a security strategy for IoT devices is extremely difficult. Manufacturing sectors are mass-producing IoT goods in order to develop low-cost IoT devices in a short period of time. Manufacturers are placing less emphasis on device security as a result of the race to capture the market as soon as possible. Furthermore, IoT device makers develop back doors that allow them to remotely access the equipment or exploit it for nefarious purposes. The majority of consumer-deployed IoT devices are linked to the network without any kind of security protection. As a result, IoT devices are readily vulnerable.

Traditional security methods are applied on two levels, namely, network and host. The host-level security method is regarded as more secure than the network-level security strategy in the current Internet era. Host-level security measures cannot be used since IoT devices are low-powered and resource limited. As a result, the network-based security mechanism is superior to the host-based security system for IoT devices.

An intrusion detection system (IDS) (Alharam and El-Madany, 2017) is a required layer of defense among the existing security measures for detecting hostile network activity. IDS are classified as network-based (examines network events) and host-based (examines host events). To defend IoT networks from cyber-attacks, network-based IDS must be educated and trained on IoT behaviors and designs. The IDS is trained on either live traffic or a collection of recorded network traffic. IDS real traffic training is a costly and time-consuming operation. The training of IDS on an adequate network traffic dataset, on the other hand, is a quick and low-cost operation. As a result, having a suitable IoT dataset for IDS training and testing is critical. Some methods, such as in, use deep learning (DL) models for feature extraction in order to identify intrusions in network traffic. Despite the fact that existing IDS technology is well established, it is insufficient for IoT devices and networks owing to processing and storage capacity limitations. Furthermore, typical IDS systems do not support common IoT protocols like MQTT (Kammüller, 2019) and Constrained Application Protocol (COAP). As a result, developing IoT-enabled IDS is crucially required.

Despite the fact that existing IDS technology is well established, it is insufficient for IoT devices and networks with limitations in processing scaling and storage capacity. Because of the unique characteristics of smart devices, such as scalability, processing, memory, and power resource limits, standard security solutions are ineffective in detecting malicious attacks in the IoT environment. IDS require an efficient IoT traffic real-time dataset including normal and suspicious traffic for training and testing. To do this, we created a real-time IoT traffic dataset for the development of IoT-based IDS in the setting of ICUs. In addition, the proposed system includes an open-source application for transforming IoT-Flock (Hussain et al., 2021). Hussain et al. (2020a,b) recorded traffic into an IoT dataset. Finally, we show how the suggested framework can be utilized to create an AI-based cyber-security solution to safeguard and defend IoT healthcare systems from cyber-attacks by applying various machine learning (ML) algorithms to the generated IoT dataset. The suggested architecture would aid in the development of IoT-ATATMT security solutions, particularly for the highly sensitive healthcare sector.

This chapter outlines a methodology for creating IoT security systems that can identify fraudulent traffic in IoT use cases, particularly in the healthcare sector. To aid the research community, the proposed architecture includes an open-source analyzer for generating IoT traffic with a use case dataset. It may also create both legitimate and malicious IoT traffic via the Message Queuing Telemetry Transport (MQTT) (Kammüller, 2019) and COAP IoT application layer protocols.

To create network traffic to capture packets and a complete payload for the dataset, we utilized the IoT traffic generator tool to build an attacking network and a typical network of IoT devices. In the IoT traffic generator tool, we created a real-life ICU use case. We generated real-time IoT traffic by evaluating real-time value ranges and creating data and time profiles for ICU devices. We took the network layer characteristics and combined them with a large number of application-layer and payload features. Finally, we employed six widely used ML algorithms to show the usefulness of the proposed framework and the generated dataset for creating IoT-ATATMT security solutions.

The remainder of the chapter is organized as follows; Section 2 represents literature review; Section 3 shows the proposed model; Section 4 represents results and discussion; and finally, Section 5 concludes this chapter.

2 Literature review

The fast advancement of IoT technology (Ghazanfar et al., 2020) has changed many aspects of life, including smart cities, smart health, smart wearables, smart industries, and smart agriculture. Health monitoring systems based on the Internet of Things are getting smarter all the time. Various IoT-based smart health monitoring systems have been presented in recent years. However, in terms of healthcare system security, IoT is still in its infancy. Because of the resource constraints of IoT devices (Rathore and Park, 2018) and the various security-level requirements, traditional network security solutions cannot be employed for IoT-based healthcare systems. Furthermore, the data created by IoT devices in an IoT environment differs depending on the use case, for example, smart healthcare and smart homes. As a result, existing security solutions and processes must be adapted to the needs of IoT use cases (Hussain et al., 2020a,b).

Rughoobur and Nagowah (2017) presented a method for detecting replay attacks on IoT healthcare equipment that is battery-powered. To identify and prevent replay attacks on battery-dependent IoT healthcare devices, their suggested approach examines the unique device id, timestamps, and battery depletion behavior. Rathore and Park (2018) proposed a semisupervised Fuzzy C-Means technique based on an extreme learning machine (ELM) to identify cyber-attacks in fog-based IoT settings. The authors utilized ELM to identify cyber threats quickly and effectively, using Fuzzy C-Means to alleviate dataset labeling problems. Similarly, Atzori et al. (2021) developed a feature engineering approach to identify abnormalities more effectively and improve the performance of standard IDSs. Alrashdi et al. (2019a,b), on the other hand, presented a methodology for identifying vulnerabilities in fog computing associated with IoT healthcare systems. In a fog computing smart house equipped with a remote patient-monitoring system, the authors employed an ensemble of online sequential ELM to identify malicious threats such as man-in-the-middle and DDoS.

The IoT Flock analyzes malicious packets in a real-time environment by exposing Common Vulnerabilities and Exposures (CVE) (Blinowski and Piotrowski, 2020). Table 1 outlines the IOT Flock Purpose and Applications.

The security shields to defend the IoT systems and networks from cyber-vulnerabilities are intrusion detection systems (IDS), intrusion prevention systems (IPS), and firewalls. The majority of firewalls use static specified rules to filter regular and suspicious traffic. IDS and IPS, on the other hand, use

Table 1 IOT Flock Purpose and Applications.

Applications	Vulnerabilities at IoT application layer	Common Vulnerabilities and Exposures (CVE) id
Generation of packet details	MQTT Publishing Flood	CVE-2018-1684
Use for stress testing of networking devices	CoAP (Memory Leak threat)	CVE-2019-9004
Use for system testing—IDS, IPS	MQTT Packet Crafting threat	CVE-2016-10523
Building of new use case models	CoAP Segmentation Fault threat	CVE-2019-12101
Used as benchmark for network troubleshooting		
Analyzes large IoT device traffic		

artificial intelligence (AI) (Rathee et al., 2020) to filter invasive efforts and are thus more trustworthy and effective than established static rules. Malicious and benign network traffic datasets are used to train and test the IDS and IPS. These datasets can be collected in one of two ways: by utilizing actual systems to produce suspicious and regular network traffic, or by employing traffic generators. The technologies that simulate real-time network traffic are known as traffic generators.

Using the network traffic (Eken and Eken, 2018) information generated by real-time systems to train and test IDS and IPS is a time-consuming and challenging task. This conundrum may be solved by using a traffic generator tool to generate the dataset. Regardless, current IDS technology is reasonably developed, but it is insufficient for IoT systems. The major reason for this, as previously stated, is the IoT nodes' limited processing and storage capability, which is the fundamental issue for host IDS. Another important reason is that the communication protocols used by IoT devices (e.g., CoAP, MQTT, and others) are rarely used in traditional networks, since various protocols have distinct vulnerabilities and IDS needs (Djenna and Saïdouni, 2018). The work creates a large and trustworthy IoT network traffic dataset so that IDS may be developed, particularly for the IoT-based ICU setting. In such a circumstance, any security compromise might have a serious impact on the patient, or even result in death (Kamble and Gawade, 2019).

There are several cutting-edge datasets that are utilized for training and testing of IDS and IPS for both traditional and IoT networks. The network traffic datasets developed in recent years have been widely used up to this point. Some are realistic datasets, which are created using real-time systems, while others are simulated datasets, which are created using simulation software. DARPA, KDD-99, NSL-KDD, DEFCON, LBNL, CAIDA, UNIBS, ISCX, and UNSW-NB15 (Hussain et al., 2021; Ghazanfar et al., 2020; Lacerda and Fernandes, 2016; Hussain et al., 2020a,b) are some of the state-of-the-art datasets.

The pioneer dataset, DARPA (Hussain et al., 2021), was suggested in 1998 at MIT Lincoln Laboratory. This dataset was created for the evaluation of IDS and comprises 7 weeks' worth of data. Emails, FTP, Telnet, IRC, and SNMP-related events are all included. The attacks (DoS attacks, remote-to-local (R2L), and user-to-remote (U2R)) were all simulated on Windows and UNIX systems. This dataset, on the other hand, lacks real-time traffic and has several flaws, such as the absence of false positives.

The KDD-99 (Ghazanfar et al., 2020) dataset was created by inspecting the IDS specifically intended to identify inbound threats using DARPA

(Ghazanfar et al., 2020). It includes DoS attacks, including pod-DoS, smurf-DoS, Neptune-DoS, and buffer overflow vulnerabilities, as well as buffer overflow attacks. Because it includes 80% of attack traffic, this dataset has great difficulty with unbalanced learning. NSL-KDD was created later to address the problems with KDD-99. It is, however, out of date because it does not include current standards and vulnerable occurrences.

DEFCON (Lacerda and Fernandes, 2016) has two versions: DEFCON-8 and DEFCON-10, which were filmed during a capture flag (hacking and antihacking) competition in 2000 and 2002, respectively. DEFCON-8 addresses port scanning and buffer overflow attacks, whereas DEFCON-10 addresses port scanning, malicious packets, and FTP threats.

In 2004, the LBNL dataset (Hussain et al., 2020a,b) was created by collecting incoming, outgoing, and routing traffic from two edge routers. It was gathered from a medium-sized website and only comprises entire header files. It has a high level of anonymization.

The CAIDA (Ghazanfar et al., 2020) dataset was obtained from a large-scale enterprise's Internet backbone and solely comprises traffic headers without payloads. Specific threats, such as DDoS attacks, are included. The data were not further analyzed to produce additional characteristics that may help distinguish between legitimate and malicious communications. Furthermore, it is unlabeled, making it unsuitable for direct IDS performance evaluation because labeling requires preprocessing.

The traffic flow (Hussain et al., 2021) of 20 workstations was recorded using tcpdump on the router for the UNIBS dataset. Only denial-of-service threats were targeted. In 2012, ISCX was created utilizing actual network settings. Simulating genuine network traffic was done by a group of people. It's a labeled dataset that includes a variety of vulnerability scenarios. It has two profiles: the Alpha profile, which is used in multistage threat situations, and the Beta profile, which is used in normal traffic. It contains complete packet payloads for a variety of protocols, including HTTP, FTP, and SMTP (Kamble and Gawade, 2019), among others. It does not, however, include HTTPS, which accounts for 70% of current-generation traffic. The UNSWNB-15 dataset was gathered by using the IXIA storm in a commercial penetration testing environment to create malicious and normal traffic.

Bot-IoT (Ghazanfar et al., 2020) is a dataset that comprises simulated IoT network traffic as well as several attack types. Bot-IoT (Rughoobur and Nagowah, 2017) is the only publicly accessible IoT dataset that comprises both regular and malicious traffic, to our knowledge, among the above-mentioned datasets. For the five IoT scenarios triggered by three types of probing attacks, DoS attacks (Ghazanfar et al., 2020; Kame and Elhamayed, 2020), and information theft attempts, the Bot-IoT dataset contains IoT traffic generated by normal and attacking virtual machines. Despite the fact that the Bot-IoT dataset comprises nearly 72 billion instances, only one IoT-specific protocol, namely MQTT, is evaluated. We can construct nearly any IoT use case, add normal and malicious devices based on the use case, and produce traffic for protocols (MQTT and CoAP) using our own traffic generating tool, IoT-Flock.

3 Proposed model

The model contains five key steps, as shown in Fig. 1, starting with IoT use case traffic generation and ending with the creation of an IoT-ATATMT security solution for malicious traffic identification in the IoT healthcare use case. The use case creation, IoT normal and attack traffic production, IoT traffic capture, IoT dataset building, and ML model construction are among the modules available.

The suggested architecture begins with the creation of an IoT use case, which is subsequently executed to create real-time IoT traffic. The resulting traffic is then collected to build an IoT dataset that will be used to train the ML algorithms. Finally, multiple ML approaches are used to train and evaluate ML models in order to efficiently identify fraudulent network traffic in the underlying IoT use case.

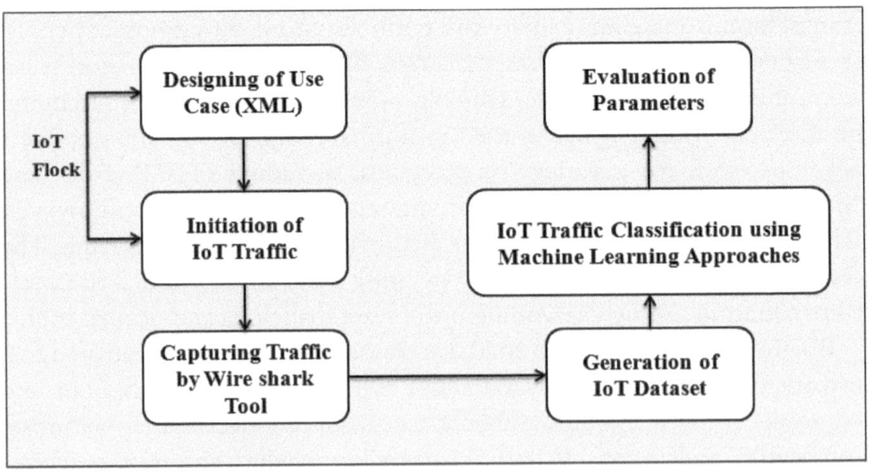

Fig. 1 Traffic analyzer model.

3.1 IoT use case generator

The suggested framework's initial module, IoT use case generator, is made up of our newly created, open-source IoT traffic generating tool, IoT-Flock (Ghazanfar et al., 2020; Hussain et al., 2020a,b).

In every use scenario, the IoT-Flock tool may create both regular and attack traffic for IoT-based devices. With IoT-Flock, one can simply construct IoT use cases based on his or her requirements and produce IoT traffic for various use cases to create traffic for hundreds of IoT devices on a real-time live network utilizing a single physical computer. Fig. 2 depicts the IoT-fundamental Flock's architecture.

In comparison to publically accessible traffic generating methods, the IoT-Flock tool offers the following unique features:

- IoT-Flock can develop real-time use cases by having a coding structure that is simple to learn and extend.
- With the assistance of a large number of devices that may be added, IoT-Flock can develop real-time IoT use cases.
- The majority of open-source and commercial traffic (Kumar et al., 2021) generating solutions do not allow for the creation of attacking entities. IoT-Flock allows researchers to develop both standard and attack IoT devices within the same use case for generating traffic at the same time.

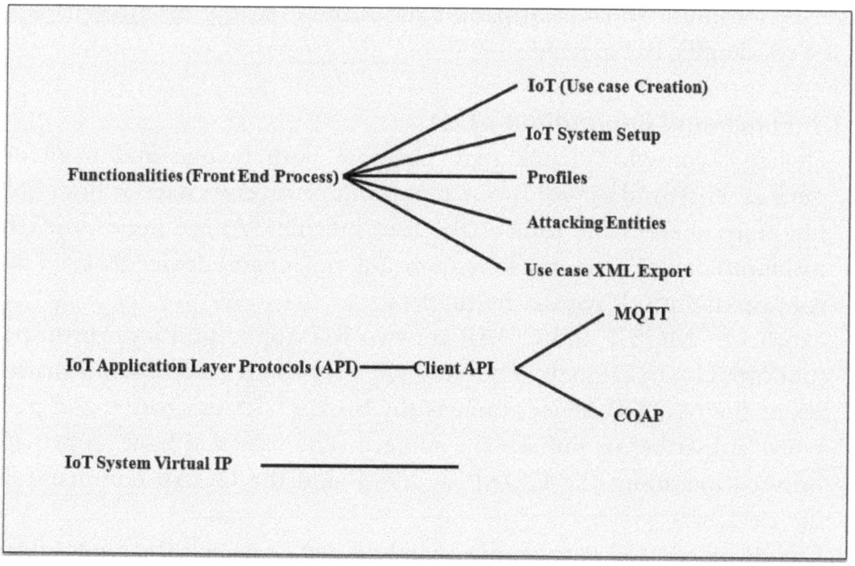

Fig. 2 IoT traffic generator model (IoT-Flock tool).

As a result, the produced traffic includes both standard and threat patterns, which can aid in the design of IDS and IPS.
- IoT-Flock supports exporting the intended use case to XML and importing the XML created by IoT-Flock or another third-party program. It may encourage researchers to design more user-friendly use cases, convert them to XML, and utilize the IoT-Flock console program to generate IoT traffic.
- IoT-Flock can generate the most recent MQTT and COAP-specific attacks. No other open-source IoT traffic generating tools currently support this. Users may choose an attack type and construct a malicious device, generating harmful traffic rapidly.

IoT-Flock works in two modes: GUI mode and Console mode. The GUI mode is intended to create IoT use cases in a user-friendly environment. Any IoT use case may be created with any number of devices. The devices that are introduced to the use case can act in the same way as real-time devices do. At any moment, a user can build a single IoT device or many IoT devices. A user must supply the necessary functional and nonfunctional information about the device in order to create a single IoT device or numerous IoT devices. An IoT device's operating behavior is defined by its functional information. It contains data about the device's kind (normal or malicious), protocol, data profile, time profile, instructions, and controls (i.e., subscribe, publish topic in MQTT case, post control in the case of COAP). Nonfunctional information about the user, on the other hand, is given to identify IoT devices.

3.1.1 Functional information fields

- Device Type—IoT-Flock may generate both benign and malicious devices. A typical device is one that sends or receives data or does both functions at the same time as the user specifies. At the same time, the malicious device is an attacking (harmful, malignant) device that can disrupt the use case's regular traffic flow.
- Protocol—MQTT and COAP are two IoT application layer protocols supported by IoT-Flock. The user will have to give further information about the MQTT device, such as the broker's IP, username, and password, subscribe, or publish the subject. The user will have to provide information about the COAP server IP and the COAP command on the device.
- Data Profile—The data profile of an IoT device depicts the types of data that can be sent by the device. An Internet of Things device can deliver

digital or analog data (values) together with a notification message. Binary values such as on, off, or 1, 0 will be sent by the digital device. The analog device, on the other hand, will send the values in a defined range as an attachment to a user's notification message. The notification message might be a short text or a large text spanning many gigabytes.
- Time Profile—The time profile of an IoT device will dictate when the device will provide data. The IoT-Flock allows for two types of time profiles: periodic and random. The data will be transmitted by an IoT device with a regular time profile after a predetermined period of time specified by the user. A device with a random time profile, on the other hand, will deliver the data after some arbitrary period within the user-specified random time range.

3.1.2 Nonfunctional information fields

A device's nonfunctional information is also required to uniquely identify an IoT device. It contains the device attributes (Mohapatro and Snigdh, 2020) (Name, IP address, and count of devices). The IoT device in traffic is identified by its IP address. Each device in the use case will have its own IP address, which will be utilized for communication.

The creation of IoT use cases can aid researchers in understanding and meeting the domain's context-aware needs. Furthermore, use cases can aid researchers in analyzing other factors, such as security needs and others. IoT use cases created in IoT-GUI Flock mode may be converted to XML format. IoT-Flock was built with the idea that any IoT use case created using a third-party tool and sent in XML format may be executed in IoT-Flock.

The IoT console mode has been developed for this reason, where the user may just supply an XML file and the entire IoT use case traffic production will begin.

We wanted to generate IoT traffic, particularly for IoT-based healthcare system use cases. We looked at an IoT-based ICU use case in this study. As a result, we must first use IoT-Flock to develop an IoT-based ICU use case. We began by examining the purpose, operating principles, and kind of data provided by the devices typically utilized in an ICU. As a result, we used IoT-Flock to construct an IoT-based ICU use case and added devices to it (Fig. 3).

Environmental-monitoring devices and patient-monitoring devices are the two types of equipment that are utilized in ICU use cases. The environmental-monitoring equipment is used to keep track of the ICU's environmental conditions in order to keep it in excellent shape. At the same

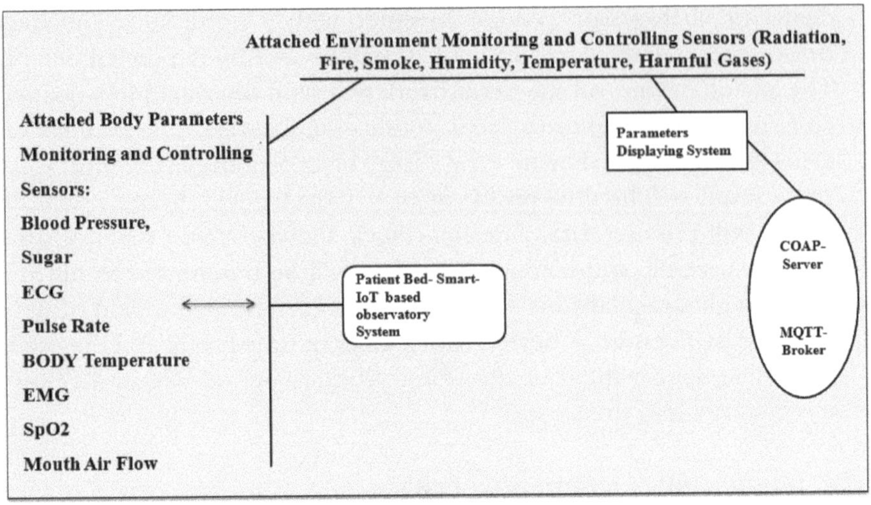

Fig. 3 IoT-based monitoring system at ICU use case.

time, patient-monitoring devices are placed in certain regions of the body to monitor the patient's health (Kamble and Gawade, 2019). Patient-monitoring devices are used to continually evaluate a patient's physical state in order to provide immediate medical assistance if the patient's health begins to deteriorate.

After a particular interval established by the ICU managers, the IoT devices placed in the ICU send a specific type of data. These qualities were given the names data profile and time profile. We selected the kind and range of data communicated by each device in the data profile, whereas we described the time interval after which each device will send or receive data in the time profile. The data profile is derived by checking each machine's datasheet, but the time profile is based on the authors' impressions. The device template (Ghosal et al., 2018) is created using IoT-Flock when the data profile and time profile of each device are provided. Once a device template has been generated in IoT-Flock, it can be used numerous times or edited as needed for a specific use case (Table 2).

We utilized an IoT-based ICU with a capacity of 2 beds, each with 10 patient-monitoring devices (sensors) and 1 control unit in our scenario. We named it Bed_b-Control-Unit, where b represents the count of beds, i.e., Bed_1 to Bed_2. Based on the physical status of the patient as detected by the patient-monitoring devices, the Bedx_b-Control-Unit is responsible for performing particular actions such as establishing the time profile, the

Table 2 Body parameters and environmental activities monitoring sensors.

Sensor	Purpose
Smoke	Smoke detection for quick action
Solar radiation	For analyzing radiations
Remote electrocardiogram (ECG) monitoring	Heart functioning monitoring
Infusion pump	Controlled medicines and defined nutrients to patient
Pulsoximeter (SpO_2)	For checking oxygen saturation in blood
Nasal/mouth air flow	Managing breathing rate
Blood pressure monitor	Managing blood pressure
Glucometer	Measuring blood glucose level
Body temperature sensor	Monitoring body temperature
Electromyography (EMG)	Monitoring of body muscles electric pulse
Air temperature	To measure air temperature with defined values
Harmful gas detection	Surroundings gas concentration observation
Fire	Fire detection for alarming
Air humidity	To measure air humidity with defined values

quantity of the dosage delivered to the patient via an infusion pump, or producing an emergency alert.

Similarly, we built another control unit named Environment-Control-Unit for environmental-monitoring equipment. To maintain the appropriate ICU environment, the Environment-Control-Unit is responsible for regulating the ICU environment conditions, such as maintaining a certain temperature, humidity level, detecting smoke, and creating an emergency alarm in case of emergency situations. Both the patient-monitoring and the environmental-monitoring sensors in our use case are MQTT-based. The MQTT protocol is connection-oriented, ensuring that the packet is correctly delivered.

3.2 IoT traffic generation

To build a large dataset, we separated the testbed infrastructure into two networks: the esteemed network and the invader network. The prestigious network is a typical IoT-based ICU network that includes a MQTT broker and several MQTT devices that communicate and receive data. The invader network is an attacking network made up of vulnerable entities capable of launching various sorts of threats against specific devices or servers.

3.2.1 Normal traffic generation

We used the IoT-Flock program to create an IoT-esteemed network for the dataset creation, which includes both patient- and environmental-monitoring MQTT devices transmitting and receiving network data under normal conditions. We developed a use case for an IoT-based ICU with 2 beds, each of which is equipped with 10 patient-monitoring devices (sensors) and a control unit named Bedx-Control-Unit. The IoT-Flock tool, which was running on a Linux computer, was used to construct all of these devices. The IoT-Flock tool built a virtual network interface for each device on a single physical computer via which these devices communicate. Furthermore, the MQTT broker and COAP server were each running on their own computer.

3.2.2 Attack generation

We built an intruder network when the regular network started producing IoT traffic. The invader network consists of 15 vulnerable devices that launch four different forms of attacks: MQTT distributed denial-of-service, MQTT published flood, brute force, and SlowITE (Hussain et al., 2020a,b). The sorts of attacks that IoT-Flock supports are described in the sections below.

- **MQTT Publish Flood**—A DDoS attack can deplete network bandwidth as well as the resources of the target system. DDoS attackers have migrated up the stack and are now attacking the application layer due to improved mitigation measures at the network and transport layers (Kammüller, 2019). IoT devices use application layer protocols to deliver data in a predefined time frame format. The periodic timeframe_device provides data to the server every b seconds. For example, a humidity sensor returns data to the server every 10s. However, with event-driven model devices, data are only sent when a certain event happens, such as when a motion sensor in the ICU detects movement in the ICU. MQTT publishing messages at a high pace can result in a denial-of-service attack. Such threats cause data transmission delays and are extremely damaging, particularly at industrial and other high levels, such as smart hospitals and smart transportation systems. Data transmission delays have the potential to destroy these assets and endanger human life.
- **MQTT Authentication Bypass Attack** (Alrashdi et al., 2019a,b)—MQTT clients submit MQTT connect requests with username and password fields to connect to the MQTT broker, which needs authentication. It was observed that by removing the password field from the

MQTT packet and simply giving an existing username, MQTT authentication may be circumvented. Even if the latest MQTT brokers mitigate this attack, a MQTT broker still needs to process this incorrect packet, which might create a delay in MQTT broker operations if it is delivered in a large quantity. As a result, the MQTT broker's delayed issue can be avoided if the IPS stops such an incorrect packet.

- **MQTT Packet Crafting Attack** (Hussain et al., 2020a,b)—MQTT packets are deliberately designed in this attack to cause an application to crash. By diverting from making connection requests toward the MQTT broker, the attacker establishes a forged connection with the transport layer by publishing it at the start.
- **COAP Replay Attack**—An intruder first scans the network for COAP client and server addresses as well as payload information in this attack.

The intruder then modifies the payload and transmits it to the COAP server using a fake COAP client IP. The seriousness of this attack may be observed in documented use scenarios where environmental sensors utilize COAP protocols to provide data to a COAP server. For example, the temperature sensor sends an ICU temperature change, and the condition is set depending on that value. If an attacker utilizes spoof IP to send an ICU temperature with an unexpected value, the ICU will be susceptible and suffer severe damage.

3.3 IoT traffic capturing

The next stage is to collect the packet flows, packets, and payload once the invader network and esteemed network devices have been formed and have begun broadcasting and receiving data. Wireshark (Ghazanfar et al., 2020) was used to capture the packets. Wireshark (Ghazanfar et al., 2020) is a well-known and free network analysis program that captures real-time packets and allows you to filter and analyze them. We created a python program to trace out the packet flows and extract the application layer characteristics from the .pcap files while recording the packet flows.

In today's world, application-layer threats account for the majority of cyber-attacks (Lacerda and Fernandes, 2016). Network and transport layer traffic information are included in the traditional publicly accessible datasets. In the conventional network realm, a distributed denial-of-service (DDoS) threat at the network and transport layer is a well-known problem, and academics have made significant contributions to its protection (Hussain et al., 2020a,b).

According to ImpervaIncapsula's Global DDoS Threat Landscape 2017 Report (Kammüller, 2019), network layer threats have decreased while application-layer attacks have increased. According to Kaspersky (Hussain et al., 2020a,b), "the crème of cyber-criminal groups is now concentrating on application layer DDoS threats." Traditional application layer protocols like HTTP are being studied for defense against the DDoS threat (Hussain et al., 2020a,b). However, no substantial effort has been made to protect IoT application layer protocols (COAP, MQTT) from DDoS threat. The lack of availability of IoT application layer attack traffic in IoT datasets is the major cause of the lack of attention. We created a python tool to extract network and application layer characteristics from IoT traffic with this goal in mind.

3.4 IoT dataset creation

To extract the network and application layer aspects of IoT traffic, we created a python tool (Alrashdi et al., 2019a,b) that analyzes pcap files and extracts features using the tshark library. In this study, we collected network and application layer characteristics from each produced pcap file and stored them as CSV files with appropriate traffic labels.

3.5 ML model development

The dataset preprocessing, feature selection, ML model training, and testing modules make up the ML model development module. The next sections go through these processes in detail.

3.5.1 Dataset preprocessing

Pcap files were used to build the dataset once the traffic was captured. We used a python script to convert the pcap files into CSV files so that we could preprocess and analyses the dataset. To make subsequent processing easier, we used Label Encoder to replace categorical characteristics of the dataset, such as protocol type (e.g., MQTT and COAP), with numerical values. Finally, we checked the dataset for missing values by authenticating it. In the dataset, we discovered several missing values and replaced them with 0. Following that, the dataset was randomly split into train and test groups using a 75:25 split ratio, meaning that 75% of the dataset was randomly picked for training and 25% for testing.

A ML model's performance is heavily influenced by feature selection. After preprocessing the data, we used the Logistic Regression (LR) technique, which has been shown to be effective in the literature

(Kammüller, 2019). We used the LR method to pick the most important characteristics for training and testing ML models: ["tcp.flags.ack," "frame.time delta," "tcp.time delta," "tcp.flags.push," "tcp.flags.reset," "mqtt.hdrflags," "mqtt.msgtype']. The specifics of these characteristics may be found in Alharam and El-Madany (2017).

3.5.2 ML models training and testing

After the data have been analyzed and the features have been chosen, the ML model must be trained. We divided the data into training and testing sets before training the ML models. Using the training dataset, we trained six frequently utilized ML classifiers for fraudulent traffic identification in IoT system healthcare contexts. Adaboost (AB), Naive Bayes (NB), K-Nearest Neighbors (KNN), Random Forest (RF), Logistic Regression (LogR), and Decision Tree (DT) are six frequently used ML classifiers. Finally, we assess each classifier's effectiveness in detecting fraudulent traffic in IoT healthcare contexts by testing the trained models against the test set.

4 Results and discussion

The performance of ML classifiers is measured using four commonly used performance metrics: precision, recall, accuracy, and F1-score. The following are the parameters that are defined.

- TP (true positive)—accurate categorization of threat flow instances as threats.
- TN (true negative)—accurate categorization of the normal flow statistics as normal.
- FP (false positive)—incorrect categorization of normal flow as a threat.
- FN (false negative)—incorrect categorization of threat flow as normal.
- FNR—false-negative rate (used to calculate error rate).
- Precision—used to measure accuracy.

The ability of the system to accurately categorize an attack packet as an "attack packet" and a regular packet as a "normal packet" is described as accuracy. It indicates the proportion of valid predictions across all samples.

- Recall—used to calculate error rate.

When a botnet threat occurs on the network, the system's ability to accurately identify the attack is defined.

- FPR—true positive rate (used to measure accuracy).
- F-Measure—mean (Harmonic) value of recall and precision.

$$\Rightarrow \text{TPR} = \frac{\text{TP}}{\text{TN} + \text{TP}} \qquad \Rightarrow \text{FPR} = \frac{\text{FP}}{\text{TP} + \text{FN}}$$

$$\Rightarrow \text{precision} = \frac{\text{TP}}{\text{TN} + \text{FP}} \qquad \Rightarrow \text{recall} = \frac{\text{TP}}{\text{TP} + \text{FN}}$$

$$\Rightarrow \text{F} - \text{Measure (F1} - \text{Score)} = 2 * \frac{\text{precision} * \text{recall}}{\text{precision} + \text{recall}}$$

Fig. 4 Parameters for research evaluation.

- F1 Score—it denotes the proportion of correct predictions in the test set for normal and attack traffic (Fig. 4).

The confusion matrices of each unique ML classifier are shown below, which was derived for malicious traffic detection across an IoT healthcare test dataset created with IoT-Flock (Table 3).

Table 4 shows a comparison of the six ML classifiers' performance in identifying normal and malicious traffic in the IoT healthcare context. The RF classifier beat all other classifiers with 99.8497% precision, 99.8968% recall, 99.6833% accuracy, and 99.7597% F1-score among the six ML classifiers.

The tests show how the suggested framework can identify cyber-attacks in order to safeguard and defend the IoT healthcare environment. One may easily create AI-based security solutions for any additional IoT use case by

Table 3 Machine learning classifier confusion matrix.

		Predicted	
Actual		**Normal**	**Attack**
NB (naive Bayes) Classifier	Normal	33,613	48
	Attack	12,175	13,853
KNN Classifier	Normal	33,623	89
	Attack	147	24,629
RF Classifier	Normal	33,846	59
	Attack	132	24,473
AB (Adaboost) Classifier	Normal	33,497	146
	Attack	132	24,386
LogR (Logistic Regression) Classifier	Normal	31,672	2612
	Attack	135	24,357
DT (Decision Tree) Classifier	Normal	33,590	59
	Attack	138	24,947

Table 4 Machine learning classifiers parameters evaluation (for normal and malicious traffic detection).

ML classifier	Precision	Recall	Accuracy	F1-score
KNN	99.7396	99.7976	99.5287	99.6169
LogR	96.8464	96.6978	99.7564	99.8745
DT	99.7387	99.8349	99.5957	99.7158
NB	81.2745	99.8283	58.3987	73.6765
AB	99.6197	99.5128	99.5387	99.5197
RF	99.8497	99.8968	99.6833	99.7597

following the suggested framework's essential stages, as shown in Fig. 1. Additionally, the experimental results and dataset created may be used to develop IoT-ATATMT security solutions, particularly in the IoT healthcare setting.

5 Conclusions

The lockdown period caused due to COVID and the world goes at online mode for conducting transactions, which activated hackers for illicit activities. The security of IoT healthcare systems is critical, since any security breach or cyber-attack in such systems might have a serious impact on human life, and in some cases, even result in death. As a result, in this chapter, we present a methodology for creating IoT-ATATMT solutions to identify malicious traffic. The proposed architecture contains IoT traffic originator tool that generates both normal and malicious traffic using an IoT-based ICU use case. The experimental findings show that the suggested framework is useful for creating efficient IoT-ATATMT security solutions.

References

Alharam, A.K., El-Madany, W., 2017. Complexity of cyber security architecture for IoT healthcare industry: a comparative study. In: 2017 5th International Conference on Future Internet of Things and Cloud Workshops (FiCloudW). IEEE, pp. 246–250.

Alrashdi, I., Alqazzaz, A., Alharthi, R., Aloufi, E., Zohdy, M.A., Ming, H., 2019a. FBAD: fog-based attack detection for IoT healthcare in smart cities. In: 2019 IEEE 10th Annual Ubiquitous Computing, Electronics & Mobile Communication Conference (UEMCON). IEEE, pp. 515–522.

Alrashdi, I., Alqazzaz, A., Aloufi, E., Alharthi, R., Zohdy, M., Ming, H., 2019b. Ad-iot: anomaly detection of iotcyberattacks in smart city using machine learning. In: 2019 IEEE 9th Annual Computing and Communication Workshop and Conference (CCWC). IEEE, pp. 305–310.

Atzori, A., Barra, S., Carta, S., Fenu, G., Podda, A.S., 2021. Heimdall: an AI-based infrastructure for traffic monitoring and anomalies detection. In: 2021 IEEE International

Conference on Pervasive Computing and Communications Workshops and Other Affiliated Events (PerCom Workshops). IEEE, pp. 154–159.

Blinowski, G.J., Piotrowski, P., 2020. CVE based classification of vulnerable IoT systems. In: International Conference on Dependability and Complex Systems. Springer, Cham, pp. 82–93.

Djenna, A., Saïdouni, D.E., 2018. Cyber attacks classification in IoT-based-healthcare infrastructure. In: 2018 2nd Cyber Security in Networking Conference (CSNet). IEEE, pp. 1–4.

Eken, C., Eken, H., 2018. Security threats and recommendation in IoT healthcare. In: Proceedings of the 9th EUROSIM Congress on Modelling and Simulation, EUROSIM 2016, The 57th SIMS Conference on Simulation and Modelling SIMS 2016 (No. 142). Linköping University Electronic Press, pp. 369–374.

Ghazanfar, S., Hussain, F., Rehman, A.U., Fayyaz, U.U., Shahzad, F., Shah, G.A., 2020. Iotflock: an open-source framework for IoT traffic generation. In: 2020 International Conference on Emerging Trends in Smart Technologies (ICETST). IEEE, pp. 1–6.

Ghosal, P., Das, D., Das, I., 2018. Extensive survey on cloud-based IoT-healthcare and security using machine learning. In: 2018 Fourth International Conference on Research in Computational Intelligence and Communication Networks (ICRCICN). IEEE, pp. 1–5.

Hussain, F., Abbas, S.G., Fayyaz, U.U., Shah, G.A., Toqeer, A., Ali, A., 2020a. Towards a universal features set for IoT botnet attacks detection. In: 2020 IEEE 23rd International Multitopic Conference (INMIC). IEEE, pp. 1–6.

Hussain, F., Abbas, S.G., Husnain, M., Fayyaz, U.U., Shahzad, F., Shah, G.A., 2020b. IoTDoS and DDoS attack detection using ResNet. In: 2020 IEEE 23rd International Multitopic Conference (INMIC). IEEE, pp. 1–6.

Hussain, F., Abbas, S.G., Shah, G.A., Pires, I.M., Fayyaz, U.U., Shahzad, F., et al., 2021. A framework for malicious traffic detection in IoT healthcare environment. Sensors 21 (9), 3025.

Kamble, P., Gawade, A., 2019. Digitalization of healthcare with IoT and cryptographic encryption against DOS attacks. In: 2019 International Conference on Contemporary Computing and Informatics (IC3I). IEEE, pp. 69–73.

Kame, S.O.M., Elhamayed, S.A., 2020. Mitigating the impact of IoT routing attacks on power consumption in IoT healthcare environment using convolutional neural network. Int. J. Comput. Netw. Inf. Secur. 12 (4), 18–24.

Kammüller, F., 2019. Combining secure system design with risk assessment for iot healthcare systems. In: 2019 IEEE International Conference on Pervasive Computing and Communications Workshops (PerCom Workshops). IEEE, pp. 961–966.

Kumar, P., Gupta, G.P., Tripathi, R., 2021. An ensemble learning and fog-cloud architecture-driven cyber-attack detection framework for IoMT networks. Comput. Commun. 166, 110–124.

Lacerda, T., Fernandes, S., 2016. Scalable real-time flock detection. In: 2016 IEEE Global Communications Conference (GLOBECOM). IEEE, pp. 1–7.

Mohapatro, M., Snigdh, I., 2020. Security in IoT HealthCare. In: IoT Security Paradigms and Applications. CRC Press, pp. 237–259.

Rathee, G., Sharma, A., Saini, H., Kumar, R., Iqbal, R., 2020. A hybrid framework for multimedia data processing in IoT-healthcare using blockchain technology. Multimed. Tools Appl. 79 (15), 9711–9733.

Rathore, S., Park, J.H., 2018. Semi-supervised learning based distributed attack detection framework for IoT. Appl. Soft Comput. 72, 79–89.

Rughoobur, P., Nagowah, L., 2017. A lightweight replay attack detection framework for battery depended IoT devices designed for healthcare. In: 2017 International Conference on Infocom Technologies and Unmanned Systems (Trends and Future Directions) (ICTUS). IEEE, pp. 811–817.

Further reading

De Michele, R., Furini, M., 2019. IoT healthcare: benefits, issues and challenges. In: Proceedings of the 5th EAI International Conference on Smart Objects and Technologies for Social Good, pp. 160–164.

Rajawat, A.S., Rawat, R., Barhanpurkar, K., Shaw, R.N., Ghosh, A., 2021a. Vulnerability analysis at industrial internet of things platform on dark web network using computational intelligence. In: Computationally Intelligent Systems and Their Applications. Springer, pp. 39–51.

Rajawat, A.S., Rawat, R., Mahor, V., Shaw, R.N., Ghosh, A., 2021b. Suspicious big text data analysis for prediction—on darkweb user activity using computational intelligence model. In: Innovations in Electrical and Electronic Engineering. Springer, Singapore, pp. 735–751.

Rawat, R., Mahor, V., Chirgaiya, S., Shaw, R.N., Ghosh, A., 2021a. Analysis of darknet traffic for criminal activities detection using TF-IDF and light gradient boosted machine learning algorithm. In: Innovations in Electrical and Electronic Engineering. Springer, Singapore, pp. 671–681.

Rawat, R., Rajawat, A.S., Mahor, V., Shaw, R.N., Ghosh, A., 2021b. Surveillance robot in cyber intelligence for vulnerability detection. In: Machine Learning for Robotics Applications. Springer, Singapore, pp. 107–123.

Rawat, R., Mahor, V., Chirgaiya, S., Shaw, R.N., Ghosh, A., 2021c. Sentiment analysis at online social network for cyber-malicious post reviews using machine learning techniques. In: Computationally Intelligent Systems and Their Applications. Springer, pp. 113–130.

Rawat, R., Rajawat, A.S., Mahor, V., Shaw, R.N., Ghosh, A., 2021d. Dark Web—onion hidden service discovery and crawling for profiling morphing, unstructured crime and vulnerabilities prediction. In: Innovations in Electrical and Electronic Engineering. Springer, Singapore, pp. 717–734.

Rawat, R., Mahor, V., Rawat, A., Garg, B., Telang, S., 2021e. Digital transformation of cyber crime for chip-enabled hacking. In: Handbook of Research on Advancing Cybersecurity for Digital Transformation. IGI Global, pp. 227–243.

Rawat, R., Mahor, V., Chirgaiya, S., Rathore, A.S., 2021f. Applications of social network analysis to managing the investigation of suspicious activities in social media platforms. In: Advances in Cybersecurity Management. Springer, Cham, pp. 315–335.

Index

Note: Page numbers followed by *f* indicate figures and *t* indicate tables.

C

D

E

F

N

O

P

Kolibri 360 GmbH
Ferdinand-Jühlke-Straße 7
99095 Erfurt, Deutschland
produktsicherheit@kolibri360.de